The House of Memory

The House of Memory

Stories by Jewish Women Writers of Latin America

Second Edition

Edited by Marjorie Agosín

Translation Editors: Elizabeth Rosa Horan and Alison Ridley

Solis Press

To Josephine, Raquel, Sonia, Helena, and Frida, the women in my life who taught me to write and to sing.

Second edition, 2022 published by Solis Press, England

First edition, 1999 published by The Feminist Press at The City University of New York City College, USA

Compilation and introduction copyright © 2022 by Marjorie Agosín.

ISBN: 978-1-910146-73-6 (paperback)

ISBN: 978-1-910146-74-3 (hardback)

Ebooks are available

⁓

Published by Solis Press, Lytchett House, 13 Freeland Park, Wareham Road, Poole BH16 6FA, England

Web: www.solispress.com | *Twitter*: @SolisPress

Contents

Part Three *On the Border: Forging Identities*

Acknowledgments

I am grateful to each of the writers whose work appears in *The House of Memory* for her beautiful writing and her generous spirit.

This anthology unites for the first time in any language the voices of Jewish women writers of Latin America, and I celebrate the courage and vision of The Feminist Press and of its publisher, Florence Howe, who made this anthology a reality. Special gratitude goes to my editors, Jean Casella, who has a privileged sensibility and a power to transform confusion into clarity, and Marna Miller, whose patience, dedication, and fine editorial work made an invaluable contribution to this anthology.

I extend my special thanks to the many translators of this volume, and especially to Roberta Gordenstein and Elizabeth Rosa Horan, for their commitment to this literature and for their gifted and respectful translations.

As always, my love and gratitude to Alida Brill and Steven Scheuer, whose generosity has made this book possible and who have allowed me to explore the rich traditions of Jewish writing in the Americas, this time through the voices of my sisters.

My husband as well as my two children serve as a constant reminder of the tenacity of love. I thank them for their presence and for their unconditional support of my work.

For this Second Edition

I thank the original authors who joined me when this first book was published and now I welcome a new generation of writers who have also joined this collection. Together they have created a vibrant landscape of Jewish women writers from Latin America.

I would specially like to thank Alison Ridley for being the translation editor for these new writers.

Marjorie Agosín
Wellesley, Massachusetts
1998 and 2022

Introduction to the second edition[1]

The House of Memory: Stories by Jewish Women Writers of Latin America was first released in 1999 on the cusp of a new millennium and amid great anticipation for the new century and what it held in store for the arts in general and, more specifically, for a community of women writers—especially minority women writers—from around the world whose work would finally be recognized.

When The Feminist Press published the first edition of this collection, it brought together the voices of Jewish women writers from Latin America for the first time. In this, the second edition, those voices have been joined by others, thereby expanding the scope of the project. I will be forever grateful to Steven Scheuer and Alida Brill for their generosity and support of the new edition.

The House of Memory is the only anthology to date that showcases, in English, this particular collection of works by Latin American Jewish women writers from South, Central, and North America. A dearth in published literature exists despite the multitude of noteworthy female authors who share the Latin American Jewish identity; writers like Angelina Muñiz, Clarice Lispector, and Margo Glantz. The long-time omission of these authors from anthologies likely reflects how they have historically been afforded less recognition and renown than their male counterparts.

It is a great pleasure to reissue this anthology with Solis Press, which is committed to publishing fine literature throughout the world and championing the works of authors such as those included in this expanded collection. The new edition incorporates chapters by a number of established and emerging writers who have contributed to the field since the anthology's original publication. The domain of Jewish Latin American literature has grown significantly since 1999, and some of these writers have gained international notoriety. One reason for this growth is the Latin American Jewish Studies Association and its annual meetings that serve as an important source of research into the Jewish presence in Latin America (which constitutes only one percent of the region's population).

1 Translated from the Spanish by Alison Ridley.

Latin American women's literature has flourished in the past two decades with the emergence of an intriguing mix of new authors who span multiple generations. I am pleased to include works from more established authors such as Carla Guelfenbein and Gabriela Mistral, as well as selections from new authors whose voices are only now being heard. These writers yearn to tell their individual and collective stories, much like the generation of women writers whose work was included in the first edition of *The House of Memory*. In this new edition, one can see a consistent need to reaffirm the past via the present—a demanding process through which these writers endure both the complexities of history and the retrieval of their families' pasts, which are often diasporic in nature due to the persecution they endured. These authors' works demonstrate a persistent desire to write about one's identity in order to create a literary geography where the personal is intertwined with the universal. They imagine and create worlds where they return to the past—to the experiences of their ancestors—in order to understand and convey those experiences with great luminosity. In this way, they have become witnesses not only to their own lives, but also those of previous generations.

One significant change that has taken place since *The House of Memory*'s initial publication is the ever-increasing antisemitism in Europe and in Latin America, which is described by two authors in this new edition: Nora Strejilevich and Perla Sneh.

Strejilevich, a native of Argentina, maintains that she never identified herself as Jewish—coming as she did from a family that was secular—until she was taken prisoner by the military junta in 1977. From the moment she was arrested, the soldiers began shouting antisemitic slurs at her and saying she would be tortured twice as much for being a Jew. Strejilevich's essay, "The Role of the Witness," which is featured in this anthology, addresses the importance of legitimizing and heeding the testimonies of survivors of the concentration camps in the Southern Cone region. Her essay is followed by an excerpt from her fictional memoir, *A Single, Numberless Death,* in which she describes the horrors of her own detainment and the abhorrent treatment she received for being a Jew.

Perla Sneh is also an Argentine writer as well as a philosopher and an expert in Yiddish literature. Following the Second World War, Buenos Aires became a vital hub for Yiddish culture and literature. In

her featured essay from the collection of first-person testimonials titled "The Art of Not Forgetting," Sneh takes on the ancient Jewish tradition of the "call to remember" and speaks about the memory of those who have gone missing, both in Argentina during the dictatorship as well as in Europe during the Holocaust. Echoing the work of Strejilevich, Sneh underscores the constant presence of antisemitism in Argentina. Upon reading her piece, one cannot help but think about the bombing of the AMIA (the Argentine Israelite Mutual Association)—a horrific terrorist attack that targeted a major Argentine Jewish community building. Many individuals perished as a result of the attack. This crime has been under constant investigation, especially by Israel, which is searching for evidence that links the attack to Iran and Hezbollah. During that somber time in Argentine history, antisemitism proliferated making it hard to find solidarity within the Jewish community. The word "Jew" became a synonym for otherness, adversity, and blame.

However, antisemitism has always existed in Latin America, as evidenced by the many nations that remained neutral during the Second World War. The barbarism of the Nazis was often praised in military circles, and some Latin American countries only joined the Allies because of pressure from the United States. One of the few Latin American intellectuals who stood up against fascism and spoke about the impending fate of European Jews was Gabriela Mistral, who, in 1945, became the only Latin American woman to date to win the Nobel Prize in Literature. While not a Jew herself, we include here one of her essays, "Message about the Jews,"—which she wrote in 1934, shortly before assuming her post as consul to Chile in Portugal—because it is a poignant testimony to her commitment to human rights and the Jewish people throughout historical times of great suffering when countless other prominent intellectuals chose silence. Mistral was also influential in assisting with Jewish emigration to Chile when, after 1939, most Latin American nations had closed their borders to desperate Jewish refugees seeking asylum.

Aída Bortnik is a noted Argentine scriptwriter and author of short stories who, like Strejilevich, suffered persecution under the Argentine military dictatorship. Included in this edition, is her lyrical story, "Julius Golden Mountain," about a Jewish emigrant from Poland who remembers his youth in beautiful Vienna. However, he is haunted by his memory of the suicide of Austrian novelist Stefan Zweig, which

represents the perpetual cycle of violence endured by Jews. Her story evokes the Jewish people's familiarity with antisemitic persecution. Often, texts such as Bortnik's create parallels between war-era Europe and life in the emigrant authors' new homelands, demonstrating how the past is at one with the present.

Myriam Moscona, a distinguished Mexican poet whose family was originally from Bulgaria, writes in both Ladino and Spanish. Her poetic meditation in this collection titled "Windmill," evokes the suffering of the Ladino community through the metaphor of a tiger in a circus that devours the audience. This story is part of a larger collection of prose and poetry aptly titled *Tela de Sevoya*, (*The Onionskin*), as one must peel back the many layers in each piece to discover the depths of its truth. In the story featured here, hardly anyone survives, echoing the annihilation of the Sephardic community at the hands of the Nazis.

In this newly expanded anthology we also feature the work of authors who have chosen to explore their childhoods from a variety of perspectives, thereby presenting the Jewish experience through an assortment of unique vantage points.

Vilma Faingezicht is a writer, painter, and the founder of the Jewish Museum of Costa Rica. Two of her stories from the collection *Tales of the Jewish Girl* are included here. In one of the stories, "Shimele," she delves into deep reminiscences about her father and his life in Poland, and in the other, "Where Did My Childhood Go?", she describes her experience in a new school as an immigrant child in Costa Rica.

Carla Guelfenbein is a well-known Chilean author and winner of several international awards. While most of Guelfenbein's writings focus on more suggestive and ambiguous themes, her very poignant story "Toward the South," deals with coming of age, trust, mistrust, and fear. Although there is no particular emphasis on a Jewish theme or a Jewish past, one can clearly see the presence of a trait common throughout this collection: the sense of nostalgia and memories intertwined. This theme continues throughout the story in the author's exploration of an episode in a teenage girl's past characterized by sensuality, fear, and foreboding, as well as her curiosity about a potentially mythical haven in the south.

Andrea Jeftanovic's parents emigrated to Chile from the former Yugoslavia where there has been a long history of persecution of the Jewish people. Andrea was born in Chile and grew up under Pinochet's

military regime. She is the author of novels, essays, and short stories. In the featured excerpts from her novel *Theater of War*, we can see how her work is infused with memories of the Shoah, especially her father's memories. This text is also an ambiguous one as we cannot really tell where the father in the story is, or what he is remembering, but he represents, nevertheless, the contested memories of war that Jeftanovic addresses passionately in her works.

Michèle Sarde is a French writer and retired professor from Georgetown University. She comes from a Sephardic family residing in Santiago, Chile and Paris, France. Like so many writers in this collection, the Holocaust is an essential element in her writings. Sarde addresses the Holocaust, its aftermath, and the way in which it affected the lives of individuals. She explores the historical fate of Jewish communities in Europe, focusing especially on the Sephardim who settled in the Balkans. The two chapters included here from her novel, *In Search of Marie J.*, describe the intertwined stories of two women, one of them the author's grandmother who perished in Auschwitz after being deported from Italy, and the other, Yvette Kalev, a survivor of the war. In the novel, the author–narrator attempts to reconstruct her grandmother's past and her odyssey from Romania to Italy (from where she was sent to Auschwitz by the Nazis). *In Search of Marie J.* is a metaphor for the journeys that a post-Holocaust generation endures through faith and memory as well as ambiguous encounters with history.

The stories found in this collection represent a multilayered vision of what it means to belong to a minority population, or more than one minority population, in countries that are predominantly Roman Catholic. For instance, the featured excerpt from Karen Codner Dujovne's novel *To Breathe Underwater*, addresses the emotional attachment a Jewish woman in Chile, Jenny, has to her mapuche *nana*, Mirna, who has passed away. She mourns Mirna's loss while searching for an appropriate way to grieve for her. The protagonist discusses how the Jews mourn someone's passing, but stresses the importance of learning to grieve together regardless of our upbringings, ethnicities, or religious backgrounds. Many such stories in *The House of Memory* address how the Jewish experience can be a universal one, transcending one's own personal upbringing and creating a moving dialogue.

All of the stories and essays in this anthology celebrate the Jewish experience in Latin America from the perspective of women writers.

Some works, like Margo Glantz's *The Family Tree* (an excerpt of which is included here), speak about the distant past and the arrival of the Jews in new lands. The works of Gabriela Mistral, Nora Strejilevich, and Perla Sneh, on the other hand, speak to more current issues in contemporary Judaism, such as the persistence of antisemitism throughout Latin America and the presence of former Nazi Party members in the same countries that gave refuge to many of the authors featured in this collection.

As we have seen, in the past, many of the authors whose work is presented in this anthology have spoken and written about their parents' lives and memories as a way of legitimizing those recollections and making them part of our collective memory. Today, in this new decade, the voices have become more personal. They speak of their own reality with very little interference from the past. There is a sense of a new affirmation about being a minority, and a desire to write about it with a sense of belonging to the new place they call their home, while still understanding that their origins and ethnicity are from elsewhere.

The House of Memory is a place where the reader can enter with openness, joy, and curiosity. Each story is crafted by an author with a passionate and genuine voice that invites us to enter the richness and plenitude of the house of memory, where we, as readers, can join these women writers on their journeys through the porous path of memory.

Marjorie Agosín

Part One

The Family Tree:
Ancestors and Traditions

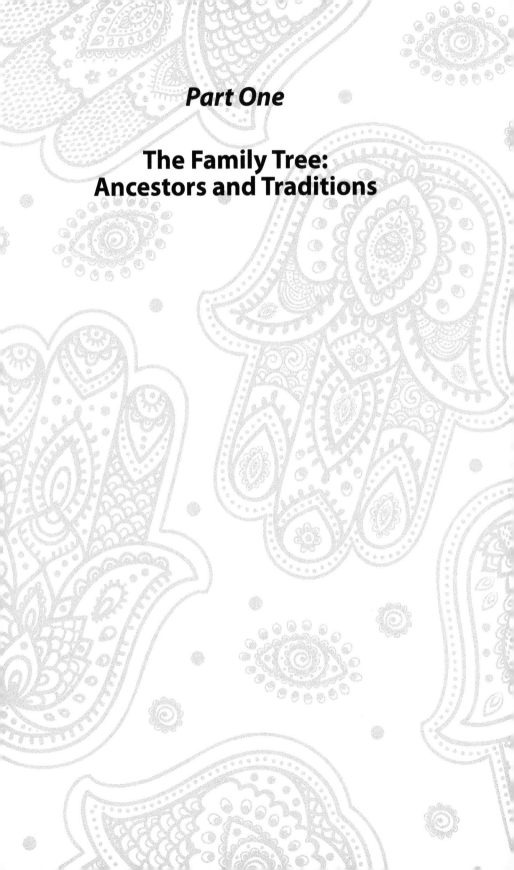

From *Musicians and Watchmakers*[1]

Alicia Steimberg

My grandmother knew the secret of eternal life. It consisted of a group of such simple rules that it was incredible that no one other than she herself knew about and practiced them. Sometimes we would participate in the ritual, thus guaranteeing ourselves, if not complete immortality, at least a good dose of it.

One of the ceremonies of this cult consisted of boiling Swiss chard and eating it immediately, sprinkled with the liquid from the concoction mixed with the juice of two large lemons. In the most perfect enactment of this rite, you would boil the chard beneath a lemon tree. When it was ready, you would make a cut into two lemons that were hanging from the tree right above the pot, so that the juice that fell on the chard would retain its vitamins, without losing a single drop of its nutritional value.

My grandmother said that ninety percent of human ills came from constipation. At home we all suffered from it, and there was a continuous coming and going of prescriptions to ward it off. Despite her wisdom in this area, my grandmother suffered from constipation more than anyone else. Whenever she managed to move her bowels, she would walk around for a while with a big smile on her face, and she would tell everyone about it. She was even known to crack a joke, or recall springtime in Kiev.

Those springs came after really hellish winters. Just when it seemed as if the cold and the snow would last forever, one morning she would draw the curtains and watch torrents of water flowing past her window. As soon as the water had passed, the sun would suddenly burst forth, everything would erupt into flowers, and the woods would fill up with wild cherries. Sweet cherries, not like the ones we get here. And that's how it would be the next day, and the day after that. Not like here, with these springtimes that don't even know what they are.

1 Published in 1998 by Latin American Literary Review Press, Pittsburgh, PA, USA. Translated from the Spanish by Andrea G. Labinger.

That's how my grandmother would describe her native land, whenever the activity of her bowels put her in a good frame of mind

I don't know if Otilia ever deluded herself into thinking she was pretty. Perhaps one summer afternoon, while she was crossing Nueve de Julio Avenue in a streetcar with her fiancé, a good-looking guy who resembled Clark Gable and was younger than she. You probably want to know how she caught him. It happened at a dance, where she and her next-in-line sister each nabbed a boyfriend.

The boys were friends. They hadn't been in Buenos Aires very long, and they earned a living as best they could. They also enjoyed the usual pastimes of bachelorhood. For thirty cents they could have a wonderful time on a sunny day: ten cents for the streetcar to the public beach, ten to get back, and ten for a salami sandwich. Stretched out in the sunshine, sporting their wool bathing trunks, their little mustaches, and their innocence, they would talk about the future:

"Hey, man, you gonna get married?" asked Clark Gable.

"Um, … no," the other one answered. "I'm gonna travel."

Nevertheless, the weddings took place only a month apart, shortly after the conversation at the public beach. Otilia got married first. (How the pretty girl envies her ugly sister's good fortune!) I witnessed Grandma's preparations. She stationed herself out on the patio of the house in Donato Alvarez, next to a bag full of little rolls. She cut them all in half and smeared them with something. On the folding tables they set up that night on that same patio, platters bloomed with little rolls, bottled orangeade and beer. I don't know if there was anything else, because I hardly even managed to get close, and when I did, I had to put up with my aunts' sloppy kisses and tell them what my name was, how old I was, and if I loved my little brother.

Nor was I able to observe the glorious moment when the brides took leave of their family homes and acquired the privilege of being supported by their husbands. The guests piled up around the bridal canopy, which was illuminated by an electric bulb. Clark Gable and his friend were tall guys; they had to tip their heads slightly to the side under the canopy, while the little lantern rested on top of their Vaselined hair. Despite this minor inconvenience, everything turned

out fine. On tiptoe, stretching out my neck to no avail, I heard the rabbi intone the praises to God which began the ceremony.

I was just a little girl, but I already understood that you were supposed to get emotional, that the jasmine-scented breeze came from the garden next door (because at my grandparents' house there were only some red wildflowers that didn't smell at all), and that more than one guest disrespectfully turned around in the middle of the ceremony to cast watchful glances at the folding tables. At the first of these weddings I learned something: I didn't have to stay until the end of the ceremony to get from the wedding canopy to the food tables. That's what I did the first time, and I nearly got trampled.

Some years earlier another marriage had been celebrated in that house, a marriage from which I was born, and three years later, my little brother (yes, I loved my little brother). After Otilia and Amanda's weddings, Grandpa got sick and I stopped going to the house in Donato Alvarez. I had no further news of him until they took me to La Chacarita cemetery (because my grandfather, an atheist, a socialist, and a vegetarian, was cremated according to his explicit wishes and doesn't repose among our other relatives in the Jewish cemetery). They didn't tell me before taking me to the cemetery that Grandpa had died so as not to upset me. We stood for a while looking at a little box which couldn't possibly have contained Grandpa. Otilia and Amanda didn't go to the cemetery on account of their "condition." My cousins were born, also a month apart: first the son of Otilia and Clark Gable. They went off to live in General Pico, and we lost sight of them for a while.

Thus ended a long and difficult period for my family, but one that was lovely and full of fun for me. I would sniff the cookies that Grandma baked in the kitchen; I would watch Mele, Otilia, and Amanda rehearsing didactic plays for the Socialist Party Theater Group; and I would see a windmill emerge on the canvas Mele was painting. The canvas didn't interest me as much as the palette, covered with all kinds of colored stains and peaks.

<p style="text-align:center">***</p>

Otilia and Clark Gable set themselves up in a room, in which they crammed a double bed and a couple of little night tables, a dining room table with chairs, a wardrobe, a cupboard, and a side table. In a vase that she called the "centerpiece," Otilia put a bouquet of artificial

flowers that she had made herself. When the Chipmunk was born (we called him that because of his chubby cheeks), they also had to squeeze in a crib.

Motherhood didn't make Otilia more beautiful, but it did make her fatter. It was no longer possible to visualize her as she had been during her engagement: skinny in her blue linen sailor dress, white spool-heeled shoes, and a mane of hair with little spitcurls on her forehead. Clark Gable, on the other hand, was even thinner than before, but still good-looking, wildly happy, and a great prankster.

Once in a while Clark Gable's mother and sister would come from Entre Rios to visit the couple. As married women, they enjoyed a certain amount of leisure and could travel for pleasure. They had screechy voices, and they practiced a form of birth control that consisted of repeatedly jumping off a table onto the floor after "having relations" with their husbands. They were famous for the number of miscarriages they provoked: in that family no one had had fewer than thirty or forty.

Otilia and Amanda, by hook or by crook, had become married ladies. Otilia chose names for her children from the social pages of *El Hogar.* The same names as the children of Senora Peralta Ramos or Senora Martínez de Hoz. She avoided those that were too obviously Catholic, such as any combination with Maria. Amanda, who had fewer pretensions and who was more sentimental and a great interpreter of tangos, gave her children more popular names. They were called Evaristo, Azucena, and Greta. This last name, which might be considered an exception, was a concession to her enthusiasm for foreign actresses.

With the business of the names, a long family tradition was broken. All Otilia and Amanda's female cousins were named Dora; all the male cousins, León. To differentiate, they were classified as Dora, Dorita, Ugly Dora, Big Dora, Little Dora, Uncle José's Dora. Then there were León, Little León, Big León, León the Watchmaker, and León the Lawyer. When they all got together, there was never any confusion: each one knew very well who he or she was and who all the others were.

With three of her four daughters already married, Grandma was happy. At other relatives' weddings, which didn't take place beneath the grape arbor, but rather in rented halls, she had her picture taken with her daughters, sons-in-law, and grandchildren, all dressed up and with new shoes. I learned to distrust the smiles that abounded at those social events. As soon as Grandma returned home from the party and

put on her housecoat, her true colors emerged. Her face reflected an existence full of suffering, yoked to the side of a silent husband and daughters who fought like wild beasts, feeding on their insatiable bitterness. The four of them were, according to what I overheard from their arguments, bitches, vipers, egotists, imbeciles, tightwads, and evil incarnate. I watched them, trying to discover those qualities in their faces, but without discerning much except that they were fat and ugly.

After each fight they would break off relations forever. But they got back together after each wedding and wake, displaying tender smiles, too much rouge, and their kids, and they eventually patched things up. For a while calm would reign. We'd organize a picnic. Everything would turn out badly, plagued by ants, mosquitoes, and packed buses. "When poor people try to have fun ..." Mele would say. She was the one who got married late. Like her sisters, she was very fond of dramatic scenes. Grandma would try to lift our spirits by telling us funny stories that happened to other people: some guy's business failed and he ended up on the street; someone else's trip got screwed up; another one had to leave school for financial reasons; yet another gave birth to a sixth daughter. She would laugh until she choked, never noticing if anyone else shared her mirth.

The same things weren't funny when they happened to her. Then she'd fall into a bitter depression, the grayish circles under her eyes would become more prominent, and she would take the event as further proof of her ill fortune.

In spite of her own unfortunate experience, she was a great advocate of marriage. She advised her girls to go to parties wearing beautiful, very low-cut dresses, with lots of jewels (real or costume, the main thing was that they should glitter), and to keep an eye out for the boys. Mustn't be a ninny. She'd say: "Young man, I'd like to introduce my daughter." The victim, taken by surprise, had no time to consider that not only did he not know the person to whom he was being introduced (which in itself is quite normal), he also didn't know the person making the introductions (not so normal).

This strategy never failed. The candidate would blush, offer his arm to the girl, and ask her to dance. Her mother would sit down next to the other mothers, who peered at her out of the corner of their eyes. It was pure envy, since their own daughters stood like wallflowers at the other end of the room, pretending to be thrilled chatting among themselves,

while the others were already trying on their trousseaux or pushing baby carriages in the park.

On certain afternoons we had visitors at the house in Donato Alvarez. My aunt and uncle from Constitución would come, give me wet kisses, etc., and ask that stuff about loving my little brother. Once they brought their grandson along to play with me, but he was coughing a lot, so I wasn't allowed to get too close. I watched him from a distance, sitting on the bottom step of the stairway that led to the terrace. When everyone was distracted, I climbed the entire staircase. When I reached the top, I lost my footing and tumbled down to the bottom, landing on top of Otilia, who was waiting for me with arms outspread. I hit her in the nose with the heel of my shoe. After that, she glared at me with hatred in her eyes, applying rags soaked in vinegar to her injury. She didn't say anything to me because I was just a child, but I'm sure that, from that moment on, I too became a bitch, a viper, an egotist, tightwad, imbecile, and evil incarnate, like all the other women.

My grandfather, the only man in the household, didn't generally participate in the conversations. Everyone remembers how he used to give orders to his daughters. Whenever he noticed them looking very happy, laughing a lot, or acting goofy, he'd give them a laxative. He was of the opinion that all strange behavior was the result of intestinal disorders. "Do you remember," Grandma would say whenever she was in a nostalgic mood, "how Papa drove you crazy with Josselin tea?" and she would shake with laughter.

When Grandma immigrated from Kiev to Buenos Aires she was eleven years old. They sent her to school, where she learned Spanish very well. She sang tangos like a sick bird:

Sca-a-ars [trill],
Indelible scars from a wou-ou-ound ... [trill].

She never spoke of how she ended up marrying Grandpa. She gave birth to her daughters quite easily, one after another. They always arrived before the midwife, anxious to be born and start quarreling. There were some very bad times. Unemployment. Evictions.

At a charity ball, money was collected, as it was for other poor families, to help them get a new house. *El Hogar* published a short article

about that ball. Taking advantage of the occasion, several of the girls made their debut into society. A few courtships began. In subsequent social notes appearing in the same magazine, there were pictures of their engagements, marriages, and announcements of their first babies' births. The young mothers selected names for their little celebrities, the same names that Otilia's children bear, even today.

Before they were married, Otilia and Amanda were salesgirls at La Piedad department store, where they extolled the beauty of the bathrobes and housecoats to their customers. Mele, the one who was slow to marry, never worked outside her home. Sometimes she would sew or do housework, and when she was done, she'd go off and paint. She painted flowers, sailboats at sunset, Dutch landscapes with tulips, and haystacks beside country houses. She copied them from some postcards she had.

On Sundays we'd all have lunch at Donato Alvarez. Otilia and Amanda's fiancés would be there. The men livened up the atmosphere: they were talkative, they'd bring bottles of wine, and they'd sit you on their laps so you could demonstrate how you were learning to read. The women didn't fight. I would recite verses, taste Papa's port, and announce that I loved my little brother

<p style="text-align:center">***</p>

Grandpa slept on a sofa in the corner. No matter how early one arrived, everything was always in perfect order: the bed made, the floor swept. Grandpa read *La Vanguardia*, books by José Ingenieros and Juan B. Justo, and essays on vegetarianism. He'd sit me on his knees and make me spell out: *l-a-v-a-n-g-u-a-r-d-i-a*. Afterward he'd send me out to the patio to play. He had a large mustache whose ends pointed up and whose shape he maintained by sleeping with something called a mustache guard.

Grandma slept in another room, which was very untidy. On top of the table, among dirty cups and bottles of medicine, you could see the twin arches of her false teeth in a glass of water, and her corset, much larger and more complicated than those of her daughters, with laces and whalebone everywhere.

Grandpa belonged to the Socialist Party. Firmly divorced from religion and family traditions, he devoted himself to instilling revolutionary ideas in his daughters. He taught them that everyone was

equal, Jews and non-Jews alike. The little girls learned to sing the "Internationale" before they knew "Rock-a-Bye Baby." He never managed to make them vegetarians. He had to content himself with eating his greens at the far corner of the table, casting an occasional disgusted glance at the stew that they devoured. He taught them to love work— not by example, however, since, thanks to a combination of bad luck, periods of crisis and unemployment, his ill health, and his brothers' selfishness, he didn't live a very active life, although it was full of all the appropriate maxims and readings. In their peaceful moments, the four girls would sing:

> The sewing machine
> sings its hurried song,
> while the good woman
> sews and sings along.

Mama was the only one of the four with any schooling. "We starved to death so you could study, bitch," her sisters frequently reminded her. "Studying is the only thing that keeps me from blowing my brains out for having to live with you, vipers," Mama would answer.

She was the first to get married, and, loyal to her father's ideas, she did so at City Hall. I was told this, since in those days children didn't witness their parents' marriages. On the wedding night, one of my classmates explained to me, the man puts his front thing into the woman's front thing and he leaves a little juice that makes a baby in the woman's belly. If he gets carried away and leaves too much juice, it could turn out to be a very big baby, like her uncle who weighed fifteen pounds when he was born and his mama almost died. It could also happen that, after nine months, when they sliced the mother's belly open and took out the baby, there might be a little unused juice left inside the mother. In that case, after a while, another baby would start to grow, and that's how you could get a little brother and always have to tell people that you loved him.

Grandpa's other daughters weren't as loyal to him as Mama was. As soon as they realized that they weren't going to get anything (I mean husbands) out of the committee meetings and the Socialist Party Theater Group they went off to look for them, without any scruples whatsoever, at Jewish parties and weddings. I don't know how Grandpa, who was always saying that religion was the opiate of the masses, must have felt, standing before the lighted wedding canopy and listening to

praises of the Jewish God at his daughters' weddings. As far as all his other ideas were concerned, Otilia very clearly and frequently said that he could stick them up his ass. Jewish husbands weren't "equal" to the others, they were better, since they didn't spend their lives playing pool at the café, and if they had a fight with you, at least they weren't going to call you a "dirty Jew."

"I'm so glad I married a Jew!" Otilia said. "You should see how Clark Gable worries about his wife and children! Big Dora's daughter married a Christian. She said she was 'in lo-ove' [sarcastic tone]. And so? What did she get out of it? She's sure sorry now, poor thing! No, not poor thing, stupid thing! Because not a Sunday goes by that he doesn't lose every penny at the races. No wonder she has to suffer so much and sew for other people, poor thing, just so they can eat!"

As she spoke, Otilia finished polishing her nails dark red and waved her hands to dry them.

Evening was falling. Like flames, Otilia's nails passed before my eyes, and from the back of the patio came the smell of the sulfur that Grandma was burning to disinfect who-knows-what.

Doctors don't know anything, Grandma used to say. "They're businessmen. They don't care about taking good care of you; they want to hurry up and finish so they can go on to the next patient."

She and the four beasts spent their lives consulting doctors, because no doctor was any good. They preferred "naturalists" and homeopaths, because, as they would say, "they cure with natural things," although they never followed any of the treatments for very long.

There was one doctor whom they respected more than the others. He had his prescriptions filled in the only pharmacy in Buenos Aires where they had the Elixir of Eternal Life, and where they displayed the following publications in the window: "War to the Death Against Toxins;" "Wheat Germ, the Germ of Life;" "The Sedative Properties of Black Molasses;" "Live to Be One Hundred with Daily Visits to the Bathroom;" and "Keep Death Away with Ten Lemons a Day."

The doctor placed the utmost importance on anything that was consumed by mouth, but he combined his dietary recommendations with general advice on hygiene, publishing both in a brochure. Each patient received one of these brochures along with the appropriate

medication for his or her ailment. It was recommended that one sleep with the windows open, even in the middle of winter; that one wash one's hands before eating; that one avoid all contact with other people's saliva (here there was a little note about the number of microbes that two people exchange with a single kiss); and that the following practice be observed: "Moisten sexual organs with cold water every day."

After having been respected and consulted by the family for quite a while, this doctor was replaced by another one (Otilia's discovery) who cured all illnesses with different sorts of enemas, a method that she found truly harmless.

It was kind of a pity, because the first one was—how shall I put it?—more eclectic.

They would sit down next to our beds, look at us sadly and move their head a certain way, bending their necks first to one side and then to the other, so that their skulls bent alternately toward each shoulder. They would listen to the details of our illness and murmur: "Poor little boy. Ay, ay. Poor little girl. Oy, oy, oy." Papa's sisters weren't like my maternal aunts at all. They were long-suffering, respectful, and they didn't engage in arguing in front of other people. Sometimes they would run into the beasts when visiting our house. "It's been so long, girls! Can you believe it?" They weren't as close to us as Mama's sisters were: we always looked upon them as the visiting team. As soon as they left, the local gang would rip into them without compunction, recalling the time when Papa's family was starving to death in the Jewish section of Entre Rios. There were nine siblings. "Nine who lived," Grandma clarified, immediately bursting into one of her paroxysms of laughter. Grandma swore that Papa's mother fed her children a staple diet of angel hair pasta in milk until they were fifteen years old, and that's why they all turned out weak and sickly (my father's premature death confirmed that fact, according to her).

I don't know if the story about the milky soup was entirely true, but I can attest that my paternal grandmother believed that this was a nutritious childhood dish. All dried up, dressed in mourning, and with sparse white hair, she'd serve it to me in her kitchen, while in the dining room the adults entertained themselves with port and cookies. It was a sweet soup with milk skin floating on top and a few bits of angel hair pasta that got stuck in my throat. With considerable effort (because she could barely speak Spanish), my grandmother explained

THE HOUSE OF MEMORY | *The Family Tree* 🐚

that the soup was good; if I didn't eat it, I was bad, and if I ate it all, I would grow up to be big and strong

You're going to kill me, Grandma said. You're going to finish off the few years of life I have left. She said this in a suffocated voice, weak and intense and tremulous at the same time, as she placed her fist on the table in a feigned blow since, according to her, she was so broken down, so worn out, that she didn't even have the strength left to make a proper fist. During these scenes she looked very hunched over, her hair in disarray, with a vacant expression and purplish circles under her eyes. After pronouncing each phrase she seemed to collapse, with her lower lip hanging out and trembling like a leaf.

Her phrases began in a low tone, almost a whisper, and rose up to a high pitch at the beginning of the last syllable, whose vowels were stretched out long enough to achieve (without losing the rhythm) an even sharper pitch than at the beginning. That is to say, an ascending tone:

> *You're going to k-i-i-i-l-l* ...
> (and in a descending tone):
> *me-e-e-e*
> (and again, voice rising):
> *You're going to finish off the few years of life* ...
> (descending pitch):
> *I have* ... *le-e-e-e-f-t.*

The fights Grandma had with her daughters were different from the ones they had among themselves. The beasts fought like equals, and none of them seemed lessened by the experience. They spoke plainly: "You want to screw up my life, you bitch, you viper, but I won't give you that pleasure." They were young, vigorous women who had nursed from none other than my grandmother herself and who had been nourished by a naturistic-vitaministic-anti-constipationistic regimen. Their mother, on the other hand, was old and quite worn down by the life she had led (always sacrificing herself to raise her daughters).

I never figured out how the fights began because I wasn't there (children should be spared violent scenes). I drew closer when the shouts penetrated the closed door and crossed the patio. Then I'd spy from behind the door, or I would go right into the room and no one took

notice of me. At those moments the accusations usually referred to very ancient matters, and Grandma would be receiving the fatal blows.

The blows were almost always of the verbal variety. Only once did I see Grandma receive a punch in the arm. I waited to see if she'd be felled by lightning, but strangely enough, Grandma seemed to calm down with the impact. She rose from her chair (she almost always fought from a sitting position, due to her extreme weakness), and she left the room, rubbing her arm.

From the first fight I ever witnessed, during which Grandma announced, as usual, that she was dying, to her actual death, twenty-five years ensued. Only in the last few years did she modify her technique a bit. She no longer threatened to die, but rather she would ask for a cup of tea, grab the cup with tremulous hands, and spill the entire contents down the front of her blouse. A daughter would have to help her change her clothes, to keep her from catching a chill. Or else she would say, "All right, Otilia, all right, don't be that way." A clear wish for reconciliation. Proof that Grandma was tired of violence and honestly desired peace. Unfortunately, the one with whom she was fighting at the time wasn't Otilia, but rather Amanda. The confusion of names infuriated her daughter even more. "You pretend to be stupid," she shouted at her. "You want me to think you don't know who I am, that you've got me confused with that other snake!"

And it went on like that until that poor mother ended her sad days. According to her, she deserved a happier ending.

From *The Family Tree*[1]

Margo Glantz

Bashevis Singer says somewhere: "The Jews don't record their own history, they lack a sense of chronology. It is as though they knew instinctively that time and space are just an illusion." This sense of elongated, gelatinous, compressed time that has a single theme with multiple variations and cadenzas resembles my parents' lives, where endlessly repeated conversations can suddenly shed a spark of light on some happening that ideal historical time has never satisfactorily explained. Time is a space marked out and filled with the ceaseless chanting of prayers by which a devout Jew measures his life.

And also his death. Then they have to say kaddish, blessing the holy name of God and remembering the departed, all seated on the ground without shoes so as to get nearer to the earth and accompany the one who has gone on ahead.

"I used to go to the synagogue next to the ritual bathhouse to pray for my father. I was the only one who was able to pray for him in the place where he died. My brothers did it in Philadelphia," [says my father].

"What did you feel?" [I ask.]

"A great warmth because I was sitting next to the stove and the old men were praying all day long, chanting psalms, and I felt less of an orphan there. First we read a chapter from the *mishnah,* the oral tradition, and then we said kaddish, praising God and remembering my father's name."

"What do you say in kaddish?"

"At least ten Jews have to come together to make up what is called the *minyan,* which is a congregation. That's the right number to hold whatever ceremony you want. "May his name be blessed forever and throughout eternity." That's what all poets hope for. There was a great poet who came from my village, about thirty or forty years older than me, Simeon Frog. Whatever happened to him, goodness knows. My brothers went to Philadelphia, I only remember the younger ones,

1 Published in 1991 by Serpent's Tail, London, UK. Translated from the Spanish by Susan Bassnett.

Moishe Itzjok who didn't want to hand over three and a half years of his life to the czar and emigrated along with Abreml who had just come out of the army where he'd served the full duration. In 1939 when I saw my elder brothers Meier, Ellis, and Leie, it was like seeing them for the first time. Leie told me that when they left they accused him of having given me a false kiss."

"Why was it false?"

"Because I didn't feel it."

"Your grandmother," says my mother, "was marvelous. When she got to the United States she traveled from one end of the country to the other to see her sons and she didn't know one word of English. She had all sorts of things written down on paper and she taught them everything and crossed the four points of the compass to see them."

"She loved your mother a lot," says Nucia rather sadly.[2]

"Yes, and I loved her too, she was a splendid woman, she never caused any trouble, she always tried to help and never interfered in a nasty way, always out of a desire to do good. Quite unlike a mother-in-law."

My grandmother is very indistinct in my memory. She was in Mexico twice, first in 1928 before I was born and then from 1936 to 1939. She died there. She was very ill in the last months of her life, while in mine she barely fills a fleeting space, one marked by a photo in which I am in the foreground and she is in the countryside. She is also part of a legend that enhances my father's life: when she was already very ill, my grandmother Sheine (or Sofia, according to her passport) waited until her youngest son, who was visiting Philadelphia, came back to Mexico before departing this life. At that time we were living in the Street of the Argentine Republic, number 96, in a three-story building with a courtyard where we used to play as children.

The new Jewish cemetery was near the Hill of the Star. The old one was near the Burial Vault of Griefs. My father remembers another cemetery when he was thirteen years old, just after the death of my grandfather Osher. Nucia was working for a wealthy relative in a mill, helping to count the sacks of grain that the peasants brought in at night

2 The author's father, Jacob Glantz, is alternatively called Jacob, Yankl, or Nucia.

My father had to keep watch, but sometimes he would nod off to sleep, sitting next to the mill. The gentiles came and to wake him up they would pee noisily, sometimes down the slipway that fed the grain into the stone millwheels, from which Jacob had saved himself with a single leap. He was in the Ukraine, in a village called Krivoy Rog, about a hundred and fifty leagues from Novy Vitebsk, his native village; it was winter, and it was 1914 too, the year the war started.

One day he was going home in a *svostchik* (a small carriage) when he came to Sofievka, a Christian village with twelve or fifteen Jewish families and a burial vault. A great storm came up, an early spring blizzard. The coach driver and his horse found shelter in a stable, and my father went to see a relation, Eizel Jilbuj, who looked after the cemetery.

"I went to look for somewhere to spend the night. I knocked and knocked. Eizel was enormously tall, and used to stoop, and had a white, white beard. He came out carrying a lantern and angry and said to me: 'Yankl? What a surprise! Come on in.'"

"I went in feeling pretty frightened, because I knew it was a graveyard. In I went, the first thing I saw was this funeral bench where they strip and wash the dead bodies, with a little broom next to it. I felt a bit panicky and wanted to get out, but I couldn't, I had the night and the snow outside and dead bodies inside."

Eizel woke up his old lady, who put on the samovar and offered my father the customary glass of tea with a lot of sugar and then showed him where he could sleep, next to a window.

"I couldn't sleep. I lay down, all hunched up. I didn't know what to do. Then I shut my eyes tight and the old lady told me not to worry. I slept a bit, then all of a sudden there was a tall figure by my side, with a piece of rope and an ax in his hand calling me and I woke up. He was shouting and telling me we had to lasso the dead first and then he would cut their heads off with his ax. I shouted too, I yelled, and the old lady got up again."

The old lady came in and restrained the crazy old man with his long white beard; then she told him off (I guess she was very small, they must have been one of those classic couples where the woman is really tiny and the man is huge, but the woman is the one who shouts loudest) and she woke him up and took him back to bed. She explained: "Eizel has started walking in his sleep. Ever since they took Yerujem off to the war."

Next day Eizel didn't remember anything about the night before. My father was still shaky, but his old relative offered him a splendid breakfast of bread and butter, herrings, semolina, tea and more tea, more bread and butter and jam; after that he took him out for a walk round the cemetery garden, showing him the paths and pointing out the children's graves, covered in flowers and almost buried in the snow, then he proudly pointed out the family mausoleums, he showed him how well laid out it all was and he said it all as though he were showing Adam round Paradise, a long time before the first sin and, obviously, a long time before the arrival of Eve.

Then he asked him if he would like to stay on for another night. My father replied hastily that he preferred to stay buried in the snow on the road home rather than spend another night among the dead.

It is seven leagues from Sofievka to Novy Vitebsk. In Sofievka there were just a very few Jews and a graveyard.

<p style="text-align:center">***</p>

When Grandfather Osher died, Yankl went to stay with his uncle Moishe Haim, an unqualified mining engineer.

"My uncle was a wealthy man, he used to work in the coal mines, which was where most of the money came from in Krivoy Rog. He was very modern, he'd shaved off his beard, not like my father who kept his long like the old-style Jews did. Your mother's father was modern too, he had a little pointed beard that you could hardly see. Before he went to work in the mines, my uncle had mills and supplied the military with food. I was with my cousin Ilusha, who was much older than me, they were very nice to me, they treated me like a poor relation. My girl cousins, I remember them well, they were tall, handsome, strapping girls, who went to private school, because in my village the state school only had six grades and they only took Jews who spoke Russian."

"Not Yiddish?"

"Not Yiddish, nor Ukrainian either. In Krivoy Rog there was a Jewish university, a yeshiva, and a gymnasium, that's what we called a high school."

"Not one city in the Ukraine," says mother, "had up to a million inhabitants. Odessa was really important, but there were only about four or five hundred thousand people living there. There were some other big cities, Kiev, Herzon, Nikolaiev, ports on the Black Sea, and

Krivoy Rog and Kremenchug where your grandmother Sheine was born."

"She was a very intelligent woman, even though she was uneducated, she couldn't read or write Russian, only Yiddish, and not very well either, but she was very intelligent. They didn't educate women in those days, even though she was born in a city. You have to remember it was midway through the last century," says my father.

"And what about the revolution. Where were you when the revolution happened?"

"That was a very interesting time in my life, the revolution caught up with me in Krivoy Rog. In 1915 I was in the village, and in 1916 and '17 I was in the city with my uncle, though the revolution didn't reach the little places, only the deserters made it out there. They went from the villages to the city too, and then because everything was in turmoil a lot of people came to our village, begging, there was no food in the cities, but out in the villages there was never any shortage of food. All those people belonged to the intelligentsia. Then some Zionist Jews came through who set up a little *ajshara* in my village, they were training settlements for those who wanted to go to Israel. This *ajshara* went on to Constantinople later, and when my mother and brothers went to Turkey in 1922 they saw them there again. They wanted to take them with them to Israel, but my mother preferred to go and join my brothers in the United States. They were very helpful to me, I read with them, I learned Russian well, and when the revolution reached our region I became a revolutionary."

Mother has been washing the dishes in the kitchen, but now she comes in and tells us to go to the table because tea is ready. We sit down and my father carries on talking enthusiastically. Before this I have spent days trying to persuade him to tell me something about his youth and he has refused because it all seemed uninteresting. Suddenly something strikes him:

"Before 1917 there hadn't been any pogroms in our villages, but everything came with the revolutionary movements. But I've told you all that."

"I've just come across something really interesting," says mother, "I think you'll be absolutely fascinated."

"Wait just a minute, Mother, Father's remembering things he's never told me about before. Let's hear what he has to say."

"Do you want tea?"

"Yes."

"The revolution. Sit down here, Margo, are you all right? The revolutionaries wanted to free the Ukraine, there were all sorts of groups, good, honest people who wanted to help and bands of bandits trying to kill us all. Oh, yes, I've certainly lived an interesting life! The world war, the revolution, what an experience! Since everything was upside down, people used to come and hide out in my village, some very well-educated, very intelligent people, who taught me a lot. I'll say they did! They made me into a revolutionary. They were young men and women too, they must have been about twenty-two or twenty-three years old."

In 1921 he was in Herzon, where he took a course to become a teacher of Marxism, which he continued in Odessa in 1922.

"Once they sent me to Moscow as a delegate for the youth of Odessa at an agricultural congress, and I met Lunacharsky and Radek, the Bolsheviks. Lunacharsky had an aristocratic background, he came to attend the lectures on cattle shows and he brought an actress with him. Lunacharsky was an interesting man, he was tall like Radek. Do you know who Radek was? He came from Galicia."

"From Poland? Was he Jewish?"

"Yes, he was a Polish Jew, but he was part of the Russian revolution. I think his name was Rosenfeld, he was one of Lenin's Bolsheviks, Karl Radek. I met Zinoviev and Kamenev too."

"And Kalinin," says mother.

"I saw Kalinin too, but what did I have to do with the likes of them? I was just a lad, I saw them from a distance, I was interested in what they had to say, but I was too insignificant to be with them. I met a lot of leaders at that time too. Kamenev and Zinoviev were both Jews."

"Zinoviev was Trotsky's brother-in-law," adds mother.

"I had a lot of diplomas and certificates dating from that time, but when I was going through the Polish Corridor at Danzig I went into the toilet on the train and tore up all my papers, I don't know why. I was frightened and I tore them all up and lost the lot."

"Not all," I say smugly. "I've got some of them, they're all in bits."

"Like our lives." ...

"A tall cossack and a short one passed by our house, their hands covered in blood, and my mother, crying her eyes out, washed their hands in a bowl." My father's mother wore broad skirts under which she hid my two aunts, Jane and Mira, girls of sixteen and seventeen.

"I was almost out of my mind, I walked (I was only a boy), I ran from one place to another and crossed the town over the little bridge that led to the baths and I tried to shelter in my uncle Kalmen's house, he was my father's brother. It was 1917, I went into my uncle's house and I almost went mad, my uncle had a long curly red beard, all crimson with blood, and he was sitting with the blood pouring down and his eyes open. The fear of death still hadn't left him, perhaps he was still breathing! Beside him, wrapped in a sheet, were all the household utensils, everything made of silver or copper, the Sabbath candlesticks, the samovar. I was scared stiff, I had no idea what to do, I just ran out of the village like a madman. The pogrom lasted several days, I went out into the country and I found an abandoned well, deep, but with no water in it, and I spent several days in it. When I heard that everything had calmed down, I came out. Before that, I could hear the terrible cries of the girls and children."

It all happened so fast that one pogrom followed another.

"In those troubled times different groups were chasing one another and as they went through towns and villages they laid waste to everything in their path."

It all sounds so familiar, it's like those revolts that our nineteenth-century novelists wrote about and like what you read in novels about the Mexican revolution, the revolts and the levies, the confusion, the sacking of towns and villages, the deaths.

"The Bolsheviks came back and we had some of the short rifles left by the bandits and some of the horses too; only those who'd been in the world war knew how to defend themselves, the rest of us were saved by a miracle. Many of the bandits were peasants who knew us, and they killed the people they stole from to make sure they couldn't be denounced."

Yasha hid in the house of a *muzhik*,[3] a friend of his grandfather's, Sasha Ribak. He had "an enormous mustache, like the poet Sevshenko"

3 A *muzhik,* from the Russian, is a peasant in czarist Russia.

(the great popular poet of the Ukraine). My father stayed hiding in a corncrib, breathing through a hole, even as bandits stuck their bayonets into it. Ribak took him food and water and let him out when things calmed down a little.

"General Budiony's Bolshevik cossacks arrived. When things were a bit calmer, I came out. When it was dangerous I went back into hiding again. I remember Sasha well, he was very good. I wrote a poem about all that, in 1920, in Russian."

"And what about your mother and your sisters, how were they saved?"

"We survived by chance, by luck. My mother and my sisters hid in the top of the house, where there was a loft used as a storeroom, in the space under the rafters. As the groups were all chasing each other they hardly had time to look. They sacked and killed everything they found in their way. My mother was saved that first time because she washed the cossacks' hands."

<p style="text-align:center">***</p>

Sometimes they show documentary movies in the Regis cinema and girls with dark curly hair file over and over again into a concentration camp, then sometimes quite deliberately they walk into crematorium ovens. Usually they look like me, and seeing those images has left me with a daily sense of guilt that clings, guilt at having escaped a number branded on my right wrist or the indelible mark of the yellow star that was sewn onto overcoats in Parisian winters. Even Max Jacob had to wear one when he went outdoors, despite the fact that he had converted to Christianity.

Someone interrupts my recollections and the guilt dissolves. It doesn't matter much whether you're a Jew or not, what matters is whether you're willing to fight against the herd instinct.

My father remembers the pogroms, my mother does not. Nucia only remembers the story of Ilusha, the brother who was to die during the Second World War through eating a potato when he was starving. Ilusha joined a group of other young students fighting bands of outlaws who were robbing and killing Jews in the villages. The group was counterattacked by White Russians who beat them savagely and decimated them, Ilusha went home suffering from tuberculosis. He was already doomed.

"During the Civil War," says Nucia, "the partisans and the bandits were interchangeable, there were red ones, white ones, green ones who followed General Zeliony (that means green in Russian), or the *kolchakovets* who followed General Kolchak, he was a White Russian who commanded a cavalry regiment. Then there was Makhno, the trade union anarchist and his Jewish assistant, Voline, who were active in the Crimea and southern Ukraine. Makhno was a real anarchist, he used to gallop by with his horses pulling little carriages called *tachanki* and waving a black flag."

His beliefs were clear enough, but when they passed through the little Jewish rural communities, his men ransacked everything, raped and murdered.

The groups may have been interchangeable and persecuted one another, and without exception, they all devastated the villages, those ten or twelve Jewish villages near the one where my father was (Zholta, Kuschinsk, Zlochistaia and the rest), organizing pogroms "officially."

In 1918/1919, some of the young men from my father's village decided to defend themselves and hoped to join the partisans in the village graveyard, building armed barricades among the graves.

"The bandits sent two or three spies to see if we had any defenses, and they saw us and came back with some cavalrymen and killed all the defenders."

"What happened to you?"

He smiles and says: "I hid behind the graves with five or six others and we all got away. Besides, the bandits were being chased by another group led by General Grigoriev, he was an aristocrat and a counter-revolutionary, and he gave his cossacks the freedom to plunder and destroy every house they came to."

Behind Grigoriev there was another group, Bolsheviks this time, who were following them to "clean up the bandits in the village." Some of the partisans were caught and shot by the river bank.

"Sometimes even the Bolsheviks killed us and ransacked the place, because it was chaos then. Later they imposed some sort of order, and when the Civil War ended, the pogroms stopped too."

When peace was restored to the region, only thirty percent of the inhabitants of those agricultural communities founded by the czar for the Jews were left.

From *Cláper*[1]

Alicia Freilich de Segal

[The Father][2] I'm happy. Through the clean mirror, as through pure crystal, I see that at last, yes, at last the sun is setting and the first evening star has come out. Shabbat ends but my night begins. All I want to do is walk and walk … .

I'm leaving you, my dear village, and you're seeing me off without knowing it. There is such excitement in your shabby narrow streets. This time Isaac and Pesha are the ones being led to the house of prayers. She will have to dance around him seven times before they shatter the glass in remembrance of the destruction of the temple in the Holy Land by the evilness of Titus the Roman. Cursed be his name! After hearing the noise and seeing the shards of glass, then and only then will they be man and wife according to the laws of our Arbiter, Creator of the Universe.

You know something? It's unusual for a month to go by without a wedding in my village. Nu? I guess even in Paradise it's not good to be alone. Why did I decide to leave at the end of this Shabbat and not another? I've waited long enough, and the moment of destiny we forge for ourselves has arrived for me … .

But I have to pretend and hurry without rushing. Thank God nobody notices as long as my mouth laughs and my legs dance by themselves, which is of course what happens to everyone in my village when there is a wedding. If I let myself be dragged into the merriment and forget my trip, I'll have to wait until next fall and that's too far away; after all, I'm no longer a boy.

Is it true what they say, that a person's nature changes every seven years? If it is, then I've already shed my skin three times and I have reached the perfect age to break out of the shell forever. Forever? Do

1 Published in 1998 by University of New Mexico Press, Albuquerque, NM, USA. Translated from the Spanish by Joan E. Friedman.

2 The novel *Cláper* is constructed of two parallel, alternating monologues—those of a father who left his village in Poland after the First World War to emigrate to the Americas, and of his daughter who comes of age in Venezuela in the 1960s. The identities of the speakers have been added, in brackets, to this excerpt from the novel.

any of us ever really abandon forever the place where we're born and play as children?

A little while ago, on Yom Kippur, as I circled my head three times with the sacrificial rooster—and yelled out the exorcism louder than a crazy man would—I offered God this animal as a substitute for my sins. The bird will go to its death, that's what *capurot* is, after all, while I shall live a long and peaceful life in America. Amen!

Oy yoy yoy! Here comes Meilaj the mute.—Whew! He just passed. Thank you, my sweet little God, for your help. That good simpleton has very sharp eyes and with this full moon Luckily he didn't see me. He was so absorbed with his whistling, announcing the wedding and inviting all Christians to come and see the beautiful bride. Have you ever seen an ugly bride? Everyone praises such beautiful happiness! So, while performing his assignment with virtuosity, the whistler didn't notice me, leaving, with a knapsack over my shoulders.

As I pass the temple, I've got to walk more slowly. Awaiting the predestined couple, the wide open main door allows me to see the Ark, which holds its treasure, the Holy Scrolls, on the very same dais where—oy yoy yoy!—so often, I've accompanied my Pappinyu at sunrise and sunset prayers.

God sits above and arranges it so that here, below, male and female may be joined at a chosen time. I know that all weddings are parties, but today the room looks more glittering than ever before. A couple of weeks ago from nobody knew where came a strange painter who decorated these blessed walls. And he never even charged us a cent! And, what's even more unbelievable, the drawings are intact!

I would look at him in silence because he was a man of few words. But one afternoon I took him some cider and sweet dough with raisins and he spoke! He was fleeing France. He just wanted to breathe once again the air of Liozno, in Russia, where his family lives. But, when he realized how far away it was, he chose to remain in Lendov with us— "Almost the same"—he said, smiling, never once taking his eyes off the enormous rooster he was coloring blue.

Magical! That's what it was. Magical! Without any books, he knew exactly how to draw the feathers of all kinds of different creatures! From his brushes emanated a violin with wings, and green priests suspended in midair above roofs, and a seven-branched candelabra flying

like a burning bramble, and a yellow lion and red cows, and gigantic moons, without a single word. Colored shapes with soul!

The entire town was shaken. So? Nu? Who was this stranger? Marcus Chagalovich or Sagalij he called himself, I no longer remember. Of course the village divided into two irreconcilable camps. One accused him of being a profligate and a sinner because of the irreverence with which he depicted the Sacred Commentaries. "Downright pagan!" The other said he had given a false name. They pointed him out as one of the anonymous Just Men who in every era come to redeem the world. Of course that would explain why he knew more about the Laws than our own venerable teacher Aaron.

Anyway, the artist was scared off by the whispers and all the gossips. After three days, probably to avoid being cursed by them—God forbid!—without even saying good-bye, or even leaving a single footprint, he disappeared into the night, just as I am doing now, along the very same long road … .

[The Daughter] Luminous was the morning of her inauguration into the world! Without crossing checkpoints or oceans, and while living under the same familial roof, she took the road that divided Neighborhood from Milky Way.

She was not moved by her parents' objections nor, for that matter, did she share their mourning over the distant, yet to them, ever present news about the Suez Canal situation. Goodness, the way they moaned and carried on! You'd think these were their very own personal problems or something … .

The tree-lined path that leads to the main building with its high oval clock is both border and path to her liberation. There is a lot to see and many to be seen by. In order to accomplish this, she'll have to sway her hips and get rid of that skinny slouching profile, that "good-girl walk," Mom would say. A brave heroine, she had dared to break out of the family padlock, the collegiate gates, and the community fences in order to go beyond this door and enter the foremost university. God, does that sound great! Now she must walk proudly and provocatively in keeping with the mood of her deed.

At last! Left behind are those gaudy reproductions of Marc Chagall that hang all over the living and dining room walls. Where does Father

get this obsession for buying any trinket that imitates the painter? Must be his small-town taste; like all hicks, he mistakes junk for real art. Real art is these stained glass windows, which, on this particular morning, shed a special light, bringing them into harmony with the modern architecture all around it. What beauty! A splendid open gallery offers her famous muralists, painters, and sculptors in quantities that go far beyond her artistic appreciation, yet is a most fitting place in which to experience this radical moment dividing her existence.

And the school building? Is it really this two-storied gray box? It looks more like a convent. What cold and penumbral classrooms! Ah, but behind the building, what a glorious field of furry green grass! Why are the walls so bare? No color, not even a line. In fact, nothing hints at the presence of young bright students everywhere.

"They put us up here in this dorm run by nuns, but it's only temporary," explains Cristina Doglio.

The animated voices of the freshmen break the still silence:

"Hey, what's up?"

"Schedule's out ..."

"Who's teaching philosophy?"

"We get to choose from English, Italian, French, and German!"

"Wow! Look at the syllabus for Intro to Literature. That's a lot of work."

Yes, it's a new and exciting pleasure. Left behind is the daily, cloistered existence of her home in San Leopoldino. Here is an open universe without walls, so varied, it offers itself unconditionally to her every wish. No wonder the school motto is "This lighthouse is here to conquer darkness."

<p style="text-align:center">***</p>

[The Father] *Oy gottenyu!* When will I finally be able to leave Lendov? From afar I see Pinchas Gros, the only one of us who lives among the Gentiles and in the very center of town. He's a common man who doesn't even know how to write his name and celebrates the Sabbath alone. I must admit he sure has a great talent for fixing watches and glasses. So why does he live alone? And with a big goat in his backyard? They even use him to threaten children and sinners; after all, who could bear being locked up with that enormous beast and all the noise he makes?

I still have to cross the worn-out wooden bridge where young lovers walk arm in arm, until around midnight, when Don Josu lets loose his dogs and the lovers rush back to the drugstore. From the street, the lovers look through the open window and enjoy the concert.—Oh, I forgot to tell you, the drugstore houses the only piano in town, a treasure that none of us ever really saw but guessed was there. We all managed, at some point, to hear its notes. Standing in front of the colored containers of the drugstore, each heard a different melody. Know what I mean? Only the town priest could enter that house of enchantment. Dressed in priestly garb, he used to go very often to the house with the piano. What did the priest do there? Was he by any chance a privileged cherub? Tell you the truth, I always thought that what interested him was the pharmacist's wife … . And now where do I hide? Out of Guitzer Street comes Batcha and her crude husband, that chicken guzzler. *Oy veis meir!* That's all I need! Bitter as bile that woman is. Why, she'd cut off my hand with her kitchen knife if she so much as suspected that I had said they're not among the best of families. Save me, sweet God! And please don't let the lovers of the mill see me either … . Ay, ay! One night, I too dreamt of love while caressing Janala's blonde braid, inhaling her clean dress, her knotted kerchief, and her bare lips! From that intimacy at the mill, thank God, not one was ever left pregnant, God forgive! …

Farewell, Pappinyu and Mommala! May no evil ever befall you. Without saying good-bye, without hugs or kisses, your son goes away but does not leave you … .

[The Daughter] She got rid of them. She never felt they were real men anyway. Little Jacobs, Moisheles, young Reubens. Always together since primary school. No comparison to these university hunks! Those others were sexless siblings. Angels and seraphs. Soulmates. Was any of them ever like these guys here? Machos with their meaningful glances and provocative gestures? That one over there, for instance, he could be in a Hollywood movie. He's got a Gregory Peck air about him! Ah! and the one next to him! Wow! He's the spitting image of Victor Mature! And what about that hunk of a professor? Exactly like Jorge Negrete! Slim, dark, elegant mustache, reminds me of my Charro singing:

Allá en el Rancho Grande allá donde viv-if-a
Había una ranch-er-iita que alegre me deci-aa
Que alegre me deci-aaaaaa.

Back there in the big raa-anch, hack there where I once liiii-i-ved
There was a rancherita who joyfully would saaaaaa-ay
Who joyfully would saaaaa-ay … .

All this guy needs is a pistol and a big sombrero! My Mexican Charro's got nothing on him … .

Ahhh, those matinee movies at the Rex and the afternoon ones at the Anuaco! Great but lasted barely ninety minutes whereas university life will be four years of handsome men parading deliciously before her. Farewell my old-fashioned parents! At last I'm a free little bird!

[The Father] Some hours earlier, during the pause between afternoon and evening prayers, as I counted the minutes, anguished by my upcoming departure, our humble house of God was a boiling cauldron. The faithful were gathering in small circles, as if they were still at their market stalls. They were busy arguing: How many had actually died in the Great War? How many had we lost when General Piłsudski repelled the Russian army at the battle of Vistula?

"We should not have participated. That was a big imperialist war and some of our people sympathized with the Bolsheviks."

"That's nonsense! Didn't we give the Polish legions a Henry Barwinski?"

"Yes, we did, so what? They paid us well for that one, didn't they, idiot?"

"Did you already forget that we were accused shortly after, and still to this very day, of spying for the Russians? Have they quit calling us rightists and anti-Polish?"

"You're the one who's an idiot. You don't even know that the Polish parliament protested that falsehood."

"Nu, so it protested, so? Did anything change? Why? Why do we have to serve in an army where we are always watched and never trusted?"

"Friends, friends. Don't insult each other, please, it's Shabbos!"

"I believe that nothing about this country should be far from our concerns."

"C'mon, we've been here for centuries and we're now citizens of the Polish Republic."

"Any alternatives, stupid? There is maybe somewhere else for us to go to?"

"Maybe."

"Yeah, sure."

"Nu, you stay here then. You'd rather put up with the slaughter of your brothers, the burning of your miserable little houses, and the fact that your sons will never be able to study in a Polish school than suffer a little hunger in the Holy Land or even over there in America. Yes, gentlemen, and in exchange for all the advantages you enjoy here, you have to give your blood to their wars! We're citizens, right? That's what you're saying, right? Sure … You poor misguided souls."

"Can you suggest a better place? Can you? Then let's leave right away!"

"There must be some place on the face of this earth where there are no swords or Cossacks or savage thieves. …"

Their yarmulkes seem about to explode with all the shouting and shoving and even hitting at times, believe me! But the cantor's deep and tender voice calls them back to prayer marking the end of the Sabbath and once again, they turn meek before the splendor of the supplication. I, on the other hand, without arguing, am leaving: Momma, Poppa, I really don't want to be either hero or martyr on the Polish battlefield or anybody else's for that matter. I want to live and die my life for me … .

[The Daughter] One afternoon, two months later, the students crowded together in the corridors to surround a bald young man with deep green eyes. At the same time, another one, thin, but with a noble expression on his face, is taken upstairs.

The group drowns them in hugs and tears. Even Professor Miguel Rosbaum, always isolated in his cubicle and covered in book dust, runs to embrace them. And Father Hernando, one of the most reserved students, talks on and on as never before.

"Who are they, Father Cornejo?"

"Famous people."

"From TV? movies?"

"The resistance. They're survivors … ."

"And what are they doing here?"

"Jesus, girl, are you Venezuelan?"

"Yes, by birth, and you?"

"Well, I was born in Spain but I, for one, know that the UN protested the exile of these young people. Also, that General Tarugo—what am I saying?—Marcos Pérez Jiménez, the president himself, was forced to grant them visas even though one is an active member of the Communist Party and the other of Democratic Action Party. But, I've already said too much, my child. Around here, by God, even the walls have ears."

For seventeen years she had been insulated from her surroundings. Who among her people took part in those passionate struggles for freedom, liberty, the sorrow of exile and jail, the excitement of a hastily called meeting against the dictator? Being a real citizen meant finding refuge for the democratic activists: distributing food and books to the opposition, whatever sublime task she might be entrusted with. Such a noble cause justified the total giving of oneself, and she would eagerly sacrifice herself for this Venezuela of hers.

Dad and Mom didn't have to find out. Why should they? What good would it do? Voluntarily isolated, they would die of worry if they knew. It was too late for them to accept the demands of a new life. How could these ignorant Polish peasants ever understand, these peasants whose work week is a universe limited to a taxi route—from Plaza La Rueda to the corner of Carmelitas—from shop to home and vice versa? How could they possibly understand?

[The Father] Dear Poppa and Momma,

I ask you: If the Polish Gentiles win all the wars they start and will start, what do I ever gain? Quite the opposite. I'm neither Catholic, Ukrainian, Communist, or even Lithuanian. I'll always be the loser because I am who I am. That's why I'm saying good-bye. So long, really. I'm leaving but am not abandoning you. And, anyway, I remain a fervent Pole in one thing: I worry a lot about the Germans

Only yesterday Pappinyu brought home from shul a guest. This one was even poorer than us! But to share Shabbat even with only a piece of onion and herring, water instead of wine, bringing a beggar to the

table, is the opportunity God grants us to praise him. No one should go hungry on his day of rest.

The paternal words proclaim the arrival of my very last Shabbat at home.

"My friend, have you ever studied?"

"Mr. David, he whose name I'm not worthy of mentioning, gave me life to go to school when I was very little, even though my clothes were patched and torn."

"How lucky, my friend! Everyone: wash your hands and let's begin the blessings!"

I envy Poppa's voice, which becomes even more beautiful during the prayer:

> And there was afternoon and there was morning. Sixth day. And heaven and earth were created and all that they contain. And having concluded His creation on the seventh, He rested and sanctified it because on that day He concluded his work. Blessed art thou, oh Eternal God, King of the Universe, who doth create the fruit of the vine. Blessed art thou, Our Lord God, King of the world, who sanctified us and graced us with Your precepts and granted us the Sabbath to sanctify the memory of Your labor of creation … .

As the prayer concludes we raise our glasses:

"Let us drink to life and for peace! Ľchaim! Dear guest, make yourself at home. Tell me, if you know how to study you're already rich, don't you agree?"

"Thank you. Yes, but dear family, you also should know that poverty sticks to your skin and is hard to get rid of. It clouds wisdom. … I did study some, but one has to live … ."

"Excuse me, but poverty is no dishonor. …"

"Maybe not, Rebbe David, but it can make you do bad things … ."

"Yes, but I believe those bad deeds can be erased with the mortar of good deeds."

"You really think so? I think that wherever you go, wherever you stop, poverty is always in the middle of everything. That's what I think."

"Will you do me the honor of eating this gefilte fish? And tell me, my friend, did you ever try to overcome it by working with a paintbrush or with a needle and thread?"

"One has to learn many things, Sir, and, no cloak is big enough to hide poverty."

"Nu, so how do you manage?"

"I manage"

A candelabra with two candles barely sheds enough light upon us, but the vast darkness is illuminated by Poppa's every sentence and the amusing answers of Haim Lisrak, our guest who is poorer than us.

Meanwhile, Momma and my siblings doze off exhausted. Since sunrise they've been throwing sawdust on the floor trying to get it to shine, rubbing out ashes, fetching water at the well, grinding and seasoning fish, getting dressed, blessing the candles Yes, Shabbos relaxes the spirit but sure tires the body!

"Have another drink, dear guest. It's cherry brandy. A little wine lightens the heart. May you never be poor of soul. May your children grow to study Torah, to marry and to do good deeds! L'chaim! As long as there is health"

"You know, Rebbe David, poverty is worse than fifty plagues combined."

"But God only hates the ignorant"

"That may be so, but there is no crueler joke of divine affection than an empty pocket!"

"Listen, Haim, even the poorest beggar with pants full of holes, with seven different coats and seven masks to go begging alms from the same rich man, can enjoy the honor of Shabbat."

"Tsk, tsk, tsk! I certainly won't argue with that, Rebbe. That's why I keep praying: Help me, God, send me the cure, I already have the ailment!"

Outside my whole village is a single chant to God. Aromas of hot cabbage soup seeping into every corner. I don't remember when I decide to put an end to the dialogue. Anyway, if people who have read Scripture and have eaten at the same table don't exchange words on Holy Laws, they might as well kneel before an idol. Besides, these two have already argued enough. Before the prayer of thanksgiving for the food we had just received, I interrupt with a not very sacred matter: I ask Poppa to use his formidable influence to have the district bureaucrats fix the public baths. "Oy yoy yoy, my poor nose, Pappinyu! Phew! I've got to cover it tightly before I can even go in to empty out the waste containers. And you know what all the gossips say? That right next to the women's ritual baths, young ladies become pregnant! Seems that the very learned, who sing sublime harmonies and sway as they extol

the glories of our lord, every night of the week, are actually reading passionate love letters that pretty young girls hand them, while emptying the leftovers into that smelly hovel … deep below this mystical village. … Poppa … .

<p style="text-align:center">***</p>

[The Daughter] Was there ever a Sunday without guests at home? First in the house in San José and then the one in San Leopoldino. Any writer, speaker, delegate, or visitor who passed through Caracas was compelled to be a dinner guest in the small and modest apartment in the Edificio de Nuestra Senora del Carmen. A pretty incongruous name for a building that housed people with unusual traditions like ours, and which many a guest had ironically pointed out to their hosts. We lived there since the time Father almost went bankrupt. It was a place full of books, magazines, and phony Chagalls. Its only luxury was an Erard piano reflected in the glass cabinet full of crystal objects. These had been gifts from the Landaus, the Sponkas, the Erders, and others, when they moved into the lovely house on the same street eight years later, the house that had to be sold in a hurry to avoid foreclosure.

Today's luncheon is one of many. This one is given for the writer Isaiah Rainfeld. As usual, Don Maximo had already taken and brought him back from the business area of town: "Because one must try to distribute the books of this known intellectual however one can. Whether those buyers read the hardbound volumes or just use them to decorate their libraries is irrelevant. It's a fundamental act of charity to help a wise man. Besides, we'll need real dollars to pay for the American edition of poems of resistance in the ghettoes.

During the week, the business on Pasaje Benzo between Madrices and Marron streets was in the capable hands of the missus. After all, isn't she the expert in buying and selling bras, half-slips, and panties! Her husband? Oh, he's something else! Culture on agile legs and convincing lips. Yeah, a regular walking encyclopedia. No denying that.

"We sold thirty-six books, Mr. Rainfeld."

"That's great, my friend."

"In three more days, we'll sell all seventy. We'll go to the big tycoons secluded in their enormous mansions."

"It seems to be easier to write books than to sell them, don't you think?"

"Nonsense. Relax. Nobody ever turns me down. No matter where I knock, you saw that yourself. They know that I have never traded with someone else's gold. I am not a smuggler. I don't charge a cent of commission for the sacred labor of helping the learned. Just as I learned from my father, David, may he have found peace … ."

The exquisite banquet the lady of the house prepared, almost at daybreak, overflows on platters. Gefilte fish, chicken soup and matzoh balls, nuts, cakes, grapes. The best of the best. "One must always honor the intellect!"

And now, the moment of truth has arrived. Could there be a better setting to bring up the issue of her great leap?

"Father, tomorrow I'm beginning my studies at the university … ."

"This isn't the moment to discuss …"

"I'm not discussing, I'm notifying."

"Tonight when there are no guests, we'll talk … ."

"Why wait? I already registered and in fact, I'm also going to be teaching at the Colegio Canada."

"I'm embarrassed in front of Mr. Rainfeld, he understands Spanish … you're so obstinate … ."

"That's a fact."

"A daughter of mine? Practically engaged? Should get involved in that dangerous place where Reds hide and the National Security guards go looking for them with guns? That's sacrilege! Please, Mr. Rainfeld, honored guest, excuse us and help yourself to more fish."

Nothing better to dissolve her anger at Father than the Louie Armstrong open air concert at the Concha Acustica de Bello Monte brought from heaven itself just for her! Instead of screams, the sensual poetry of Gershwin's Summerti-i-me and the living is e-ea-sy … .

[The Father] Over there in Lendov, how many strangers had Friday and Saturday meals at my parents' humble table? Impossible to count. Occasionally, the guest might even be a modern freethinker from the city.

"But, Mr. David, Charles Darwin already proved that man is just another animal … ."

"What are you saying, young man? If that's so, then how come not a single animal ever produced a Darwinich, or whatever his name is?"

"Rebbe, he's an English naturalist who, after observing the animal species, determined their degree of evolution. … No, sorry, nothing to do with our God."

"If a horse had something to say, he would speak. …"

"That's not what we're discussing, Mr. David. Beasts have their own way of expressing themselves."

"Yes, yes, they have tongues, that's true, but they cannot say a single blessing!"

"They express themselves in sounds and gestures."

"Young man, the ignorant is not the one who does not know, but the one who scorns divine knowledge. And don't you forget that! A goat has a beard, but that doesn't make it a priest. Does it?"

"Ah! Finally we agree on something. Sir, you do admit then that we are the higher ranked in the animal kingdom?"

"You said that, I didn't. Anyway, before you become too big for your own breeches, young man, remember that butterflies precede you in the kingdom of divine creation! …"

And so they might continue until the moon descended and the sun dazzled us … .

[The Daughter] Ahhhh! Her intoxication continues with the music of Jelly Roll Morton. … The mixture of sweet wine and wrathful words at the end of Mr. Isaiah Rainfeld's reception fueled her tenacious will to face her opponent and pursue the confrontation:

"Father, I beg you! Please try to understand my wish to have a career."

"I understand and cannot tie you to the house, or prohibit you from having an honorable profession. Quite the opposite, I want you to amount to something, not be like me, who never got a diploma, who could not study and so had to earn a living knocking on doors, peddling, selling schmates. What do you want from me, Kindele? I'm afraid for you! In that political environment of atheists!"

"But, Dad, you're not even religious!"

"Yes, I most certainly am, in my own way. It's true I no longer pray every day and I don't do a full fast on Yom Kippur and no doubt because of that my Poppa is turning in his grave. But, I practice my tradition every moment of my life. And, as you well know, I've made a sacred cult

of my mother-tongue, Yiddish. Have you ever known me to sleep away from home, even one night? Do I have children on the streets? Do I get drunk? Gamble? Other women? That's what you're going to be exposed to out there. I'm afraid for you and for your sisters. ..."

"Please, please, try to understand. We can't stay locked up forever. Each of us has to forge her own life! You did it, or have you already forgotten? You broke with your family and crossed oceans!"

"That was very different, young lady! Don't confuse the issues! I stayed back in Lendov, just my feet left! Can you understand that?"

"No, not at all. Anyway, why not just pretend that I'm not leaving San Leopoldino either, just my beautiful legs are running in search of other roads?"

A seemingly never-ending dialogue was being repeated, but she decided that as of this night it was ending. Max's moist eyes and Rifka's long sad face, marked with silent resentment, her leave taking at breakfast.

Would it have been wiser to go to another country? With what money? Maybe she just lacked the courage to cut, really cut that heavy cord

[The Father] As I was telling you, at the end of Shabbat, I'm leaving, without a word. I have a foreboding that I'm saying good-bye forever to Nune the carpenter, Toiba the cripple, and Leib the hunchback. *Oy gottenyu*, how deeply my heart aches for Momma, the blanket that covers all my weaknesses.

And when at last, Lendov is behind me, I jump, practically fly to Magelnitze without spending even a minute in that ugly little town where I used to come so often to buy yarmulkes. Its very smell upsets me. You see, when someone from my village closes their eyes forever, he is wrapped in his talith, covered in straw, and then sent in a carriage to this overcrowded cemetery. Its stench freezes my bones!

"Magelnitze is sacred because it's where the eternal house is," my father used to say. "It's the good place," my mother usually added. You know what I think? I think it's the only place in the entire world where someone from our village has a right to his own little piece of land! That's what I think. And anyway, this business of putting the dead in face down, boy, that really buries a person! Even if they swear to me

that it's the real garden of Eden, and it's where all the dead will be resurrected, I still prefer gardens that are above and not below ground. Above, always above. You know what I mean? Even with all the hunger, plagues, pogroms. Nu, what can I tell you?

I don't stop at Vialorovsker either, because I know for sure that one-eyed Zina lurks right behind that window. Poor girl, she's been waiting for me to become engaged to her for four or five years now. ... I point my face to heaven and cross the main road like a thunderbolt. I couldn't bear to feel her rancorous gaze.

"Get married? But Poppa, I'm just fifteen years old!"

"So what? I got married at the same age and I'm just fine, no?"

"But that's not good enough for me. From a cat a scratch; from a child bride nothing but damnation."

"What are you saying, my boychick? To get up early and marry early never hurt anyone. You'll have a good dowry and time to study Scripture."

"Pappinyu, you know why the bear dances? Because he has no wife. Give him one and he'll stop dancing. They sing that one at the market, Poppa."

"But it's a lie, because a husband is like a king and all couples are fine after a year or so."

"No, no, and no. It's never too late to marry or to die, Pappinyu."

"*Oy veis meir!* May the one whose name is blessed forgive your affront, my son! You're very stubborn and I worry night and day about how you'll end up."

And while he wails, pulling hairs out of his long black beard, I run away to help Momma with the town fair where she buys us used clothes

[The Daughter] That whole week was full of tension and whispers. Finally, on Friday night, when the rest of the family sleeps, he speaks. He looks worried.

"Where does one begin such unpleasant business? My dear sweet daughter, I want to consult you on a very delicate matter." In a low voice: "Please don't get upset. But ah ... Manuel Rabinovich, the engineer, destined to be your husband, and from such a good family too,

grandson of wise people! Well, anyway, he asked for a dowry, a house, car, office, and if possible, some cash. ..."

The father, knowing full well his daughter's wickedly complicated personality, has to tell her the whole truth. ... Should he get a bank loan? What does she think?

Well, I'm not surprised. It is customary, after all. The problem is I still like him even after six months. Elegant, handsome, first kiss and out together, in a group, of course, to places like that fabulous Montmartre in Baruta with its European music and the naughty Pasapoga with its mambos and guarachas.

"Thanks for the warning, Dad. If I were you, I wouldn't do anything." Of course in historical terms, a dowry was after all a justifiable institution even under a Marxist focus ... but it had nothing to do with love. "Tell me, Dad, how much did you make when you married?"

"Your mother with three cotton dresses. ..."

"Well, that's just about what I think you should fork over ...

At times, Max could seem primitive and abrupt in his reactions, but he had never been a good peddler. He was unable to sell his daughter. His smile, overflowing with impishness, signed a pact of complicity On that point at least, there was never any argument.

[The Father] It's a long way to Warsaw. And to be honest, it was none too sweet. But then again, I guess it could have been worse. On the way to Przytyk and Góra Kalwaria, I befriended a couple of coachmen. I've heard it said that God should protect us from forced exile and from coachmen, but, even though these were pretty rough guys, I could tell they weren't totally stupid. Look, these unfortunate men travel for so long facing their horses, after a while they themselves become like animals.

Anyway, I really liked Nisale, the frisky one. After listening to all my Oy yoy yoyings over my calf pains, one afternoon he asked me: "Tell me, young sir, you seem quite learned, what do we really need our legs for? After all, to Hebrew school we are taken, to our wedding we are driven, to our grave we are carried, to the temple we never go, and in front of all pretty Gentile girls we prostrate ourselves So, what do you think, do we need them for anything?"

"Yes, Nisale. We need them to take us to America the Golden!"

He remained pensive. Probably not half as old as he looked with those smooth toothless gums. I took great care to keep to myself my ideas about the feet being the very center of a penitent's soul. Like Joel, the bearded one dressed in rags, who showed up one day at my village. "May his body be feverish for nine years!" "A pox on him!" "He should only grow like an onion, with his head buried in the ground!" they all cursed him. Only a few of the women gave him some stale bread and water, moved by his misfortune.

To make a long story short, Momma, teary eyed, tells me about the great Joel, born in the big city of Vilna, whose voice, at thirteen, was already legendary throughout the country. He sang the prayers with the virtuosity of the chosen. One day a famous Gentile composer hears him at an event and, overwhelmed, begs the parents to allow him to be the child's teacher. Years later, while in the capital singing profane tunes, Joel meets Katiuska, a Polish princess. They fall madly in love. So at the age of twenty-two, Joel abandons his singing career and, rejected by his people, he who had been so pious and devout decides to atone for his sins. He goes from village to village dragging himself to each and every little broken down house until he gets to ours. What grief his broken down body bears! And even you two, my very own parents, watch him suspiciously between the slits of the window shutters.

Dear parents, in this letter I can finally tell you that as I felt his child-like face and white hair wandering feverishly around the alleys of my childhood, I was more frightened than I had ever been in my life. A leper without sores.

I was reminded of the story of the king and the two men who guarded his orchard, one blind and one crippled: "I see some delicious ripe fruit but I can't reach it with only one leg," says the cripple.

"So what do you need two legs for? If you stand on my shoulders, we'll both eat juicy apples. I don't need eyes to taste them. Why should you need two legs?"

And that's exactly what they did. When the king found out, he questioned his guards.

"Your Highness, how could it have been me? I can't climb or walk."

"Do you believe, your Worship, that I could have picked them without seeing?"

The king ordered the cripple to get on the shoulders of the blind man and then sentenced both to die.

THE HOUSE OF MEMORY | *The Family Tree*

Body and soul must always go together, Poppa. I have finally realized that if succumbing to pleasure sickens one's head, then one ends up with pain like Joel's and in an asylum in Warsaw. I will never be a cantor like my brother, nor a mohel like you, Pappinyu, much less one of those chosen to study God's words fifteen hours a day. Now and with this letter, I can finally tell you one of the reasons I left home without kissing you good-bye. Please try to understand. Just like you can't dance at two weddings at the same time, I don't want to separate my heart from my head. Poppa, Momma, dear little brothers and sisters, please don't cry when you think of me … .

"That's what we need our feet for, Nisale, to save ourselves in America … ."

From *The Book of Memories*[1]

Ana María Shua

Almost Like America

Grandfather was skinny when he crossed the ocean. He was real skinny and young, too, and he wasn't a grandfather before leaving Tomachevo to cross the ocean. Grandfather didn't want to come. No one wanted to come here. This wasn't exactly America. It was a poor runner-up. It was dangerous for women. They were put to work as whores. But Granny wasn't a whore, she worked as a seamstress. Back then, men here wore large white scarves that were embroidered.

"You mean handkerchiefs that you put in your pocket? Embroidered handkerchiefs for blowing your nose?"

"Large handkerchiefs like the ones you wear around your neck. White scarves, they said. Can't you hear?"

Grandfather was never persecuted. Grandfather wanted to build America, but not this America, the other one, you know, the real one, the one up north. He was a tailor's apprentice and he was always well dressed. He'd wear those Russian smocks buttoned at the neck and the baggy pants buttoned down at the ankle (like the Cossacks wear in the Russian ballets), made of thick, well-tailored cloth.

And that's the way you'd find Grandfather dressed in Poland, where it was always cold and where everyone ate potatoes. But he was also a deserter. Potatoes on Monday, potatoes on Tuesday, potatoes on Wednesday, potatoes on Thursday, potatoes on Friday, and on Saturdays … ah!, that was something different! Saturdays! On Saturdays, fried eggs and potatoes. One would think that Grandfather would've hated potatoes and, with all that meat in America, he'd never have to eat potatoes again. But potatoes are what he liked best. On Saturdays, fried eggs and potatoes.

1 Published in 1998 by University of New Mexico Press, Albuquerque, NM, USA. Translated from the Spanish by Dick Gerdes.

"Which army did Grandfather desert from?"

"Who knows? Poland was full of armies. There was the czar's army, the Red army, the Polish army, the Polish National Guard. And the Poles supported the Red army and the German army. They all came and went and fought among themselves."

Then one day Grandfather was drafted. It was wartime. Grandfather didn't want to go to war, he wanted to go to America. His fiancée didn't want him to go either, she wanted him to marry her. So he deserted and hid in her house. He hid there for a year, right in her bedroom. And in her bed, too? Grandfather did that? What was he waiting for? He was waiting for the right document. He waited for anyone who got sick, or who might have an accident and die. He was always wearing his nice suit, hiding in his fiancée's house, and waiting for someone to die young so he could buy his identity papers, a nifty legal document belonging to someone who hadn't deserted.

"And what was his fiancée's house like on the outside?"

"It was a house just like any other house."

"And what was his fiancée's house like on the inside?"

"There's a picture of it in the Book of Memories. There's a rug on the ground, and on the rug there's a table, and on the table there's a sewing machine, and around the table there are some chairs, and behind them there's a large piece of furniture made of dark wood, maybe an armoire. And to one side of the table there's a rocking chair and on the other side an armchair."

"Are there pictures on the walls?"

"There weren't any pictures because there were no walls. And around the rug, everything was white, pure white, because it was sitting on the snow. And that's the way his fiancée's house was on the inside. There wasn't enough light inside to take a picture, so they took everything outside and put it in the snow."

Gedalia Rimetka died fairly young and he had a mustache. Grandfather took his identity papers to the American consulate, the real one, the one up north, but they turned him down. Gedalia hadn't died young

enough; he just wasn't young enough to be my grandfather. It was always cold in Poland, and it was always snowing. When the snow melted, everything turned to mud. Even the mud was cold.

Grandfather crossed through the mud in Tomachevo, but he really wanted to cross the ocean. So he went to the consulate of this poor America where, he was told, they didn't pay much attention, they didn't understand anything, it was all the same to them. That's America too, but not quite. What's important is to leave Europe, to be able to cross the ocean. Then it'll be easy to get from one America to the other America.

They didn't pay much attention, or they didn't care, or they didn't understand anything, and so Grandfather got ready to cross the ocean. Grandfather Gedalia Rimetka—always elegantly dressed but a little too skinny—boarded the ship in Odessa and started the crossing. They ate the skins of the potatoes, too. Potatoes, however, are full of carbo-hydrates. Why, then, was Grandfather so skinny? Because he only ate potatoes, and only a few at that.

"Are you sure it was Odessa? Immigrants didn't leave from Odessa? Check the Book of Memories, what does it say?"

"The Book of Memories says that when Grandfather Gedalia board-ed ship he was seventeen years old and wore a short-brimmed hat."

The ocean was wide, the ship was Italian. The men slept together in the hold. Was it called the bilge? Grandfather Gedalia didn't know the word *bilge*. Everyone but he vomited everywhere. Gedalia, who was tall and skinny, watched his ship-brothers vomit. There were Polish and Russian travelers, and Italians who had gotten on in Genoa. They ate a lot of pasta on board the ship. Lots of macaroni and potato dump-lings, but no ravioli. Round pasta, flat pasta, Bologna-style fettuccine with meat sauce, or pesto. That's why by the time Grandfather reached America he wasn't skinny anymore. He gained forty pounds in twenty days. Grandfather ate a lot of pasta but he never got sick. After they reached Brazil, he also ate a lot of bananas.

They arrived first to Pernambuco, where there were lots of black and Indian people, and it was hot. Grandfather didn't like it there. "This is America?" his fellow travelers asked. They felt deceived. Give up

that mud for this mud? Doesn't look promising. Hot mud in America instead of cold mud in Poland? And so they loaded up with bananas. At first they were green, then they turned yellow. Large bunches of mysterious bananas. And that's how a young, skinny, adventurous kid left Odessa and how a dour and fat Grandfather Gedalia arrived in Buenos Aires. He always refused to eat strawberries. They're everywhere in the forests. Bananas are another matter.

"And those on the ship who ate according to the Jewish religion, what did they eat?"

"Those on the ship who ate according to the Jewish religion didn't eat."

And, finally, they arrived. Buenos Aires was a much more acceptable America. It was comparable to Warsaw. It was a real city. He stayed at a hotel for immigrants. Friends were waiting for him. It was cold, not as bad as Poland, but a lot colder than it is now. The cold that the immigrants felt was another type of cold. They would stuff newspapers inside their clothes to stay warm. Newspapers kept you warm, like this, underneath your shirt, yep, whole newspapers.

He lived for a short time in Entre Rios, where the Jewish communities had been established. It was cold there too, especially in the mornings. His fingers would get stiff, numb from the cold, as he milked the cows. Yes, Grandfather wasn't elegant anymore. Grandfather Gedalia was good at making suits, he knew how to cut cloth and sew, but he didn't know how to milk cows or harvest flax. On the other hand, he knew how to ride a horse. And he quickly learned how to eat barbecued meat.

Afterward he went to the city. Then he sent for Granny, who had been waiting for him in Tomachevo, and he didn't put her to work as a whore but as a seamstress. Then he earned a lot of money. Then he collapsed and died.

"What do you mean, collapsed? Didn't Grandfather Gedalia survive that collapse? Applying hot and cold presses?"

"Grandfather Gedalia survived one collapse but died from another. That's life for you."

Grandfather, said Aunt Judith, was a son of a bitch and he shit all over us. Uncle Pucho said Aunt Judith was a liar and had a dirty mouth. Uncle Pucho never did like women with dirty mouths.

The Name Rimetka

The original Gedalia, the one who died in Poland, the one whose identity papers Grandfather purchased, the one who had died fairly young so that Grandfather's face would coincide with the one in the picture, but not sufficiently young enough to convince the consulate authorities of the real America, the one up north, well, that Gedalia was never called Rimetka exactly.

The surname Rimetka was the result of a combination of auditory expertise and orthographic arbitrariness of some civil servant who attempted to decipher a document written in another language by providing his own interpretation of a surname that he thought a foreigner from Poland should have, which occurred at the time he was taking down Grandfather Gedalia's personal information for the purpose of making his Argentine identification card.

Like so many other immigrants, the Rimetka family had acquired an intensely national name, a truly indigenous product, much more authentically Argentine than a correctly spelled Spanish surname, because Rimetka never existed in Grandfather's homeland, or in the original language or, for that matter, in any other country or time in history.

About Grandfather Gedalia's Personality

Grandfather Gedalia never wavered in his habits. Every day at five o'clock in the afternoon he would have a cup of English tea at the Richmond Café on Florida Street, where he would sit with his friends and watch the women go by.

Not once did he ever set foot in the Richmond on Florida Street. He always went to the Lion Bar instead.

It's possible that Grandfather never set foot in the Richmond on Florida Street (to set foot inside, in the strictest sense of the word) because he always sat at a table on the sidewalk outside. Perhaps he might have set foot inside the premises because he had to go to the

bathroom. You might think he would have sat inside when it rained, but that's not true either. He simply didn't go there when it rained because the women wouldn't be out walking.

Grandfather Gedalia would go to the Richmond Café and the Lion Bar because he was a moneylender and he had clients at both places. He would meet his Jewish clients at the Lion Bar and the others at the Richmond Café.

Grandfather Gedalia never charged interest on loans to Jewish people because it simply didn't look right. But he also never loaned anything to anyone without charging interest.

They never let moneylenders frequent the Lion Bar.

That's not true.

After he got older, Grandfather Gedalia would meet with his clients in the Pumpernickel, a snack bar that sold hamburgers. Grandfather Gedalia didn't like hamburgers, but he liked the Pumpernickel, mainly because they didn't have waiters and he could spend as long as he liked there without having to buy anything.

Pumpernickel almost rhymes with *kuentenik*. *Kuentenik* means something like moneylender.

Kuentenik doesn't have anything to do with the word moneylender.

Kuentenik is a type of peddler.

In addition to being a moneylender, Grandfather Gedalia was also a *kuentenik*. But he earned more money as a moneylender. As a *kuentenik* he had to do his work on a bicycle until he could afford to buy his first car.

Let's say Grandfather Gedalia would meet with other men in a bar or a coffee shop. They were probably his clients because Grandfather Gedalia never had any friends. There is no doubt that he would watch the women go by. Is everything right so far? Do you agree with what we've said?

No. Grandfather Gedalia was quite charming. He had lots of friends. Most of his friends were immigrants, like him, but he also had some Argentine friends. He was especially proud of them. Not every immigrant had those types of friends.

Many years later, when Grandfather Gedalia would meet someone who was a son of an immigrant he would immediately ask his name and then go on to say that when he was coming over on the ship he had met someone by that same name. Whoever talked to him for the first

time found him to be quite charming and would begin questioning him at length about this person he had met in order to see if he or she was part of their family.

Grandfather Gedalia was always terribly stingy.

Grandfather Gedalia was not always terribly stingy.

When Grandfather Gedalia was young, he was very ostentatious. Only after the Crash did he become an Uncle Scrooge.

Grandfather Gedalia became a miser after his children had grown up.

When Grandfather Gedalia bought the Old House he was a real miser about some things, but in others he liked to flaunt his wealth.

Grandfather Gedalia had a Hispano-Suiza automobile and he would take us out for rides in it. And he had a winter coat of beaver skin made for me and we would vacation in Uruguay. In Pocitos. And if you don't believe me, there are pictures to prove it.

It wasn't a Hispano-Suiza, it was a Packard coupe and we called it "the Packard." We always spent vacations in Mar del Plata. And if you don't believe me, there are pictures to prove it.

If you can't see the statues of those seals, you won't be able to tell if it's Mar del Plata.

You can't tell if it's Pocitos either.

Grandfather Gedalia was an admirer of the Kaiser and that's why he gave Uncle Pucho the name of Isaac Guillermo. He also admired the Germans in general until, that is, the Second World War.

After the Second World War he hated and feared the Germans but he still continued to admire them.

Grandfather Gedalia was for Yrigoyen and that's why he named Uncle Silvester Hipólito, after Hipólito Yrigoyen, who was president of Argentina from 1916 to 1922, reelected in 1928, and deposed in 1930. He originally named him Shloime but the civil servant didn't understand, or he acted like he didn't understand.

Grandfather Gedalia wasn't interested in politics.

In Poland, Grandfather Gedalia was a Communist. After he got to Argentina, he became a materialist.

How was he going to be a Communist and still follow the dictates of his religion? After you become a Communist, there's no going back to your religion.

After that he just stopped being religious. But he followed tradition. Mainly to keep up appearances.

If so, then why did he throw Aunt Judith out of the house?

Aunt Judith always annoyed everyone, she was unbearable, she was foul-mouthed, so Grandfather Gedalia gave her the boot using her disrespect for our religion as an excuse. In reality, he was the one who wasn't religious.

That's a lie.

What's a lie? If he didn't give a hoot about religion or politics, why did he give Uncle Pucho a name like Hipólito? Because he didn't care one bit about politics. But he was for Yrigoyen just the same.

When Granny would say something, Grandfather Gedalia would always add: she has a big mouth and so she talks. Other times he would say: there is a saying in the Talmud that goes something like this: when people are born stupid, they'll be that way all their lives and the more they talk the more you can tell how stupid they are. Then he would repeat the saying in Hebrew.

Aunt Clara's grandchildren went to a school that taught Hebrew. After that, whenever he would quote the Talmud, he wouldn't repeat it in Hebrew anymore.

Grandfather Gedalia and Granny loved each other very much.

Grandfather Gedalia and Granny had their own special way of loving each other very much.

When Grandfather Gedalia was hiding in Granny's parents' house in order to escape from the Polish army, he never said "she has a big mouth and so she talks too much."

Whenever Grandfather Gedalia didn't like her food, he would throw it on the floor, say, for instance, when there wasn't enough salt or it wasn't hot enough.

When Grandfather Gedalia would be talking and Granny interrupted him, his eyes would well up with tears and he'd look at her as if to say "Now that I'm finally old and decrepit doesn't anyone show respect anymore?" When Granny would be talking, Grandfather Gedalia interrupted her all the time.

Grandfather Gedalia sold things on credit.

What kind of things?

Anything. It didn't matter what it was, he just had to sell it on credit. Is that what it means to be a peddler?

Yes.

At first he peddled his wares on the street, then he went around on a bicycle. But when he got his first car he didn't use it for work, only to take rides.

Grandfather Gedalia used to say that after riding his bike around all morning, a working man had a right to ask his wife to put salt on his food. This meant that if the food didn't have enough salt, a working man had the right to throw it on the floor.

When Grandfather Gedalia got very old, he couldn't eat salt because it was bad for his blood pressure. But he continued to eat hot food.

Selling things on credit was a peddler's life. All the peddlers belonged to a peddlers' co-op. The wives of the peddlers would take things from the co-op and pay for them at cost. But they never bought anything on credit.

Whenever Grandfather Gedalia would tell a lie, he'd pat his left knee.

Grandfather Gedalia suffered from arthritis in his left knee, which had become swollen and deformed, so he'd pat it all day long.

Grandfather had a business selling cloth in La Boca district. Back then, the cloth stores sold more than just silk, even though there were stores that sold fine yard goods.

Whenever the rainy southeast winds would hit La Boca, everything would become flooded, so Grandfather Gedalia would have his Great Inundation Sales.

He would always put his bolts of cloth high up on the shelves so they wouldn't get wet.

In order to sell the cloth at his Great Inundation Sales, he'd wet them down with a bucket of water from the back of the store.

Was he in business in La Boca before or after?

It was after Grandfather Gedalia quit as a peddler but before he became a moneylender.

Grandfather Gedalia was always a moneylender, even in Poland.

Grandfather Gedalia couldn't have been a moneylender in Poland because when he came over he was still very young.

There are people who charge interest while they're still in their mothers' wombs. There are people who, as they're being born, make mortgage loans to the midwives.

Moneylender is just an elegant way of saying loan shark.

There is nothing elegant about being a moneylender.

Grandfather Gedalia was a loan shark and a moneylender. And ever since he quit making his own clothes, he was anything but elegant.

Grandfather Gedalia favored Uncle Silvester because he always got up early and they'd play dominoes together.

Uncle Silvester was the only one of Grandfather Gedalia's sons with whom he preferred to talk; for instance, he would go into Silvester's bedroom, look at all of his books, and then ask him how much they'd fetch at the flea market.

I've also heard that one Sunday afternoon he took Silvester on the trolley and then bought him a ham sandwich.

Grandfather Gedalia never ate pig's meat because it was against his religion.

Grandfather Gedalia never ate pig's meat in public.

Grandfather Gedalia was a pig.

From *In Search of Marie J.*[1]

Michèle Sarde

On December 19, 2005, sixty years after the event, the author received an email containing a few details regarding the deportation of her grandfather Moïse Benrey, but almost nothing about his wife Marie Jerusalmi. Both were Sephardim—Jews whose ancestors had been banished from Spain at the end of the fifteenth century. The author–narrator set out to discover and reconstruct the tormented journey of her paternal grandmother, from her native Romania and her husband's Bulgaria to Italy. The latter country proved to be an illusory haven from Nazi persecution, from where she was to be deported to Auschwitz, never to return. In two intertwined stories, the narrator travels to many countries to meet with witnesses to the events, and she seeks to retrace the drama-filled life of a young Sephardi woman from eastern Europe in the first half of the twentieth century. The rediscovered story of Marie J. is based on what Jenny (the central figure of an earlier book, *Returning from Silence*[2]) told her daughter, the narrator. Jenny herself intervenes in the narration, while Marie J. and her shadow, the "Lady in Black," comment on the unfolding saga; both are ever-present in this quest.

The two chapters presented here describe the narrator's encounter in Plovdiv with Yvette Kalev, a Bulgarian woman—also a Sephardi—who describes how she and her people survived the Second World War, when Bulgaria was Germany's ally. The people of Bulgaria refused to hand over their citizens to the death camps, although the government did send Jews in the Bulgarian-occupied territories of Thrace and Macedonia to the camps.

Parallel fates: Crossing Nazi Germany

This genetic law engenders a ring of grandmothers, hand in hand down the centuries, beginning in Toledo on the banks of the Tagus, and

1 First published in French in 2019 as *A la recherche de Marie J.* by Editions Julliard, Paris. The publisher is grateful to Editions Julliard for its kind permission to reproduce these translated extracts of the book. Translated from the French by Rupert Swyer.
2 *Revenir du silence*. Paris: Julliard, 2016. To be published by Swan Isle Press in the spring of 2022 with the title *Returning from Silence*.

then across the whole of Europe as far as Plovdiv, on the banks of the
Maritza. My grandmothers started out as pretty young Jewish girls.
[...] They ended up as old Jewish women.

Angel Wagenstein, *Far from Toledo*

*It's a film in black and white, where we see two Jewish women in trains
passing each other, crossing a Germany already turned Nazi. One
is Yvette Kalev, a twenty-year-old Bulgarian off to study literature in
Strasbourg before it's too late. The other is the Lady in Black, a woman
of fifty-six, who is journeying to embrace her sister in Bucharest, before
it's too late.*

SAYS JENNY: WHEN SHE WAS IN PARIS, YOUR GRANDMOTH-
ER NEVER TOOK THE METRO UNESCORTED, THEN SHE CROSSED
EUROPE ALL ALONE IN 1938 TO SEE HER SISTER IN BUCHAREST.
SHE SENSED PERHAPS THAT THIS MIGHT BE THE LAST TIME.

Sunday 11 September [2011]

She arrived around midday in the wisteria- and rose-filled garden of
the hotel in the historic quarter, a tiny lady with piercing black eyes
beneath a hood of white hair. Although she was ninety-two, she had
picked her way through cobbled streets of the old town, wearing an
elegant embroidered red silk jacket. The Lady from Plovdiv kissed me
and drew a gift for me from her bag. An orange and yellow rose, which
she herself had crocheted for me. I was very moved. She too.

I told her about my visit a couple of days earlier to the History
Museum in Sofia, discovering the DNA of Bulgaria's story, between the
"Ottoman yoke"—absent from the official version—and the "National
awakening," much in evidence here in the architecture of the city of
Plovdiv.

I told her how surprised I was to find in this historical memory an
authentic Esther, the heroine of Purim, a fourteenth-century Jewish
queen, this Sarah who emerged from her conversion as Theodora. She
was the mother of the last king of Bulgaria and her daughter, who
became a Muslim, married the Sultan and averted an invasion of the
kingdom.

I did not tell her that this story dovetailed with my constant pre-
occupation: conversion. For Sarah converted to Christianity out of love,
or to become queen. Tamara, her daughter, converted to Islam to stop
the Turks from invading her brother's realm. Paris was worth a mass,

so said our good King Henry IV when he converted to Catholicism. And so did I, the little girl baptized in 1947!

We sat down and Yvette told me straight away that Salomon Benrey would not be coming. He was to be operated on the next day and had gone into hospital. But she said she would tell me everything. First, she wanted to know if we liked her city, the oldest still-inhabited city in Europe, Thracian Philippopolis, the Macedonian king's city, standing on the banks of the Maritza River, which imparts an aura of femininity to this town dozing on its memories.

I recounted our journey the day before along the ancient road to the east, our entry into the town, haunted already by the Myceneans in the second millennium BC, and our arrival at the hotel where we were now meeting. It was a mansion with a shaded garden, adorned with statues and tables where, against a background of daffodil yellow tablecloths, reigned a Byzantine blue, an Ottoman blue profound as a summer's night illuminated by a crescent moon.

I recounted our stroll along Alexandrovska Street, the Roman theater, the church of Sveti Konstantin i Elena with its iconostasis and bishop's throne; our pause in Lamartine's House, where the French poet stayed for three days with his Bulgarian hosts. The French president, François Mitterrand, paid homage there to the renowned nineteenth-century poet and uttered prophetic words for a country then still under Communist rule: "With the other Europe, I feel the doors of the next century will let in the air of freedom, which will enter through the doors and windows."

I told her how we had wandered along the avenues and through the alleys dreaming of lost worlds, with their Byzantine reminiscences and their Christian oratories, their synagogues and mosques, their magnificent *fin de siècle* residences with sculpted ceilings, and wooden shutters on the overhanging upper floors and pediments. I talked of Plovdiv, still Turkish yet wholly Bulgarian, where the parents of our grandparents chatted in old Spanish and read in French. I told how in that moment, in a moment, the awful disappearance of Marie and Moïse had vanished into thin air, in this city from another age, as if nothing had changed, as if the totalitarian regimes with their imprescriptible horrors had never occurred, as if the dead lay in peace in well-tended cemeteries and their ghosts mingled in all simplicity.

The Lady from Plovdiv listened. Then she spoke to me of Salomon, the first Benrey I was due to meet in Bulgaria. "He belongs," she told me, "to a branch that probably shares a common stem with you. He wants to tell you that he had done some research. He is not a direct relative of yours but of Lisa and her sister, whom you will be meeting in Burgas. There was indeed a Moïse in that family, born in a small town near Burgas. He is not your grandfather but a cousin of the father of the two Benrey sisters."

Salomon's itinerary consists of two words: Communist faith. His father was sentenced to fifteen years in prison by the Fascists, not as a Jew but as a Communist. He wanted "to die on his feet." The son had inherited that commitment. He had been happy under the Communists and with them. When they fell, he left for Haifa and his non-Jewish wife had followed him there. They returned to Bulgaria "to grow old and for the healthcare." Of his Judeo-Spanish identity, all he would say was: "We kept the tradition, not the religion."

The Lady from Plovdiv wanted to know everything about Marie and Moïse. She agreed to let me record her on my little tape recorder. She settled into the armchair between two cushions embroidered with geometric figures in the blue of her city, and began speaking.

"I, Yvette Kalev, am the living history of Plovdiv, one of whose streets bears my father's name.

"I was born on December 25, 1919, on the day Jesus was born, but a few centuries later. My father and mother both came from highly respected families in the city.

"My grandmother died when I was four years old; her tomb is still in the Jewish cemetery in Plovdiv. That's lucky, because the Communists got rid of the oldest graves to make way for the tombs of partisans. But we no longer take up much of their space, since there are now barely one hundred and five Jews in the whole town.

"My mother was born in 1893 to a woman who was a citizen of Plovdiv; she too was a Kalev. She did her schooling in French with the Alliance Israélite Universelle. Because she had an artistic temperament, with a talent for painting as well as being highly musical, her parents sent her to Zurich, to the boarding school later described by (Elias) Canetti in his autobiography, *The Tongue Set Free*, which you've no doubt read. My mother studied there for three years.

"When she returned to Plovdiv, it was during the Balkan War and it was time for her to marry. She met Eliezer Kalev and in marrying him she found herself with her grandmother's name. Doubly Kalev. My father was born in 1892, ten years after your grandmother Marie. He too studied at the Alliance. And then he pursued his studies at a school in Vienna.

"My parents were wed in my grandmother's house in 1915. And I now live in the attic of that house. If you close your eyes to what's missing, you can come. It's a place filled with memories ... Both my parents were Italian citizens, like the Canettis. We loved everything from Italy, the songs, opera. We children went to bed in the evening to the sound of music, with the pieces Mama played on the piano to send us to sleep. Italian nationality became problematic with the outbreak of the First World War. All those Jews who did not hold a Bulgarian passport, like my father, were grouped together in Bucharest.

"I was born in 1919 and registered as Yvette Vida Eliezer Kalev. That name is important to me, because later I was obliged to change it. When I was little, we had a big house in Plovdiv with wrought iron Stars of David on the railings and a magnificent garden. We had a lot of servants—ten at least—to help Mama run the house.

"Then came the 1929 crisis, the Great Depression. My father was beside himself at the thought of being unable to repay his debts. I thought of him when you spoke of your grandfather who wanted to repay his in non-devalued money. He went to see the Bulgarian prosecutor and declared himself unable to pay. He was so upset he couldn't express himself properly. I must say, he spoke French, English, Turkish, Italian, Russian, and German perfectly, but he spoke Bulgarian with an accent and didn't pronounce certain letters well."

Yvette spoke the word "sun" in Bulgarian with and without an accent to show how her father spoke.

"In fact, a later audit showed that everything was in order and that he had got his sums wrong. But it was too late."

Yvette did not say why it was too late.

"So, we left our home in the smart neighborhood and abandoned the eight bedrooms, the piano, the beds, the rugs to the creditors. Now it's all in the museum.

"In 1933, we moved into a very modest apartment. My brother had gone to Rome for his final year of medicine. And it was I who bore the misery and the attacks against my father, who had been so naïve, in no

way born to be a banker. I even had to leave the Jewish school because the students, even the professors, made fun of him.

"Because the Alliance no longer existed, I completed the Bulgarian gymnasium for girls with the highest grade, in 1938. After that, I wanted to continue my studies, but without Bulgarian nationality and with my Italian papers, I could not enter the university. So, my mother wrote to the head of a hostel for Israelite girls in Strasbourg. And that's where I went in October 1938, to start my higher education.

"I went with my father to the French embassy in Sofia to complete the formalities for entry into France with an Italian passport. But we were told we did not need a visa. Papa accompanied me to Sofia, I boarded the train without a qualm. We had no idea what was going on in Germany!

"To get to France, I had to change trains in Munich. I said a few words in German and I was allowed to switch to the other train with my suitcase, which contained just one thing: a dictionary. I sat down and watched the scenery as it went by. Shortly before reaching the French border, I got into conversation with my seatmate, who inspired confidence because of his dark eyes and an expression … that looked familiar. You know, in those days there would be kind of mutual recognition. The look? Or instinct? We chatted in French. His family had been arrested, but he had managed to escape. And I told him that I too was Jewish, from Bulgaria.

"At last, we reached the French border, in the little frontier town of Kehl."

— Monsieur, your baggage?

— Mademoiselle, your passport? Italian? You cannot enter France. You don't have a visa.

— What do you mean? I did everything I had to do at the French consulate in Sofia.

— I'm sorry. You've been misinformed. Italian citizens can't enter France without a visa. That's the rule.

— My God, what am I to do?

— There's a French consulate in Karlsruhe. If you've filled in the forms in Sofia, they'll issue you a visa.

"I was terrified, but I tried to stay calm. I asked my fellow traveler:"

— When you reach the other side, would you mind seeing whether there's an Israelite hostel waiting for me? Tell them I've stayed on the other side.

"And there I was, all alone in the middle of nowhere, in this little border station, with no money, with nothing but my dress, my overcoat and the fat dictionary in my suitcase. In *Nazi* Germany.

"And all of a sudden, I remembered that before I left, my mother had knitted me a cardigan—you know how mothers are, Jewish mothers especially—and that she had slipped something inside it. Just in case.
...

"So, I took out my cardigan, found the inside pocket, which I quickly unpicked. What a woman, my mother! There was a tidy sum inside. Then, I noticed everyone was watching me. I went out of the station, walked, and I spotted a little inn. I went up to it. There was a sign that said 'No Jews or dogs.' But I went inside. I asked for a room. I paid and went upstairs, more dead than alive.

"At midnight, there was a knock on the door:"

— Police! Your papers!

"I handed over my Italian passport in the name of Yvette Kalev. And I held my breath."

— It's alright! Good night!

"Early next morning, I still had some money left over. I took the train back to Karlsruhe and took a cab to the French consulate, where I was welcomed like a queen; they embraced me and fed me and everything. They called Sofia, checked that we had gone through the formalities, and in a twinkling of an eye they stamped the visa and wished me a safe journey. This time, crossing the border was a piece of cake. Luckily, because I was stone broke. In Strasbourg, I hailed a cab, gave the address and told the driver they'd pay at the other end.

"At the hostel they were in despair, having heard from my fellow traveler that I was all alone in the heart of Nazi Germany. You can imagine how they welcomed me. The first thing they did was send a telegram to Mama: 'Yvette is safe and sound with us in France.'

"I began studying French literature at the University of Strasbourg two days later. At the Israelite hostel I found a director and an assistant directress, and new acquaintances. I made friends with another student, a Polish girl who invited me to spend the Christmas vacation with her in Warsaw. Her family had money, and it was she who paid for the books, which we shared. I even wrote her name alongside mine in the textbooks from which we studied excerpts from Balzac, Flaubert, and Zola. I still have them as keepsakes. For she never came back. Not

she, nor the director of the hostel, who ended his days in Birkenau, like your grandmother.

"Here, in Bulgaria, we were safe all the same ... But not right away! And I'll tell you what happened next. Our Odyssey."

Yvette took a breath, asked for a coffee, closed her eyes for a few minutes, then took up the story.

En vida kontarlo, *Marie whispers to me. It's an old adage where we come from that means: "Provided we remain alive to tell the story."*

The Ghetto's Little Fiancée

I was glad to see my Yako getting married before the war, says the Lady in Black. I loved Jenny from the start. She was Yvette Kalev's double. Educated and strongminded. And I was happier still when you were born, a month after war was declared. I knew you would outlive me, and not just because it's natural for a granddaughter to outlive her grandmother.

Says Jenny: In Salonica, in 1943, when they realized they were all going to be deported, young couples, whether engaged or just in love, wanted to marry right away so that they would not be alone when they went away. It was a kind of reflex, a life-affirming reflex.

Yvette went on:

"At the start of the 1938 academic year I was able to enroll at the University of Sofia. I lived with a Macedonian family, with all the modern conveniences. But the war came. And then came the persecution, with the Law on National Security. First of all, I was made to change my name. I was called Yvette Kalev. Well, I became Vida Kalef. Why this change of one letter? Because Kalef, in Bulgarian, sounds really Jewish. Kalev, on the other hand, no. So, Kalef. One consonant could govern life and death.

"And then all the prohibitions you know about. Like in France and the other countries in Europe ... On our front door they stuck a little square white card topped with a Star of David, saying: 'Here lives the Jew Kalef'. Oh, and I forgot: forbidden to travel inside the country without police authorization. So, fleeing to a neutral country? Forget it. The Turkish, Swiss, Swedish, Spanish consulates, all closed.

"From April 1941 onward, German planes were allowed to fly through the air space above Mount Vitosha heading west. From that

moment on, as residents of Bulgaria we were enemies of the Allies, and, as Jews, enemies of the Bulgarians. I had to quit my room in Sofia and move into the house of a Jewish family near the synagogue. I had to ask permission to go back to see my parents in Plovdiv. Each time I went to the police, I was treated worse than a dog, threatened that I would 'end up over there,' in the Nazi camps, which were transitioning from concentration to extermination. Luckily, though, we didn't know that.

"At the end of 1942, I left Sofia and went back to Plovdiv, where the old Jewish quarter had become a ghetto. We all had to live together in the Kalef house. I had just one examination in Italian literature to pass in order to graduate. I prepared for my exam in the public library. I would turn up at the door punctually at eight in the morning. Unlike others, the director was well-disposed toward me. He would shut me in a room where he prepared all the books I needed to study. I left the library at closing time and went home on foot, despite the curfew.

"On March 10, 1943, I was awakened at around four in the morning by the sound of soldiers' boots. And I looked out of the window. Opposite, I saw an eminent Jewish physician who had been forced to hand over his home and doctor's office to accommodate the Jews from other districts pending deportation. There were lots of rooms, and in each room lived a family, children, grandmothers, babies, who had been forced out of their homes. Gendarmes with rifles dragged them from their beds, slapped the little ones to wake them up. I can see it still … haggard women in their night shifts, children clinging to them … There was crying, wailing … unbearable.

"My uncle shouted to me through the window: 'Quick, go warn Mr. B., tell him to alert everyone!'

"I rushed outside. Mr. B. was a rich Bulgarian, a very good man who knew lawyers. They gathered immediately and wrote a protest note to the king. Meanwhile, they'd assembled everyone, including my entire family, in the courtyard of the Jewish school, threatening them."

— The railcars are ready. In a few hours, you'll be in them.

"But, thanks to those good people who'd gone to see the king, the prime minister, and the government, early in the afternoon, all the Jews were able to return to their homes. And they weren't likely to forget what had happened to them.

"Nor was I likely to forget …

"At the end of May, I sought permission to go to Sofia to sit my final exam in Italian ..."

— *Nyet.* Finished! You can't travel anymore.

"I went to see the Commissioner, not the inspectors. And I pleaded:

— I'm begging you! It's my final examination. For my diploma!

— What's the use of a diploma? You won't end up in Bulgaria!

"So, I went to the train station and took the train to Sofia. Without permission. Once there, where to go?

"I had a Jewish friend, the daughter of a distinguished attorney who exceptionally had been allowed to go on practicing. My friend greeted me very coolly, saying:"

— We only have four beds. For my father, my mother, my sister and me.

"And her father called the police to inform them that Miss Vida Kalef, not Kalev, had come to stay with him.

"Two hours later, I was summoned to the police precinct by the chief inspector."

— You are an undesirable element. Why are you in Sofia?

— Just to pass a final examination. Please, call my professor of literature. You'll see I'm on the list of candidates.

"And the inspector phoned, and the professor confirmed. So, he said:"

— The barges are waiting to take you away, you, the Jews. And I'd send you there right away. But if you graduate, then the police will take you to the train station and you'll take your train to Plovdiv. After that, it's out of my hands.

"The next day, during the exam, I couldn't utter a word. Everything I had learned slipped away. The examiner looked at me long and hard. Then he gave me a 3.3 out of 6. Enough to pass.

"Forty years later, I went to thank him and honor him. He replied: 'What teacher would not have done as much for the freedom of a human being!'

"A few days later, in Plovdiv, I received my diploma. I'd begun my studies as Yvette Kalev. I graduated as Vida Kalef. But I still have the certificate.

"Meanwhile, the young man who was shortly to become my fiancé had been mobilized in a labor camp, and he was smashing rocks to build roads, like the brother of Hannah C. He too had heard the terrible cries of the Jews from Salonica, Skopje, Kavala, and Pirot, coming through

the open slats on the sides of their cattle trucks. He was a medical student. He cared for the injured, bound up wounds, treated people. It was he who went to Sofia to bring back medicines. Once he couldn't get back on time—he was forbidden to return home till the end of the year. All the others were freed in November, and he didn't come back till the first of January, 1944. When he got back, he told his mother he was sick of being a bachelor. And he heard the young Yvette Kalev was unattached."

Yvette said no more about the beginnings of this relationship. One does not discuss love.

"So, every morning at eight he sent me a signal, I came outside, and we strolled together along the banks of the River Maritza, without kissing. We had two hours before the curfew. In the end, we decided to get engaged. My mother was against it because we came from a prominent—if ruined—family. They, they were richer, but less noble in her eyes. My fiancé was a qualified dentist, but he couldn't work. He lived with his whole family from Plovdiv plus those from Sofia, who had taken refuge with them.

"That day, we had our walk as usual, still without kissing, and well before the 10 a.m. curfew we went into his family home. Opposite the synagogue. And there we came face to face with his mother.

— Mama, we're engaged.

— How lucky you are, *ijiko*, to have won such a learned woman! But come and sit for a moment.

"Everyone in Plovdiv knew I was the only girl to have graduated from college."

— No time. We have to go to Yvette's.

"There, my fiancé asked my parents' permission to kiss me. The Jews have strict morals. Yet, I was almost twenty-five.

"And then we went to see his brother, who made us stay for lunch. I fell asleep at the table. While I dozed, my fiancé asked his sister-in-law's brother—who was allowed to move around the ghetto—to go out and buy all the flowers he could find. And when I awoke and was able to go home, all the balconies were decked out with sprays of exquisitely-scented spring flowers. And everyone embraced me, congratulated me. It was the big event in the ghetto.

"Two months later, my fiancé received a summons. He had to be at the train station on June 13, to be sent to a camp. So, he said to me:

THE HOUSE OF MEMORY | *The Family Tree* 🔖

— We must get married. They're surely going to deport us to Germany. I want to be able to hold your hand till the last minute.

"Married? But where? We couldn't go to the synagogue any longer—even though it was right opposite his house. So, the chief rabbi of Plovdiv decided to hold the religious ceremony at my parents', on June 2 at two in the afternoon. And since we weren't allowed to be outside at that time, we asked for a permit. But not for a marriage, for a funeral, because that, that was authorized.

"I'll show you the Kalev house later. It's still there, even though all the others have been destroyed. An old house with staircases on either side. That's where we were blessed. The groom wore a threadbare old suit and his brother's necktie. We spent the night in a little hotel, dying of hunger because there was nothing to eat. And at midnight, the American planes sent their congratulations ... by bombing Plovdiv ...

"A few days later, I accompanied my husband and my brothers to the train station, with no idea where they were going. And they began their forced labor, building roads. And we waited as the vise slowly loosened its grip.

"On September 9, 1944, the war was over for the Bulgarian people. And for us.

"Why stay in Bulgaria after 1948? Both our families had gone to Israel. We found ourselves alone with our two sons. But my husband was a dentist. He loved his profession. We did make inquiries, though. And then my elder son, who had to give his consent, refused. He was a Communist, like Mr. Benrey. He didn't want to leave ... Now, I'm going to show you the site of the old ghetto."

We follow her into the very ancient Jewish quarter, locked within itself during the dark years; where Jews had been happy, then dispossessed of everything.

— Here is my grandmother's house, now a butcher's shop ... And there ... look ... that's the front porch of my home, where I lived for part of my childhood and where we had to return with the whole family, where I married clandestinely because we weren't allowed outside.

I lay the orange and green rose, which Yvette had knitted for me with her ninety-two-year-old fingers, before the Star of David on the Kalev house, and Rodrigo takes a photo.

— There is the home of the Jewish physician when I gave the alert ... and here is where my husband lived, opposite the synagogue, which

can't be seen from the street but has a garden around it. I have planted a tree in it, and I've fought to have the synagogue restored … . Imagine this tiny ghetto, just a handful of streets teeming with people stifling in overcrowded houses, even sleeping in the toilets, under threat of deportation, not allowed to work, nor to study, to love or to live.

On the square where the lumber merchant used to be, wretched Roma people with children in rags occupy rundown houses, abandoned by their former occupants in the migration of 1948.

— You must excuse me now, but I'm exhausted.

We walk with Yvette back to her street. Suddenly, she stops, turns around, hugs me and whispers:

— The Shoah haunts me … more and more …

— Me too!

— Adieu.

— Adieu.

Then she goes on her way without looking back. I gaze after her a long while, her tiny fragile silhouette, gradually disappearing into the radiant sunshine of this lovely morning in Plovdiv, once the capital of ancient Thrace, where once there were Jews, then none, only Bulgarians.

These two days are as if we had spent our whole lives together, as if she had been my mother, as if we had shared this memory and this dog's life, day after day.

Adieu, Yvette. I vow I'll never forget you and will tell your story, the story of our people, implacably persecuted yet reborn from its thousand-year-old ashes, arising anew.

Marie, for her part, insists on accompanying her right to the end. Then, once more beside me, she whispers:

— You heard that? She was liberated on September 9, 1944. And we, we had just been arrested by the Gestapo. If I had followed her!

— But you were gone already, Nonamali. From Sofia. And from Burgas … where I'm returning you.

From *Tales of the Jewish Girl*[1]

Vilma Faingezicht

Shimele

Shimele!
 Where is Shimele?
 Who is kicking the ball?
 Although he is no longer here, his echoes slip through the air!
 We lived in Alajuela. There, the days were hot and sunny and we, my sister Sharita and I, held the hands of *Shimele*, our father, and a football to hand over at the game that they had dedicated to us. They dedicated many to us, so we had to go all dressed up in our Sunday dresses and, of course, always hand over the ball with which they played. Sunday mornings we met up with the players in a plaza in front of the church.
 Shime belonged to two worlds. Behind him was Poland, his native country. He had not lived in Costa Rica for many years, having arrived as an immigrant from faraway lands. He came from a small city called Zellechov. After much pain and suffering, he became one of the survivors of the Second World War. Life had reserved him this prize, so that during his youth he had to fight, survive, emigrate, start over, work, and always be grateful with what life offered him. Shime was a grateful man, but he was also very young and had always played football. That was one of his passions.
 In the city of his birth, the differences between Jews and Christians were very evident. Nevertheless he, despite being just a boy, had relationships with all the groups who played in the plazas and thus made innumerable friends, but sporting friends, because once the games were done, he returned to his house and all those groups of young footballers looked forward to their next match, as well as their next day of practice. Playing football was one of his great passions, probably because he knew from the start that he was very good on the field: he dominated the ball and was the fastest, he was also agile and strong,

1 First published in 2016 by Editorial Clubdelibros. Translated from the Spanish by Cristina de la Torre.

not to mention daring, exactly that, he was intrepid and immensely courageous. He immediately managed to get everyone to respect him and reserve a special spot for him when forming the town's teams.

With those town teams he toured other nearby cities, to play and defend the local honor, that honor that Jews and gentiles shared as one of the few things they had in common, because religion and prejudices placed them in very different environments and situations in everyday life. Sports, or better said, football, united them and made them feel equal. There were many years of sharing, years of youth, of joy and successes, because they were good, some even said they were very good, and they always won and left the name of the city, as well as their own names, in high esteem, which I believe is really what moves each individual deep inside.

Thus passed the years of Shime's youth, who in the day to day worked in all the family businesses, small stands in Rinek or the market in which they sold merchandise and clothing to farmers. But there were also what he called market days. Those were days on which my father was in charge, from a very young age, starting at twelve years, of loading carts with merchandise, then departing at dawn to go to the places that had market day. Farmers arrived from nearby with all the fresh produce from their farms and many other traders with a great assortment of goods to sell. He remembered those days as times of very hard work for a small boy. He told us how hard it was to prepare and pull those carts with all the merchandise and he told us that the days were long and boring, starting at dawn and ending very late. But they were times of family work, of sacrifice and commitment. The family consisted of everyone and each person was responsible for his or her tasks, whatever they were. Shime did not complain, he always was grateful for the life he had to live. Of course, he also possessed some skills with which life had favored him and that made him feel very proud: he was a great athlete, but he also had a magnificent voice and so sang and prayed like an angel, and he was aware of his talents.

Prayers, in the house and in the synagogue, were part of his curriculum: he always liked to sing, he liked to sing almost every day and, given this gift, he decided he was going to teach Sharita to sing, as it seemed she had been endowed with a good voice.

That is how he brought his love for football from Poland—no one can ever take our loves away from us. Moved by that predilection, he

took my sister and me to public plazas on Sundays so that we could hand over the balls at the games that were dedicated to us, and he would jump in and play for a while. From his native Poland, he had also brought his voice, which could never be taken from him. That voice always grew richer; it was part of his patrimony.

I've arrived at the conclusion that true patrimony is that which no one can take away from us, that which we carry in an intrinsic manner and that which we ourselves can develop and perfect. We have it within us, no one can touch it or suppress it.

This is how we saw him sing, pray, and play football. Through the years, my father became integrated using the qualities with which he created a world first in Poland and then in Costa Rica. He lived in both places, in small towns like Zellechov and Alajuela, cities that I have turned into sister cities, with so many destinies in common and so many witnesses affirming "that Shimele passed through here and he was my great friend."

That is what the owners of the pharmacy in Zellechov told me when I went to visit in the years of peace and liberty. Without me needing to ask any questions, they began to tell me about the games and successes of the football team, both on the town's soccer pitch and in neighboring cities. And the stars, of course, were Shimele and his great, great friend, the owner of the pharmacy. These are indeed marvelous memories of life!

Where Did My Childhood Go?

Where did my childhood go? Where did that small girl, shy and smiling, gentle and affectionate, go? That is how my mother said I was, that is how she remembered me. She remembered so many episodes that did not register in my memory. With my mother's reminiscences, I began to recognize stories and events that helped me discover a little more about that girl, memories that helped me to find out details about her personality. With her memories I began to know myself. What more can you tell me of that girl, of that girl who was me?

I see myself in school on the first day of classes. I had to be strong. I had to say that I was not scared. My mother took me all the way to the desk. I can still see every corner of the classroom. I can still feel the cold that ran through my entire body when she left me sitting there. She

asked me sweetly if I was okay, and I told her of course, not to worry. These words were my customary answer so that she would not suffer and so that she could leave tranquilly. As soon as she turned the corner and left, as soon as I knew that she had gone, I lay my face on the desk and began to cry.

How clearly I can still see that moment! It is one of those memories that marks us for our entire lives. It is the moment in which we begin to face the loneliness of our existence. There we are, facing the world alone, alone in the midst of unknown people watching what we do, what we say, and how we behave.

I was so frightened, and in addition to not being very talkative, I found the classroom space—with its four walls and its many desks occupied by scared little girls about to begin wailing—to be terrifying. And at the front an unknown lady, a lady who said she was the teacher and whom we had to call "niña". Niña Delfinita was her name.

I remember a window beside the teacher's desk, very close to the chalkboard, with violet plants in bloom. That was surprising! As surprising as the memories of the anguish I experienced at that moment which remained recorded in my soul. At the same time, all those memories bring with them a certain feeling of salvation. Those purple shades of the violets brought joy to my life forevermore. Suddenly, amid my weeping and sadness, someone took hold of my shoulders.

— Blimale, Blimale, what's wrong? Why are you sad?

My mother had returned. She hugged me and caressed me. She knew that I needed her, she knew all along that my apparent bravery was usually an act. Thus my soul was marked for eternity, with her hugs, with her affection, and with the color of the violets.

She remembered her school years, when she was a little girl in Zellechov, a small town in Poland. In those times and in those countries, not all Jewish children attended school. Some parents preferred to leave them at home, because they were also afraid, very afraid, but that was a different fear ... and she remembered it.

In the schools in Poland, the Jewish children were intimidated and beaten by the Catholic children. That was a rather regular custom. They had to go prepared and see who would be the brave one who dared to be the defender, the one who was not afraid and could face the Poles who attacked them.

This was indeed a different kind of fear, and my mother knew it. But upon leaving me alone at the school she could not avoid the uncertainty of not knowing what I would experience among so many strangers.

But Costa Rica was different and she immediately began to realize this. The people were friendly and affectionate and in the school the teacher was like a second mother, attending to and protecting her students. I rapidly adapted and began to love Niña Delfinita.

After the first day of classes, I see everything happen as if in a dream. Then I am holding my mother's hand and it is the end of the year already and the school's closing activities are about to begin. Those moments were so exciting that they cannot be forgotten. I am dressed in costume like a cute little animal and she takes me to the performance hall, in an important theater in the city of Alajuela, located behind the Institute, a famous and prestigious education center in the city. But the best part of that night and what remained etched in my heart was the search for the bag of gifts at the end of the ceremony. Each girl had to bring a little memento for each of her classmates, and the teacher prepared a bag with each of our names on it on it and put all the presents that had been brought for us inside it.

The emotion I felt while looking for my bag still makes me tremble with joy, the moment I saw the enormous brown bag full of gifts, with my name written in big letters on it, I grasped it in my hands and went back to my mother; she hugged me and we began to walk down the sidewalks, passing through Central Park on the way to our house.

—Blimale, are you happy? Did you like the end-of-year party? She asked me.

My child's face said it all. I clung with one hand to my mother and with the other tightly held my bag of presents and she … she thought that it was like a dream to be able to walk freely and tranquilly through the streets of Alajuela hand in hand with her young daughter, and so she gave thanks again to life for having permitted her to arrive and live in these tropical lands.

Sailing Down the Rhine[1]

Sonia Guralnik

The air is warm and still there is no breeze, the trees hold their breath; everything is motionless waiting for the last passengers.

At the end of the dock a bus appears, advancing slowly until it stops by the boat.

A very tall woman is the first to step down. She wears thick-lensed glasses.

"Good morning, Frau Braun."

"Good morning, Captain."

"Allow me. I am going to count the tickets."

She notes his blue jacket, his white cap, under which some gray hair peeks out. The captain has fine lips, which are sketched between two vertical folds. He is young still, in this youth of gold buttons—just how old might he be? He has just grown a fine mustache, which he dyes black, that's for sure.

The little old women appear at the bus's door and begin to step down with great difficulty. Some lean on canes, others walk two-by-two, in a slow march. All wear lace-up boots, all have twisted legs, but each one presents her deformed hips in a different manner: at times the knees come together, at others they are incredibly separated. Those who have long legs wear short boots like a child's and those who have legs like short parentheses wear tall boots like a hunter's.

"I'm not getting on board!" one of them says. "The Rhine's water isn't as clear as it used to be. It's dirty." And she crosses her arms.

Another whispers, "I don't want to go. I get so seasick on boats."

An old woman uses a parasol to keep the sun, glaring from the street, away from her face. She squints constantly.

"Hurry up! Hurry up!" orders Frau Braun, clapping her hands. "The boat is waiting for us."

There's a yellowish old woman who wears a wide-brimmed hat and gloves. Someone makes fun of her.

1 Translated from the Spanish by Martha Manier.

"I never go outside unless I'm correctly dressed," she says, straightening out her gloves, "or else I could be confused with the servants."

They have placed four wheelchairs on the deck.

Madame Grete is quite fine. She wears a tiara in her hair and an ocher-colored shawl on top of her overcoat.

"Everyone here?" the captain asks.

"Everyone!" shouts Frau Braun from below. And she pushes onto the gangplank the old woman who gets seasick.

The old women sit in two lines on the main deck. They have been promised hot chocolate if they behave themselves. They hold hands and begin to sing with shrill little voices as the boat departs.

Their voices, growing faint as the noise of the motor increases, are suddenly drowned out.

The boat has left behind the houses and the suburbs with their chimneys, parks, bridges, and sown fields.

A young woman on board sells postcards to the tourists. Approaching the old women, she suddenly seems to grow older.

"They are postcards from the war. This is how Cologne was after the bombing raids. Only the great cathedral was saved," she tells them, and she passes the cards close to their eyes so they can see but not touch.

At noon, Frau Braun holds her chin high and makes the old women move on up to the top deck to get some sun. They all hold hands: "Hänschen Klein, ging allein," they sing as they move along. Madame Katz goes through her purse: her glasses must be there in the bottom. Madame Ursula hasn't been able to locate her teeth. Someone has taken them. How is she ever going to sip chocolate and nibble pastries?

They have stolen Madame Grete's watch.

"There's a thief among you," Frau Braun says, shaking her index finger. Then she turns to the captain, explaining to him, "they get confused, they imagine days, things, dates, they forget ..."

"I don't forget," thinks Madame Katz. She bows her head to rid herself of the formless memory that has hounded her ever since she entered the nursing home. She has seen this woman somewhere else. Where? How can she remember? "Wasn't it in the spring of ..."

Suddenly her memory is invaded by the warmth of her daughter's body, and everything clouds over in a rush of unstoppable tears. She sits up quite straight. Again she goes through her purse. Who could

possibly have taken my glasses? She is sure she had opened the drawer to get them before she left on the outing.

"I can live without my glasses. I no longer read," she thinks. And thinks.

Frau Braun converses with the captain.

She is sixty, tall and strong; her short hair grows quickly. No one knows she was a torturer in the concentration camps. Nor does anyone have any reason to know. The old women fear her. That helps her maintain discipline. She is capable of tiny tortures that leave no telltale marks: she hid Madame Ursula's dentures, and she just threw Madame Katz's glasses into the river. Up her sleeve she has Madame Crete's watch and soon she will drop it into the milk. She will add salt to the chocolate, but no one will find out because old women frequently imagine things and besides, they never say anything during the commission's annual inspection at the Paradise Home.

Madame Katz continues to contemplate the captain. There is something about him that seems false, like this boat and this sunny, happy day. She looks at him more intently and suddenly a light illuminates her old eyelids: the black mustache is a fake. Mustache. MUSTACHE. That's it! The jailer at Bergen-Belsen. They called her Mustache. My God. They say she shaved every day, but even so a shadow appeared at noon. It's noon now. Hardly daring to do so, she looks over at Frau Braun, who has the sun in her face. …

"She took Annie from me," Madame Katz thinks with great difficulty. She pushes back the thick tears that come up from the pit of her stomach, the sharp-edged sobs that pierce the feelings of everything she has lived.

"No, you just can't imagine how they are," Frau Braun is talking to the captain. "They forget their way, it's difficult to manage them. At times they become mischievous like mice. …"

The captain looks at her.

Madame Katz has made up her mind. She shouts: "Frau Braun is the torturer at Bergen-Belsen! Frau Braun is MUSTACHE!"

Like the rustle of dry straw, the old women's voices begin:

"Where were you during the war?"

"In many places. And you?"

"I was also in Bergen-Belsen."

"In Auschwitz."

"I was in Dachau."

The old women roll up their sleeves.

"In Ravensbruck."

"I was also in Auschwitz."

"My parents were never buried."

One of the women tries to stand up. She is the one with the bowed legs and short boots. She falls. Madame Ursula begins to cry and shout.

Madame Grete stammers, trying to get the situation in hand, so that they'll listen to her, that's why she's the queen. She will do the talking.

They all mill around Madame Katz, while the old women farther back keep asking questions, still not understanding what is happening. Madame Katz drills on with her voice low and her perfect punctuation, each syllable distinct: "*She* is the one who mixes up our boots, *she* is the one who takes away our fresh bread and leaves us the scraps before we enter the dining room, *she* steals and destroys our glasses, *she* is the one who puts salt in our chocolate, *she* is the one who turns off the heat when you are shivering in the darkness. Ursula, *she* is the one who shouts behind our backs, the practical jokes, she calls them. *She* is the one who cuts the historical items from the paper, she is the one who tore my Annie away from me through the bars, in pieces she tore her from me.

In the distance, Frau Braun pounds her hands together, distractedly. Definitely, this captain is very nice.

"Go wash your hands," she orders halfheartedly. And she turns back to the captain, commenting, "Look how their hands are stained with freckles. There is no way to hide these women's age once you see their hands."

The captain has gone up to the bridge.

Madame Katz keeps talking in a hoarse quiver. The old women nod to each phrase. Finally, she says, "It will be after lunch." The whisper travels throughout the boat, the wrinkled whisper that is not heard.

Once again, the old women have taken each other by the hands. But this time a current of life runs through them. The old branches straighten in the storm. Where were you, Auschwitz, my brother, Bergen-Belsen, my brother, on the third day they broke our legs. "Rheumatism," the reports called it after the war, what a laugh, rheumatism, my legs, the ones I used to show off and get whatever I wanted, and now they are turned outward.

Madame Ursula, afraid, her new skirt dragging across the floor, repeating, "Quickly, quickly, she's coming." They pull her up and head off to the dining room. They can't wait any longer. All follow the movements of Madame Katz.

"Would you all please do me a favor and hurry up!" Frau Braun howls, planting herself before them with her hands on her hips. Madame Katz approaches and with her sharpened wrinkles says: "No. First we will form a circle and sing a round. Ready!"

> Hänschen klein
> Ging allein
> In die weite
> Welt hinein! ...[2]

The captain and two crewmen have looked for Frau Braun for a long time now and with no luck. The captain has to take charge of the old women. The boat has arrived in Koblenz.

2 "Little Hans/went alone/into the wide/world! ..."

Rojl Eisips[1]

Teresa Porzecanski

Well, that's why I'm still carrying that awful letter in my pocket. Now and then its existence fills me with a dark longing to hold it again, to grasp the worn-out envelope in my hand. Then I slide my hand in, bit by bit, terrified, as if it were a trap. Since I really don't want to find it, I wish that my pocket's shapeless emptiness would push my hand into a corner.

But when I get home in the middle of the dense, rush-hour traffic, and an incomprehensible buzzing zigzags through my ears, and I know that I'm about to give in, that I'll really give in, I head straight for that envelope. I search for it quickly in my jacket. Touching it gives me an almost sanguine feeling of peace and quiet.

I silently repeat the name of Rojl Eisips, as if doing so would wing her on back, and I could see her again, in the flesh. Over and over I read the Hebrew letters, almost indecipherable now, as if its writer were forgetting, little by little, the strokes of the remote alphabet, the mazy signs flying from the pen. The envelope—what's left of it—is covered with the traces of fingerprints, with ridges inextricably intermingled and blended.

It's all because I found Rojl Eisips. I found her through the ambiguous directions that a close-lipped Lithuanian cobbler gave me. He managed to recall that he used to have a distant relative with that name, who was paralyzed, or deaf, or a hopeless case, probably the mother of a distant cousin he barely knew, or the child of a disagreeable aunt who used to work in a bank—he couldn't recall the name—on the third floor, accounts department. And I found that old guy, in turn, through a lonely seamstress who specialized in stitching lapels for suits, while I got her address from an former haberdasher, who remembered that once upon a time she had a neighbor—it was when she was living in a pension on Blandengues Street—and the neighbor's name was Rojl Eisips, a cook, and maybe she was still there, full of life and raring to go.

1 Translated from the Spanish by Elizabeth Rosa Horan.

All that, ultimately to come across this moldy woman of indeterminate age. Opening a single eye, suspicious, she stabbed the rancid air of the hallway. "And why would someone be wanting to see me? Me!"

The visiting nurse didn't bother to answer. First she looked over to me, her glance both guilty and sarcastic, with a grimace that curled up and settled in the left-hand corner of her mouth. A minute later, she made a gesture of indifference and left. There I was, facing the wheelchair, while the nurse moved away, unaffected by the clammy corridor.

And then we were alone, Rojl Eisips and I, in that contentious orphanage, the "Asylum for the Old." At that moment the old woman pointed to a chair for me, and made herself comfortable in hers, and I understood that we were, the two of us, looking onto eternity.

"In Jerusalem," I whispered, "right in the oldest part of the stone city," I added, "an old man, selling carpets, handed me a letter with your name and address on it. And he told me: 'It's very urgent. It must reach the hands of Rojl Eisips as soon as possible.' "

"You say it was a stone city, but very, very old?" asked the old woman, in an accent transformed by a variety of origins. And then, suddenly, as if struck by a subversive idea, she said, "Come, tell me everything, the whole truth."

Perhaps her deafness, the sleepy way she had of looking at me, made me realize that she would never understand.

Firmly, I insisted, "I have a letter for you. A letter sent by a simple carpet seller in Jerusalem."

But there suddenly came from her, from some unexpected place within her, a new voice—dark, like a barrel—with which she repeated and repeated her own question, even as she was circling in on some vague plot woven far back in her memory. Then, as if conquered by sudden and credible truth, Rojl Eisips invented laughter—laughter that rose from the pit of her stomach, as if suddenly something in her might split open, giving birth to a whirlwind of light and harmony.

"But of course, of course I know you, Anele," she said, with her new voice. "How could I forget my oldest granddaughter, the slenderest of all the daughters of my daughter Frida, who died in Latvia? Why, that's her face you have, just like your mother's. And those eyes. The very same eyes your foolish father had, God keep them in His glory. Amen."

"No!" I shouted, much upset. "I'm not your granddaughter. I only came to give you this letter." And I extended to her the envelope, an

action that then struck me as ridiculous, even absurd, in the gloominess of that place.

"A letter?" she laughed, motioning it away. "What letter?" Now she was showing her gums, which were almost empty, and as moist as those of a newborn baby. "I don't need any letter to know you. I know very well who you are, Anele. How many times did I feed you and tell you stories, while your mother returned to Latvia to search for that foolish father of yours. He wasn't going to leave Riga until they dragged him out. And they did. In '39."

Suddenly, the indefinable age of the old woman had gone back in time. Her entire body had now expanded, and the beginnings of youth swept over her—over her eyes, small but limpid, and her smile, which became more and more pastoral, until her words were now rushing out all at once, one after the next, scarcely intelligible. Almost without stopping they flowed out, soft and foamy, from between her girlish gums. All her relatives, long since gone, were returning through her in a mad rush for life, suspended in the eyes of Rojl Eisips, which were at once irridescent and flaming with love's ghosts unleashed.

I still managed to gasp: "An old man I met in a store, selling rugs … when he learned that I was returning to Montevideo he scribbled out this letter, and he asked me, he begged me, 'Deliver it to Rojl Eisips. It's urgent,' he told me, 'Rojl Eisips.'"

But now a group of Cossacks had invaded her birthplace, plundering religious objects, setting fire to it, her parents trapped inside. And now her aunt, who sold pastries in a market in Vitesk, had raised the little girl on her own. And now Rojl Eisips reached the port of Montevideo in January of 1922, with a pair of shoes and a small bundle of belongings, enough for her needs, to be a cook on a ranch in Colonia, and later moved to the capital, apartment 8 on Blandengues Street, then giving birth to five wise children by a ghostly husband, now deceased.

It was getting dark outside and Rojl Eisips kept on talking. A vague litany lent rhythm and movement to her words. Over and over the Cossacks were killing her parents. Once again the aunt from Vitesk was making pastries to sell in the market. Then a ship appeared on the horizon of the port, and a fifteen-year-old girl wearing a head scarf descended, toiling in a multitude of dishes and kitchenware, then becoming pregnant, then bearing five wise children. What had it all

been? Nothing but this summary, spun over and over, with the rhythm of a fable, as afternoon wore into evening.

Sometimes it was Rojl Eisips who was selling the pastries, but at the market in Vilnius, not Vitesk, and her parents were being killed by the Polish police, not in a fire set by Cossacks. Then it was her aunt who arrived in America, with the bundle of clothing and the shoes, and it was the five children who gave birth to Rojl Eisips.

I don't know why I didn't escape. I had to stay. There I remained, hour after hour, hypnotized, until night took over and managed to silence Rojl Eisips. Two obese, machinelike nurses moved her chair. It slid along without a squeak. And as she was leaving, the very last time, head tilted to one side, eyes still glowing, those childlike gums were still spread wide, still telling stories.

And that's why the crumpled letter is still in my pocket. That's why I haven't been able to deliver it. I really don't know why I'm still keeping it, there where I put it the first time, and handling it over and over. Maybe I'm afraid to open it and prove that Rojl Eisips is still here and I'm nestled within her. And the two of us are irretrievably sinking into one sweet, drawn-out sentence.

The Portuguese Synagogue[1]

Angelina Muñiz-Huberman

In Amsterdam the words "Violence has a certain unity of form" suddenly came to me.

In Amsterdam I left the others and walked to the Portuguese synagogue. As if fulfilling a promise. As if seeking solitude: the nostalgia of a place. A place that can only be the center of the universe.

There with the enormous iron candelabrum in the ceiling: that was the exact spot. Where all acts converge. Where such an appointment with destiny is undeniable.

You cannot put off what you know is to happen. What else am I doing in the synagogue but waiting for the encounter?

Sitting on the bench of dark, dense wood. Polished by centuries of clothes rubbing against it. (No one sits down anymore. The visitors stick their heads in quickly and disappear.) (I do sit. I've been sitting for quite some time. So much time that the caretaker grows suspicious. He doesn't know what he suspects, but he suspects something just the same.)

I run my fingers along the smooth wood. I rest. I hear the sounds of the full synagogue. Packed with recent arrivals from Spain and Portugal. After the edict of expulsion.

1 Translated from the Spanish by Martha Manier.

What would have occurred during the Nazi occupation? Silence. Silence. Silence. After all the windows and the urns were broken, one by one. Shattered, smashed to bits, crushed to pieces.

Etty Hillesum walked near the Portuguese synagogue before joining the condemned.

The appointment was sacred.

What are the sounds I hear? Those of half a millennium ago, or those of forty, fifty years ago?

Both.

Etty Hillesum approached God in her own way. But her confusion was great. She didn't know what to do with the evil of the world.

She decided to accept chaos.

To wound herself in order to become part of the nightmare.

Where I am sitting another "I" could have been sitting. One of those women who emigrated and attended the inauguration of the *esnoga* in 1614.

Things can happen or they can not happen.

Here, in the silence of an unvisited temple, the emptiness of God remains. Those who fled the Inquisition found their place and prayed. No one could flee the Nazis.

Two diaries, among others, remained, that of a girl and that of a young woman: Anne Frank and Etty Hillesum. Both interrupted.

I would rather be the woman who sat here centuries ago. Because Anne and Etty are too near. They scratch and tear at me.

That's not true. I wouldn't have wanted to be here in 1614 either. I wouldn't have ever wanted to be in any temple or in any other house of God. And yet, here I am, sitting in the Portuguese synagogue, an empty museum.

I'm the one who's empty.

I no longer have a time in which to live. History has shattered me. I do not believe. I do not think. I do not feel.

And what's worse: I'm not even an automaton.

And the appalling part: I still possess a weak moral code.

If I have no time, it's because I have no place.

I probably shouldn't stay in the synagogue. The caretaker is so anxious and so eager for me to leave that when all is said and done he will have his way. Because what am I doing here?

I am just occupying a small section of a long bench made of solid wood. I have installed myself here and I'm not going to move.

I'm beginning to feel my muscles relax, to feel a laziness, a forgetfulness. As if my body were merging with the wood. As if I were no longer myself. As if I had ceased to exist.

I float and am transported.

I could pass through the glass and become part of the blueness of the sky. The iron bars framing the air prevent me from escaping.

Would the victims have escaped this way?

From the prisons of the Inquisition, from the boxcars, from the barbed wire?

No.

No one escaped.

The executioners escaped.

Although she was a girl, Anne was more mature than Etty. I don't know that for a fact.

Etty was still deceiving herself. She clung to prayers and poetry. To let herself finally be dragged down the path of denial.

Is it true that she tried to pray in the closed Portuguese synagogue?

She could still believe. I no longer can.

Despite the presence of the sacred enclosure: a monument to the divine absence.

I had drawn away from the others: from those who run down the streets, through the museums. And, of course, who pedal their shiny bicycles.

In order to rest in the simple light of the synagogue.

And to take flight.

Images captivate me, and from them I get my ideas. From glass and mirrors (even those veiled by black cloth). From kaleidoscopes and from stained glass windows.

Even though I confuse my memory with the memory of others. Did it happen to you or did it happen to me? Is it your memory or mine?

I don't know my limits very well either. I don't know where I begin and where I am the others. I surprise myself with an imitated gesture, with a word belonging to someone else.

I go from one mimesis to the next.

So I don't know who I am. I just am. One of these possibilities. Nothing that can be concrete. A sketch of a person. Ambiguous, half-traced.

Ah, but it bothers me that they might recognize in me something that is not mine. After all, it's robbery.

Etty aspired to mystical perfection. I can't believe in it. In the midst of the horror, she became as transparent as air.

When she was able to escape, when it was still possible, she avoided it. She said: if my people die, I will die with them. She didn't want to be a survivor or a witness.

She thought to leave a final testimony: squeezed together with the hundreds of Jews who were going to meet their death, through some crack

in the moving train she threw out a card on which she had written: "We go singing to the concentration camp."

But I don't accept it. Today, in this temple of so many tears, I don't accept going off to death singing.
Because it was not a chosen death.
It was an imposed death.
Violence on a whim.
Agony in the name of fun.
Blood spat out.
The body carried to new depths.
The naked scorned.
The soul slashed.

And yet, in the abandoned synagogue there is peace. Prayers are still suspended. In the air.

It's silence.
What else can it be?
Silence.

In the Portuguese synagogue in Amsterdam there are no walls. The space is as vast as the heavenly dome.

Destruction is present.
The end of the world is hanging.
The armies of darkness polish their high, black boots.

The polished, black boot comes down hard on the bare foot.

The soldiers' excrement spreads over the roundness of the earth.

The perfection of the circle is lost.

The Portuguese synagogue of Amsterdam remains.

Those who desecrated humanity descrated themselves first.

They were the ones who swallowed their own vomit.

From the shit they proclaimed purity.

Etty was easily deceived.
 Anne saw the truth.

With a faint breath, both of them shook the paper army.

In the synagogue I want to explain the unexplainable. To reason out the unreasonable.

An invented existence could be so peaceful. Simply to let life go where it ought to go. Follow the natural order of things. Instead of having lived this wretched present moment, to resign myself to imagination.

Not to compare. To choose total separation from reality. And thus, to erase history. No issues, no anecdotes. To sink into the flow of mental images. To turn out the light forever. To turn on the darkness.

Since language doesn't serve to explain. Since the word has been broken. Since systems and institutions are hollow scarecrows. Since the ten just men are nowhere to be found. To what heaven do I rise?

To the one creating the rupture?

From chaos, what can arise?

It's true that I drew away from the others. From those who were traveling with me. From those who are still babbling.

And I sat down here, in the Portuguese synagogue. For such a long time. Such a painful time. To think that one day I would think again, that one day I would understand.

That light would begin to shine in my darkness.

That, like the mystics, I would be granted a revelation.

So that just that idea might endure: I would write on black paper one dark night.

What a desperate coming and going. Gropingly. With the walls receding. Blindly. With the tips of my fingers not feeling a thing.

To think it is possible to embrace the whole world in this warm space of precious woods that is the Portuguese synagogue of Amsterdam.

Amen.

The "Golem"[1]

Rosita Kalina

On the day of his death we all went to see him because we remembered his enormous platinum beard and his black hat, that angular figure of a good-hearted man, like Don Quixote, battling the windmills.

Rebbe Israel always received us without really seeing us. He had a halo over his head and a strap in his hands. He prepared us for our Bar Mitzvah, killed the hens, chickens, and roosters that we brought him twice a week, and when he drank alcohol that was ninety-five proof, perfumed with a few drops of mint extract, from a glass tumbler, just like that and all of a sudden, he'd even dance the *sherele* sometimes. Rebbe Israel lived a block away from the Battleship Spain grocery store in a tumbledown shack with a courtyard for the hens who thrashed around in the middle of their death throes, pools of blood spurting from their jugulars. The courtyard where the animals were dying was grooved and narrow. Toward the back stood a cement basin, always trickling water from a spout to wash away the blood.

Not everything was red at the rebbe's house. Neither could we say that everything was white. When we sat in the schooldesks of the *cheder*,[2] some days the boys and others the girls, papers would fly through the air, fountain pens would dance over our heads, and water would fall from the sky without our knowing how. Everything was miraculous in Rebbe Israel's house, even the big lumps on our heads that he gave us when we forgot to put on our yarmulkes, and the tugs at the long *peyes*[3] of the most religious boys when they did not move earnestly enough while they prayed, or when they made a mistake in pronouncing some word, especially the name of God in reverse, which provoked the fury of the rebbe, who relied on angels to punish us with a wooden rod about half a meter long.

In the rebbe's house no common language was spoken. He spoke to us in Yiddish and we half understood him in Spanish. He trans-

1 Translated from the Spanish by Roberta Gordenstein.
2 A *cheder* is a Jewish religious school for younger children.
3 *Peyes* are long, uncut locks of hair worn in front of the ears, traditionally worn by orthodox Jewish boys prior to their Bar Mitzvahs.

lated the blessings from Hebrew into Yiddish for us, and we acquiesced and repeated, repeated and acquiesced, as if we understood everything completely. In Hebrew we repeated like parrots the passage from the Torah that we'd have to read, and in Yiddish, like parrots, we'd learn the speech that would follow our confirmation when we became thirteen years old.

Sometimes we took revenge on the rebbe's magic and applied our own to him. Rebbe Israel used two talithim,[4] one for everyday use, and another for special prayers. The everyday one was smaller. Talith katan, he called it. He passed it over his head, making it rest on his shoulders, and didn't take it off, even during the summer. When the rebbe sat down, we tied the four long fringes to the seat, and you should have seen the commotion. The hens cackled, the ones who were jumping around in their death throes became quiet in order to hear better, the air wet itself laughing, and the angels discharged their fury with the magic wand, which was sharper and sharper, or with suddenly strengthened hand-slaps, instead of the usual blows.

One day a more elaborate revenge occurred to us: a hen that our mamas squeezed into a sack for us to take to the rebbe, a hen that miraculously passed over a Gillette razor that we pretended not to see between our trembling fingers. We kept the peseta for ourselves in order to go to the Teatro Moderno on Sunday, and it never entered our heads that the poor hen, sacrificed that way, ceased to be kosher, because we had thrown its neck backwards without removing the small feathers, or because we had not recited the brocha before passing her over the blade.

The series of films at the Moderno were like fables: *Rin Tin Tin*, the *Phantom*, the *Lone Eagle*, and *Dracula against the River Lizards*. When Fu Man Chu—the magician—appeared in person, we had to save more money. Then we took fewer hens to the rebbe. Our mothers were happy; they praised our eagerness to carry the bundle for them. They didn't know that our magic was making the hens from the rebbe's house disappear, immediately transferring them to the Friday night table, well-seasoned, tender, and cool, after spending a single night in the refrigerator with a block of ice from our house.

4 A talith is a traditional prayer shawl worn over the head or shoulders by men during morning prayers.

As we were saying, things became very complicated at the rebbe's house. We were twelve boys, all given to magic, and between the rebbe's miracle-working and our own, our Bar Mitzvah preparations were delayed. Of course, we needed six months of study. We had already spent three, and nothing had entered our heads. The pencils continued making pirouettes in the air, the notebooks lost their pages, and every time more water slipped in through the walls, because the rebbe made water spring from the wall at the touch of his magic wand. We always returned home soaked like nocturnal frogs, and our mothers asked, "What happened? You bunch of bums!"

"No, Mama! It's just that the rebbe's basin overflowed and we helped him hold back the waterfall."

We were already halfway through our apprenticeship and we understood less and less each time. Suddenly, a new person appears in the rebbe's house. We look at him with distrust. A rival who knows a lot and has already left us in the dust. He was a small boy, quiet, with a mark on his forehead. Even when we asked him a question, the boy pretended not to understand. He was either very quiet or very foolish, so we did not worry about him and tried to pay more attention to Rebbe Israel's gibberish.

What a curious thing! From the time that boy appeared, we began to place phylacteries[5] on our left arms and on our foreheads. We began to understand the Hebrew a little more, and even what we would have to say in Yiddish. We even asked Mama if she had placed the *mezuzah*[6] correctly on the right-hand side of the door because we discovered that she had put it on backward, so we took it down, opened it to see what it said inside, closed it again to return it to its proper site, and began to kiss it when we entered or left the home.

Meanwhile, the strange boy kept growing and growing each day by leaps and bounds. We realized this because he was stretching out rapidly and we were not. In six months we did not grow even a centimeter, and he, on the other hand, was getting taller with the power of a beanstalk. *Caramba!* We invented a story: we baptized the boy

5 Phylacteries are a set of small leather cases holding slips inscribed with Scripture passages, traditionally fastened to the forehead and left arm by men during morning prayers.

6 A *mezuzah* is a small piece of parchment inscribed with Scripture, placed inside a case and attached to the doorpost of the home, in accordance with Biblical instruction.

"Golem,"[7] because although he understood what we were saying, he never spoke, not even a word. Surely the rebbe had created him with the earth from the little courtyard and the water from the basin, in order to help us with our notebooks, inkwells, and pencils. Unobtrusive, the "golem" moved among us, placed our pens in our hands, kept the pages of our notebooks in order, and even helped the hens to die quickly.

While the "golem" was growing, Rebbe Israel was becoming shorter. Each day he shrank by two or three centimeters, until he managed to measure the same as we did.

But the "golem" grew disproportionately and already managed to touch the ceiling. The reddish stain on his forehead did not disappear, but it no longer caused us any curiosity. We had lost our distrust of him, and his figure did not frighten us. Everything was magic in Rebbe Israel's house.

Finally the long-awaited day of our Bar Mitzvah arrived. Seated with our coreligionists in the first row of the synagogue facing the Canada Dry plant, we waited our turn to be called to read the Torah. Rebbe Israel, at our back, administered affectionate pinches and shoves. We read with devotion the passage where the prophet Elijah rises to heaven in a chariot of fire, and we addressed the congregation in good Yiddish, as good as that which Rebbe Israel spoke and taught.

When days later we went to visit him to bring him a little token of appreciation, the rebbe had recovered his stature, but we did not see the "golem." We wanted to ask him, "Rebbe, where is the 'golem'?" but we thought that perhaps he had died suddenly because there was a great mound of dirt near the basin.

We learned later that the same thing that had happened to us had happened to other groups of young boys. They also saw the "golem." It's a shame that we have already forgotten the Yiddish and the Hebrew, and that Rebbe Israel has died. They covered him with white sheets, and twelve burning candles kept watch over the body, which was laid out on the floor, alongside the desks of the *cheder*. They say that when he died, a red mark appeared on his forehead, like the letter aleph.[8]

But we did not believe it.

7 A golem, in medieval Jewish legend (and associated with cabala, the mystical system of Scriptural interpretation), is a robotlike servant, usually made of clay and brought to life by means of a charm, particularly the name of God.

8 Aleph is the first letter of the Hebrew alphabet, and a powerful sign within the cabalistic system.

Camera Obscura[1]

Angélica Gorodischer

Now it turns out that my grandmother Gertrudis is an important person and it is forbidden to speak badly of her in this household. So, in spite of the fact that I and my entire family have always spoken badly of her, what I have had to do is shut my mouth and not say anything, not even mention her name. I ask you, who understands women? But I really can't complain: my Chaya is the very best there is. Next to her, I'm worth nothing; you have only to see her—like everyone in the community, who began to look at her with desire as soon as she turned fifteen; she was so blond and with those eyes and those manners and the way she has of raising her head, that there was not a single *shachant*[2] who didn't think of marrying her off in a good match, but a very good one, at least to one of the sons of old Saposnik, the one with the automobile repair shop, and by the time she was sixteen my mother-in-law was out of her mind with offers of this, that, and the other, and one had to aim very high. And that same Chaya, who married me and not one of those rich guys—although, frankly, I don't do so badly myself—is prettier at thirty than she was at fifteen, and you'd never know that she has two grown children, Duvedl and Batia, the spitting image of her, except that they have my black eyes; that very Chaya, who is always so sweet and gentle, turned into a wild animal when I said there was no reason the picture of my grandmother Gertrudis had to be on top of the fireplace in a gilded frame with decorations that must have cost her a pretty penny, don't deny it. And that particular photo, too.

"Don't mention that subject again," Chaya told me when I told her to remove it. "Don't even think about it. I put the picture there and that's where it's going to stay."

"All right, fine," I said, "but at least not that photo."

"And what other, tell me that, huh?" she said, "since it's the only one she had taken in her entire life."

"Thank goodness," I said. *"Zi is gevein tzi miss!"*[3]

1 Dedicated to Chela Leyba.
 Translated from the Spanish by Roberta Gordenstein.
2 A *shachant* is a matchmaker.
3 "She was too ugly!"

I don't even want to remember what she replied.

But it's true that my grandmother Gertrudis was ugly, profoundly ugly: short, skinny, dark, bowlegged, cross-eyed, with round glasses that had blackened metal frames and a broken earpiece held together with some pieces of cord twisted together and tied in a knot, always dressed in black from the scarf on her head down to her slippers. In contrast, my grandfather Leon, so handsome, so huge, with that mustache like a king's and dressed like a gentleman, he seems to fill the entire photo, and his eyes gleam like two lanterns. You can barely see my grandmother next to him, which is an advantage. To top it off, she is surrounded by all her children, who were also tall and good-looking, the six boys and two girls: my uncles Aarón, Jaime, Abraham, Salo, and Isidoro, and Samuel, my father, who was the smallest of the boys. And my aunts Sara and Raquel are seated on the ground near my grandfather. And behind them you can see trees and part of the house.

It's a very large photo, on Bristol board, sepia-toned, the way they were in those days, so that the gilded and decorated frame must have been very expensive, and it's not that I pay attention to those things: Chaya knows that she can indulge herself and I have never denied her or my children anything, and as long as I am able, they will have everything and will not be worth less than others—the very idea!

That's why it hurts me to have the photo on the marble fireplace mantel, but of course I can't protest much because it's my fault and only mine for going around talking so much. And why shouldn't a man be able to tell his wife things about his family, you tell me; you could almost say that she has the right to know everything that he knows. And nevertheless, when I told Chaya what my grandmother Gertrudis had done, half in jest, half seriously—I mean in a funny way in order to lessen the importance of the tragedy, and somewhat indignantly, as if to show that I know that what's right is right and that I haven't inherited my grandmother's evil tendencies—when I told her the story one summer night as we were returning from an air-conditioned movie theater and we had bought ice cream cones and were eating them in the kitchen, just the two of us because the children were sleeping, she stopped eating and when I finished she pounded on the table with the spoon and told me she couldn't believe it.

"But it's true," I said. "Of course it's true. It happened just as I told you."

"I know," said Chaya, and she got up and stood next to me with her arms crossed, looking at me angrily. "I know it happened like that, you wouldn't have invented it. What I can't believe is that you are so heartless as to make fun of her and say that she was an evil woman."

"But Chaya," I managed to say.

"No 'but Chaya's' or anything," she shouted at me. "It's a good thing that I didn't learn about this before we got married. A good thing for you, because as far as I'm concerned it's a disgrace to find out at this stage of my life that I'm married to a brute without feelings."

I didn't understand anything, and she left, slamming the door and leaving me alone in the kitchen, alone and wondering what I might have said to make her so furious. I went as far as the door but changed my mind and returned. We've been married ten years and I know her very well, although rarely had I seen her so angry. Better to let her calm down. I ate up what remained of my ice cream and the other one, almost all there, that Chaya had left, placed the ones we had brought for the children in the freezer, wiped the table with the dishcloth, and left the dishes in the sink. I made sure that the door and window opening onto the yard were tightly closed, put out the light, and went to lie down. Chaya was sleeping or pretending she was sleeping. I got into bed and looked at the ceiling, which appeared gray with the light entering through the open window. I touched her lightly: "Chaya, *mein taier meidale*," [4] I said to her, as I did when we were newlyweds.

Nothing. She didn't move or answer me or breathe more deeply or anything. All right, I thought, if she doesn't want to, she doesn't want to, she'll get over it soon. I put my hand back and closed my eyes. I was half asleep when I opened my eyes and saw the gray ceiling again because it seemed to me that I had heard her crying. But I must have been mistaken, it wasn't so serious. I fell asleep for real and by the following morning, it was as if nothing had happened.

But that day, when I return almost at nighttime from my business, tired and hungry, what do I see? That. The portrait of my grandmother Gertrudis, in its gilded frame with decorations on top of the fireplace.

"Where did you find that?" I asked, pointing my finger at it.

4 "Chaya, my dear little girl."

"It was on the shelf above the closet," she told me with a big smile, "with all the photos of you as a child that your mother gave me."

"Oh, no," I said, and stretched out my hands as if to remove it.

"I'm warning you about something, Isaac Rosenberg," she told me very slowly, and I realized she was serious because she always calls me Chaqui like everyone else does, and when she says Isaac, it means she is not very happy, and she had never said it before with my last name, except for one time. "I warn you that if you take that picture away from there, I will leave this house and take the children with me."

She really meant it. I know her. I know she really meant it because that other time she had called me by my first and last name she had also threatened me with leaving, she did that a lot, and we didn't have the children yet, and to tell the truth, things were not the way she thought they were, but it's better not to discuss that subject. I lowered my hands and put them in my pockets and thought that it was just a whim, and all right, let her do whatever she wanted, and that I would try to convince her soon. But I didn't convince her; I never convinced her and the photo remains there. Chaya got over her anger and said, "All right, let's eat. I made a rice kugel."

She makes it with my mother-in-law's recipe, and she knows that I like it enough to eat three servings, and I know that she knows, and she knows that I know that she knows. That's why she had made it that day. I ate only three servings but I couldn't stop wondering why Chaya had behaved that way, why she wanted to have the photo on top of the fireplace, and what was the matter with my grandmother Gertrudis that she caused such an uproar in my house.

Nothing, she had absolutely nothing, not even a name, a good, honest, Jewish name, Sure or Surke, like other people's grandmothers, no, sir: Gertrudis. She never did anything right or on time, not even be born, since my great-grandparents came by ship with three children and my great-grandmother pregnant. They came from Russia, but they had left Germany for Buenos Aires on the *Madrid,* and when the ship docked, at that very moment, my great-grandmother's labor pains began and they thought that my grandmother was going to be born on deck among the trunks and baskets and packages and people coming and going, although they still did not know that the one who was about to be born was a girl. But my great-grandfather and his children had to disembark because almost everyone else had already done so, and my

great-grandmother remained above writhing and watching her family already on Argentine soil, and then it occurred to her that it would be best for her also to disembark so that her son would be an Argentine. Very slowly, little by little, grabbing the railing and with a sailor helping her, she descended. And in the middle of the gangplank, what happens? Yes, just at that moment, in the middle of the gangplank, my grandmother was born. My great-grandmother let herself sink onto the beams and right there, with the help of the German sailor who shouted something that no one understood except the other German sailors, and a woman who ran up the gangplank, my grandmother Gertrudis, my great-grandmother's last child, arrived in the world.

From the very beginning there were problems with her. My grandmother, was she Argentine or was she German? I don't think my grandmother's nationality mattered a bit to either Argentina or Germany, but the immigration officials were overwhelmed with regulations, which said nothing about any similar case, and thus did not know what to do. Besides which it seems that my great-grandmother was becoming more and more of a problem and in spite of having just given birth, she began to shout that her daughter was Argentine—as if anyone could understand what she was shouting and as if with that she were making a gift to the country where she had just arrived, and what a gift.

In the end, she was Argentine—I don't know who resolved this, or how, probably some civil servant who was in a hurry to go for lunch, and they recorded it at the port as an Argentine arriving from Germany, although she had never left there for here, and there was another problem when they asked my great-grandfather her name. They had intended to call the baby Ichiel if it were a boy, but with the pressures of the voyage it had not occurred to them that it might be a girl and a girl also needs a name. My great-grandfather looked at his wife, which it seems he always did whenever he had to make a decision, but her energies had been exhausted with the pains, the pushing, the descent down the gangplank, and the shouts over the nationality of her daughter, who through all this was bellowing on a counter while wrapped in her father's jacket.

"Call her Gertrudis, sir, it's a pretty name," said the immigration official.

"What?" asked my great-grandfather—in Russian, of course.

"My fiancé is named Gertrudis," said the man.

My great-grandfather found out shortly afterward, upon leaving the port with his family, the luggage, and the newborn, what the official had said, because Naum Waisman who had gone to meet them with his two children and car had translated it for him, but by then my grandmother was already named Gertrudis.

"Yes, yes," said my great-grandfather, somewhat disturbed.

"Gertrudis, do you understand? It's a pretty name," said the official.

"Gertrudis," said my great-grandfather, as best as he could, pronouncing the *r*s badly, and so it remained because that's how it was recorded in the port.

About the other troubles, the ones that came after with the civil registration and the birth certificate, it's better not to speak. However, for a time all was quiet and nothing else happened. That is to say, things happened, but my grandmother had nothing to do with it.

It turned out that they stayed with Naum for a month until they got adjusted, and afterward they left for the countryside. There my great-grandfather worked as a farmhand, but in a few years he bought the little farm and made it prosper, at first with the entire family working from sunup to sundown, but later things improved and with hired laborers all went well, so well that he bought a few hectares more until he wound up having a good-sized piece of property.

At that time, my grandmother Gertrudis was fifteen years old and was already horrible-looking. She was cross-eyed from the moment she was born on the gangplank of the German ship, but now she was emaciated and bowlegged and seemed to be mute, so little did she speak. My great-grandfather had a ton of friends in the neighboring countryside and in the town where they went every Friday morning to stay until Saturday night at the home of a first cousin of my great-grandmother. But neither he nor his wife had great hopes of marrying off that ugly and disagreeable daughter—until my grandfather Leon appeared like a blessing from heaven.

My grandfather Leon had not been born on the gangplank of a ship, German or otherwise. He was born as he should be, at home, or more precisely, in his parents' house, and from that moment on, he always did what he should, when he should, and therefore everyone loved him and respected him and no one laughed at him and no one thought he was a disgrace to his family.

He was a widower, childless, when he appeared at my great-grandparents' house, the widower of Ruth Bucman, who had died a year before. It seems that they must have informed my great-grandmother of what this was all about, because she washed and combed and perfumed her daughter and advised her not to speak, although there was no need for that, and to always look at the ground so that he might not notice her crossed eyes, which was useful but also unnecessary, and so that he might see at the same time that she was an innocent and timid girl.

And that's how my grandfather Leon married my grandmother Gertrudis, not in spite of the fact that she was so ugly but precisely because she was so ugly. They say that Ruth Bucman was the prettiest girl in the community, in the entire province, in the whole country, and in all South America. They say she was redheaded and had almond-shaped green eyes and a sinful mouth and very white skin and long, fine hands, and they say that she and my grandfather Leon made such a pair that people would turn around in the street just to stare at them. They also say that she had a devilish temper and she made life impossible for her father, her mother, her sisters and brothers, her sisters-in-law, her nieces and nephews, her neighbors, and the whole town. And for my grandfather Leon as long as he was married to her.

The worst thing was that she bore no children, not even one was she able to give her husband; maybe it was just to spite him, because it seemed that the poison of that woman reached even that far. When she died, my grandfather breathed a sigh of relief, slept two solid days, and when he awakened, he dedicated himself to resting, to polishing his mustache with brilliantine, and to going to town every day on horseback to visit the friends that Ruth had alienated from his house by way of her shouting and bad manners.

But things could not go on that way for long; my grandfather Leon was a real man and he was not made to be alone all his life, besides the fact that the house was falling apart and needed a woman's touch and the fields looked practically abandoned and some people had already begun to take a look calculating that my grandfather was going to sell for almost nothing. That's why, a year after the funeral of his wife, my grandfather decided to get married, and remembering the hell he had experienced with Ruth, he decided to marry the ugliest woman he could find. And he married my grandmother Gertrudis.

The fiesta lasted three days and three nights at my great-grandfather's farm. The musicians took turns playing in the barn and the women were not able to keep up with the cooking, even with the kitchen in the main house, the servants' kitchens and two or three stoves and ovens that had been improvised outside. My great-grandparents outdid themselves gladly. You have to understand that it was a cause for celebration, since they had managed to get out from under such a burden and marry her off to the best candidate for a hundred miles around.

My grandmother did not spend the three days and three nights at the party. The very day after the ceremony, she set to work to put her husband's house in order, and nine months later, my uncle Aarón was born, and a year after that, my uncle Jaime was born, and eleven months later, my uncle Abraham was born, and so on. But she never stopped working. You have to hear the stories my aunt Raquel told of how she got up before dawn and prepared the food for the entire day, cleaned the house, and went out to work in the field; and how she sewed at night while everyone was sleeping and she made their shirts and their trousers and even her sons' and husband's underwear and the daughters' dresses and the sheets and tablecloths and all the linens for the house; and how she prepared candies and preserves for winter, and the way she knew how to drive the animals, bale hay, pack the bales together, and help to load the carts. And all this without saying a word, always silent, always looking at the ground so no one would notice her cross-eyedness. You have to admit that she lightened my grandfather Leon's workload, as small and skinny as she was, because she had the endurance of two men put together. By afternoon my grandfather no longer had anything left to do: he decked himself out and left for town on his best horse, with the deluxe harnesses my grandmother had already fastened on, and since she didn't like to be around people, she remained at the farm and continued her routine, day after day. And so time passed and eight children were born, and my aunts say that even with her labor my grandmother never stayed in bed or missed a single day of work.

That's why what happened was even more terrible. Of course my grandfather Leon was no saint and he liked women and they liked him, and of course some ill-intentioned neighbor woman went to my grandmother with tales, and she didn't say anything or cause a scandal or cry or yell, of course. And the fact that my grandfather suddenly

remembered Ruth Bucman and went around for a few days with his tail between his legs didn't mean that my grandmother should have blamed him for his past deeds. I don't say that he was right, but those are things that a woman knows she has to forgive in a man, and frankly she didn't have the right to do that to my grandfather, she who ought to have been more than grateful because my grandfather had married her. And everything was crueler still if you think about the irony of fate, because my grandfather tried to surprise them all and give all his sons and daughters a present. And I suppose my grandmother Gertrudis too, of course.

One day, while the eight children and my grandfather Leon were eating and my grandmother was coming and going with the casseroles and the platters, my grandfather told them that a traveling photographer had arrived in town, and everyone asked what he was like and what he was doing and how well he took pictures and whose pictures he had taken. And my aunts begged my grandfather to take them to town to take a picture of each one of them. Then my grandfather laughed and said no, he had already spoken with the photographer, and the next day he was going to come to the farm with his cameras and his equipment to take pictures of all of them. My aunts laughed and clapped and kissed my grandfather and began to chatter among themselves to see what dresses they were going to wear, and my uncles said this was all women's foolishness and fancy ideas from the city, but they smoothed their trousers and looked at themselves sideways in the window glass.

And the photographer went out to the countryside and took a picture of all of them, that brown photo on Bristol board that is now on top of the fireplace of my house in a gilded frame with decorations and that Chaya does not allow me to remove from there.

He was blond, the photographer, blond, skinny, not very young, with curly hair, and he limped a lot on his left leg. He sat them all down outside the house, with their best clothing, combed and polished so that it was a pleasure to see them. All of them except my grandmother Gertrudis, who was dressed as always in black and had not even bothered to put on a decent dress. She didn't want to be in the picture and said no so many times that my grandfather Leon was almost convinced and didn't insist anymore. But then the photographer approached my grandmother and said that if anyone had to be in the picture it was she; and she said something to him—I don't know if they told me what it

was and I forgot, or if no one heard and they didn't tell me anything—
and he answered that he knew very well what it was not to want to be
in any photos, or some such thing. I've heard the story many times but
I don't remember the exact words. The thing is that my grandmother
placed herself next to my grandfather, surrounded by their children,
and they remained posed there for a long while and they smiled and
the blond, skinny, and lame photographer took their picture.

My grandfather Leon told the photographer to stay there that night
so that he could develop the photo and the next day he could take some
others. Thus my grandmother fed him that night also. And he told sto-
ries about his work and the towns he had visited, what the people were
like and how they received him and the strange things he had seen or
experienced. And my uncle Aarón always says that he looked at her as
if he were speaking only to her, but who knows if that is true because
he would not have been the only one who realized something was
going on. What definitely is true is that my grandmother Gertrudis sat
down at the table with her family, and that was something she never
did because she always had to have everything ready in the kitchen
while the others were eating in order to serve it on time. After they
finished eating the photographer went outside for a smoke because no
one smoked in that house, and my grandmother brought him a shot of
liquor, and it seems to me, although no one told me this, that the two of
them must have spoken of something.

The next day the photographer spent the entire morning taking pic-
tures: first my grandfather Leon alone, then with the boys, then with
the girls, then with all the boys and girls together, then my aunts alone
with their well-ironed dresses and curled hair. But my grandmother
Gertrudis did not appear, occupied in the dairy and in the house as
always. But I imagined that—I who did not know her, I who had not
been born since my father was a little boy who hadn't met my mother
yet—I imagine her that day, hidden, spying on him from behind some
door left ajar, while the meal was burning on the fire. These are only
my own imaginary wonderings because according to what my aunts
say, she never burned a meal or ignored anything in the house or in
the field.

The photographer developed the photos and ate lunch in the house
and in the afternoon he mounted them on the cardboards with an
engraved border and the date, and my grandfather Leon paid him.

When they finished eating it was already night, and he said good-bye and left the house. He had already loaded everything into the shabby carriage in which he had appeared in town, and from the darkness outside he again shouted good-bye to everyone. My grandfather Leon was happy because the photographer had taken some very good pictures of them, but it did not warrant his accompanying him beyond the door because he had already paid him more for his work than anyone else in town or on the farms. They all went inside and you could hear the horse moving away and then nothing else.

When someone asked about my grandmother Gertrudis—which until today my aunts and uncles argue about because each one says that he was the one who asked—my grandfather Leon said that surely she must be around doing something outside, and a little while later they all went to bed.

But the next morning when they arose, they found the lamps still lit on the tables and the gates left ajar and the door unlocked and unbarred. There was no fire or dinner prepared or breakfast ready or cows milked or water for drinking or for washing or bread baking in the oven or anything at all. My grandmother Gertrudis had run away with the photographer.

So now I ask, am I right or not when I say there is no reason for that picture to be on top of the fireplace of my house? "And if the children ask about it?" I said one day to Chaya.

"We'll see," she said.

They asked, of course they asked, and in front of me. Fortunately, Chaya had the sense not to explain anything. "It's papa's family," she said, "many years ago, when his grandparents were alive. You see? Zeide, Bobe, Uncle Aarón, Uncle Isidoro, Uncle Salo."

And so she continued naming them and pointing to them, one by one, without making any comments. The children got used to the picture and no longer asked anything else.

Even I became accustomed to it. It's not that I agree, no, not that, but I mean that I never notice it anymore, it doesn't attract my attention, unless I am looking for something over there and I have to move the gilded frame with the decorations. One of those times I asked Chaya, who was nearby messing up the shelves of the cupboard: "Are you going to explain to me someday what possessed you to put that picture there?"

She turned around and looked at me. "No," she told me.

I wasn't expecting that. I was expecting a little chuckle and that she would tell me yes, sometime she would tell me, or that she would tell me right now.

"What do you mean, no?"

"No," she told me again without laughing. "If you need me to explain it to you, that means you don't deserve for me to explain it to you."

And that's the way it remained. We found what we were looking for, or maybe not, I don't remember, and Chaya and I never again mentioned the photo of my grandmother Gertrudis on the fireplace with its gilded frame with decorations. But I keep on thinking that it is an insult for a family like mine to have in such a prominent place the photo of someone who seemed like such a good wife, so hard-working, so involved in her home, and who one day ran off with another man, abandoning her husband and children just for spite, for no reason.

The Yom Kippur Light Went Out[1]

Rosa Palatnik

It was dawn on the day of erev Yom Kippur. Just as they did every morning at this hour, church bells pealed mystically through Mirel's low window. A fond memory pressed against Mirel's heart, and she searched longingly in the pale morning sky for a hint of this heartache. It seemed to Mirel that today the dreamy church bells sounded different from the rest of the year ... these bells that she met so gladly every other day seemed today to have an urgent tremor in their peal:

Gim gum gom, gim gum gom ...
It seemed to Mirel that they were calling out:
"Go to shul, go to shul ..."

Mirel had never been an observant Jew, not even in the Old Country. Quite the opposite—out of all the children who lived in her home, she was known as the irreverent one. She was not punctilious about the laws of *kashrut*, she didn't maintain Jewish laws, she did not observe the commandments directed at women. Nevertheless, as a child she had absorbed the majestic trembling of the approach of the High Holy Days, and this remained with her like a holy mystery every year.

Mirel, who had only been in Paris for a short while, still vividly remembered her father's white hands spread over her braided head, blessing her as she ventured into the wide world. His pious lips murmured, "Don't forget who you are ... always remain a Jewish woman."

Mirel went to Paris with a two-year-old child in her arms. She came fighting for her life, quarreling with her own destiny. For weeks and months, she wandered along the happy boulevards of Paris, searching for work that could be brought home. Only eight days ago, a non-Jewish factory owner had taken pity on her. Looking her over from head to toe, he asked her about her background and finally agreed to give her some work to take home. Since that time, her child played

1 Published in 1953 by Monte Scopus, Rio de Janiero, Brazil as part of *Kroshnik-Rio: Dertseylungen*, pp. 194–8. Translated from the Yiddish by Jessica Kirzane.

much more happily, cooing in the dawn like a joyful dove. Her childish laughter cheered the dark hotel room.

In the Old Country, Mirel could always sense the approach of Yom Kippur in the sky's appearance. Even if the sun was shining in all its glory, for her the sky seemed full of sad clouds that were drawn gloomily toward the Seat of Glory to be judged together with all of the sinning souls on the Day of Judgment.

This morning Mirel saw the same Yom Kippur sky of her past, and she thought of how the Jews from home, with their damp *peyes* and white *kitels*, shuffled in their slippers through the streets, drawn to their houses of study. And the women, in colorful dresses with white sashes in their combed wigs, hurried with thick prayer books and thin volumes of *tkhines* under their arms, preparing themselves to cry loudly to everyone they met, wishing everyone they met, even their enemies, a *gmar khsime toyve*.

She also remembered the Yom Kippur eves of her childhood. Her mother brought her to *Kol Nidre* services. When the rabbi from Lublin, Reb Shloymele Eyger, arrived at the *shul*, he was clouded in a religious awe. His pale face with its narrow beard took on an unworldly appearance. With his lyrical voice he sang out the opening tone with pointed sharpness, like a confident conductor certain that he stood before a well-trained orchestra: "*Or Zaruah LaTsadik!*"

Soon, the rabbi raised his pale, gentle arms in supplication: "Master of the Universe, have mercy on Your people Israel!" …

He held his pale face in his white hands. The congregation could sense a cry welling up in his throat. He could no longer speak, and his voice broke apart like a burning spark tossed into a dry barn.

This is how the rabbi's voice kindled the white-clad congregation: "*Or Zaruah LaTsadik!*"

Everyone cried together. The Jews, wrapped in their white *talitot*, bowed and sighed with the rabbi's holy prayers like strong trees bending and creaking under the gathered momentum of a hurricane.

Mirel relived that image in her mind again this morning, and from the impression of that memory she decided to find out how they prayed *Kol Nidre* in Paris.

All day long, Mirel prepared to take part in the passionate prayers. She recognized again the sad clouds, like family, that she remembered from Yom Kippurs past. She decorated her poor room with white curtains, spread a white tablecloth over her little table, and put on a white dress. She prepared Yom Kippur food, and in the evening, when a Yom Kippur mood covered everything, Mirel brought out a large Yom Kippur candle and set it on a box of sand on top of the covered table, remembering how her mother would bless the children before the Yom Kippur wine. She went to her sleeping child's bed and wordlessly held her warm little hands to her breast. Burying her head in the child's little pillow, she quietly sobbed as she fulfilled her *mitzvah*.

Just as she was praying for a better fate for her little girl, a knock on the door tore apart the quiet Yom Kippur scene. A tall non-Jewish man stood by the half-open door with his blond hair tossed to the side, holding a package of women's scarves under his arm. He ordered her with a gruff voice, "Here's your work ... these have to be ready by morning."

Mirel stammered fearfully, "I wanted to go, I must go, I can't do it ..."

Her boss's tall messenger winked at the Yom Kippur candle and spoke ironically, "If you are a worker in Paris and you don't want to go to the factory, then you have to work when your boss asks you to, and not whenever you feel like it. *Au revoir!*"

Mirel stood, frozen, and stole a longing glance at the holiday table, which had been newly sanctified by the earnestness of her God-fearing preparations. She looked at the sewing machine resting quietly in a corner. And then her eyes fell on the disheveled package of work that lay there with the severity of a decree. It made her remember, despite herself, the hungry days and the sleepless nights spent wandering the streets and factories fruitlessly looking for work. And then her gaze fell on her crying, scared child sitting on the little bed. Mirel looked deeply into her child's innocent blue eyes and finally spoke in a raw voice: "I am doing this for you."

Stumbling as though drunk, Mirel approached her covered sewing machine, took off the cloth, and began to turn the wheel, watching as the spool of thread suddenly unraveled. She began to thread the bobbin that stubbornly began to sew. Her eyes fell upon the mirror hanging across from the machine. From there she could see the rising flame of the Yom Kippur candle that suddenly started to spark. And in the

sparks it seemed to her that she saw a world of eyes looking at her, begging something from her. With quick and certain steps Mirel rushed, fleet as a deer, to the covered Yom Kippur table. She hurriedly blew out the Yom Kippur candle.

From *To Breathe Underwater*[1]

Karen Codner Dujovne

To God for the silence.
To the Mirnas's of the world.
To Mary.
And to you, for believing in me.

2:55 a.m.

It is almost three in the morning. Two fifty-five. Alberto snores, I know I will not fall back asleep. I walk into the bathroom, turn on the light, hopefully he does not wake up, put on my robe and slippers, the exact same ones I have worn ever since we got married. I cannot stop thinking about you, your enormous casket, so big it filled half of your living room. Did you know they dressed you in white as if you were finally a bride? You looked stunning, important, something you never wanted, they made you up so much, so much.

In a few hours the sun will rise. In a few hours when the sun starts shining, I will have to let you go, start a new life.

3:01 a.m.

I turn on the boiler, I fetch the chamomile. It is cold, this bench, I stir the tea and think about us, about the times we were here, staring at the sunset while drinking the honeyed infusion. Here I have the yellow notebook, to think it was yours, that once I saw you writing the shopping list on it, you barely could, with your round, tight letters, like you still were in third grade. Now, now I want to let you go, like I did with my brother. At your wake, Chochi insisted so much that I approach the casket, me, the one who had never seen a dead body, we Jews don't look at them, we just wash them. I did not say goodbye to Richi either, you know, I was at the hospital when his *shiva* begun, the mourning days of the Jews. That *shiva* I didn't experience, Mirna. We sat on the floor,

[1] First published in 2015 as *Respirar bajo el agua* by Editorial Cuarto Propio, Santiago, Chile. Translated from the Spanish by the author.

we covered the mirrors and did not even bathe. This is my *shiva* for you, Mirna. I need to say goodbye in my own way, the way only Jenny Goldstein can. How can I let you go without honoring you? I really did not expect to see you dead. Well, I don't know what I thought, but to see you there in the casket in the middle of your living room with Mati's teddy bear, Willy, in your arms, your mother crying …

I just found the aquamarine pen I write with, it was thrown on the floor outside Dana's room. I turned off the lights in the hallway and the silence became louder. Suddenly Matías woke up, mom, what are you doing with that notebook? Go to sleep, I told him, I can't, he said. I took him to bed, lay a while with him. The darkness was absolute, far away I saw a shimmering light.

I saw you dead, Mirna.

I've had it hard these last six months without you here at home, they've been heavy. I knew what was coming, but I couldn't avoid it, I needed you, you made me feel good, at peace, together we spent hours in the kitchen, I think that's why I'm coming up with this *shiva*.

My *shiva* for you. Tonight I will celebrate you.

But, Mirna, I cannot cry for you for seven days, nor can I cover up the mirrors and pictures, sit on the ground, rip my clothes, much less recite the *kaddish* like I did with Richi. I need to do something to let you go forever, that's why I have my *shiva* for you, I will share my world, here I will write life.

Windmill[1]

Myriam Moscona

In the main tent of the circus, the animal tamer lights a wheel on fire so that the tiger can jump through the circle of flames and land on the other side without getting burned. Two benches are arranged, one higher than the other. As in medieval rituals, the people beat their chests. There are men holding monoculars and women wearing hats covered in tulle. The tiger bypasses the obstacles with a grace that is recognized by the hundreds of spectators who scream with pleasure.

The tamer gestures that the final act will commence, and she introduces her head between the tiger's jaws. This is why I ask my father to carry me because I want to feel his arms embracing me in the rising tide of fear. Her luck running out, the tamer falls down on the ground with the tiger on her back ... The scene continues: the tiger remains on the woman's back and is attacking her. An agitated and panting voice can be heard over the loudspeakers: "Ladies and gentlemen ... a doctor, we urgently need a doctor! Can someone in the audience please help."

A river of blood begins to gush from one side of the woman's body. The tiger devours her. The people begin to swarm towards the exit doors, transforming into a violent mob. I don't know how much time passes. A confused sensation of fear floats in the air when an agitated yet falsely tranquil voice erupts from the loudspeakers once again: "Attention everyone. Ladies and gentlemen, the danger has been contained. The show will go on. Return to your seats. You are invited to go back to your places."

The tiger, having already smelled the blood, moves away from the body, its reddened snout beats against the canvas walls. The voice that

1 From the collection entitled, *Tela de Sevoya* (*Onioncloth*), published in 2017 by Les Figues Press, Los Angeles, California, USA. Translated from the Spanish by Celeste Kostopulos-Cooperman.
In the original version, the grandmother, the ringmaster and the inner voice of the narrator speak in Ladino. Their exact words are as follows. Ringmaster: "Senyoras, senyores. No podemos fuyir de muestros destinos, todos estamos moertos, ninyas, ninyos, domadores, fieras. Todos moertos." Grandmother: "Sentites kualo dijeron? Estamos moertos. Nadien te va a matar, sos moerta i tu ... Tu padre está en los ornos, ijika, ande keman a las linguas del avlar". Inner voice: "Sos la última kreatura".

requested calm speaks again: "Ladies and gentlemen, we cannot escape from our destiny. All of us are dead. Children, tamers, and beasts. All are dead." I don't know what more the voice says. I cling to my father's legs so that we can leave the circus as soon as possible, and I feel the tiger closing in on me. I look up to ask him to carry me, but I quickly lose him in the crowd. Instead, I see my grandmother Victoria almost in front of me, and she very gently speaks to me: "Did you hear what they said? We are dead. No one is going to kill you because you are already dead."—"Where is my father? I want to go with him."—"Your father is in the chambers, my child, where they are burning the speaking tongues." I don't know what she is talking about. From there I see the tamer, facedown and wrapped in a crimson cloud. There is no one left. The tiger, the people, my father, my grandmother, everyone has suddenly disappeared, except for me and the dead tamer. A voice deep inside says, "You are the last creature."

And then among the different girls who make up my being, the frightened one stands up, the one whose voice I hear more than I should. As usual, I place my hand on my throat to hear her speak.

Terror speaks inside with an altered voice like that of the *dibuk*, those spirits that are the souls of dead people who occupy the bodies of living beings, forcing the person who is possessed to behave as "other," and speaking through her in different voices.

The voice whispers to me in a raspy but high-pitched tone: "The things you run away from the most are the hardest to avoid."

And then I curl up next to the dead tamer, until I fall asleep.

No More Worries[1]

Clarice Lispector

— Everyone knows that sprinkling salt on the fire or hiding a broom behind the door can get rid of unwelcome guests.

— Everyone knows that a red ribbon tied round the patient's waist can arrest the progress of erysipelas.

— Likewise, if you hang a red handkerchief up in the bedroom, it can cause a vicious attack of measles.

— There is nothing better for curing hiccup than to take nine sips of water without pausing for breath. Or to turn up your sleeves. In the case of an infant, a tiny piece of damp cotton-wool should be placed on its forehead.

— If you bury chayote in the soil early in the morning, it will remove warts.

— If you spill sugar on the table, sprinkle a few grains on your chest and you will almost certainly come into money.

— Spilling salt brings bad luck, unless you throw a little over your left shoulder.

— Touching wood to ward off all evils is something everybody knows.

— To make sure that duck turns out tasty when cooked, it should be plucked in total silence. And to make sure that chicken is really tender and succulent, put three chickpeas or a clove into the pot.

— A seahorse, on the other hand, relieves asthma.

— And anyone with sweaty hands need only catch a toad and hold it for a few seconds and the perspiration will vanish.

— It is common knowledge that crossed knives can provoke a quarrel and the same is true if one passes salt across the table.

— A broken mirror should be thrown into the sea.

— Hats should never be placed on top of a bed or shoes placed under a chair.

— It is always better to put the right shoe on before the left one.

— A lock of hair should be tucked into the hem of a bride's dress.

1 Translated from the Portuguese by Giovanni Pontiero.

— On departing, one should always leave by the same door one entered by.

— Anyone who sweeps the house at night and throws out the rubbish is also in danger of throwing out good fortune.

— When the hem of a dress gets caught accidentally, it is advisable to bite it in order to get a new dress.

— Yellow is the color of leap year.

— In order to safeguard the health of young children, one should tie a tiny sachet round their neck filled with tiny lizards' tails.

— A stolen statue of St. Anthony will get any spinster to the altar.

— Itching in the right palm is a sign that money is on the way.

— One should pay in coin when given a handkerchief or a knife as a present.

— A glass of cold water with three pinches of salt will ward off the evil eye.

— Certain looks can cause sweet peppers to shrivel up.

— When you lose something, tie a ribbon or piece of string to the arm of a chair or the leg or a table, to the handle of a jug, round a lamp, or whatever, and keep the little demon tied up securely until the lost object is found.

— Crosses marked with chalk on the soles of your shoes can prevent them from squeaking.

— A piece of cork in the frying pan turns the food a golden brown.

— Never open an umbrella indoors.

— Any little black bird coming through the window brings misfortune.

— A St. George's cross on the right-hand side of one's front door keeps trouble at bay.

Now then, if you start putting all these precepts into practice, you will have no more worries.

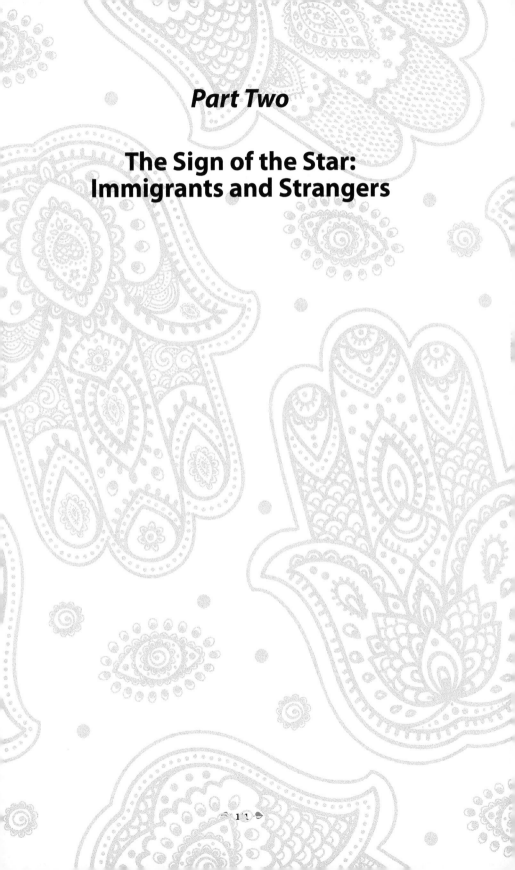

Part Two

The Sign of the Star:
Immigrants and Strangers

The Sign of the Star[1]

Ana Vásquez

"Iliusha, Iliushenka, precious little angel … Wake up! … You have to go to school." Through his eyelashes he glimpsed her smile, so familiar yet at the same time bewildering. He felt the caress of her black hair on his cheeks. He hugged and kissed her.

"Mommy! Mamushka."

"*Colecho, colechito, colechón,*" she hummed, imitating his way of speaking when he was a little child and could not yet manage to say *colegio* or *tejido.* But with time, imitation had transformed itself into a language loaded with secrets, which She used to awaken him, wrapping him in her warm tenderness, and tickling him on the soles of his feet to wake up his tiny toes, and placing a cozy sock on his little left leg.

How many times would he evoke that morning, the one when She said to him for the last time, "Iliusha Iliushenka," when he had to take the first step—in spite of himself—to abandon that translucent and marvelous world and enter that other world of suspicion and aggression, the world of the grown-ups. He was at the door, holding Rosalía's hand, when She ran to hand him the avocado sandwich, wrapped so carefully in stiff white paper that it always seemed like a present to him. She straightened his tie and kissed him on the forehead.

The class began with its habitual murmur of voices. They sang the tables, "twice one are two … ." Miss Guire reviewed the assignments and afterward stood on tiptoe to place the piece of chalk on the uppermost edge of the blackboard, and with that large, round handwriting that Iliusha tried so hard to imitate, wrote, *Pairs of Words,* and traced a vertical line dividing the entire space. She spelled each word, wrote *hair* here and *hare* there.

"What kind of sandwich do you have?" Jimmy asked him.

"Show it to me!"

"Avocado."

1 Dedications: To little Paul, who, one wintry day in Paris, had to battle the demons and assume the sign.
To Luna María, budding, may she grow putting forth roots in memory.
Translated from the Spanish by Roberta Gordenstein.

He was saved by the bell. Miss Guire stood up. "Come on, children, straighten the benches before going out for recess."

Small, Iliusha was one of the first in line. Jimmy and Fernando Flores were among the biggest; they went out at the end. "Wait for me, shrimp," Jimmy shouted at him. But Iliusha was wise to him, and, hurrying to join a group of teachers who were chatting in the sunshine, he unwrapped the white paper and cleverly stayed near them as he ate his sandwich.

Ever since they had been in kindergarten, two years ago, Jimmy and Fernando had found their special places. Fernando was the best fighter and he liked to make fun of the smallest ones; Iliusha learned quickly not to pass near him because he was an expert at tripping and there was nothing Iliusha could do, on the ground and bruised, facing an oversized bully who was laughing at him besides. And he also learned to guard his colored pencils and to gobble up his sandwich quickly. Freckle-faced and fat, Jimmy was the favorite of Miss Guire and all the teachers. He was son of the English vice-consul, and for Queen's College, which aspired to be an authentic English *colegio,* having someone from *the* embassy as a student was something like having a coat of arms whose prestige reflected upon everyone. Jimmy could forget his homework; it didn't matter. Besides, he already spoke the "correct" English of his family. He could knot his tie with the colors of Queen's any way he wished, and no one would scold him. And when he behaved too badly, Miss Guire would let his father know and go out with a smirk of satisfaction to wait for him at the entrance of the school. An exclusive deference automatically gave Jimmy a special position: he was untouchable.

Almost all the children in the class gathered at the rear of the schoolyard, near the quince trees, where the teachers hardly ever went and where no one could surprise them. There they were, stamping their feet on the ground to shake off the numbness. Iliusha approached slowly, savoring the last bite of his sandwich.

"... I can't go because Sunday morning we always go to Mass," Fernando was explaining.

"Me, too," said Marisa. "We go to Mass at noon."

Rubbing his freckled nose, Jimmy asserted that they were Protestants, and that was different.

"It's the same, but another way," someone said.

"It's better to be Catholic!"

"It is not!"

"Because …"

"Where did you get that idea?"

"It's just that Protestants …"

Jimmy, who was shouting loudest, dominated the argument. "And my father prays before we start to eat. It's a sin to eat if you don't pray first."

"Of course, you'll get sick!"

"That's God's punishment!"

"What is praying?" asked Iliusha in his delicate little voice. Fernando pointed at him, scandalized. "Lying midget, how can you not know what praying is?"

A wave of heat swept over Iliusha's face until he began to feel dizzy. "Liar! Liar!"

Those staring eyes, pursuing him, interrogating. Why did he have to ask, as if he were at home, with Her, who always said to him, "Ask me all the questions you want." When would he learn to bite his tongue, to hold back? Now he felt even smaller, almost insignificant, under Fernando's accusing finger. "No," he answered, with just a thread of voice, "Really I don't know …"

"But aren't you Catholics?"

"No," he replied, softly.

"Then you're Protestants!"

"No, not that either."

"But you can't be nothing! You must be something!"

And then, from the depths of memory, a word reached his lips: "I'm Jewish."

"That's impossible," declared Marisa flatly. "Only dogs are Jewish. Because, of course, in the song about who killed Jesus, you have to answer, 'the Jewish dog'."

Fernando began to jump up and down. "You're a dog, bow wow, a Jewish dog …"

"And you don't pray?"

Iliusha shook his head. He had already admitted he didn't know what that was.

"Don't you go to church?"

He continued to shake his head: "Rosalía goes sometimes," he said, "but we don't."

"Who is Rosalía?"

"The servant." She was the only person he had heard complain, "Hurry up and eat, I'm going to be late to church." She had shown it to him, with its tower and the clock that never told time. But Mass had nothing to do with it. Rosalía went to church to meet her boyfriend.

"And you don't believe in God?"

"Who?"

"God!"

He hesitated, not knowing what to tell them. "I don't know him," he stammered, trying to excuse himself.

"Stupid!" Fernando shouted at him. "You're a stupid dog. No one knows him, you idiot! But people believe."

Iliusha was bewildered. Why was he the only one who had not heard of this man? "I don't know him," he repeated. He didn't understand.

"Come on, children," shouted Miss Guire. "Hurry up."

Believing. Why would you have to believe? Once, in kindergarten, he had gotten involved in a terrible argument about Santa Claus. "He doesn't exist," Iliusha asserted, because She had said so and She never lied to him. "It's Daddy who brings the presents."

"Can Father come down the chimney?"

"Those are just stories; in my house there is no chimney, and they bring me presents without any problem."

Fernando (who was already bigger) shouted at him, "Liar! I saw him, and I have a photograph. A photo with him, understand? And he has a white beard like this ..."

"That's just a man who dresses up like Santa Claus, but he's not real." She had shown him when She took him to choose his bicycle.

"Liar! He had a sack with gifts and everything."

Iliusha was positive; he stated over and over that Santa didn't exist, but he couldn't find arguments to contradict the evidence of the photo, and the other children also insisted that they had seen him.

"You have to believe," said Marisa. "If not, he gets angry and won't bring you anything."

She never lied and for that reason he was certain, but the others didn't want to hear it, the presents were more important. But when they finished first grade, no one believed in Santa anymore. "That's for

babies," they asserted contemptuously, because now they knew how to read and they felt grown up. But no one remembered that Iliusha was the first to say it. Maybe this story about God would be forgotten also, just as they'd become convinced about Santa Claus. Rosalía talked about God and included him in everything, like something that is repeated over and over until it means nothing, scattering "heaven's sakes" and "oh, my God" between sighs and grumbles. Because She didn't talk that way, and because he loved Her, Iliusha tried to speak like She did and not like Rosalía.

All through the class he couldn't concentrate, worried about that man who seemed so important. He would tell Her about it as soon as he arrived home. Then She would take him in her arms and everything would be simple again.

At noon, the children got together again, trampling the dry leaves of the plane trees, telling each other stories, exchanging pictures and stamps. Iliusha walked distractedly, between Marisa and Carlos Cariola, asking himself why they talked about a Jewish dog in the song. Maybe there were Catholic dogs?

The house was surrounded by a little garden where there grew three trees, which She cared for as if they were old friends. There was the medlar, which was covered with orange fruit as bright as a picture in his storybook, a walnut tree, and in the back the noblest tree, as She always said, removing the ripe damson plums carefully, "Try it, Iliusha, how sweet!" On the ground floor was the workshop with its machines, the room where his father dampened the hides and stretched them, stapling them across an enormous table, the entrance with two armchairs where the ladies might wait, the fitting room, and the office. Next to the walnut tree, an exterior stairway led to the house. On each step She had placed flowerpot stands with flowers. He ran up, two steps at a time, shouting "Mamushka, Mommy."

"She went out," answered Rosalía, sulking as always. "She said to tell you to eat all your supper—and don't dawdle."

"Where did she go? Tell me!"

"She went to get your little brother."

Finally, finally, he was arriving! Iliusha had waited so long for him! He went running into the room. Everything was just the same, the cradle next to the window. On the pillow he left his old teddy bear; it

would be a present for his brother. He ran down the stairs and entered the shop. "Daddy! ..."

The machines were silent. The seamstresses were warming their dinner in the kitchenette and putting their plates on a corner of the great table where they cut the hides. They smiled at him, as always. "He took your mommy to the hospital." The odors from downstairs were disturbing, strange: the damp hides, the distinct seasonings. "Don't worry, he'll be back tonight."

He forgot about the Jewish dogs, and about the man, the one in whom he had to believe but whom he didn't know. He ate with Rosalía, in the kitchen. "If you eat everything, and quickly, I'll let you listen to the radio play with me."

She didn't like this, and since his parents did not allow him to listen, he was sure it would be entertaining. He ate everything as quickly as possible. He even swore by God, placing his crossed index finger and thumb on his lips, as Rosalía showed him. If he ever betrayed her, he would burn in Hell, and that was the worst fate.

"Jacqueline is a nurse in Switzerland, remember? She has to take care of a very rich young man who is locked up in a clinic. It seems that his stepfather wants to kill him little by little. A matter of inheritance," she added to explain to him, but he had no idea what that meant. While the two eagerly followed the adventures of poor Jacqueline, hiding from the wicked stepfather in the Swiss mountains, Iliusha thought that it wouldn't be so terrible if they were a few days late in bringing his little brother home. That way he could find out what happened to Jacqueline. "I think they'll get married in the end," said Rosalía.

The stepfather approached the bush where Jacqueline was crouching. Would he discover her? "We're late!" shouted Rosalía. "Oh my God, run! Run to school!" He arrived almost breathless as Miss Guire was closing the classroom door.

"Reading class. Open the book with the blue plastic cover." A passage from *David Copperfield*, illustrated with a sketch of London, into whose dark streets Iliusha immediately ventured. "Since you arrived last, Elías, you are going to read first."

He stood up. He didn't do badly, but it was hard to make himself heard over the ones in back. This time his voice broke, and he finished the paragraph with difficulty, moved by the adventures of poor David, helpless and alone. He felt he was going to burst out crying because

of the pain the character was suffering, wandering about the sinister London of the engraving.

"Louder, Miss," ordered the tiresome Fernando.

"Come on, Elías, read it again, very loud!"

Iliusha held back his tears because that was just what Fernando wanted, to persecute him later, shouting that he was a sissy. After reading he sat down, losing himself in a daydream, a mixture of the adventures of Jacqueline and the drama of David Copperfield. Jacqueline was like his Mamushka, with Her smooth black hair. Instead of seeking his little brother, She was running over the mountain, with Her white apron and nurse's shoes, with the same frightened eyes She had had when he was dazed after falling off the swing. Iliusha looked like the handsome rich young man from the clinic, but it was David. Only She could save him; She had to descend the Swiss mountain—which he imagined as steep and violet-colored as the Andes—to search for him in the mysterious alleys of London "And maybe they'll get married in the end," said Rosalía.

The bell signaled them to put away their books and go outside. Iliusha walked like an automaton, following his companions, still possessed by the dangers threatening poor David, trying to imagine how She would arrange things in order to arrive on time. Again they stood next to the plane trees, quiet, watching him approach. He smiled at them, distracted.

"Elías," said Rodolfo Sánchez, the best student. He spoke as if his good grades authorized him to represent the others. "We want to tell you something." Iliusha continued smiling, without responding, without being completely present. "We've decided not to speak to you anymore," continued Rodolfo. "From now on, no one will be able to talk to you."

"Why?" asked Iliusha, brusquely forgetting the dangers David was risking.

"This morning you told us you were Jewish, right?"

"Of course, why?"

"My father says you belong to the race that killed Christ."

While Rodolfo pushed him out of the world, Fernando began to howl, "Jewish dog, Jewish dog."

It seemed like a nightmare to Iliusha. He was sure it was not true. "But I haven't killed anyone," he whispered.

"Not you, your family, they were the ones."

"But ..." He couldn't continue, he didn't know what to say. He was invaded by an impression of unreality, as if it were not he who was there, next to the plane trees, hearing his condemnation. "But ..." he repeated, and then he was silent, doubting. Perhaps it was true.

As if they had all agreed, they turned their backs on him. Sticking out his tongue, Jimmy made a face at him: "Ha, ha, ha, you're in trouble."

He didn't know how he returned to the classroom. All he wanted that afternoon, what he desired for a long time, was to be born again. Not in his own house, but to another family—to be the son of Marisa's mother, for example, or of Mrs. Flores, even if that meant being as dull as Fernando. He would even have accepted being red and freckle-faced like Jimmy, as long as he had a respectable father. To free himself from that infamous heritage, to cease being Her child because She was a murderer. But then he would have to renounce Her tenderness, lose that marvelous voice which sang to awaken him. No, not that! It was too much. He was ashamed to have even thought it. He preferred not being at all, changing himself truly into a dog. He would no longer go to school. He would remain in the garden, beside the medlar tree, wagging his tail whenever She approached. But Iliusha knew that no matter how much he wished, he could not be someone else. If only he could go back in time, no further than this morning, when they were talking about praying. He would bite his tongue until it bled, he would clench his teeth with all his might, so that the cursed words would not escape. And if they asked him what he was, he would answer, "Catholic and Protestant, both at once. We go to all the churches, we pray all day long." And God? Of course, he knew him, certainly he believed. He concentrated in order to return to yesterday, and his head ached so much he became nauseous. But nothing changed. It was today, in the afternoon, or it could have been any day after "it" happened. He had already said "it"; the abyss had opened.

Almost as if it were a game, they all took pains to respect his exile, and if someone accidentally spoke to him, another would give him a shove, to say, "It's forbidden." At recess they turned their backs on him deliberately. They walked faster in the street so that he couldn't catch up with them. Their glances slid over his as if he didn't exist.

Now Aunt Debbie was sleeping at his house. She kept him company in the afternoons, and what was even worse, she ate lunch with him.

Not only was his Mamushka missing, but now he couldn't listen to the drama with Rosalía either, and poor Jacqueline remained hidden from him forever beneath the bushes. Daddy wasn't in his shop, he almost never saw him. He returned late at night. Half asleep, Iliusha asked him about Her. "Soon she will come back. She sent you a kiss ..."

Why didn't he break out in tears when they ignored him? Why didn't he run to Miss Guire to tell on them? Why didn't he say anything to his father, or tell Aunt Debbie when the two of them ate together, accompanied only by the sighs of his aunt, who blew her nose all the time? A frightening sense of shame swept over him, invading him. He observed his aunt, his daddy, he remembered Her, and he was certain, positive, that none of them seemed like the murderers in the movies. They couldn't be evil or kill anyone. It couldn't be true. In the depths of his being, he hated himself for believing them, for having doubted his Mamushka. Although he had not confessed it to anyone, he had wanted another family, and that was betrayal. "You must be patient," sighed Aunt Debbie. But she was lying to him; he knew that if She was not there, it was because of him. In bed at night, he asked Her to return and forgive him.

Something was preventing him from complaining, from accusing them. And not for anything in the world would he have asked them to accept him again. He was Jewish, and he couldn't and wouldn't erase what he was. He never learned to fight or defend himself, and it never occurred to him that perhaps there were other Jewish children in the school. He thought he was the only one. He returned home alone, pretending that he could only step on the center of the sidewalk tiles, that if he walked on the edges a horrible disgrace would occur. Sometimes children from other classes who were going his way would approach him, but if they spoke to him, he wouldn't answer. He didn't want to give them the opportunity to turn their backs on him. Somehow he had to make it obvious that he was Jewish, as if he were marked with a mysterious sign.

Recess was when he suffered most. It no longer bothered him to be alone except that he didn't want the teachers to realize. As the mornings were still cool, he invented a sore throat. "My mommy doesn't want me to go outside." He remained in the empty classroom. If Miss Guire returned in the middle of recess to correct the notebooks and found him there, alone and bored, it didn't matter. Because she didn't

have to know that the others refused to speak to him. He opened the white package, ate his whole sandwich, carefully collected the crumbs scattered on the cloth covering the bench, and stood up noiselessly to throw them in the wastebasket next to the blackboard. Afterward, since he was bored, he reread his lessons.

In the afternoon it grew hot, and Miss Guire did not let him stay in the room. How could he pretend? How could he hide what should not have been seen? Half the school was fascinated by the spinning tops; they competed to see who could make them dance best. Iliusha observed them from a distance, playing in the corner by the quince trees. He strolled about, hands in his pockets, moving slightly closer to groups of children from other classes so that the teachers—who were observing distractedly while they chatted in the center of the school-yard—might think he was with them. He listened to them momentarily without saying anything, for fear of a new denunciation, and then drifted away slowly to continue his walk. It occurred to him as he was wandering about this way that the others pointed to him behind his back: "That's Elías, the one who's an outcast because … ." He walked looking down at his shoes, wrapped up in himself, as if hiding his eyes would prevent them from identifying him and he would become truly transparent, invisible. Afternoon recess became interminable. He would have liked to invent another illness for himself, but he only knew about sore throats. And he didn't want to exaggerate because then Miss Guire might not trust him. Sometimes he questioned whether she also knew he was Jewish. If so, why did she speak to him?

They were starting geography. Miss Guire drew something like a brown empanada and painted a thick sky-blue border around it. Underneath she wrote *island* and below that, *An island is a piece of land surrounded by water.* "Copy this in your notebooks!" Iliusha took pains to make his empanada just like the one on the board, and he copied the sentence meticulously. During recess he reread it, humming, as he did to Her songs. The next day Miss Guire added new and complicated drawings with several colors: a peninsula, a strait, a mountain, and a valley. Iliusha invented a distinct melody for each one of the defini-tions, while the others made the tops spin in the yard.

Monday, surprisingly, they had visitors in class. The children stood up and greeted them with a bow. "What is an island?" asked Miss Guire. No one knew, not Jimmy (who was English) or Rodolfo. Then

Iliusha raised his hand and repeated exactly the definition from the notebook. It would not have occurred to him that an island could be one like Robinson Crusoe's; for him, "island" was something similar to "*Colecho, colechito, colechón*," a song made of nonsense words.

"And the mountain? ... The valley?" Iliusha knew all the definitions. "Very very good, Elías, excellent."

"He deserves the Honor Board," said the gentleman visitor, with a good-natured smile and a very hoarse voice. The Honor Board was the maximum aspiration and pride of all the children and all the classes at Queen's, reserved for the best. Each class competed to have the most Honor Board students. Not even Rodolfo Sánchez was on the Honor Board for this month; Iliusha was the only one in the class.

"The representative," said Miss Guire. "An example." He continued sitting on the bench with his hands folded, without looking at anyone, pretending he didn't hear the whispers behind him.

He returned home, running, his heart beating louder than a locomotive. "Rosalía, Rosalía! Mommy's back ..." She must have returned, certainly now. She would be waiting for him, She who divined everything. She would have forgiven him. Now She would be proud because the name of her Iliusha, Hers, appeared on the Honor Board. She would kiss him on the forehead, laughing, take him in Her arms, and they would dance, humming their secret songs. He would cling to Her neck while She spun around in a whirlwind. He would kiss Her. "Never leave me again; don't stop loving me." He almost felt Her smooth hands caressing his cheeks already. "Rosalía!"

"Why are you shouting at me; don't you see that I'm busy?" She turned her back on him just as the others at school did. "I'm behind with the meal."

Then he couldn't stand it any longer; he threw himself to the floor sobbing, pounding the boards with his clenched fists. It was essential that She and only She come to calm him. "I don't want to wait anymore. Let Her come back now. Now!" He heard his own yells. And Rosalía's, calling Aunt Debbie.

He sobbed desperately. It was impossible for him to swallow a mouthful. Aunt Debbie insisted that he drink a glass of warm milk with honey. "Your mommy told me you like it a lot. Come on, drink it and make her happy. You mustn't cry like that. Eat an orange, and this little chocolate bar." It had a salty taste.

She brought him to school. She took him by the hand, walking rapidly, and he was terrified because he couldn't walk in the center of the sidewalk.

"Auntie … what if I went to another school?"

"Queen's is one of the best schools in Chile. It's expensive but …"

"But?"

"Your father works very very hard to pay for it."

"Then if I changed he wouldn't have to work so much."

Aunt Debbie moved her head, smiling. "He does it out of love for you, so that you can speak English well … and for friends."

"Friends?"

"At Queen's you can make good friends."

Suddenly he realized he had forgotten to tell her about the Honor Board. He opened his mouth but his lips felt stiff, his tongue rebellious and immobile. He didn't feel like it any longer. His prize was for Her, not for Aunt Debbie. He wasn't even proud, as if nothing were important any more. Aunt Debbie straightened the knot in his tie and smoothed his hair with her hand. He went running into the school so his aunt couldn't touch him, there in the street, in front of everyone.

He remained standing next to the door, observing the yellowing gama grass, not thinking of anything, sad. He didn't want to explain why he wasn't returning.

"Teacher's pet," Fernando Flores insulted him, with a shove, "You'll do anything to get good grades!"

Iliusha didn't look at him; he barely heard him, concentrating on his battle with those black ideas that pursued him. It seemed to him that the episode of the Honor Board hadn't happened that morning, but a long time ago, in that other life where he could still ignore what he didn't want to know. They did the Pairs of Words again, and even though he knew them by heart, he didn't raise his hand or say anything. But when someone made a mistake, Miss Guire asked him, "And now, Elías." He would spell the word in English and give the translation correctly and without enthusiasm, with his eyes fixed on the cover of the bench. Absent. "Bright boy," commented Miss Guire. "Very good."

Just before going out for recess, they passed him from behind a folded paper with his name in red letters. He opened it: "JEWS TO THE CREMATORIUM." He paused, spelling out the unknown word. Miss

Guire was waiting for him to close the door of the room. "What is a crematorium?" he asked her in his timid little voice.

"They are the ovens where they burn stray dogs." But faced with his frightened eyes, she took his arm. "It's for wandering and sick dogs; don't worry, they don't make them suffer. First they give them a shot to put them to sleep. Go out to play, Elías, you don't look good."

They were sending him to the crematorium. With the dogs. Between the flames and the dogs, asphyxiating him with smoke, like the inferno Rosalía always talked about. Blindly, he ran toward the rear of the schoolyard, where the group was, where Fernando was laughing. With his fists clenched. He wanted to push him out of his life, kill him, never see him again. Being a murderer didn't matter, since he was one anyway. He ran in slow motion, in a kind of nightmare where his legs could not move as quickly as he wished. Stripping himself of fear, he ran as if he were crossing a border.

He hurled himself on Fernando in a whirlwind of blows and kicks. He lashed out any way he could, blind with rage. David against Goliath. They rolled in the gama grass, shouting and insulting each other. Iliusha barely heard the teachers scolding him as they separated them. The two were bruised, faces bleeding, and Fernando's shirt was torn. They took them to the nurse's office to wash up, and then they returned to class.

"Now you're going to shake hands like two real gentlemen," ordered Miss Guire. "Come on!" In front of the whole class. Neither one moved. Iliusha did not feel the tears or his face burning. "Come on, fair play." Ritualistic words. Fernando stretched out his hand, "like a gentleman." Iliusha crossed his hands behind his back and stared directly at him. With hate.

"This can't be. Elías, you are disappointing me. Don't you want to shake hands?"

"No." For the first time, they heard him in the back of the room.

"Come on, apologize, shake hands and it will be settled." Fernando stepped forward. Iliusha backed up.

"No," he repeated.

"What's the matter, are you angry?"

He was not able to explain that anger is the last resort of the defeated, of the weak, of those unable to express themselves. Fernando could permit himself those noble gestures because he was strong, and because the whole class was on his side. Iliusha had only his anger to help him

survive. Later, when he was a doctor and successful in life (as they say without knowing what they are talking about), he would still feel that ache in his chest, that anguish. As though at any moment they could again turn their backs on him, exclude him because of what he was. Maybe by then the cells of his body would no longer be the same, but at the bottom of his secret pain, in the deepest part of the adult Elías would be huddled little Iliusha, with his wound always open.

"Come on, Elías," insisted Miss Guire, "be nice." He squeezed his eyes shut to concentrate and remember Her. He knew She would be proud. Perhaps now She would decide to return. "If you don't apologize, Elías, I am going to have to punish you."

He stayed after dismissal, writing fifty times, *Good boys are always polite.*

"What did Fernando do to you?"

"Nothing, Miss."

"He must have done something, Elías." He raised his head and returned her look without lowering his eyes, concentrating on biting his lips and holding his tongue because he had learned it was always best to keep silent.

"You have never been a fighter, Elías, that isn't like you. Tell me so I can fix it. ... Answer me, Son." Hearing her his heart began to melt. She was the only one to call him "Son"; Miss Guire didn't have the right. He shook his head, with his lips shut tight and his eyes moist. He showed her the notebook with the fifty lines, took his bookbag, and fled without saying good-bye.

If Aunt Debbie was still in the house it meant that She had not returned.

"I was going to jump and I slipped on the grass, he explained."

"But how?"

"It was a game of running and jumping. Since I was winning they pushed me."

"They're so jealous," grumbled Rosalía. He accepted the hot chocolate his aunt served him. He could barely do his homework. He fell asleep, exhausted, and continued fighting in his dreams. Against everyone—dogs, dragons, demons. All of them, the others.

It was Friday. In the morning the entire school went to the movies. An English film. Wisely, Iliusha stationed himself in front of Miss

Guire and slept through it. As they left, Fernando Flores passed by his side, bumping into him. "Scaredy-cat."

Elías turned toward him with an opaque glance: "It's forbidden to talk to me."

His aunt had prepared gefilte fish. Everyone said she was a famous cook. Even though he was only a child, she awaited his praise with a triumphal smile. But Iliusha had gotten so used to not speaking that now it was difficult for him to produce any sound; he had to swallow some saliva first and then let it go, like someone who hurls himself into freezing water. He didn't comment but ate it all up. "Do you want more?" He nodded his head. He ate a second serving and she smiled at him.

"Aunt, do you believe in God?"

"No … we don't believe."

"Why?"

"We have other ideas. There are so many discoveries, progress, science …"

Iliusha understood her small disparaging motion more than the meaning of what she was saying.

"Maybe we don't have one?"

"Of course we do, Jehovah. But we don't believe in those things."

"Aunt, Catholics, they believe, they go to Mass, they pray and everything. That's why they're …"

"Oh, Elías, what questions, what questions, You're right, a Catholic who does not believe in God and who doesn't go to Mass stops being a Catholic."

"But those of us who don't believe in God, are we still Jews anyway?"

It was too complicated. The only thing he understood, although he already knew it intuitively, was the certainty that he was different. He didn't know why, but that's the way it was.

"And if you don't believe, why do you wear that?" With his index finger he gently touched the six-pointed star that she wore hanging from a little chain, and at that moment he remembered that She also wore one. "This is something else. It's the Star of David." Like David Copperfield—and he imagined that David, small and alone, like himself. He remained quiet, lost again in his daydream.

Aunt Debbie sighed, drank her little bit of coffee, lit a cigarette. "Do you want to know why I wear it?" Iliusha nodded his assent. "Because your grandparents died over there, far away …" With her eyes fixed on

a distant space, beyond Iliusha, she was not speaking to explain to him, but to herself. "It's my history, what ties me to them." Then she noticed his disturbed expression and took his hand. "A long time ago, on the other side of the ocean, some very bad people, very bad, forced the Jews to sew a star just like this one on their clothing, and they put it here—you see?—right on their heart. Then, when these evil men were in a bad mood, or things were not going well for them, they blamed the Jews and searched for those wearing the star to beat them … or kill them."

"And aren't you afraid to wear it?"

His aunt smiled, "Sometimes, but I ignore it and wear it anyway."

The sky was covered with huge black clouds. The heat was oppressive. "An earthquake is coming," forecasted Rosalía as she accompanied him to school.

A boring class. Miss Guire talked about honor and loyalty, assuming they would realize she was referring to the previous day's battle. Iliusha was gliding in a kind of dream populated with fleeting images that escaped from him every time he attempted to retain them for an instant. A white wing, the backyard of his house filled with garbage, shining stars sticking to his clothing, thousands of little stones tumbling down on him, landing on him like a stinging waterfall. Images that galloped by, returning over and over, until he was exhausted.

He wandered, half asleep, through the schoolyard, and it was perhaps that mixture of worry and tiredness that prevented him from realizing the danger. Amidst the clamor of familiar noises, the students approached, lining up to return to class. The teachers surrounded the director, still commenting on the morning's exit. Absorbed, Iliusha walked at the back, automatically maintaining the distance between himself and the others, as if excluding himself were his personal obligation and no longer theirs. He discovered that one could believe and not believe. And at any rate, he didn't understand why, he would always be a Jew. He didn't hear them come close. When Fernando and Jimmy grabbed him roughly by the arms he couldn't manage to shout. As soon as they subdued him, Rodolfo Sánchez covered his mouth. He struggled but two others grabbed his legs and between the five of them they dragged him toward the rear, to that space between the quince trees and the wall where the gardener piled up the dry leaves. "We're going to burn you, damned dwarf," whispered Jimmy. "You'll die in sin. Heretic."

He believed them. How could he not believe them, if the day before they had sent him the paper about the crematorium, and just recently Aunt Debbie had told him the story of the evil men who killed those who wore the star? He didn't want to die. With all his strength he tried to free himself, desperate. They were panting. Somehow, he managed to set one leg free.

"Outcast!"

"Jewish dog. Hold him tight!"

"Grab his leg!"

They punched him in the face.

"First we're going to brand you with a *J* so you'll know why."

"Poor animals," She always said when She saw cows branded With the initial of the ranch owner. Poor things, how it must hurt them. He saw the pencil point coming closer; it was upon him, between his eyes. He twisted backward, terrified. "No, not that!"

And suddenly nothing.

He didn't know what they did to him, or how they found him, or the punishment Fernando and the others received. He came to in the nurse's office. What was his father doing there next to the director? "Mamushka," he murmured, and fainted again.

He lost consciousness, plunging into a deep and empty sleep, rising up at times, carried by delirium, sinking again into a slumber without memories. He barely felt Aunt Debbie washing his hands. "And these red marks, poor little thing ... what could they have been playing?"

Afterward, or maybe before, he opened his eyes and saw the doctor, motionless, as if he had always been there. He struggled on precipitous slopes, pursued by a Fernando, who had turned into a dog and was spitting flames. He fled through moving mountains that were suddenly fenced playgrounds and dead-end streets. He smelled the smoke, escaping from the crematorium. She was beyond. And then, *An island is a piece of land surrounded by water.* Who was singing? Was it She, encouraging him? Or was it Miss Guire, shaking the rod to punish him? Go back Iliusha! Hide! Flee from the devils. And he continued his wanton race, almost breathless, no longer knowing whether he was running to tear himself away or because he wanted to find Her.

He was hot, vomiting. "Poor little thing," said Aunt Debbie's voice. How many days? How much fever? Suddenly it seemed to him that Miss Guire was also in his room, next to the doctor, making faces at him.

Now the wall was moving. It wasn't a wall but Fernando and many others just like him, menacing. Beyond, She stretched out her arms toward him, smiling, "My Iliushenka." The wall grew and grew, preventing him from seeing Her. His heart was beating madly as he searched for Her always, between the packs of hounds or in the yard with the quince trees, getting closer to Her. He was next to Her, under the blankets; he could almost touch Her … But no, now She was waiting for him beside the samovar, next to the blurry photo of his grandparents.

When the fever began to leave him, a cold sweat overcame him, chilling him to the bone. If he opened his eyes he saw a six-pointed star shining in the center of the lamp. He squeezed his eyelids shut, exhausted, trying to fall asleep again, to continue searching for Her. He was certain that if he found Her he would be saved. They would return together; they would never be separated again. And the pack of hounds would cross the space with stars on their foreheads and howls of joy.

Half awake, or maybe still asleep, he wished with all his might, with his whole being; he tried to catch his star. But if his father gave it to him it was because She would no longer return. Then he burst into tears because he didn't want to, couldn't, accept that. Dying, what a frightening thing. He cried because She was not at his side, because suddenly he realized that Her absence, while he was sick, was the confirmation of that horrible thing.

His father opened the blinds, and the brilliant light invaded his room, illuminating the blue of his blanket. He felt the warmth of the sun like a caress. They set him between the large cushions. They fed him broth. He managed to swallow a mashed banana with honey. How could he explain that mixture of impressions and feelings, the joy of the light, the taste of honey still on his lips. He breathed deeply. "I want my Mamushka's star," he begged his father, sure that he had it. His father shivered, hesitated, sat down on the bed and took his hands— "Her star …"—and embraced him.

He would wear it when he returned to school. Maybe, just maybe, it was a way of keeping Her, of feeling less alone, of being with Her forever. "And that way they'll all know what I am," he said.

From *May You Make a Good Bride*[1]

Rosa Nissán

Second Grade

Every night I kneel down next to the window, gaze at a star (which is probably my guardian angel), and say the "Our Father" for God, and a "Hail Mary" for the Virgin Mother. Even though I'm the daughter of Jews, I hope that I have a guardian angel who follows me around all day long, just like my classmates have. Today I prayed that I won't have to change schools; they want to stick me in an elementary school with only Jewish kids. (Where do they get so many of them?)

> Dear Lord, make it so that I get to stay forever at Guadalupe Tepeyac Elementary. Don't let them take me out for anything in the world, especially now when I'm going to go into third grade—the most difficult year of primary school. Only here at this school, and with your help, will I be able to get through it. I promise you that I'll do whatever you ask of me: follow the Ten Commandments, go on Saturdays to catechism classes, and then, the day that I die I will be the guardian angel of whoever you say.
>
> In the name of the Father, the Son, and the Holy Spirit. Amen.

At eight o'clock in the morning, before beginning our studies, we always pray. We put the palms of our hands together near our mouths, we close our eyes, and then we all recite our prayer in unison. And Our Heavenly Father hears us. With our right hands we make the sign of the cross, and then we sit down to study. Our desks are really nice; the top lifts open and inside we store all of our school stuff. I have the top of my desk lid decorated with stickers: in the middle is Saint Theresa (I adore her), and on all four sides are other saints with flowers all around them. I spend all day giving them little kisses so that they watch over me.

When we complete our assignments or behave ourselves, the misses reward us with another sticker. I'm one of the best behaved, and among

1 From *Novia que te vea*, first published in 1992 by Editorial Planeta Mexicana, Mexico. Translated from the Spanish by Dina Castillo-Mendoza.

those who have the most stickers. I just have to hide them when I'm at home because my mom doesn't like them very much. Sometimes she catches me making the sign of the cross in the morning. The other day she told me, "I would prefer it if you would leave the classroom when the others are saying their morning prayers." But I couldn't possibly do that. The rest of the kids would ask about me, and besides, I like saying prayers.

Yesterday during recess everybody was making sand castles. I was backing up to make mine a little bigger when I stepped on another girl's castle. She got so mad, and then threw sand in my eyes and screamed, "Jew girl, Jew girl!" Hearing that really surprised me, 'cause most of the girls don't even know that I'm Jewish.

A whole bunch more came around and then they started yelling "You people killed Christ!" and they made the sign of the cross in my face, and just stared at me like I was the Devil himself.

I yelled back, "That's a lie. I'm not a Jew. I say my prayers and make confession just like the rest of you."

It's almost one o'clock in the morning. I can't sleep. I keep thinking about how they threw sand at me.

This dream of Hell keeps haunting me. Last week I dreamed the same thing. The fire kept coming back to my bed to visit me, over and over. The yellow flames lit up the darkness, waves of orange and red fire. Then tombs opened up like manhole covers. People came out of them to walk toward God—he's going to reward or punish us. I can see the lids opening up, the resurrected people starting to walk. "The final judgment. We'll all be there someday," said Mother Mary. "Then we will know whether we'll make it to Heaven, or whether we'll end up with a tail and horns." The ones that go to Hell will make little kids do bad things.

Last night the neighbors came down from the second floor and we played Lottery. I got the playing card with "The Devil," and I lost because that old bad guy just never got called. That awful little red demon was dancing around with his evil eyes in my sleep last night. He's got this big iron fork that he uses to sweep the cinders around; he

just comes and goes, wherever he wants. He gives me this look out of the corner of his eye, shows me his horns, and sharpens his talons on the burning edge of his blade. It just scares me to death to imagine that this could happen to me. Oh, I hope it doesn't come to that!

And why is it that we've got to go around naked? And with all those resurrected dead people no less! Oh, I would just die if they saw me naked, and if I then had to go out like that and have everybody see me. What an awful punishment! I'd run into all these people that died like a thousand years ago: Benito Juárez, Napoleón, Miguel Hidalgo y Costilla, my other grandma, Cinderella, Cuauhtémoc … And how in the world is he going to be able to walk anyway, when they burned off his feet?[2] It must be that we come back all in one piece; they say nothing is impossible for God. It might actually be fun, if I get to meet all of these people, but … naked? Oh, not that! How embarrassing! And without even anything to cover yourself up!

> Love God over everything else. (I love Him and I pray to Him.)
>
> Don't take the Lord's name in vain. (I'm not going to swear anymore. But if I do swear something that's not true, I'll cross my fingers behind my back, and it won't count.)
>
> Honor your father and mother.
>
> Keep the Sabbath and the Holy Days.
>
> Don't kill.
>
> Don't fornicate. (This one I'm skipping. Who even knows what it means?)
>
> Don't steal.
>
> Don't bear false witness or lie. (I don't tell too many lies. Besides, it's the worst thing I could do to my mom.)
>
> Don't desire someone else's wife. (I don't understand … whose wife?)

2 Benito Juárez (1806–72) was president of Mexico (1857–65, 1867–72), particularly revered as a champion of Mexican independence and democratic reform and as the first national leader of indigenous heritage. Miguel Hidalgo y Costilla (1753–1811) was a priest who led a rebellion against Spanish rule; he was eventually defeated and executed. Cuauhtémoc was the son of Moctezuma, who was emperor of the Aztecs when the conquistador Hernán Cortés arrived in Mexico in 1519. It is believed that Cortés's men tortured Cuauhtémoc by burning off his feet in an attempt to make him reveal the location of Aztec treasures.

Don't covet someone else's belongings. (That's an easy one, 'cause I
never want what isn't mine.)

If I just follow these, I'm sure I'll go to Heaven. The thing that I really
like about the Ten Commandments is that they're the same for Jews
and Catholics. Finally, something that's the same! I can recite them
at home just like I can at school. At least I have that. It's easy to fol-
low them, too, 'cause that business about me going to Hell is just too
horrifying.

I want to go to Heaven and be an angel like on my stickers. I'd sure
like to be one of the invisible ones. How fabulous to be invisible! Go
everywhere, flying from here to there, seeing everybody without them
seeing me ... now if I could just get up close to kid's ears and tell them,
"Don't pay any attention to the Devil! Give your Sundays over to the
nice Old Man. Let other kids borrow your crayons, even if they break
them." They say that the Devil comes and tells kids in their left ear to
misbehave, and their guardian angel tells them in their right ear to
behave themselves.

Those blond angels with the baby-blue robes and transparent wings
live up in the sky and they get to see God, the Virgin Mother, and all
the Saints, and talk to them. "Holy Cross, Holy Cross, make the Devil
go away and Jesus come." Ol' pot-bellied demons—don't come around
me—get out of here! Go away forever! I know that those little devils are
really pushy and they keep coming back to your ear and saying, "Steal
that pen, hit your sister, pull her braids, make fun of her!" Sometimes
they convince you, because the Devil only teaches you bad habits, and
those demons are very tricky.

My robes would be white; I'd fly around from here to there. I'd tell
all the kids to be good, no matter what country they're from ... but
I'm not sure I'd want to be the angel of a Jewish kid, I'd rather have
a Roman Catholic. Someday I'd take the highway up to the sky; I'd
sprout beautiful wings like a butterfly, and from the clouds I'd throw
buckets of water so that those below would feel like it was raining.

All the girls at school get presents and parties twice a year; once on
their birthday, and then on their Saint's day. But Jews don't get to cel-
ebrate the day of their Saint. The teacher asked me when was my Saint's
day. The only thing that I could think of answering was that I would

ask my mom. I'm sure there's no Saint Oshinica. I'll look in the calendar; if there's a Saint Eugenia, I'm saved.

<div align="center">***</div>

Since we live on Guadalupe Boulevard we get to see all the processions that come by every day toward the Basilica.[3] They go by singing and dancing and laughing; they drink arm in arm, carrying their children, their sick people, their food, their blankets. Each group has a guy in charge that watches out and makes sure that they don't go so slow that the procession behind catches up.

When we can just barely start to hear them, we run out to the balcony; we don't seem to ever get tired of watching them. Sometimes the groups are three or four blocks long, and when they pass us by, that's when it starts to get sad. But on the days close to the Holy Mother's day, they come by one after the other, bearing different standards, all with the image of the Virgin of Guadalupe—the Mother of all Mexicans—framed in threads of gold.

They must be having fun, coming from places like Toluca, Querétaro, Pachuca, and lots more. When they pass by our house they start singing "Mañanitas," so happy because they're about to get to the place where the Virgin of Guadalupe appeared for the first time. Many of them are so full of emotion just from being so close, their eyes fill with tears. Others are already on their knees, even though there are still fifteen blocks to go.

<div align="center">***</div>

The whole area smells like *gorditas*. And all around the Basilica there are women sitting on their little steps off the street, warming up these corn tortillas on clay dishes. They're small, about the size of a quinto coin (well, maybe a little bigger), and come in packets of ten, wrapped in colored tissue paper.

3 The Basilica of the Virgin of Guadalupe, which sits atop a hill in Mexico City, is the nation's most famous cathedral, dedicated to its most beloved native saint. The faithful believe that it marks the spot where, in the sixteenth century, the Virgin Mary appeared to an indigenous peasant, Juan Diego, and requested his help in bringing his people to Christianity. It draws thousands of pilgrims each year.

I wonder why it is that they sell so many of those special candles all around down there. They're the really long and pretty rose-colored ones, and they're decorated with little golden flowers.

Sometimes we go inside the church to hear the mass. And sometimes we just walk around the vendor stands. Then we go up the little hill that you can just barely see from the window of our house. At the top there's a little white house with a cross on top. It's right there where the miracle happened to the Indian, Juan Diego. He sure was lucky! I hope that someday she can appear to me. If it's a miracle, then it could happen to me, too. Later on we come down from the hill, and to get back home we take the train that goes all the way up Guadalupe Boulevard. That way we're not gone too long and Mom doesn't notice that we went down there again.

I believed them. I believed my parents when they said that it wasn't the Jews that killed Christ. "If they bother you again, tell them that Jesus was Jewish, that he made his Bar Mitzvah."

"Oh yeah, right, Dad," I said. "Like they're going to believe that! They'll just get mad."

Since my mom was to going to Monterrey to see my grandpa, Micaela hurried up with her chores and she took us down by the Basilica again. We met up with some of her friends. After a while, I heard one of them say, "I'm telling you, Mica, you shouldn't be working for them. The money they pay you isn't enough—it runs out just like water."

I pretended not to hear this. The truth is, I don't know what to say when I hear that kind of talk. And then, what if they start in with the whole thing about killing Christ, too? Everybody must know about that. We went into the church on the hill and I just stared at the crucifix. Really, look how they left him! Some lady who was kneeling by us was crying 'cause he was dripping blood. That poor guy! How could you not hate whoever did that—what terrible people! It's been so many years since it happened, but you still have to feel awful about it. If this lady who's crying by me knew that I was a Jew, I really think she could kill me. The good thing is that Micaela likes me and she's not going to go around gossiping and telling on me. And besides, you can't tell if

someone is Jewish just by looking at them. Frankly, I'm glad I'm Jewish rather than Black. But even I feel pretty sad and guilty about it. Look how they nailed him to that cross! What horrible people.

<div align="center">***</div>

On the corner where we live there's a fine goods store, and the owners Berta and Bicha are friends of my mom. They live in the back of the store on the ground floor. They make the most beautifully decorated cakes. Sometimes I just sit for hours watching how they do one layer and then the next. They even make the little figurines, with paint and wires, then the flowers—different colors like blue, yellow, and pink. I think the prettiest ones are the wedding cakes. But I can change my mind when I see the ones to celebrate a *quinceañera*, with its little figurine coming down the steps of a circular staircase.[4] I spend a lot of time looking at them, and at the yellow, pink, and blue powdered sugar.

Actually, the figurines don't look that great until we make them a little dress with a piece of tulle and attach it with a bit of frosting around the waist. Then we cover the pleats with the frosting from the decorating bag, and it looks just like a little waistband. That's when they really look elegant. Then we apply a little paint to make them dark or fair-skinned, and they end up looking just like we want them to. Poor things! But they're always pretty.

Bicha and Berta are friends with a priest who gives catechism classes on Saturdays at the church closest to my home. A lot of kids go there; we learn how to pray, and ever since I learned how to cross myself I'm better at knowing which is my right hand, 'cause it's the one you have to use to make the cross. When we're all done they give us those licorice candies that I love so much. I've never missed a class because they cover for me and tell my mom that I'm with them helping decorate the cakes. I really want to make my first communion, and they're the only ones who can help me save myself from the final judgment; and even better, maybe God will forgive my whole family.

<div align="center">***</div>

4 In Mexico and other Latin American countries, girls' fifteenth birthdays, or *quinceañera*, are marked with especially lavish celebrations that welcome them into adulthood.

In our neighborhood, Colonia Industrial, there are a lot of other Jewish families; they've been my parents' closest friends since even before they were married. My mom introduced Max and his wife Fortuna. They've got kids, too, but I'm the oldest—we all get along great. Today my mom and some of the other ladies decided to go to a Jewish school that's over in another neighborhood, Colonia del Valle, to see if maybe all of us get together, the school will send a bus to pick us up. When we got home from school, we found out they had registered us.

Third Grade

All of these kids killed Christ too? They seem all right to me. They don't seem like they could have done it. Maybe they don't remember doing it. They play marbles and tag and freeze tag—everything I played in the other school. Could they really be like my old friends? You can't tell at all that they're Jewish.

Gotlib, Bombero

Barbara Mujica

Ernesto Gotlib lit a cigarette and put it to his lips. He inhaled fitfully, then coughed. The cigarette tasted bitter. He rapped on the side of the table with his right hand—an edgy little rap—and mashed the cigarette in an ashtray.

"Rebeca!"

Rebeca knew what he was going to say.

"You think they've got to me yet?"

"You just asked me that two minutes ago."

"So? That was two minutes ago. What about now? You think they've got to my name yet?"

"How could I know?"

Gotlib got up and looked out the window, but he did not see the brown and gray rocks clutching at the sky like gnarled hands. The rugged coastline extended in either direction in front of him. Waves smashed against craggy knuckles, then shattered. Slivers of seawater caught the fading light as they sprayed upward. Gotlib sat down in a different chair and lit a new cigarette.

"Just tell me what you think."

Miriam came in with dishes and started to set the table.

"Move your arm, please, Papá. It's in the way.

Gotlib moved his arm off the table so that Miriam could put down a dish.

"I don't feel like having tea today," he said.

"Teolinda baked *alfajores*."

"I know, sweetheart. I'm just not in the mood. My mind's not on food."

"But you should eat something, Papá."

Gotlib shook his head.

Miriam set a teacup by his dish anyway. He would change his mind, she thought. Papà loved the sticky, nut-filled cookies that the Argentine cook prepared.

"Come on, Papá," she coaxed. "It's five o'clock."

Miriam finished setting the table and went back into the kitchen.

"You should eat something, Ernesto," said Rebeca. "Whether you have a cup of tea or not won't influence their decision either way."

Ernesto sighed. "You think they've got to me yet?"

Rebeca shook her head. "God knows. How many of you were there?"

"Seven, I think ... Me, López ... let's see ... Martinelli ... that's three ... Valenzuela ... that's four"

"What about Tomich? Wasn't he coming up this time?"

Miriam had come back with a plate of *alfajores*.

"Marcela Tomich told me they were going back to Santiago, Mamá. She said her father wasn't a candidate."

"So that's only four," said Rebeca. She tried to make her voice soothing as she reached over and squeezed her husband's wrist. "One less to worry about."

"No," said Gotlib. "I never counted Tomich. I knew they were leaving Antofagasta. His brother is in Santiago. They have a business there."

"Well, so ... four. López, Martinelli, Valenzuela, and you."

"There's Petersen."

"He'll have a good chance. They're always impressed with an English name."

"Swedish."

"Whatever."

"Just as long as it's not Jewish. Just as long as it's not Rosental or Vainberg or Gotlib or something."

"Ernesto, stop it. This is Antofagasta, Chile. This is not Nazi Germany."

"They've never elected a Jew. Never!"

It was true. There had never been a Jew in the Volunteer Fire Department of Antofagasta.

"Papá, don't get yourself worked up."

But Gotlib was worked up. Tonight the entire department had met to vote. Only the most respected men in the city were invited to join the fire brigade, and since boyhood Gotlib had dreamed of being a fireman, a *bombero*.

As a child he had watched the incandescent fire engines racing down the streets. On either side, the proud flame tamers stood tense and bold. When they reached the burning building, they yanked out their hoses and shoved their ladders up against the blistering walls, then hurled

themselves into the asphyxiating black haze to pull out endangered men, women, children, even pets. It was like a movie.

Don Mauro Mujica had been head of the brigade for as long as Gotlib could remember. A successful businessman who had rebuilt the family fortune that his mother had squandered on horses, Don Mauro had a reputation for tough-mindedness and hard dealing. At work and at the club he was reserved. He wore English-cut suits and smoked imported cigarettes. But the sound of a siren transformed him. The mask fell and the cool caution that characterized his business style gave way to temerity. He rushed into the flames, balancing on teetering beams, yanking out victims, securing walls, hauling up hose, yelling orders. At a fire, old Don Mauro—he had seemed old to Gotlib back then, although he must have been in his forties—turned bold and resolute. He had grit. He led his men into the most vicious fires. They respected him, and they elected him chief term after term.

After a victory, the fire trucks would return to the station, moving slowly now, but with sirens screeching, as the townspeople grouped on corners to wave white handkerchiefs and hail the firefighters as heroes.

On September 18, Independence Day, and on other festive occasions as well, the firemen paraded through town in their gleaming engines, led by the fire chief in his bright red car. Don Mauro was at the height of glory as he led the noisy procession with his young son seated beside him. Sometimes Maurito would ride with his father to a fire on an engine. Gotlib was about eight or ten when he began to envy Maurito, who was the same age as he. Gotlib had longed to sit on one of those huge, gleaming trucks just once—not beside his father, of course, for his own father could never be a fireman. But by that time, he had already realized that he was not of the same breed as the tall, fair, slim boy with the wide smile whose admittance into the elite brigade was a foregone conclusion.

Sometimes Gotlib hung around the fire station on a Sunday. Mauro Senior would have the Victrola on, and the firemen, many of them of Italian extraction, would listen to a tenor sing "Santa Lucia." Don Mauro was at ease on those Sunday afternoons, surrounded by his men. He poured burgundy from his uncle's vineyards while Maurito, in those silly shorts that all schoolboys wore and unanimously hated, galloped around the station house. Then someone would coax, "¡Canta, Maurito!" and the others would chant, "¡Canta! ¡Canta!" They kept a

huge Mexican hat with silver trimmings on a peg in the office and Maurito would put it on and sing "Jalisco, no te rajes." All the men would laugh, not only because they thought Mexican songs were hilarious, but because Maurito was the fire chief's son and he was a great little clown. Ernestito would laugh with them, but he would keep a little to the side, a little out of the way. No one ever told him to go home, but no one ever invited him to come again next Sunday, either. Someday, he thought, Maurito would be a fire chief just like his father.

"I suppose there isn't much of a chance," Gotlib was saying. "It's an honor even to be a candidate, Ernesto. And to have been nominated by Mauro Mujica, the chief's son!"

"That's right, Papá," said Miriam. "I'd say you stand a very good chance."

"So what do you think? You think they've got to me yet?"

Rebeca would have preferred to have her tea and *alfajores* and not talk about it anymore, but she knew that her husband's self-esteem was riding on this vote and that his nerves would not let his mind off the subject.

"Let's see … Tomich is going to Santiago … Santamaría … he'll get in. He's Don Mauro's son-in-law, and his father has been a *bombero* for years … . That makes six … ."

"What about Carrera?" asked Miriam.

"That's it, Carrera! Good girl, Miriam. How could I forget Carrera?"

Rebeca smiled at her husband. He adored the girls. His daughters were the most important thing in his life, far more important than this ridiculous vote. That's why, Rebeca thought, it was a shame he was making himself so sick over this business.

And yet, she understood. To be a fireman was to be one of them.

"Well, if they went in alphabetical order, they took Carrera first, then Gotlib, then López, Santamaría—no, Petersen, Martinelli, Santamaría, Valenzuela. They started at three-thirty. It's after five now. They've already considered your candidacy, Ernesto. They've probably all gone home for tea."

"Sometimes the debates go on into the night."

Rebeca sighed.

"What if they didn't go in alphabetical order?" Gotlib said.

Rebeca stood up and went to call her other two daughters. "Tea, girls! Teolinda made *alfajores* and there are buns and sweet rolls!"

She sat down again and turned to her husband.

"If they didn't go in alphabetical order, then I don't know."

"So," said Gotlib heavily, "maybe it's already been decided."

"Maybe. So go ahead and eat."

She poured tea into his cup. Two giggling teenage girls collided with each other and the railing on the stairs. They tumbled into the dining room. One kissed Gotlib on the forehead, the other kissed him on the cheek.

"*Hola*, Papá. How's the future fire chief?"

"Don't make jokes, Emi," said Miriam. "Papá's nervous."

"Nothing to be nervous about," said Emilia. "You're as good as elected."

"They probably laughed themselves silly, to think a Jew wanted to be a fireman," said Gotlib.

Miriam suppressed a guffaw.

"C'mon, Papá," said Sara. "Don't get melodramatic."

This time Miriam laughed out loud. "After all this family has been through, Papá! Do you really think the Gotlibs of Antofagasta will fall apart if you don't get elected to the fire brigade?"

Gotlib smiled and squeezed her hand. He knew she was right.

Logic told him she was right. But there was more to it than that.

The Gotlibs had been in Antofagasta for more than forty years. Ernesto's father, Joseph Gottlieb, had come to Chile right before the war. Hitler was showing his fangs, and Joseph's brother Herman, who had seen his neighbors slashed with knives and broken glass, insisted that to wait would be fatal. Joseph didn't think so. He had started out as a tailor, but had expanded into ready-to-wear. He had a shrewd head for money and had built up a thriving business, importing cheap goods from Italy and turning huge profits. He had six stores in Munich alone. To up and leave everything behind would be devastating. Herman said that if Joseph didn't go, he would go alone. He had friends in Switzerland and France, and he could get false documents.

Herman did not need to harp. Events convinced Joseph that his brother was right. Late one night in September, hoodlums hurled a bottle filled with blood through Herman's front window. The crash was deafening. Shards of glass flew crazily through the room. They

mixed with crimson on the opposite wall and slid, carried by streams of blood, down the painted surface onto the floor, where red and glass formed splintery pools that glistened eerily. Trembling, Herman called for his brother. Joseph stood and looked for a long time. Then he held his brother Herman in his arms and both men cried.

Joseph returned home and helped his pregnant wife pack two light bags. They took a change of clothes, a few items of jewelry that had been in the family for generations, and pictures of their parents. Joseph went to the store on Winkler Street and took all the money out of the safe. Then he lovingly straightened the stacks of sweaters, the rows of jackets, the skirts, the scarves, the wool stockings. Before he left, he turned out the light. Joseph felt as though a cleaver were lodged in his chest.

There was hardly time to say good-bye to cousins and friends.

In the train, Joseph's wrists went limp and he felt nauseous, as though he were sinking into a sea of vomit. Eventually his wretchedness became so intense that he stopped feeling it. He looked out the window at the tiny farms and drab sky, and allowed himself to be lulled to sleep by the monotony of the movement and the landscape.

Herman, Joseph, and Joseph's wife, Constanza, arrived in Le Havre before dawn. They got on the first ship crossing the Atlantic in which there were accommodations available. They did not ask where it was going because it didn't matter. Later they found out they were headed for South America, and thought that this was as good a destination as any.

The crossing was smooth, but Constanza's pregnancy made it tedious. Constanza was in the stage at which even the smell of fresh cooked vegetables made her ill. The odor of fuel and seawater sickened her to the point of paralysis. The cramped cabin and the rocking of the vessel—slight though it was—made her feel as though she were caught in a rapidly spinning canister. She did not complain, but in those rare moments in which her head was clear, she saw herself running through a pasture hand in hand with the child that would soon be born. Under her feet she imagined the grass to be soft and dry.

The first port of call was Rio de Janeiro. There was a crowd of dark faces at the docks and Joseph thought that maybe they had detoured to Africa, although the steward assured him that he was in Brazil. The swarm of black and red and green and yellow seemed foreign and frightening to Joseph. Multitudes of black people in brightly colored

shirts ... ripe produce in crates and baskets ... throbbing rhythms of portside musicians ... smells both pungent and rancid. Joseph knew that Constanza needed fresh air and solid ground, but he and Herman decided to stay on board until the next stop: Buenos Aires.

Argentina appealed to them. There was already a German-speaking Jewish population there. There would be synagogues and schools for the children. But a man on the boat named Eisenberg said that there was more money to be made in Chile, and besides, Chileans were tolerant of Jews. Argentina was full of Italians, and who knew what to expect of them? There were Italians in Chile, too, but they were a small minority, and besides, most of them were from earlier immigrations and so had fewer ties with the homeland. In Buenos Aires, according to Eisenberg, not only were there more Italian surnames than Spanish, but there were sections where the only language spoken was Italian.

Joseph and Herman considered the situation. Mussolini had helped Hitler bolster Franco in the Spanish Civil War, and now there was talk of a formal Rome–Berlin axis. Where there were Italians with close and recent ties to Italy, there would be anti-Semitism, the brothers reasoned. Eisenberg said that he had a cousin in the north of Chile, where there were lucrative copper mines. It was an area of vast wealth that attracted thousands of Chileans from other cities every year, and this new, affluent population needed goods: clothes, food, furniture, medicines. There was plenty of cash, but nothing grew or was manufactured in the north. Everything had to be brought in from outside. It was, Eisenberg said, a land of opportunity for a shrewd businessman.

Joseph and Herman disembarked in Valparaiso. There, they contacted friends of relatives of friends, who recommended them to a German wholesaler in Antofagasta who supplied the mines at Chuquicamata. His name was Uwe Rissel.

Joseph went to work for Herr Rissel, but Herman, who had been trained as an engineer, found work at the mines. Joseph was an excellent salesman, with years of experience, and although he was not pleased with the idea of working for another man, news from relatives in Europe made it clear that he was lucky to be alive and working at all.

Rissel had access to a huge inventory; he sold everything from radios to toothpaste, from refrigerators to perfume, from auto parts to ladies' panties, from penny novels to screwdrivers. His orders tripled and quadrupled within a year of hiring Joseph. By then, Constanza had had

a baby girl named Ana Noemí, and Joseph was glad of the increased commission that Rissel gave him.

Joseph learned Spanish quickly. At night he listened to soap operas on the radio and practiced pronouncing the names of the characters in front of the mirror: "Roberto … Rrrroberto … Rrrrrroberto … Raúl… Rrrraúl … Rrrrrraúl … He bought a dictionary and read lists of words out loud to Ana Noemí. (When she started babbling, he discontinued the practice for fear she would imitate his imperfect pronunciation.) He went to the local school and offered to pay a young teacher by the hour to give him lessons. The fellow gave him a child's book of grammar exercises and every afternoon during siesta, Joseph would write them out, letter by letter: *Tú vas. Quiero que tú vayas. Tú vienes. Quiero que tú vengas.*

Joseph had a knack for convincing the miners that they desperately needed products that they had never even heard of. He sent the neighborhood children to the mine stores to ask for Milagro de Lourdes Elexir or Melena de Oro Shampoo, products unknown in Antofagasta. A few days later, he appeared at the store announcing that he was the sole representative for Milagro de Lourdes and Melena de Oro.

In the meantime, Herman had begun investing in the mines. With the demand for metals caused by the war, he was soon making money by the fistful. He was the first of the two brothers to buy a home—a small pink villa by the beach, with a spectacular view of the sea from the living room and a spectacular view of the mountains from the master bedroom. Within a few years, he married a Chilean-born girl named Ester Anita Shapiro, and they had two children, Jaime and Meyer.

Joseph's son Ernst was born a year and a half after Ana Noemí and a month after his brother's son Jaime. Joseph and Constanza named their son Ernst Heinrich: Ernst after Constanza's father, who had died of cancer years before, and Heinrich after a Nazi torturer.

The child's middle name was a compromise. Rissel admired Hitler, although that did not prevent him from hiring shrewd Jews to make money for him. When he heard that Gottlieb's wife was expecting, he demanded that his employee name the baby Adolph. Joseph refused, arguing that tradition dictated that he name their son after a deceased relative. Rissel's color rose. It was a little thing to ask in return for all he had done for Gottlieb, he said. He might just have to look for another sales manager, he said. Gottlieb thought that Rissel was bluffing. The

German had never made as much money as now. But Joseph Gottlieb could not take a chance. As a conciliatory gesture, he gave the boy a middle name that was acceptable to his boss.

Heinrich Himmler was just beginning to make a name for himself in Europe as head of the *Schutzstaffel*, or Black Shirts, but with luck, not even the boy himself would ever associate the Nazi's name with his own. Joseph had had an Uncle Heinrich who had died years before. Officially Ernst Heinrich was named after him.

By the time he was four, Ernst was accompanying his father to Rissel's. By the time he was seven, it was he who went pestering store managers for the products that his father was promoting. At nine, Ernst Gottlieb had mastered one of the fundamental principles of business: create a need.

Joseph got his big chance when Chile broke relations with the Axis in 1943. German nationals were being forced out of the country and Rissel had to sell cheap. Joseph got a loan from his brother and took over Rissel, SA. He renamed the firm Antofagasta Wholesalers, the most neutral, un-Germanic tag he could think of. Constanza stayed home and took care of the children and kept the books while Joseph hustled. By the late 1950s, Gottlieb had built Antofagasta Wholesalers into one of the biggest companies in the country.

Herman prospered as well. He had invested his earnings in beachfront property and was now the owner of houses, apartment buildings, and a hotel. He urged Joseph to put his money into land, but Joseph preferred to stuff cash into the mattress. "Where I can get at it easily if I need it," he said. Herman thought his brother was thinking like a Chilean peasant instead of like a clever European businessman, but nothing he said made Joseph change his mind.

"This isn't Germany," Herman prodded. "It's not like you'll have to make a quick getaway."

Joseph accumulated sacks and sacks of escudos. Soon there were too many to fit into the mattress, so he hid money behind pictures, under floorboards, in wells, in holes dug beside trees, and in a secret compartment under the roosts in the chicken coop. When Chile went into an economic crisis and changed from escudos to pesos, Joseph was left with bags of money that wasn't worth the paper it was printed on.

Joseph's son Ernst was a teenager when he started writing his last name *G-o-t-l-i-b* to make it conform to its Spanish pronunciation. At

the same time, he changed his given names to Ernesto Enrique. Joseph did not put up a fight. In fact, he was glad. At last, he was done with Himmler once and for all.

Ernesto was articulate about his identity. He was a Chilean, he said, not a German, and he didn't want anyone mistaking him for a foreigner. He was proud of Chile, which had taken in thousands of Jewish immigrants before, during, and after the war. It was thanks to Chile's open-arms policy toward refugees that, instead of being thrown into a gas chamber, he had been educated in good private schools and had studied business at the Catholic University of Valparaíso. (Wealthy Jews, like wealthy Masons and other renegades, had a tacit working relationship with the Jesuit fathers. The Catholic schools were the best in the country. Jews and Masons supported them generously; in return, the priests educated the infidels' sons. Each side kept out of the other's hair and neither asked too many questions.)

By the early sixties Ernesto had completed his degree and gone into his father's business. He no longer loved Chile because it had taken in immigrants during perilous times; he loved Chile because he was Chilean. Unlike his father, he spoke Spanish without an accent and with dialectal variants; he said *uté* instead of *usted*, *etái* instead of *estás*, *paco* instead of *policía*, *porotos* instead of *frijoles*, and *living* instead of *sala*. He ate empanadas on Sunday afternoons and had tea every day at five. Yet Ernesto Gotlib sensed that he didn't quite fit in. No one had ever said anything to him about being Jewish, but at the Colegio San Luis he had felt pangs of embarrassment in the locker room when his circumcised penis was in full view. He felt awkward at Mass and in religion class. When they talked about the one true faith, it mortified him. The first time he had to line up with the other little boys for confession with Father Reblando, he lost his composure and had to be sent home. He was certain that Father Reblando was going to call him an anti-Christ and blame him for the death of Jesus. After that, Joseph arranged for his son to be excused from some of the rites. Joseph had made sizable contributions to the school, and the fathers agreed to the arrangement. They were a tolerant bunch.

As a university student, Ernesto had been invited to parties, and friends often had him to dinner—and sometimes even to baptisms, first communions, and weddings. But whenever a classmate introduced

him to his parents, he suspected that they were thinking, "Ah, Ernesto Gotlib, the Jew."

Ernesto noticed, or thought he noticed, that his friends never presented him to their sisters.

After college, when young men began to join their fathers' clubs—the Club de la Nación, the Auto Club, the Club Italiano—he began to feel excluded. Joseph belonged to the Unión Hebraica, and that was all right, but Ernesto yearned to attend dances at the Alianza Italo-Española, where the fire chief's pretty daughter Graciela rocked and rolled with the sons of the men who formed the elite of Antofagasta: the firemen. To Ernesto's mind, those boys were real Chileans. Some of them had foreign grandparents—Martinelli, Petersen, López (whose grandmother was Yugoslavian)—but Gotlib was sure that they never felt like outsiders. Gotlib felt like an outsider because Gotlib was a Jew.

Joseph and Herman Gottlieb did not share Ernesto's discomfort. They knew who they were: German Jews who had fled Nazi Germany in order to save their lives. They spoke German or Yiddish at home and walked down the street with yarmulkes on their heads on Friday nights. On the Sabbath, their wives lit candles. They were grateful to their new country for taking them in, but they knew that they were foreigners, not Chileans. They were perfectly content to have dinner at the Unión Hebraica on Sunday night, and they encouraged their sons to attend dances there, make friends with Jewish girls, and settle down.

After the switch from escudos to pesos Herman lent Joseph money to rebuild his financial base. This time, he invested in gold. Herman was rich and Joseph would eventually be rich again, but what was money for, Joseph asked Herman, if not to pass on to children and grandchildren? The Gottliebs looked at their progeny and smiled.

But in 1970 the world of Joseph and Herman Gottlieb shattered. Salvador Allende was a candidate for president, and violence was erupting in the streets. When Allende was elected, Herman's fears mushroomed. The new chief of state set out to revamp Chilean society, nationalizing industries and enterprises—including the mines.

Herman, like others who had invested heavily in copper, lost everything. Joseph would have been pleased to give his brother money, but money was not the real problem. Herman's life was in shambles. He had started from scratch in Germany and built a business, only to lose it. He had started from scratch again in Chile, and now the prospect

of starting over yet again was overwhelming. Herman was no longer a young man. The sleeplessness was wearing him down. The strain showed on his brow and in his voice, which frequently cracked and trailed off. Herman was sinking into depression.

In the streets, rock-throwing mobs attacked anyone wearing a business suit. Herman and Joseph Gottlieb did not consider themselves perpetrators of economic crimes. They had not inherited their fortunes; they had earned them through sweat and ingenuity. But the firebrands saw no difference between Joseph and Herman Gottlieb and the idle rich.

Herman and Joseph had the impression that they were reliving a nightmare. Herman became afraid to go outside, not only because thugs and hoodlums of all persuasions used politics as an excuse to throw potatoes with razor blades embedded in them at passers-by, but because squatters were taking over homes. It was dangerous to leave a house unattended, even for a few hours. And who knew if you could trust your servants?

In the following months, inflation soared and strikes spread. In the stores, there was no kosher meat or any other kind of meat. For a ration of rice, housewives queued up from five o'clock in the morning once a week, on Thursdays. Before long, women were beating their empty pots in the plaza to protest the scarcity of food. Toilet paper became a luxury item. Shoes were unbuyable. Rumors spread that Chile, an important manufacturer of leather goods, was sending its shoes to Cuba. Herman bowed his head and with a meat cleaver slashed the toes out of the shoes of his grandson, Jacobo. Meyer's boy was growing, Herman explained as though he had to justify his actions. Jacobo's little foot needed room.

It was a September night when a bottle filled with blood crashed through Herman's front window and shattered against the opposite wall, splashing crimson over the lamp, the sofa, the cream-colored carpet. Herman had been sitting at the piano, picking out a polka he remembered from childhood.

Herman did not move. He sat for a long, long time and watched the blood stream down the wall before he felt his muscles contract and his throat grow tight and dry. His head ached terribly. He had lived this scene before. He wanted to cry, but he didn't. He just sat watching the blood serpent creep slowly, slowly down the wall.

When Herman's wife, Ester, came back from visiting with Constanza that afternoon, she found the living room a wreck. In the bedroom, she found her husband sprawled over the bed, his head blown to bits, teeth and hair stuck to walls and furniture, and blood, great pools of viscous black-red blood, seeping through the white bedclothes onto the floor. His note said simply that he had been through it all once before. He couldn't bear to go through it again.

On September 11, 1973, Allende fell. Some in the country rejoiced, but Ernesto Gotlib was in mourning. His father, Joseph, had died only two days before. The doctors said it was a heart condition, but Ernesto knew it was grief. Joseph and Herman had always been inseparable.

By then, Ernesto was married and all three of his daughters had been born. He, like many others who had opposed Allende, assumed that the country would return to democracy. When it did not, he ranted at the dinner table and drew up protests that he read at meetings of the brotherhood of the Unión Hebraica. But with time, his furor cooled, Pinochet was a dictator, but the country was prospering. Store shelves were filled with imported goods and there was a huge demand for everything from radios to toothpaste, from refrigerators to perfume. Pinochet wouldn't last, he told himself, and in the meantime, he, Ernesto, was cleaning up. He had inherited his father's business, and ran it with the expertise of a person who had known how to sell before he had known how to walk.

Gotlib was a rich man. He owned not only Antofagasta Wholesalers but retail stores as well. And he did not hide his money in the mattress. He invested it. Over the years, he accumulated houses, condominiums, office buildings, an interest in a shipping company, and a tourist boat. He had three beautiful daughters and a wonderful wife. But still, something was missing.

Gotlib had influence because he had money, but the pangs of the locker room had never subsided. Did those men who were recognized as the city leaders appreciate his merits, he wondered, or did they consider him a pushy, crafty, upstart Jew? In the middle of the night, as the waves rolled softly onto the beach with a steady swish, Ernesto felt the eyes of his classmates on his circumcised penis. He heard the voice of Father Reblando. He saw the soft, blond curls of Graciela, the fire chief's daughter, resting on the lapel of … Aníbal López.

Now that his father and uncle were dead, Gotlib had loosened his ties with the Jewish European community in Chile. After the war and during the following years, waves of Jews arrived from Germany, France, England. But they were not like Gotlib. They were foreigners. Gotlib was Chilean born. Not only for himself, he felt, but for his dead father and uncle, he needed to be accepted as a real Chilean. He needed to validate their choice. He needed a sign for all the world to see that he was not only a citizen, but the best of citizens. He needed to be a fireman.

Miriam put down the tray of breads and cakes and massaged her father's shoulders.

She's a beautiful girl, thought Gotlib. "It's for her—for all of them—that I want this so much," he said to himself. "So that they shouldn't feel like outsiders. So that they should be comfortable mingling with the best of them."

Of his three daughters, Miriam was the one to whom he felt closest. Emilia, the eldest, was exotic and talented. She had huge brown eyes and curly chestnut hair that framed her darkish face, and she played the piano like Arturo Rubenstein. (Well, Gotlib conceded privately, maybe not exactly like Arturo Rubenstein.) Gotlib smiled at his first-born child, and she smiled back at him.

Sara, the youngest, was pert and sassy. The beneficiary of the battles Gotlib had fought with Emilia and Miriam and lost, Sara was allowed to wear makeup at thirteen and go on overnights with the Girl Scouts of Antofagasta. Her sisters had wanted to do those things; he and Rebeca had said no but had wound up giving in. By the time Sara was a senior member of Antofagasta Troop 1034 and began wearing lipstick, her parents had stopped resisting. Even so, Sara had grown into a fairly well-behaved girl, although more spirited and stronger willed than her sisters. She had long, light brown hair that she refused to cut, although Rebeca said it looked messy, and a few barely-there freckles that she tried to cover with makeup, even though Gotlib said they were cute.

Miriam was taller and thinner than her sisters. She had soft, blond, shoulder-length hair and eyes whose irises were blue on the rim and amber within. Her facial structure was less than perfect, but Miriam had an incandescence that brightened a room. Gotlib felt her fingers

knead and soothe the tight muscles of his neck, and knew that God had truly blessed him. It was, perhaps, too much to want to be a fireman, too.

Sara was speaking: "It's not the end of the world if you don't get in."

"She's right, of course, Papá," confirmed Miriam.

"Anyhow," said Emi, "if you don't make it this time, maybe somebody will nominate you again next year."

Gotlib basked in his children's love for a moment.

"You know," he said, shaking his head, "it gives me a funny feeling to think that at this very moment they may be talking about me. They may be deciding about me."

"Probably not," said Rebeca. "They probably decided hours ago."

But Rebeca was wrong. At the station house, Don Mauro had just presented Gotlibs name.

"Any discussion?"

"A good man," said Don Dionisio. "In spirit he's been one of us for a long time. Since he was a kid, really."

"Anything else?" prodded Don Mauro.

No one made a move to speak.

"Are you sure?"

Don Ricardo looked rather sour. He was getting hungry and he wanted to go home.

Don Héctor scratched his eyebrow out of boredom.

Don Ignacio shook his head, but said nothing.

Don Mauro waited in silence for someone to come forward. Don Agustín yawned. They had been at it for a long time.

"Then let's vote."

The men placed their ballots in the box. When they were done, Don Alejandro, the brigade secretary, read them aloud, one by one.

Gotlib had finished tea, but he and Miriam remained at the table talking. Rebeca sat with them a while, then got up to get her sewing; with three girls in the family, there was always something to mend. Teolinda was clearing the table. Sara and Emilia had gone upstairs, but bolted down when they heard a knock at the door.

Gotlib jumped up, then forced himself to sit back down. One of the servants would get it.

Virginia, Teolinda's niece, came into the room.

"Señor," she said, "there are two gentlemen here to see you."

"Who?" Gotlib's voice was controlled. He was making a great effort not to appear upset.

"Don Mauro and his son."

Gotib took a short, tight breath. He hadn't expected a visit. He had expected a telephone call.

"Have them come in," said Rebeca.

"I'll see them in my study," said Gotlib.

But Don Mauro was peeping through the dining room door.

It was an indecorous thing for the fire chief to do, and Gotlib was confused. But Don Mauro was grinning widely and the younger Mujica was bounding toward Gotlib as though he couldn't wait another instant. Mauro—the son—embraced Gotlib before a word was spoken.

"Congratulations, Ernesto," said Don Mauro.

"Congratulations, *compadre*! Welcome to the *bomberos*!" The younger Mauro's smile was even bigger and warmer than his father's.

Gotlib was fighting back tears, but Miriam was making no pretense to self-control. She was crying openly. Sara and Emilia were laughing.

"See, Papá?" giggled Sara. "What did I tell you?"

Emilia, then Sara, then Miriam kissed their father.

Rebeca was last of all.

Gotlib hugged his wife close as he turned to Don Mauro and his son.

He opened his mouth to speak, but his throat was tight. Finally, he said, "Thank you … thank you. …"

Rebeca was the first one to regain her composure.

"May I offer you some tea and *alfajores*?"

"Thank you, but we can't stay," said Don Mauro.

"Just a cup of tea?"

"All right, just a cup of tea."

Rebeca signaled Teolinda to bring clean cups and to refill the pot.

"Can you … can you tell me if there was a lot of discussion?" asked Gotlib.

"No," said Don Mauro. "There was no discussion."

"Everyone knows you, Ernesto. Christ, you've been hanging around the station since you were in short pants. You've always been a part of the *bomberos*. That's what they said—that you've always been one of us. It was unanimous."

"Unanimous! But didn't they mention ... anything else?"
Father and son both looked puzzled.

"No," said the younger Mauro. "Nothing."

Rebeca felt a new surge of joy. She got up and went to help Teolinda with the tea. She did not want to cry in front of her guests.

Miriam got up, too, to keep from laughing. "Silly old Papá," she said to herself.

Gotlib smiled, but a new worry was gnawing at his brain.

"I wonder if they really wanted me," he said to Rebeca later, as he got ready for bed. "What I mean is, did they really want *me*, or did they just think a token Jewish name would look nice on the roster?"

Alcira in Yellows[1]

Alicia Kozameh

To all those who,
with respect and fondness toward their origins,
emerge from themselves.

Cadmium yellow the sun at the end of the summer of 1958, a March stained with darkened blots, when in some part of her brain, in the process of understanding, Alcira has deposited the certainty, the conviction of her five years: *I can feel them, I feel all of them, they are five, five years they say I am completing, and I believe it.* Filtered by vapors ascending from chimneys, distanced from any possible abstraction, adding mustard-colored waves of heat to the industrial and mortal sky of Rosario, the air observes Alcira. It examines her closely, describes her for itself, and tries to understand her. It animates itself to question her and analyze her parts and return her intact to her origins. *Thanks, Alcira, without alternatives, must feel, thanks to this air I remain whole, thanks to the air that circulates, that comes and goes,* that wanders through the neighborhood of her five years, thanks to this air she can recognize herself, have a certain idea of herself, in spite of the ambivalences, in spite of the multiplicity of messages, of stories and signs.

Search, Alcira, between the dark and parallel lines that cross the sky from one corner to the other, *between those electrical cables that terrify me when the rain lets go but that move me inside and fill me with those desires to laugh, to shake myself with joy, because they are musical staffs, they are my score, the last one they bought for me; those electrical cables are a gigantic staff that surrounds me and spins around me, goes crazy and wraps me up, makes me dizzy; the cables carry within them the movement, the speed with which my ten fingers move on the piano; they put that madness into my hands and shake them, make them vomit up the music.* The scores that Alcira loves because they are music, and the scores that are intolerable for her because they are the instrument that her piano teacher brandishes, waves, in order not to permit her to

1 Translated from the Spanish by Roberta Gordenstein.

interpret her own melodies. The ones she invents in the middle of those nights in which not a single sound is heard.

Search, Alcira. She searches for moments, situations, in the sky of her neighborhood, in which there may appear some similarity with the words she hears each day: from her father's mouth, from her mother's eyes. With the food she eats and the food she enjoys. With the faces, almost always round, of her cousins. With her mother's insistence on bathing her portion of meat with several scoops of milk curd under the satisfied gaze of her father, and the tense and lowered eyelids of her grandmother, descending as if to neutralize offenses, place results at a distance, change the direction of thought, during the long supper on the long dining room table of her house.

Alcira searches between her two feet squeezed against the grooves of the wide sidewalk, the sidewalk extended between the shadows of the tall trees open to above, searches for *why, why did grandmother sink her finger covered with rings into my belly, near my belly button, and say to me a little in Spanish, a little in her Arabic of Aleppo, and another little bit in Yiddish: "You listen to me well, Alcira. The ridiculous ideas of your father, who is meshuggene, don't have to matter to you. They don't matter to you. You have to marry a Jew, do you understand? A Jew."* Alcira, without a reply. With a certain strength she scrutinized the eyes of the old lady; with more strength she followed the movements of the old ringed finger to be certain that it was not going to perforate her empty, defenseless stomach again, and she ran to the table, which was already laid.

And the following day she committed the error. The error of the word. She committed the error of those who have words at their disposal and use them: she approached her mother and asked her the meaning of the episode and the reason for her grandmother's so-lively interest. Alcira's mother, Raquel, very Raquel, all of her, and filled with fears, settled a dry and worried gaze on Alcira, like the gazes of people who have words but do not always use them, and slowly approached the father. And after a moment of doubt she decided to be honest with him, decided not to hide from him her daughter's ingenuousness or her mother's desires (although she left buried, compressed between the walls of some of her most personal orifices, her sentiments, secret but never forgotten), and she told him the story completely and in detail. She declared: "My mother told Alcira that when she grows up she has to marry a Jew. How is it possible that she does not appreciate the conces-

sion you make, permitting her to visit us, to remain in this house for days? It seems that behind our backs she is trying to convince the child. What do you think about that?"

And Alcira's father certainly had a very clear opinion of the facts. He said to Raquel, the very much Raquel: "How do you think I am going to feel about that? This is all your fault. Your mother is trying to convince Alcira of this foolishness because you allow it. Because you are as Jewish as she is. Shrews, the two of you. Dirty Jews. That's what you are. Now get out of here before I grab the three of you and kick you out of this house."

Like tempera, the sun, thick, melting simultaneously over the entire city, all-powerful, infiltrating itself between the grooves, plugging the openings. Injecting itself into the breath of those who run desperately, of those who walk slowly, of those who wait patiently, and of those who sleep for just a few hours. Into the breath of the plants. Of the insects. Of the corpses, stretching out in a skinlike and powerful mantle of undetainable flows and energies swelling the distinct natures of the earthly cortex with vitality.

It's killing me, Alcira feels. What's killing me is the stuffing. That makes me think that the bulky gray object that lies motionless in the middle of the street, where cars pass every once in a while, is a dead cat or a very furry little dog, struck by a truck or a motorcycle. That's why I hate the trucks that carry stuffing for the mattress manufacturers and lose it along the way. Because my mind skips from thoughts of my grandmother and the Jewish husband to the fear of what the stupid stuffing might be instead of stuffing, and it's hard for me to return. But what I want is to think about what my grandmother said, with her finger covered with thick rings entering me through my belly button, inserting itself where all the food is gathered and going down through what my mother calls the intestines, which is where all the caca is waiting to come out. My grandmother's finger, growing longer and coming out with the caca when I go to the bathroom, although I don't know what would happen, because either she jerks her hand back and takes it out and afterward washes it, I mean, before she begins to cook my mahmules *and my* mehche uaraa enab, *or else my grandmother's arm and head and body enter also, and then, just like that, all at once, she falls into the toilet.*

What can she have meant with that business of the Jewish husband? Better that she doesn't fall into the toilet, because she is good, my grandmother, and sometimes it seems to me that I love her.

The air, which still observes her and examines her closely, the winds of Rosario and its outskirts exerting pressures on the every day more ample surfaces of Alcira's torso. Of her arms. Of her feet, which hold more weight and too much mental turmoil, when, more or less in the winter of 1965, Alcira was battling with her more or less twelve years, and the different words of her father distributing themselves, penetrating into the smallest crevice, like the sun, solid and persistent, chrome yellow, exhausting. Her father hurling his words at her: "This girl is changing schools right now. You're taking her out of public school and enrolling her with the nuns. Today. And as a boarder. Board-er. I won't hear of her leaving every day. From Monday to Friday, boarding. This very day."

And another voice, the voice of the every day more Raquel, ascertaining quietly, "And now what's the matter? Why is she going to go to Catholic school, and on top of everything, as a boarder?"

And the exasperation of that father, that father and not another, *why not another, why isn't it possible to exchange a father for one more suitable to the needs of each child,* sinking into her pores and hardening itself like cement, paralyzing any intention of flight, dismissing: "Because I say so. Because every visit of this old woman is the same story. She comes here to meddle in our private life, to try to change the decisions we made years ago. She doesn't understand that you were married in the Catholic Church to a Christian. They disowned you, they forbade you to enter your house forever, they wished that all your children would die or be born sick, they shouted this in your face. That family is no longer your family. You are a Christian, not a Jew. There are no Jews in this house. Alcira is baptized. She is a Catholic. But of course, the old lady insists. I heard her talking with Alcira in the kitchen, repeating that shit about having to marry a Jew. Why, tell me that? So they will insult her in the street? So they will shout 'dirty Jew,' which is, after all, what you and your mother are? This is not a country for Jews. Let the Jews look for another place. My daughter is not a Jew. And tomorrow she is changing schools, so there will be no doubt. And you'll

speak to the nuns so they will make her take communion and give her a bed. And don't come to me saying that you take communion at eight. You can take it at any age. Leave now and register her. Now."

And a thread waving in the air, in front of Raquel's face, which is the succession of her words: "And you, since when are you a believer? From the day I met you I've heard you say you don't believe in God. What has turned you into such a practicing Catholic all of a sudden? I think the only thing you want is to humiliate us all. You ought to be a little more strict, so much strictness are you demanding of others, and follow what the Greek Orthodox Church, your family's church, commands you. And leave others in peace."

And waving in front of Alcira's father's face, not a thread, but a rope, which is the succession of his words: "I want them to let us live. That's what I want. I don't want anyone to point at us. I don't want anyone to consider us different. We are already the anti-Peronists of the neighborhood. We don't need anything more to be the target of all these ignorant fools. And on top of everything else, you, playing at being a Jew. Get out of my sight, will you?"

They have continued conforming, reorganizing the powers, the counterposed forces, in the air that Alcira still breathes. Each time with bronchial tubes more blocked, with asthmatic sparkles in her big eyes, which begin to clamor for fresh air. Air less populated with caustic, divisive sounds. Air without any irritating particles, air that does not produce excessive phlegm in the respiratory passages, in the souls. Air only for Alcira. That only Alcira can breathe. On a yellow afternoon of that winter. Chrome sun.

That's how it seems to me. It seems to me that a person is not what others decide. You are what you are. If I was born with chestnut-colored hair, filled with curls, why do there exist people who would do anything so that I would become a straight-haired blond? What happens if the grandson of the lady on the corner, who everyone says is Muslim, one day invites me to go out? What is my grandmother going to say? And my father, what is he going to do? Are they going to wish me dead? Are they going to kill me? Because it seems to be that a person who is neither this nor that is nothing. Or maybe, is no one. And whoever is no one is dead. Or something like that. At least that is what my mother's father told her when he found out that the reason she had escaped from the house was that she was planning to get married the following day to a goy: from

that moment on, she was no one. She was nothing. And that's why, as far as he and his whole family were concerned, she was dead.

<p align="center">***</p>

When you are twenty years old in a year like 1973 in Argentina, when what you have is a country inundated with social injustice, a city with ocher skies, a Semitic-Judeo-anti-Semitic family, a sad experience of long adolescent years among nuns who wash their hands of reality and live in repression, in hypocrisy, and in resentment, some very well-known artistic inclinations and a sense of justice that grows stronger every day; you are the only thing you ought to be: a young person sensitive to everything and totally prepared to surrender even your life in pursuit of a country, a world, that is equitable and just. Or more or less that.

The sun, ocher, the skies of the first half of the seventies in the cities, in the suffocating crowds, in the exterior and interior deserts, in the mountains. Inflammable and ocher, lucid and open to the great struggle. And to the illusion of possible survival. The sun.

You will always have to defend something. That is why we are here. We exist. Because there is always someone who needs to take something from another to protect what he has or to add something to his wealth.

Defending. That idea invades my mind; defending, it invades me, spreads out in me. I feel it take charge of me and it does me good. Defending what keeps me in a certain space in this world. Defending the right to follow my impulses toward Edgardo Fridman, who is two years older than I and has such green eyes that I cannot stop from staring. Defending my right to him without my father repeating the same old story he has told so many times before, always so redundant, and without him slapping me in the face, shouting, "You are not a Jew, and you're not going to get involved with that dirty Jew." The sun ocher, low, each time lower, and about to turn itself upside down on the world and suffocate it gladly with breaths of mustard. Of *sambatyon*.[2] Of mud. Taking refuge and solidifying itself in all the orifices forever.

If Edgardo were the great-grandson of Siddhartha Gautama I would feel the same. When I met him and liked him, I didn't know anything about him. What's the difference? We talked about it, and I told him

2 *Sambatyon* is, in Jewish folklore, a river that seethes with hot stones every day but the Sabbath.

the truth: I am an atheist. I don't see any god anywhere, nor am I look-
ing for one. Neither is he. What am I? A human being. And I have the
impression that that is enough. Our responsibilities are myriad, and it
doesn't seem to me that all the energies we have at our disposal ought to
be invested in beating children to avoid their marrying someone of one
or another religion. It doesn't seem to me. That fanaticism. As if they
had a magnet in some zone of the body and they moved to the rhythm of
the movement of another. They don't use the power of reason to take a
step aside, to separate themselves, to observe their surroundings. To ask
themselves if the reasons why they moved to that rhythm were their own
or whether they reached them from another direction. To question them-
selves about that enigmatic authority that decides for them to whom they
belong. They don't question themselves. I don't know if they give them-
selves a reply.

I feel like crying.

What is the difference between aiding a Jew in an accident and aiding
a Buddhist? I need an explanation. But it is not within my family that
I am going to find that response. In myself. Only in myself am I going to
find it. And I have it: there is no difference. And returning over and over
to the subject is squandering the few minutes we have at our disposal in
this life. That never return.

I certainly feel that there might be other differences. It would be much
more difficult for me to aid an Argentine or Chilean or Uruguayan sol-
dier, whether or not he has tortured or assassinated any of my friends
with his own hands. There is where I live the contrasts. There is where,
for me, things begin. Where the distinct roads begin, that each one opts
to take or not. The road toward destroying one's peers or toward contrib-
uting to their basic joy of being alive. Toward being in favor of or toward
being against humanity. Why am I going to want to favor those who
deprive others of food, of freedom, or of life?

There is a lot of sense in the newspapers' report that more than forty
percent of the Left in this country is of Jewish origin. Why not, I ask
myself? Opposing these military men means fighting against a repetition
of the Holocaust. Of course they, the oh, so prolific statistics, are the least
subtle manner the authorities have of establishing the two targets, two in
one, of the repression that is approaching.

It overwhelms me to feel positive toward my people, to have that clar-
ity embracing me. And it liberates me not to have any uncertainty about

what the religious origin of my militant companions might be. Nor that of any of the millions of inhabitants of this country for whom I seek equality so much. For whom so many of us seek it.

I need to breathe deeply. Deeply. So that the air puts pressure on my esophagus. And my stomach. My organs, the pieces of my body. My very own.

Ocher the yellow that invades and defines everything. Not cadmium, not chrome. The years accelerate the speeds, and existence is saturated with history.

"In this house we eat pork. Po-ork. And we mix it with milk. Mi-ilk. And whoever doesn't want to work on Saturdays is a bum. Bu-um. And if you don't like it, go back to your family. No one is forcing you to remain here. And don't think that I am so stupid as to not realize that what you are hoping for most fervently in what remains of your life is for me to die, so that you can go running off to the synagogue with your sisters. Jew. That's what you are: a Jew."

The eternally Raquel absorbs the sounds, the timbres going up and down, hoarsened by the emphysema from which the words spurt forth. She no longer questions: "Since when are you a practicing Catholic?" She no longer asks questions like that. Or like others. But she absorbs, she internalizes the sounds, in which the old stubbornness makes itself tangible. And she knows that the words that pile up and stifle themselves at the end of the sentence and at the sides of her half-opened mouth must make some sense.

Terra sienna, the sky that Alcira does not have the possibility of questioning. The basement of the prison fades everything to sepia, to browns that long for those old yellows, those jaundiced tones of the afternoon. Of the afternoons of unchanging Rosario, city with sulfurous clouds, industrial, never completely free. The Rosario saturated with family, filled with the grandmother with golden rings. The Rosario replete with insults and demands.

Toasted *terra sienna*, the air that presses against the physical surfaces of Alcira, that examines her closely, observes her, describes her and tries to understand her, that analyzes her parts, that returns her, intact, to her origins. The air that gives her form and places her in front of herself. And puts her in front of the past, which is neither more nor

less than the present. The prison of her twenty-two years, the prison of her five, and the prison of her ten. And always, then and now, the same necessity of leaping toward the unforeseen and freeing herself. The sepia air of closed dampnesses and circular motions gives her form in the space of the cell and tries to impose on her the memories, images, sometimes mutilated, of her history. Of a long and meticulous film that has lasted twenty-two years now, without cuts and without ambiguities. Of an unmistakable faithfulness toward its initial model, toward the first figure of the series on a long paper, folded and overlapping, cut out with exactitude and painstaking care, so that all the figures of the frieze are maintained identical and united.

It is so repetitive, the experience is different and the same every day, there is something like a commandment in so many minds, you ought to belong to someone, to something, it is necessary to be part of a group. The idea makes me afraid. And it seduces me. But I want to be able to bring about my independence. And have the inner strength to take a leap and break away, without having disappeared from history, for that reason. And from outside, to observe my movements, my growing insanity, my mastery. I want to be myself and I want to be she, I want to be the one to whom I speak every day, and who is my you, my she, and my self.

And who else am I? More or less, besides being Alcira, I am the obsessive writer, the curious one, the one determined to try for justice, the delirious, the crazy, the impossible, the obstinate, and the curly-haired one. I am whoever I want to be. And I am Alcira.

The darkened air of the cell observes her, divides her in sections, examines her closely, and does not forget the order in which she was connected in the beginning. It studies every element that comprises her, introduces itself into her smallest corners. It analyzes her, reads her, interprets her. It reorganizes her in a different order, observes her from a distance. It attempts very diverse ways, and none seems to give satisfaction. It seems to think profoundly. Goes on rejecting, one by one, all the options. Searches. It's trying to find her eyes. And it places them: brown and lively. And it begins the reassembly of her parts. The reconstruction in all its details. Which continues returning Alcira, in tones of yellow, to her genuine and complete forms.

Exotic Birds[1]

Reina Roffé

During the bitterest days of my European exile, I turn to the photo album where I keep, along with more recent memories, a few images from my childhood—images that enlarged and corrected, come back to me in dreams and in disturbing moments of insomnia. That is when I see the child I was and the people I loved, and when my first and perhaps only home comes clearly into view. In that house, as if on stage or in a boxing ring, everyone defended his or her own territory with blood, sweat, and tears. Aunt Reche, however, seemed to stay behind the scenes: she didn't want to fight over the space; she wanted to leave it. I secretly shared her desire. We both believed that beyond the walls of that house a kind of salvation awaited us.

Aunt Reche waited for several years, passing up many incidents that would have given her more than enough reason to leave, until she finally found the right opportunity. One never knows when a dead branch will sprout flowers. In fact, I never did find out how that particular argument started in the kitchen, the epicenter of all the daily quarrels. I am convinced that it was nothing serious because only a few words and shouts were exchanged, but it was the drop that made the glass overflow.

I remember watching a bird trying to fly across the patio in the oblique drizzle that had been falling since morning, when I heard a clear, forceful voice:

"I'm leaving for good."

After making the announcement, Aunt Reche ran through the hallway heading toward the stairs.

She was finally running from the house and from herself. What was she like? What had she been like just moments before some alien power took over and put her in motion? That motion was now suspended in its own impulse, in the fury of escaping, in her legs, her feet, her step, in the slight sway of her entire body.

1 Translated from the Spanish by Margaret Stanton.

She was a tired woman. Her tiredness was not new, it was as much a part of her as was her pale skin, her slight smile, and the eyes that revealed her disgust, her tedium, the smothered cry, and the conviction that nothing was worthwhile.

When she was little she used to walk along the dirt streets of a pretentiously named town in the province of Santa Fe, until she reached the train station where she would hide and dream of getting on the train that would take her to Buenos Aires. However, when the family finally did move to the capital, she was interested only in the port where the Sephardic Jews from Morocco used to disembark, among them her own young parents, who arrived at the beginning of the century.

As I remember her, I find it difficult to attribute her permanent air of melancholy to her nomadic appearance (she always seemed to be somewhere else). None of the stories about her provides a reason to justify her absence, the withdrawal into herself that made her invisible to everyone else.

No one ever saw her. Her apprenticeship for becoming invisible must have started very early, when she was still a child and spent long hours following the paths of the ants along the cracks in the flagstones. There must have been something in her infancy, in the solitude of her childhood days. But in her case, it was a different kind of solitude, one without which nothing was possible for her.

In the Jobson-Vera mansion, where she was born around 1925, her parents and siblings ignored her, not because they didn't love her, but because of her determination to be ignored, to become a colorless spot, an imperceptible filigree on the floor or on the walls. The teachers used to give her very high grades in school, but they complained that she was like an extension of the bench she occupied in the classroom: dull, quiet, doing what was required.

She was compliant. I know she was especially dedicated to the Friday afternoon chore she assumed when she still lived in the small town. Lacking a synagogue, the Sephardic community of Jobson, consisting of three or four families at that time, had improvised a prayer room in the back room of the store that belonged to her father, the grandfather that I never met. Seldom did the ten men needed for the rabbi to begin the ceremony appear. Aunt Reche had the job of going in search of those who were missing. She didn't understand this law but, although I can imagine her indignation at the fact that women's presence didn't

count, I am convinced that she took her weekly duty very seriously. According to her older sister, who never kept secrets for her, once when Aunt Reche couldn't find the tenth man, she decided to take his place. She put on the cast-off clothes of the men of the house, covered her blossoming curves with a large coat, greased down her hair, put on a yarmulke, and took her place next to the other men.

She went unnoticed on that occasion and also again at the age of twenty, when she repeated the feat, needlessly, in the temple on Piedras Street in Buenos Aires, no less, which was always full. These are the only mischievous things or transgressions she is known to have committed. Later on she lost interest in everything and decided to act like a robot whose actions were preprogramed.

And in spite of that, her heart beat quickly. Even today I believe I can hear her rapid, furious puffing on the day she ran toward the stairs with the intention of reaching the last door of the house. I have her image frozen in my memory: Aunt Reche moving against a cobalt blue background; Aunt Reche who felt emotions, who felt love and anger although she was submerged in death. Certainly, she expected more than anyone else did. How much more? A little more affection, a little more tolerance, the little extra promised by the lottery, the illusory bonuses of the business of life? I suspect that the magnitude of what she hoped for had become a burden, all out of proportion to what she could bear.

From there, perhaps, came her sleepless nights and the premature knowledge of failure and sorrow—a primordial, pre-existing, unyielding sorrow that nevertheless made her rebel against her own knowledge that life was only life passing by. Could her relentless, barren insomnia have been the cause of these impressions? How could she fill the void, flirt with the darkness without going crazy with the thought—first innocent and then obsessive—that all effort was in vain, that love was a meaningless fiction, nothing more than an et cetera that justified all the theories that popular philosophy at once proposed and rejected in sayings, proverbs, songs, and movies. The only real connection for her was the tick-tock of the clocks, the predictable church bells, the emergency sirens, the cat fight on the roof, the pulse of the night pounding in her head.

Her silence also added to her invisibility. Words left her mouth with great difficulty. She pronounced them one by one in a low voice, with

resistance and with a savage blush on her pale cheeks that made people very uncomfortable. For Aunt Reche words must have sounded worn out before being spoken, trivial and unnecessary. She didn't say words, she threatened to say them; in truth, they became entangled on the tip of her tongue and turned against her in an interior mumble.

The few people who could see and hear her felt little more than a platonic veneration toward her. There were never any rumors about her being in love or having a lover; she maintained her virginity intact.

In my memory and in the photos Aunt Reche seems as attractive as most of the girls of her time and social class. What's more, between the age of twenty and thirty she radiated a surprising charm that made her stand out from the prettiest girls. Perhaps in the subtlety of her ways and in her depths there was a dissuasive touch that intimidated the men, that impeded their approach, and dissolved their initiative. Those who might have wanted her quickly exchanged desire for respect.

It was a respect she probably longed for in a different order of things: in her everyday negotiations, in the most immediate reality which, to her dismay, was hostile and dull. Everything affected her, leaving its mark on her like a whiplash: the ferocity of her mother, who called her a piece of meat, the domineering men of the house, her sisters' selfishness, the neighbors' stupidity, the intolerance of certain members of the community. She didn't cry because she knew it was useless, but she acknowledged receipt with a tangible desperation. If someone had extended a hand toward her, they would have felt the tense net in which she was wrapped.

I can imagine, based on my own experience, that it was in the darkest hours, the hours of insomnia and lucidity, that all the pieces joined together to form the jungle where the trees were in flames and the beasts were screeching as if it were the end of the world. And so the day's smallest discomfort became a sharp pain. By the time night had ended, all of this anguish had left her empty, unable to share her feelings with anyone. She was uninhabited, but not dead, and that was her worst defeat.

There was a time when she did want to live like everyone else. They say that she looked for a job, begging her parents to let her work outside of the home. They permitted it; she was already twenty-five and they knew that she would be an old maid. I can imagine her on the bus, watching tired people blissfully dozing in their seats. How she

would have loved to change places with the fat woman whose nostrils quivered from her heavy breathing as her energy yielded to the deep, refreshing sleep that would allow her to wake up smiling like a baby.

A pat on the shoulder, followed by a kind of envy of the lightness with which others went through life, would awaken in her the need for intense physical activity. They say that she would often walk thirty blocks to work. In the office she did her own work and that of two or three colleagues. She ate in the noisiest bars so that the chatter, the exuberant gestures and voices, the simple, spontaneous happiness flowing from the other customers would stick to her bones and break her silence. The noise enlivened her, made her eardrums tingle, her bones vibrate, her tongue click, her teeth chatter until she exploded within, mute, more alone, more abandoned than before. Some days she would end up exhausted. But she slept little; three hours was a major accomplishment. And the following morning she would be doubly tired—from her natural fatigue and from the extra physical exhaustion—thus becoming even more a phantom figure.

There was no solution. An unfailing inversion of values was at work in her. Every project she took on in an attempt to be like other people went in the opposite direction, it went astray. I am sure that with time she learned to laugh at herself, which perhaps afforded her the only intimate satisfaction that she was capable of fully enjoying. Although she was able to enjoy her own personality, which her family had declared incurable, her comings and goings began to assume the self-assurance of a saint. Rather than a transformation, it was the full deployment of the dominant traits of her temperament. Her calm manners, so habitual in her, became static. Her naturally white complexion took on a porcelain look. She seemed sculpted in marble or plaster or, more precisely, glass. Because of this transparency, she truly looked like an image carved in crystal, through which other bodies were visible in the light, as if she were an open window. When someone looked and spoke to her, they didn't address her, but rather the person behind her.

On one occasion—Aunt Reche told me this herself—she saw her younger sister in the street and, believing she was waving at her, responded by waving back, but her sister walked by without recognizing her, to meet someone else. The episode made her laugh to herself, a laugh she swallowed like a bittersweet morsel. The fact that she was still invisible at the age of forty, even when she did not want to be, tasted

like a liberating elixir on the one hand (she could pass by imperceptibly like a fly's eyelash and laugh at everyone), but, on the other hand, it was like the aftertaste of the poison that had made her insignificant, like a flash that disappears at the speed of death.

Death? She showed some sparks of life at times, although they only lasted as long as a falling star. Because that day, when her mother again told her that she was nothing but a piece of meat, and Aunt Reche answered that she was leaving for good, her entire body shook with a flourishing vehemence. She ran through the hallway toward the stairs, a crucial area of the house where all the profound arguments and the most violent rejoicing took place. At that instant the steps that led to the street, as I remember them, stood out from the rest of the house like a redeeming space of arrival and departure.

It was raining, and near the back of the house a bird was flying over the patio. Aunt Reche had reached the foyer and then the first step without losing her courage. I was trying to push her along for her sake and for my own. But she needed to catch her breath on the landing. This brief pause before opening the screen door and going down to the main door stopped her, stopped her definitively.

Perhaps during that decisive moment of hesitation it occurred to her that it was better to stay with her own than to risk living among strangers. The familiar solitude had a tone less desolate than the solitude of exile. Or maybe she thought that it really didn't matter where and with whom she lived: a woman who resides only in her private world is a stranger for everyone, everywhere.

As she retraced her steps, Aunt Reche was still trembling, but she possessed the serenity of a surrender to her own battle, as if she had accepted a verdict, as if she had had a revelation. Her look was that of a game warden surveying exotic birds.

Kaddish[1]

Graciela Safranchik

It's Reina who's coming over here. She does it so slowly that she seems to be stopping with each step. She brushes her cheek against mine, and we're so close now, one woman to another, that I can see the tiny wrinkles around her eyes. I also smell the thin, delicate perfume that hovers, ever so slightly, over her own scent, the scent of a mature woman. She murmurs something that I don't manage to understand, something about fate, and she takes me by the hand.

She too will return, with the others, to the center of the room. From there she'll look at me, she'll say, My mother is old, now what are we going to do with this old woman? And as soon as she can she'll forget me again.

Reina. My younger daughter. When did I stop wondering, What kind of woman is this, this daughter of mine?

Reina drops my hand. She lets it fall into my lap. Maybe she's surprised by this small, dead weight that she's just cast aside, which offers no resistance, because she shudders and looks away. It's cold, Mama, you should rest awhile, she tells me. She offers me a coat, a shawl: she wants to cover me up. She tries to pull her arm over my shoulders, but something stops her. The horror, I think. Let's hug Mama, cover her up, quick, she's cold. What will we ever do with her?

It's all right, dear, I tell her. It's been years and years now that my hands have been getting cold. It's age, I tell her.

Then I look directly into her eyes. I surprise her.

I'll be back, dear, Reina says, and finally she leaves me and joins the others, completing that close-knit, homogenous group of grown-ups who watch me from the middle of the room. All my children.

You have to keep watch over the corpse all night, the coffin closed, draped in the ritual black cloth.

Then the funeral procession. The widow and children first, then the rest of the family, friends, and neighbors.

1 Translated from the Spanish by Elizabeth Rosa Horan and Martha Manier.

You have to go to the cemetery and let others wash the body, every-one quiet by the gates of the garden where the tombstones bloom like flowers, they bloom beautifully, I think. And the men lift the coffin, various men, among whom are my sons.

Maybe they will be the ones to bring it to its assigned place. I can't remember this particular detail. Then they sing. A voice intones the familiar melody that will start the funeral cortege and stop by the open grave. The sons will say their prayer and tear their clothes just as the ground has been torn to receive him, their father. We will hear their chanting, in an avalanche. One chant or song will build on another and another in a measured counterpoint, like the complaint of a child who's been left irremediably alone.

We'll hug each other. Someone will come for me. Together we'll all get into the black automobiles. Other cars will come behind ours, in a procession. We'll return to the house.

There all the mirrors will still be covered.

She's put on all her jewelry—her rings, her earrings, the pearl necklace.

She's decked out in all her most costly things, her best dress, fur coat, patent leather shoes.

Anyone would say that she's about to flee, or that she's ready for a party.

She has also tinted her hair with a blue rinse that fills her face with shadows when she lowers her head. She still has a beautiful head, it's perfect, short hair scrupulously trimmed from her collar.

She's as old as anyone can get, but she nevertheless seems solid, like a building that could have been there forever. We're used to seeing her like this, it's been ages that she's looked just like herself. But Mama is old, so old that we don't know what to do with her. How to take care of her now, I mean. How to help her die without life touching her ever again, so that no other pain ever reaches her.

So many years alongside Papa and now, so calm, so fresh. Maybe she doesn't understand what's happening, not yet. It's even possible that she's happy to have us all together. Her children. Poor thing, how very sad.

I take her hands. It's cold, Mama, I tell her. Your hands are icy. Can I get you a coat, a shawl? I hug her and she suddenly looks at me, right in the eyes, like a bird.

Why am I feeling this terrible shame?

It's enough to go through the door, to get the picture.

A lot of grown-ups, horrified by a dead man's coffin. And that old woman, illuminated in a corner, holding the hands of the prettiest daughter, like someone carrying a flower that could break at any time.

I hear a radio, or the flooded engine of a car. What else sounds like that?

My eyes seek out my brother who roams the room like a master of ceremonies. Seeing me, he smiles, makes faces, and shrugs his shoulders.

If he'd let me take his hand again, returning to the place where the living speak and touch, I'd go to him, my brother. But I'm planted like a tree at the door, and I can't go back or move anywhere, for that matter.

When we were little, he'd plop down on all fours, saying, Up, Sahib! Climb onto the elephant! I'd clamber on and raise my arm. Opening and closing my fist, I'd make the trunk, while he produced strange noises with his mouth.

Sometimes we'd run through the whole house like that, him shouting, me holding onto his hair. Every so often, Mama would watch us, alert, raising her eyes from her book, with such disapproval that her eyebrows, knitted together, would form a long, hard wand.

Now he looks at her tenderly. He doesn't seem ashamed to see her there, cornered, like an insect.

No matter how long someone's been alive, memory is always an amazing thing. Ultimately, everything settles down in a single place, as if we were looking at a photo album.

It's impossible to know where we were, when we stopped to catch a moment. Why that moment and not another? It's like reading stories, I think. In the beginning we fly behind the action. Then it doesn't matter, the eyes alight at random; everything's become confused, upside down, inside out, no difference.

Now I remember my father, playing on the bluff above a river. I don't know if it really happened. I mean, I don't know if I really did see my father there, if I shouted, Be careful, you could fall.

Maybe I'm confused, and it was a movie, or a photograph someone else took.

I imagine a noise, a loud buzz, the water maybe; it's as if I were really remembering it. There's my father, smiling at me. I look at him and yell, Be careful, you could fall into the river.

At this very moment I want to cry for him. For my father, who died more than fifty years ago. Not for my dead father, but for the young man in the photograph, who smiles and stretches out his hand as if he were trying to keep his balance, as if he had suddenly discovered that he was about to fall.

I don't know if I shout to him that it's dangerous, or maybe he's the one who's shouting, telling me not to come any closer.

Like this other image that returns again and again today. So close, of course, but so slow that it takes the course of a lifetime to reach me.

He's still in bed. I hear his labored breathing. He breathes with great difficulty and his wheezing grows louder. It's so loud that it shakes the room. It's the death rattle, I tell myself, I've just understood it.

Standing, facing the bars of the hospital bed, I look at him. The white bedspread ripples, barely tracing the outlines of a body consumed by illness. He is all shriveled, but his feet are growing. I can see them clearly, positioned here in front of me.

I throw myself on his feet, trying to stop them: they are growing so much I think they make him look really ridiculous. Then my older son pulls me away. He walks around the bed and approaches his father, holding the old razor in his hand.

He's going to kill him, I shout.

Time has passed, it's some other moment. My son is sharpening the razor against a strop of worn-out leather, he's humming something. He's crazy, I think. My son has gone mad.

I see how he slowly, scrupulously covers his father's face with a white mask. He covers his face with foam. Only the tiny hollow of a mouth remains, from which the maddening noise of death escapes. He'll be suffocated, suffocated, suffocated.

I don't fall because I am still standing by the bars of the bed, next to those feet. From there I suddenly see two strange men busy with their own ritual.

An old man is dying, resounding like thunder, and the other one, in shirtsleeves, is shaving his father for the last time as if there were nothing else to do in this life.

What's this agitated breaking that I feel so close by, so near? God! I'm the one, the woman who's suffocating! I breathe, I breathe. I have to control my body. I withdraw into myself. I sweat, tremble, throb, what a racket, what a lot of noise, of smells, all packed into me, under pressure. I'm going to explode. Up, Sahib! Can they hear me? How crazy. I have to control myself. It always happens this way, and when it doesn't, when we want to intervene, to say, now I'm going to breathe, Now I'm going to move this way, everything turns out badly, and I have to forget, forget, no one is listening.

It happened before, on the train. I thought I was supposed to wait for Reina at the station. I didn't want to take the car. There were so many people squeezed together into the aisles that you couldn't breathe. I wanted a cigarette so badly, it was torturing me, my hands trembling. I was suffocating. I'm going to die, I thought, this very day.

I tried to make myself comfortable, but the mass of bodies was packed in tighter and tighter. Then I remembered the mail car, that it should be close by. I began pushing with all my strength, moving in that direction, but with so much difficulty that I squeezed between legs and scrunched-up arms, until I finally came to the open car.

There were so few of us, you could see the dust floating in the sunlight. I lit a cigarette, inhaled, and the smoke burned my throat. I could feel the rumbling of the train. It sounded different from there, like the noise of water scouring rocks, tree trunks, things that don't float and that pound surfaces with a dry muffled thud. Like drums.

The guard was next to me, an enormous bulk in his dirty uniform.

Rigid against the closed door, he seemed self-absorbed, off somewhere else. He's as a bored as I am, I said to myself.

I took a better look at him. The clear outline of his toes pushed against the dead leather of his shoes. He had his hand in the pocket where he kept a ticket-puncher. I heard him click it, again and again,

a dry, insistent click that he accompanied with convulsive shoulder movements. He'd planted himself there, as if he were expecting to trap a criminal and had forgotten about it for the moment.

Standing nearby, a boy stared at him. His face was twisted, ready to scream, his mouth half open and his crazy man's eyes glued to the guard's pocket. I couldn't resist the compulsion to reproduce his expression with my own mouth, until my jaws ached.

The boy suddenly turned toward the guard and showed him a ticket no one had asked to see. He looked at him, his forehead so furrowed that an infinite number of wrinkles were outlined, like on a fetus. I heard a dog bark, the wheels clacking against the tracks, the water flow, the drum. The jolting movements shook me. The boy had disappeared and the guard, who hadn't moved one centimeter from his spot, dangled the ticket-puncher from a finger, like a trophy.

The shadows of the railyard buildings began filtering, in streaks, into the car. We were arriving. Once again light, noise. I walked like a robot to the central hall. There was Reina. A world of people milled about, close by, without crossing the imaginary circle that contained her, like the spotlight that follows the acrobat across the circus ring. She hadn't changed in all these years. She was wearing a long skirt that billowed with the wind and then glued itself back against her body, dissolving. It was like a blue sail held up by her hand on her waist, her gesture so slight that the patterned cloth seemed a watery reflection.

My heart jumped. I could hear the commotion on the railway platforms, the screech of the locomotive, the constant hammering of the wheels and pistons. Here I was, confused by the magic of the dress that clothed and unclothed my sister's innocent body. She was looking off into the distance, toward some other spot. I wanted to call out to her, but then I discovered the sketch unfolding on the skirt. Against the blue fabric, stretched out, I saw bodies and more bodies, with soot-blackened faces and rounded, uplifted eyes, watching.

They were prisoners, remains snatched from an old silent movie or from a scene by George Grosz. Someone shouted my name, Judith, and the skirt came toward me, unstoppable, it took me by the neck and hung onto my life, once again, like a prison term.

These rooms where we keep watch over our dead have the atmosphere of a hotel or a station.

People stir up words; they move predictable images. If you let them do that, there's nothing else, they'll all be the same. That's why I only look at what's inevitable, it's the only thing that sometimes reveals who we are. That's how I learned to recognize my children, too. Smoke signals, fragments. In the world I come from, many came to this conclusion: humanity has died.

One can learn to read fragments. This is possible. Everything else, at my age, is pointless.

Humanity, humanity: what an illusion. We used to believe that we could believe in ourselves. Then it came to an end: the gods, the teachers, the victims. It's pure chance. Humanity came to an end, that's all. I mean, death is something that employees administer. A human being lives, keeps apart, shares, tries to get attention, and today, here he is, jammed into a coffin and surrounded by a bunch of people saying a lucky thing it's his turn. It'll be the poorer ones next time, the oldest ones, thank God there are others, others even older than I am. That woman who's collapsed in her chair, for example. She'll go, take our place. It'll be her turn first.

Everything's decided beforehand. A place assigned from far away, in no-man's land, one name after another, all in rows, we'll count on our fingers.

But it's not so easy to predict, today this one, tomorrow that one, and they know it. The inevitable also plots torturous pathways. This is just what I like to see. The pieces that never fit so well that we can think finally we've got everything in order.

Here comes my son Jonas. Now the place is packed. They must all be doctors, I'd recognize them with my eyes closed. They accumulate their self-assurance like prophets, like crazy men. Even Jonas, who wanted to be different, a homeopath. He's still poking around in his wizard's book, to come up with the perfect, the right combination.

Jonas brings the bitter metallic smell of the street. He says it's raining; the rain is hellish. Not much is happening inside. We don't know if it's raining, for example. Here, death has brought us all together, in one place. To get it over with, that's what we came for. To get it over with and then show, right away, how life goes on even with the grief, even with the tears. May the ritual of grief show us the way, with each of

its prescribed steps. Still, it really doesn't matter how, someone always knows what to do from one moment to the next.

With the rain, Jonas says, everything will be ruined. He's satisfied that, in his own way, he's found something to communicate, something to keep himself busy.

He arranges the procession's order, determines the order of kinship, takes care of the bill, because he's discovered that his father hasn't left him anything else to deal with. No tomb, no wound. His father took care of everything before he collapsed. His place in the cemetery, even mine, too.

And although he might dispute it, Jonas, my firstborn, carries the only name and the only position possible, the one his father loved.

Now he worries about the umbrellas, about all the mud. There's nothing else for him to worry about. He runs to the window, pushes the others aside, looks out. There he can come into contact with certainty, with what happens in a determined manner, with what can be sorted out or controlled. Natural phenomena.

Since time began, that's something we can still busy ourselves with: the end of night, rain bursting from the sky, what we like to call time.

On his way, he encounters Judith. She can't move. She's anchored there, waiting to be chosen once again. And it's Jonas who takes her by the arm, my poor child, he says something to her, he makes her laugh against her will, like an idiot. She has her mouth open, gasping. She hopes her brother will soon disappear, that all of us will disappear.

May they die, may they all die. That's what Judith says, suspended there like a scarecrow, like a figure from the Annunciation. Nevertheless, she doesn't stop laughing.

It hasn't gone well for her, it's no easier for her. My place is the one she still fights for. Only Rudy, sweet Rudy, the one with the small hands, can save her from dying, drowned in hatred.

He'll go put himself in front of her, burnished like a mirror; he will intervene between Judith and her old mother, between Judith and her beautiful sister, and he'll love all of us women just the same.

Reina is the only one who doesn't know anything about anything. She keeps sliding along, as if she were a ballerina on a polished floor. Anyone would adore her perfect, well-ordered body, offered. Nevertheless, Reina is precisely the one who most resists.

How could she escape from herself when everyone is ready to save her, to let her die.

Sometimes I think I've always known. Before they were born, from the very moment I loved him and knew I was loved. I had to give him these children, which he loved, in order, one after the other. I had to resign myself to looking at the inevitable.

I think, It's no small matter after all. What more could a woman from the world I come from take for herself? Hardly anything, hardly anything at all. A place on the sidelines. I work as tightrope walker or as worm: there's no big gap, no great difference. Depending on how one looks at it, the glint of the embroidery needle can be like that of that of the scalpel.

Suddenly it comes to me. I'm talking like him.

It's just that we've lived so many years together. Now there's not much left of me, just the little bit of myself that I could steal from him.

I demand attention, too. I knead a bit of life, like a bread crumb, grimy, but eager.

In a show of works by prisoners, I've seen incredible things done with pieces of bread. This is our art, perhaps, that survives.

I knew it earlier, when I tried to write in secret, when I was raising children, when I was keeping house. For centuries and centuries the steadfast resentment continues, as if we hadn't taken a single step forward since then. I mean everyone, all of humanity. What a brief existence!

People have started to come back to life. Their voices are rising. It's beginning to feel less cold.

I think about all this while I clasp hands, while I brush my cheek against more-or-less warm faces, while I smell the remnants of strange perfumes coming from all over the world.

Dear, dear Yeny, say the mouths that are moving like puppets, naming me.

Put in its proper place, a quiet world is something that attracts me.

This is new, I think. The din of the crowd used to please me. The plazas, the market, the bars, all that movement, that confusion of words that at times stood out in high relief. A single phrase like a shout, or the

permanent sawing of a complaint, of an explanation, of a story told for whatever ear.

Not now. Suddenly I can't stand the noise. Perhaps because my own voice consoles me, or because I no longer want to let myself be knocked about. I'm becoming weak. I lose my equilibrium.

I easily lose patience.

The storm came, here, and brought my grandchildren and great-grandchildren. So many people, milling about with the doctors.

They don't know if I'm sleeping, if they can draw near.

I raise my head a little more and look out so they can see me. They kiss me, they rearrange me as if I were a big pillow. They bring big children, small children, and repeat the names I may have forgotten. But names are something I easily remember, although I might not know exactly to whom they belong.

I still remember anecdotes, far better than names.

Until he became sick, they came to tell me things. No one much likes to visit a sick old man. Visits from the doctor, then from doctors. This is what we receive in the last years. But there are always books to read, memories to invent. In this sense I don't err.

I can clearly remember many faces from my childhood, some stories, which they've told me and which I myself have told again and again. Later, the desires of youth, marriage, the birth of children, the form that each of them was taking in the group.

The rest has been a long wait. I don't know for what. I never wanted to know.

We argued. I felt I couldn't make myself understood. That everything I said was held against me. I wanted to pound on something, but I didn't have the strength, not even for that.

I wanted to escape, to flee far away. But I didn't know how and there was no longer a place to go back to. Nor could I flee to any place, to some unknown site.

That's when the telegram arrived. Papa was dying. I had to do something about that. I cried all night long, huddled up against the pillow.

The possibility of Papa's death wasn't making me desperate. Rather, it was the mental paralysis that didn't allow me to understand anything at all.

Papa was eighty-seven years old. He had to die sometime. Mama was also very old but we never thought of her as having any age. I never worried about how I would take care of them. On the other hand, I wanted someone to come take care of me.

I was self-centered. I cried that night and all the next day and didn't move from the hotel once.

I also drank. I drank too much.

I didn't want to go home like this. I didn't feel that I was in any kind of shape to be meeting the others. The same old stories, and Papa dying, an old man with all his children around him. The idea made me want to puke.

Jonas called someone who called someone else who called someone else. They finally reached me. I couldn't not talk to him.

I was still crying when we had that awful phone conversation. You couldn't make out the voices very well. Jonas was shouting and his voice came and went like a ghost.

He said it was necessary for me to come, it didn't matter what I might be doing or what might be going on in my head.

Nothing's going on, I told him, absolutely nothing is going on in my head. And I cried, and cried some more. I thought my heart would break in two.

Reina, he said, in a few hours you'll receive an airplane ticket and I hope you'll be in Buenos Aires this week. Buenos Aires. A gray, dirty, noisy place. Corrientes. La Paz. San Isidro. The river. I would see the river, I thought. The house. It's a beautiful house. Now who's going to live in that big house? Does Mama still climb all those stairs? Who takes care of the garden? Who removes the dead leaves from the swimming pool? What am I doing with my life? I don't want to go back.

And I repeated that thirty, forty times: I don't want to go back. I'm afraid. I'm afraid.

It was a little after Jonas's call that Amanda knocked at the door.

I didn't want to let her in. I couldn't stand the idea of hearing her say those awful things again.

You don't know how to love, you're as empty as a shell. I hope you die. I hate you. And I am silent, as always, so she can continue. Who do you think you are, she'd say, How do you think you could do this to me? This. I was sleepy.

Amanda pounded on the door and pounded and I threw myself on my bed. Finally I opened the door. A lot of time had gone by. An eternity. She entered silently. She sat on the bench next to the bed. I want to hear you out, she said. I couldn't put one sentence together.

I'm not going to sit here all the livelong day, she insisted. It's time that you talk.

What could I tell her? My head was empty.

My head is empty, I said.

Well, then, speak with your mouth, she countered.

I said I was leaving, that my ticket would arrive soon. What for, she asked. To bury Papa, I said. I started to cry.

It was a low blow. I didn't want to do that. I know it was a low blow. However, I wasn't lying. I was only giving myself a little time.

Very well, she finally told me. They say Buenos Aires is a beautiful city.

My granddaughter lifts the baby from behind and hands him to me, his arms flailing. He is purple and crying as if he had just been born.

I don't want to take him, I tell her, but she insists, as if I were speaking to someone else.

I remember a photo, and who knows who showed it to me. A fat woman with strong, enormous hands, like a washerwoman, holding a baby by the arms.

She was looking at the child with a peculiar expression and her headdress, carefully placed so that it would gracefully fall, was gathered there on her hair as if it were a bride's veil.

The baby threw its head backward, stubbornly, as if it were trying to escape from the picture.

Below, the caption read, "England's Queen Victoria with her granddaughter." But I only saw a fat milkmaid, horrified by the convulsions of the starched tadpole they had left in her arms.

Her rings appeared as spots on her fingers. The diamond brooches fastened at her collar resembled spaces of light beneath her hungry, froglike gullet. Perhaps for that reason the child contorted itself, restrained as it was by those squalid arms, sticking out from under the pleats and the foam of lace.

The child in my arms cries. I wrap him up in his blanket. Softly, I cradle him until he calms down.

Maybe we'll fall asleep together. Anyway, we both have to wait.

You anxiously awaited the spell the river would cast every afternoon, when the dense vapor arose, devouring our feet and even crawling in under our skirts, as if someone had opened a boiling pot at that very moment, when the sun set behind the porticos of Prague.

It's a circus magician's trick, you'd say, the old dry ice trick.

But the spell was repeated unceasingly, although we'd run away, as far as we could, and pretend not to be surprised. Then you'd say, It's the river ghost. It would arrive wrapped in its transparent sheets to wail through the streets, wanting to cover them so as to confuse our path.

If you can now see, here the fog doesn't nip at your ankles like a dog. It has found a way to squeeze in under pressure, to make us panic.

Where we are going, where we come from: we don't know. We barely move, amid the bandages. Half ghosts.

We lose weight and float like angels wrapped in webs of spittle, in filters of light.

I no longer have you, and words come back at me, as if I weren't the one speaking.

Judith is crying beside me, and Jonas stares at the auto's mirror. He looks at the silence bringing us together. He sees we have nothing to say to each other.

To advance under these conditions will probably be impossible. The fog has swallowed the city. We can barely see the hood of the car. We are going so slowly that it seems as if the cars are refusing to take us there, to his grave. And it rained buckets, all night long.

They'll have to bail water from the grave before they lower the coffin.

I don't know if there's some system to let it drain. A ditch or something, I guess. But they'll have to get the water out. We're not going to drop him into a puddle, into the mud.

We shouldn't have to waste any more time. We're going so slowly, it's dangerous to be on the road like this.

Cemeteries are farther and farther away from the cities these days, from the life of the city. But how to imagine this delay? Back there, inside, we couldn't know the fog was so dense.

I hope they have it all ready, that they give us time, that they take the situation into account. This sick climate, just like London's.

We always think about London when there's fog, we fall into the old cliché. But the two times I went there the sun was shining. An exception, to be sure. It must've seemed ridiculous to everyone else when I praised London's weather.

This is pitiful. Why would it happen to us, today of all days? Here we are, stopped in the middle of the road, can't see a thing. On a day like today you can't see past the end of your nose.

If we stop and get out someone could hit us from behind. You have to go along slowly, very slowly, one right after the other.

The dead man up ahead leads us toward the nothing that envelopes him. What irony! Papa would enjoy it if he could see it. Perhaps he does see, why not grant him the possibility?

He might have created this bottleneck for us. You want to come with me to the cemetery? Okay, just don't take the wrong road. And above all, make sure it's me you're following.

<p style="text-align:center">***</p>

I'm cold, he said. The blanket your mother threw on top of me is very light.

His voice came from some joint behind the wall. It sounded hollow, as if he were shouting from some other room.

I ran into my room to look for covers but found only the baby blue crib quilt. How am I going to warm him up with this tiny thing, I shouted. I could hear how he'd laugh. When I returned to the room I called him, Papa, Papa, but heard only my own voice fade into the distance. Papa, I insisted, and he moaned, I clearly heard his moan. I looked from one side to the next and soon I saw the bed hanging from the ceiling with its huge brass frame and round black casters.

Papa, you're going to fall, I said, my voice thin. I'd barely said this when the ceiling began to move and I awoke in such a panic that it took me some time to calm down.

Why did I ever dream anything like that?

It's frightening to lose someone, it's frightening not to find someone you know has to be there, to see he's no longer there, and suddenly someone looks at you, the one who's there is someone else, or else you don't know or can't know if it's really the same person.

I run to buy Papa roses, but they tell me not to. That he only wanted stones on his grave.

The roses are so dark red, so intense. I can't stand the idea of not buying them.

Mama gets angry when I select a bouquet. But finally she smiles and holds them in her arms. We'll keep them on the table for several days, she says. They're very fresh roses.

Next to the tables with flowers, flocks of children mill about, waiting for handouts from those who arrive.

They remind me of the ducks on the Moldau, the ones that chased us along the bank with no reprieve, quacking crazily whenever someone drew too close. We used to throw stones to make them go away, and they threw themselves onto the rippling water to eat them, the stones.

There are no ducks like that here, I think. Although it wouldn't surprise me to see them anywhere.

This isn't the gravedigger, it's the man who washes the bodies.

People don't approach or touch him. He's unclean. Dragging a fireman's hose and wearing a pair of rubber boots that rise above his knees, he comes out to strut before those who are waiting. It's his moment of glory, he's going to carry out his part of the ritual before these people, now halted, can complete their own.

He leaves once, twice, to look about. He carries his hose here and there before carrying out his task. Without his secret magic that no one should witness, the funeral party cannot proceed.

It will barely be an instant.

He'll open the coffin where my father is, and he'll look him in the face. As if he were a god.

The drizzle is so fine, so soft, that it feels like a silken thread against your face.

They are waiting inside, all of them, for someone to do what must be done before carrying him off to be buried. I stand at the gate. I look at the trees, like hills that undulate and spatter their green here and there against the whiteness that devours everything.

It must be the glint of the bones, I think, and I know it's nonsense. But I can't keep from seeing them gleam as they deteriorate.

Here she comes, carrying those flowers, so red that you can see them miles away.

Pale but unabashed, she resembles a Japanese doll with its mask of rice powder.

She has her head wrapped in a shawl because of the rain and the cold and she keeps her hands in opposite sleeves of her coat while holding the bouquet against her body with her arms. They are blooming on her, the buds burst open. Reina doesn't seem to belong to us. She has gone off to one side, almost mixed in with all the other people who are waiting. She looks at a child, who returns her gaze. In her hands the child holds red roses that she extends to Reina.

The woman in the shawl and the girl in the blue hood are both so beautiful, so beautiful, that the mirror containing their image fills with fear.

Even here, where tears are necessarily cried for other reasons, beauty can soften us.

I feel wounded, doubled over like a giant who has nothing over which to reign.

The men are praying and they begin to lower him. I can hear how the hinges creak, how the pulleys squeak and the ropes grow taut. The wood hits the earth. He has arrived.

They say I can cast my handful, my first, to begin covering him.

It is a moist, strongly scented earth that sticks to my palm.

My dearest one, clinging to me, the earth I cast upon you contains blades of grass and shining grains of sand. What I extend to you is a world, albeit a small one, but large enough to fill a woman's hand.

I know it will reach you even in death.

Grief is so intense and at the same time the happiness accompanying it is so new. I ought to stay here forever, close my eyes, and listen to

the rustle of the trees against the wind or run to greet those who are arriving.

In the end, it's like inhabiting the cities that I wandered like a ghost. The same incessant way of piling stone against stone, in an explicit, recognizable order. The men facing the women, the suicides in front of the wall, one beside the other, so many names I had forgotten: Yentl, Jane, Schloime, Libe, Abraham, Rifke, Itzjak.

I don't want to go back.

I put my small stone on top of the mountain covering him. A smooth red stone used in construction. They will remove it when they place the gravestone or it will stick to the mud and be forever mixed in the earth containing him. His scab of eternity.

Inside, his bones will rot, and on rainy days glimmers of light will burst forth.

I don't want to go back. Now that he is dead, let him be the one who flees from me.

What's the mouth? The seat of the soul? Or is the soul found in the eyes?

I hold my breath while the clumps of earth mixed together by the rain bounce around. I can hear the hollow sound of the wood as if he weren't there, as if he had already been consumed while waiting to be brought to his definitive place.

It's so cold that we are trembling like animals. We're stiff, glued to the task of the man with the shovel.

We see how his knotted hands slide along the handle while he wipes the drops of sweat foaming around his eyes. Like tears.

Doing this and hanging onto the fur of my mother's coat, I look like a monkey. I don't know how much time has gone by. I don't feel my feet, I can't see, my mouth hurts.

She says, Let's go, dear. Judith, it's so cold in this place that if we don't move they are going to have to cover us, too. Then I walk.

My mother drags me along, as if she could. She, so tiny, pulling along my very being. She talks and talks to me. She tells me that at home, she has to treat the tree trunks so the ants won't devour them.

There were a lot of us. Perhaps someone has counted the number of people, so many young folks, so many old ones, until coming up with an exact number.

I see them, my relatives, what else? I have followed their trail for too long a time to give up now.

Judith is sticking to me. She doesn't want to fall. I say, Let's all go home. I'd like to go lie down. I need my bed. Yes, Mama, she answers. It's been at least forty years since I've thought of her as docile, so like the child she was.

<p style="text-align:center">***</p>

Mama wants to rest, I tell Reina. Let her be the one who busies herself, the one who moves them along. But she says there are too many of us.

Who's going to feed all these people, she asks, horrified. She doesn't understand a thing.

Jonas won't lift a finger, I tell her. He's just buried his father and now he'll have to fuss at his mother until he's convinced.

No way can we get away from him.

What would he have to convince him about, Reina asks. She knows perfectly well what he wants.

For that very reason, I say, he'll never stop. He has to control, to prevent, I think. Falls, broken hips, memory lapses, mistakes, accidents, gas leaks, fires. He won't stop. He won't stop, I say. Not until she dies, I think. I can't say it, though.

Reina shrugs. How pale she looks.

You look pale, I say. You look like a corpse.

It's the place, she laughs. When you're here, history comes down on you, the history of all humanity. Here, there, everywhere. The world is plagued by hollow castles, tombs crammed with corpses. I'm sick of it, she cries, sick and tired of it all!

You're crazy! Don't shout! I shout in turn.

I can't believe what I hear. She, who rode about for years in carriages paid for with the money Papa sent, and now the world's too small for her.

You talk like you're full of it, I tell her. You always lived like a duchess.

Like a queen, *una reina,* she corrects me, and her crazy laugh breaks through the cemetery's forced silence.

Sometimes I would like to be like her. Turn my back on everything and then nothing could ever hurt me again.

I had forgotten these streets, or maybe they've changed some, in recent years. How much wealth is here, how much security. So many dogs, policemen, posters.

I'm falling, stumbling, asleep on my feet. Mama nods too, hunched next to me.

Poor thing. She must be exhausted, sleeping so poorly all these nights, at her age, and everything else, of course, there's also everything else.

I hold onto her arm. She has clamped onto her purse with both hands. I can see them, her hands with the enormous age spots. Now that the light bathes them, so near me, I can see how much they've changed. Her knotted fingers are thick at the knuckles. They are no longer the hands that played the piano, that combed hair.

These hands now clutch the purse as if there were nothing else around to hold. As if she were running the risk of someone snatching it away from her.

I tell her: a lot of trees have fallen. I never understood how these trees, seemingly so solid and strong, can be uprooted by the wind.

The storm did a lot of damage, I tell her, this mother of mine.

They're old trees, they had to die sometime, she answers. But we're almost there, Reina, we're near. Near what, I wonder.

She grows agitated, opens her purse, sorts out an enormous bunch of keys. The gate key, the one to the front door, and others that no longer serve a purpose. She wants to know if I kept my duplicates.

Of course not, Mama, I say. I don't have much chance to use them.

That's true, she answers. We can always ring the bell. We have an intercom now. You'll see. Your father saw to it before he fell ill. He had to take care of things, that's the way he was.

How was he? What kind of man was my father? Sometime I'd like someone to tell me.

<center>***</center>

The car stops, we've arrived. At last. There's an enormous wrought-iron fence around the house. I have to work some to get my bearings. I might have gone by without having recognized it.

We all get out of the cars and approach each other on the sidewalk. Mama tries to go ahead with her keys in her hand, but Jonas rushes the gate and takes out his own key case with an excessive, deafening noise.

She shudders. He takes his time about it.

That's enough, Jonas! Judith shouts, but he turns his back on us and opens. We all enter, women last.

Judith has taken Mama by the arm. The two of them hang back. They walk up the gravel path, looking at the mushrooms, the trees, as if seeing them for the first time.

I don't understand what unites them now. I can't understand.

Jonas is still opening doors when Mama reaches us. Go on in, Son, she says. You're home now.

My children are still here, seated around the table. This resembles a very formal gathering, this gathering in my dining room.

Suddenly, I don't think I understand what they're doing here. It's barely a moment, but I'd like them go out into the world. I'm thirsty, I say. Can someone serve me some tea. In the small china cups, I say.

These cups are normal-sized. They're ordinary. They aren't appropriate for passing time. The woman who sold them to me spoke of others, smaller ones. For tea, when you're old, she said.

Two old women sit down, she explained, nodding. They have a large teapot with hot water and a smaller one with tea leaves, and they fill the small cups. This is an old woman's tea.

My tea is bitter, biting. It's an excellent tea. Not yellow, but green. Completely green.

It's true that you need at least two old women for the ceremony to make sense.

She still hasn't cried. I know she cried before, when she held his hand and said tender things to him. She cried in private.

But now she can't, she can't. She doesn't know how to cry for him dead.

I'm afraid for her, and I don't want her to notice my fear, my weakness. She expects us to think of her as determined as always, ready for

everything, and that we'll leave her alone. For the first time, I think we shouldn't do it. But no one can tell her anything.

Mama, dearest Mama, it's too late to begin. It's even too late to keep on being the way we were.

You're going to realize what happened, and I won't be here then, to look you in the eye.

We say good-bye, now we kiss. Don't behave, Rudy, she whispers. You've behaved your whole life.

Do you think you could stay with her a few days, I say. Until she's more comfortable, until she can look around, all this emptiness.

Reina says, Only a few days. She says that all her things are in Prague, that she doesn't have money or clothes, that she's come with a suitcase filled with useless things. I offer some coats, whatever she wants. She hopes that you'll stay, I say. She can't get along with me. We can't talk. I fight her, you know. I don't think.

I'll hand her over to you, I think, she still cares about you, still says what one needs to hear, and she'll say it many times, Reina. She'll not ask anything inappropriate. Not from you, her beloved daughter. Nothing that can bother you. Later, you can go away forever. No one will ask you to stay, no one will hold you back.

A few days, at least, I tell her, that'll be enough. Then Rudy can take her, perhaps. We'll see.

Let her have you near for a few days, so she won't be alone.

Reina is looking at me wide-eyed. She's not worried. It's more like a look of astonishment.

What surprises you so, I ask. I didn't know you loved her so much, she says.

A woman phones. A woman for Reina.

She's speaking French. At first it throws me. Someone speaking to me in French isn't the norm. I feel important and answer courteously. Just a moment please, if you'd be so kind. That's the important part when it comes to languages.

Reina comes downstairs like a whirlwind, like when she was girl and skipped down the stairs, two at a time. She snatches the receiver from my hand. She's flushed.

Maybe because of the physical exertion. She doesn't move around much and suddenly to come down the stairs like that. No, I don't think so. It's the emotion of it all.

Go, Mama, please. I want to talk, she says. And she starts up in that language. She says sweet things, such sweet things. She speaks like a pampered child, she almost purrs, look at Reina.

Anyway, I go. It's none of my business. Ten, fifteen minutes go by. A half hour. Reina is still talking. Chuchuchú, chuchú. French sounds like that. Those lessons at the Alliance Française have served her some good, at least. To think she always went against her will. And French suits her.

One could imagine speaking each of the world's languages. But few words. Nevertheless, here she is long-distance.

I can't help being curious. I love you, she says.

A person loves everything in French. One loves ice cream, whipped cream. You know I love you, she says.

I shouldn't be here, listening. I never did it before. I don't understand. I don't understand the words. She says, I'm jealous, or maybe I'm pretty.

Jealous. No one says I'm pretty, just like that. Not even Reina.

We women have always been jealous. Ever since they locked us up at home and told us all those lies. Jealous of looking at the world through peep-holes, through *jalousies*. That must be where the world comes from

Don't make me suffer she says. I hear her clearly. Suffer, she says!

That's it! Her fleeing, her confusion, her upset state when we ask her things. She's upset most of the time. ... It was that! That kind of suffering!

She says, don't go. Wait for me a few days. I have all my things in that damn place.

I listen from behind the door, like a thief. I'm afraid, like a thief of lives.

To be a mother is to play ignorant. I told myself that many times. Why is it so difficult now?

It was that! Something as simple as that!

Please, I beg you, she says. She grows humble. This daughter of mine has reason to be humble. Her pride. Please, I beg you, I implore you, she says.

I don't want to hear any more! I don't want to see anything!

But I look at her, so beautiful, pale now, speaking that language of love, to whom does it matter with whom? I look at her from the keyhole in the door, as a servant would look at her, on the sly, like a mother, well, that's what I am, and she's been gone for such a long time

Reina says that the woman who called is a photographer. She's my friend. We were in Prague because a publishing house contracted us for a book, she says. Photographs are important, I say. You wouldn't know who you were if you couldn't see yourself in pictures.

Do you still have that old box filled with photos, the one we'd pull out every summer to play with, she wants to know. Then she laments: We always had so few, because of Papa's wild idea. ... That's something I could never understand. Why did he resist being in pictures? Why did he hate them so? Perhaps because he'd lost his family's, I say, but I don't know, I never wanted to ask. It was his secret. For the first time, I tell her that when we got married he didn't want them to photograph us together. But he took me aside and asked me to write on a piece of paper, I'm happy, I feel beautiful. While I was writing, he looked at me so intently that I really was, I really felt like the most beautiful woman in the world. He always did things his way, I smile.

Reina wants to see the old photographs. My dear daughter, I say to her, why dig up so many dead people? But if they're still here, she becomes enthusiastic, Let's, Mama. Show me at least one of them, the first one you take from the box ... ! Let's play again ... !

She climbs up onto a chair to hand down the hatbox. That hat, I tell her, the one that came in this box, is in a photo. Three young women in ridiculous hats with enormous brims. Identical hats and identical dresses. It was Pearl's idea. She thought if we looked alike they wouldn't take us for foreigners. We had fun doing it. That youthful madness was a sheer joy.

Here it is! Reina shouts as if she had found a treasure. We'll both look. Yes, it's Italy, I think. Whatever has become of them? This is the very place where we separated, when I met him. Who are the others, my daughter asks. I point out Pearl, a cousin, and Amalia, my friend from childhood. In the photo the three of us are smoking. It wasn't

something just anyone would do, I mean, that women would do. The three of us with the same hat, like uniformed store employees.

Tell me about them, about the others, Reina says. Amalia went to the United States to marry some rich guy. We wrote to each other two or three times and then I lost track ... I think I forgot about her, that's all. Pearl must have died ten years ago: I don't remember having met any Aunt Pearl, Reina says.

Never a letter, nothing, I think. Whatever became of her? We were very close; nevertheless, something happened, something that seemed so terrible that we never spoke again. Someone told me that she was dead. I was sorry. At my age you are always sorry when you learn of a friend's death.

You have so many friends, she continues. Do you still get together every Tuesday to play cards? No, dear, not anymore, I say. There isn't anybody to play with anymore.

Reina puts the photo in the box and stops the game. Why do you keep the box from that hat, my daughter suddenly wants to know. Because I was wearing it when I met your father. The three of us, dressed like that, saw him and set our eye on him. I wasn't the prettiest, I think, but he liked me.

At best, he went after the others and struck out, or so I now believe. Oh, I don't know. The three of us never again talked about him. Whenever he appeared, we'd grow silent. I'm still here, silent, and he's dead.

<p style="text-align:center">***</p>

Everything here is so quiet. Tonight the dogs aren't even barking. The garden seems empty, with no soul. I can't open the window to listen to the trees whisper because it's too cold. Or because I can't stand the silence.

Nights like this one, beyond the reach of clocks, shouldn't exist. I'm afraid, as if I were a child. I'm so afraid that I would like to die and I don't know what that means: to want to die.

It's not the first time I've felt this way. I have experienced the sensation before, many times in my youth, but now it's not something I can think about easily, that I get excited thinking about. At my age, the encounter with death is all too close at hand, too threatening to seek its company voluntarily. Yet here I am wanting to die, for no reason. No reason.

Before he … before losing him, I also thought about this, that I want to die. I saw him suffer, writhing in bed. I didn't know what to do. I was desperate. I think I hated him for suffering so. I hated his suffering that way. It would be better for him to die, I thought. Let it be over once and for all. Let me die too. That's what I thought.

I went to sit in the waiting room. The nuns walked past like terrible angels, scraping the rubber soles of their slippers against the waxed tiles. I hated the nuns, too. Again, I thought: I want to die. I felt so alone. I spent a great deal of effort trying to remember things that could make sense of that grief that took hold of me like a prisoner. Not only the grief of losing him, but grieving for myself, for my emptiness, for my own distress.

I chose the right word: remember. It was something from the past, something that was already there, that I needed to find to defend his life. I mulled the idea over and over. What did dying mean to me? I didn't want to lose him. I couldn't stand the idea that he might stop breathing. I was controlling his breathing like one who permanently looks at a clock. I only wanted his suffering to end. I didn't know what it meant to live without him. Nor what it meant for him to stop living.

Over the years I made myself think that it would all end sometime. What good did it do me? Didn't my own death always appear as a scene? I could see my dead body perfectly, my children's grief, even my own, caused by this death of mine, parading before my very eyes.

According to my state of mind while I was having this fantasy, I either felt sorry for myself or I thought, Well, that's it, let them do something about it, their mother is definitely dead.

It was a kind of vengeance. A small one because I didn't dare risk too much in my fantasies. How do I get up my courage to represent such a spectacle of their indifference? But when it was a question of him being left behind dead, it was different. Suddenly I knew. Death wasn't what I wanted, rather, it was the end of life, of some form of life. I couldn't bear the tension my heart had to withstand when it was so overburdened, so slow to comprehend, so laden with unspoken words. I wanted the resentment to cease, the hatred of grief to cease. I wanted to be someone else.

It was difficult, but I returned to that room where he was given over to suffering. I drew as near as I possibly could. I looked at him. I tried to recognize him under the mask that this type of life, this agony, had

placed on his face. He was saying something. I thought he was deliri-
ous. Everything is going to be all right. I lied to him and held his hand.
He turned his head, disproportionate for what remained of his body. He
looked at me with the eyes of a crazy man, as if my presence by his side
might break the mystery that made him a person, the mystery that was
taking him away toward death. He clung to me with all the strength he
had left, and crying, he shouted: Mama! Mommy! Yes, my dearest, I cried
along with him. And I thought, here comes death to cover his mouth,
nothing will be left, nothing of him, just like nothing of me is left for him.

Now I think I might have been afraid that the silence would take me
away, too. But I'm being cruel to myself. It wasn't only that. I was afraid
of the presence of the body that was starting to harden in the hollow of
my hand, afraid of that thing that was there … a violent desire that they
not snatch him from me.

The garden is immobile, mute. I would like to unglue myself from the
window and crawl under the covers, but I can't. Here I stand, shivering,
terrified. I don't want to go to bed. I can't stand the idea of being still.

<p style="text-align:center">***</p>

When I enter Mama's room, I find her seated in front of her dresser,
as rigid as a mummy. Mama, are you okay? I ask. She is annoyed, as if
I had come upon her doing something terrible. She turns around and
looks at me with eyes grown small from anger. Why didn't you knock?
she barely whispers, because her anger won't let her talk.

I'm sorry, I say, and I flee from there. My face burns with shame.
I've come across her at an intimate moment. I didn't think that Mama
would have anything to hide because she's an old woman.

I'm in my room when she calls me, shouting. I run to her door, but I
can't gather the courage to enter. Shall I come in, I ask from outside. Of
course, she says, aren't I calling you?

She's still there, motionless before her dresser, but now she looks at
me as if she were looking at herself. She wants me to come closer. I take
a few steps, until I'm behind her chair. Not there, she says, and taking
me by the wrist, she draws me to her side. She pulls on my arm without
letting go until we're next to each other, glued.

Bend down a bit, she whispers. But Mama, I start to complain.
What's the matter? You frighten me … . Don't be silly, she smiles. I
only want to look at you in the mirror.

There we both are. She has stuck her face next to mine. A cold face that has wrinkles on her chin, around her eyes, in the smile lines by her mouth. She smells of cosmetics, rouge, expensive perfume. She smells as my mother has always smelled.

We are together, looking at our faces in that strange way, but we do not see ourselves. Relax your mouth, she says, softer. Mama, I start to protest, but she looks at me again with that new fury, almost shouting, For once do what I tell you, I'm not asking much!

Then I became silent, and we look at ourselves, just like that, our heads together. I try to soften my mouth, to let it open a little in the mirror image, but my lips tremble. She asks me to pull my hair back. Now she speaks softly, sweetly. I hold up my hair with one hand, without moving from her side. My legs ache from the unnatural position I must adopt, but I don't dare change it.

That's it, she says, that's it! Although the look is sadder. Sadder? I ask. That's right, she says. I never had that sad look.

Thanks, dear, she finally says. She closes her eyes, as if tiredness were suddenly devouring her. Do you want something from me, she whispers, asleep in her chair.

No, Mama, I answer, as I walk to the door, I don't want anything that I can't wait for.

Everything around here is one big confusion, a tremendous confusion. I want him to look at me, to see me as I am. That's what I want. The world doesn't scare me. It has simply ceased being of interest. I'm out of place. Could he have known this? Could he have lingered so long because he knew that by leaving, he was abandoning me to this absence of myself? I'm tired. No one is looking now. No one can see into the past.

My mother told me that once upon a time there was a beautiful woman. She was so beautiful that all the young men of the village were in love with her. She received their letters, their requests, their sighs. She would always think about those young men whose love she would never be able to reciprocate, and her heart was breaking. So great was her pain that she killed herself.

For the first time I think I understand the story. Today, faced with life, while my heart is breaking.

After Papa's expected death, Mama's unexpected death has unsettled all of us. I'd wandered around the house all day, not daring to speak to her. I called Judith because I was afraid. Mama seems strange, I told her, and Judith came flying. But she was afraid, too. She was always afraid when it came to Mama. The two of us stayed in the kitchen drinking tea, like when we were girls and had something to hide.

Mama didn't leave her room. I went up first, but she didn't want to open the door. After a while, Judith went up, and she told her to wait a little, it wasn't time yet. Time for what, Mama, she wanted to know. It's not time for anything, she said, her voice so clear it hung there in our ears.

At last she called us. She was lying in bed, wearing the same dress she wore for Papa's funeral. Once again she'd put on all her jewelry, and had tried to put on makeup, but her tears made the mascara run, staining her cheeks.

Sometimes it's best not to understand so much, my dears.

We were paralyzed, the two of us. Seeing her there, wearing that dress, really impressed us. She said that she loved us, that she loved Rudy and Jonas, but she didn't have the will to wait any longer. Everything was in its place. That anything we might do was okay, if it was what we wanted. I think she said this for me, although she was looking at Judith at that moment. She said she'd never believed in advice because she, for the most part, had never taken it. Life was marvelous, she said, and she regretted not having given it more of herself, of her heart.

We tried several times to interrupt her, but she stopped us by taking our hands, squeezing them tightly. I could feel how her enormous diamond ring was digging into my palm. I thought she'd deliberately turned it around so that I would feel it jab. I don't know how I could have that idea. Then she asked for tea. In the china cups, she said. I went downstairs to prepare it myself. Judith stayed with her. From the kitchen I heard her singing. I hadn't heard Judith sing in years. Mama asked, she said. Let's have our tea. It won't be an old lady's tea, but, she slyly added, neither of you is young either. That put her in a good mood. We all laughed. She told us where we would find the other cups, like the ones we'd used. She thought it a good idea that we both have some. That any tradition at all would do, when a person felt alone. Papa and

I weren't too generous with traditions, she said. We kept them for ourselves. Anyway, we might not have done them the right way, she said. One always does things poorly when doing them for others.

I think this was the last thing she said. Do you want to sleep, Mama? Judith asked her. She seemed so tired. She only closed her eyes, and with a smile and a wave of her hand indicated we should go.

We never saw her alive again.

Once again those chants are rending our souls, perhaps that's why she made me sing when we were alone, to imagine how they'd sound when we brought her here. The two stone markers will be facing each other. Papa reserved the plots. He wanted her with him, soon, as soon as possible. But I don't believe she was quite ready to follow him. Is he what she's following? Is that why she chose to die so abruptly? Is it something you can decide? To die like that? Of what? Of fear? Of boredom? What made her so suddenly tired? Did we, her children, wear her out? Anything a person does is all right, if it's what you want, she said. Even dying? Did you mean it's more worthwhile to die, when you don't want anything else? That's what you told me, yes, me, although at that moment you were looking at Reina. I know you were saying that to me. Did you know I wanted to die, too? What else did you know? One always does something poorly when it's done for someone else, she said. Was she afraid we'd do something with her, something she might not want? I wasn't going to let Jonas drag her through life. Was that why she said it? I don't understand. But it's not good to understand so much, she said. Was she speaking about Reina? Did trying to understand Reina wear her out? Did she know something? Something about Reina? About Papa? About me, perhaps?

I would've liked to have had the time to learn how to love her differently.

Mama dies and the birds sing. I never heard so many birds singing all at once. It's a marvelous day; the sun has come out, all of a sudden. Now they are both together, one facing the other, like Papa wanted. We wanted that, too. What a way they had of bringing us together—Judith, Rudy, Reina, and me. Together like before and so heartbroken.

Julius Golden Mountain[1]

Aída Bortnik

He nearly escaped from his sister Genya's grasp that first bright morning, wearing his dark velvet suit with the silk bow and pressing his brand-new notebook against his quivering chest. The street was clean and smelled unfamiliar. The horse-drawn carriages were deafening at times, but he did not shut his eyes in hopes that his brothers Filo and Muni wouldn't sense his fear of the city. Everyone had told him that Vienna was beautiful. He would have liked to remove his hat and greet the ladies whose perfume enveloped him. But he didn't have a hat like the one his father wore so gracefully. He didn't yet wear a cap like his two older brothers. He was too young that day when, along the same streets Stefan Zweig walked eleven years earlier, he first went to that large building where they taught about how to understand the world.

Twenty years after that wondrous morning, having left that school as a teacher of Polish and German, with outstanding grades in Russian and Slavic, Julius Golden Mountain shared a tenement room with two friends on the corner of Corrientes and Junin and found the work he was seeking: janitor in an orphanage.

This was his first job since disembarking from the boat at the port of Buenos Aires. He never sought any other work. He never left the children. He never ceased being a teacher and a father to generations of men.

He was nearly eighty years old when he retired. That big old house where he got his start as a janitor was now a small village under his direction. He canvassed it on bicycle starting at six in the morning: mediating, consoling, listening, teaching and, as he himself would say—now that, besides the children, he was also responsible for the lonely elderly—learning for when he himself would be old.

Julius was born in the countryside, far from beautiful Vienna, at the close of the first spring of the new century. Though he was the youngest of his father's four children, he was the first to abandon what was Austria at the time of his birth and Poland by the time he left, and

1 First published in 1983 in *Hum®* magazine, Buenos Aires, Argentina. Translated from the Spanish by Annette Prekker Levine.

he was the only one in his family—of his parents and brothers, of the vast network of freckly boy cousins and awkward girl cousins, of pious aunts and uncles, of lively and confusing relatives who seemed to extend infinitely toward Germany, toward Poland, toward Russia, toward the Slavic countries, toward the sunny south—he was the only one of all of them, who survived revolutions and pogroms, invasions and reconquests, local and world wars, final solutions and ethnic cleansing … . That endless chain of the Golden Mountain family, that endless tapestry of love and hardship, of memories, of arguments and celebrations, had disappeared from the face of the Earth.

In 1942, Stefan Zweig—his compatriot who had taken that same route toward gaining understanding of the world eleven years prior, a writer loved by his whole generation—died by suicide upon learning that, along the very streets where Julius once walked in a velvet suit with a silk bow, toward the school, Zweig's books were being burned in bonfires of hatred. Julius Golden Mountain understood him, cried for him and for the children they had once been and for the entire universe they had both lost. But he found a means of survival, a means of eternal affirmation that resisted the bonfires, the hatred, and death.

Ever since I can remember, I have witnessed this scene repeat itself: a man somewhere between the ages of thirty and sixty, runs out of a bar or a home, or stops and leaves his car in the middle of the street, or simply shouts, shouts Julius's name and embraces him. A sustained embrace. Some cry, others suddenly go quiet with a childish and uninhibited smile that brings them to life. He always knows their names, always remembers their achievements, always recognizes the children still there inside these men with tearful eyes.

I have seen them embrace him countless times throughout my life. Some search for words and others don't even attempt to find the language to express the gratitude they can hardly contain: he heard them, he understood them, he explained to them or he embraced them in silence one time, one unforgettable time that they treasure as the moment that a man was able to help them become men.

Julius Golden Mountain, the only survivor of that endless chain, has sowed the world with an indestructible seed. Though none of the children to whom he gave love bear his name, together they form a mountain range so high and so vast that no amount of hatred could ever erase his family from the face of the Earth.

From *Theater of War*[1]

Andrea Jeftanovic

I'm the Same Age as Dad

I'm the same age as Dad. He's stuck at age nine, which was how old he was when the war began. I don't want to get any older either. I want to stay with him in his nine-year-old sadness. Dad sleeps with the light on just like me. In the darkness, he says, the black trees might creep in. Dad is frightened by the siren at midday, when a moustached officer greets him with an outstretched arm. Dad is a six-foot-tall child, size XL, with wrinkled sleeves. I am the same age as Dad. It's just that he's turned the same age several times.

Dad always has the same nightmare. He's inside an empty train station. He thinks the hand of God placed him on the wrong platform: *When I turn my head, the faces of the lost children multiply. The vacant eyes of the women. The hunched backs of the men. I clench my fists. They make the pilgrimage through this atomic landscape with their heads bowed. There are hundreds, thousands of them, shuffling between the rails. And my fists are clenched. The beings board the trains. My fists are still clenched. A shrill whistle sounds. The iron wheels begin to turn. I walk with my fists clenched. The shadows of the boxcars slither across the ground. I see them move away, their arms stretching from the narrow windows, gesturing wildly. I bound over the sleepers with my fists clenched. I watch until the darkness of a tunnel finally swallows the shapes. I run and run after the train, but it's stopped halfway, facing the wrong direction.*

Dad is absent as he reads the newspaper and thinks about the war. He does the maths, adding, subtracting, calculating the length of that period. I tell him to forget it, that there are only tin soldiers and water guns here. He says that barbed wire surrounds his dreams. Dad is stuck in time, remembering the war. A march of boots gallops in his ears. He always carries bread in his pockets. He has forbidden me to read his-

1 Published in 2020 by Charco Press, Edinburgh, UK. Translated from the Spanish by Frances Riddle.

tory books; he writes a year on his leg. He doesn't know that I hide an encyclopaedia under my bed and know what that date means. He takes stock of the pantry, counts the non-perishable food items: each jar of preserves, package of rice, bag of beans lengthens his list. Every day he inventories the contents of the lockbox.

I have the urge to hug Dad and reassure him that the war is over, but we each cry alone in our own rooms. Two thousand four hundred and fifty-seven, is the number that Dad unknowingly writes on my arm the day I turn nine. This is the figure that sears my skin: the number of days the war lasted, all the tears Dad has cried. I commemorate my ninth birthday with four digits. I add the two, the four, the five, and the seven. I watch Dad spend the day opening and closing the newspaper. Two thousand four hundred and fifty-seven is the number of days they owe him.

From the rooftop of his childhood home, Dad watches as two soldiers knock on the door. The men speak to his mother in low voices. As he waits on the roof, he paces nervously from one side to the other. He feels the hot tar beneath his feet. From on high he watches them take his father away, arms bound. There's a gnash of fire on the horizon. He will always remember that summer afternoon when he couldn't find the voice to ask his father where he was going, what time he'd be back. He couldn't say goodbye to him either. In the following weeks he would ask every man in uniform about his dad, showing them an old photo. His boyhood muteness still drums steadily in his chest. It's the reason why he'll never again walk with a straight back. It's the reason why he moved to another country he had never even heard of.

Dad sleeps in the room next to mine, but when he closes his eyes he's lying in a cockroach-infested cellar beside his two brothers and their last fourteen cans of food. He remains perfectly still. Dad is so small that he can hide behind the wallpaper and let his eyelashes brush the wall. The three boys hold their breath because they hear strange footfalls in the hallway. The day before, they'd found the front door smashed in. The wood ripped from the hinges, a note in another language on the floor. Their mother spends hours cleaning out the closet. She shines shoes, brushes suits, folds shirts. She moves dressers and chairs. She changes the position of her bed, tidies the dining room. She wears black. At night they read the secret lists by candlelight. They do

not find their father among the typed-out names. Fat drops of semen erase entire lineages.

Dad says there is a mournful rain inside him. He dreams that God kneels on his shoulder and asks him for forgiveness.

The Memory of the Senses

Dad as a boy, his stomach bloated with hunger. When I say *I'm starving to death*, he gets nervous and opens the cupboard. He rummages through packages, counts containers, jars and boxes. He rotates the stock. He crosses something out in his notebook of provisions. Without looking me in the eye he holds out a handful of raisins.

In Dad's city, three boxes of food could be exchanged for information. A litre of gasoline for a meeting with an officer. A family jewel for a fake passport. The streets were lit by enemy spotlights hovering over his neck on his walk home from school. The men wore tattered uniforms. They walked barefoot because they'd already sold their last pair of shoes. The dogs let out guttural growls as they rooted around in the garbage, licked the wounds of the dead. The sewers were destroyed, the toilets all leaked. Excrement on the sidewalks, street corners, impregnating clothes, furniture, lampposts. Intestines choked with terror. To walk on the street was to step in your own shit, the excrement of your neighbours and everyone else, all living in fear. A coagulated river of waste and faeces. The faeces flowed into the shape of an *S* that was intersected by *Z*s and *H*s. A chain of excrement that snaked through the city.

I'm closing the bathroom door behind me when I hear Dad's anxious voice. I stand in the middle of the hallway, my back to him.

'Tamara, did you flush the toilet?'

'Yes,' I answer, and my legs tremble as I walk away. 'Then why does it smell like shit?'

I sniff but I don't smell anything. I know he's tormented once again by a stench that exists only in his mind. From my bedroom I hear him flush the toilet several times; the water rushes and he sprays air freshener. Dad still smells the acrid, rancid odours of his hometown. He gags from the stink lodged in his nostrils. That night I dream that I

open the bathroom door and I find Dad dead, sitting on a toilet over-flowing with excrement.

The kids spend their afternoons standing outside the candy shop. Dad watching at the window, as if it were a movie, caramel dripping under the heat of the lamps. The colours of the sweets form a rainbow. Through the glass, he savours a lollipop that melts in his mouth and his cracked tongue writhes. He removes the cellophane from the warm chocolates and lets them slide down his throat. But his daydreams are interrupted by the rumbling of his guts. Hunger fills his head; the cavity of his abdomen contracts. Amplifying the memory of the day's lone mouthful. A scrap of bread chewed with a few motions of his mouth in an infinite mental loop.

At the table, Dad eats quickly, not a single crumb left on the plate. He checks that all portions are of equal size. He glances sidelong at the other bowls, gathers the leftovers into his. Dad scrapes at the dish until the porcelain squeaks. Then he sops up the gravy with a piece of bread, drawing circles on the plate. He finishes before anyone else.

'Is there any more?' he asks.

'You've had enough,' Mum answers.

'Is there any more?' he asks as if he hasn't heard her.

We all sit in silence as we slowly move the forks to our mouths.

'I want more!' he insists.

Mum hands him a piece of bread, which he covers in butter and desperately devours. He hasn't even finished chewing the crust when he breaks the silence.

'Who's going to share with me?' he asks in a tone somewhere between sweet and threatening.

'But ... you haven't even finished,' Mum says, nervous.

Dad carefully watches the other eaters. He rescues my leftovers, pushing them noisily onto his plate. He continues chewing after we've all finished and are slumped languidly against the table. He eats non-stop because war could break out at any minute.

When Dad looks out the window, he is hypnotized by the horizon ... soldiers file by in brown uniforms that display the metal butts of their rifles. They march in double lines with their impassive faces, trailed by tanks. Dad sits on the sofa. I call out to him but he doesn't hear me. He has erected a wall of news. He reads the paper in an alphabet without history. He reads in silence as a soundtrack plays on repeat in his ears.

He turns the page: he's in another time, thinking in another language. Dad is constantly invaded by the same sounds: footsteps on cobbled streets, the scrape of a shovel on pavement, the high-pitched whistle of the bombs, the death rattle of a dying man. If he keeps reading the newspaper, he hears the squeals of the train axles, the dry slam of a wooden door. Then he remembers another use for it. In his eyes, dead bodies lie on the streets, covered in sheets of newspaper.

I Learn to Write by Copying Other Kids

I learn to write by copying other kids, in a concerted effort to fill the blank page. Dad's unanswered questions guide my research into things I'll read about later. I come to answers after connecting fragments, codes, excerpts from books, old magazines, letters from family members. I lay out Dad's questions together with my findings and attempt to put the puzzle together. I look up the meaning of strange terms in the dictionary. I write down mass grave, epidemic, deportation. There are some words I can't find, opening a new abyss.

The things that Mum says not to say I take down in my notebook so I won't forget them. I combine words that sound good together, writing their definitions in careful handwriting. I mix long words with short ones, consonants and vowels, verbs in past and future tenses. I want to finish a sentence, but I get distracted by the latest fight. I'm still writing, I'm full of ideas. I live in a timeless space. Lost in an era that doesn't belong to me. I inhabit places I've never been. Dad, on the other hand, has never left that distant time.

Dad is still thinking about the war. He forbids me to read history books and scribbles a year on his legs. I record the same date like a tattoo on my brain. One day he discovers the encyclopaedia I have hidden under my bed and says nothing. I keep searching, getting lost in other books. I run my fingertips over the drawing of that continent and I stick pins into the cities I'll visit someday. A stain on the centre of a world map. I never knew if we were from here or from there. So I founded my own country in a blue notebook where I'm not a minority. Mum and Dad want me to be ignorant. They don't want me to study, to read so much. They say that just a few words are enough; that history is for those who have no present. I copy paragraphs from books, dates, heroic figures. I witness events I wasn't present for. I come across names I've heard countless times at home. As I read, I cover my mouth

to hold back my horror. I study the faces and the expressions that mask so much hate. I draw everything I think. Now I can name the places, the people, the dates that hurt me. I'm terrified to continue reading, but I need to understand my parents.

Dad and Mum come from so far away. It's visible in the distance they keep from other people. Their remote cities assert themselves through record albums in other languages, through peculiar expressions coined. At home we pray to another God, we celebrate other holidays, we speak in a language both familiar and incomprehensible to me. Our house smells different, the kitchen sweeter, the oven always warm.

In the living room there are other kinds of decorations, objects that can't be found in the neighbours' houses. There are bronze ashtrays with Turkish stones; coloured glass. A pair of candelabras on the mantle. A map with cities I don't recognize. A plaque on the left side of the door. My last name is hard to pronounce; I have to spell it out. People approach me with questions. But most of the time in the classroom or while reading I'm not there, I choose other destinations. I want to live under a table, inside a closet, between the lines.

It's December. The neighbourhood kids are out on the streets with their new things: aluminium bikes, stylish clothes, battery-powered toys. I feel a sudden fire in the pit of my stomach. The metallic spokes rotate around the twenty-four-inch wheels. They ask about my presents; I don't know what to say. I don't have any new toys to show off. They surround me and ask why my parents talk so strangely, where their accent is from, if I've been to their country. As they interrogate me, the world spins, like when I look at the bike tyres whirling around the axle spun by the gear. I hear laughter and more laughter. Their bodies rise over their bicycle seats; they pedal fast but don't move away. They ring their bells. Ring ring. Their laughing floats on the air as they turn the corner. I'm standing in the middle of the street, my shadow thrown over the sidewalk and part of the wall. I watch myself moving endlessly over a conveyor belt. My feet tire from this lonely treadmill race.

Family From Another Continent

We're a captive audience. Our parents learned the art of performance on another continent. The showing begins after midnight. Dad is always delayed by his memories of the war. We all hide the same watch under our pillows; the one Mum uses to measure his tardiness. We

hear his key in the door and we move to the living room. The blue plush sofa offers front-row seats. The rug is the main stage. We settle in for the show and my parents take their places. My mother wears a red robe that shows her voluptuous cleavage; her face looks gaunter without makeup. My father seems distracted, slightly more stooped, with one hand in his pocket. The wood floor creaks, the ceiling lamp swings in their tears. Sheathed in deformed pyjamas, my siblings and I lean our heads together and our pupils dilate.

The show continues backstage. Lying in our beds, we hear Mum's shouts, Dad's hoarse exclamations. The rattle of drawers opening and closing. The floor shakes, they race around their bedroom, dented voices shuddering the walls. The foundation trembles. A movement that opens a chasm between us and within each of us. We don't want to listen to any more. We pull our wool blankets tight around our heads until we can no longer hear; our cheeks burn, our eyes fill with fluff.

We never applaud after this show. Night after night, the same scenes play out before our hollowed eyes. When everything is over, we go back to sleep. No one will speak of the performance in the morning, not that day, not ever. The only evidence is the impression left in the sofa by our bodies sunk into the cushions for so many hours. Suddenly a fleeting doubt: did we really see it or was it just a dream? We are left with phrases that float down from the upstairs bedroom like an internal echo, *leave, I don't want to see you ever again, you're a tyrant.* The words flutter, twirl, repeating over and over, threatening to drive us mad.

For a while now the refrigerator has held only a tub of margarine, half a lemon, and some empty bottles. I find three wrinkled apples in the crisper. I go into the bathroom; the flame inside the hot water heater is off, soot lining the hole like metal fangs. The pipes squeal when we turn on the hot water. Envelopes stamped with the word URGENT arrive, but my parents don't open them. The school principal calls my siblings and me into her office to tell us about the unpaid fees. My loves, tell your parents that the last chance to pay is next Friday, she smoothly intones through painted lips. I stare at the cloth flower pinned to her dress. We leave the office, our hands scratching at pockets filled with sand and crumbs. I return home to find Dad with a pile of bills on the unmade bed, banging the numbers of an old calculator.

Mum is agitated. She says there's no money in this house, we're going to starve. She paces back and forth as she speaks, shaking her costume jewellery. The house in complete disarray, damp towels strewn across the floor, the sink overflowing with dirty dishes, the blinds closed. Everything smells musty. Adela asks about the cleaning lady. They've fired her. The three of us look at each other and tacitly agree not to say anything about the school fees they owe. I count the money I have hidden in an empty chocolate box; it's not enough, we wouldn't even be able to survive a couple of days.

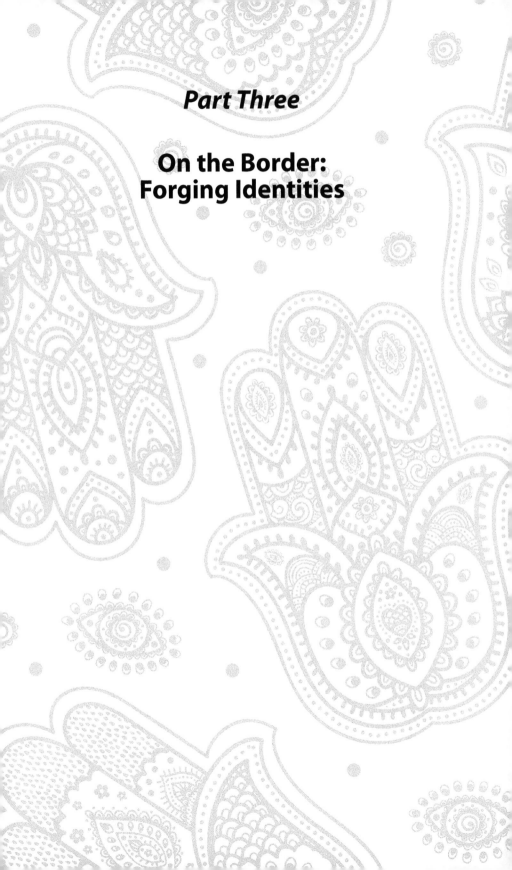

Part Three

On the Border:
Forging Identities

Message About the Jews[1]

Gabriela Mistral

Antisemitism

Beware of not seeing this clearly: the persecution of the Jews, especially in highly cultured countries, is just one example of Europe's animosity toward the Asiatic. Henri Massis,[2] as well as Charles Maurras[3] and his ilk, abhor with close-minded hatred the oriental influence from which all Western culture freely emanates. The talented intellectuals as well as the extraordinarily gifted ones[4] (Maurras being an example of the first, and Massis, the second), do not want to consider—or perhaps they already know it and have kept it to themselves—that if they were to endeavor to scrape off the oriental from European thought since the latter's inception, their great matron would be left stark naked. Europe was suckled by the Greek lioness brimming with Asiatic viscera, and then it was suckled by the Roman she-wolf, a great and noble hybrid beast. Later still, it voraciously gobbled up Christianity, an oriental food if ever there was one. And if Europe were to rid itself of its oriental roots, it would remain devoid of mystique, a stark dry bone, no more than some systematized moralistic whitewash.

They abhor the Jew for being a detached but integral member of the germinal body of Asia. They detest him for representing a contrary order, and one might also say as a different kind of Adam.

We will not follow in their satanic venture. There is more Asian flesh on the expanse of our continental crust than we realize, and the

1 First published in *El Mercurio*, Santiago, Chile, June 16, 1935 and reprinted in 1987 in *Prosa Religiosa de Gabriela Mistral*, edited by Luis Vargas Saavedra, by Editorial Andrés Bello, Santiago, Chile. Translated from the Spanish by Alison Ridley. We thank the Gabriela Mistral foundation for their support with this essay

2 Henri Massis (1886–1970), a French Catholic nationalist and intellectual who saw the East as the enemy of the West. Among many other writings, he authored the 1927 book, *Défense de l'Occident (Defense of the West)*.

3 Charles Maurras (1868–1952), a French nationalist, intellectual, and anti-Semite.

4 In the original text in Spanish, Gabriela Mistral uses "talentoso y talentudo" here. These terms, which on the surface appear positive, are meant to be derogatory. The "extraordinarily gifted ones" should be understood to mean something negative, such as "conceited."

American *mestizo* who denies this fact has everything to learn about his own personal geology.

When it comes to the pure white segment of our countries (Spanish and Italian), there is too much Orientalism in their blood and their culture, though its presence may be more obscure, for it to be dismissed offhand in disgust and anger. While there are individuals who assert that Asia began in Greece, others know that its origins can be found in Sicily, Venice, or Morocco.

It would be foolish for our America to latch onto the filthy tail of this antisemitic campaign. We have enough to do in our own nations—where everything is still in a state of primordial chemical soup—without distracting ourselves with French antics or absurd ventures in Berlin.

Envy

Next comes the second cause of antisemitism. Europe does not want the Jews, because the Jewish people, whether Spanish, Dutch, or Germanic in origin, have always been considered a formidable competitor. Keenly skilled at whatever task he tackles, the Jew is resilient and accomplished in the jewelry business as well as in moneylending and banking enterprises. He is also a veritable genius in metaphysics and is accomplished in letters. Like a catapult, he knocks down anything that is put in his way, whether unscrupulously or as a test. The mystery of his effectiveness has been explained as follows: "He has suffered so much that pure spirit courses through his veins." Human metal more tested by blowtorch or hammer does not exist on this planet so rife with pain. No weave of flesh so pierced by needle or spike has ever lived. What is more, we are dealing with a special kind of suffering, a dreadful type of pain invented for the Jew more so than for the Chinese or the Zulu. It is suffering by way of humiliation, taunting, and disgust. The Jew was received, wherever he went, with blatant enmity. He prospers all the while observing the green face of envy of Christians or pagans, his neighbors or colleagues. His successes, his comfortable home, and his standing in society are never praised without an accompanying gnashing of teeth. It is as though whatever he harvests or amasses is snatched from him by way of theft or plunder, as though not even one square meter of soil or light will ever belong to him, because he constantly has to cede it to mediocre upstarts or idiots from who-knows-where.

To us, he is seemingly a Selenite or a Saturnine,[5] a being from another planet who inexplicably fell to ours and who eats our flour, our suckling pig, and our fruit against the natural order of things. This reality is so absurd as to appear fantastic; we would think it a myth or a fable if we were reading about it for the first time. However, this universal act of silent or vociferous protest is the plain and arrogant truth when we, the favored children of God in heaven, are faced with living alongside the Jews.

Religion

The old reasons, which were never really reasons, for repudiating the Jewish people because of their religion that was considered acutely different from our own, have been invalidated as being spurious. Those must have been medieval times when, red, black, or white, the uncircumcised wore his religion like someone wears his skeleton—as the backbone of his entire being. He stood tall because of it, was intoxicated by it, and was almost febrile with it. But now ... there is great laxity among the faiths, but especially the Western faiths. We are faced with a type of endless carnival, a vile holiday from any kind of spiritual rigor. The commonplace Jew, on the other hand, is now considered an atheist; as much of an atheist as a false Christian, as icily rational as the stuffy, lackluster works of Spencer and his followers.[6]

And, nevertheless ... if we examine European and North American culture[7] closely, and if we look carefully at their philosophies and letters, we will discover something intriguing: The man who here or there manages to preserve some spiritual foundation in his thinking or his art will—if we touch on the matter—reveal to us his Jewish core. That man is called Henri Bergson, a steadfast proponent of the existence of the soul, or Stefan Zweig, a biographer brimming with well-nigh religious views on the lives of heroes, or Romain Rolland, an advocate of Asia in Europe.

5 The word "selenite" comes from Selene, the goddess of the moon in Greek mythology. Here, the context appears to be, someone from the moon, while a Saturnine refers to something or someone related to, or from, Saturn.
6 Herbert Spencer (1820–1903), the nineteenth-century English philosopher credited with coining the term "Survival of the fittest" and developing social Darwinism.
7 The original text uses the word "escultura" here, which means "sculpture," however, "culture" makes the most sense in this context."

In any event, the only supposedly valid justification for our displeasure with and rebellion against the great heretic—no longer that he believes differently from us, but rather that he *does not believe at all*—has become hackneyed.

We must add that this tainting or leveling of the Jew befell him because of our contamination of him, which came about as a result of the Positivist school of thought, our collective life lacks any moral quaking, and the foolish contempt of anything spiritual in our culture. As a consequence, we temporarily destroyed or broke the European and American Jew's prodigious religious foundation. We have infected him with our fetid breath of materialism and attached to its fiery flank our cold-as-ice repudiation of him. This has been a long, slow, and odious enterprise born of Japheth's science and letters inflicted upon God's spirited Shem.[8]

At the very least we should not continue, in the manner of the Pharisees, using the ancient proclamation against the Jew who has been thoroughly undermined by us. Moreover, we should, at a minimum, desist from exclaiming in plazas or in our homes the rebuke that was heard in the Middle Ages: "Hunt[9] the Jewish dog for being an infidel." Jesus Christ, in his infinite nature, would surely be infinitely disgusted upon hearing us utter such words as his supposed advocates and the sentinels of his doctrine.

American Decency

Day by day, Europe supplies us with records and evidence that should make us, like a siren, rise up in alarm from the level ascribed to us by that continent in order to surpass it in certain aspects of decency and civility that it used to possess but is rapidly losing. Once Europe was saturated to its marrow with culture, it began to see itself as liberated from such primitive virtues as tolerance and respect toward pious men, and from Christian society, which used to be awash in civil rights.

The Latin American, who has matured as an innocent creature, feels his moral honor—which he thought to be complete—redouble when he

8 Japheth and Shem were two of Noah's sons.

9 The word used here in Mistral's original is "Halalí," which has differing meanings. It has been said to be a cry used to rouse dogs, but it is also associated with the hunt (or a hunting horn) in German. Either could work here, but the idea of the hunt seems to fit well with the theme of the piece.

reads the list of German or Ukrainian abuses against the Jewish people who were expelled from their home countries. It is as though one is leafing through a picture book filled with obscene and demented images, all because a certain type of distinctive cruelty takes a lewd turn and a nation in a fit of xenophobia becomes a kind of orgy in Suburra.[10]

The old Russia allowed Jewish women to live in certain cities only if they registered as professional prostitutes.[11] Many young female students adopted that role in order to be able to finish their studies ... Civil rights have been afforded the Jewish masses nominally, but without actually protecting them. Those rights were taken away from them or violated in a number of places and ways before Nazism—which was more definitive in its actions—completely annihilated them. The Jewish genius of the consummate Renaissance man—that quintessential being who is the essence of competence and is called Einstein in the sciences and, a few rungs below, Zweig or Remarque in letters—has been worthless during times of plundering. The German, Polish, or Lithuanian Jew has been deprived of the sacred right to escape and be free. For instance, he is often denied a passport and, if he is clever enough to discover a way to escape, he is considered a special type of pariah, one known to consulates and police as the man who arrives at the border without papers, the individual without a nationality who appears not to have been born anywhere on the globe. As I mentioned before, it seems he has fallen to Earth from Saturn. The Jew, a traditionalist seven times over and a reactionary half of the time, will arrive in the country of his refuge branded, like an animal, as an indisputable "Bolshevik."

A Lesson for Us

Our America continues seeking out, inviting, and at least accepting European immigration. I know very well that our America prefers other races over the Jewish race, at times arguing our greater similarity to those other races, and other times, I suppose, our greater dissimilarity

10 Michael Herzfeld refers to the Suburra as "the 'red light district' of ancient Rome" in his article, "Small-Mindedness Writ Large: On the Migrations and Manners of Prejudice." *Journal of Ethnic and Migration Studies*, vol. 33, no. 2, p. 265, 2007.

11 For more on the topic of old Russia and the prostitution of Jewish women, see Nelly Las's "White Slavery" in the *Shalvi/Hyman Encyclopedia of Jewish Women*, June 23, 2021. https://jwa.org/encyclopedia/article/white-slavery.

... if one considers certain regions in Argentina and Chile. Let's not ask our countries to accept a massive number of desolate Jewish immigrants. But let's do ask that they—with little rational effort, which is to say, with basic humanity—accept a small-agreed-upon quota of Jews who Europe has spewed from its twisted Christian viscera. Argentina has established—and I believe quite comfortably—its portion of the quota. If our twenty countries can follow through on this great act, which can only be termed an authentic act of decency, we will have accomplished an effective, honest, and generous feat. One should weigh and measure such adjectives carefully as they are very important to those who safeguard the continent's honor.

By way of this act, we will have returned to Europe some of the culture and Christian policies that it originally imparted to us. In its stance toward the East, Europe has marred and debased its bimillenary rule. Let us cast back to Europe, from our side of the world, a collective gesture of an integral and inclusive Christian right that we learned from that continent during its purer era and that we have strengthened rather than squandered.

Shoes: Andante, with Variations[1]

Margo Glantz

1. With the passage of time, the word *shoe* loses its original associations and etymology. Who remembers that the Spanish word *zapato* comes from the Turkish? It dates, then, from the Renaissance, and it didn't exist before then, in Spanish: other words, such as *calzas* and *calzado,* were used. In the *First Dictionary of the Spanish Language,* compiled by Covarrubias, *calzado* means someone who wears *zapatos,* as opposed to monks and nuns, whose profession involved not wearing them, in the examples of Saint Teresa of Ávila or Saint John of the Cross, commonly known as the Discalced (that is, barefoot) Carmelites.

2. The great Egyptian colossi are barefoot. The Homeric heroes, too, however we might doubt it. Moses, on the other hand, in Deuteronomy, can take pride in saying to the Hebrews: "I have made you walk through the desert for forty years, and your sandals have not worn out under your feet." This is the first written mention of footwear. Although if we reflect on this, God, when creating us, had already thought about needing to equip us with a good foundation on earth: our first shoe is what anatomy provides; the soles of our feet guarantee us a firm step. The softness and elasticity of this first footwear owes particularly to a marvelous combination of little bones, the sesamoids, located under the first metatarsus.

3. And this preamble is necessary for anyone who wants to write the story of a woman whose greatest ambition was to walk life's road wearing a pair of designer shoes.

4. She wasn't born on silk sheets or with the proverbial silver spoon in her mouth supplying her first taste of food. She worked in a provincial shoe store that sold city styles, that is, imitations or copies, at reasonable prices. This store specialized in the Elizade low-heeled pump (shiny black; austere, perfect cut) for the comfort of matrons. It also had thin-soled shoes in styles combining red and beige, or gray and black,

1 For Beatriz Aguad.
 Translated from the Spanish by Elizabeth Rosa Horan.

or white with brown and navy blue. These were especially designed for ambitious young women in a working-class *barrio*.

5. It's time to confess that this story is autobiographical and, therefore, profoundly sincere.

6. The designer preferred by the protagonist is Ferragamo. He was born on June 6, 1898, in Bonito, Irpinia, the eleventh son in a family of fourteen children. His parents owned some farmlands. From the time he was quite small, he was obsessed with footwear, but his father (like my mother's father) regarded it as an undignified profession. One night he worked to make a pair of white shoes for his favorite sister's first communion. It was fate. Just as Leonardo da Vinci was born to paint the *Mona Lisa* and design revolutionary inventions, so was Salvatore Ferragamo born to design shoes.

7. When I began to write about my life, I became unsure, even though I, too, had an unassuming childhood. After I read Nabokov's memoirs, my doubts have grown stronger.[2] Truth be told, when I read things as profound as what he writes, I feel diminished, useless, and what's worse, my obsessions become somewhat inferior, like the natural history of the Americas was for Buffon.[3] How can someone whose only tragedy in life has been childhood exile from one working-class neighborhood to another compare with an exile from the aristocracy, from a country that produced Gogol, Dostoevsky, Chekhov, and of course Nabokov ... *afterward*? My story deals with a woman who loves hopelessly, and the consequence of this fatal love is not suicide, in the style of Anna Karenina throwing herself onto the train tracks, or Madame Bovary taking arsenic because she can't cover her debts, or even the Princess of Cleves, who entered a convent to avoid carnal love. No, my heroine's tragedy consists of a slowly evolving deformation of the left foot, which produces a persistent but middling pain, lessened by analgesics. It's like the pain of a callous or an infected molar, pains wholly incomparable to the lacerating pain inflicted on Christendom's holy martyrs: the amputation of a breast, the mutilation of a limb, flaying, crucifixion. In Nabokov, tragedy often degenerates into subtle parody.

2 *Speak, Memory*, the 1951 memoir by Vladimir Nabokov, recounts his childhood and youth in Russia and his eventual exile from his homeland.
3 The Count of Buffon (Georges Louis LeClerc, 1707–88) made the scientific knowledge of the French enlightenment accessible to readers, and formulated theories on the foundation and evolution of the universe.

In my case, parody lapses into farce, a fate similar to that of the wretch-
ed natives who were reduced to underlings when Columbus discov-
ered they didn't have a cent. And my parents were already underlings
in their own right (Russian Jews)—didn't Hitler determine that and
exterminate them? My parents didn't even go to America, the real one,
but to Mexico, south of the Rio Grande, where we're all deemed worth-
less. Had I been born in New York, I would have studied at Cambridge
or Harvard and my English would be impeccable, like that of Carlos
Fuentes. I insist: I was born here, south of the Rio Grande, and I insist
on recounting the tragedy of a woman who loves too much. What could
be more foolish?

 8. Nabokov believed in God, a god formed by a kind of choir of spir-
its flitting about like butterflies. What kind of God could I believe in,
since I don't even come from Russia, and my inheritance is only a sec-
ond-rate exile? When all is said and done, my parents were the exiled
ones, and their exile was less productive than Nabokov's or even that
of some of the conquistadors. The other day my mother handed me
the key to why she didn't return to Russia: she had nothing to boast
about. If she wasn't rich or famous, why emigrate? Stalinism hadn't yet
reached its height, although it was taking shape, but the act of going
into exile was something grandiose, and my mother only went into
exile to follow an adventurer who didn't even have a beard in those
days. Things would have been better if we'd had an unusual destiny,
but my father had a series of small shops, a series of moves, a series of
books, a series of daughters, a series of trips, and a series of paintings
and sculptures that were awaiting recognition as works of Art, like the
work of the pre-Raphaelites, which were fashionable again in England.
The war didn't touch us closely at all. We heard about it on the radio
or we saw it on the newsreels shown at the movies, while my uncles
and cousins in the Soviet Union were dying in combat, or from hunger
and exposure. Perhaps this obsession with shoes that I am trying to
make heroic to compensate for my lack of family heroism originates in
my Uncle Ivan's line of work. He was my mother's older brother, and
a shoemaker—a nefarious trade, shameful for the family, especially
considering that this uncle didn't even produce a complete pair, but
just barely the upper parts of shoes, no soles, and what's more, it's not
even known if he made men's or women's shoes. My uncle Allosha,
who arrived in Mexico sent by my grandparents to protect my mother

from exile and from my father, was also employed in selling shoe parts: he sold only the sole, made from the inside part of the hide, not even a good sole. So with the two uncles (who sold shoes, of course, in a shoe store in a mediocre neighborhood, shoes with downtown styling but at popular prices), could in no way compare ourselves to the famed Ferragamo, who turned the creation of shoes into an art as famous as that of Yves Saint Laurent with his dresses, or Bach with his fugues.

9. It should be evident, then, that there wasn't anything high-class about us. To elevate the level of my story about unfortunate love, to make it tragic, I have to construct a Herculean universe. I will try to do so. I already said that my uncle Allosha came to Mexico sent by my grandfather to take care of my mother, and when he arrived here he fell into this odious profession—or better put, he sniffed it out, since he had a leather store (cheap leather) on Jesus Carranza, a street obviously not at the height of elegance, and what's worse, he sold what shoemakers for the masses disparagingly call butchered goods. To complete the picture I must draw before proceeding to narrate my story of the woman who loved too much: my very own parents often had shoe stores in the town of Tacuba, where they sold city styles at Tacuba prices, and what's more, where they copied to perfection and without ceremony the shoes of my idol *avant la lettre*, Salvatore Ferragamo (who *par dessus le marché* was a Fascist). Amid my readings of Faulkner and Dos Passos I sat, forlorn, in the shoe store, praying to God no more customers would come so I could finish *Sanctuary* or *Manhattan Transfer*; how could I have known that later on, Ferragamo would be my idol? How could I have known that I would subsequently sink so low as to buy shoes only by that designer? Back then, or maybe when I was too young to be able to read in the shoe store, I could perceive the sadness my mother sometimes felt when she had to sell shoes and my father did nothing more worthwhile than write poetry. However, in spite of being so young, I already knew how to appreciate the elegance of those shoes (unwitting Ferragamo knockoffs) that we sold at 23.50 pesos a pair, lovingly constructed of strips of leather in green and gray, white and black, brown and beige, red and navy blue, with a marvelous, lovely, winged heel. Shoes, as I well know now, inadequate for traveling those streets, which during the rainy season filled with mud as deep as the old lake at Xochimilco, through which you passed in canoes, or on the back

of a native porter (a *tameme*) for the modest sum of fifty cents, or one *tostón*, a colonial coin.

10. As I was saying, the shoes that my mother sold were conscientiously made by hand and unwittingly imitated the Ferragamo designs then sold in Dallas's Neiman Marcus for about $40, an exorbitant amount if one thinks that we sold them for 23.50 pesos a pair when the dollar was worth 2.45 pesos. But doubts again nag at me. How can I write a book about such trivia?

11. *The Times* of July 1989 reports that the reviled and guillotined Marie Antoinette has become the darling of the French, who have absolved her of her sins some two centuries after the fact. And at an exhibition that the Caen Museum has organized to celebrate the bicentennial of the French Revolution, the most-visited object is a shoe that the unfortunate Queen lost as she climbed to the scaffold. Three architects have been commissioned to create six abstract spaces to house, in turn, that most precious piece of footwear. Curators dressed as the Queen's *Guard des Corps* carry it, protected by their white gloves, from one space to the next. The public must kneel on a white sheet, to venerate it.

12. Today I have decided to call this book: *The Story of a Woman Who Wanted to Walk Life's Road Wearing Designer Shoes …*

13. I must begin telling the story at the precise moment when the woman (me, that is) is walking down a street of shoemakers, perhaps that street in Lisbon, there behind a plaza, where they sell cheap shoes, similar to those sold in the shoe stores abounding in Tacuba. I would like to write a text as refined as the refined shoes designed by Ferragamo, and I can't, because the woman (that is, I) only knew neighborhood shoe stores specializing in copies for the lower middle class and for the beggars who came by every Saturday with an empty tin can to collect the prescribed small change and who on weekdays came wearing worn-out shoes, no socks or stockings, asking for work shoes at 7.50 pesos or for old women's low-heeled pumps in a shiny black with a tiny strap at 5 pesos. Only my piano teacher, chubby, wearing cotton knickers the color of lemony *mamey* cactus, bought shoes in a grayish green that scrupulously matched her pearly-colored purse. Shoes were the only item we sold: once, *in illo tempore*, in the heart of downtown, we had a boutique called Lisette, where my mother sold hats, purses, and gloves: obsolete objects.

14. A reliable antiques magazine lists an exceptional find: a pair of seventeenth-century shoes, from a house belonging to the Lords of Northampton, sold at public auction for £20,000. And here I should add, the extraordinary thing isn't in the mere fact that they might have discovered shoes from the seventeenth century. The extraordinary thing is that the pair in question is in a perfect state of repair. Remember: Marie Antoinette, like Cinderella, lost only one shoe when she climbed to the guillotine.

15. A woman walks by a store window several times. Rather, she walks down a street where shoes are sold. Her obsession is twofold, fixed on shoes and on a novel relating to the road to be walked, an obsession shared by Saint Teresa, Saint Ignatius, Saint John, and, in Mexico, by the seraphic Franciscans. The idea is to trace a comparable and allegorical parallel between the woman who must walk an amorous road, or the road in *mezzo del camin di nostra vita*, let's say, along with the seraphic friars, Saint Teresa, and Saint John, who walked unshod or with very poor sandals. I keep writing the text in which a woman wearing designer shoes walks life's road, her zeal contrasting with a martyr's calling, thus her nostalgia for Saint Teresa of Ávila and the seraphic Mexican friars; she finishes it off with Saint John of the Cross, the most important of the mystics. It should be underlined that this obsession will, perhaps, totally change the plan of her novel.

16. First she walks along streets where there are shoe stores, and when she looks at them her thoughts are indissolubly linked to the beginning of the novel, seen as a long road to walk, a road that becomes impossible to travel if her feet are not shod in special shoes, the most marvelous and soft pair, the most aesthetic ones in the universe. In her travels she comes across a shoe store in which there is a pair of shoes that fascinate her: they are on sale; nevertheless, they seem far too expensive, for she is accustomed to installment purchases, to buy in bits and pieces. Her parents were also fond of installments, as they say, because when they arrived in Mexico their first encounter on the train headed off into the unknown was with a Jewish man wearing thousands of ties around his neck and thousands of hats on his head and I-don't-know-what on his hands, but he spoke to my parents in Russian and told them not to speak Russian but German, and that marked their lives. It started my father down the credit road carrying a basket full of bread on his head. Then he bought himself a horse—and where did

he get it, if he had no money? I never found out, but you have to agree that in Mexico he started out down life's road on the right foot and on a horse, and this horse was to carry the bread, but while my father was riding horseback like a conquistador, an Indian, who to be precise was called Serafín, carried the basket on his head, and Serafín was like Cortés's slaves, because my father preferred to read poetry while Serafín loaded, sold, and collected the monthly payments because, although it may seem improbable, the bread was sold on the installment plan. And if I go down life's road on foot and wearing designer shoes—Ferragamo or Maud Frizon (not Christian Dior, nor Yves Saint Laurent)—then things will surely go well for me, especially if I keep my former ancestral habits, those of a person who relies on credit, and if I can get, on sale, the last pair of fatigue green Ferragamo shoes, make that demiboots, with a medium-sized heel and a cunning little buckle, a divine pair of shoes that fulfills a double function: to allow me to keep going through life in designer shoes that are elegant, perfect, and—a fundamental point—not too expensive.

17. It didn't occur to me before, but wouldn't her feet be pinched and sore because she never wore designer shoes until now? Nonetheless, I go on, and she goes on, down Bond Street, passing Armani, where she especially gasps before his suits, when she touches the fabric's texture; Ungaro, exquisite dresses, but too young (she no longer has such a narrow waist); Yves Saint Laurent, marvelous, but where could she wear such shoes? She could buy herself an Armani suit, she has the money now that they're on sale, but she's used to spending money on trifles. Her clothes take up so much space in her closet that after having totaled the cost of all of them, she could have bought herself something marvelous, but she doesn't, and she does the math again because she has the mentality of someone who buys in installments. Her blind steps lead her again to Ferragamo, where she has seen the shoes; she knows that she won't be able to write if she doesn't have good shoes to wear, she has already proven that: at this very moment she is wearing shoes from Oxford Street, from Ravel, a cheap store for out-of-towners like herself, people who don't have much money or who, like me, have the mentality of someone who buys on installments, besides feeling an immense, tango-like nostalgia for those shoes made of colored strips, green and gray, red and gray, navy blue and white; high, narrow heels— from the shoe store of my childhood, the one Mama had—next to the

shiny Elizondo pumps for old ladies that we went to Tacuba to find with Papa, when the vampish ones cost 23.50 pesos, and those for little old women cost 12.50. Perhaps I should buy myself some shoes like that: I remember a taupe pair from Christian Dior, very high-heeled, t-strap pumps like those from the 1920s, shoes I had to give away the other day, although they were still in very good condition, but I could no longer wear them, for I have bunions, and having bunions fits perfectly with the mentality of a person who buys on the installment plan, and not with stylish shoes.

18. A foot as deformed as a worn-out shoe, down-at-the-heel, no longer covering the misshapen foot, the dents or wrinkles showing a part the foot can never fill. Nothing receives the impact of reality so much as feet, in shoes or on the ground. That's why, as a girl, I wore black patent leather t-straps, flat, with a rubber heel, or white ones, and during the first days I didn't want to walk in them so as not to dirty the soles, and to avoid such a thing I walked on newspapers. That maneuver stops the effect of reality: it keeps beauty intact, as happens in still life paintings in which a few table scraps establish balance, never deteriorating because they are painted.

19. Her blind steps lead her again to Ferragamo, where she has seen the shoes; she knows she won't be able to write if she isn't wearing good shoes. She enters, inquires about the shoes; they show them to her: they are a greenish gray, with a silvery reflection produced by the treatment they have given the leather; the heel isn't too thin; it's medium-sized, with a slight curve toward the instep, like those in the Ferragamo shoe catalogue now on exhibition at the Victoria and Albert Museum. She went to the museum; she has passed through innumerable rooms piled high with erratic collections of medieval statues, blue ceramics, Persian rugs. She thinks she should stop, because Persian rugs are definitively associated with shoes, or rather with the lack of shoes, because one should never walk on them; you have to take your shoes off before entering a mosque or a home; nevertheless, she continues on her way without stopping, the thought is useless as she treads this road trampled on by shoes: the rugs are on the wall, not even sandals could reach them. Finally she finds—oh how wonderful!—the room where the brilliant Ferragamo shoes are on exhibit. Back in the store, she tries on the shoes they've brought her after she pointed them out, there, on the round table where the sale objects are displayed. They tell her it is the

only pair. She tries a shoe on the left foot, the one with the bunion; she verifies that the fit is perfect, simultaneously solving the problems of beauty and of comfort. However (and she can't avoid it) they seem too expensive, even though they're on sale. She returns to the other stores and no other shoe pleases her as much, but they still seem too expensive to her. She is used to spending her money on less expensive things, cheap things; it seems to her that those are the only things she deserves, but, and this is for sure, she also knows that the novel she wants to write can't be written if she doesn't decide to buy the Ferragamo shoes; they are her open sesame, the glass slipper from her fairy godmother.

20. At that moment what bothers her the most is the fact that she's eating too much *turrón de yema* candy, drinking too much sherry, and getting fat, and besides, she can't wear Ferragamo shoes, not even to the beach, to take them off to feel the sand, because she has bunions and, unless the sand covers her feet, her deformity is visible. She thinks about other shoes Ferragamo has made, and about those lasts made to the size of each diplomatic, imperial, artistic, or jet set foot. Then she wants to have feet like Mangano, who belonged as a child to the lower class, just as she did, and who probably wears fashionable brands, just as she does, and who has, just as she does, a bunion. Why not think about that? Ferragamo could have fashioned her a shoe last, sized to her bunion.

21. This afternoon, I thought Ferragamo's life interesting. What an odd idea for someone who has deformed feet and is at the beach, barefoot. I don't know how I could be interested in the life of a fat man who was always bent over, measuring feet and building wooden shoe lasts. Although, of course, those lasts were unique, one for each foot, because just like fingerprints, our footprints are unique, as in life or anatomy, a singular design of nature. Besides, on each one of the lasts that he made, Ferragamo inscribed the name of the owner of the shoes that allowed that person to walk solidly on the ground. The lasts were perfect, made of an exceptional quality of wood. Now those lasts are sold at the price of gold, but you have to buy them if you want to keep your shoes impeccable. I never get tired of thinking about it; the prints of each foot are exceptional, as unique as fingerprints; but in this democratic era no one wants to admit it, and buys ready-made instead of tailored clothing: *pret à porter*, and it's redundant to repeat it, the same thing happens with shoes.

22. While she thinks about her shoes, she knows she will write a text that has to resemble an opera, one that stops both history and the sentiments, immobilizing them. In the theater those sentiments are aroused; in the opera, what seems tragic becomes grotesque, on account of the voice, the gestures, and the costumes; also because, she thinks again, she has deformed feet and they become more and more deformed each time she sings her triumphal aria, an aria in which her male companion, who loves her, always falls asleep because he can't stand opera and the scene is repeated, degraded in the shoe store, in her mind, while the music swells on the impeccable compact disc where Aída, like Nefertiti, begins her descent to Hell with her intense pure soprano voice.

23. I stop, this is very important: her main obsession comes from the idea of fame, the honor of a name. Convinced, she returns to Ferragamo, she tries on the shoes again, the clerk comments, "You were here earlier." She nods, it's decided, she buys them, but before doing so, she utters a vow, a promise made to Saint Teresa: to wear them only when she sits down at her typewriter, like she is doing now, with her shoes on, with hose of the same shade (later in Fogal she will buy several pairs, designer hose for Ferragamo shoes) and finally, solemnly, the time has come; seated like a seraphic Franciscan before the typewriter or at the computer, smoking a cigarette, listening to Bach, eating *turrón de yema* candy and drinking a glass of port, she begins the most heroic act of her existence: to write *The Story of the Woman Who Walked Through Life Wearing Designer Shoes.*

The Melancholy of Black Panthers[1]

Luisa Futoransky

Let's imagine a hailstone thawing. It slides along because of gravity—a force to which all of us animate and inanimate beings pay tribute to this day—the winds and accidents of the terrain; with its heart, its cordial hard center of ancient minerals, and a periphery that grows with weeds, obstacles, small objects that join with it, like aids to memory, or anecdotes about the terrain, until it flows together with others into a violent river, which like all rivers goes to the sea, but as the Bible proclaims, the sea does not overflow. So do I present, gather, and observe the voice of the minorities of the diaspora within the great channel of Latin American literature.

Within that palpitating and singular conglomerate that comprises the words written to tell, recount, and dream in this century of our vast literary cartography, I pause, intrigued, with the greatest respect regarding a particular period—the one between two wars—and a distinct segment of the population, which I choose to call "the mute women." I am referring to our grandmothers and great-grandmothers. The ones who were forced from their torched little villages to the *goldene medine*, innocent translation of Eldorado into Yiddish. I do not wish to signal a real absence of the word, because at times they shouted like wild animals, but the written testimony, especially that produced by the women themselves, is practically nonexistent. Of those women there remain few birth certificates, those that were not sold off or traded. Only those of death are extant and intact, which obviously they did not write.

Their first and last names, Castilianized by their children or grandchildren, appear in pitiless struggles for shares of inheritances in the registry of deeds.

I want to talk about the women because the great crime of our age, because it is not codified by theological or secular laws, is omission. Lying is a sin, sometimes a crime, but guiltily omitting, silencing, laying aside, is not.

1 Translated from the Spanish by Roberta Gordenstein.

I belong to the generation of the children of Jews who came to Argentina because, between one war and another, pogrom and pogrom, they fell off the map into ships, just as the Albanians, Malaysians, Cubans, or Haitians are doing now in their own way and before them the Vietnamese; in short, the shipwrecked of all times. Those who lived from hand to mouth, and be thankful you have hands.

For those who may be familiar with the painting of the Old World that depicted the tatters with which the new one constructed its modernity in order to return them to the old in ellipses and in spirals of courage and blood, I remind them of the pictorial work of Lazar Segall, a central European from Brazil. His scenes take place mainly in cesspools crammed with people, almost as brown as the waters of the deltas and the swollen timber of those ships. The climate breathed in his canvases is the fragile and the precarious. Even so, the picaresque of nostalgia continued building bonfires, making smoke signals in order to be understood, or simply to make the outpourings of the soul a little bit warmer.

Anxiously, the immigrants wished to become part of the country, and rapidly: that country of which they were totally ignorant and of which they demanded so much, to which the combative fury of foreign hussars and their own mad hunger had led them. It is easy to understand them, because how human is the desire to be understood quickly, or to stroll down a street whose pitfalls and ruts are known. One needs a country in order to read between the lines, to be familiar with the degrees of jealousy, the wrinkles of good and evil in the faces of the others, I mean, our own.

My relatives were not city-dwelling Jews from the capital. Neither had they been city dwellers in the places where they were born, and neither had the parents of their parents been in the impoverished sites from which they in their turn had also escaped. After arduous periodic interrogations and investigations of my relatives, almost always with negative results, I found a vague point on the map which, then as now, changed its name and flag with a certain frequency, but which always remains near a river, perhaps the only reliable and domesticated fixture of the geographical landscape. From the shores of the Dniester, it seems that some of us reached the Spanish language, the way my cousins say they reached the Portuguese of Brazil or the English of Brooklyn. None

of these people—my people—imagined seeing the ocean, just as none imagined being lost, forever.

In Argentina, at that time called "the Queen of the Plata" they came, as always, to the periphery. The ones on the periphery, aren't they, perhaps, the only ones who make the center evident? And searching for who-knows-what secret dream of redemption and Promised Land, they settled down in a place called Santos Lugares and wound up selling shoelaces and strings of garlic and onions in the town marketplace, and sewing linings for ties and corded seams for pajamas. To recreate, in short, the shtetl, the center of the imaginary, the main street of the rich and the poor, the well-read and the foolish, lunatics and saints. From the dreams of Eldorado they sensibly lowered their sights to those of silver, copper, and minerals of lesser nobility and alloy. Ending by reducing them to two: a little home of one's own, "of substance" and the son, "a doctor." And they left behind them the words of a dying language, Yiddish, on the greedy coasts of the Atlantic in order to consolidate their passage, sometimes paying in raw flesh, from utopia to the predominant culture. Like the generation that came with Moses to the Promised Land and nevertheless had to wander forty years in the desert in order to enter. That's why the second generation of immigrants, that is to say, that of our parents and our own, is just beginning to produce the saga of their future after their families had experienced, voicelessly and breathlessly, decades of poverty and trials, which they survived out of pure stubbornness. Perhaps also because the Europe they had abandoned was a conflagration where only hunger and all the familiar plagues prospered, plus other new ones of still-unknown cruelty.

Among the many things that I still have not written but would very much like to write is to give at least a pale glimpse of the life of those young women who came from villages harsh in patriarchal customs, who were reduced to the level of chattel in dialectical languages, to the pampa, the unheard-of distances, madness. They changed, altering their shtetls as best as they could, at the risk of populating the asylums with melancholy or violence, and the cemeteries with suicides. Those, the ones who were ostracized, watch from the sidelines, with their crooked gravestones, the "natural" deaths of the others.

When I say melancholy, I think of those exaggerated and obligatory mourning periods of my childhood. For years, the women of my family

and the neighbor women dyed the season's clothing with black aniline in great tubs of zinc, in order to respect their rigorous mourning customs. Chronicles of entire districts were inscribed in the memory of the people because of their respect for or violation of mourning rituals. Three long years of monochromatic circumspection, which then gave way to the gamut of grays of partial mourning. At times the deficient quality of the operation recalled, because of large grease spots, the earlier print of the dress. It would tenaciously reappear in strange, superimposed designs, bringing to mind comparisons with old, exciting times that flourished despite the circumstances. A situation analagous to when I once surprised myself in the zoo, noting the backs of the black panthers. From up close their leopard spots shone through, the family memory of their origins. From that experience comes this title, because perhaps my women, in their apparent strength, distilled a dense, nostalgic "Melancholy of Black Panthers." Incapable of accepting losses. Too many, perhaps, for a single life.

Nowadays, the axe blows and stabs of the rag-picker (which furnish at any moment the fragments and splinters of our own existences) make me widen the optics of my *compatire*, of my own sharing, to experience, like my poor old mother, aunts, grandmothers, and neighbor women similar dwellings in the catalog of passion: ostracism and exile.

The women I talk about did not fit in—but they must have fit in as best they could, or supposed that they did—the suppositions of an urban imagination. Like the survivors that they were, they must have sharpened their ingenuity in the perception of the immediate. Without keys for translating the New World, they must have forced their way in with pick-locks. Repopulating life with new gestures and words. But what words. How to defend the body and oral traditions they were carrying, holding fast to them from the Middle Ages into the New World, how and when to compromise with the new realities, which required unheard-of relationships between man and work.

The fissures began to make themselves felt when all the fears within and without could not pass through the same coordinates of thought and word. These excisions tend to be fecund for opening precious treasures in the realm of the fantastic in literature and in art in general, but not in the struggle for life. Men's daydreams can give rise to a blazing inferno or to the sublime flying buttresses of Notre Dame. ¡*Helás!* There's only one Notre Dame, while Hell, public and private,

is innumerable. So did the closets begin to be populated with the dead and with the living men and women who could not cope with the new reality. Most of them were profound melancholics, although there also were some violent ones, those who ended up in the madhouses with the most terrible of punishments, the strait jacket: once put on, there was no going back. Less dramatically, more amusingly and modestly, most of our women dreamt of a golem, a zombie domestic who would relieve them of the oppressive tasks of the home and defend them effectively in the hazardous world of transactions with the goyim. To calm the children of turbulent schooling, from their innermost being they invented the fear of the dark, of the unmentionable, by means of the bogeyman. This was achieved, sometimes with the opportune presence of the gypsies pronounced with *tz*, the abstract *tziganer* who would steal us away, condemning us to wander with them. Since the threat of living in absolute freedom did not instill sufficient fear in the intractable, they added the notion that they would sell us to be ... the word "slaves" was not pronounced. The concept of white slavery, together with a panoply of sexual terrors and taboos, they inculcated into us girls much later.

Every family knew, in private, new alliances and unspoken wars in the marketplace, where husbands and boyfriends were always scarce. Unequal combat when faced with the fascination exercised by the goy, the gentile, the other. Those wars, subtle or ferocious, took place in the intimate, secret language, Yiddish.

Bashevis Singer reminds us that this language is the only one in the world that was never spoken by the powerful. A harsh destiny met this language, which arrived over waves of desperation and fury at the coasts of the Atlantic, which metamorphosized itself as best it could and knew how, passing from New York through Rio to Buenos Aires, only to expire, in an almost irremediable fashion, in the open air of its beaches.

If we observe at close range the baggage of these people, we see that in the beginning they brought rancor and alienation because of the expulsion to which they had been submitted. Under such conditions they looked at the others, who in turn looked at them, as hostile. Hostile because of their respective appearances, for not having the custom of living together, for their different devotions and sacrifices to the Divinity: exile, from the time of Babel (to not depart from the first

reference in Genesis), has doubtless been and continues to be a punishment, like translation.

Because what is translating and being exiled but taking an arbitrary block of words, a planetary system of ideas, phonemes and fantasies, and transplanting it to a different, unknown planetary system. Frequently the orbits do not fit. Many words and laws, generally the greatest, the most profound and secret, remain bouncing around like worn-out springs, out of their orbits; for that reason, translation and exile are always synonyms of loss.

Arriving in one language, living in another, and writing in a third is the literary experience of the contemporary novel; Singer, Kundera, Conrad, Nabokov, Beckett, Kosinski, Gombrovickz, or Kafka themselves confirm it. Their written language is not the one that others speak. For the great transfer of communication they realize limited pacts with language, almost impossible to translate, because sarcasm is the only inalienable weapon in the hands of the exile. Irony is capable of absorbing hatred and piety without poisoning us too much. As a result of producing such disfranchisement, the world has become a shambles inhabited by all the barbarians.

An image persists in my scenario as I ramble through these pages; it is of a painting by Francis Bacon. From a chaotic circle of greens surges a massive tree, unarmed, torn out by its roots. Without anesthesia. Like a wisdom tooth. Its roots in the air. I have a premonition that from them some grafts will bear fruit, other shoots will inevitably perish. About that line blazes, like a road, a yellow point, in full view. It might seem to be the head of a man. A little horse perhaps. The title of Bacon's work is irresistible: *Portrait of Van Gogh.*

No one better than ourselves to stand in front of the mirror of cities without hope, the jungle of all exiles. One must observe always, in order not to presume anything, that path from which we originate; it may be enough to consider, although only superficially, the treatment that the metropolises offer to each new wave of immigrants: at one or another moment of their lives, along with all the humiliations, everyone passes through this, waiting on tables and cleaning the sidewalks of the others in order, much later, to empty their pails of trash, their rubbish. It falls to the recently arrived to maintain tidied up, in short, the unconscious of the city. *On est toujours le juif de quelqu'un.*

If I am quite in agreement that's for a writer, "homeland" is where one writes, not about what or whom one writes, it is essential to poke around in the exile of those who belong to us in order to understand also our own expatriations. The fears and tremblings of those panthers of our blood, their whispers and laments through which they sift their glories and sorrows that infiltrate the imagination of the great channel of this, our Latin American writing, to which we, in their honor, also belong.

In the Absence of Love

Ruth Behar

> "When I say that I no longer loved him, I mean
> to say that you have no idea to what lengths one
> can go in the absence of love."
>
> "Give me some idea."
>
> "I can't."
>
> —Marguerite Duras, *The Ravishing of Lol Stein*

In the absence of love, I am going to Cuba again. It's my seventh trip. I no longer have a reason to return. There is nothing left to find, nothing left to bring back. I have taken pictures of the forlorn houses in Old Havana where my mother grew up, where my father grew up. I have walked through the rooms of our apartment and sat on the edge of the bed where my parents once made love. I have sat on that bed with the striped bumpy spread that's under a window looking toward the sea. I have stood again under the brass lions of the Patronato Synagogue. I have stood on that same spot where a picture was taken of me when I was four, a Cuban flag half slipping out of my hand. I have gone as far as the town whose sugar slopes cannot stop weeping for the Indians and the slaves. I have gone as far as that town where my great-grandfather brought the family from Poland, only to spend nights of oblivion hunched before his account books, writing stories in Yiddish of his childhood.

I don't understand anything.

My marriage has ended, but we're staying together because neither of us has the time or energy to do anything else. We have a son who's more attached to his father than to me. Whenever he needs anything, he calls out "Daddy!"—a wail as desperate as a shofar sounding in the desert. It's the price I've paid for being a professional woman. All of my son's friends are being raised by single mothers, divorced or never married, and they watch us like hawks. They flirt with my husband and wait for me to join them.

I'm going to Cuba for two weeks. I've lost weight, so I won't feel bad this time about looking fat while everyone else goes on a national Weight Watcher's program because of all the shortages. From the sale

rack of the store that has all the rayon Javanese clothes, which I usually can't wear because it's too cold here, I've picked out a short dress with a drop waist. It has thin spaghetti straps that I'll need to tie into bows to keep them from falling off my shoulders. The dress is pale gray embedded with pale pink flowers. I don't know yet what shoes I'll wear with it. Everything I have is black and too heavy for that paper-thin dress with its little girl flounce. I need sandals. And I'll have to paint my toenails a shade of dusty rose.

I don't expect anything to happen in Cuba. I mean, a love affair or something like that. I'm too cautious. I won't let myself be used by some guy who needs a plane ticket to Miami. Politically, who knows what could happen? I've always suspected I'll end up there in the midst of the final chaos, during the last chapter of the Revolution. As the book is being closed. That's the price I imagine fate expects me to pay for returning after there's nothing left to find, nothing left to bring home.

He always said it didn't matter if I didn't love him. He had enough love for the two of us. More than enough for the two of us. I wanted him to prove it to me. I don't like false promises. That's why I held back. Gave little. I think he was lying. His love wasn't boundless. It ran out. Or maybe he just got tired. Men get tired, my mother always said. I guess I pushed too hard. But I won't blame myself. It's the cultural differences—what in the world could have brought together a Jewish Cuban woman carrying too much history on her back and a bashful guy from Texas who thrives on peanut butter and sliced banana glued together with mayonnaise? Pure madness, nothing but madness.

And yet I know our good-bye at the airport will be so tender that I'll believe I almost love him. I'll beg him to wish good things for me. As I step onto the plane, my heart will shatter like glass under my feet.

Just like last year, I'm going to Cuba on a Jewish humanitarian mission. It's one of the few ways to get into the country. All expenses paid in advance, staying at the best hotels. Bringing dried milk, powdered eggs, and potato flakes, stuff you eat in times of famine or war. For the last thousand Jews still living on the island. We're enchanted by the idea of helping the Jews who stayed behind, guarding over the palm trees. It makes us feel better about having left.

The first day in Cuba, it will be the same as always: we'll visit dead Jews first. In an air-conditioned bus they'll take us to the Jewish cemetery in Guanabacoa. I've gone many times, taken many pictures of the

moldy graves and their salty Stars of David. But I will put on my new gray and pink dress and go again.

I'll leave a stone at the grave of my cousin, who died of leukemia.

I'll leave a stone at the grave of my great-uncle, who died of cancer.

I'll leave a stone at the site where they buried that sliver of soap made of sorrow and bitterness.

And before I wash my hands, I'll leave a stone by the gate.

For the losses I can't name. In case I don't return.

On the Border: Essential Stories

Miriam Bornstein

Dondequiera que vayas verás
cosas diferentes, pero el
pueblo será el mismo.

Wherever you go, you will see
different things, but the
people will be the same.

—Abraham Bornstein, El Llanto del Vistula (Cry of the River Vistula)[1]

I. The Desert: Tierra Santa/Holy Land

I come from a land of ancient mesquites; *péchitas* hanging from my
mind like poems, simple in their sweet taste on children's tongues play-
ing *a la casita*.[2] A land where *laureles* bleed as bold as Southwestern
history. I have forgotten when it was that I left; but I keep returning
como una culebra mordiéndose la cola; devorándome las entrañas para
encontrarme otra vez en mi desierto. Regreso al polvo antiguo después de
acumular otro polvo. Huellas de otras voces; uñas incrustadas en el alma
como la espina del sahuaro orgullosa de habitar su presente mile-nario. /
I have forgotten when it was that I left; but I keep returning like a snake
biting its tail; devouring my entrails to find myself again in my desert. I
return to ancient dust after gathering other dust. Imprints of other voic-
es; fingernails inlaid in the soul like the thorns of the sahuaro,[3] proud

1 Abraham Bornstein, *El Llanto del Vístula*, Ediciones de América, Mexico, D.F., 1944, p. 158.
 In his short life (1916–52) my father became a writer in Mexico and, although there are
 several unpublished manuscripts, this novel as well as a children's play were published
 in Mexico City. This novel is written in Spanish and it deals with life and the characters
 that lived in his small rural hometown, Żelechów, right up to the Holocaust. It ends with a
 description of resistance efforts in the defense of Warsaw against the Nazis, an expression
 of gratitude and love for his adopted country, and a lyrical cry for freedom on behalf of the
 oppressed and the poor.
2 Mesquite (from the Nahuatl *mizquitl*) is a tree native to the southwestern United States and
 Mexico, which bears *péchitas,* beanlike pods that are sweet and edible. *La casita* is when
 children play house.
3 The saguaro or sahuaro is a giant cactus native to the southwestern United States and
 northern Mexico.

to inhabit its millinery present. I return to my Mexican and Spanish desert, to the land of my Indian ancestors; cultures intertwined in me like my great-grandmother's long mestiza braid and wisdom.

I now ask for her blessing and kiss her hand one more time as I remember words with memory clinging to them. Words with the essence of bones, beings dancing in the soul, working their way out through the eyes creating other eyes and more. They come like furrows to flesh and ocotillos.[4] Emptying ghosts ready for harvest under a full moon. Remembering scattered pieces of the self over sacred pyramids, fished from the sky by *sacerdotisas*; words with full headdress and filled eyes.[5]

II. Mother is a Way of Remembering

Some of my memories of my mother include an image of her hanging clothes out to dry in the sweltering heat embracing the land; an August net cast in the still Mexican Arizona Desert. Who was to say that the glory of her red hair and the loyalty of her fair hands would be pinned to my memory, distorted by time and heat arising from the very same desert in our backyard. Her delicate fingers hanging clothes are in her children's memories like pieces of love facing the sun and truth. There, quietly, with eyes turned inward searching for life. Awareness standing on a line, like so many of the lines my family has had to cross before arriving here, on this page with this voice.

Words that have flourished against the wind behind barbed-wire fences and cement walls thick with prejudice. Memories coming to the edge of being, standing at the edge of the well. Surfaces broken over and over again by the crossings. It seems as if I have always been crossing borders, lines, fences, barricades, hedges, railings, oceans, rivers, *fronteras, sueños, miedos, tapias con vidrios puntiagudos que amenazan los ojos, castigan antes de llegar a la orilla de la esperanza.* / It seems like I have always been crossing borders, lines, fences, barricades, hedges, railings, oceans, rivers, borders, dreams, fears, walls with sharp-pointed pieces of glass that threaten the eyes; punishing before arriving at the edge of hope. Undocumented memories and histories find their

4 Ocotillos are spiny, woody, furrowed shrubs found in the southwestern United States and arid regions of Mexico. They produce a long, bright red flower in the spring.
5 *Sacerdotisas:* priestesses.

birthplace and slip through all the ancient holes in the night and the soul and the fence, splitting hearts in the passing between one and the other.

III. En Polonia, Abraham/In Poland, Abraham

Eres de un país donde las esperanzas se quedaron congeladas en el hielo, en las pupilas de un pueblo. El lago donde la abuela Mamishi lavaba la traviesa experiencia de tu infancia guarda las huellas de tu correteo de niño. Tus risas aun hacen eco en los recodos del bosque y en los puños de tu gente gue como tú atravezaron la historia para seguir luchando.

Eres de ese país que no conozco donde igual que tú el sol jugaba asustado a las escondidas para sobrevivir la pesadilla de ser judío en esas tierras. Polonia antigua y fría desborda su corazón y te recuerda en el tañer de las campanas de Żelechów, tu pueblito al sureste de Varsovia. Atrás se quedaron las palizas de los "goím" cuando ibas por la calle jalando tu carrito vendiendo carbón y combatiendo las garras del poderoso inviemo y del prejuicio. Al final del día ibas también cargando con el peso de la pobreza hasta tu cama en la vieja casa de la calle Nalewsky frente al Rynek. Regresabas a bordar recuerdos con palabras de humo en la transparencia de aquella tierra blanca y silenciosa; despertando al amanecer como el corazón de los antiguos castaños que revientan cerca de los pastizales. /

You come from a land where hope remained frozen in the ice, in the pupils of a town. The lake where grandmother Mámishi washed the mischievous experience of your childhood holds on to the imprints of your running around. Your laughter still echoes in the twist and turn of the forest and in the fists of your people, who, like you, crossed over history to continue their struggle.

You come from an unfamiliar country where, like you, the frightened sun played hide-and-seek in order to survive the nightmare of being Jewish on this land. Poland, ancient and cold, overflows its heart and remembers you in the sound of bells in Żelechów, your small town southeast of Warsaw. The beatings of the goyim remained behind as you walked on the street pulling a cart selling coal and fighting off powerful winter's paws and prejudice. Also carrying at the end of the day the weight of poverty to your bed in the old house on Nalewsky Street, across from the River Rynek. You would return to dream and embroider memories with words of smoke in the transparency of that

white and silent land, waking up at dawn like the heart of the ancient chestnut trees bursting near the pastures.

My father Abraham Isaac Bornstein Engel, an eleven-year-old boy in 1927, facing poverty and the rise of fascism, packed only the most essential memories and the necessary words in his eyes. Mámishi would take her children, Michalina, Lea, David, and my father, like a bouquet of flowers to "Meksiko," where for six years the old lion with the sweet and tender gaze, *mi abuelo* Mordecay Joseph Bornstein Goldboaum, *hijo de* Nehemiah Bornstein Bielawski and Yenta Goldboaum, had earned their passage southwest across the River Vistula by selling ties on the street to gentlemen with dark eyes who stroked their land in their pockets as they too crossed a river and sent for their own families. Men who carried their need to the other side and offered the toil of their hands, enduring humiliation with *familia* strength. Men like *mis tíos*, braceros returning to Aztlán, the heartland of the ancients in *el norte*,[6] a line that I too was to cross in 1964 at age fifteen, holding on to my mother's dreams, the childhood of my little brother Abraham, and the work of my oldest siblings, Frida, David, and Rebeca.

IV. From the Land of Abuelos: Weavers/From the Land of Grandparents: Weavers

Una cigüeña stands on one leg on the roof of the synagogue surrounded by the white countryside of winter and hope.[7] It witnesses the turning of the land red with anger and hate. Balancing on the border of identities and religions, this time between Nazi and Jew, my family migrates again. Mámishi and Tatishi wove their hope out of the forest and across an ocean. Their yarn spun an unknown future and a boat carried their dreams like a prayer shawl over their heads. In their hearts they carried a blessing and the most sacred thought from Jaime Mayer Horovich Engel, my great-grandfather, and his wife, Lea Felner. In his novel, my father remembered:

6 *Mis tíos*: my uncles. The term *braceros* derives from the word *brazo* or arm. To meet the labor shortage of the 1940s, the United States and Mexico set up a program in which Mexican citizens worked as hired hands or laborers. By the time this form of cheap labor ended in 1964, close to five million braceros had worked in the United States. Aztlán is the original Aztec homeland in what is now the Southwestern United States. *El norte*: the north, in reference to the United States and to Aztlán, the Aztec's ancestral homeland.

7 *Una cigüeña*: a stork.

"Nunca olvides que eres judío."

El Rojo no aguantó.

"¡Qué broma! Vines en un estado feudal, en plena siglo veinte y en el corazón de Europa; ghetto escolar, pogroms, vejaciones, Hitler de vecino ... ¡y olvidarse de que es uno judío ... !"

"Never forget that you are a Jew."

El Rojo couldn't stand it.

"What a joke! You live in a feudal state, at the height of the twentieth century in the heart of Europe; student ghetto, pogroms, mistreatment, Hitler for a neighbor ... and not to forget that one is a Jew ... !"[8]

I am sure that my father carried this sentence in his proud and kind heart for the rest of his life. I see it in my children's eyes when they are called "Meskins" and told to go back from where they came even though their birth is rooted on this land.

It is said that the quota of Polish citizens immigrating to the United States was filled and in spite of having explicitly invited the tired, the poor, and the huddled masses yearning to be free, Lady Liberty pointed south. "No more Jews allowed in here," she signaled in the night, and today she is still pointing south across the river, bridge, fence to political and economic refugees speaking Spanish.

My father was to take the Żelechów of his childhood to the warmth of ancient rites and poetry, *la tierra mexicana* / the Mexican land, where he was to write in Spanish and knit sweaters for his firstborn, his daughter Frida.

V. Abraham y Cristina: My Parents

No sé dónde empezaron tus ojos, ni ese amor capaz de cruzar un océano para acurrucarse como paloma en el pecho de una mexicana, mi madre / I do not know where your eyes began, nor that love capable of crossing an ocean to cuddle up like a dove on the breast of a Mexican woman, my mother, María Cristina Gómez Sánchez, daughter of Margarita Sánchez Ortiz, my mestiza grandmother and her Spanish husband, Andrés Gómez Peral.

8 Bornstein, p. 156.

Mámishi almost died of a heart attack when she learned that my father was to marry outside of the faith—to a woman named Cristina *para colmo de sus males, "oy gevalt!"*[9] She wanted her to change her name to Ruth and create a melodramatic Jewish soap opera. Cristina held her ground and Abraham married her anyway in a little church, holding on to his Jewish heart, where he promised his God to stand by her, to support her in the bearing of her five children. She in turn, promised la Virgen de Guadalupe that she would support the bearing of his literary work and journeys.

It was on one of those journeys, at age thirty-six, that the car veered to the right on a stretch of highway near Lagos de Moreno, Mexico, turning and tossing my baby brother, Abraham, out the window and killing my father, killing my mother's passion. To this day I remember how deep her sorrow was, how profound her pain, always, in spite of time and grandchildren in our ancestor's land. This event has always been part of me even though I was only three years old.

En Estos Tiempos

Quizá este poema sea una elegía
o simplemente
 se me antoje recorder
 entallarme las palabras.

Así
lanzo el anzuelo por la memoria,
tal vez recobre la imagen velada,
 oscura tierra entre mis labios.

Hoy
solamente me quedan:
 algunas hojas polvorientas
 (posiblemente huelen a ti)
 unos jirones de piel esparcida
 inclinados al pasado
 una voz tardía
 alargada por el tiempo
una mano implícita que acaricia mis poemas.
No, la verdad es que no te recuerdo

9 *Para colmo de sus males*: to make things worse.

así, con el inventario intacto de tus huesos
pero quisiera acordarme
de tus pasos cotidianos
de tus amigos, tus quesos, tus cigarros
y tu amor definitivo a México.

Sólo me queda tu perfil en un sueño
y en el hueco de la mano
 estas inútiles palabras.

In These Times

Perhaps this poem is an elegy / or I simply feel like remembering / trying on words. / So / I cast the fishhook through memory; / maybe I can retrieve the hidden image, / dark land between my lips. / For now / I only have left: / some dusty sheets of paper / (perhaps they smell like you) / a few shreds of scattered skin / leaning toward the past / a belated voice / extended over time / an implicit hand caressing my poems. / No, the truth is that I don't really remember you / with the entire inventory of your bones / however, I wish I could remember / your daily steps / your friends, your cheeses, your cigarettes / and your definite love for Mexico. / I only have your profile in a dream left / and in the palm of my hand / these useless words.[10]

VI. Mother Border Struggle

At thirty-two years of age, my widowed mother headed north to a small border town, where my little brother and I watched American tourists with curiosity and pretended to speak English by twisting our mouths, making strange faces and sounds, and then rolling on the floor laughing, holding our aching bellies.

For practical purposes, *mami* got used to widowhood, just like her mother with her six children and her grandmother with her own six children. For three generations, the curse of the widow's peak.[11] Curious strands of inherited hair became an art as she fed all of us by combing ladies' hair in the living room of our humble house in Nogales, Sonora.

10 Miriam Bornstein, in *Donde Empieza la Historia*, Spanish Press, Sacramento, California, USA, 1993, p. 27.
11 It is believed, particularly in Mexican culture, that when a person's hairline forms a peak on the forehead, he or she will eventually become widowed.

Pushing aside her constant tiredness and the rude remarks because her clients' straight, dark Mexican hair did not conform to the curled, blond beehive of the woman who appeared on the worn-out pages of a magazine written in English, she worked spinning smiles in her eyes as she watched her children eat with gratitude in their hearts. *Arroz y frijoles* were her offering to our future.

VII. Crossing Rivers: Vistula and Rio Grande

In spite of the kindness of our people and the fire of her fierce spirit, the harshness of life for a widow with five children and a grandchild proved too much for my mother. Again, my family headed north, this time across that boundary that only welcomes working hands, agricultural hands, hands to smooth wrinkles on clothes, hands that wash the shame of hoarding so much, invisible hands that service, feed, and clothe a nation that takes so much from so many and offers prayers on television and says grace in "English Only."

I remember my mother's hands, long and delicate beings of love and devotion. Hands that brought sustenance to the soul with every meal no matter the struggle of the day. Hands that appeared over and over again, offering the bounty of unconditional love until crossing the border to *al otro lado*,[12] where my mother folded the Mister's underwear, cleaned dirt, and kept her designated place in a *House and Garden* home. Her hands allowed *a los del otro lado* to live without the weight of daily life, to fill their lungs with the luxury of pride, and to not ever learn the kind of dignity that simple work can bring to the spirit. Sometimes, if mother performed her duties well and there were no social engagements for which to prepare, *la Misis*[13] would grant my mother permission on a Sunday to run to the edge of Mexico and reach across the border to her children, who were not yet allowed in this country.

I remember my mother's hands, becoming small, soft, and new like baby's kisses, sneaking past uniformed, vigilant "legal" eyes through the chain-link fence, reaching for my budding adolescence and my little brother's perpetual innocence. She kissed our fingers and our hands

12 *Al otro lado*: the other side of the border; in my case, Nogales, Arizona, USA.
13 *La Misis*: the Mrs., the woman of the house who employed the domestic workers.

linked, hungering for each other across our pain, our need staring at us like *púas desgarrando el corazón* / thorns tearing into the heart. A line imposed long before us by history, war, and greed now splitting the most sacred union between mother and child, our being.

All this sacrifice to become "legal aliens," but "aliens" nonetheless in our ancestor's land.

I still remember my mother's hands, now filled with the Arizona Desert, eternal time and silence.

VIII. Talking of Struggles

I have always known that I had relatives of fire like an omen hanging from my neck. Ashes stuck to the epidermis fallen to this land like living molecules of long ago. Who would have said that, unfamiliar as I am to their sky, I would trace the footsteps of their words back into their Jewish eyes and learn to step around unearthed bodies scattered like forgotten residue of madness, a hate unadorned and open. I can't help but think that considering the history of my people and those who have survived across borders, rivers, boundaries of bigotry … my very own life could be considered a miracle. In the same context, *me impresiona imaginarme que en otro espacio, en otro tiempo mi sangre judía me delataría, mis hijos marcados por sus abuelos que no conocen serían convertidos en cenizas desperdigadas en un bosque sobre las alas de pájaros que abora llegan a mí, a esta pápina, como el bumo de aquellos seres arremolina-dos en el rincón del miedo* / I am deeply moved upon imagining that in another space, in another time, my Jewish blood would give me away; my children designated by their great-grandparents, whom they do not know, would be converted to ashes scattered in a forest on the wings of birds that now come to me, to this page, like the smoke of those beings crowding around each other in the corner of fear.

From my father I inherited the word like the strands of *cuentos de espantos* given to my childhood by *la viejita del barrio,* the ancient storyteller who dished out images and *cocoricos* as big as *la luna llena.*[14] Holding the hand of *mi hermanite,* the way home was long, under the

14 *Cuentos de espantos*: ghost stories; *la viejita del barrio*: the elderly neighborhood lady; *cocoricos*: a type of cookie made with corn flour in northern Mexico; *la luna llena*: the full moon.

eye of that moon, with her ghost stories still rattling in our bones and imagination.

Finally, I would return to my mother's arms to dream of words left dancing in my eyes. Words like rivers entwined with memories as ancient as *paredes de Israel y pirámides* / walls of Israel and pyramids, where rituals assured the survival of the sun, and it is still that way.

This is my ritual, my way of keeping alive the bloods in me, given to these hands to weave a precious prayer shawl, this time a woman's cloth, a rebozo, with the colors of our own history and culture, to cross over the pain and reach the song within each of us.[15] Inherited fierce mother courage given to me to survive what is left behind and struggle for what must continue.

From *Always from Somewhere Else*[1]

Marjorie Agosín

The Deep Breath of Exile

All exiles are like deep breaths, imperceptible in uninhabited land-scapes. We abandoned our country at night. No one saw us take off. Like fugitives we gazed one more time at the Andean cordillera as the wind created ridges and scars in the dampness of our tear-drenched faces.

The Melody of Exile

My father always told me that he was always from somewhere else and that he looked at maps to invent cities. He also said that his parents had told him that he was always from somewhere else and that he was a child of the diaspora. But when he spoke to me, in 1968, about leaving Chile, this idea of belonging to a community of foreign exiles stirred within me a fear that came from vacant tables and broken mirrors.

I felt that my body was covered with a green layer of scales and bad omens. I felt cold when I heard the paper maps rustling in the hands of my parents. I didn't want to see anything new. I loved my country, its shores and its melodic language like the sweet rippling rivers. Yet I heard a voice that said: We will go to look for other islands, to surround ourselves with other seas.

My mother balanced herself within a dark and magical circle, telling us that Jews lack a national identity, that we are the most orphaned and exiled people of the earth. But I didn't want to be an orphan. I wanted to have friends and to accompany them while they left flowers for the Virgins. I wanted to sit in the folded skirts of the old shepherd who sweated in his heavy woolen garments in the summer months.

Sometimes I used to hide in my pockets *milagros*, the little mass cards bearing colored pictures of the saints. But I knew that Jewish girls didn't have saints to protect them.

1 First published in 2000 by The Feminist Press at The City University of New York, New York, USA. Translated from the Spanish by Celeste Kostopulos-Cooperman.

This time my best friends told me that I would return to the land of the Hebrews. The word *Jews* seemed too harsh, and not the least bit subtle. In fact, we were not going to Israel, the homeland of the Jews, but to the United States, the last stop on so many immigrant trails of tears.

Once again, we prepared to depart. My mother carried a handful of dirt from the southern regions of her childhood, and my father his skeletons, which accompanied him on his nights of shadows. I, on the other hand, did not know what to take with me. My cache of possessions seemed like a depository of lost objects. Memory seemed to stick to me like a covered tattoo. But I left with them and accepted the condition of being from somewhere else and from nowhere in particular.

In the evenings sometimes, I still wake up sweating, as my father does, and I don't find the maps or the suitcases, only the nightmares of being a traveler without a place to go. The experience of exile is like a sinister rainfall. No one recognizes my name or the fragrance of my skin, and no one caresses me because I am alone in a place where no one even recognizes my voice. This is how the lost and ephemeral memories of exiles are.

Suddenly, the voice of a messenger or an angel tells me that memory is right here, that it is like a music box that needs only to be opened in order to begin the process of recall.

Nostalgia

From the nostalgia-laden past, we invent countries like dreams; we sketch false rivers, imagine certain aromas, and speak the language of the homeland as if it were a ring sealing love's alliances.

Letters

Seated by my side with an old and distant gaze, my father asks me if the letters have arrived—those letters from Chile that foreshadow the happiness of newlyweds and the peace of the dead, those letters that we have waited for, daily, for nearly thirty years. They are letters from distant friends, who talk to him about his dilapidated laboratory and

about our house, now inhabited by the noises made by the footsteps of others.

People in exile adjust to foreign landscapes. They hold onto letters with much eagerness and passion—a passion for memory, for past experiences, and for usurped time. I contemplate my father waiting for the letters. He has the gaze of an absent man who interrogates beings from other spheres, from countries close to an also distant sky. Exile is a state of crude recalling, of being and not being anywhere, of waiting for the arrival of the familiar in foreign places, of feeling oneself always remote.

Living Translation

Our life in the United States has always balanced itself between the frontiers of return and the misty memory of flight. When we arrived in Athens, Georgia, we bought few pieces of furniture because we were always hoping to return to Chile. We talked about our country, wrote letters, and dreamed about the cordillera, knowing that we lived too far away from it. We ate our tasty foods seasoned with garlic and herbs, our fresh vegetables, and never tried to become part of a culture that was so foreign and distant from our own, where people greeted each other with caution, where time was a slender border of fear, and where no one dared to ask about the health of the sick. We lived in a borrowed zone, knowing that at any moment we might have to leave, as if we were waiting for the end of the war, the surrender of our furniture, and the glorious return to life.

Chile's military dictatorship lasted almost twenty years. We lost friends who disappeared clandestinely and who now have disappeared from the memory of those who knew them. We missed births and funerals. Our identity lay confused, suspended between imaginary and real borders. We lived in translation.

Now all of us reside in a type of atemporal land, in a region lost between the memory of what was and what we have fabricated across distances. We are Jews without a country. Every day we learn other languages and live in borrowed houses. I believe that if they were to blindfold us, we would find the road home.

From Belarus to Bolondron: A Daughter's Dangerous Passage

Ester Rebeca Shapiro Rok

In telling the story of my Cuban Eastern European Jewish American self, I listen closely to a competing cacophony of ancestral voices carrying 150 years of oral history and living memory, because among them I discern the currents of my own life. I must reconstruct the dislocated narrative of a family life unfolding in a turn-of-the-century Russian–Polish border shtetl village and then transplanted across three continents, two world wars, two revolutions, and five languages. Contrary as always, I insist on scrambling the official story and casting my central protagonists in contradiction to the cherished myths our family still lives by. From my earliest memories in Havana, Cuba, I grew up in the hothouse atmosphere of my father's profound attachment to his parents, Abuela Berta and Abuelo Lazaro, and his brother, Tio Noel. My father's family formed intense ties of mutual protection and loyalty in the long passage from the shtetl in Rubyshevish, Belarus, to the rural Cuban village of Bolondron. You would never have known from the way we lived our daily lives, as patrilineal as any Bedouin tribe, that my father had a sister, Tia Consuelo, whose story I carefully studied as a daughter's cautionary tale.

In Abuela Berta's family mythology, stories of shtetl hardship paved the way for the family's creation myth, her decision to undertake the arduous journey out of Eastern Europe in 1936 and book passage to Cuba. The family's voyage, like any heroic quest, required that we outwit a cruel, arbitrary fate whose small coincidences and near-misses obscured the enormous consequences. If we could catch the appointed train, we could begin a passage ending in a land of palm trees and plenty. If we missed the many necessary connections, we would leave the shtetl on a different train, and remain forever in Poland, strewn as smoke and ashes in Hitler's crematoria.

To hear Abuela Berta tell our family stories, her daughter, my exuberant Tia Consuelo, was a source of eternal danger requiring constant maternal vigilance until she was finally married off and became her husband's concern. Why, I wondered, was Consuelo so cruelly left out

in the cold of her own family's inner circle? She herself never stopped protesting the enormity of her own family's rejection, even as she married the men they chose for her, twice by the age of seventeen. Consuelo lived a difficult life by the side of my explosively sentimental Tio Isaac, whose profound loyalty to his own sister was forged by the crematoria fires that left them sole survivors of their Polish family. Her marriage created the haunting irony of Consuelo's life: for her husband, his sister always came first, reminding her cruelly of her invisibility to her own brothers in her own family. She lavished her generous soul's love on her son, Leon, and daughter, Leye, her six grandchildren, and her four great-grandchildren. All her thriving family are loyally devoted to the cause of making Consuelo, at long last, feel loved. At her husband Tio Isaac's funeral, Consuelo, then age seventy, told me that not a single day goes by when she doesn't remember the violence and pain of her childhood, hard as she tries to forget those bitter memories and enjoy the outpourings of love from her children, grandchildren, and great-grandchildren.

But I don't want to make it seem that Consuelo was a shrinking and pitiful presence. On the contrary, it was precisely her passionate intensity, her vivid curiosity, which overflowed the borders of our otherwise constricted shtetl family. Abuela Berta could tolerate expansive strivings on behalf of her sons, but could not make room for Consuelo's downright dangerous sensuality. Abuela Berta might have known how to manage her daughter Nachame—the name meaning "consolation" in Hebrew—under the strict rules of their shtetl life. Now, their lives were utterly unbounded by old traditions, transported into a new world that could hardly be imagined but was unquestionably filled with the dangers that had always followed Jews on their many diasporic voyages. Consuelo, as eleven-year-old Nachame, began the voyage to Cuba in 1936 and later she recast the story as a picaresque tale. At the age of adolescence, she experienced the family's terrifying train trip across an increasingly dangerous Europe as the finest adventure of her cloistered, claustrophobic shtetl life. As they waited for the ship that would cross the Atlantic to Cuba, Nachame evaded her parent's watchfulness and took her little brothers wandering in London. Family legend tells the tale that they only made it back to the hotel by capricious chance because she located a passerby who spoke Yiddish and was able to direct them. My father's version of this story betrays his eternal conflict

between a younger brother's admiration for his adventurous sister and his anxiety turned to terror that they could, at any point along the journey, be lost and surely perish as children alone in a dangerous world. When Abuela Berta related this portion of the journey she added the moral of the story to her cautionary tale, reminding us that in our family quest for survival, we could only count on fellow Jews.

Once the family arrived safely on the boat, new dangers awaited. The long trip in the ship's crowded third-class hold terrified our landlocked shtetl family. My father Jaime, still six-year-old Nachemie on that trip, and his nine-year-old brother Neiach, soon to become Noel, were free to roam the ship in Consuelo's wake, ostensibly to watch over her dangerous sense of adventure, but actually to reap the benefits of her intense sociability. Consuelo so charmed the crew and first-class passengers that she obtained far better accommodations for them, including regular access to first-class meals, the fear of hunger always a looming detail in my father's stories. After their long voyage across a darkening Europe and a turbulent Atlantic Ocean, Nachame arrived in Cuba as Consuelo, now a fully developed young woman. Her name still meant consolation, but that apparent continuity masked a world of difference and marked the ironic tensions between old world and new that characterized her growing up as well as my own.

Consuelo ripened into a voluptuous young woman, a full-faced, full-bosomed Russian beauty, with a pale yet rosy complexion, softly wavy blond hair, and lively green eyes that showed her alert curiosity and intense emotionality. Consuelo was short yet round and big-breasted as a young girl—what we would call *zaftig* in Yiddish, conveying a generous motherliness, or what we could call *sabrosa* in Spanish, conveying a generous and enticing sensuality. Consuelo's presence was further enlarged by her voice. Her speaking voice seemed to be broadcast out of larger than usual lungs, or maybe was amplified and resonant in her massive frame. She became bluntly outspoken, in an inimitable blend of Polish shtetl coarseness and Cuban *chusmeria* (slang specializing in salacious double-meanings), shattering the silence of a family where most feelings were expressed indirectly, if at all. Consuelo always seemed to be in some excited uproar. She had replaced her shtetl Yiddish with a countryside Spanish, and her voice inevitably took on a powerful, expansive quality that filled the room, punctuated by picturesque obscenities. During my own growing up between cultures,

this time in Miami after we left Cuba, Consuelo became a cherished source for scarce family images of a woman with passions and appetites. While my ascetic mother treated sexuality as a secret that reduced her to stuttering silence, Consuelo was an exuberant cook, her food fragrant with excessive garlic and cumin, her language peppered with obscenities: she sought any opportunity to call a *pinga* by its proper name. Consuelo's zest in evoking sex with its concrete, vivid intimacy remained a referent in my clandestine sexual awakening, wedged between Havana and Hollywood, in the end closely mirroring her own.

My favorite story about Consuelo's growing up as the bridge between two worlds was the family legend about her brief first marriage at the age of sixteen. To me, the circumstances of that marriage, one of those family secrets that everyone knew, captured Consuelo's history and place in the family, which I feared could so easily become my own. Mostly, the story of the brief prelude to her first marriage, which was itself of even briefer duration, captured my imagination and explained something essential to me about the family forces that denied her control of her own life. Consuelo presented my practical and implacable Abuela Berta with the terrible dilemma of bringing her daughter up as a proper young lady in an unfamiliar foreign land. She found the period after Consuelo's puberty especially demanding and treacherous, coming so soon after their immigration. Abuela Berta told me once, part proudly and part fearfully aware of the great dangers involved, that all the young and eligible young men, as well as others not so young and eligible, had fallen in love with Consuelo, including the town's chief of police. Consuelo was being asked out by a number of passionate suitors and frequently serenaded at night, in the fashion of Cuban romance. Curious as always, Consuelo found these suitor's attentions compelling proof of her attractiveness and value. Yet her interest in the local young men was completely forbidden; since there were no other Jewish families in their village, Consuelo was expected to wait patiently for an arranged marriage.

More quickly than the family could handle, Consuelo's intense curiosity and sexuality presented the problem of finding a suitable young man among the Ashkenazim of Cuba, the Eastern European, Yiddish-speaking Jews, all of whom were referred to as *polacos,* whatever their national origin. Cuba was profoundly foreign to my family that even its Jews were unacceptable. The Spanish Jews, the Sefardim, were

called *turcos* and were considered foreigners, of a different race, and hardly Jews. They might pray in Hebrew, but in the intimacy of their homes they spoke Ladino instead of Yiddish, the intimate language of our homes. One of the family's concessions to American assimilation has been accepting Sefardic Jews as permissible, although still slightly suspect, marital material. In Consuelo's time, with Ashkenazic immigrants so recently uprooted, the Sefardic Jews of Cuba were too alien to provide a needed sense of shared kinship and culture. I consider it one of the great ironies of our tribe's diasporic dispersal that my ancestors, in their inevitable transculturation with their Polish neighbors, absorbed both a far paler skin and a greater portion of Polish racism than I would have desired on behalf of my own Cuban Jewish identity.

In spite of the limited acceptable pool of potential suitors, a match was made for Consuelo through the island network of Eastern European Jewish families; this was done without the intimate knowledge of family background that characterized generations of shtetl life. The young man, whose family lived in Havana, was introduced to Consuelo, and they became betrothed, My grandparents had traveled the seven hours by bus and train from Bolondron to Havana to meet with him and his family and evaluate their suitability. They found them to be apparently well-to-do hotel keepers, which probably provided additional appeal to Abuela Berta, since her mother's father had been an innkeeper in Rubyshevish. She was relieved that this mutually acceptable family match also pleased her headstrong daughter.

Now, I have heard many conflicting versions of the story of this ill-fated marriage's abrupt dissolution, embellished by each speaker according to his or her own point of view. Abuela Lazaro told me his remembered story thirty-five years later in Hollywood, Florida, his smoke-roughened voice and thickly Russian-accented Spanish adding to the intensity of his already agitated retelling. My grandparents wanted desperately for me to appreciate their side of this sad story and had long ago accepted that I had lost my Yiddish in our United States transplantation. Spanish was now the shared language of family intimacy. Abuela Berta let him take the lead, but inserted necessary details to fill out the narrative and persuade me that they had done all they possibly could for their wayward daughter. As my grandparents told the story, Consuelo arrived in Havana after a proper Jewish wedding in Jovellanos and at some early point discovered that her new husband

and his family were the owners not only of hotels, but also of brothels, which were legal though not respectable in Cuba. Abuela Lazaro angrily remembered that Consuelo had called them in tears, telling them what she had learned about her new husband and in-laws and asking that they take her home. Abuelo Lazaro even suggested that this man expected Consuelo to help out in the family business (as a receptionist or record-keeper?)

Abuelo Lazaro and Abuela Berta's brother-in-law, Tio Loba, married to her sister, Tia Anita, went into Havana together. They severely beat Consuelo's husband and his father, and they brought Consuelo home. According to Abuelo Lazaro, they were taken to court for assault but fully vindicated by the judge, who confirmed that they had acted appropriately in defending the family's honor. Abuelo Lazaro was furious and indignant at this terrible deception and blow to the family's reputation. As a secondary concern in his approach to the court, our family demanded the dowry paid for Consuelo returned, and was vindicated by the court in forcing the money's return. Through the haze of remembered outrage, Abuelo Lazaro proudly recalled the opportunity to rescue his daughter, avenge the family's dishonor, and receive return of the money by his own decisive action. The courts of this exotic new land did deliver a familiar justice.

I later asked my father what he knew about the story of Consuelo's first marriage, and told him what Abuela Berta and Abuelo Lazaro had told me. Father laughed and said my grandparents were either misremembering the story or deliberately re-embroidering it. He had been told by Consuelo herself, when she came home weeping, that her new husband had told her he loved another woman but his real love had been unacceptable to his family. He had agreed to the arranged marriage with Consuelo to satisfy his parents, but he did not love Consuelo and would continue seeing the woman he truly loved. Since, my father continued, Consuelo had been in love with this man, she was heartbroken and refused to continue in the marriage. To me, my then eleven-year-old father's version sounded suspiciously like what Abuela Berta would come up with as an acceptable way of explaining the situation to her impressionable youngest son. The key dramatic elements of my father's version—the young man torn between filial loyalty and romantic love and, of course, choosing filial loyalty—provided precisely the

explanation of events that Abuela Berta was most drawn to, as I learned over the years.

More recently, when my cousin Edith, my Uncle Noel's older daughter, was visiting Boston, she inquired about my writing and I mentioned that I was still working on our family stories. I told her that the best story so far described the family's arrival in Cuba and Consuelo's brief first marriage. Edith, eager to set the facts straight, responded quickly, "Oh, my mother told me that story." Consuelo went to her marriage bed, her husband discovered that she was no longer a virgin, *era ana puta*—she was a whore—and he sent her back to her parents. She added that her husband, Joel, was friends with the first husband's son from his second marriage, and could confirm these facts. The story of Consuelo's marriage as seen through my aunt's eyes did not surprise me, because I recognized in it the kind of moralistic cautionary tale used to terrify Edith into protecting her own virginity in the turbulent permissiveness of our shared North American adolescence. I was instead astonished by the extraordinary news that Joel knew a version of the story from the divorced first husband's son. I was frankly shocked by the evidence that our intergenerational lives had continuity, did not drop off the edge of time like amber photographs of a vanished shtetl, of a vanished Cuba. We immediately asked Joel, "So what do you know about this story?" Joel dismissed as fiction the story of Consuelo's lost virginity. Consuelo had been too hurt that her husband had agreed to an arranged marriage while loving another woman, and she had insisted on her right to a love of her own. The story of her lost virginity had been generated by the young man's family, who had been trying to keep Consuelo's dowry payment after the marriage was dissolved, claiming that Consuelo and her family had committed a breach of the arranged marriage contract, which was all about social obligations and mentioned nothing at all about love.

While disagreeing on the motive, everyone agreed that following these events a divorce was quickly arranged. Consuelo immediately met and married Isaac, in 1943 a recent arrival from Poland whose heart and eyes burned with the fires and ashes of the crematoria. Hitler had destroyed all but his sister Rivkeh, the sole witness to a vanished world. As I remember Isaac from when I was growing up, he was a black-haired, mustachioed, portly man, effusive and affectionate in a maudlin way that was embarrassing to us as children. Father and Noel

always regarded Isaac as a sentimental clown in the classic Russian style, not to be taken too seriously. Over the years they were often on and off of speaking terms with him because of Isaac's frequent objections to their failure to give their sister her fair measure of love, respect, and financial support.

After her marriage, Consuelo moved in with her husband and his sister Rivkeh's family, and from that time on was more involved with her husband's family than her own. Yet Consuelo never stopped trying, in the face of repeated failure, to feel more included in the tight family circle that Berta, Lazaro, and their two sons became over the years. Consuelo's relationship with her family finally changed during the months of Abuelo Lazaro's illness and in the period after his death in 1984. At age fifty-seven, Consuelo finally began to feel included as a potentially valued member of her own family, an inclusion still interfered with by Isaac's combative temperaments and by Consuelo's own anguish at a lifetime of rejection. At age seventy-one, so recently a widow, with Abuela Berta's recent death marking the end of a generation, Consuelo may finally be offered a more substantial place in her family as this installment of our shared story continues to unfold.

While I was growing up, the story of Consuelo's marriage and the turn her life had taken terrified me, even when I was too young to understand my fears. I was horrified, as I reached adolescence, of an early marriage within the approved Cuban Jewish family circle and of the claustrophobic life that would follow. As an oldest daughter who had been disappointing to the family for failing to be a firstborn son, I identified with Consuelo. I was destined to share her character, disrespectfully outspoken and with a dangerous tendency to disobedience. By early adolescence I also shared her unhealthy interest in boys, goyim and North American Jews alike. I had been taught, as a Cuban Jewish girl, that whatever my intelligence (regarded suspiciously as related to my disobedience and family disloyalty), my contribution to my own and my family's future well-being would come with my success at attracting a suitable mate. Fully part of my own North America world, I could not at that age visualize myself married, although my competitive self felt that vying for the sexual attentions of men was a fine idea. I ended up applying this family principle rather farther than was acceptable, resulting in violent struggles over my sexual behavior during my adolescence.

In what was my most intense encounter with Consuelo at the inter-
section of our lives and fates, she talked to me at some length about
her attempt to be a loyal daughter and obey her mother's wish that she
marry Isaac. The conversation took place in Consuelo's apartment in
Queens, where she lived down the hall from her two married children
and her sister-in-law's family. My sister, cousins, and I had all gone to
visit Consuelo and her family during Christmas vacation of my senior
year in high school.

During that entire visit, Consuelo plotted to engineer my betrothal
to her daughter Leye's brother-in-law Enrique, linking me more close-
ly to her family through a marriage within her own extended family.
Enrique was a very bright, affectionate, serious older man, an alluring
twenty-five to my rebellious seventeen. I enjoyed the romance and the
satisfying sense of conquest in our relationship for as long as my ado-
lescent attention span held out. For everyone else in that branch of the
family, the whole affair had the serious weight of courtship. During that
endless two-week visit, Consuelo would take me aside to explain mar-
riage as it really was, so as to better prepare me for this next, imminent
stage in my life. At one point, she was telling me that marriage was a
matter of yielding to practical realities. She herself had not known what
marriage really demanded when she married Isaac, but she learned to
make the best of things.

Warming to her words, as always, she began to speak increasingly
loudly and to race around the small apartment, throwing her weighty
body from room to room as she seized props to better illustrate her
points. As she tried to tell me that marriage involved intimate relations
with a relative stranger who often had disgusting habits, and condi-
tions and compromises of that sort, she ran into the bathroom and
came out with a towel, screaming, "I even wipe my face with his towel,
which is soiled with the pus from the sores on his skin!" She rubbed
the towel on her face, exemplifying wifely devotion and sacrifice, which
presumably would soon fall to me as well.

It seems extraordinarily ironic, looking back on it, that Consuelo of
all people should have tried hardest of all to marry me off at the sig-
nificant age of seventeen. I'm not sure if she was aware of my parent's
despairing, futile attempts to control my sexual relationships with boys
to the limits of proper feminine virtue. Perhaps she felt an early mar-
riage would in my case, as in hers, succeed in channeling my sexual

energy and curiosity to the proper object, before my virtue was lost. (Little did she know how lost it was already.) Maybe she felt my parents and grandparents would be grateful to her for providing me with such a good match and at the same time saving me from the dangers of my impetuous character. After all, my cousins were already talking about my disobedience and sexual effrontery, saying *"que se portaba como une puta"*—how I behaved like a whore. Consuelo became absorbed in taking control of my life at the same age and in the same way that others had taken control of hers, by arranging an early marriage.

At the time of my visit to her home I felt a peculiar sensation of being party to a Russian courtship. The unfamiliar winter setting in a snowy New York added to my eerie feeling of participating in the romantic rituals of another world, as if the lost world of the Polish shtetl had been parachuted into Queens. In Consuelo's living room, thick, red velvet curtains were always drawn, and the ornate lamps cast a darker glow against the heavy furniture. My American ideas about my place as a liberated woman reminded me that this scene could not possibly be for real. Yet the strain of ancient expectations collided with my own view of my life and began to seem too close to a possible reality, no longer a hilarious cross-cultural romp I could later share with my hippie friends. For the first (and last) time, I called my father and begged to return home early.

Consuelo and I have remained close, and she understands how deeply I appreciate her indomitable personality and the dilemmas it created for her in our constricted Shapiro clan. Consuelo has developed an intimate relationship with her own daughter, and has never repeated her own sad history by devaluing her older daughter in favor of her younger son. Consuelo's children's and grandchildren's filial loyalty and capacity for expansive expressions of love for one another has always seemed to me to be Consuelo's enduring legacy.

When I saw Consuelo at the wedding of her then twenty-two-year-old granddaughter, Lisette, I went to sit with her for a brief while, she huge and resplendent in a white lace hand-beaded dress, her blond hair carefully lacquered, her diamond and gold jewelry bountiful evidence that she had made material success of her married life. I remembered that we had recently seen each other at a family event, and she had contemptuously looked at my ethnic beads and asked me in her characteristically brusque way, *"Oyeme, chica, cuando tu marido te va a*

comprar joyas de verdad?"—when is your husband going to buy you some real jewelry? Two years later, I was divorced and at the wedding alone. We had one of our customary, searingly intense talks about our intertwined lives. She asked me if I was planning to have a child on my own, as it was too important a piece of living to sacrifice, with or without a man, and to hell with what people thought. I told her I was planning to do exactly that if I remained single much longer, and she offered her approval and support. I mentioned that I had continued to write about her and the family, and wondered if I had her permission to publish this work sometime. She said that she had always been proud of her ability to live her own life rather than be dominated by her parents, with their fears and prejudices. "*Yo siempre hice lo que me dio la gana*"—I always did what I felt like doing—she said proudly. "I don't care who knows it." I thanked her for this gift of her life, made with her customary generosity and seasoned with her *picardia*, her sense of mischief, sharing her desire that in our self-important, self-protective family, all hell should break loose.

Toward the South[1]

Carla Guelfenbein

I clearly remember, before passing through the doors of the Hotel Delfín, when Mama stopped, brushed her hands over my shoulders as if she were removing a layer of dust, knotted the ribbons of my braids, and told me again what she had repeated endless times in the taxi: "It'll only be two hours, dear, three at the most."

Two girls entered the hotel, dressed to draw attention, their heels clicking; Mama watched them out of the corner of her eye and continued her task; their unrestrained laughter hung suspended in the air. Mama was thirty-three years old. My father had left us around eight years ago, and despite the fact that she still kept her natural elegance and attractiveness, the tough work, the hard times, the effort of providing for us in that dry dusty city—all of it had begun to leave its marks. She worked behind the window at the Central Post Office receiving packages and, from time to time, some stranger passing through, dazzled by the discovery of her beauty in such an unexpected place, would invite her to go out. Maybe what most excited my mother was the opportunity to glide through the doors of the Hotel Delfín. It had been built a decade before and its glass structure, tall and narrow, stood out in the sweeping plain like the promise of a world to come.

"I'll be in room 1810, like the year of our independence. But don't move from this spot, you hear?" she indicated as she slipped a bill into the palm of my hand.

After a few minutes, I was seated in the lobby and my mother, with her black glossy hair, her green eyes, and her false eyelashes, was disappearing behind the golden doors of the elevator.

The sun had withdrawn beneath the edge of the plain and through the tall windows I could see the red glow that it had left behind. In the vast expanse of sky a lone cloud was heading south. I had brought my homework from school and for a long while, preoccupied with complicated mathematical calculations that weren't going well at all, time's passing had become imperceptible. When I raised my eyes, in

1 Translated from Spanish by Nicole Bell.

the shadowy depths of the large floor-to-ceiling windows the first stars had begun to twinkle. I was hungry. I picked up my bag with its notebooks and school supplies and I headed toward the bar on the top floor. I knew the way well. Mama didn't like to leave me alone in the room we rented. It was in the house of a widower who was a little odd, so every time Mama had one of her dates at the Hotel Delfín, she brought me with her.

I sat down in a stool at the bar and ordered a ham sandwich with an orange juice. From their tables, men in dark suits were looking toward the corners where small groups of girls were exchanging murmurs and laughs. I could hear their voices, their whispers, I sensed the perfume emanating from their sinuous bodies. One of the men made up his mind and, gathering his courage, moved toward the girls, only to disappear shortly after behind the bar's doors with one of them. And I didn't let those glances that most of the men threw toward me like lassos go unnoticed, either. I was thirteen, and my mother took great pains to make sure I didn't appear older than that. But even so, I was conscious of the attraction that I exercised over men, an attraction that I knew woke forbidden desires that, by their very nature, turned against the men with desperate intensity. I crossed my legs, encased in girls' socks, gave some tugs on my braids, and passed my index finger smoothly over the tip of my nose while at the same time taking small sips of my orange juice through a straw, knowing the effect that each one of these gestures provoked in the human specimens observing me. Seated next to a boisterous group of office workers, a man was looking at me with more insistence than the rest. He was a bit younger and wore a close-fitting suit with thin lapels, like Elvis Presley wore. He had a certain charm. Maybe it was his long eyelashes, his rebellious air, or the insistence with which he stared at me. For a while I played around with my braids for him, without looking at him, of course, but I soon lost interest. In front of me on the other side of the bar, a man dressed like an explorer took a seat. He had graying hair and features my mother would have classified as "attractive," and, in that short amount of time, he had already downed two whiskeys. A pair of heavy bags hung beneath his eyes, giving him the appearance of an old raccoon. He looked tired. He was different from all the others, not only because he was unaccompanied and wasn't wearing a suit, but also because he seemed to be heading to another world, a place where

he didn't want anyone to follow him. Without looking away from his glass, which he held with both hands, every so often he half closed his eyes and murmured, as if he were talking to someone residing within the depths of his being. A pudgy man with a shining bald patch and steel-frame glasses started the Wurlitzer, and the pleasant sounds of trumpet music flooded the room.

When I finished my sandwich, I was still hungry. But I didn't have any more money. Anyhow, Mama should be arriving soon. I rested my elbows on the bar and while I was thinking about my own things, I found myself looking at the bar's bottles, suspended upside down, which gave off flashes of color. Mama had promised me that we would go to the south to visit my grandmother this summer. There the land was fertile, damp, and the air was light. I liked to dream about that expanse of trees without dust, and also about my grandmother, who I had never met. Sometimes I thought that maybe neither one truly existed, and that the "south" was just a place that lived in my mother's imagination. A place that waited for her and that, in the middle of this wasteland, granted her a horizon on which to rest her gaze so she wouldn't get lost. A type of neon sign in the middle of the empty freeway, marking the existence of a place where she would finally be able to rest. When I looked up, the man with the long eyelashes was in front of me. His body was swaying slightly.

"Is it all right if I sit down?" he asked me. His voice was smooth. I lifted my shoulders in a gesture of indifference, but the man sat down anyway.

"I put 'Volare' on the Wurlitzer for you, do you like it?" he asked me.

"Yes," I responded. Although to tell the truth it was a song that I detested. My mother usually listened to it on her gramophone, making a stupid face and taking little leaps like a quail.

I felt his drunken breath. Eluding his gaze, I rested my eyes on the wall. A silver ball hung from the ceiling, throwing flickers of light over him, which moved around like fairies. I tried to think about the trees in the south that had names like myrtle, boldo, ulmo, larch. The man pulled his seat closer to mine. Now I could not only feel his breath, but also the heat emanating from his body, and although no one had told me, I knew that he had an erection. I began to drum my fingers on the bar top as a sign of impatience. If only I knew some spell to make people vanish, like how I could usually make painful thoughts disap-

pear. But what was happening wasn't part of my imagination. A man had his hand on mine. I jumped up. Eyelashes also got to his feet and taking me by the shoulders, said, "You like to play, huh?"

I lowered my eyes. He took me by the chin and made me look at him. I was scared. But mostly, I felt a sense of loss. This man, with his hard hands, had brought me to this side of life. And I didn't like it.

"Let her go," I heard a firm voice say from in front of us at the bar. It was the explorer.

Eyelashes looked at him derisively and, without letting me go, exclaimed that it didn't concern him. The explorer got up from his seat. He must have measured six and a half feet tall, and there at the top, at the end of his neck, his face seemed lost. Eyelashes let go of my chin, but not before squeezing it hard enough to hurt me. He looked at me with contempt, turned around, and left the bar. The explorer returned to his seat without glancing at me, and with a bewildered look ordered another whiskey. I wanted to thank him for what he had done for me, but within a few seconds he was already deep in thought again.

Little by little the bar was emptying. Mama should have picked me up a while ago. I closed my eyes and called to her in silence. But somehow I knew that she couldn't hear me. Her image had become so distant, like everything that surrounded me: the last faces bloated by alcohol, the subdued sound of the music, and the lights that barely shone in the darkness.

"Don't you think it's time you went to bed now?" I heard the explorer's voice all of a sudden.

I couldn't tell him the truth. I would leave to go cry. I wasn't going to cry in front of a stranger.

"I was just leaving," I said. I grabbed my book bag, said good-bye to the man with a gesture of my hand, and left the bar.

The same pianist as always was playing alone at one end of the lobby. He was getting on in years and his hands landed on the keys like two battered wings incapable of taking flight. I sat down on a cushiony armchair and curled up into a ball. The music put me to sleep. I don't know how much time had passed when I heard his voice again.

"You're still here," the explorer pointed out, and he passed both hands over his face with a bewildered gesture. He sighed deeply and added: "You should be sleeping."

"I know. I was just leaving," I said again.

"I'll come with you," he insisted annoyingly. "Next time I wouldn't want to find you floating in the pool."

His words sounded mournful and I felt scared, because of what fate could have in store for people without them knowing it.

"I'm in room 1810," I mentioned, remembering what Mama had told me.

"The year of our independence," he declared and he let loose a dry laugh without a shred of cheerfulness.

We went up in the elevator in silence. Deep wrinkles made furrows around the explorer's light-colored but now reddened eyes, and although he moved about steadily his movements were slow and cautious. He had drunk a great deal.

"I'm also on this floor," he said when we arrived at the eighteenth floor. "I'll come with you."

Endless lines of rooms snaked the length of the hallway and an orchestral version of a Cole Porter song was playing from the ceiling. I stopped in front of room 1810 and knocked on the door. We stayed there a few seconds, but no one came to open it. From an adjacent room someone slipped a hand out and deposited a tray on the hallway floor with the remains of some dinner.

"You don't have a key?" he asked me. Again he had that same bewildered expression as before, as if everything had suddenly intervened in his path in the most bothersome way.

I shook my head no. I was tired. I leaned against the wall and slid down to the ground. At the end of the corridor, some footsteps could be heard.

"I can wait. My mother is in there," I said, and closed my eyes.

The explorer sighed and sat down next to me.

"I can't take you to my room. They would accuse me of who knows what."

It was strange to see a man of such dimensions in that position: his curved spine, his bent knees, like a warrior watching from a crook in the battlefield as the enemy annihilates his comrades. We stayed like that, silent, in the semidarkness. Now Cole Porter himself was singing "Begin the Beguine." The explorer listened without saying a word. I felt cold. As if a subterranean wind had suddenly wrapped around my bones and tissues.

"My name is Gabriel, and you?" he asked.

"Nieves."

"Yuki," he said. His voice sounded broken down, as if something inside of him was withering away with each passing moment.

"What did you say?"

"You have the same name as the girl in a novel. Yuki. 'Snow' in Japanese."

"Do things end well?"

"Who cares," he said brusquely and fell silent. He had his elbows resting on his knees. Then he grabbed his head with his hands and wiped one of them forcefully across his mouth.

"You don't have to stay here with me," I told him.

I got up and knocked once more on my mother's door with both fists. I put my ear against its cold surface. The silence on the other side was dark and lurched along, like the beating of a heart. I sat down again.

"I'm sorry, Nieves," the explorer said. "It's just that I had other plans. Things haven't turned out like they should have."

"A girl?" I ventured to ask.

"I had enough girls in my life," he said with an ironic smile.

"You're talking in the past."

"Am I?"

"You said 'I had'."

"Maybe because I don't need any more in this life."

"But there are other things besides sex," I whispered. It's what I heard Mama's coworkers say.

He looked at me without smiling and said:

"What do you know." And we returned to silence.

From one of the bedrooms came a sharp noise, similar to that of a hammer. But then it stopped. Some of the white ceiling lights trembled, as if they were going to go out. We heard the elevator cables squealing as they moved.

"I haven't slept for eight days," he let out suddenly.

"Eight days is a long time," I said.

"One hundred and ninety-two hours to be exact. And twenty-two bottles of alcohol."

"I suppose you must be tired."

"Very tired."

"And you want to sleep."

"Yes. That's what I want. Forever." A slight tremor passed over his face.

Although I could only see them from the side, it seemed to me that his eyes had become like ice. He muttered some words that I didn't catch. And then he fell silent. I thought that I should say something, to break that frigid silence that had settled around his body.

"How can you think about sleeping forever when you can't even manage to sleep for a few hours?"

He let loose a hard laugh that echoed in the hallway.

"There are many ways. They aren't things that you would want to know. Or understand."

He rested his cheek in the palm of one of his hands and closed his eyes.

From the ceiling an overly sweet orchestral song played.

"I understand," I said in a whisper.

He lifted his head and looked at me. There was something imploring in his gaze. His body shook. Then he buried his head in his hands.

I don't know how, but I had understood. I thought maybe he was carrying a weapon or a blade in his pocket, or maybe those were waiting for him in his room. But while we kept talking, while he stayed next to me, the explorer couldn't use them to end his life. It was then that I spoke to him of the south, of my grandmother, of her dogs that had Russian names, of the leaves of the larch trees that rustled with the afternoon breeze. And although I was scared, although I didn't know what was happening on the other side of the door, or why Mama wasn't coming to pick me up, I experienced a rare happiness, as if suddenly my life, insignificant until that moment, had stood out from all the others with a meaning bigger than its own.

I don't know when we fell asleep. I woke up when a woman emerged from a room with a pair of heels in her hand and then disappeared around a turn in the hallway. It must have been getting light out. The explorer was still next to me. I jumped to my feet and knocked vigorously on the door to Mama's room. Time and time and time again, shouting her name, until the explorer took me by both arms and stopped me. I let my head fall against his chest and he slowly rubbed my back.

"We need a good breakfast. You'll see, after a hot coffee everything will look better."

"Mama doesn't let me have coffee," I said, while I dried my tears with the sleeve of my jacket.

"Whatever," he muttered. He started to walk toward the elevator and I followed him.

When we went down to the lobby, there was a commotion. At least five officers in uniform were questioning travelers, and the bewildered bellhops were coming and going like small scurrying prehistoric animals. A woman shouted hysterically with a dog in her arms, while a man with a little gelled moustache tried to calm her down. The explorer asked me to wait for him there and approached one of the concierges. While they talked, the explorer didn't take his eyes off of me. I sensed that something very bad had happened. After a few minutes he returned to my side and took my hand.

"There's a café on the corner. The concierge says they make some spectacular scrambled eggs."

I didn't question in that instant why we didn't have breakfast in the hotel, or the reason why the explorer's expression had changed. Now in place of weariness, his tired coarse features had taken on an expression of worry and a touch of humanity. His blue eyes rested firmly on mine, as if they were trying to reach the bottom of my heart. While he drank his coffee and I my chocolate milk, I asked him about Mama. He averted his gaze to the window, brought his index finger to his temple and moved it, as if trying to adjust something in his brain. After a few seconds he said: "We're going to the south, where your grandmother is. How about that? Your mother will catch up to us in a few days."

Before noon, without carrying any luggage or making any preparations, we got in the explorer's white Impala. I asked him again about my mother and he told me again that she would follow us soon. When we left the city I looked back: the great tower of the Hotel Delfín emerged on the horizon. I felt sick. I must have been very pale because the explorer parked the Impala on the side of the highway and urged me to get out. I vomited on the side of the road. A cutting breeze blew over the desert plain, coming from the north. In the distance, the mountains sank into a deep sleep.

It's possible that in some remote part of my being, I already sensed what had happened. While the last of the viscous liquid left my mouth, I saw again the elegant figure of my mother disappearing behind the elevator doors. I imagined that she raised her arm, and that with a smile

she said good-bye to me. Maybe she already knew that the anonymous man she had a date with would kill her that night, that she wouldn't be in room 1810, the year of our independence, but in another much more sumptuous room, one on the top floor, one which that guy, under another name, had reserved for both of them. Maybe my mother knew that the explorer would be there and that he would be the one to take me back to the paradise that she had lost. When we started off again, the desert was entirely covered in a cloud of dust that undulated slightly. I looked back again and the Hotel Delfín had disappeared.

The Role of the Witness: Writing and Memory[1]

Nora Strejilevich

> The memory of horror entails less a set of abstract definitions than the enquiry of those meanings imposed upon us by extermination that shape our present. We can still, therefore, call their objection "resistance."—Perla Sneh

Introduction: Disappearance and Writing

> Had I really returned somewhere, here or somewhere else, to my home, to wherever? The certainty [...] that I had not really returned, that an essential part of me would never return, this certainty sometimes took control of me, disrupting my relationship with the world, with my own life.—Jorge Semprún

The memory of my forced disappearance into, and reappearance from, Club Atlético, the Argentine Clandestine Center for Detention, Torture, and Extermination (CCDTyE), where I spent less than one week of my life, or all of it, makes me rethink ideas and keep recalling that past from a present that always propels me to revisit narratives of that experience. I don't choose the texts; they come to me. Neither do I attempt a thorough exploration—I trust that others will be able to continue to inquire into the writing that insists on putting horror into words.

It is hard to consider this text finished because questions don't end, and answers unsettle, contradict, and step on each other. They say and retract what they said—there's always another argument that challenges and disturbs any order. I know that thinking doesn't lead to solutions; it barely finds paradoxes that can't be solved. That's precisely why we can't put an end to it. There isn't an end. We wander among endless narratives that, as Laura Estrin says, can do it. And in this wandering, which is shared, common ground and rejections emerge that have different perspectives (the first, comfort and reassure; the second, irk and cause controversy). That's why I make way for other voices by interweaving my writing with quotes and excerpts I incorporate, whether or not I agree with them. They help me untangle the indelible subjective

1 First published in 2019 by LOM Ediciones, Santiago, Chile. Translated from the Spanish by Judy Filc.

aftermath of an atrocity that keeps demanding attention, whose marks still prevail because they surpass us.

I don't intend to classify the writing that inspires these pages: testimony, concentration camp narrative, concentration camp memoirs, plain literature? If I join this debate, it's because other topics are being settled on the way.

I'm concerned, moreover, with the questions that stem from the intimacy of life in the camps, from the coexistence with this mark that is an identifying feature, whether we like it or not. I wonder, for instance, if survivors write so as to return to the world from which they were extricated; if they write to open another space by dint of words (another space that, unlike the camp, will be habitable); and if they will succeed, and if so, how and when.

Like certain novels or philosophies, certain testimonies remain topical—they don't abide by calendars. And it doesn't matter if they precisely describe the events to which they refer, since a text never transcribes the experience it recounts; it doesn't produce literal versions of what is real.

These writings aim neither to gather data nor to reconstruct true events. Witnesses recall from their present and, in doing so, discover new aspects of the deadly logic that still comes first in the contemporary world. Every testimony aims to retort and challenge with its weapons, which are its letters, the attack that humankind perpetrated on itself.

The Invisibility of the Witness

If, like any artwork, these texts outlive their times, their reception won't stop at a certain historical period. Nonetheless, we survivors are viewed, above all, as remnants of a particular past or repositories of information; as living evidence. For this reason, our story is valid in trials involving crimes against humanity. Yet outside this realm, we continue to be an Other who, since she epitomizes the victim of the crime for which nobody wants to take responsibility, is dismissed.

While Argentina is challenging in myriad ways, the sinister dimension created by former Commander Jorge Rafael Videla[2] with his noto-

2 Jorge Rafael Videla was the head of the first military junta that led the coup on March 24, 1976. He was condemned to prison during the trial of the junta in 1985. In 1990 he invoked the pardon that was declared by President Carlos Menem. In 2010 he was sentenced to life in ordinary prison for having committed crimes against humanity; in 2012, to fifty years for the systematic appropriation of children of disappeared people. He died in prison in 2013.

rious dictum ("They're neither dead nor alive, they're disappeared"), the story of the "reappeared" hasn't gotten the seal of approval. And it hasn't gotten that seal, even if such story is essential to prevent this ghostly dimension from being mythicized. Watching concrete women and men suffer from up close and thinking together with those who have experienced the most exacerbated form of biopolitics can give us the key to understand what we are enduring today—power relations whose matrix still exists.

Albeit spectral, the void left by the catastrophe is full of faces, of human beings with names and histories who inhabited that limbo of exclusion called camp.[3] Why are their voices still unheard? One potential answer is that anesthesia comes first, and that is why witnesses, considered as standard bearers of pain, are not appealing. In addition, these stories challenge members of society who don't question their tacit acceptance of a horror that, being naturalized, secures the required approval to delete the Other, whether the "subversives" (who object from their emancipatory power) or those who typify the blame for all our misfortunes.

I don't expect suffering to draw a crowd. I am only refuting those who claim that unlike fiction, testimonies can neither symbolize nor create meaning; that they impose a univocal sense to their narrative and do so with scarce or nonexistent literary development. I'm against such confusion between criticizing and condemning, between challenging and setting oneself up as a judge. I'd like, instead, to give survivors' testimony its fair role and recognize its irreplaceable contribution.

In the twentieth century, the Southern Cone region was destroyed by a disappear-making power (as Pilar Calveiro puts it) that transformed the entire region into a fateful laboratory for the human condition, whose effects are looming over the present. By keeping its word, the language of reminiscence stages, develops, and resists. As they recount their stories, survivors become witnesses, and no one can testify for the witness. "I experienced it, believe me" does not invoke truth as a coincidence with a referent; it invokes the account of one's own experience.

3 In this book I use both nomenclatures: *Clandestine Center for Detention, Torture, and Extermination*, widely used in Argentina and *camp*, a term that refers to Nazism and links various methodologies of forced disappearance that have left similar marks at the symbolic level.

The survivors' narrative goes against the grain of history—it is the history of the defeated. It is a way of calling attention with body-word. As Estrin puts it, testimonies bite; they affect.

When democracy had already returned, Videla complained of "the constant aspiration to keep rummaging through the past." Moreover, having forgotten his integral participation in planning and implementing the systematic extermination plan, he stated:

> [W]e must find a solution to the well-known problem of the disappeared and offer it to the Argentine society. Are they a real thing, a fib, a political or financial speculation? What are they actually?
> (*Página 12*, March 5, 2012)

I can answer the question about *who* they are—the commander never asked. The disappeared are my generation, the preceding one, and the next; my family, my friends, and my friends' children. My interest in the subject, therefore, surpasses academics. Is it possible to address genocide with the detachment of theoretical discourse? Each testimony embodies its vision of the camp—that inhabitable habitat, in Ignacio Mendiola's words, whose mission is to destroy subjectivity. Hannah Arendt called it *the corpse factory*. How could one refuse to listen to those who speak of and from the mark left by that factory, instead of distancing oneself from them based on adopting an objective knowledge that died decades ago? Each testimony is a journey of emotion and thought, without which we fall into instrumental reason whose coldness leads to disaster.

The Communal Wave

While it isn't included in the canon, this narrative is read in certain spheres, circulates in alternative circles, and joins a movement that, in Argentina, abruptly emerges in the post-dictatorship era with an intense human rights activism that strengthens with the onset of democracy. Fernando Reati shows the significance of this network to which, it's worth repeating, survivors owe their survival after the camps, even if in this case he is speaking, above all, about Mario Villani. To the question about the reason for remaining alive, Villani answers:

> Perhaps leaving the camps alive was the easiest part [...] The hard part was choosing what to do with those traumatic memories. And this is where other survivors, victims' relatives, Mothers and Grandmothers

of Plaza de Mayo, members of H.I.J.O.S.[4] [...], human rights activists,
and the ordinary people who supported him were an integral part
in his inner drive to spend the following decades bearing witness in
any trial he could, granting any interview requested, and speaking
at any forum that was made available to him. Without that gigantic
communal network of friends and comrades who encouraged each
other to keep recalling and denouncing [that wouldn't have been
possible], especially in the tough 1990s, when it seemed that the rest of
society was turning its back on him. ... (Reati, 2017, p. 182)

This wave, moreover, has generated a lengthy, fruitful debate on past
events and their political and ethical meaning, which has led to years
of making, staging, and writing films, plays, essays, and fiction—a
powerful *"figuration work*, an *effort to frame* a way of speaking that
is being detroyed" (Sneh). These were years of establishing museums
and transforming former camps into places of memory; years of fierce
controversies over the way to approach such a change (should we re-
signify these spaces or leave them as untouched symbols of dread?
Should we explain horror, or might it be that, by rationalizing atroc-
ity, we would run the risk of naturalizing it?) During these years, the
post-dictatorship state, which after its historical trial of the juntas had
backed down and passed the so-called impunity and pardon laws, is
finally promoting public trials for crimes against humanity commit-
ted by the civil–religious–military regime. Nonetheless, the witness's
voice, which is essential within the legal sphere, is still subsumed under
the courts, which aren't the only spaces where we can assimilate *what
happened and is still happening to us*. It is indispensable for the court
to have a binary language that distinguishes the guilty from the vic-
tims. Witnesses, however, can also create plots that aren't determined
by such ritual or categories. It's obvious that these are not enough; that
it is imperative to inquire into the power relations making up our soci-
eties and the ways in which state violence is still exercising destruction
(issues that are settled outside the court).

4 The word means "children," but is also an acronym for "Hijos e Hijas por la Identidad y la
 Justicia contra el Olvido y el Silencio" (Sons and daughters [fighting] for identity and justice
 against forgetfulness and silence). It's an organization made up by children of disappeared
 people that is engaged in reconstructing the history of the dictatorship and the fate of the
 disappeared and imprisoned activists. Its goal is to secure the trials of those responsible for
 crimes against humanity.

While the trials constitute an irreplaceable pillar for the *res-publica*[5] to be viable after extermination, the survivor accounts (among others) are critical to identifying the mechanisms in which we continue to be entrapped and involved. That's why I agree with Alejandro Kaufman's statement that "horror, and the break of the bonds of responsibility and indebtedness it produces, requires a deep cultural conceptualization".

Such conceptualization entails a cultural change that has consolidated, to a certain extent, in some Southern Cone societies, with a different scope according to the country. Nonetheless, the pressure to end this process is ferocious. In Argentina the current government ignores every claim;[6] in Chile there has been a resurgence of student and social fights, but the scarce trials for crimes against humanity have suffered a step-back; and Uruguay hasn't implemented yet any policy that fosters this type of trials.[7]

Beyond the legal aspect, from 2015 to 2019 authoritarianism reemerged in a republican suit, devoted to destroy what postdictatorship governments built. And it's our responsibility to reflect on this plot. Nobody can view themselves as removed from it; for terror devices to persist in different forms, exclusion must be tolerated, must be accepted to ensure survival. How is it possible that so many could agree that a section of the citizenry was erased and then later deny their erasure? Is there a connection between consent, as Kaufman calls it, and the reap-

5 The author does a play on words with the Latin *res publica*, public thing, and *república*, republic in Spanish.

6 The government that considered human rights as state policy between 2003 and 2015 has been followed by one whose interest is exactly the opposite in this and other senses. Survivors and activists have promoted public trials with great effort by collaborating with the prosecutors in the search for evidence and information. While these haven't stopped, their progress depends on institutional change; no legal fight can be maintained without cultural change. Such a change was insufficient to guarantee the continuity of the welfare state, but manifests today in a fight that is expanding its demands. A paradigmatic example is women's striking and taking action under the slogan "ni una menos" (not even one [woman] less). This was the first explosion of the feminist movement which, according to journalist Horacio Verbitsky, "represents the origin of a phenomenon such as the rounds of the Mothers [of Plaza de Mayo]" (*Página 12*, October 23, 2016). The women's movement has erupted in Chile with identical strength.

7 In the case of Uruguay the legal fight was left behind compared to civil resistance. In former prosecutor Mirtha Guianze's statement to *El Universal* journal, "after forty-five years since the military coup in Uruguay, on June 27, 1973, hundreds of legal trials and investigations are at a 'standstill' because there hasn't been a 'political will to progress toward the truth' [...] I think there has been scant progress. Actually, what has progressed has been the acknowledgment of civil society'" (*El Universal*, June 27, 2018).

pearance of right-wing parties determined to create new figures of the *homo sacer*, a being that can be murdered and whose murder isn't even equal to a sacrifice? These questions, which Agamben, above all, raises, reverberate strongly in our region, where camps coexisted with everyday routine; underground centers were often located in cities—such as the Libertad prison in Uruguay, 38 Londres in Chile, and ESMA (the army's mechanics school) in Argentina—and kidnappings happened in broad daylight. While the 1970s resistance, state terror, and postdictatorships differ in each nation, I focus particularly on these communicating threads. I think that it's essential to spread the story of the survivors of the camps, who can report in minute detail the way in which saturnine states devour their children. That's why, when the question of whether these testimonies make a particular contribution to the culture of memory, I answer, yes and this book shows the nature of that contribution.

Literature, Testimony, or Testimonial Literature?

The texts I'm presenting here can't be classified: document-novels? Non-fiction narratives? I call them testimonies to emphasize that they recount borderline experiences (that's why they straddle genres). The "testimonial" category is so uncertain, that some authors reject it: Susana Romano-Sued, who survived several camps, prefers her book *Procedimiento. Memoria de La Perla y La Ribera* (*Procedure: Memory of La Perla and La Ribera*) to be considered simply literature, without a restrictive adjective. Hernán Valdés, on the other hand, advocates for the testimonial nature of *Tejas Verdes: Diary of a Chilean Concentration Camp* when it's classified as a novel, to underscore its denouncing power. The truth is that there are fictionalized and poetic concentration accounts, and others where orality and literary narration coexist. If we define all of them as *testimonial* it's to make them visible, since their contours stand out from the opaque background where everything looks the same. The main thing is to highlight that this writing exists and that reading it is essential, especially in these times, when a subjugating power (the continuation of a murdering power with a different mask) is being legitimized again in the region.

From *A Single, Numberless Death*[1]

Nora Strejilevich

We shall not permit death to run rampant in Argentina.
—Admiral Emilio Massera, 1976

A certain perverse magic turns the key to the front door. Steps rush in. Three pairs of shoes practice their disjointed stomp on the floor, the clothes, the books, an arm, a hip, an ankle, a hand. My body. I'm the trophy of the day. A hide with a hollow head, eyes of glass. The make-believe hunters step on me. *Step on a crack, break your mother's back.*

This ritual exorcises my sins inside their temple: a green Ford Falcon with no license plates speeding through red lights up the wrong side of Corrientes Street. No one bats an eye. It's business as usual.

But it's not every day (or is it?) that the laws of gravity are broken. It's not every day that you open the door and four rooms are ripped apart by a cyclone that shatters the past and yanks the hand off the clock. It's not everyday that you stumble and fall, hands behind your back, trapped in a night that tosses about shreds of daily life. Dizzy you whirl in a vortex of scraps of yesterdays and nows crushed by orders and decrees. You get lost amid chairs overturned, drawers emptied, suitcases torn open, colors blanched out, maps slashed, roads severed. You barely make out the echoes reverberating "You thought you could escape, bitch" as an enormous mouth devours you. Familiar voices perhaps whisper, "She hasn't done anything, neither has he." But you are here, on this side, in this precarious body: soles tattooed on your skin, boots on your back, a gun at the nape of your neck.

"On your feet!" and you stand up, meek, confused, stunned, defeated, and you shriek, "They are taking me away, they're taking me away!" as claws of steel dig into your flesh. Shoved with impunity into the elevator at two in the afternoon, dragged out of the building, space vanishing under your feet. On the sidewalk you kick and scream against a nameless fate in some mass grave.

1 Published in 2002 by University of Virginia Press, Charlottesville, Virginia, USA, pp. 3–4. Translated from the Spanish by Cristina de la Torre.

I hurl my name with every last fiber—with lungs, with guts, with legs, with arms, with rage. My name fails wildly on the edge of defeat. The animal trainers order me to jump from the high platform into the void. They push me. I land on the floor of a car. Blows rain down on me. "Take that for screaming in Jewish, and this for kicking." And this, and this.

"You Yid piece of shit, we're gonna make soap out of you." I'm a toy to be broken. *Step on a crack, break your mother's back.*

The Art of Not Forgetting[1]

Perla Sneh

> When disappearance and torture are presided over by those who speak
> like us, have names like ours and attend the same schools [...] the
> abyss that opens in our conscience and in our heart is infinitely more
> profound than any word that professes to describe it.—Julio Cortázar

I begin by sharing that I grew up within a tradition that makes memory
a precept: "remember and never forget," is something we would repeat,
"from generation to generation." These words left me somewhat per-
plexed when I was a child because they commanded me to remember
precisely what is unforgettable to the point that even those who did
not live through the events of the past can remember them in detail.
However, what was back then, dwelled in other languages; in Spanish
things were easier, less serious. After all, here the trains went to the
beach.

I overlay these meditations with an image, a photograph: the black
and white denounces its antiquity; a bunch of boys and girls are hud-
dled together around a desk in the cramped space. Behind them is an
enormous blackboard. The smiles illuminate a transpired seriousness
of ties and jackets. The headbands and the gathered hair brighten the
grey of the jumpers. Amid all of the gazes directed toward the cam-
era, there are two that pass through me, the one who is looking at the
photograph, and not the one who is in it. One is of Q, a friend whose
name I hold with affectionate modesty. He is there, in the background,
stretching to stand out among so many heads plastered with styling gel.
Neither he nor anyone knows that the voracious incandescence of ter-
ror is waiting for him around the corner. The other gaze is of someone
that I refuse to name; I see him squatting in the foreground. Neither he
nor anyone else knows yet what will become of those who feed—with
bodies like that of Q—this imminent voracity.

I imagine that they looked each other in the eyes, and that they rec-
ognized one another on that indescribable flight from which only one
of them returned. Nothing can assure that things happened exactly

1 Translated from the Spanish by Celeste Kostopulos-Cooperman.

this way, but I borrow from the poet's words: although some circumstances may vary, the story is substantially true. I mention these partially dreamt memories because it is easier to talk about them this way. There in the photograph we are all together, at the edge of that abyss into which the language some of us were raised in was thrown, understanding that "homework" was a school obligation and "parsley," an inexpensive condiment. From there the language emerged, forever poisoned by the operationality of an assassin, plagued with expressions that, like abscesses about to burst, cannot—to paraphrase Martínez Estrada—be said without fear.

Since then, we share a language that separates us, but not in the sense that all languages separate, spreading debris and misunderstandings that permit us to continue talking. No. What separates us in this language is not a misunderstanding, but a fierce and unequivocal materiality, deprived of any metaphorical nuance; that which gave form to what I prefer to call the "National Terror."

Terror: not a feeling that overwhelms a subject, but rather a set of specific actions, contemplated and planned to destroy another. Although it is nourished by inherited languages,[2] it does not lack its own originalities. To use a term that is dear to the language of the perpetrator, in order to qualify all thought: this terror is not "foreign;" it is as much ours as *mate*. A terror that appropriates meanings and identifies those destined for annihilation, organizes actions to carry out this "task," and deploys extermination techniques that have as a necessary condition, subjective decimation prior to physical annihilation. The "National Terror," as when one says "national question" or national mourning, or doctrine or security or national catastrophe; that is to say, a tragic, universal, and radical State at whose level the public thing becomes the private thing of each and every one.[3] In this sense, terror and its language are and cannot, not be, a national question.

Reading the words, "plane and river," in a title by Nora Strejilevich should be enough to make us all shudder. Likewise, everyday terms like "hood" and "grill," should also makes us tremble profoundly. Even in

2 How to ignore the Franco-Algerian heritage or the undisguised returns of a translated Nazism?

3 Vladimir Jankelevitch, *Lo imprescriptible*, Muchnik editores, Barcelona, Spain, 1987. Translated from the French.

translation, the "National Terror" carries its own sting, because while looking at the river, how can we pronounce Primo Levi's desolate term, "the sunken," without a dire materiality rotting away our tongue?

It is not about requesting documents from words. No vigilance is worth anything when the tongue loosens; speech is not regulated ... except in terror. Let us try, rather, to listen to the words that remain in our mouths, whether we know it or not. Interrogating them is a way of speaking with the memories.

It isn't an easy task, since ours is a language that nationalized death: the disappearance of people followed by torture and death is internationally recognized as "Argentine death," says Osvaldo Bayer.[4] "Any of the many people who disappeared in Argentina during the period of military rule between 1976–1983, presumably killed by members of the armed forces or by the police."[5] A clear sign of the systematicity of the terror is in the use of plural markers when describing both the victims and the perpetrators.

However, this entry is incomplete: it only mentions those who were presumably killed in the reign of the "National Terror," but says nothing about those who, on the contrary, and with all certainty were born in its bosom. Extermination is not only a matter of putting to death, but also of bringing to life. That there are still hundreds of people born in darkness who are unaware of their own origins is evidence of the extent to which future generations have become detached from the terrors of the past.

"Mothers and grandmothers" are names that—far from familiarizing politics—highlight how extermination persists in the filial modes it imposes. "Butcher filiation," is how Pierre Legendre defines it. The elementary forms of kinship—which Levi Strauss considered basic—were injured and must be rewoven in the face of that sinister force that puts history in suspense, because everything remains in suspense while not only the dead, but also the living remain disappeared.

That is why the "National Terror" shows up from time to time, reminding us that it is still among us: the mortuary bags thrown into the Plaza de las Madres were that and nothing else; to clear up doubts, one of them bore the name of Estela de Carlotto.

4 Presentation of the book, *Music and the Holocaust*, de Shirli Gilbert, November 2010.
5 Vladimir Jankelevitch, 1987.

Theatrical explanation of the threat: "We are still here," "We will return for you," "quickly, quickly, at any time"—these bags depict disappearance and not death because an extermination does not end. It is barely interrupted because its objective remains in force. The survivors are those who—for whatever reason—have managed to avoid their fate of obliteration; but do not be deceived, they are still in the cross-hairs; they/we have only managed to be barely punctual at the time of annihilation.

To this persistence, let's oppose memory: a warm shelter of reiterated stories, a plot of narratives made up of shredded words rescued from oblivion; a discourse that, although it does not suture the abyss (today disguised as electoral merchandise under the commercialization of the term, "crack"),[6] seeks to sustain itself and to sustain us in the disturbing sphere of a truth.

If we wish to engage in the difficult art of not forgetting, we cannot spare ourselves the anguish of attempting it.

6 *Crack* is a recent term in Argentine political discourse that reflects the polarization of the country into pro- and anti-Kirschner forces and is viewed by many as synonymous to dissent.

Biographical Notes of the Writers

Marjorie Agosín (Chile, 1955) moved permanently to the United States in 1968 with her parents, who were themselves the children of exiles from Eastern Europe. She is a poet, essayist, critic, and international activist. Her many books include *Always from Somewhere Else: A Memoir of My Chilean Jewish Father* (1998), *A Cross and a Star: Memoirs of a Jewish Girl in Chile,* (1997), *Dear Anne Frank* (1994), and *Scraps of Life: Chilean Women and the Pinochet Dictatorship* (1987), among many others. Winner of the Letras de Oro Prize and the Latino Literature Prize, Agosín is chair of the Spanish department at Wellesley College.

Ruth Behar (Cuba, 1956) came to the United States in 1962, immigrating with her Cuban parents. Her love for the island of her childhood has been a central theme of her writings. She is professor of anthropology at the University of Michigan and has won many awards including a MacArthur grant. Her works include *The Vulnerable Observer: Anthropology That Breaks Your Heart* (1996) and *Translated Woman: Crossing the Border with Esperanza's Story* (1993), an account of her friendship with a Mexican street peddler. Behar is the editor *of Bridges to Cuba* (1995) and coeditor of *Women Writing Culture* (1995), an anthology about the creative writing of women anthropologists. Behar is currently writing a memoir.

Miriam Bornstein (Mexico, 1950), a poet and literary critic, was born in Mexico to a Mexican mother and a Polish father, whose family fled Poland just before the Nazi takeover. Bornstein's family immigrated to the United States when she was fourteen, settling in Arizona, where Bornstein earned her Ph.D. This bicultural border experience continues to influence Bornstein's poetic voice. She is the author of *Bajo Cubierta* (1976) and *Donde Empieza la Historia* (1993). Her poetry has appeared in national and international anthologies, including *Daughters of the Fifth Sun* (1995) and *Floricanto Sí: A Collection of Latina Poetry* (1998). Bornstein is associate professor at the University of Denver, where she teaches Chicano/a and Latin American literature and culture.

Aída Bortnik (Argentina, 1938) was renowned for her contributions as a feminist journalist, playwright, and screenwriter. She lived through repression and censorship in Argentina and was forced into exile dur-

ing the military dictatorship of 1976–83. Bortnik's depiction of the dictatorship period in the Oscar award-winning film, *The Official Story* (1985), is a landmark representation of the era. She wrote the story included in *The House of Memory* for the satirical magazine *Hum®* while she was banned from writing for television, film, and radio. Her play, *Papá querido*, was integral to the Teatro Abierto movement in protest of the censorship of the arts.

Karen Codner Dujovne (Chile, 1972), a journalist, master's in comparative literature, author, and podcaster. Her first fiction novel *To Breathe Underwater* (Cuarto Propio, 2015), narrates the relationship between the lady of the house and her nanny, who passed away at very short notice. She is also the author of "Cuadernos de escritura: con estos ejercicios escribo" (2021), a booklet for aspiring writers. She is the conductor of Espiral, tu podcast de literatura y creatividad since 2018. She is a board member of Memoria Viva, a Chilean nonprofit organization related to the Holocaust and its remembrance. Codner lives in Santiago de Chile along with her four children and husband. Her personal website is at https://karencodner.com/

Vilma Faingezicht (Costa Rica, 1947), is the daughter of survivors from the Shoah whose family came from Poland. Faingezicht has traveled the world, living mostly Costa Rica and for short periods of time in Mexico, Puerto Rico, and Israel, where she studied history and Latin at the Hebrew University of Jerusalem. She has dedicated many years to the plastic arts: oil, acrylic, collages and has presented these in several exhibitions, in Costa Rica and elsewhere.

Alicia Freilich de Segal (Venezuela, 1939), daughter of Yiddish-speaking journalist Máximo Freilich, grew up in a home filled with Venezuelan Jewish writers. After receiving her Ph.D. in literature from Venezuela's Universidad Central, she began publishing critical essays and cultural journalism in leading newspapers and magazines. The author of two prize-winning works of fiction, *Clapér* (1987; tr. 1998) and *Colombina descubierta* (1991), Freilich de Segal also represents prominent Jewish organizations in Venezuela.

Luisa Futoransky (Argentina, 1939), a born traveler who often calls herself a perpetual gypsy, is a poet, novelist, and short story writer. Futoransky, who typically considers Jewish themes in her work, has

received several international prizes as well as a Guggenheim fellow-ship and the Chevalier des Arts et des Lettres granted by the French government. In Spain she received the Carmen Conde Prize for her book of poetry, *El divan de la puerta dorada* (1984). She is also the author of one novel, *Son cuentos chinos* (1983), the story of her life in Peking as a radio announcer. She currently resides in Paris and is a translator for UNESCO.

Margo Glantz (Mexico, 1930) is a writer, essayist, and professor of lit-erature at the UNAM, the National Autonomous University of Mexico, in Mexico City. Glantz is the author of many books of essays and short stories. *Las genealogías* (1981; tr. *The Family Tree*, 1991), an auto-biographical memoir about her father, Jacobo Glantz, is her most well-known work. Others include *Erosiones* (1984) and *Síndrome de naaf-ragios* (1984). In addition to her prolific writing career, Glantz is also cultural attaché to London.

Angélica Gorodischer (Argentina, 1930) moved to the city of Rosario after studying at the University of Buenos Aires. She is a prominent cultural figure and activist in her adopted city. Also a short story writ-er, novelist, and essayist, Gorodischer is the author of ten novels. She is best known for her science fiction writing, in particular for her char-acter Trafalgar, an extraterrestrial being who converses with Rosario's writers in cafés. She has received much acclaim for *Trafalgar* (1990), as well as for her novels *Mala noche y parir hembra* (1983) and *Bajo la jubeas en flor* (1973).

Carla Guelfenbein (Chile, 1959), has lived in England for eleven years, where she was awarded degrees at the University of Essex and Central St. Martin's in London. Returning to Chile, she worked as art director for the magazine *Elle*, until she decided to become a full-time novel-ist. She is the author of eight novels acclaimed by the public and crit-ics. Her literary thriller, *In The Distance With You*, won the prestigious Alfaguara Prize. Siri Hustvedt, author of *The Blazing World*, says: "Guelfenbein's elegantly structured, psychologically astute novel moves with the urgency of a detective novel, but its real mysteries turn on questions of authorship, reading, interpretation, and the strange power of fiction to enter the speechless realm of human erotic desire." The Nobel prize winner J.M. Coetzee has said about her writing: "Subtle, clearsighted, compassionate."

Sonia Guralnik (Chile, 1924) has lived in Chile for almost sixty years. Although her native language is Russian, she began writing in Spanish when she was almost forty years old. Guralnik has published numerous short stories in Chilean newspapers, a book of stories called *El Samovar* (1984), and an autobiographical novel, *Recuento de la mujer gusano* (1991). Most of her work deals with issues of Jewish identity in Latin America. Guralnik, who is also an acclaimed chef, lives in Santiago.

Andrea Jeftanovic (Chile, 1970), is a sociology and PhD graduate in literature from the University of California, Berkeley, and is a novelist, storyteller, and essayist. The inheritance of loss, the violence of desire, and the inner urge to find a sense of self count among her chief subjects. Her extensive literary work ranges from novels, *Theatre of War* (*Escenario de guerra*, Alfaguara) (which won the Gabriela Mistral Literary Award and the National Endowment prizes for the best novel published), *Love in a Foreign Language* (*Geografía de la lengua*), to nonfiction and short storytelling (*Escribir desde el trapecio, Hablan los hijos, Conversaciones con Isidora Aguirre*). Her widely celebrated collection *Don't Take Candy from Strangers* (*No aceptes caramelos de extraños*, Seix Barral) won the Best Literary Work Award by the Circle of Art Critics in Chile and has been translated into several languages. Jeftanovic's most recent story collection is *Roving Destinations* (Tajamar editores). Jeftanovic is a theater critic at the newspaper *El Mercurio de Chile* and she combines her literary work with academic research and at Universidad de Santiago de Chile.

Rosita Kalina (Costa Rica, 1939) trained in comparative literature and received her master's degree in English literature, she then became professor at the University of Costa Rica. Kalina's poetry, essays, and fiction have appeared in several of her country's newspapers. Her book *Los signos y el tiempo* (1988) won the National Prize for Poetry. Other books include *Esa dimensión lejana* (1997) and *Cruce de niebla* (1980). Currently, she is director for cultural affairs at the Department of Education.

Alicia Kozameh (Argentina, 1953), born to a Jewish mother and a father whose family belonged to the Greek Orthodox Church, was baptized a Catholic and sent to a Catholic boarding school. Her political activities led to a three-year prison sentence in Rosario and Buenos Aires, a period of her life detailed in her novel *Pasos bajo el agua* (1987; tr. *Steps*

Under Water, 1996). In addition to novels, Kozameh writes short stories, memoirs, and screenplays. She now lives in Los Angeles, California.

Clarice Lispector (Brazil, 1925), who was born in Ukraine, arrived in Brazil when she was two months old. A well-known author, Lispector was also a journalist, contributing numerous essays to Brazilian newspapers. Among her many books are *Laços de Família* (1960; tr. *Family Ties*, 1972), *Maçã no escuro* (1967; tr. *The Apple in the Dark*, 1986), and *Agua viva (*1973; tr. *The Stream of Life*, 1989), which was recognized by the French philosopher Hélène Cixous. She died in Rio de Janeiro and was buried in the city's Jewish district.

Gabriela Mistral (Chile, 1889), was self-schooled in her early years and then became a rural school teacher. In her twenties, Mistral began to write her powerful poetry and also continued to work in public education. The Mexican government invited her to work on educational reforms. After her time in Mexico, she began a diplomatic career and became consul in several European nations. Her poetry and essays, as well as her compassionate voice towards children and women, became influential in the Americas. In 1948, at the end of the Second World War, Mistral was awarded the Nobel Prize for Literature; the only Latin American woman to have received this honor to date. Mistral is a great influence on American writers and her human rights legacy is an important one, and especially so in the Chile of today.

Myriam Moscona (Mexico, 1955), is an author of several books. *Ivory Black* was awarded the Landom Morton price by the American Academy of Poets and also the Pen International for best translation. Her latest books include *La muerte de la lengua inglesa*, Ansina poems in Ladino and *Tela de sevaya*, a book published in Mexico, Argentina, Spain and the USA. Moscona is also the winner of the Premio Xavier Villarutia for her *oeuvre*.

Barbara Mujica (Chile, 1949) is a novelist, short story writer, and critic who has lived much of her life in the United States. Her book-length fiction includes *The Death of Don Bernardo* (1990), *Affirmative Actions!* (1999), and *Far from My Mother's Home* (1999), a collection of stories. A two-time nominee for the Pushcart Prize, Mujica won the E.L. Doctorow International Fiction Competition in 1992 and has received a number of grants for her work. Mujica writes extensively on Spanish

Golden Age literature and is professor of Spanish at Georgetown University. She also directs El Retablo, a Spanish-language theater group.

Angelina Muñiz-Huberman (Mexico, 1936) was born in southern France while her parents were escaping the Spanish Civil War. The author of almost thirty books including novels, essay collections, and poetry collections, Muñiz-Huberman has won many prizes in Mexico including the Xavier Villarutia for her work *Huerta cerrado, huerto sellado* (1972; tr. *Enclosed Garden*, 1988), and the Sor Juana Ines de la Cruz Prize. Among her works are *De magias y pródigos* (1987) and *De cuerpo entero* (1991). Muñiz-Huberman teaches at the UNAM in Mexico City.

Rosa Nissán (Mexico, 1939) grew up in a Sephardic household in the Jewish community of Mexico City. The mother of four children, Nissán went against family tradition by enrolling in journalism courses. She went on to participate in workshops directed by famed Mexican writer Elena Poniatowska. Beginning in 1983, Nissán published sixteen short stories, followed by two novels, *Novia que te vea* (1993) and *Hischo que te nazca* (1996). She continues to live and write in Mexico City.

Rosa Palatnik (Poland, 1904), was a prolific Yiddish author. Palatnik began to write in Yiddish as a young girl, and her career grew as she migrated, first to Paris and then to Rio de Janeiro. She told stories of Jewish immigrants struggling to integrate into new lives in her three home countries, as they confront their past and assimilation. Her stories were witty and rich, with a complex relationship to the Jewish tradition, especially after the Holocaust. She also tried to confront the racism in Brazilian society, although she did not confront the racism in her own community. She died in Rio de Janeiro in 1981.

Teresa Porzecanski (Uruguay, 1948) is a writer, anthropologist, and professor of cultural anthropology at the Universidad de la República in Montevideo. She is also a poet and an essayist. Her recent fiction includes *Invention de los soles* (1981), an erotic novel, *Ciudad impune* (1986), and *Historias de vida de inmigrantes judios al Uruguay* (1986).

Reina Roffé (Argentina, 1951) studied journalism and literature at the University of Buenos Aires. In 1979 she won the Borges Prize for her first work, the short story "Profanation." She traveled and studied in

Europe and the United States and began to write nontraditional novels that question stereotypes of sexuality and gender. Among such works are *La rompiente* (1987) and *El cielo dividido* (1996). Roffé, like so many of her generation, left Argentina in 1976 and moved to Madrid, where she still resides and works as a journalist and writer.

Michèle Sarde (France, 1939), is a French writer and professor emerita at Georgetown University, where she taught French literature, gender studies, and intercultural studies. She presently resides in Chile and France. The key themes of her work are the women's cause, intercultural issues, and the interweaving of personal and historical memory. Her books have been translated into several languages, won several literary awards, and given rise to academic studies. Sarde has written biographies of Colette and Marguerite Yourcenar, and is co-editor of the latter's correspondence. As an essayist, she is the author of two volumes on the history and sociology of women in France. As a novelist, her most recent work is a cycle of remembrance devoted to her Sephardi family—from the Ottoman Empire to the Holocaust—aiming to bring back to this world the lost who have marked her life and left traces of themselves in her books.

Graciela Safranchik (Argentina, 1953) lives rather reclusively in Rosario. Her published works include *Cruce de niebla* (1995) and *Kadish* (1993).

Ester Rebeca Shapiro Rok (Cuba, 1952) was born in Havana to an Eastern European family that had arrived in Cuba shortly before the Holocaust, and left it for Miami shortly after the revolution. She is associate professor of psychology at the University of Massachusetts, Boston, and director of health resources at the Mauricio Gaston Institute for Latino Research, Pubic Policy and Community Development, and has published several books in the field of psychology.

Ana María Shua (Argentina, 1951) writes novels, short stories, children's books, and essays. Among her many books are *Soy paciente* (1980; tr. *Patient*, 1997) and *El libro de los recuerdos* (1994; tr. *The Book of Memories*, 1998). The grandchild of Jewish immigrants from Poland and Lebanon, Shua often writes about relations between first- and third-generation Argentine Jews. The recipient of a Guggenheim fellowship in 1993, Shua has also worked in journalism, advertising, and film.

Alicia Steimberg (Argentina, 1933) has received numerous literary awards throughout her career. In 1983 she was awarded a Fulbright to join the International Writing Program at the University of Iowa. Her many works include *Músicos y relojeros* (1971; tr. *Musicians and Watchmakers*, 1998) and *Cuando digo Magdelena* (1992). Steimberg, who lives in Buenos Aires, continues to conduct frequent lectures and workshops at universities in the United States and Latin America.

Perla Sneh (Argentina, 1952), is a psychoanalyst, writer, and tenured professor at the National University of Tres de Febrero. She is a senior researcher at the Center for Genocide Studies and head of the Jewish/ Jewish American Specialty Career at the PhD program on cultural diversity. Sneh studied at the Bezalel Academy of Arts and Design, the Universidad de Buenos Aires, and the Angel Garma Institute. She was awarded the Premio Nacional by the Ministry of Culture of the National Government of Argentina in 2013 for her book *Palabras para decirlo—Lenguaje y exterminio* (2012). Sneh has also published, *La Shoah en el siglo* (1999), *Ciudad autónoma* (2004), *Bíblicos* (2006), *Buenos Aires ídish* (2006), *Jarabe de pico* (2011), and *Lengua vespertina* (2018).

Nora Strejilevich (Argentina, 1951) is a writer and professor of Latin American literature. She was granted the Letras de Oro Award for Hispanic Literature in the USA for *Una sola muerte numerosa* (1997), later translated to English (*A Single Numberless Death*), German and Italian, and adapted for the stage (Michigan, 2002). Her more recent books are *Un día, allá por el fin del mundo* (2019) and *El lugar del testigo. Escritura y memoria: Uruguay, Chile y Argentina* (2019).

Ana Vásquez (Chile, 1947) was born into a German-speaking family. She studied psychology at the University of Chile and practiced until 1973 when she left the country during the Pinochet dictatorship. After settling in Paris, where she specialized in rehabilitating victims of torture, Vásquez began to write in both Spanish and French. Among her works are *Abel Rodríguez y sus hermanos* (1981), a novel about political betrayal and exile written during the Pinochet period, and *Mi amiga Chantal* (1991). Vásquez still resides in Paris and writes for feminist journals and human rights periodicals.

Credits

Mullahs on the Mainframe

MULLAHS
ON THE MAINFRAME

ISLAM AND MODERNITY
AMONG THE DAUDI BOHRAS

Jonah Blank

THE UNIVERSITY OF CHICAGO PRESS
CHICAGO AND LONDON

By the same author:
Arrow of the Blue-Skinned God: Retracing the Ramayana through India

The University of Chicago Press, Chicago 60637
The University of Chicago Press, Ltd., London
© 2001 by The University of Chicago
All rights reserved. Published 2001
Printed in the United States of America

10 09 08 07 06 05 04 03 02 01 2 3 4 5
ISBN: 0-226-05676-7 (cloth)
ISBN: 0-226-05677-5 (paper)

Library of Congress Cataloging-in-Publication Data

Blank, Jonah.
 Mullahs on the mainframe : Islam and modernity among the Daudi
 Bohras / Jonah Blank.
 p. cm.
 Includes bibliographical references and index.
 ISBN 0-226-05676-7 (cloth : alk. paper) — ISBN 0-226-05677-5 (pbk. :
 alk. paper)
 1. Ismailites—India. 2. Ismailites—Pakistan. I. Title.

 BP195.I8 B55 2001
 297.8′22′0954—dc21

 00-057686

⊗ The paper used in this publication meets the minimum requirements of
the American National Standard for Information Sciences—Permanence of
Paper for Printed Library Materials, ANSI Z39.48-1992.

Contents

Acknowledgments

My first thanks are due to Syedna Muhammad Burhanuddin, without whom this study would have been impossible. My conclusions and analysis are not always in accord with those of the Bohra clergy, so I am very grateful that Syedna kindly gave community members his blessing to cooperate with an outside researcher for the first time. I have tried to portray orthodox society as accurately as possible, but this book is an independent ethnography unendorsed by any dawat organization. To permit such an uncontrolled, uncensored undertaking was, I believe, an act of trust—a trust I have tried my very best to honor.

Other members of the Daudi Bohra Qasr-e Ali to whom I owe a debt of gratitude include: Shahzada Qaidjohar Bhaisaheb Ezzuddin, whose kind attention greatly facilitated my project; Shahzada Shabbir Bhaisaheb Nuruddin, who was a source of guidance and encouragement from the very beginning of my fieldwork; Sakina Behnsaheb Mohyuddin, who arranged for my first audience with Syedna; and Ayman Behnsaheb Kalimuddin, director of the Burhani madrasa system, who enabled me to distribute my questionnaires and who personally demonstrates the educational achievements of so many Bohra women.

I would like to offer very special thanks to some of my personal friends within the Daudi Bohra community. Over the past seven years, Abduz-Zahir Bhaisaheb Mohyuddin has spent countless hours answering a constant stream of inquiry, with seemingly limitless patience and good grace; as a new father (with more important claims on his time), Abduz-Zahir displayed tremendous generosity of spirit. In a similar vein, I am pleased to credit my close friend (and college roommate) Ayaz Shaikh for introducing me to the Bohras more than fifteen years ago. He, his brother Aizaz, his wife Sunita, and all the members of the Shaikh and Gunja families not only assisted my fieldwork, they became my own surrogate family during my sojourns in Mumbai.

Bohra custom mandates deep respect for the dispensers of learning—in traditional parlance, "mullahs" (hence the title of my book). It is particu-

larly appropriate, therefore, that I give thanks to my academic mentors: to Stanley J. Tambiah, my thesis advisor, who kept my feet on the Straight Path through long years of doctoral study; to Nur Yalman, whose voluminous knowledge and magnanimity of spirit were an inspiration to me both as a student in his seminars and as a teaching fellow in his lectures; to David Maybury-Lewis, who taught me anthropological theory and (through his work with the organization Cultural Survival) provided an excellent example of how to put theory into socially engaged practice; and to Ali Asani, who not only showed great patience and forbearance as my Urdu teacher, but who gave his time generously in correcting my errors of Gujarati translation.

To these Harvard mullahs I must add one more: Mullah Shabbir Muhammad Mansoorbhai Jamali, of the Mumbai Burhani Madrasa, who served as my instructor in Lisanu-Dawat, and general guide through the various *zahir* aspects of Musta'li Ismaili doctrine. I am similarly beholden to Shaikh Mustafa Abdulhussein, who righted many potentially embarrassing mistakes. All remaining errors are entirely my fault, and they would have been far more numerous without Dr. Abdulhussein's vigilance.

For providing the funding necessary to complete my fieldwork in India and Pakistan, I would like to thank the Fulbright Foundation, the Academy for Educational Development, the National Security Education Program, the Mellon Foundation, and the Harvard University Department of Anthropology.

My research, however, would have remained nothing more than a private endeavor if not for my editor, T. David Brent. Publishing a work that aims to reach both an academic and a general audience requires great editorial skill, vision, and courage. I am profoundly indebted to Dr. Brent, to my superb copy editor, Carol Saller, and to the rest of the staff at the University of Chicago Press for turning a raw manuscript into a finished book.

During the course of my writing I have greatly benefited from informal conversations with many experts on Islam, India, and other matters. Space precludes my mentioning all of them, but the scholars and friends whose erudition has enriched my work include Fouad Ajami, Walter Andersen, Stephen P. Cohen, David Diaz, Wendy Doniger, Diana Eck, Ainslie Embree, John Esposito, James Fallows, Šumit Ganguly, Pranay Gupte, Michael Krepon, Sulayman Nyang, Bartholomew Ryan, Riaz Hussain Shah, Shashi Tharoor, Ambassadors Howard and Teresita Schaffer, Shirin Taher-Kheli, and Ashutosh Varshney.

My final acknowledgment is to the people of the Daudi Bohra community. For your welcome, your guidance, and your willingness to put up with a ridiculous stranger asking a lot of painfully obvious questions, I offer my deepest and most sincere appreciation.

Introduction

The mosque is overflowing with several thousand Daudi Bohra worshipers, and every man present is dressed exactly the same: white *kurta* and pajama trousers, with a white and gold pillbox skullcap. Every man is bearded, and pounds his chest in unison with the Ashura self-flagellation of his brethren. In a screened gallery above, women perform the same rites in *burqas* and veils that cover them from head to modest toe. What is most remarkable about this highly traditional scene is not its antiquity, but its novelty: as recently as a generation ago, relatively few of the participants (residents of the cosmopolitan Indian city of Mumbai) would have been physically distinguishable from their non-Bohra neighbors.

Over the past two decades the Bohra clergy has attempted—with great success—to establish a communal identity that is at once universally Islamic and unique to the denomination. Moreover, it has done so not by rejecting modern or Western ideas and technologies, but by embracing them: the Bohras have used modernity as a tool to reinvigorate their core traditions. The case study of the Bohras should serve as a powerful refutation to those who would essentialize Islamic revivalism, or even (to use a more ideologically laden term) Islamic fundamentalism.*

The Bohras uphold most aspects of Islamic orthopraxy as faithfully as any Taliban pietist could wish. In all matters of prayer, dress, physical comportment, and even avoidance of financial interest, they are highly conservative. At the same time, they eagerly adopt any and every aspect of modern or Western culture that is not specifically forbidden. Far from displaying the anti-Western attitudes sometimes found among other revivalist groups, Bohras proudly send their children to Britain or the United States for education, exhibit greater gender equality than most communities of the subcontinent, and have become Internet pioneers uniting

*I use the controversial appellation "fundamentalist" here and throughout the study not to suggest that the Bohras have recaptured the fundamentals of Islam, but to describe a group that attempts to make Islam the fundamental foundation for its daily existence. See p. 262 for a discussion of the uses and meanings of this problematic term.

members of their far-flung denomination into a worldwide cybercongregation.

Is this unusual? Perhaps, but there is no reason that it has to be. Most aspects of "modern" society that the Bohras reject are not really modern at all. The Bohra clergy urges the faithful to renounce alcohol, drugs, and sexual promiscuity. But are these truly the hallmarks of modern society? People all over the world have been brewing liquor, ingesting all manner of narcotics, and engaging in every conceivable sexual practice since the dawn of recorded history. Rejection of these practices is antimodern only if modern society is defined solely by its vices.

With Islamic fundamentalism in the forefront of both scholarly and nonacademic discussion these days, the goals (and audience) of this book will naturally be twofold. A professional anthropologist or a regional specialist may take as given the argument that Islamic traditionalism need not be antimodern, and concentrate instead on the discussion of theoretical points arising from the case study of hegemonic institutionalization of a uniform communal identity. A more general reader, however, may choose to give the theoretical sections a cursory glance and skip to the ethnographic description of a community—one never before studied by outsiders—which confounds nearly every stereotype of what fundamentalist Islam can and cannot be. I hope the book will hold something for the cloistered scholar and the intellectually curious lay reader alike.

FOCUS OF STUDY

The case study I present is, at its most basic, a description of how "tradition" can not only be maintained, but resurrected and even created anew. A unique denomination of Gujarati Ismailis, the Bohras[1] are led by a *da'i al-mutlaq* (apex cleric, generally referred to by the honorific title "Syedna") and *dawat* (clerical hierarchy). The community had been far more secularized and assimilated during the later part of the tenure of the previous da'i (Taher Saifuddin, d.1965) and the first decade of the reign of the present da'i (Muhammad Burhanuddin) than is the current norm. The dawat's carefully planned program of cultural retrenchment was launched in the late 1970s, and the "tradition" in question is (like most resurrected traditions) a blend of antique and neoantique custom. The central elements of this neotraditionalist reform program have been: (1) enthusiastic embrace of modern communications technology to standardize culture across a wide geographical area; (2) mandated codes of personal appearance, dress, and language to delineate the boundaries of the community and fortify group cohesion; (3) wholehearted encouragement of Western edu-

cational ideology and practices to foster a unified societal identity while keeping ambitious, freethinking members within the fold.

The dawat has built on the spiritual hegemony inherent to Ismaili theology, and used thoroughly modern methods to translate this moral authority into de facto sociopolitical control sufficient for (and bolstered by) a concerted program of identity reification. The careful balancing of old and new is by no means a hidden agenda: it is a constant refrain in clerical pronouncements. "The modern age has destroyed or weakened many religious groups," warns one dawat tract, noting that Syedna "is loath and averse, as a religious duty, to countenance a change in fundamental Islamic principles."[2] But the clergy advocates a forward-looking program rather than a hidebound return to the past: "We must learn and derive benefits from Western societies without becoming enslaved by them," the current da'i has said. "While we focus on worldly and material success we must at all times remain aware of our religious obligations. *Deen* [religion] and *duniya* [the secular world] must coexist within us in harmony."[3]

THEORETICAL ISSUES

The example of the Bohras, I would argue, demonstrates the viability of a modernistic manipulation of tradition by a premodern elite, and the possibility of such an elite gaining widespread community acceptance of its mandated orthopraxic norms within a relatively brief period of time. The means by which the Bohra program has been carried out should be of theoretical interest not only to anthropologists, but to any social scientists investigating such issues as identity formation, religious or political authority, and the modernization of tradition.

The group identity promulgated by the Daudi Bohras is in many respects a neotradition, but this does not imply that it is an ersatz creation. As Eric Hobsbawm and Terence Ranger (among others) have noted,[4] the very notion of "tradition" is an elusive concept: it can be manipulated by elites for their own ends, and never exists in historical stasis. I leave investigation of whether any particular cultural practices are "authentic" or "novel" to other researchers, and focus instead on the means by which such practices are reified and perpetuated. The Bohra dawat has largely succeeded in solidifying its concept of identity, I would argue, not by winning over the entirety of the populace, but by securing the support of a critical mass of followers who have then been able to establish enough of a societal norm to gain compliance from the rest of the group. To do this, the dawat uses both carrots and sticks, employing a full range of modern ideas and techniques to keep its followers in the fold.

Inherent national traits and cultural essentialism have become theoretical straw men: since the essentialist model was effectively debunked by Benedict Anderson and Ernest Gellner almost two decades ago, it has been commonplace to note that ethnic identities are socially constructed rather than organic.[5] Far less commonplace, however, are examples of such identities being fostered by a specific, deliberate program: a top-down effort to bolster traditional (or neotraditional) culture in a modernist context. The Subaltern historians have skillfully highlighted the artificial nature and colonial provenance of sharply delineated Muslim and Hindu identities on the Indian subcontinent, although most (properly) stop short of labeling such identities as solely the product of intentional manipulation.

The Islamic world has seen innovators try to replace indigenous or traditional practices with Western or "modern" ones: Turkey's Mustafa Kemal Ataturk, for example, or Iran's Reza Shah Pahlavi. Some colonial-era Muslim reformers attempted to refashion Islamic orthodoxy itself so as to align it with Western ideals: Sir Syed Ahmad Khan took this approach in India, and Muhammad Abduh followed a similar path in Egypt. More recently, the Taliban of Afghanistan and the conservative wing of Iran's *ulema* have put a reactionary spin on modernization: they have sought to resurrect anachronistic identities by pairing the use of certain Western technologies (particularly military ones) with wholesale rejection of Western ideology. Throughout the Islamic world, however, very few communities have attempted to foster a group identity that is thoroughly "traditional" and at the same time thoroughly "modern." This has been the aim of the Daudi Bohra clergy: to solidify an Islamized group ethos in a community with significant exposure to the ideas and the lifestyle of secular Indian society.[6]

The dawat can compel a certain degree of orthopraxy merely by fiat, but the imposition of ideology on an unwelcoming populace could hardly provide a sound basis for long-term success. The clergy's strategy, therefore, combines hard and soft elements, both sanction and suasion. Clifford Geertz notes the inherent conflict between science and faith, and contends that religions can respond either by denying science or by wholly accepting and virtually sacralizing it.[7] The Bohras (I suggest) have done something like the latter: using the tools of modernity to bolster core values that were in danger of erosion, coopting—and in some cases even sacralizing—all elements of modernity that are not deemed a direct threat to core doctrine.

A discussion of Islamization in India cannot help but provide material for the debate between scholarly camps that Charles Lindholm has aptly

described as "dualist" and "essentialist." The former includes Imtiaz Ahmad, T. N. Madan, and Veena Das, who argue that Muslim practices on the subcontinent are generally characterized by a high degree of syncretism and are thoroughly woven into the multicultural fabric of the region. The latter camp is most closely associated with the writings of Francis Robinson, who contends that Indian Muslims are and have historically been moving closer to conformity with "visions of perfect Muslim life" held in common throughout the Islamic world. The debate has been heated at times: Das, for example, has accused Robinson of "taking a somewhat polemic stance against not only Ahmad but also the entire anthropological understanding of Islam." While I favor the syncretistic viewpoint, I recognize that various parts of the following case study could be grist for either side's theoretical mill.[8]

Ravindra Khare has persuasively argued that Weber's postulation of a basic incompatibility between traditional and modern values does not hold up on the subcontinent: "In historical terms, India has been interacting with diverse aspects of Western modernity for about two hundred years" and "India has not been a passive recipient of the values and processes of modernity."[9] The example of parallel modernization and Islamization in the Khojah community demonstrates that these two competing ideologies can indeed coexist, although it must be noted that among the Khojahs modernization has been rapid while Islamization has been far more modest. Describing another Indian example of religious reformulation, Louis Dumont wrote, "In our own times Hinduism has repelled the onslaught of Christianity by integrating those Christian values which are most dangerous to it."[10] I suggest the Daudi Bohras have achieved the very same goal in relation to the basic ideology of Western modernity.

LARGER ISSUES

In addition to providing the basis for theoretical academic discussions, the Daudi Bohra case study can add to intellectual debate on much wider social concerns. In the areas of ethnic conflict and cultural preservation there is much to be learned from the example of a community that is simultaneously devoted to quietism, modernism, and traditionalism. Why has this particular Shi'a minority—fundamentalists by most meaningful definitions of the term—shunned sectarian violence throughout its history, while groups with similar ideological pedigrees (the Ismaili Fatimid-descended Druze of Lebanon and Syria, for example) have turned to political bloodshed?[11] What factors have enabled the Bohras to come to terms

with modernity better than many other groups? What lessons can other culturally threatened communities seeking to preserve their heritage in the face of modernist onslaught learn from the Daudi Bohras?

The entire phenomenon of religious revivalism requires a more nuanced and sympathetic treatment than that commonly given in academic circles. The observation of Ashis Nandy in reference to the very different issue of Hindu nationalism has broader relevance: "Modern scholarship tends to see zealotry as a retrogression into primitivism and as a pathology of traditions. On closer look it turns out to be a byproduct and a pathology of modernity."[12] Without sharing Nandy's characterization of firm religious devotion as pathological zealotry, I would agree with his contention that the way secularist scholars view religious communities says more about their own preconceptions than about those of their subjects. The Bohra case study, I suggest, makes this secularist bias—equally ingrained in many academics and casual watchers of the evening news— abundantly clear. Only in a modernist state can the very idea of tradition be revolutionary.

Since the end of the cold war, Muslim fundamentalists seem to have replaced Soviet Communists as the West's bugbear of choice. Both in academic and in popular circles, the core values of traditionalist Islam are commonly portrayed as inherently hostile to those of a modern, pluralistic society. When a professor as highly respected as Samuel Huntington posits a "clash of civilizations" between the democratic West and the supposedly reactionary forces of Islam,[13] he is merely giving scholarly voice to an opinion all too prevalent throughout America. The characterization of Muslim fundamentalists according to strict stereotype is one of the only points on which most politicians, journalists, and think-tank pundits seem to agree. The image of Islam generally presented to the public is that of its most extreme and militant fringe: Iranian ayatollahs, Taliban mujaheddin, or Hezbollah terrorists. And the response of Western academics—some of the few non-Muslims with firsthand knowledge of what Islam is and is not—has been surprisingly weak: an array of platitudes against essentialization, with little attempt to tackle mischaracterizations of traditionalist Islam head-on. One of the foremost goals of the ethnography that follows is to provide some balance to the equation: to present a case study of a community, numbering up to one million, in which traditional Islamic values and modern Western practices coexist harmoniously. In fact, I suggest, the Daudi Bohras have used the very tools of modern society to strengthen and reinstitutionalize the fundamental core of their faith.

Further study would be required to determine the extent to which less privileged segments of Bohra society subscribe to the values of the elite

stratum that provided the statistical basis of my survey. At least within this upper segment, however—this little leaven that leaveneth the whole lump—the quest to combine modernity and tradition seems to be a clear success: 90.1 % of my respondents said that traditional values were stronger throughout the community now than they had been for several generations—and they said this was largely due to modern, Western-inspired education, technology, and ideas.[14]

METHODOLOGY

The Daudi Bohras take their religious guidance from a single centralized clergy with a strictly hierarchical organization. At top of this structure is the daʿi al-mutlaq, whose absolute primacy in all matters of faith is not questioned even by the small group of dissidents who dispute the daʿi's authority over mundane affairs. Central control extends well beyond the realm of theology to encompass all aspects of a believer's life. It is the strictness and effectiveness of this dawat control that has prevented any previous ethnographer from making a study of the denomination. As a re-sult of their sequestration the Bohras are one of the few major communi-ties left to which Marcus Banks's dictum of tainted evidence—"the mani-festations of ethnicity we study today contain within them the ghosts of previous academic formulations"[15]—does not apply.

An attempt to conduct research in an orthodox Bohra community any-where in the world would be virtually impossible without the active or tacit cooperation of the religious authorities, and the clerical official respon-sible for contact with outsiders (a brother of the daʿi) notes that no such re-search had ever been authorized prior to my study. My own ethnographic study idled for over a year before earning the duʿa (blessing) of the daʿi al-mutlaq Syedna Muhammad Burhanuddin (the duʿa was for believers to co-operate with my research—it did not and does not imply official endorse-ment of my conclusions). For the duration of my fieldwork I was given full freedom to attend all community rituals, and frequent private access to many important figures in the royal family and the clerical hierarchy. It would have been impossible for me even to have spoken with Syedna—let alone to have sought his permission for research within the commu-nity—if not for the generous efforts of friends and patrons within the Daudi Bohra community, and my comments in the Acknowledgments do not begin to express the depth of my indebtedness to these individuals and to others whom I have left unnamed.[16]

The basis for most of the information contained in this study is par-ticipant observation during eighteen months of fieldwork, primarily in

Mumbai (as Bombay has been known since 1995, when the Shiv Sena/ Bharatiya Janata Party government in Maharashtra officially changed the state capital's name to its Marathi spelling) but with significant portions of time spent in Surat, Karachi, and other sites. Attendance at ritual and community functions was complemented by private interviews with scores of sources of varying degrees of orthopraxy. Some of these sources I have named in the text, others I have left unnamed in the interest of confidentiality: while I hope and expect that this research will be well received within the Bohra community, I wish to make certain that the blame for any controversial information rests with me rather than those who have helped me. This is all the more important for members of the Bohra clergy, a group closely bound by family ties and famously wary of outside investigators.

This study does not aim to present all aspects of Bohra society in detail: the picture I attempt to paint is primarily that of the orthodox paradigm. The society I describe is that of its most devout members, those Bohras whose lives are centered on the person and teachings of the da'i al-mutlaq. How representative these circles are of Bohra society at large remains an open question. I believe, on the basis of several years of intensive observation of Bohra communities in India, Pakistan, and the United States, that the orthodox paradigm represents a standard that most Bohras acknowledge as an ideal, a standard that most do not attain, but that most reach for to the extent they are able. On the defining issue of the centrality of Syedna—the da'i's place as fundamental touchstone for all spiritual questions in life—there seems to be remarkably little divergence of opinion: while many Bohras place less emphasis on his role as an ethical or practical guide, only the most alienated renounce their allegiance to him. Overt opposition is limited to a group described even by its own leader as minuscule. While I do not claim that the orthodox circles are fully representative of Bohra society, there is ample reason to regard any divergence of core values as one of degree rather than essence.

In order to create a statistical framework for both my anecdotal observations and the paradigmatic information provided by orthodox sources, I obtained questionnaire responses from Bohras living in four geographically disparate locations (Mumbai, Nagpur, Karachi, and Calcutta).* This was an attempt to measure the dawat's success in maintaining a unified code of orthodoxy and orthopraxy among Bohras far

*While I use the spelling of Mumbai instead of Bombay (with exceptions explained in the next chapter), I have retained Westernized spellings for other cities (Calcutta and Madras for Kolkatta and Chennai, for example) when indigenized nomenclature would cause undue confusion.

removed from their central location in Mumbai and Gujarat. The universe for this survey was 169 households containing a total of 1,068 individuals.

Since my questionnaire was distributed with the cooperation of the dawat, I present its findings through occasional references in text rather than a comprehensive set of tables. I offer the survey results solely to supplement and quantify my ethnographic observations, not to make any claim of systematic, statistically determinative data collection. The participating families were those with children in dawat *madrasas* (schools), the devotional elite of the group. They represent only one segment of the Bohra community, but a vitally important one: the critical mass of orthodox practitioners whose strict adherence to dawat teachings is crucial in establishing such norms throughout the wider community. One noteworthy aspect of the survey results is the close alignment of responses from all four sites. I wish to emphasize, however, that the most important element of my fieldwork was participant observation rather than survey data. I have complemented my primary ethnographic research with these figures because no other quantitative data on mainstream Bohra attitudes is available, but a truly independent survey of the community would be a fruitful area for future research.[17]

The techniques I employ in my examination of the Bohras are those common to most anthropological researchers and ethnographers, but are supplemented by the experience of more than a decade's work (on and off) in the field of journalism. In the past I have worked in cultural reportage and the sociology of religion, with anthropology serving as an underlying foundation.[18] Here I present a work of academic anthropology, with journalistic experience serving as a supporting pillar. It is my hope that the combined approaches will convey a deeper, more complete, and finally more truthful portrait of the Bohra community than either approach by itself could provide.

It is also my hope that by examining one particular group of Ismaili Shi'a based in Mumbai I will be able to cast some light on issues applicable to a wide array of other traditionalist communities struggling to come to terms with a rapidly changing world. I hope that my observations on the mechanics of a neotradition being crafted by a spiritually hegemonic elite may be of interest to other academics, but that is only part of my goal in this work. The Bohras have taught me a great deal, and I believe their story can provide surprises and useful lessons to many people outside the walls of academe—people who consider terms like "mechanics of a neotradition" and "spiritually hegemonic elite" to be so much eggheaded gobbledygook.

In every part of the world there are traditional-minded individuals and

societies attempting to cope with the surging onslaught of of modernity, struggling to uphold ancestral customs and identities without merely becoming fossilized in an archaic past. For these people, and for people who care about these people, there is much to be learned from the example of the Daudi Bohras.

Part One

Ethnography

CHAPTER ONE

Historical Background:

The Roots of the Faith

To understand the present, one must first understand the past. Nowhere is this adage more true than among the Daudi Bohras. The culture of modern Bohra society, the faith that gives Bohras their fundamental identity, the structure of the clerical establishment that governs all facets of daily life—each of these is an outgrowth of the history of the denomination. To explore any ethnographical or theoretical issues related to the Daudi Bohras, therefore, it is best to begin at the beginning.

POPULATION AND ORIGINS

The Daudi Bohras are a denomination of Ismaili Shiʻa of Gujarati descent, with 470 major communities spread out over forty nations around the world. Both dawat and dissident sources place the worldwide population at one million, but this figure (like most big, round numbers) should be treated as a very rough estimate.[1] As post-Independence censuses in India do not provide denominational data, the main statistical basis for speculation remains censuses of the colonial era. The 1931 census rated the community at 212,752, but all Shiʻa groups tend to be undercalculated in Indian censuses. The matter is further complicated by separate categories for "Shiʻa," "Bohra," and "Muslim," raising the possibility of many respondents identifying themselves as non-Bohras out of confusion.[2]

Since the 1930s all figures bandied about have been extrapolations from earlier data. They range from 317,844 to 560,000 to the ever familiar one million. The dawat itself is rumored to have very precise figures, but if such data exist they have never been made public. In pre-Independence court testimony, Syedna Taher Saifuddin estimated his following at 300,000, but for the past thirty years dawat sources have cited the figure of one million. A more conservative guess might be somewhere between 700,000 and one million worldwide. In any case, at least two-thirds of the total population live in India, with the largest concentrations residing in the Western states of Maharashtra (particularly Mumbai) and

Gujarat. If one calculates Muslims at 12% of the Indian population, and Shi'a at about one-fifth of Indian Muslims, one reaches a rough estimate of Bohras comprising something like 2.5% of Indian Shi'a and 0.5% of India's Muslims.[3]

As a community of indigenous converts rather than an elite ruling class of extrasubcontinental ethnicity, Daudi Bohras fall into the *ajlaf* rather than the *ashraf* category of Indian Muslims. The name "Bohra" is generally presumed to be derived from the Gujarati verb *vohrvun* (to trade), reflecting the occupation of the overwhelming majority of Bohras throughout their history. While certain Bohra families (including a dynasty of da'is al-mutlaq in the eleventh-thirteenth/seventeenth-nineteenth centuries)* claim Rajput Kshatriya descent and other aristocratic clans posit Brahmin ancestors, the bulk of the community seems to have been converted from the mercantile *jatis* of the Vaishya *varna*.[4]

ISMAILI HISTORY TO THE END OF THE FATIMID CALIPHATE

PRE-FATIMID HISTORY

Until the second quarter of the twentieth century the unavailability of primary source documents made any academic study of Ismailis a highly speculative endeavor: centuries of Sunni repression and the resulting practice of *taqiyya* (dissimulation) had kept any authentic texts from being circulated outside the most restricted of Ismaili circles. All non-Ismaili scholars writing before the 1930s, whether Sunnis, Shi'a, or Western Orientalists, had to piece together accounts from information found in the documents of the Ismailis' enemies: thirdhand information gleaned from medieval heresiographies or polemical Abbasid tracts. The rediscovery of genuine Ismaili documents in India, Central Asia, and Yemen, however, provided a wealth of material for scholars of history and theology alike, most notably Wladamir Ivanow and Henry Corbin.

While the history, theology, and philosophy of the Ismailis up to the end of the Fatimid period are beginning to be satisfactorily examined by scholars of various disciplines, the ethnography of present-day Ismailis of the Musta'li branch (i.e., Bohras) is still virgin terrain. In the following chapter, I briefly summarize about 1,400 years of history as background for my discussion of the Daudi Bohras. A reader seeking a more complete histor-

*Paired dates are given in the form "after Hijra/Common Era." Unless otherwise noted, unpaired dates are in the Common Era of the Gregorian calendar. Also unless otherwise noted, ranges of dates given for an individual are those of his tenure as imam, da'i, or holder of other title.

ical account of the Fatimid and pre-Fatimid eras (the period during which Bohra history and Nizari Ismaili history are coterminous) might refer to Farhad Daftary's magisterial text and other sources noted in the Bibliographical Discussion.

Early Shiʻism: 10–148/632–765

From the very start, even before the two branches of Islam formally split, the struggle between Shiʻa and Sunnis might be described as a struggle between purity and practicality. What began as a dispute over succession soon became a fundamental difference in outlook. The immediate question of earthly governance—should rule be entrusted to the most saintly candidate or the most effective one?—grew into a timeless question at the heart of the faith: Is God's guidance channeled through man or through text?

When the Prophet Muhammad died in 10/632, he left no universally recognized successor. Ali ibn Abi Talib, the Prophet's son-in-law and first cousin, was seen as a candidate of exemplary virtue, but power brokers deemed him too young (and perhaps not sufficiently forceful) to lead the community. They settled on Abu Bakr, the father of the Prophet's wife Aisha. He was a safe choice (both an early convert and a member of the predominant Quraish tribe), but an elderly man who died two years later.[5]

The next two caliphs (the title, *khalifa*, literally means "successor") established what would become the Sunni paradigm for political leadership: a ruler whose legitimacy stemmed from strength and decisiveness more than piety or spiritual charisma. Umar, a bold, ruthless warrior of intimidating height and bulk, expanded the Islamic empire to Egypt, Syria, and Persia. Uthman lacked his predecessor's physical presence, but had the benefit of a strong family: the Quraishis were the most powerful tribe in Arabia, and the Umayyads were the most powerful clan in the Quraish.

While Uthman himself was not viewed as corrupt, by reserving choice governorships and other plum positions for his own kinsmen he aroused a certain degree of resentment among members of the *umma* (community of Muslims). Early converts—some of them companions of the Prophet who had fought against the Umayyads at the disastrous battle of Uhud— now chafed at the dominance of their old adversaries. Many remembered when the clan had been Muhammad's most implacable enemies, how they had renounced paganism for Islam only when Muslim troops were on the verge of capturing Mecca. During Umar's reign new conquests had directed hostilities outward, but a tapering-off of territorial expansion left demobilized warriors dissatisfied with the scant prospects for booty. When a group of these soldiers murdered Uthman in 35/656, community leaders chose Ali as caliph.

A member of the same Hashemite clan as Muhammad, Ali had grown up in the Prophet's own household. While many Umayyads were seen as barely reformed polytheists more concerned with privilege than righteousness, Ali (even his enemies would have had to concede) was a true believer. Sunnis still regard Ali as the last of the Rightly Guided Caliphs, and contend that he freely accepted the authority of his three predecessors. In Shiʿa historiography, however, the Prophet anointed Ali as his successor while returning from pilgrimage to Mecca just before his demise, and Ali never surrendered his claim.* The Shiʿat Ali—"the Party of Ali," of which the word Shiʿi/Shiʿa is an abbreviated form—had been politically marginalized until the death of Uthman, and even during the five years in which his caliphate was broadly recognized Ali experienced very few days of peace.

The first challenge came from Aisha, whom Ali defeated at the battle of the Camel; he permitted her to retire to Medina, with all of the honor due to a widow of the Prophet. Umayyad clan leader Muawiya, the governor of Syria, was more successful. Refusing to surrender his office, he accused Ali of complicity in Uthman's murder and claimed the caliphate for himself. Ali marched against Muawiya at the battle of Siffin, but was foiled (Shiʿa tradition holds) by the Umayyad commander's ruse of attaching copies of the Qurʾan to his soldiers' clothing. Ali agreed to arbitration by a panel of elders, a compromise that would lead to his own death: angered at his decision not to crush the Umayyads when he had the chance, some of his more militant supporters broke away and set up yet another rival caliphate under Abdullah al-Rasibi. Shiʿa forces defeated these Kharijites (as they were called), but one of the extremists assassinated Ali with a poisoned sword inside a Kufa mosque. He died on 21 Ramadan 40/661, a date that is still a major Shiʿa remembrance.

The community at Kufa chose Ali's son Hasan (d.49/669) as its imam, and the decision was approved in Mecca, Medina, and Iran. Half a year later, however, Hasan abdicated in favor of Muawiya, on condition that he and his followers be permitted to preach their doctrines without hindrance. Eight years afterward, the new caliph had Hasan poisoned. Muawiya reigned unchallenged for twelve more years, during which time the name of Ali was cursed every Friday in congregational prayers throughout the Umayyad empire. This dynasty would last nearly a century (41–132/661–750). Hasan's brother Husain did not challenge Umayyad

*This designation (not acknowledged by Sunnis) at Ghadir Khumm on the eighteenth of zyl-Hajj is the basis for the institution of *nass* in both the Ismaili and Ithna-Ashari branches of Shiʿism. Daudi Bohras commemorate the event by holding their recommitment of the mithaq pledge annually on this date.

might during Muawiya's lifetime, but when the caliph died in 61/680 Husain agreed to raise his standard.

On the plain of Kerbala, in what is now Iraq, Husain and seventy-two of his companions were slaughtered by the four thousand soldiers of Muawiya's son Yazid. The year was 61/680, the date was Ashura—the tenth of Muharram, a pre-Islamic fast day that has since become the defining historical event for Shi'a of all denominations. Every year in Ashura rituals, Bohras (like all Shi'a) both mourn and commemorate the martyrdom of Imam Husain. The line of imams of all major surviving Shi'a groups trace their descent from Husain's only son not massacred at Kerbala: Ali Zain al-Abidin, who had been confined to his tent owing to illness. While Ali Zain adopted an outwardly quietistic attitude after the death of his father and does not seem to have openly claimed community leadership, later Shi'a tradition considers him the imam for the period 61–95/680–714.

Although many of the initial supporters of the Party of Ali were motivated by political rather than strictly spiritual grievances, within a century of the Prophet's death this movement had developed its own distinct theology. Its basic outlook was radically different from that of the Sunni mainstream. The Sunni framework for religious interpretation was essentially communal: the revealed text of the Qur'an was available for all who wished to read it, the compilations of ahadith (traditions; sing., hadith) clearly set out the example of the Prophet himself, and any disagreements about how to apply these guidelines were to be settled by the ijma (consensus) of the ulema (clergy; sing., alim) using the tools of rai (reason) and qiyas (analogy) available to any educated person. The four major Sunni schools of fiqh (jurisprudence)—Maliki, Shafii, Hanifi, and Hanbali—all arose approximately contemporaneously with the crystallization of Shi'a belief, and all four Sunni madhhabs sought to establish a broad-based uniformity of law and custom.[6]

The Shi'a conceptualization of Islam moved in precisely the opposite direction: it posited spiritual inspiration as a top-down rather than a bottom-up process. The traditions of the Prophet's life provide ample foundation for either approach. On the one hand, Muhammad tried to express God's revelation as clearly and simply as possible, to broadcast the divine word as widely as he could, and to provide a living example of the conduct expected of every good Muslim. On the other hand, during his lifetime Muhammad was the sole source of guidance for his umma, the sole channel through which God conveyed instructions to the fledgling community, the sole moral touchstone for any question of spiritual doctrine or daily practice.

It was this latter model that the Shi'a adopted, postulating a continuation of Muhammad's spiritual authority in the person of his blood relatives. Divine revelation was deemed a truth far beyond the realm of human understanding: If the Qur'an was the actual Word of God,* how could mere fallible mortals ever hope to comprehend its true meaning? To suggest that God could be bounded by the limits of human intelligence would be blasphemy, so the only way even to approach the Almighty would be through the mediation of some greater-than-human agent. That agent was the imam, a concept that remains the central distinction between the Sunni and Shi'a views of Islam.

In Shi'a belief as formulated by Imam Jafar al-Sadiq (see below), the imam is *ma'sum* (sinless and infallible), perfect, the essential bridge between Creator and created. God has sent a succession of prophets to the world, each with a revelation appropriate to a particular time and place. All revelations are the same, but their manner of expression is tailored to the specifics of a progressively developing human understanding. The function of the imam is to interpret the revelation of the prophet of his age and disseminate it to society at large.

A prophet (*nabi,* or *natiq*) is sent to deliver divine revelation only at particular times in human history, but there must always be an imam present in the world to interpret the teachings of the prophet. The imam can look behind the surface meanings of mere text and deliver the true message hidden within. As such, the words of the imam carry far greater weight not only than such human tools as rai, qiyas, and ijma, but even than *sunnah* (the example of the Prophet, from which Sunnism takes its name), ahadith, or the text of the Qur'an itself: while the Qur'an is perfect, human beings who read it are not. Any approach made to divine revelation except via the imam is necessarily tainted by the fallibility of human reason. Only through the agency of the infallible imam can mankind hope to approach the inconceivable Oneness of God.[7]

Initially, various Shi'a groups defined the *ahl al-bayt*—the Prophet's family from which the imam could emerge—in fairly unrestricted terms. In line with pre-Islamic Arab kinship patterns, many viewed the bounded unit as the entire Hashemite clan, accepting not only all direct descendants of Muhammad, but descendants of his uncles Abi Talib and al-Abbas as well. Other early Shi'a accepted any descendant of Ali, whether by Fatima or by al-Hanifiyya. Not until the Abbasid caliphate—when the Hashemite dynasty abruptly turned upon the Shi'a groups who had helped

*Harry A. Wolfson has labeled the Islamic parallel of the Christian doctrine of incarnation (divinity taking the form of flesh) as "inlibration" (divinity taking the form of text).

it overthrow the Umayyads—was the prevailing definition of the ahl al-bayt limited to descendants of Fatima and Ali through Husain.[8]

Zaidis, followers of Zaid al-Shahid (ibn Ali ibn Husain), rebelled against the waning Umayyad rule, but faded to the periphery of the Shi'a movement when their imam was killed in battle in 122/740. In Zaidi doctrine the imam is not infallible, and the imamate is neither hereditary nor dependent on *nass* (designation): any descendent of Husain can claim the office by launching a righteous rebellion. This qualification rules out the concept of a hidden imam, which has been a staple of both Ithna-Ashari* and Ismaili Shi'ism. In Zaidi terms, a true imam must publicly champion his imamate.[9]

Zaid's half-brother Imam Muhammad al-Baqir (95–114/714–732), meanwhile, adopted a policy of political quietism that would be made a point of mainstream Shi'a doctrine by his son Jafar al-Sadiq. This quietism supplanted Zaidi insurgency by a Darwinian process of natural selection: during the years of Abbasid rule (132–656/750–1258), Shi'a leaders who advocated open rebellion were killed off before they could pass their militant doctrines on to the next generation of believers.

Imam Jafar (114–148/732–765), son of Muhammad al-Baqir, was the figure who consolidated much of Shi'a doctrine, for Ismailis and Ithna-Asharis alike. He is the source of the preponderance of ahadith accepted by Twelver Shi'a, as well as most of the ahadith deemed normative by Ismailis, and is even cited in the *isnads* (chains of transmittal) of many Sunni ahadith. Respect for Jafar's scholarship and piety extended far beyond Shi'a circles. Not only did Jafar found the madhhab of jurisprudence still practiced by Ithna-Asharis, he is said to have provided instruction to Abu Hanifa al-Nu'man and Malik ibn Anas, founders of the Hanifi and Maliki madhhabs of Sunni law. Jafar created a consensus for nass as the mark of an imam's legitimacy, ending the preceding chaos of competing Alid contenders attempting to justify their claims by recourse to arms.

This disassociation of spiritual authority from temporal rule would be crucial to the survival of Shi'ism: from that time forward, imams would be able to provide religious leadership without having to prove their credentials in futile uprisings against vastly superior forces. Jafar's emphasis on the imamate as the sole path to God would be a hallmark of both Ismaili and Ithna-Ashari doctrine: "[W]hoever dies without having acknowledged the true Imam of his time," one hadith attributed to him proclaims, "dies as an unbeliever." By the end of his imamate, Jafar had succeeded in win-

*Also called "Twelver" or "Imami" Shi'a, the Ithna-Asharis represent the most populous branch of Shi'ism.

ning the recognition of virtually all Shi'a factions. It would be the first such period of unity since the death of Ali ibn Abi Talib—and the last such period in all Shi'a history to follow.[10]

Early Ismailism: 148–297/765–909

After twelve centuries of Sunni misrepresentation of Ismaili belief, it is useful to remember that contemporary descriptions of pre-Fatimid Ismailism are based almost entirely on the accounts of sectarian opponents. The only significant surviving texts of this period are the *Kitab al-rushd wa'l-hidaya* written by the Ismaili missionary Mansur al-Yaman ibn Hawshab (d.302/914) and the *Kitab al-alim wa'l-ghulam* either by ibn Hawshab or his son Jafar. The only comprehensive Ismaili history by an Ismaili author prior to the modern era is the *Uyun al-akhbar* of Idris Imad al-Din ibn Hasan, the nineteenth da'i al-mutlaq of the Musta'li dawat in Yemen. This work, covering the entire period from the life of the Prophet until the concealment of the twenty-first imam, Imam Tayyib, draws much of its material for the pre-Fatimid period from the Fatimid text of Qadi al-Nu'man, *Iftitah al-dawa*—itself a work written centuries after many of the events described.[11]

Far from the extremist image summoned up by its enemies, early Ismailism seems to have been very much in the doctrinal mainstream of orthodox Shi'ism. Bernard Lewis describes the entire Shi'a movement as a "revolt of the depressed classes, Persian and Semite alike," while John Norman Hollister terms the Ismaili branch as "essentially Shi'ism on the march, to establish a theocratic and therefore truly Islamic state." Ivanow, whose position as the foremost non-Ismaili historian of Ismailism has not been eclipsed since his death in 1970, calls the denomination "the most catholic and highly developed form of Shi'ism." The high degree of congruence between Ismaili and Ithna-Ashari doctrines is shown by the fact that the *Da'a'im* of Qadi al-Nu'man (the basic compendium of Fatimid theology) is drawn largely from the teachings of Imam Jafar al-Sadiq, and that Twelver theologians have even tried to claim al-Nu'man as one of their own.[12]

The great schism of Shi'ism arose on the grounds of succession rather than doctrine: Ismailis believe that the imamate was passed to the descendants of Jafar al-Sadiq's son Ismail, while Ithna-Asharis believe it was inherited by the descendants of Ismail's brother Musa. Doctrinal divergence followed, but initially the split centered on avenue of spiritual authority. Ismail was born circa 100/720, and was about twenty-five years older than Musa. He received nass from his father, and this nass was never clearly revoked. As Daftary notes, "There can be no doubt about the au-

thenticity of this designation, which forms the basis of the claims of the Isma'iliyya." According to a theologian of the high Fatimid period, Imam Jafar made his nass in public, declaring of Ismail: "He is the Imam after me, and what you learn from him is just the same as if you have learnt it from myself." The crisis for Shi'a occurred when Ismail, having been declared the next imam by infallible decree, predeceased his father Jafar by about a decade. During Jafar's lifetime this cast doubt on the imam's own infallibility, and laid the seeds of a bitter struggle for succession on Jafar's death.[13]

Three of Jafar's surviving sons claimed the imamate, but none had clear evidence of nass. Musa emerged as the consensus candidate backed by a majority of the Shi'a notables, but a determined group of partisans championed the cause of Ismail's son Muhammad: nass was irrevocable (this camp held), and the imam is infallible in his choice of successor. Modern Bohra clerical sources do not dispute Ismail's premature death, but they contend that this event did not change the legitimacy of succession. This position has been articulated by Musta'li theologians for at least eight centuries (possibly much longer). The third da'i al-mutlaq after the occultation of the twenty-first imam, Syedna Hatim Shamsuddin (d. 596/1199), wrote that according to prophesies attributed to Ali ibn Abi Talib himself, "The eldest of these [sons of Imam Jafar] shall die in the lifetime of his father, appointing as his successor the seventh imam." The early Bohra cleric Hasan ibn Nuh of Broach (d. 939/1533) is even more explicit: "The sixth imam was Mawlana Isma'il b. Jafar, Abu Muhammad, surnamed al-Wafi. He died during the lifetime of his father, but not before the latter had appointed him as his successor . . . [Ismail] bequeathed his position to his son, Muhammad b. Isma'il, with the consent of his father, transferring to him the office of the imamate by his father's, Imam Ja'far's, order, and in his presence."[14]

Another Ismaili view—as articulated in later centuries, at least—was that Ismail had *not* died before his father, but that his death had been staged as a scheme to protect the true line of imams from Abbasid plots. In the words of the ninth/fifteenth century Musta'li da'i al-mutlaq Idris Imad al-Din, "[T]he time came for Isma'il to dissemble death, using this ruse against his enemies who were full of hatred, enmity and the ardent desire to extinguish the Light of God"; the imam permitted Musa[15] to be acknowledged only "as a 'screen' for the real successor." Jafar ibn Mansur, writing during the Fatimid ascendency, expresses the same belief: "His body was made to disappear during the lifetime of his father, as a mystery intended to protect him from his enemies and as a test for his followers." Imam Jafar al-Sadiq is said to have gone to extraordinary lengths to "prove" Ismail's death, even parading a procession of witnesses past the

open coffin to testify that the body it contained was that of his son. Five years later, Ismail is said to have appeared in Basra—and even to have cured a paralytic. Whether or not the ruse succeeded in fooling the Abbasids, it certainly succeeded in confusing the Shi'a.[16]

Some accounts claim that Jafar withdrew his nass from Ismail on discovering that his son was a drunkard, but such speculation appears to be Ithna-Ashari and Sunni polemic rather than history. If nass was revoked during Ismail's lifetime, a more plausible charge would have been association with heretical *ghulats*. Lewis and other scholars argue that Ismail was closely linked to Abu al-Khattab, a ghulat who made such extreme claims that Imam Jafar was forced to curse him. In addition to raising issues of *batini ta'wil* and numerology that would later find their way into orthodox Ismaili belief, al-Khattab is said to have placed himself outside the bounds of Islamic doctrine by preaching the divinity of the imams. He was eventually crucified by the Abbasids, expressing his loyalty to Jafar and Ismail to the very end.[17]

After the death of Jafar al-Sadiq, Muhammad ibn Ismail fled Medina and settled in Kufa. Early Ismaili devotion centered on Imam Muhammad rather than on his father Ismail: to a sect called the Qarmatis, and perhaps to most Ismailis prior to the Fatimid caliphate, he was referred to as *al-Mahdi* or *al-Qaim* (The Riser), and expected to return from seclusion to usher in a new cycle of prophesy. While Mahdism is a concept dating back to the first century of Islam, Ismailis have tended to prefer the term *al-Qaim*.[18]

Muhammad ibn Ismail was succeeded (modern Ismaili doctrine holds) by his son Abdullah al-Mastur, the first of the "hidden imams." During this *dawr al-satr* (period of concealment), the imams carried out their spiritual duties while living lives disguised as simple merchants. They traveled from place to place, or tended to business in one site for as long as was safe, communicating with their followers through a secret network of da'is.* Early in the Fatimid caliphate, Imam al-Muizz billah is said to have searched out the remains of all the hidden imams and transported them to Cairo for reburial.[19]

Modern scholars have noted that the idea of an imamate passed down in secret from the second/eighth to the fourth/tenth centuries[20] seems to have been first articulated during Fatimid times: if such a doctrine was propagated contemporaneously, the veil of taqiyya prevented it from appearing in the documentary record. During these two embattled cen-

*The term is used here in its original sense of "missionary" rather than shorthand for da'i al-mutlaq.

turies, Ismailism was primarily a peasant and Bedouin movement with little urban presence. In such a context, and particularly when laboring under the burden of Sunni oppression, a certain vagueness in doctrinal theory is to be expected. Abbasid vigilance forced the movement deep underground, and according to legend Imam Abdullah al-Mastur concealed himself so well that for several years he was completely lost to his followers. After an exhaustive search throughout much of the Muslim world, Ismaili loyalists are said to have found the imam at a site named "the monastery of sparrows."[21]

The second hidden imam, Ahmad al-Mastur ibn Abdullah, is said to have authored the Ismaili theological text *Rasa'il Ikhwan al-Safa*. He was succeeded by Husain al-Mastur ibn Ahmad, during whose tenure missionaries are said to have had great success in the dissemination of the faith. His representatives gained a firm foothold in Yemen, and among the Berbers of the Maghrib his da'i Abu Abdullah al-Shii laid the foundation for what would soon become the Fatimid empire. According to Syedna Idris Imad al-Din, "He organised the propaganda, spread it further afield, broadcast instructions to his followers, making it manifest . . . and dispatched his da'is everywhere. He thus made the true religion visible to those who were in search of it."[22]

The policy of *satr* protected the imamate from external Abbasid threats, but exposed it to threats from within. The next (and last) hidden imam, Husain ibn Ahmad, had to rely on his brother Muhammad Habib to communicate his directives to the community at large. As Husain's death approached, Muhammad Habib tried to transfer the imamate to his own line by claiming that nass had been conferred on his own son. Soon after, the son died of mysterious causes. The regent claimed nass for his next son, and that candidate also passed away. In all, according to legend, Muhammad Habib anointed ten of his sons, and watched all of them die before he acknowledged Husain's son Abdullah al-Mahdi as the legitimate imam.[23]

It is with Abdullah al-Mahdi[24] (268–322/881–934), the eleventh imam, that the dawr al-satr ends and the Ismaili community reemerges into a period of open, verifiable history. During the terms of the preceding imams, da'i Abu Abdullah al-Shii had succeeded in converting the Berbers of what is now Tunisia to the Ismaili cause. He had already established a rigid theocratic rule, with strictures including death for the sale or use of alcohol, and invited Abdullah al-Mahdi to rule over the kingdom that had been set up in his name. The imam was publicly proclaimed caliph in 297/910, and with his arrival in the Maghrib the Fatimid period of Ismaili history begins.[25]

As mentioned above, the history, theological interpretation, and even the mere existence of the hidden imams cannot objectively be determined to date from a period prior to the Fatimid caliphate. Until the year 286/899, Daftary states, "the early Ismailis, or at least by their overwhelming majority, originally recognized only seven Imams." In that year al-Mahdi declared himself the imam, and retroactively declared his three predecessors imams as well. Prior to this time, all Ismaili leaders had used the title of *hujja* (proof) rather than *imam*. Al-Mahdi's declaration caused an immediate schism with the Ismaili Qarmatis, who had previously maintained allegiance to him as the hujja and vehicle for communication with the hidden Qaim. The genealogy of the Fatimid caliphs has been a matter of bitter polemical debate between Ismailis and their Sunni or Ithna-Ashari rivals. During the dawr al-satr, imams were seldom referred to either by name or by title, and generally mentioned only through vague pseudonyms and obscure allusions. The enemies of the Ismailis allege that al-Mahdi created the entire lineage of hidden imams out of whole cloth, while the Ismailis argue that the genealogy had always been carefully preserved but kept in strict secrecy until it could safely be made public.[26]

Even now, after the rediscovery of many authentic Ismaili primary source documents, the pre-Fatimid period of the movement remains shrouded in mystery. Contemporary Ismaili writings are generally too vague to provide a picture of the community with historical precision, while contemporary Sunni and Ithna-Ashari texts lump Ismailis together with any number of real or imagined heretical sects. The most common name by which they are denoted in Sunni texts is simply *malahida:* "heretics." No distinction was made among the various types of unorthodox belief, and the actual or supposed doctrines of one sect were freely associated with any of the others. The very label of *Sabiyya* (Sevener), which has come to be widely applied to the Ismaili movement as a whole, was never used by the theological ancestors of today's Ismailis themselves. The term was coined in reference to the Qarmatis, who accepted a line of only seven imams (Ali, Hasan, Husain, Ali ibn Husain, Muhammad ibn Ali, Jafar al-Sadiq, Muhammad al-Qaim). To make matters even more confusing, the denomination now called Ismailis did not generally use the term "Ismaili" either—they referred to themselves merely as *al-dawa* (the mission) or *al-dawa al-hadiya* (the rightly guiding mission). Such vagueness of nomenclature further complicates the task of sorting out truth from fiction.[27] In a link to its pre-Fatimid past, the modern-day Bohra clergy still refers to itself by the term *al-dawa al-hadiya*.

Confusion between Qarmatis and the line of Ismailis today deemed orthodox, moreover, is an accurate reflection of the hazy boundaries of

the community at the time. The Qarmatis were a messianic Ismaili movement drawing their appellation from their early leader Hamdan Qarmat, whose surname is said to stem from an archaic Aramaic word meaning either "red-eyed" or "short-legged." Initially the Qarmati da'is considered themselves (and were considered by others) to be part of the overall Ismaili mission. They established strong footholds in parts of Yemen, Bahrain, Persia, and Iraq, and for a time posed political challenges even to the Abbasid and Fatimid empires. The Qarmatis preached radical egalitarianism, and seem to have been quite genuine in their program of social leveling. As was the case for early Christian communities, an egalitarian, communalist doctrine gave rise to charges of libertinism and antinomianism. For the Qarmatis, as for the early Christians, the charge seems to have been false: Lewis argues that the Qarmatis may well have shared their possessions, but probably not their wives.[28]

In the late third/ninth century the Qarmatis attempted to ally with the Zanj rebels, former African slaves who were enjoying notable military success in the period 255–270/869–883. The rebel leader, Ali ibn Muhammad al-Zanji, declined the invitation, and both movements were eventually suppressed by the imperial powers. It is interesting to speculate on what might have happened had these two groups of radical social revolutionaries succeeded in combining forces. Instead, the Qarmatis took an action that guaranteed their alienation from Muslims of all persuasions: in 317/930 they attacked and plundered Mecca itself, carrying away the Black Stone of the Qa'ba. They are alleged to have killed 30,000 men, enslaved an equal number of women and children, and filled the well of Zamzam with corpses. Al-Mahdi is said to have sent a letter to the Qarmati leader Abu Tahir rebuking him in no uncertain terms: "You have marked down for us a black spot in history, which you will not erase. . . . You have brought on our dynasty, our sect (Shi'a) and our da'is the name of unbelief and Zandaqa and heresy by your shameful deeds."[29]

Al-Mahdi ordered his pseudosubordinates to return the Black Stone immediately, but the holy item was not restored until the Abbasids agreed to pay a heavy ransom in 339/950. Shortly after the desecration of the Qa'ba, Abu Tahir recognized a bizarre Persian pretender as the awaited Qaim; the pretender, who is said to have been a Zoroastrian, mandated the ritual cursing of Muhammad, the destruction of the Qur'an, and the worship of fire. By the time the Qarmati leader recognized his mistake and ordered the Persian killed, the movement had already suffered an irreparable loss of legitimacy. The Qarmatis would still challenge the Abbasids and Fatimids alike, but during the fourth/tenth centuries they were gradually absorbed into the Fatimid Ismaili fold.[30]

A more dangerous source of confusion, in the early years at least, was that of the ghulats. The term *ghulat* (exaggerator) was coined by early Shiʿa as a label of abuse for extremists who pushed the envelope of devotion to the imams past the limits of Islamic orthodoxy. Many ideas of various ghulat groups would eventually be integrated into mainstream Shiʿism, both Ismaili and Ithna-Ashari: Mahdism, *ghayba* (occultation), and *taʾwil* (esoteric interpretation) all seem to have had their genesis in ghulat circles.[31] Some ghulats were strongly influenced by Manichaeism, and their notions of gnostic duality would later become a basis of Fatimid speculative philosophy. Other ghulat notions, however, were more directly in conflict with core Islamic belief. Some ghulats denied the very existence of paradise and hell as they are described in the Qurʾan, and posited instead a form of reincarnation reminiscent both of Hinduism and of later Druze belief: after death, the soul of a good person was believed to migrate to the body of a human being of a higher spiritual level, while the soul of an evil person might be reincarnated in an animal. A wide array of *ibaha* (antinomian) practices and beliefs were ascribed to the ghulats, some of them authentic and some merely the "exaggerations" of the heresiographers. The Sunni writer Amir Khusrau, in his *Khazain-ul Futuh,* describes persecution of early Ismailis/ghulats in terms that reflect a supposed divergence of both mores and doctrines:

> It was discovered that among these shameless wretches, mothers had cohabited with their own sons and aunts (mothers' sisters) with their nephews, that the fathers had taken their daughters for brides and there had been connections between brothers and sisters. Over the head of all of them, men as well as women, the saw of punishment was drawn. The saw with its heart of iron loudly laughed over their heads with tears of blood. Those who by a "secret stroke" (*zarb-i-pinhan*) had become one, were now openly sawed into two and the soul that had sought union with another soul was now compelled to leave its own body.[32]

In these circumstances, it is hardly surprising that the early Shiʿa in general (and Ismailis in particular) adopted a policy of taqiyya—mandated public dissimulation of belief. The doctrine is said to have originated with Imam Muhammad al-Baqir, while his half-brother Zaid was engaged in a futile attempt to challenge the might of the ruling powers head-on. The Qurʾanic basis for taqiyya is generally given as 3:28 ("Let not the believers take unbelievers for friends rather than believers; and whoever does this, he shall have nothing of the guardianship of Allah, but you should guard yourselves against them, guarding carefully.") and 16:106 ("Whoso disbe-

lieveth in Allah after his belief—save him who is forced thereto and whose heart is still content with Faith—but whoso findeth ease in disbelief: On them is wrath from Allah.")[33]

Taqiyya was formally incorporated into Shi'a practice by Imam Jafar, and it accounts for a great deal of the uncertainty surrounding Ismaili history and belief. In theory, no articulation of any aspect of doctrine available to a person outside the faith can be accepted as wholly genuine: Ismailis are obliged to shield their beliefs from the observation of all but those pledged to obey the imam and his deputies, and any document or public statement must be examined in this light. Even the most clear-cut of formulations may well be intentionally deceptive, as a matter of religious policy. Perhaps the only thing an outside observer can state with certainty about Ismaili doctrine is that nothing about it can be stated with certainty.[34]

THE FATIMID CALIPHATE: 297–567/909–1171

From the tenure of Imam Abdullah al-Mahdi until nearly the end of the visible imamate (as recognized by Musta'li Ismailis), the line of imams would be coterminous with that of Fatimid caliphs. At its height, the Fatimid empire encompassed North Africa, Sicily, Egypt, Sudan, Palestine, Syria, and the Hijaz (including Mecca and Medina). The Fatimids never succeeded in converting Egypt to Shi'ism, nor did they make a great effort to do so,[35] but their rule marks the high point of Ismaili history.

The first three Fatimid caliph-imams ruled from Ifriqiya in North Africa. Abdullah al-Mahdi dealt harshly with those of his new subjects who refused to acknowledge his theological supremacy, and many recalcitrants (among them groups of Kharijites) were imprisoned or executed. One Kitama Berber shaikh, deliberating whether or not to pledge his support to the newcomer, sought an audience with Abdullah al-Mahdi and requested the imam to demonstrate his legitimacy by performing a miracle. The caliph showed him the miracle of life and death: he had the shaikh executed on the spot. The da'i Abu Abdullah al-Shii, who had personally established Ismaili rule in the Maghrib and handed the state over to al-Mahdi ready-made, may have initially entertained hopes of serving as de facto ruler. He soon learned that Abdullah al-Mahdi was no puppet: the da'i and his brother were charged with sedition and promptly killed.[36]

Abdullah al-Mahdi's son Muhammad al-Qaim (322–334/934–946) imposed heavy taxes on his subjects in order to fight largely futile campaigns of expansion and territorial consolidation. He briefly captured Alexandria but was soon forced to withdraw. Late in his reign a rebellion broke out

among the Kharijite Berbers that came close to toppling the fledgling dynasty. Al-Qaim's successor al-Mansur billah (334–341/946–953) eventually crushed the revolt, and found a novel means of dissuading any other potential challengers: he let the rebel leader Abu Yazid die slowly and painfully of his wounds, then gutted his corpse, stuffed it with straw, and paraded it from town to town, in a cage with two monkeys.[37]

Imam al-Muizz

Al-Mansur billah's successor, Imam al-Muizz li-Din Allah (341–365/953–975), codified both Fatimid law and religious doctrine. The chief text produced was the *Da'a'im al-Islam,* written in the name of the imam with al-Muizz as the putative author, but in actuality the work of chief qadi and hujja Abu Hanifa al-Nu'man. The *Da'a'im,* together with al-Nu'man's *Asas al-ta'wil, Iftitah al-dawa, al-Majalis wa'l-musayarat,* and other works, laid the foundation for all later Fatimid thought and practice. The *Da'a'im* remained the only true work of Ismaili fiqh, laying out the standards of jurisprudence that would remain in force until the fall of the dynasty. On the authority of Imam Jafar al-Sadiq, the traditional tools of Sunni fiqh were excluded from use: *ijtihad* (interpretation) relying on rai and qiyas was regarded as liable to human error, and therefore invalid. Even *sunna,* the example of the Prophet as documented in ahadith, was strictly limited. The only ahadith deemed absolutely normative were those transmitted by one of the imams, generally Muhammad al-Baqir or (in most cases) Imam Jafar himself.* Replacing these fallible techniques of fiqh was the infallible judicial judgment of the imam himself. A reigning caliph could be guided by the precedents of earlier imams, but no text could challenge the authority of a present imam.[38]

Six years after his ascension, Imam al-Muizz saw his name replace that of the Abbasid ruler in the Friday *khutba* read in Mecca and Medina—symbolically granting him leadership of the Islamic world. The Fatimids would retain control of the holy places of Islam, with a few brief interruptions, until the end of the dynasty. When the last Ikshid ruler died before his son was old enough to take over the throne, local authorities made a virtue of necessity and invited al-Muizz to extend Fatimid rule to Egypt. Soon Syria fell too, and the armies of al-Muizz took the old Umayyad capital of Damascus. In 362/972 al-Muizz transferred the seat of his empire to Cairo, a city built especially for the purpose. Within two years, al-Muizz

*Modern Bohras are more willing to accept the validity of generally recognized ahadith. The library of the Jamea tus-Saifiya in Karachi, for example, contains the same edition of the ahadith of al-Bukhari that I have cited as a bedrock source for Sunni tradition throughout this manuscript.

had to repulse a Qarmati invasion that nearly reached the outskirts of the new capital. The confrontation, however, shook the Qarmatis' hold on Ismailis outside the Fatimid domains. Al-Muizz brought many of these scattered eastern Ismaili communities into the Fatimid fold for the first time.[39]

Imam al-Aziz

It was under al-Muizz's successor, Imam Aziz billah (365–386/975–996), that the Fatimid empire reached its greatest extent: from the Atlantic Ocean to Sindh in present-day Pakistan, from the Red Sea up (briefly) to Mosul in what is now northern Iraq. Al-Aziz is generally acknowledged to have been the ablest caliph of the Fatimid dynasty, and his accomplishments were due in part to the highly capable management of his *wazir* Ibn Killis. Imam al-Aziz was known as a great builder of mosques and monuments; perhaps his most notable work was al-Azhar: although this school—the world's first university—had been founded in his father's reign, it was al-Aziz who completed the construction of the campus and brought the institution to its full glory. The seeds for future turmoil were sown, however, when al-Aziz brought in Turkish soldiers to supplement the Kitama Berbers who had previously comprised the bulk of the Fatimid armed forces. The infusion of Turkish mercenaries maintained caliphal power for another generation by offsetting the growing strength of the Berber troops, but opened the door for the later ousting of the Fatimids by the Ayyubids and Mamluks, their Turkish titular servants.[40]

It was also under Imam al-Aziz that the Fatimid tradition of religious tolerance reached its greatest height. While the practice was honored by some caliphs in the breach, on the whole the Fatimids accorded their subjects more latitude in matters of conscience than did many contemporary regimes. As a small elite ruling over a population composed primarily of Sunnis with a sizable Christian minority, most of the Fatimid caliphs were careful not to trample the religious sensibilities of their subjects. The very first person to hold the powerful office of wazir—in effect, the day-to-day administrator of the empire—was Ibn Killis, a convert from Judaism. He served as wazir first to al-Muizz, and more notably to al-Aziz.[41]

The last wazir under al-Aziz was Isa ibn Nasturus, a Christian. Under later caliphs several other Christians and at least one Jewish convert held the title of wazir, and members of both faiths held high offices in the reigns of al-Aziz and of some of his successors. Al-Aziz permitted the Coptic patriarch to rebuild the church of St. Mercurius near Fustat, and actually encouraged a public theological debate between his chief qadi and Severus, bishop of Ashmanayn. Personally a firm supporter of Shi'a practice, al-Aziz promoted the Ashura rites which had been initiated in Baghdad c.352/963

and brought to Egypt under al-Muizz. His support for Ismaili orthodoxy, however, did not conflict with his deep-seated toleration. Imam al-Aziz took a Christian woman in marriage, and she seems to have been the mother of his only surviving son and successor.[42]

Imam al-Hakim *

This controversial successor ushered in a rather uncharacteristic religiously repressive period in Fatimid history. Only eleven at the death of his father, Imam al-Hakim (386–411/996–1021) spent the first four years of his reign under the control of his tutor, the eunuch slave Barjawan. Shortly after puberty, Hakim ordered the execution of his guardian and assumed power directly. His reign was characterized by allegations (often unproven) of such erratic behavior and episodic cruelty that some Sunni and Western historians have suggested that the caliph may have suffered from mental illness. He ordered members of his court killed for the most minor of infractions—wazirs and qadis, aristocrats and concubines, anyone who happened to offend him in any way. In a fit of anger directed most likely against his sister, he forbade all women in his realm to leave their houses, or even to look out of their windows.[43]

At one point al-Hakim issued an order that all Christians in Fatimid domains wear a five-pound iron cross around their necks, and all Jews wear a five-pound metal bull. He commanded that several thousand churches and monasteries be razed in a single year. In 400/1009 al-Hakim ordered the destruction of the Church of the Resurrection in Jerusalem, an act which helped stoke passions leading to the First Crusade. Nor did Sunnis escape his whimsy: al-Hakim had curses against the first three Sunni caliphs painted in gold calligraphy onto the walls of his mosques.[44]

At the same time, al-Hakim was a lavish patron of architecture and theological learning. He reopened the Dar al-Hikmat (Hall of Knowledge), which provided free education, room, and board to scholars in training to be Fatimid da'is. Its library of law, astrology, and medicine was one of the finest in the world. His Masjid al-Anwar, still one of the largest mosques ever built, was refurbished and restored in 1980 by the Daudi Bohra da'i Syedna Muhammad Burhanuddin.[45]

Without espousing such unorthodox doctrines himself, al-Hakim inspired a heretical movement that soon moved so far from the Shi'a main-

*The portrayal of Hakim is drawn primarily from non-Ismailis historians. Bohras and other Ismailis reject this version of events: they regard Hakim as a strict ruler rather than a repressive one. In their interpretation, Hakim cracked down on prostitution, usury, and the sale of alcohol—actions that historians (influenced by Abbasid propaganda) misportray as acts of misogyny and religious intolerance.

stream as to depart altogether from the realm of Ismailism (and possibly from Islam). In the early years of the fifth Islamic century, a Persian by the name of Hamza ibn Ali began articulating extravagant doctrines about the spiritual status of al-Hakim. He had been preceded by al-Hasan ibn Haydara, but it was Hamza who would turn out to be the motivating force of the movement. Hamza was joined by a Turk from Bukhara named Muhammad ibn Ismail al-Darazi, and Darazi was the first to declare publicly the full divinity of al-Hakim. Darazi preached antinomianism, and was considerably less guarded in his words than Hamza. For a time al-Hakim is said to have come under the influence of Darazi. According to some accounts (the legitimacy of which Ismailis reject) he stopped going to *masjid,* withdrew from all religious observances, even ended support for the upkeep of the holy places in Mecca and Medina and forbade pilgrims from making the *hajj.*

In 410/1019 Darazi was killed, either by an orthodox Mamluk or on the orders of the capricious al-Hakim. Around this time al-Hakim took to asceticism, dressing only in black, growing his hair long, riding unescorted through Cairo on an ass. On the twenty-seventh of Shawwal in 411/1021, al-Hakim departed alone to a hilltop retreat for an evening of meditation. He never returned. His clothing was found, laced with dagger-holes, but the body was never recovered. Al-Hakim's sister, Sitt al-Mulk, is said to have arranged his murder to support the imam's son Zahir, who had inexplicably been disinherited in favor of a distant relative named Abdul Rahim.[46]

The modern-day Druze are descended from the group loyal to al-Hakim as a manifestation of divinity. Although named for Darazi, they are said to revile him for misrepresenting the nature of al-Hakim. It was Hamza who fled Cairo after al-Hakim's disappearance and spread the word that his master had merely entered occultation. The Druze of today are 300,000 strong, concentrated primarily in Syria and Lebanon. Their doctrine is strongly influenced by ghulat beliefs, neoplatonism, Khattabi batini gnosis, and the expectation of the return of both al-Hakim and Hamza. The Druze era of time begins with the proclamation of al-Hakim's divinity in 408/1017, and the community has remained closed since 435/1043: no converts are accepted, no apostates permitted. In the view of many Muslims, both Sunni and Shi'a, Druze beliefs fall outside the realm of Islam.[47]

Fatimid Decline

Al-Hakim was succeeded by his son al-Zahir (411–427/1021–1036), after Sitt al-Mulk had Abdul Rahim summarily executed. Al-Zahir remained a mari-

onette throughout his entire reign, dangling on strings pulled first by his aunt and after her death by his wazirs. In his name, however, some measure of religious toleration was restored. Christians who had been converted by force under Hakim were permitted to resume their former religion without being sentenced as apostates. Because of continued Abbasid hostility, however, many discriminatory restrictions on Sunnis were kept in place.[48]

Al-Zahir's son al-Mustansir billah (427–487/1036–1094) reigned longer than any other Fatimid caliph, saw Fatimid suzerainty acknowledged in the Abbasid capital itself, and (at least in the selection of his functionaries) restored the tolerant ecumenicalism of al-Aziz. This open-mindedness provided a rhetorical opening for his enemies: Mustansir's employment of many Jews in high positions (including the convert Sadaq ibn Yusuf as wazir) led to Abbasid propaganda that the Fatimid line was of Jewish descent, a charge that would be echoed in many later Sunni polemical tracts.[49] It was a non-Muslim by birth—Badr al-Jamali, an Armenian Christian slave whose conversion would have been something less than wholly voluntary—who turned out to be the most powerful figure in Mustansir's entire reign.

Badr rescued the dynasty from a state of virtual chaos, and in the process created a de facto dynasty of his own. The period 454–466/1062–1074 was a time of great distress for both the Fatimid caliph and his subjects. Earlier in his reign, during the ascendancy of his mother (who was herself a Sudanese slave), Mustansir imported large numbers of bonded Sudanese soldiers to assure himself of a loyal base within the unruly military. The act only served to turn the Turkish and Berber troops from confrontation with each other to united action against a common foe. It was a Turkish general, Abul-Harith Arslan al-Basasiri, who occupied Baghdad in 450/1058 and for a year had the khutba read in the name of the Fatimid caliph. But the victory would not last long: after refusing to send the Abbasid ruler to Cairo as a captive, al-Basasiri was abandoned by the Fatimids. Seljuk Turks drove him out of Baghdad and returned the Abbasid caliph to his throne. In Egypt, Turkish mercenaries turned against the Fatimid imam's African soldiers, and after five years of fighting they emerged victorious. The Turks proclaimed their allegiance to the Abbasid caliph, pillaged the royal palace, and destroyed most of the irreplaceable Fatimid libraries. In 462/1069, the *sharif* (custodian) of Mecca transferred his allegiance to the Abbasids and the Seljuks.* A seven-year famine had reduced the people of Egypt to eating dogs, and even to cannibalism. The caliph himself was a virtual prisoner in his castle, having surrendered both his power and his crown jewels to the Turkish commander.[50]

*Fatimid sway would be restored, but only briefly: 467–473/1074–1081.

In 466/1074 Mustansir summoned Badr, a successful general and governor commanding a force of Armenians not beholden to any other authority, to rescue him from his own army. Badr's troops restored order, and Badr himself became the first wazir to wield true power in his own right rather than merely as the agent of the caliph. He was the first to take the title of wazir al-sayf: vizier of the sword. From his tenure onward, wazirs would not only be the supreme civil authorities, but would enjoy de facto supremacy in the military and even religious spheres as well. This was the case even for wazirs who were unconverted Christians: an Armenian named Bahram, wazir just after the Tayyibi secession (529–531/ 1135–1137), actually held the title of Sayf al-Islam, the Sword of Islam.[51]

While Mustansir's reign saw a precipitous decline in the power of both the Fatimid empire and the Fatimid caliph himself, it also saw the peak of activity and effectiveness of the Ismaili dawat. Missionaries were particularly effective in Central Asia, continuing the work of earlier daʿis and laying the foundation of communities that would follow the Nizari branch and flourish to this day. In Bukhara, the father and brother of the great philosopher Ibn Sina (known in the West as Avicenna: 370–428/ 980–1037) were adherents of Ismaili doctrine. Ismaili daʿis were successful enough to cause Nizam al-Mulk, de facto ruler of the Seljuk empire, to appoint Abu Hamid Muhammad al-Ghazali as a court theologian; al-Ghazali's most important anti-Ismaili tracts would be produced after Nizam al-Mulk's assassination by Persian Ismailis two years before Mustansir's own death. In order to propagate the faith, Mustansir relied particularly on the efforts of al-Muayyad fʾil-Din Abu Nasr Hibtullah, the daʿi al-dawat, whose *Majalis* was a massive compendium of Fatimid theological and philosophical thought. An important local daʿi of this period, Nasir-i Khusrau, wrote a series of Persian texts that would later become extremely influential among Nizari Ismailis.[52]

From the standpoint of the Daudi Bohras, however, the most important act of al-Mustansir was the sending of missionaries to Gujarat. While the tales of the miracles performed by these daʿis must be considered mythical, the conversion of Gujarati Vaishyas to the Ismaili faith does seem to have begun under al-Mustansir.[53]

Mustaʿli/Nizari Schism

The death of Imam Mustansir brought about the greatest schism in Ismaili history: that of the Mustaʿliyya and the Nizariyya, the followers of two rival sons of Mustansir. Those who believe that the imam bestowed nass on his younger son Mustaʿli would become known as Western Ismailis (because of their initial strength in Egypt and Yemen), and are today repre-

sented by the Bohras. Those who believe that nass was bestowed on the elder son Nizar would become known as Eastern Ismailis (because of their initial strength in Syria and Iran) and are today represented by Khojahs and other followers of the aga khan.

When Imam Mustansir died, his supremely powerful wazir al-Afdal put Musta'li billah (487–495/1094–1101) on the caliphal throne. That the wazir had already married his daughter to Musta'li could bolster either side's claim to nass: perhaps al-Afdal forged the marriage alliance because of Musta'li's nass, or perhaps the wazir defended Musta'li's claim because the young prince was his son-in-law. This question is one I leave to the Ismaili faithful and to historians of Ismailism.

Nizar, who had been away from Cairo, returned to find his brother's accession a fait accompli. History is written by the victors, and Musta'li and al-Afdal had emerged victorious. Nizar died in prison, but his followers would remain strong in Persia long after Ismailism of all stripes had virtually died out in Egypt itself. The caliphal throne that Musta'li inherited must not have been an especially comfortable seat: the dawat was faltering even in its heartland, the First Crusade inflicted humiliation on the tottering empire, and the imam himself was little more than a puppet manipulated by the heavy-handed wazir.[54]

The Persian followers of Nizar would go on to form the sect known to the West as the Assassins—the legendary band of supposed fanatics who would provide the basis for much of the misinformation about Ismailis throughout history. The myths of their appetite for murder have been highly exaggerated. Selim Hichi, a modern scholar, has presented a tally of all the executions commonly attributed to the Assassins—from the first in 465/1072 to the last in 671/1272. A close look at this list shows that during the entire two centuries of the Assassins' activity there were only forty-four deaths ascribed to the group, and of these only four seem motivated by religion rather than politics.* Several victims, such as Alp Arslan (465/1072) and Nizam al-Mulk (484/1092) are clearly anachronistic attributions, having been killed years before the Nizar-Musta'li schism.[55]

Moreover, the legends surrounding the very name of the Assassins seem to be based on fantasy rather than fact. According to medieval myths brought back to Europe by the crusaders, the Old Man of the Mountain whipped his followers into a fever pitch of zeal by drugging them with hashish and then bringing them to a magnificent garden filled with fine food and beautiful women—a vision of the paradise that was said to await

*The assessment of which are political and which are religious is mine, not necessarily Hichi's.

all loyal martyrs. As Bernard Lewis has persuasively argued, however, this story probably owes more to overactive crusader imaginations than to actual historical events. In all likelihood, *hashshashin* (users of hashish) was merely one of the many terms of abuse tossed indiscriminately at Ismailis by their Sunni adversaries.[56]

The Eastern Nizaris clung to their political independence until the Mongol invasion of Hulagu Khan, and afterward remained an important community in Persia up until modern times. In the nineteenth century they attained new prominence when the line of living imams took on the title of aga khan and transferred the seat of the imamate from Iran to India in 1839. The Nizari tradition is today upheld by Ismailis loyal to the aga khan: the most notable community is that of the Indian Khojahs, but there are other significant Nizari groups in upper Pakistan, Central Asia, and Western China. European confusion between the Nizari and Musta'li branches of the Ismaili faith has continued long after the medieval period. James Baillie Fraser, a Scotsman traveling in Iran during the early part of the nineteenth century, reported the murder of the first aga khan's father with the following observation: "The Bhoras [sic], from India, were particularly devoted to their saint; and many that day sacrificed themselves in his cause."[57]

End of the Fatimid Caliphate and Concealment of Imam Tayyib

Back in Fatimid Egypt, Musta'li's son al-Amir (495–524/1101–1130) was only five years old when his father died. For the next twenty years al-Afdal continued to wield power as wazir, until he was murdered—either by Nizari partisans or by the young caliph himself. After taking the reins of government in his own hands, al-Amir was himself assassinated, by a cabal of ten Nizaris. Depending on which account one chooses to believe, al-Amir either died without leaving an heir, or left an infant son who was killed by a rival claimant to the caliphate, or left a pregnant wife who escaped—or (as Bohra doctrine holds) left a son named Abu al-Qasim Tayyib, aged somewhere between two days and two years, who succeeded him as the twenty-first imam.[58]

The caliphal seat was seized by al-Amir's cousin al-Hafiz, whose son and two grandsons followed him in a succession unrecognized by Tayyibi Musta'lis or by Nizaris. The line of Hafiz seems to have been acknowledged as legitimate caliphs and imams by most contemporary observers, but Hafizi Ismailism did not survive long after the fall of the dynasty. The last Fatimid wazir finally dispensed with the fiction of an independent caliphate, and established his own dynasty under the auspices of the Abbasid empire: Salah al-Din Yusuf ibn Ayyub, better known to the West as Saladin, officially ended Fatimid rule by having the khutba read in the

name of the Abbasid caliph in 567/1171. On the death of his master Nur al-Din, he established the Ayyubid dynasty in his own name. Under the Ayyubids and the later Mamluks, Fatimid libraries were destroyed and Egyptian Ismailis were persecuted until nearly all of them either converted or fled to exile.[59]

The Mustaʻli line of imams, however, continued (and is believed still to continue) in secret. At the death of his father al-Amir, the infant Imam Tayyib was protected by the most important woman in Mustaʻli history since the death of the Prophet's daughter Fatima. Al-Malika al-Sayyida, the wife of the Fatimid daʻi of Yemen, had been appointed to carry on the work of her husband in his later years, and after his death Imam Mustansir had even promoted her—in her own right—to the still loftier title of hujja. During the rule of al-Hafiz, she ran a rival dawat out of Yemen in the name of the infant Tayyib. The baby imam was hidden away from public eye, thus instituting a second period of satr. Al-Sayyida personally selected Zueb ibn Musa as the daʻi al-mutlaq, elevating this office to the highest visible rank of the Fatimid dawat. The line of Tayyibi daʻis began in 526/1132, and with al-Sayyida's death six years later the office of hujjat passed to oblivion.[60]

The period of satr continues to the present day, with the line of imams continuing (Bohra doctrine holds) from father to son, through the descendants of Imam Tayyib.[61] The present imam, like all those since Tayyib's time, lives anonymously in the world, utterly unknown to those around him, periodically in contact with the faithful through his daʻi al-mutlaq. Bohras know neither his name, nor his age, nor anything about him whatsoever—he may be an Internet entrepreneur or an honest street vendor selling vegetables from a handcart, and the faithful may walk past his glittering office building or ramshackle stall without ever realizing it—but they consider his presence in the world absolutely essential for the perpetuation of mankind.

MUSTAʻLI ISMAILI HISTORY FROM THE FATIMID DOWNFALL TO THE PRESENT

MUSTAʻLI ISMAILIS IN YEMEN AND INDIA: 450–946/1067–1539[62]

Origins of the Community in India

Satish Misra pays eloquent tribute to the rise of the Bohras (and Khojahs) under difficult historical circumstances: "[N]owhere else was the penetration of Islam as peaceful or the rise of the new communities so imper-

ceptible. No other Muslim community in India suffered more at the hands of the iconoclastic Sunni rulers."[63] The story of the Bohras in India is indeed one of a nonconfrontational mercantilist community, which has achieved great prosperity and cultural strength while staving off the twin threats of internal schism and external religious persecution.

The first part of the Indian subcontinent to experience a significant Ismaili presence was not Gujarat, but Sindh. Ismaili daʿis—both orthodox and Qarmati—had been active here since pre-Fatimid times, and the region was a refuge for Ismailis and other dissidents of the Abbasid empire. The ruler of Multan seems to have been converted in 347/958, although the level of doctrinal congruence between the Qarmati-influenced local daʿis and Fatimid orthodoxy remains unclear. When the traveler Shams-ud-din Muhammad ibn Ahmad Bashshari Muqaddasi visited Multan in 375/985, he reported that the Friday khutba was being recited in the name of the Fatimid caliph, indicating that the region was a Fatimid vassal state. This outpost of Ismailism would be short-lived: In 396/1005 Mahmud of Ghazna invaded from Afghanistan and forced the king of Multan to transfer his allegiance; five years later Mahmud annexed the territory completely and massacred Multan's Ismaili population.[64]

The faith fared far better to the south, in the neighboring western Indian region of Gujarat. As discussed above, missionary activity was initiated here by Imam al-Mustansir, whose surviving correspondence documents the historical (rather than solely mythical) provenance of early conversions.[65] The year traditionally given for the beginning of the Ismaili mission to Gujarat is 450/1067. According to legend, a daʿi named Ahmad was responsible for the first dawat contact, but was unable to make much progress owing to difficulties of language. He is said to have brought two Gujarati orphans (Abdullah and Nuruddin) back to Cairo with him for training, and returned them to their homeland after extensive instruction on all aspects of Ismaili doctrine. Bohra myth credits Abdullah with planting the lasting roots of the faith in Indian soil. His first two converts (tradition holds) were an elderly couple named Kaka Akela and his wife Kaki Akeli,* to whom he showed the power of God by causing a well to fill magically with water in the midst of a drought. (Water, it should be remembered, is a common Islamic metaphor for spiritual knowledge.) Kaka Akela was the gardener of the local monarch's vizier, who became Abdullah's next con-

*The names are explicitly mythic: In Bohra kinship terminology, "Kaka" is the paternal uncle of Ego, and "Kaki" is the wife of Kaka. In modern usage the words "akela" and "akeli" can mean, "alone, only, sole," although it is not certain that this is the derivation of these characters' names.

vert when he saw his own garden suddenly burst into miraculous lushness while all other vegetation in the kingdom withered away.[66]

Although the mass of the converts were of Vaishya background, tradition attributes the major impetus to the conversion of the Rajput raja of Patan himself. According to myth, Siddharaj Jayasingha (also known as Bharmal) sent an army to capture Abdullah, only to have his forces turned back by a mysterious wall of flame. Another legend has Abdullah making one of the icons in the royal temple speak—and declare the truth of Islam to an astonished court. The most famous story of Bharmal's conversion is less overtly mythological. Abdullah is said to have won the king away from Hinduism by showing him the emptiness of the magic practiced by his court pandits. A huge icon of the elephant-headed deity Ganesh is said to have been miraculously suspended above the floor of the temple, permanent proof of the mysteries of the faith; Abdullah, legend goes, found that the trick had been accomplished by embedding four powerful magnets in the walls of the temple. He removed the magnets, sending both the icon and the monarch's devotion to Hinduism tumbling to the ground. It is said that when Siddharaj accepted Islam in 1143, so many other twice-born Hindus followed his example that the pile of discarded sacred threads weighed 260 pounds.[67]

While Siddharaj Jayasingha was a verifiable historical figure, there is no textual evidence that he ever gave up his Shaivite faith. Not only do the Khojahs claim conversion of Siddharaj, but three different Sufi *tariqa* also lay stake to him as an early initiate. The earliest dynasty of Bohra *walis* (chief da'is for India during the period of the Yemeni dawat) claimed direct descent from Bharmal, as did the Rajput dynasty to which most da'is al-mutlaq from the late seventeenth to the early nineteenth century belonged.[68]

Bohras and other Gujarati Shi'a suffered little persecution under Hindu rule, but during Sunni regimes there were periods of tranquility interspersed with times of severe repression. The first such time was ushered in by Zafar Khan Muzaffar, who invaded Gujarat in 793/1391 as the proconsul of the Tughluq shah Muhammad III. Zafar Khan established his own sultanate in Gujarat, which remained independent for nearly two centuries (810–991/1407–1583) until its annexation by the Mughal badshah Akbar. Under Zafar Khan and his son Ahmad I (the founder of Ahmedabad) the Bohras began the practice of taqiyya, which they would maintain up to and during the Mughal era.

Jafar Patani and the Shi'a-Sunni Schism

Oppressive policies of the Gujarati sultanate provided the spur for the first major schism of the Bohra umma: the secession of a large segment of the

population from Shi'ism to establish a Sunni Bohra community. During the early ninth/fifteenth century, a Bohra theology student by the name of Jafar of Patan sought permission from the Gujarati wali for advanced training under the da'i al-mutlaq in Yemen. The wali denied him permission, on the grounds that he had not yet finished his basic preparation at the local school. Jafar flouted the wali's wishes, and went to Yemen on his own. When he returned to Gujarat two years later, the congregation at Cambay asked him to serve as their prayer leader. When the wali refused to give his permission, Jafar angrily renounced his allegiance to the Ismaili dawat and declared himself a Sunni. He soon received the support of Sultan Ahmad Shah (1411–1442), a religiously intolerant ruler who introduced *jizya* (tax on non-Muslims) to Gujarat for the first time. Under a campaign directed by Jafar, Bohras and other Shi'a were persecuted ruthlessly. Whether persuaded by Jafar's oratory or the sultan's depredations, a very large segment of the Bohra community converted to Sunnism, possibly in the year 1426. An early twentieth-century Bohra writer puts the proportion of converts at 80%, while a Sunni historian writing four years later places the total number at a highly improbable 1.2 million. After leading the drive against Shi'a for two years, Jafar was assassinated in 845/1441.[69]

For nearly a century, however, the schism seemed to be more a matter of appearances than a true social cleavage: the Shi'a and Sunni Bohra communities continued to maintain close ties, even intermarrying with great frequency. The final split was, coincidentally, brought about by another Jafar: Syed Ahmad Jafar Shirazi, a Sunni missionary who had migrated from Sindh to Gujarat. Working first for Sultan Mahmud Shah Begada (1457–1512) and later for Sultan Muzaffar Shah (1512–1526), Syed Ahmad Jafar instituted a renewal of repressive measures. Under his guidance, Muzaffar Shah (to whom Gujarati chroniclers have given the somewhat ironic sobriquet of Halim—"the Clement") executed the Bohra wali, Mullah Raja Saheb Jamaluddin. At this time intermarriage between Sunnis and Shi'a ceased, and the two communities have had no significant social interaction in centuries since.[70]

At some point after the Jafari schism, the Sunni Bohra community seems to have given up trading in favor of agriculture. Colonial gazetteers and secondary sources following them describe two different Sunni Bohra communities, one mercantile and one agricultural, with only the agricultural segment descended from the Jafari seceders. It is not clear whether this distinction holds up to close scrutiny: there has been considerable confusion between Sunni Bohras and Sunni Vohras, the latter term more properly applied to various mercantile Gujarati Muslim communities unrelated to the Ismaili Bohras.[71] A work on Indian Muslims published in

1832, purportedly by a Muslim author named Jafar Sharif, describes two rather than three divisions of the original community: "The Bohra traders of Gujarat and other parts of central and western India are representative of the Ismailiyya Shi'a sect. . . . At present the Bohras have both a Shi'a and a Sunni branch, the former including most of the city traders, the latter the rural agriculturalists." A late nineteenth-century account of the Jafari Bohras, probably written by the Daudi Mian Bhai Abdul Husain, states that "[i]n appearance they differ somewhat from the Daudis, resembling Memons and other Sunni Musalmans," but that in the matter of social custom, "[e]xcept that they are stingier and more given to tobacco and opium, they are much like the Daudis."[72]

THE BOHRA COMMUNITY IN INDIA: 946–1200/1539–1785

During the centuries after the end of the line of visible imams, the importance of the Indian community of Musta'li Ismailis had grown steadily in comparison with that of the Yemeni community. While the dawat enjoyed good relations with the local Ayyubid emir and other Sunni political figures of Arabia, it was forced to engage in near-chronic warfare with various Zaidi shaikhs. Some figures, like the third da'i Hatim ibn Ibrahim al-Hamidi (557–596/1162–1199), were celebrated for their leadership in battle as much as for their spiritual achievements. During the Yemeni centuries, clerics like the second da'i Ibrahim al-Hamidi (546–557/1151–1162) and (especially) the nineteenth da'i Idris Imad al-Din (832–872/1428–1468) worked to refine and explicate the finer points of Fatimid theology and cosmology. Their writings represent the most recent Western Ismaili texts to have received significant analysis by scholars outside the dawat.[73]

While the Yemeni Tayyibi community was often fractious and loathe to submit wholly to the authority of the da'i, the Indian converts were far more accepting of central clerical control. Syedna Idris Imad al-Din took a special interest in the progress of the mission in Gujarat, and had a particular fondness for the Indian believers. Once he is said to have tested the loyalty of the Indian community by commanding his wali, Adam ibn Sulaiman, to let a lowly *bhishti* (water-carrier) lead the congregational prayers. Despite the intense humiliation that such an act would have brought to Gujaratis still influenced by Vaishya ideas of caste purity, the order was obeyed without hesitation.[74]

Transferal of the Dawat to India, and the Sulaimani Schism

Syedna Idris's grandson, the twenty-third da'i Muhammad Ezzuddin ibn al-Hasan, was so impressed with the scholarly abilities of a Gujarati cleric

at his court that he designated him his successor. On Muhammad Ezzuddin's death in 946/1539, Yusuf Najmuddin ibn Sulaiman became the first Indian to hold the office of daʻi al-mutlaq. Syedna Yusuf spent the first five years of his reign in his hometown of Sidhpur before returning to Yemen to finish out his term. His successor, Jalal ibn Hasan, served only a few months, but he transferred the seat of the dawat to India permanently. Syedna Jalal was also an Indian by birth, as would be all future daʻis with the exception of the Yemeni Ali Shamsuddin (1041–1042/1631–1632). The decision to move the dawat was influenced not only by the importance of the Indian community, but also by the fall of Yemen to the Ottoman Turks and the persecution of Ismailis that followed.[75]

In marked contrast to the tightening of Ottoman ideological control in Yemen, Gujarat experienced a rare period of near-total religious tolerance with the ascension to power of the Mughal badshah Akbar. Policy enacted at the center, however, was often thwarted at the local level: Mughal officials continued to take anti-Shiʻa measures long after such actions had been banned by the ruler, so Syedna Daud ibn Ajabshah (975–999/ 1567–1591) traveled to Akbar's court to plead his case before the emperor personally. He was successful in getting all discriminatory measures lifted. During his absence from Gujarat the daʻi had left all community affairs in the hands of Daud Burhanuddin ibn Qutbshah, an act that Daudi Bohras point to as proof that nass was legitimately conferred on Daud. On the death of Daud ibn Ajabshah, Daud ibn Qutbshah became the twenty-seventh daʻi with no outward signs of dissent in the community.

Four years later, however, Shaikh Sulaiman ibn Syedi Hasan al-Hindi, a grandson of Syedna Yusuf Najmuddin who had been serving as the dawat's *amil* (deputy) in Yemen, produced documents purporting to show that nass had been conferred on him rather than Daud. The Daudis regard these documents as a forgery, and note that the seal of the previous daʻi was stolen around the time of his death by former servants engaged in a bitter legal battle over property. The succession dispute was brought before Akbar in 1005/1597, and the badshah appointed a tribunal to decide the case. The panel decided in favor of Daud, and Sulaiman died shortly thereafter; his supporters continued to regard his successors as the legitimate Mustaʻli Ismaili clerical line. Both rival daʻis are buried in Ahmedabad, and their tombs are the sites of parallel pilgrimages for Daudi and Sulaimani Bohras to this day.[76]

The schism, unlike that of the Jafaris, is one of succession rather than of doctrine: Daudis and Sulaimanis maintain nearly identical sets of doctrines and beliefs. The Sulaimanis contend that Daud was only supposed to be the placeholder for Sulaiman, to hold office temporarily until it would

be safe for the true da'i to ascend, but that once in power Daud refused to relinquish his station; the judgment of Akbar's tribunal is ascribed to prejudice in favor of an Indian claimant over a Yemeni one, and Sulaimanis believe that their founding da'i was poisoned by his enemies at the time of the verdict.[77]

The Sulaimani Bohras took on Western ideas and practices considerably earlier than did their Daudi counterparts. The Mumbai businessman Tyabali became the first member of either community to accept the principles of Western education, sending his sons to boarding school in England as early as 1851. Tyabali's descendants, the wealthy and prominent Tyebji family, have been the social leaders and trendsetters of the Sulaimani community ever since. In 1894 the Tyebjis and the Fyzees (another prominent Sulaimani family, closely linked to the Tyebjis by multiple marriage alliances) took all their women out of purdah. Justice Badruddin Tyebji became India's first Muslim barrister, the first Muslim judge to sit on the Bombay High Court,* and the first Muslim president of the Indian National Congress. In the late nineteenth and early twentieth centuries the Tyebji-Fyzee clan produced many lawyers, doctors, and engineers, as well as one of India's most celebrated scholars of Islamic jurisprudence, Asaf Asghar Ali Fyzee.

Writing at the turn of the century, a colonial gazetteer noted that "[t]he Sulaimanis have almost given up Gujarati Bohora [sic] dress and turban," speak both Gujarati and Hindustani, and intermarry with Sunnis, but apart from that "do not differ much from the Daudi Bohoras, with whom they associate but do not intermarry."[78] Today the Sulaimanis comprise some 10% of the overall Bohra population. The seat of the Sulaimani dawat has remained in Yemen since the time of Sulaiman himself. In India, the Sulaimanis are concentrated in Baroda and Mumbai, and speak Urdu rather than Gujarati as their first language. They tend to wear Western dress, intermarry with Sunnis, and adopt more assimilationist policies than their Daudi counterparts. The Sulaimani da'i has a much weaker societal position than the Daudi da'i, and does not possess nearly the same degree of authority over his followers.[79]

Alia/Nagoshi Schism

About three decades after the Sulaimani schism another group of dissidents left the Daudi fold, again over succession rather than doctrine.

*I retain the spelling "Bombay" (rather than "Mumbai") when it is used as part of a pre-1995 name, or in other instances where the Marathi spelling would be unduly anachronistic.

Syedna Daud ibn Qutbshah was succeeded by his aide Shaikh Adam Sai-fuddin; nine years later, Daud ibn Qutbshah's son Abdul-Tayyib Zakiuddin succeeded as the twenty-ninth da'i. His nass was challenged, however, by Ali ibn Ibrahim, a grandson of Syedna Adam Saifuddin. When the case was brought to Emperor Jehangir for adjudication, the Mughal badshah ruled in favor of Abdul-Tayyib and ordered all parties to reconcile peace-fully. Ali agreed, but once he returned to Ahmedabad he revoked his acquiescence and claimed the title for himself in (or shortly after) 1034/1624. The Alia Bohras have, like the Sulaimanis, maintained a sepa-rate line of da'is ever since, while holding to the same basic doctrines as those of the Daudis. At the beginning of the twentieth century Alias were said not to intermarry with Daudis but to be similar to them in appearance and behavior. The seat of the modern Alia dawat is Baroda, where Syedna Tayyib Diya al-Din holds the office of forty-fourth Alia da'i (the lineage is identical up to the time of the Aliad schism). The community is now said to number only 5,000, and has never comprised more than a tiny fraction of the Bohra population.[80]

The Alias themselves experienced a schism during the tenure of Syedna Shamsuddin Ali, the thirty-seventh da'i of their lineage. In 1204/1789 a group of antinomians broke away from the Aliyya, preaching that the era of Islam had ended and all practices enjoined by *sharia* were no longer necessary. They espoused a number of Hindu notions, including vegetarianism, and for this reason were labeled Nagoshiyya (from na-ghosh, "no-meat").[81] As of 1897, they were said to have dwindled to a mere four households (all in Baroda) and to have intermarried with Aliyya but not with Daudis. Twentieth-century references[82] to Bohras almost in-variably refer to the Nagoshis as "practically" extinct, but there does not seem to be any firsthand account of this group for at least a hundred years. The ultimate reference point for all twentieth-century citations is an 1899 gazetteer, so unless some researcher documents the present-day exis-tence of Nagoshiyya, perhaps the subsect should be treated as historical rather than contemporary.

Persecution under Aurangzeb

Some repressive measures against Shi'a were reintroduced by Jehangir and Shah Jahan, but never on the scale of pre-Mughal oppression under the Gujarati sultans. The worst oppression suffered by the Bohras, how-ever, would come at the hands of Aurangzeb—first as governor of Gujarat, later as emperor.

The whip cracked almost immediately after Aurangzeb's arrival in Gu-jarat in 1055/1645. Among his first actions as new governor were to con-

fiscate six cartloads of Daudi Bohra literature and throw the thirty-second daʿi, Syedna Qutbkhan Qutbuddin, in prison. The daʿi, who had assumed office only the previous year, was brought before a kangaroo court at which he was not permitted to testify. According to the *Mausam-e bahar*,* the authorities kept the daʿi in his cell during proceedings out of fear that his eloquence might win over the members of the court. The case against him consisted of an account of the denomination's theology—as presented in the coached testimony of a young Bohra boy. Syedna Qutbkhan was tried in a single evening, and executed the following morning.[83]

Sunni imams were appointed to supervise worship at all Bohra masjids, and attendance at these converted mosques was compulsory for all members of the community. Heavy taxation was imposed, with unofficial extortion by local officers adding an additional burden. Bohras reverted to taqiyya, attending Sunni services in public while carrying on their own rites in secret. Four months after the martyrdom of Syedna Qutbkhan, Aurangzeb left the governorship of Gujarat for military campaigns further afield. Although his successor, Shaistah Khan, adopted a more tolerant attitude, the Bohras were still not free of constraint: Aurangzeb took Syedna Qutbkhan's successor, Syedna Pirkhan Shujahuddin, with him as a hostage to insure the outward compliance of the community. Shaistah Khan was himself succeeded by Ghayrat Khan, whose oppressive measures were mitigated only by the intervention of Shah Jahan himself. During this time, the Rajput dynasty of Daudi Bohra daʿis was ushered in by Syedna Ismail Badruddin (1065–1085/1655–1674), who transferred the seat of the dawat from Ahmedabad to the safer site of Jamnagar. Syedna Ismail, the thirty-fourth daʿi, claimed descent from the legendary Raja Bharmal (Siddharaj Jayasingha), and the line of Rajputs would hold the office of daʿi with only a few brief interruptions for the next 200 years.

The period of relative peace ended with Aurangzeb's ascension to the throne of the Mughals. The new badshah's attempts to impose Sunni practice throughout his domains stemmed from deeply held personal conviction, but was further complicated by his experience of warfare against the Shiʿa sultanates of the Deccan. Grinding years of battle against these states had established the paradigm of Shiʿa as political as well as theological adversaries, and Aurangzeb forced his conquered foes to remove all Shiʿa inscriptions from their coinage and replace the name of the Safavid shah with his own name in the reading of the Friday khutba. That Ismailis had

*This Gujarati chronicle, written in the late nineteenth century, is probably the single most important source in Bohra historiography. While much of its information is mythical, the *Mausam-e bahar* synthesizes earlier histories of the denomination, and remains the foundation upon which nearly all later accounts are based.

no ties to the Deccan sultans or the Safavids earned them no mitigation of Aurangzeb's harsh treatment. Bohras were forbidden to observe Eid al-Fitr and other rites according to their own calendar, to make pilgrimages to their shrines, or to practice Ashura rituals. Sunni *pesh-imams* (prayer leaders) were reintroduced to all masjids, and any congregants failing to attend were punished with flogging. All marriage and death ceremonies were required to be performed by Sunni qadis rather than Bohra amils, and large sums of money (both official taxes and unofficial bribes) were extorted from community members at every possible occasion. Repression peaked in 1093/1683, tapered off the following two years when a massive famine drew Aurangzeb's attention away from ideological concerns, but rose again in the last decade of the emperor's reign.[84]

Systematic persecution eased with the decline of Mughal power, but Bohras continued to be subject to the whims of Sunni rulers and petty local officials. A rare—almost unprecedented—instance of Bohra resistance occurred in 1730, when Sarbuland Khan attempted to squeeze more money from the Bohra community than even the lax standards of the time seemed to permit. The Daudis' feeble attempt at rebellion was quickly crushed, and Sarbuland Khan raised his level of extortion as punishment for the merchants' disobedience.[85] In an attempt to escape the depredations of greedy local overlords the dawat shifted its seat from Jamnagar to Mandvi-Kutch, Ujjain, and Burhanpur.

Hibtia Schism

During the Ujjaini period the dawat suffered another schism, this one less disruptive than those of the past. In 1171/1761 Syedna Hibtullah was challenged by a young shaikh who (coincidentally) bore the same name. Shaikh Hibtullah claimed that his father, Shaikh Ismail, had been in contact with the hidden imam, who had given him the title of hujja. In the old Fatimid hierarchy the hujja outranked the da'i al-mutlaq, so Shaikh Hibtullah claimed supreme authority over the entire community. Such a claim might ordinarily have been treated with derision, but both father and son were scholars of high standing in the community: a catalogue of Ismaili texts that they compiled would later form the basis for much of the bibliographical work of Wladamir Ivanow. The Daudi da'i, however, enjoyed excellent relations not only with the Mughal emperor Shah Alam (he held the title of Mughal Qadi of Ujjain) but also with the Maratha leader Sindhia and with the British East India Company as well. The dissident cause, moreover, lost all hope of mass support when Shaikh Hibtullah inexplicably decided to marry one of his father's divorced wives.[86]

Various attempts were made at reconciliation, but the rebels were

adamant. Eventually the dawat apprehended Shaikh Hibtullah and cut off his nose as a mark of humiliation. Describing the incident from the standpoint of the early twentieth century, dissident Abdul Husain acidly observed, "Apparently, the mania of the orthodox Bohra fanatics of Ujjain for cutting the noses [sic] of a dissenter is getting hereditary, for recently they have cut the nose of a suspected dissenter who had joined the Mahdibagh camp."[87] The Hibtia schismatics survived into the nineteenth century, and twentieth-century texts describe the sect as being still represented by a few families in Ujjain, but these accounts (like those of the Nagoshiyya) all seem to stem from information in the 1899 gazetteer.

THE COLONIAL PERIOD: 1200–1366/1785–1947

The advent of British hegemony in India proved highly beneficial to the Bohras. Where other Indian communities saw (at least in retrospect) imperialistic encroachment, the Bohras saw relief from Sunni persecution. During the reign of the forty-second da'i Yusuf Najmuddin ibn Abdul-Tayyib Zakiuddin (1200–1213/1785–1798) the dawat moved its headquarters to Surat, to take advantage of the protection offered by this East India Company trading post. Surat had been an important Bohra center for nearly a hundred years prior to the move. In the early eighteenth century, in fact, a Bohra merchant by the name of Virji Vora maintained economic dominance over much of the city's trade. He owned the pepper monopoly for the entire region, ran a mercantile empire stretching from Ahmedabad to Agra to Golconda (Hyderabad), and had the port of Surat locked up so tight that the East India Company itself was forced to treat him like an independent princeling. During the latter part of the eighteenth century, the Bohras of Surat were exposed to many aspects of Western culture for the first time. The use of liquor and tobacco grew within the community, prompting efforts of eradication by Syedna Abdul-Tayyib Zakiuddin and Syedna Yusuf Najmuddin, the forty-first and forty-second da'is. The forty-third da'i, Abdul Ali Saifuddin, forbade extreme *matam* (self-flagellation) during Ashura, banning not only the infliction of wounds with weapons but also excessive wailing or breast-beating. He is better known, however, for his 1814 founding of the Saifi Dars, the precursor to Surat's Jamea tus-Saifiya academy.[88]

The early nineteenth century witnessed several major instances of sectarian violence within a single year. On December 17, 1824, and February 18, 1825, simmering tensions between Bohras and Sunnis in the town of Mandapur erupted into bloodshed. In the earlier of the two incidents, a Sunni mob surrounded the house where the Syedna Tayyib Zain-

uddin was staying and caused so many deaths that East India Company troops had to be called in to restore order. On September 15, 1825, Bohras at a *ziyafat* (feast) held in the da'i's honor were attacked in the city of Gwalior: the feast happened to fall during the Jain festival of Paryushan, and the local Jain community was politically powerful enough to have prompted the local raja to institute a ban on animal slaughter for the duration of the holiday.[89] By Bohra custom it would have been disrespectful to offer the da'i a feast that did not include sumptuous meat dishes, so the hosts had arranged to butcher some goats privately. This unlucky congruence of events led to a highly unlikely confrontation: the Bohras, who maintain apolitical quietism as an article of faith, were attacked by an angry mob of Jains, who uphold uncompromising nonviolence as a cardinal point of doctrine.[90]

The Growth of Mumbai as the Denomination's Focal Point

The Bohras helped create Mumbai, and Mumbai helped create the Bohras. Neither the city nor the community would have precisely its present-day form if not for the presence of the other. Moving to the rapidly developing metropolis in the early nineteenth century, the Bohras (like the Khojahs, Memons, and Parsis) quickly took up work in professions traditionally shunned by caste Hindus: most often, selling hardware, glassware, plumbing supplies, paint, stationery, or soap. They avoided the more traditionally polluting occupations (butchering, sweeping, leather working, or selling spirits) but within the confines of mercantile trade they concentrated on niches not customarily filled by Hindus. Since Mumbai was a city built by and centered on trade with Europe, there was an ever increasing number of these niches to be filled. As the Indian Industrial Commission would write during World War I, these Gujarati entrepreneurs distinguished themselves "as contractors, merchants, financiers, and shipbuilders, and have throughout shown themselves little, if at all, inferior to the English in enterprise, and usually in command of more capital."[91]

Modern-day Mumbai is the capital of the state of Maharashtra, but until the creation of this state in 1960 the city had always been at least as closely linked to Gujarati as to Marathi culture. During most of the colonial period, Gujaratis held the preponderance of economic and political power. The 1881 census shows only a bare majority of the population speaking Marathi as a first language (50.2%, compared with 26.8% Gujarati speakers and 11.6% Hindustani speakers); in 1911 the percentage of Marathi speakers would reach its highest point before or since: 50.9%, still barely half of the total. By 1961, the percentage would drop to 42.6%.[92]

In this cosmopolitan milieu, therefore, the Bohras were able to leave

behind their stigmatized minority status and become full-fledged members of society. In 1808 records show some Bohras branching out from their customary occupations so far as to join the army of the Bombay presidency. Most, however, remained in trade. While the bulk of the community opened shops and small businesses, from the early nineteenth century onward a substantial number entered banking and larger industry as well. Absolute numbers are difficult to come by until the later part of the colonial period, but by way of comparison the Khojah community (which displayed similar demographics) was said to number three thousand households at the time of the arrival of the first aga khan in 1840. The Daudi Bohras were so successful in their new environment—both in Mumbai itself and in the various Gujarati cities administered by the Bombay presidency—that by the end of the nineteenth century a colonial gazetteer would write, "the trading Bohoras, originally all Shiʿahs of the Mustaʿli branch of the great Ismaili sect, are the richest and most prosperous class of Musalmans in Gujarat."[93]

Post-Mughal Crisis of Muslim Identity

In the wake of the defeated 1857 uprising, Indian Muslim intellectuals engaged in considerable soul-searching on the topic of Islam and modernity. The final dissolution of the long-moribund Mughal empire caused a crisis of identity for Sunni Muslim elites. Some, like Sir Syed Ahmad Khan, advocated the wholesale adoption of Western technologies, ideologies, and educational practices in order to prevent the usurpation of power by the Hindu masses. Sir Syed's viewpoint made the West the standard by which all else was judged:

> I can truly say that the natives of India, high and low, merchants
> and petty shopkeepers, educated and illiterate, when contrasted
> with the English in education, manners, and uprightness, are as
> like them as a dirty animal is to an able and handsome man. The
> English have reason for believing us in India to be imbecile
> brutes.[94]

Figures with less self-hatred, like Syed Amir Ali, tried to forge a path incorporating modern thought and technology but remaining firmly grounded in Islamic tradition. Unlike Sir Syed Ahmad Khan, Syed Amir Ali rejected the notion of Western superiority: he saw Muslim culture as merely fallen from its original heights, corrupted first by the venal Umayyads, then by the Sufis, and later by the rigidity of the Hanbalites and Wahhabis. While Syed Amir Ali advocated a return to the rationalism of the Muʿtazila school of thought, Muhammad Iqbal used modernistic ter-

minology to preach a more traditionalist revival. He praised the Wahhabis and rejected the Mu'tazila, arguing that their rhetorical excesses had led to a reactionary Hanbalite backlash. Although Iqbal broke with orthodoxy in regarding the ahadith as outdated and nonbinding, he opposed any type of Westernization in matters of custom: "[E]ven the immutability of socially harmless rules relating to food and drink," he wrote, "purity and impurity, has a life-value of its own."[95]

The Bohras remained almost entirely aloof from these debates of the Sunni intelligentsia. They had never identified with the Mughal elites (quite the contrary), so the widespread Muslim crisis of identity did not affect them. The Bohras continued to follow a policy that was simultaneously more and less open to Western influences: they were far readier than the Sunnis (or most other segments of Indian society) to enter new lines of business, to use and sell Western products, to fill the social niches created by the arrival of the Europeans. At the same time, they were less anxious than many of their neighbors to ponder the larger issue of how their culture fit into the overall balance of power on the subcontinent. While the Sunnis agonized over how best to escape the forest of modernity springing up all around them, the Bohras contented themselves with carving out a small clearing in the trees.

While very few Daudi Bohras adopted Western education, ideology, or customs in the nineteenth century, more than a few filled their homes with the material comforts of European modernity. Sir John Malcolm, writing in 1823, noted that "[t]he Bohras have brought in European improvements in constructing their houses and furniture," while another observer wrote that the homes of Bohras in Sidhpur were "half European in form," and the editor of a gazetteer added, "In Surat many of the best of the modern houses belong to Bohoras."[96]

The Daudi Bohra dawat suffered a constitutional crisis in the years after 1255/1840, when the forty-sixth da'i, Syedna Muhammad Badruddin, died under suspicious circumstances. Muhammad Ali ibn Jiwabhai, author of the *Mausam-e bahar,* writes that this last of the Rajput da'is was thought to have been poisoned with a powder of finely ground diamonds—on the night before he was scheduled to announce his successor. The ascension of Syedna Abdul-Qadir Najmuddin (who was of the same lineage as the forty-fourth and forty-fifth da'is, and whose family has supplied all of the da'is from his reign forward) does not seem to have been challenged at the time. Fifteen years later, however, Abdul-Qadir's nass was called into question: since the designation had never been made in public, critics charged that the preceding da'i had been killed to prevent him from anointing a different candidate.[97]

The cloud of doubt overshadowing the nass of the forty-seventh da'i did not lead to outright schism, but continued to cast a pall over the dawat for the rest of the century. In 1876 a group of shaikhs, believing that the uncertainty over the da'i's legitimacy signaled the end of the period of satr, traveled to Arabia in hopes of finding the imam; they searched the holy places for any sign of the imam's emergence from concealment, until Ottoman authorities threw them in prison on suspicion of espionage. According to the *Mausam-e bahar* (which ends its narration with Abdul-Qadir's reign) Abdul-Qadir spent dawat funds extravagantly, ran up huge debts, and debased the standing of the Bohra ulema by bestowing the title of shaikh on friends, relatives, and wealthy donors rather than reserving it for learned religious scholars; the historical account also charges the da'i with intentionally starving the Surat Jamea of funds in order to prevent the education of scholars able to challenge his nass.[98] Whether by design or by happenstance, the Surat academy suffered a marked decline in the late nineteenth century: even the late Yusuf Najmuddin, brother of the current da'i and rector of the Surat Jamea, acknowledged that during this period the academy was little better than a *maktab* (primary school).[99]

Syedna Abdul-Qadir was succeeded in 1885 by his brother, Syedna Abdul-Husain Husamuddin, whose most notable achievement was the establishment of *musafirkhanas* (pilgrims' inns) at many important Bohra shrines.[100] By founding these lodges, Syedna Abdul-Husain fostered an institution that is today one of the more popular and widely utilized dawat services.[101] The forty-eighth da'i also campaigned against superstition, which is said to have been rife. Among the Gujarati folk beliefs common at this time was ascription of auspiciousness to the performance of certain tasks on certain days of the week: Sunday was said to be good for naming a child, eating a new dish, wearing new clothes, tilling land, or learning a new skill, but bad for buying a house or setting out on a journey; Monday was good for laying the foundation for a house, sending a bride to her husband's home, or bartering an animal; Tuesday, lucky for business or for taking a bath after an illness; Wednesday, good for shaving, changing residence, or learning a new lesson, but bad for buying a cow. Thursday, same as Wednesday, except bad for buying an elephant; Friday, ditto, except bad for buying a goat; Saturday, same again, only bad for buying a camel.[102]

Syedna Abdul-Husain was succeeded by his nephew Muhammad Burhanuddin, the son of the controversial forty-seventh da'i Abdul-Qadir (and not to be confused with the current da'i of the same name). Under his stewardship the office of the da'i declined to its lowest level of power and community influence in modern times. The legitimacy of the entire dynasty was challenged by, of all people, Muhammad Burhanuddin's own

younger brother Syedi Abdul-Qadir Hakimuddin. The da'i was subjected to the humiliation of a civil suit brought by one of his own amils, and even when accused of financial impropriety by one of his underlings he was unable to hand down a writ of excommunication. A series of stipulations was imposed upon the da'i by the powerful Bohra industrialist Sir Adamji Pirbhai, who demanded that the power of dawat officials be curtailed at all ranks. Pirbhai's sons would carry on the tradition of opposition to dawat authority, and form the foundation of the modern dissident movement.[103]

The reign of the forty-ninth da'i saw the last Bohra schism, that of the Medhibaghwalas. In 1897 a man named Abdul-Husain ibn Jiwaji claimed he had been appointed to the office of hujja by the hidden imam. The assertion, coming at a point when the da'i's legitimacy had reached a low ebb, was given more credibility than such a claim might otherwise have received. About one hundred families broke away, taking their name from the Nagpur neighborhood that became the headquarters of the new denomination. Shortly thereafter a splinter group split from this splinter group: the Atba-e Malik Vakils. Also called Artaliswalas (Forty-Eighters) for the point when they believed the line of da'is came to an end, this group was said to have given up all Muslim rituals and observance of sharia in expectation of an imminent apocalypse. The main branch of Medhibaghwalas (also known as Nagpuris) displayed less pronounced antinomianism: they too looked for the Day of Judgment in the immediate future, but regarded *namaz,* hajj, and other aspects of sharia as laudatory (though not obligatory) rather than as wholly superseded. The present community is said to consist of some one thousand individuals residing in Nagpur and Mumbai, under the leadership of a cleric by the name of Maulana Hasan Nurani.[104]

It was during the reign of the forty-ninth da'i that the gazetteer of the Bombay presidency included an eleven-page account of the Bohras that would form the basis (generally the sole firsthand basis) for all ethnographic accounts published later.[105] The account seems to have been written by a Bohra named Mian Bhai Abdul Husain, who would become a dissident by the time he published a work under his own name two decades later. The descriptive passages provide a valuable window into Bohra life of the late nineteenth century, but a careful researcher should not (as authors citing the same information in Abdul Husain's own book have generally done) mistake them for twentieth-century ethnography.

The author writes that most "Daudi customs do not, so far as has been ascertained, differ from those of ordinary Musalmans." Despite their adherence to Islamic norms, Bohras maintained a rigid barrier of identity between themselves and other Muslims:

They are attentive to their religious duties, many both men and women knowing the Kuraan. They are careful to say their prayers, to observe Muharram as a season of mourning, and to go on pilgrimage to Makkah and Kerbala. They strictly abstain from music and dancing and from using or dealing in intoxicating drinks or drugs. Though fierce sectarians, keenly hating and hated by the regular Sunnis and other Musalmans not of the Daudi sect, their reverence for Ali and for their high priest seems to be further removed from adoration among the Khojahs.[106]

Most spiritual shortcomings were said to be punished by fines, with more serious offenders (such as adulterers or drunkards) subject to flogging or excommunication.[107] But the daʻi's role was not merely that of an overseer: "[T]he head Mulla spends large sums in feeding and clothing strange and destitute Daudis, and in helping the poor among his people to meet the expenses of marriages and other costly ceremonies."[108]

In 1323/1906 Syedna Muhammad Burhanuddin ibn Abdul-Qadir was succeeded by Syedna Abdullah Badruddin, the last of the relatively weak, reactionary figures who had held power since the mid-nineteenth century. He conferred nass on his second nephew, Taher Saifuddin, who held the office from 1333/1915 until his death in 1385/1965.

Syedna Taher Saifuddin spent the first half of his reign rebuilding the legitimacy and authority of the dawat, fending off powerful challenges from dissidents, and by the time of Indian Independence his position was stronger than that of any daʻi in a century. Boldly reversing the policy of his immediate predecessors, Syedna Taher Saifuddin actively encouraged both modern education and the adoption of a wide variety of Western customs, technologies, and practices. The policies of Syedna Taher Saifuddin and his son and successor Syedna Muhammad Burhanuddin are the subject of much of the rest of this study.

Rituals of a Daudi Bohra Life ⸺⸺⸺

ETHNOGRAPHIC SOURCING

While reliable primary and secondary sources for Ismaili history and doctrine are no longer the rarities they once were, ethnographical accounts of the Bohras remain virtually nonexistent. Textual information must be gleaned from partisan sources rather than academic ones. Most cultural description previously published (generally as part of more widely ranging works) is derived almost entirely from a single source: the dissident Bohra writer Mian Bhai Abdul Husain, either through his *Gulzare Daudi* or his authorship of the segment on Bohras in the late nineteenth-century *Bombay Gazetteer*. Nearly all later source material by non-Bohra writers is essentially recapitulation (directly or via another text) of Abdul Husain.[1] In the ethnographic portions of this study I have consulted all available textual sources, but based my comments and description on participant observation, explication by authoritative dawat officials, survey responses, and interviews with community members of all degrees of orthodoxy.[2]

Most Bohra rituals are variants of pan-Islamic practices, but in all cases find a unique denominational expression through the central place of Syedna in even the most private and intimate family ceremonies. In this respect, Bohra ritual life mirrors the community's larger identity: Daudi Bohras share a basic Islamic ethos with Muslims all over the world, and have been emphasizing universal Islamic orthopraxy with increasing rigor in recent decades, but the Bohras are clearly demarcated from all other denominations by centering their spiritual lives on the person of the da'i al-mutlaq.[3]

RITES OF BOHRA CHILDHOOD

BIRTH AND INFANCY

The life of an observant Bohra is guided and shaped by the pronouncements of Syedna even before the moment of conception. A couple wishing to have children will often seek the advice and blessing of the da'i, either in person or (with ever increasing frequency) by fax or e-mail. Some would-be parents ask the da'i to pray for the health of their baby; others request a supplication specifying the child's gender. During the time they are trying to conceive, the couple may make a gift of money or food to a *fakir* once a month. In Syedna's family and other particularly traditional households, the donation takes the form of a monthly goat sacrifice with the meat distributed to the poor.

A couple experiencing fertility problems may even ask the da'i to suggest a day and time to attempt conception. In such a case Syedna would consult astrological charts and provide an answer as specific as 9:48 P.M. on the fifth day of the month of Rajab. The use of astrology in determining auspicious times for many important actions dates back to the Fatimid era, and is regarded as different from Gujarati folk belief in universally auspicious days for certain activities.

Once conception is confirmed, the couple may ask Syedna for prayers against ectopic pregnancy, miscarriage, or stillbirth. Among the more traditional segments of society, all preparations for birth might be the responsibility of the pregnant woman's sister-in-law: not only are birth procedures outside the domain of the husband, but the wife's own female relatives typically do not live in her household and the expectant mother herself is already carrying a heavy enough burden. Today, however, informants in more cosmopolitan circles (even in staunchly orthodox clerical families) report that these duties are performed by whichever relatives might happen to be available.

Selecting a Name

The only task that remains squarely the responsibility of the sister-in-law is the finding of a suitable name. In many (if not most) cases the child's name is not selected by the relatives, but bestowed by Syedna. The sister-in-law may request a name by fax or e-mail, but if possible she will seek a brief audience with Syedna and make the request in person. She (or a proxy sent in her stead) first tells Syedna the names of the other members of the family; this lets the da'i select a name with links to previous generations, and prevents the confusion of having two siblings inadvertently given the same name. Syedna makes his decision on the spot, and the par-

ents willingly accept whatever name they are given. Several times I have seen family representatives approach the daʿi after a religious ceremony, recite the list of their relatives' names, and have Syedna give them his decision—all in the space of about a minute. In most cases, Syedna will provide two names: one for a boy, one for a girl. Occasionally he will provide only a boy's name. This is regarded as a sign that the baby will definitely be male, since a name given by Syedna cannot be discarded at the parents' whim. Even Bohras who select their children's names without Syedna's guidance limit their choices to those traditionally considered Muslim. Like other Shiʿa, Bohras avoid the names of the first three Sunni caliphs: Abu Bakr, Umar, and Uthman. Hindu, Western, or Parsi names are not deemed acceptable.[4]

The number of families asking Syedna to choose their children's names seems to have risen considerably in recent decades. This is due partly to a heightened sense of the need for orthopraxy felt throughout the community since the late 1970s, but principally to the increased availability of modern means of communication. Two generations ago, Bohras who lived anywhere but Mumbai or Surat had far greater difficulty merely making the request: before the rise of domestic air travel the daʿi made fewer trips to cities outside Gujarat or Maharashtra, and inhabitants of far-flung communities made fewer trips to sites of Syedna's audiences.

Even before the advent of widespread Internet access, an overwhelming 84.8% of my survey respondents had asked Syedna to name their children. Spiritual guidance in selecting children's names is clearly seen as an important dawat service, but not as an absolute necessity. Only 3.5% of those providing rankings cited the naming of children as their first priority, while 16.0% rated it as one of the top two dawat services.[5] One measure of the Bohras' eager use of technology is that the percentages of households requesting children's names do not vary significantly with the community's geographical distance from the dawat center: respondents from Karachi and Calcutta (farther away, but more likely to own telephones) requested names slightly *more* often those from relatively nearby Nagpur.[6]

Birth

As the time of birth approaches, the sister-in-law or her proxy may approach Syedna for a gift of dried dates and holy water. These are believed to speed a late birth: if the baby is long overdue, the mother eats the dates and drinks the water. If she gives birth on or before schedule, she passes the dried dates to another pregnant woman and pours the water onto a patch of soil.[7]

In small towns childbirth is still performed at home, but in Mumbai and most other large cities Bohra women generally deliver their babies in hospitals. Those who can (there is often a long waiting list) go to Bohra clinics such as Mumbai's Saifee Hospital, where doctors' fees, room, board, and all other expenses (with the exception of medicine) are paid by the dawat. Others go to public hospitals or to private Christian or Parsi institutions, and there is no stigma attached to this.

While at the hospital, rules of gender segregation are essentially the same as those of everyday Bohra purdah. A woman is expected to refrain from physical contact with men other than her husband or blood relatives, and likewise to keep her body and hair covered whenever in the presence of men outside her family. One observant woman reported that during her pregnancy she taped a note outside her hospital door reading, "NO MEN." This was not an absolute prohibition (she would have had no objection to any necessary male medical personnel), but merely a convenience to save her the trouble of dashing for modest clothing whenever an orderly or hospital administrator might barge in unannounced.

Once the expectant mother begins her labor, however, no men or boys except the husband (and any essential medical staff) are permitted to enter the room. Female family members sit at her bedside and recite verses of the Qur'an. A professional obstetrician (female, if possible) delivers the baby, but many Bohras observe the traditional custom of having an older woman from the mother's family lift the infant to the mother's chest.

The very first words that a Bohra hears upon entering the world are those of the *adhan* (the call to prayer) chanted into his or her ear. This is a custom common to many Muslims, but has particular significance for the Bohras owing to its tie to the birth practices of the ahl al-bayt (family of the Prophet): according to ahadith, a credible eyewitness reported, "I have seen the Prophet proclaiming Azan into the ears of Hasan when he was born."[8]

A hallmark of Bohra attitudes toward birth is the complete complementarity of traditional and modern practices. In all matters relating to the health of mother and newborn, Bohras avail themselves of every modern medical tool, drug, and practice. This separates them from many Indian Muslim communities, who often rely on traditional midwives from the same "polluted" Hindu jatis that serve the Hindu majority.[9] In matters with no direct bearing on health or hygiene, however (such as insistence on female medical professionals whenever possible), the Bohras maintain their traditional customs.

Birth rituals are considered important, but not as central as other aspects of orthopraxy. My survey respondents ranked their importance only

seventh out of ten practices listed, and more than one-third did not even place them in the top ten.[10]

Circumcision

Rituals surrounding *khatna* (circumcision) are given significantly less prominence by the Bohras than by many other Muslim groups.[11] The operation itself is generally performed at the hospital shortly after birth, by a medical professional rather than a traditional practitioner. When questioned, sources said this was simply a commonsense precaution: modern surgical methods offer better hygiene and fewer health risks, and are therefore preferred to more traditional techniques. "After all" (one male source noted) "this is not an area where you can afford to make a mistake."

The ceremony accompanying circumcision is performed long after the surgical operation. It is commonly delayed until the boy is seven years old, but can take place at any convenient time during childhood.[12] While all male Bohras must be circumcised, the accompanying ritual is not accorded paramount importance and is tacked onto any other major celebration. It commonly consists simply of the boy wearing a veil of flowers around his brow and being led through the family's *chawl* while seated on a horse. As is the case with all Bohra rites, it is considered particularly desirable to have the khatna ritual presided over by Syedna himself. In many Bohra communities the boys will all be circumcised immediately after birth, but hold a joint khatna celebration years later, at whatever time the da'i happens to visit their city.

Female circumcision among the Bohras, as among some other Muslim denominations, is a matter of great controversy. The Bombay census report of 1911 noted the practice of clitorectomy in the Bohra community, but the reliability of this information is difficult to gauge. Sources within the community have given me wildly conflicting testimony: I have at various times been told the custom is absolutely forbidden, that it is occasionally carried out in secret, and that most Bohra girls are subjected to it. Whether the custom is extinct, extremely rare, or still widely practiced, it is a topic on which no male researcher (particularly one outside the community) can speak with real authority.[13] An issue of such seriousness, however, would be an important area for investigation by a sensitive researcher, particularly a female community member.

Khak-e Shifa Mahti

Each day for three days the newborn is fed a tiny pinch of *khak-e shifa mahti*—soil taken from the holy ground at Kerbala. Every Bohra who makes the pilgrimage to this site brings back a supply of soil for any future

births in his or her extended family. The soil is ground into a fine powder, then dissolved in water and given to the infant in a small spoon. It is believed to have not only spiritual benefits, but medicinal ones as well. As a concession to modern medical practice, today this ceremony takes place only once the doctor has given her approval. Instead of the first three days of life, it is generally conducted on the first three days after the newborn leaves the hospital.

Chatti

On the sixth day after birth the *chatti* ceremony is held at home, for close relatives. This is the time when the sister-in-law announces the name she has solicited from Syedna: until the chatti ceremony she has not told anyone else in the family, including the parents themselves. The sister-in-law whispers the name into the infant's right ear while facing in the direction of *qiblah*. For the next five or ten minutes the relatives all try to guess the new name, until the sister-in-law tells the mother, who tells the rest of the family. The parents then give the sister-in-law presents (often articles of clothing) as thanks for her diligent work over the preceding nine months.

The chatti ceremony ends with the baby receiving its first clothing, a tiny kurta sewn by the sister-in-law. She will have obtained the material for this kurta (the "sixth day's cloth") from the da'i: if at all possible, a piece of fabric cut from clothing worn by Syedna himself. The da'i makes a point of wearing and discarding a great number of kurtas to make sure that there is always a plentiful stock of sixth day's cloth, but demand far outstrips supply. Material from Syedna's own clothing is distributed to the da'i's relatives and individuals of great importance, while Bohras with less influence are given material blessed (but not previously worn) by Maulana.

As is the case for so many Bohra customs, several generations back the sixth day's cloth was a practice often limited to Surtis* and families with close personal ties to the da'i. Again, rapid spread of modern communication has enabled a greater cross-section of the Bohra population to seek the religious favors that once would have been beyond their reach. Today many Bohras living overseas ask a friend or relative in Mumbai to obtain the sixth day's cloth and send it to them by Federal Express or DHL. Until recently, the idea of entrusting blessed material to the untender mercies of the Indian postal system would have run dangerously close to blasphemy.

*People whose ancestral origin is in the city of Surat. This group comprises the de facto aristocracy of the Daudi Bohras.

Aqiqa

The major ritual of childhood is the aqiqa ceremony: it can be held on the seventh, fourteenth, or twenty-first day after birth, but to give the new-born a chance to gain strength the latter two dates are preferred. If the ceremony is not held by the third week after birth it must wait until the child has entered adolescence. Where the chatti ceremony is small, informal, and limited to the close family, the aqiqa is a large, ritualized, semipublic affair. All of the baby's hair is shaved off, weighed, and buried in the ground. Later, the family will present a fakir with a bar of silver equivalent in weight to the baby's shaved hair. Today coins are generally substituted, and the sum is nominal: with a gram of silver costing no more than 20 rupees in Mumbai at the time of my fieldwork, the typical gift was less than one dollar.

After the hair is shaved and weighed, the family sacrifices a flawless goat and daubs the infant's forehead with its blood. The aqiqa goat must be without physical defect, strong and healthy, with four sound limbs and two good horns. This ceremony is in part a reenactment of the legendary episode in which Ibrahim's sacrifice of his son Ismail is avoided by the divine substitution of a goat for the infant (cf. Qur'an 37: 102–113). The sacrifice generally takes place in the chawl of the *mohalla*[14]—not in the family's own apartment, but not at the masjid or at a butcher's shop. After being slaughtered the goat is skinned, dismembered, cooked, and served to the assembled relatives. Since the typical aqiqa kid is often too small to feed all of the invited guests, several other goats are served as well. These need not be slaughtered on the spot, nor need they be up to the aqiqa kid's standard of physical perfection.

Both the hair shaving and the goat sacrifice are pan-Islamic rites. The codifying Sunni theologian al-Ghazali states: "It is sunnat to give in charity gold or silver to the weight of the hairs of the child." He stipulates, however, that the ceremony be performed on the seventh rather than the sixth day after birth, and cites a hadith in which the Prophet orders his daughter Fatima to perform this ritual for the newborn Husain.[15] As for the ritual of aqiqa (in Arabic, *ʿaqiqah* = sacrifice), Ibn Hanbal held its performance on the seventh day after birth to be obligatory, while the founders of the other three Sunni schools of law regarded the rite as less than wholly mandatory. Al-Ghazali suggests the sacrifice of one goat after the birth of a girl and two after the birth of a boy.[16]

Anthropologists (most famously, Structuralists in the tradition of Claude Lévi-Strauss) sometimes examine religious ceremonies for universal symbolic meanings unknown to the participants themselves.[17] At first

glance, the aqiqa ceremony might seem a rich lode for such mythograph-
ical excavation: since the aqiqa goat is often a young, frisky kid, it might
be considered a symbolic substitute for the newborn child. Such interpre-
tation would be bolstered by the fact that the baby's mother (alone among
all the family) is forbidden to partake of the feast. If the breast-feeding
mother were to eat, the baby (in effect) would be eating its symbolic self.

Closer examination, however, demonstrates the dangers of trying to
second-guess one's own sources. In this case, the plain facts showed a
certain ethnographer that he wasn't nearly as clever as he'd thought: many
of the same rules that govern the Bohra aqiqa ceremony also apply to
the goat sacrifice at Eid al-Adha. The hajji performing his ritual duty is like-
wise forbidden to eat the meat of the goat he has slaughtered, so in this
instance the animal must have some other symbolic meaning. As it hap-
pens, the puzzle needs no Structuralist deciphering—the mother at aqiqa
and the hajji at Eid al-Adha both refrain out of ritualized selflessness. As
generous, openhanded hosts, they cannot partake of the feast until all of
their guests have eaten their fill. Once the first goat has been consumed,
aqiqa mother and hajji alike are free to dine on mutton from any other
goats slaughtered to round out the meal.

My Bohra friends were gentle in disabusing me of my carefully con-
structed notions. When seeking explanations for other rituals I have since
tried to set aside attempts at societal psychoanalysis, and simply ask.

CHILDHOOD

First Words

Children begin learning how to speak after about a year. Some Bohras try
to insure that the first word out of their child's mouth be "Allah"—the be-
ginning, middle, and end of a pious Muslim's life. Where Western parents
often prompt their infants to say family nicknames like Mama or Dada,
Bohra parents may teach their children the names of the family central to
their faith: Muhammad, Fatima, Ali, Hasan, and Husain.[18] This custom is
far from universal, however. As the religiously observant father of a new-
born explained, "Sure, we'll be pleased if the first word our son utters is
'God'—but an infant is not a tape-recorder."

Salaam-e Syedna

An observant Bohra makes personal *salaam* to Syedna as often as an op-
portunity presents itself. The salaam-e Syedna consists of kissing the daʿi's
right hand and asking for his duʿa. The first time a child makes salaam is

an important rite of passage, the culmination of much parental coaching. Some children make their first salaam at a public function, but private sessions are also scheduled periodically for groups of children to make their first salaam together. For Bohras living far from Mumbai, a child's first salaam can be more difficult to arrange: in more remote towns, all the children of the community, regardless of age, make their first salaam whenever the da'i happens to visit the city. Babies too small to kiss the hand of the da'i are placed on a pillow, and Syedna gently rests his right foot on the child's body.

Namaz

Learning how to say namaz (Arabic: *salat*) marks a major step in the development of every Bohra child. The content of the daily prayers differs little from that of other Muslims. Like all Muslims, Bohras pray five times each day. Like most Shi'a, they say the five obligatory prayers at three times: *fajr* (dawn) prayers in the morning, *zuhr* and *ashr* (midday and afternoon) prayers in the middle of the day, and *maghrib* and *isha* (sunset and night-time) prayers in the evening. This practice has the support of some Sunni hadith tradition as well. The Bohras take a short break between their zuhr and ashr prayers, and between their maghrib and isha prayers, thus maintaining the orthopraxy of five distinct salats each day.[19]

Adolescence: Mithaq

The central rite of passage for Bohras is *mithaq*,* the only major ritual unique to the denomination. This ceremony, obligatory for every Bohra who wishes to be part of the community, is a covenant between the believer and God, effected through his wali. In addition to spelling out the duties a believer owes to Allah, it includes an oath of allegiance: a vow to accept the spiritual guidance of Syedna wholeheartedly and without reservation. Before mithaq, a Bohra is a child. After mithaq, he or she is an adult, with all the rights and responsibilities of any mature member of the community.

The mithaq oath is first taken at whatever age a child is deemed to have reached maturity: most commonly, thirteen years for girls, fourteen or fifteen for boys. During early puberty, a child will be brought by his or her parents for an interview with the local amil. The amil asks the youth a series of questions about the Bohra faith, and only after providing adequate answers will the child be accepted for mithaq.

*The name of this rite is often transliterated "misaq."

Mithaq can be administered individually or in a group induction, depending on the number of adolescents a local community may have. In small towns it may be given for a single child, while oaths administered by Syedna himself typically draw thousands of inductees. Usually the mithaq ceremony is held at the local masjid, but it can also be held in a private home or a rented hall. Boys and girls go through the half-hour mithaq ritual together, but for the first time in their lives they are segregated by gender.

Until mithaq, Bohra children of both sexes are permitted to wander freely between the spheres of men and of women. Even during the holiest of religious functions it is not uncommon to see a father taking his young daughter to pray in the men's section of a masjid. After mithaq, however, a girl is considered a woman, and must be certain to keep purdah. While purdah in the Bohra community is far less restrictive than in many other Muslim groups, its observance in such ritual settings as the masjid is obligatory.

On the eighteenth day of the Islamic month of zyl-Hajj, every Bohra congregation renews its mithaq vows together. The ceremony takes place on this date because (Shi'a tradition holds) it was on the eighteenth of zyl-Hajj in the year 23 A.H. that the Prophet Muhammad and his son-in-law Ali received an oath of mithaq from 70,000 new Muslims at Ghadir Khumm on the road from Mecca to Medina. The oath is said to hearken back to a verse from the Qur'an: "God purchased from all the faithful their souls and their property in consideration of Paradise."[20]

The amil administering the oath recites a series of questions, after each exhorting the congregation to "say yes." Every question is a specific promise, a specific vow to God and to the imam (and, during the imam's occultation, to the da'i). To every question, the congregation replies with a resounding "Nam," Arabic for "yes."[21] The wording of the mithaq oath, it should be noted, is a source of great internal controversy: since the vows explicitly bind the inductees to obey all of the da'i's instructions in both spiritual and temporal matters, they are central to the issue of dawat hegemony. Mithaq is the foundation for the legitimacy of dawat control, so dissidents have challenged the authenticity of the oath itself. The only published texts of the mithaq oath are identical versions printed in a variety of dissident works, all of them ultimately traceable to a text of 1920.[22] The dawat has not authorized publication of the modern-day text and does not allow the tape-recording of religious ceremonies without permission, so I cannot provide an alternate transcript for the service I attended. The substance of the oath, however, does not seem to be in dispute: orthodox and dissident Bohras disagree on the precise wording and the provenance of the mithaq oath, but agree that in its current form it requires inductees to swear unfettered obedience to God and to Syedna.

Once the group reaffirmation of mithaq is over, all the new oath-takers step forward to make their pledges separately. Until fifteen or twenty years ago, Syedna used to spend many hours on the eighteenth of zyl-Hajj personally accepting mithaq from every first-time oath-taker. Now, owing to his advanced age and the increasing numbers of inductees, he takes mithaq from a dozen or so carefully selected youths but delegates another high cleric to accept the pledges of the others. Outside Mumbai (or wherever Syedna might be on that date), it is the local amil who accepts the mithaq pledge on his behalf.

The eighteenth of zyl-Hajj mithaq ceremony that I observed at Saifee Masjid began after a long *majlis* with open-palm matam. Syedna was out of Mumbai, so the *mukasir,** Syedi Husain Bhaisaheb Husamuddin, served as prayer leader. The replies of "Nam" to Mukasir Saheb's questions were unanimous, if more restrained than the full-throated roars of "Ya Husain" which had echoed through the masjid during matam a few minutes before. The mithaq lasted about twenty minutes, just prior to midday namaz. The mukasir spent a few minutes with each first-time mithaq candidate, pressing to insure that he or she was taking the oath freely and with full knowledge of its meaning. Male candidates held the mukasir's hand while answering, but female candidates (in the first mark of their new status as women) held one end of a piece of string while the cleric held the other.

Dissidents view the oath of allegiance as an infringement on their rights: some Bohras refuse to take the oath, and some others take it unhappily. The vast majority of my informants, however, did not regard mithaq as oppressive: some saw it merely as a symbolic gesture, while most viewed it as a sacred covenant.[23] Whatever private reservations some members of the community might have, mithaq remains a central ritual of the faith. Not only is it the fundamental rite of passage from childhood to adulthood for boys and girls alike, it also continues to be a pledge renewed—to outward appearances, at least, quite voluntarily—by all observant Bohra adults every year.

RITUALS OF ADULTHOOD

MARRIAGE

The legal institution of marriage for Bohras, as for all orthodox Muslims, is *nikah*. Strictly speaking, this is less a religious sacrament than a personal

*"Mukasir Saheb" is the honorific form commonly used when referring to the office-holder by his title.

contract, a negotiated domestic alliance between two individuals and between two families. The theory of nikah is similar for Bohras and other Muslims,[24] but the da'i's absolute centrality in all aspects of life serves to sacralize marriage to a greater degree than in most other denominations. In practice, the area of marriage customs shows the Bohras' syncretic melding of universalistic Islamic and local Hindu traditions: while nikah formally "makes" the marriage, informal *shadi* rites (generally borrowed, like their name, from Hindu usage) are the focus of more lavish celebration.

There is no confusion over which of the two is more important: the Bohras are Muslims first and foremost, so nikah trumps shadi. But Bohra attitudes toward marriage are indicative of the larger theme of this study: the openness that Bohras currently display toward Western ideas, practices, and technologies is thoroughly in line with their age-old openness to outside influence even on customs as pivotal as those related to marriage. A central portion of Daudi culture and identity is native Indian rather than pan-Islamic in origin: Gujarati language, eating at the communal *thal,* and dressing in kurta and pajamas, to name but a few elements. With marriage customs, as with modernity in general, anything not deemed contrary to the basics of Islam may be embraced wholeheartedly. The union of old and new custom is itself a marriage: sometimes rocky, sometimes in need of individual accommodation, but generally (one hopes) harmonious in the end.

Respondents to my survey rated marriage rites only of intermediate importance as a basic marker of faith: less important than contact with the da'i, pilgrimage, manner of dress and eating, or funerary rituals: while considered among the top ten values of the faith by 67.9 %, marriage rites were ranked only sixth on that list. This highlights the essentially contractual rather than sacral nature of the institution—while not considered a primary religious obligation, it is clearly the centerpiece of almost every Bohra's life.

Engagement (Nizbat)

Arrangements for marriage begin soon after a youth has taken mithaq. Unlike some Indian communities (both Muslim and Hindu), Bohras do not permit child marriage or betrothal. Keith Hodkinson notes that throughout much of the Sunni world nikah can take place as soon as both parties have entered puberty, which in some communities can be reckoned as twelve for boys and nine for girls. Children younger than this can be wed provisionally, but are free to repudiate their (presumably unconsummated) union upon reaching legal adulthood.[25] Until the decades prior to

Indian Independence, child marriage was widely practiced by Ithna-Asharis.[26] Colonial authorities attempted to curtail the practice with the Child Marriage Restraint Act, but as late as 1943 a dawat attorney could set out the rules governing child marriage in matter-of-fact terms: the guardians of both boys and girls could make legally binding unions, even without the explicit consent of the parties involved. "A minor boy on attaining puberty may divorce his wife," Abbasali Najafali writes, "but a girl on attaining puberty cannot revoke her marriage."[27] Among today's Daudi Bohras, however, any childhood matchmaking is merely speculative: relatives may dream up advantageous unions for children fresh out of the womb, but serious discussions wait until the youths have passed the age of mithaq.

Regardless of how soon it follows the oath of allegiance, for most Bohras, nizbat is the next life ritual after this coming-of-age ceremony. Even if the engagement is made while the parties are in their teens, the actual wedding is generally put off until both the bride and the groom have finished as much schooling as they intend to complete, and until the groom has enough financial security to start a family. With high-school education becoming the minimum norm and higher education increasingly expected of both spouses, a couple will typically marry when the groom is in his early to mid-twenties and the bride in her late teens or early twenties.

The age of marriage among Bohras is marginally later than that of other Indian Shi'a, but well within the statistical mainstream. In a nationwide survey of Shi'a, 99.5% preferred boys to marry after the age of 18, with 70% expressing a further preference for delaying until the early to mid-twenties.[28] Opinions about the optimal age of marriage are directly related to education: 62% of illiterates cited the ages 15–20 as optimal for boys, while more educated segments of the population favored later weddings to allow the boy to finish his schooling.[29] Another survey found northern Indian Shi'a were somewhat more traditional than the national average: 86.2% listed the preferred age for a groom at 18–26, while 91.2% said the prime age for a bride was 12–20. More than one-quarter cited the ages 9–14 as ideal for a bride, despite the illegality of child marriage.[30]

Despite its dominant position in most aspects of Bohra life, the Daudi clergy plays a remarkably small part in the process of matchmaking for members of the community. Fewer than one-third of my survey respondents reported even seeking dawat assistance, and a mere 2.1% listed matchmaking as one of the two most important dawat services. These rates are significantly lower than those for musafirkhanas, naming chil-

dren, no-interest loans, and even business contacts. Perhaps even more telling: while barely one-quarter of respondents considered the dawat helpful in finding marriage partners, nearly three-quarters acknowledged the usefulness of modern technology (phone, fax, air travel) in matchmaking. Over half of the respondents explicitly noted that technology had served them better than the dawat in the search for mates, while a mere 3.7% said that the dawat had been more helpful than technology. Surprisingly, members of clerical *khidmat** families reported *less* dawat assistance than did members of nonclerical families: a mere 14.8% of khidmat families reported dawat help, while 55.6% (marginally higher than the norm) reported only technological aid.[31]

Mahr

Like other Muslims, whether Shi'a or Sunni, Bohras give *mahr* (dower) at every wedding.[32] Mahr, the Bohras are quick to point out, is quite different from dowry, an institution that has caused the ruin of many a Hindu family. Dowries in India are often a crushing financial burden on the family of a bride: dowry is commonly equivalent to two years' wages for the father, and if a groom is particularly sought-after the sum can easily run up to several million rupees. As John Esposito notes, dowry has no textual basis in Islam, but is firmly rooted in the tradition of some Muslim communities; it is not uncommon for the bride's family to provide clothing, money, and jewelry that are theoretically still the property of the bride but become the de facto property of the husband and his family.[33]

Mahr, by contrast, is paid by the groom—to the bride herself. This should not be confused with a bride-price paid to the *family* of the bride, which in Islamic terms would be forbidden as an act equivalent to purchasing a wife. Mahr is an Arabian custom that predates Islam and was specifically advocated by the Prophet Muhammad as a disincentive to divorce.[34] The dower (in theory, at least) becomes the inalienable property of the bride, a payment for her virginity (*nafs,* or "self") and an insurance policy for the marriage's survival. The husband will have rights over all other marital property, but the mahr is the bride's alone. In previous generations the mahr may have been a guarantor of the wife's independence, but owing to inflation the traditional sum has been reduced in value to a symbolic rather than actual deterrent to divorce.

In the Bohra community the amount of the mahr is often Rs 786, a number equivalent to the numeric value of the letters in the Arabic tran-

*Khidmat ("service") is the term employed for any type of dawat work. Members of the clerical hierarchy, from the highest to the lowest, are all described as being in khidmat.

scriptions of the word *bismillah* (In the name of God). This figure is not automatically determined, however, and must be negotiated by the two families prior to the nikah. In the mid-twentieth century, mahr could be Rs 40 or 41, Rs 100 or 110, or even a service such as teaching a chapter of the Qur'an.[35] Ismail Lambat reports that among the Sunni Vohras of South Gujarat mahr is set at Rs 127.50, for no known reason.[36] This same unusual figure of Rs 127.50 is the mahr reported for other Gujarati Muslim groups such as the Chhaparbandhs and the Mansuri-Tantgaras. Still other Gujarati Muslims have nearly identical rates: Rs 127 for Bhands, Dhobis, Khatris, and Hajams, while the Maliks and the Marwadis set mahr at Rs 125.[37] In the present-day Daudi Bohra community, acceptable figures for mahr apart from Rs 786 include Rs 452, Rs 552, or any other number ending in the digits 52. This number is chosen because the present da'i, Muhammad Burhanuddin, is the fifty-second da'i al-mutlaq of the Daudi Bohra succession.

Throughout the Shi'a world, a low or nominal mahr is generally deemed more meritorious than a high one.[38] This preference is based on the example of the Prophet Muhammad, who is said to have demanded only a token dower when he gave Ali his daughter Fatima in marriage. Such a tradition would have significance for all Muslims, but particular strength for Shi'a because of their special reverence for the ahl al-bayt. A token mahr is therefore referred to as "sharia-mahr" or "mahr-e-Fatimi." The practice of setting the mahr at a numerically symbolic value is not unique to Gujarati Muslims: Ithna-Ashariyya in other parts of India set the sharia mahr at Rs 1,100, a figure believed to equal that of Fatima's dower.[39]

This appears to be another example of the Bohras maintaining orthopraxic norms more scrupulously than many other Muslims of the subcontinent. In their survey of Shi'a throughout India, Hasnain and Husain report that nearly one third of respondents paid more than Rs 1,100, and 4.1% paid mahr in excess of 1 *lakh* (Rs 100,000). It is noteworthy, however, that in the two states where Bohras are most concentrated—Maharashtra and especially Gujarat—the general Shi'a population paid considerably lower mahr than the all-India average.[40]

Likewise, Bohras seem to stick closer than other Muslim groups to traditional avoidance of dowry. The practice is forbidden by the dawat, and this ban appears to be widely obeyed. No Bohras I met acknowledged giving or taking dowry, or even hearing of the practice within the community—although there is sometimes a fine line between a dowry per se and a generous wedding present given to the couple by the parents of the bride. By contrast, 30.2% of Hasnain and Husain's Shi'a respondents acknowledged accepting dowry. Bohra practices in dowry (as in dower) are

much closer to those of other Shi'a in Maharashtra and Gujarat than to Shi'a elsewhere in India: 90% of survey respondents in Maharashtra eschewed dowry, as did 95% of the Shi'a in the Bohras' ancestral home of Gujarat.[41]

Nikah

Under the provisions of the Special Marriages Act of 1954, any Indian Muslim has the option of marrying either by nikah or by civil law. Those who opt for a civil marriage are bound by the secular provisions that apply to the rest of the civil population, while those who select nikah are governed by the *shariat** of their own community.[42] The shariat for Bohra nikah is in basic accord with that of other Muslim groups—with the crucial addition of Syedna as the ultimate sanctioning agent.

In order for a Muslim marriage to be acknowledged as legitimate, the woman must give her free consent in front of two *shahideen* (witnesses). The shahideen can be anyone, but are usually relatives of the woman. They must sign a document attesting to the woman's acquiescence, because the bride herself (in a ritual manifestation of purdah) will not be present during the actual nikah ceremony. Apart from the requirement that both bride and groom must have already taken mithaq before receiving permission to marry, a Bohra nikah contains most of the same elements found in Sunni or Ithna-Ashari nikahs.[43]

Generally the amil will take the bride aside just before the ceremony and spend a few minutes talking with her in private. He makes certain that she is agreeing to the marriage of her own free will, has full understanding of what it means, and is not being pressured or forced into the decision. The bride is perfectly free to back out even at this late date: one source who knew his fiancée well enough for the union to be classified as a "love match" confided that many grooms experience a moment of trepidation when, with all the guests assembled and waiting, Syedna or his amil takes the woman aside and gives her the opportunity to call the wedding off. At very least this indicates that female consent is more than a mere formality. By way of contrast, in Abrar Husain's survey of Uttar Pradesh Shi'a in 1976, 65% of respondents said they did not think it necessary for the bride to give her consent to a union.[44]

The public nature of the marriage union, demonstrated by the necessity of witnesses and clerical supervision, is a point on which Bohra practice diverges from the Shi'a norm. Since the late nineteenth or early twen-

*Shariat, Islamic law relating to marriage and other family matters, is a subsection of sharia, Islamic law in general.

tieth century, marriage documents have been filled out in four copies: one for the groom, one for the bride's guardian, one for the local jamat, and one for the central dawat records.[45] Whereas Sunni custom requires witnesses of a marriage's formation but not of its dissolution (a man may utter the triple *talaq* in a fit of passion at home, for example), mainstream Ithna-Ashari Shiʿa practice requires witnesses for a divorce but none for a wedding.[46] Provided both parties agree that the marriage has taken place, it is generally regarded as a purely private affair. In this respect the Bohras differ from both branches of Islam: virtually no aspect of personal life is treated as a purely private affair. The guidance, permission, and blessing of Syedna (directly or through his local amil) are fundamental aspects of every important action an observant Bohra may undertake.

This central role of the dawat adds a sacral element to nikah that is largely absent in most other branches of Islam. While Hinduism and Christianity treat marriage as a sacrament, almost all Muslim denominations regard it as a civil contract (albeit with strong religious overtones).[47] In orthodox Bohra doctrine, however, any marriage that is not affirmatively blessed by the daʿi or his representative is null and void. As textual justification the dawat cites a saying of the Prophet authenticated by the Fatimid jurist Qadi al-Nuʿman: "Every nikah wherein the khutba is not recited and performed is like a leprous hand."[48]

Colonial-era dawat attorney Shaikh Abbasali Najafali, in a work aimed at clarifying Bohra personal law for the cases decided in public courts presided over by British judges, argued that the very concept of marriage was different among the Bohras than in other denominations: "According to this sect, nikah is primarily a sacrament," he wrote in 1943; "it is only secondarily that nikah is a contract."[49] This position, however, is debatable. Bohras commonly seek the blessing and guidance of Syedna when starting a business, buying real estate, making a voyage, sending their children to a new school, or beginning any other major secular undertaking. In marriage, as in all aspects of life, the daʿi is looked upon as the ultimate source of instruction, advice, and spiritual sanction. The line between affirmative blessing and tacit permission of nikah is a fine one, and has (informants tell me) been blurred in the recent past. Since the daʿi's spiritual authority reaches all corners of Bohra life, in a sense there is no aspect of existence that is *not* primarily a sacrament. Whether this is more pronounced for nikah than for other important facets of life is a question I will leave for the theologians.

The ritual of nikah is limited to men and boys. In part this is due to a symbolic maintenance of purdah, but since gender segregation is far less strict today than in previous times it may also be interpreted as a reaffir-

mation of wider kinship principles.* Nikah is a union of families more than of individuals, a wedding not of two people but of two bloodlines. The bride, therefore, is represented by the head of her patrilineal bloodline: her father, grandfather, or other male relative.[50] Female members of both families observe the ceremony from a screened-off enclosure, but they are not part of the nikah rite itself.

Mahr is generally paid at the nikah itself: among Shi'a this form of mahr payment is termed *muajjal* (prompt payment), and is distinguished from *muwajjal* (deferred payment), which seldom occurs among the Bohras. Muajjal is preferred among most Shi'a, because Ali paid his full mahr at his wedding to Fatima.[51] Once the amount of the mahr is agreed upon publicly (well before the wedding), the nikah certificate is signed by the bride, the groom, and two witnesses. One copy is given to each family, and one copy is sent to the office of records at the local *jamatkhana* (community office). Then the wedding party goes to the masjid to seal the *nikahnama* (marriage contract) with a religious blessing.

At the masjid, the groom stands to the right of the amil and the bride's father stands to the left. They clasp their right hands together with fingers interlaced, and the amil wraps a handkerchief around their wrists. He praises God and the imams, and says that he recognizes the union according to shariat. The amil makes the groom promise to accept the bride, to keep her happy, never to beat or mistreat her, never to abandon her or divorce her without good cause. The groom so promises, then the father of the bride says to him, "I give you my daughter in God's name, and accept X amount of mahr [on her behalf]." The mahr is then given, and the families exchange whatever gifts they wish, sometimes using the amil as intermediary.[52]

The point on which a Bohra nikah differs most strikingly from those of all other Muslim groups is the oath of allegiance. A basic and absolutely necessary requirement of every Bohra union is mithaq: not only must the bride and groom have made their pledge before nikah can be finalized, but their parents must have done so as well. Nikahs were sometimes celebrated without mithaq in the recent past, but since the retrenchment of orthopraxy instituted by the current da'i in the late 1970s no cleric is permitted to perform nikah rites for any individual who has not offered mithaq. This is a powerful tool in the enforcement of clerical hegemony: even the fieriest dissidents must think twice before opposing the dawat when they have children's weddings to consider.

*An equally valid case could be made that the symbolism upheld is patriarchal dominance rather than patrilineal kinship structures. The relative importance of gender politics versus kinship patterns is a question I will leave for the social theorists.

Quite frequently, several families will arrange a joint marriage cere-
mony to save on expenses. Often there will be some sort of kinship tie
linking the participants: the grooms will all be brothers or cousins, for ex-
ample. In smaller *jamats,* families with no connections of blood may cele-
brate their weddings simultaneously for reasons of economy or conven-
ience. The most sought-after type of nikah is a ceremony at which Syedna
himself officiates. To be married under Syedna's auspices is one of the
highest honors a Bohra can hope to attain, and weddings are often delayed
by years or shifted to cities far distant from either family's home in order
to find a space on the da'i's calendar. Even so, it is a privilege generally re-
served for Syedna's blood relatives and members of other highly influen-
tial families.

Shadi

Despite the deep Islamic roots of an obligatory marriage banquet,[53] the
Bohra wedding feast is generally associated not with the nikah, but with
the complementary custom of shadi. The word is taken directly from the
Hindu community, and means "wedding" in both Hindi and Gujarati. It
seems likely that when the Bohras converted from Hinduism they retained
many of their traditional social customs for marriage while adopting the
Islamic nikah as a legal standard of legitimacy. This syncretism is well
within the mainstream of subcontinental Islam: as Imtiaz Ahmad notes,
while the nikah universally establishes the legitimacy of a union, in Mus-
lim communities throughout India it is often completely overshadowed by
shadi festivities.[54]

While nikah is a private contractual matter between two families,
shadi is an occasion for public celebration and ostentatious display. Few
relatives (let alone strangers) attend the nikah, while everyone with even
a passing acquaintance of either family is invited to the shadi. Marriages
in the humbler ranks of society often bring together all members of the lo-
cal Bohra population, while those of elite families tend to attract friends
and relatives from all parts of the Bohra world. In past generations the
feast would have been held at the jamatkhana or a private house, catered
by Bohra chefs specializing in such affairs, but today a shadi is equally
likely to be held in the banquet hall of a large hotel. In Mumbai the shadi
usually lasts only one day, but in smaller villages or in royal circles it often
encompasses three or four days of continuous feasting and festivities. The
Hindu religious rituals of shadi are eliminated in the Bohra community,
leaving the custom as primarily an exercise in the prodigious consump-
tion of delicious foods. At royal shadis held in Saifee Mahal, it is not un-
common for the number of guests to exceed 5,000.

Other Indian Shiʿa, particularly in the North, celebrate a *walima* feast on the day after the nikah. The significance of this rite is that the Prophet held a feast for Fatima and Ali the day after their marriage, but the Bohras celebrate virtually every holiday of note with a large ziyafat. Among Uttar Pradesh Shiʿa surveyed by Abrar Husain, nearly three-quarters considered the walima to be compulsory, though opinions on its obligatory nature varied with educational level: 91.7% of illiterates but only 44% of college graduates deemed it vital. Whether or not the walima was seen as a *hukm-e-shariat* (holy obligation), 94% said they had had such a feast after their own weddings.[55]

In the past a Bohra groom would ride a horse around the mohalla, both rider and mount draped in fresh flowers. In Mumbai and other congested cities this custom is fading owing to the pressures of urban life: cutthroat vehicular traffic on Muhammad Ali Road, for example, makes horseback riding a problematic endeavor. It is still fairly common in royal families and other wealthy, suburban, or traditional-minded circles. One of my close friends in the community celebrated his shadi in this manner in Mumbai during my period of fieldwork, but the wedding was a royal affair, and the horseback procession took place within the courtyard of Saifee Mahal. Another close Bohra friend rode to his shadi on a pure white horse bedecked with flowers—in the middle of Augusta, Georgia.

In a direct holdover from Hindu custom, the groom is often daubed with turmeric; the bride and all women in the wedding party paint their hands and forearms with elaborate *mehndi* patterns that stay on for days, or even weeks. As is the custom in many Hindu communities, during the shadi festivities the mother of the groom tosses sweets or money into the assembled crowd of well-wishers. In yet another holdover, once the feasting is over, the bride (joined by the women of her family) may pour out loud crocodile tears as she is led away by her new husband. Even in the royal families of the Bohra clerical hierarchy, few of the practitioners know the source and meaning of all the shadi customs. Some practices, such as the breaking of coconuts to symbolize fertility and vibrant offspring, are unmistakably Hindu in origin.[56] Several clerical sources told me they had no idea what the rationale was for most shadi customs: the bride and groom place themselves wholly in the hands of elderly female relatives, who debate the proper order, execution, and symbolism of each ritual among themselves.

This parallel practice of Islamic nikah and Hindu social custom is common to other Indian Muslims. In Gujarat, syncretic marriage rites are reported in many (if not most) Muslim communities. In Uttar Pradesh, the poorer segments of Shiʿa society tend to opt for a shariat marriage (purely

nikah, with token mahr paid on the spot), while the wealthier inhabitants celebrate elaborate *urfi* weddings (customary celebrations, with mahr often running into the lakhs of rupees paid out over many years. As Nadeem Hasnain notes, "among a vast section of the Shi'a of eastern Uttar Pradesh and Bihar, Nikah and a couple of other ceremonies are the only Islamic part of marriage. The secondary rites and ceremonies have been derived from the local Hindu customs."[57]

The Bohra community of Surat is particularly traditional in most social customs, and shadi practices are no exception. Horseback processions here are more common than in many other sites. At one Surat shadi I attended, the groom (who had earlier in the day celebrated his nikah in a joint ceremony blessed by Syedna) was seated on a pure white horse, covered from head to toe in white and red flowers. Only his face was visible, with every other part of his body blanketed in a thick layer of petals. The arrangement of wedding wreaths is a task traditionally provided by Bohra artisans solely devoted to this trade. The groom's mount was led by its bridle—the rider would have had a difficult time controlling the horse without disturbing his floral arrangement.

Behind the groom came a brass band dressed in blue tunics, white trousers, and gold caps. Amid the drums, horns, and tubas was the band's centerpiece: an electronic synthesizer, its sound amplified by two powerful speakers pulled along in a wooden oxcart. The musicians were Hindus specializing in shadis of many communities: they even carried a banner with their name—New Bharat Band—in *devanagari* rather than Arabic script. For half an hour or so that evening the wedding party made its way through all the streets of the Bohra mohalla. Bringing up the rear of the procession was an item emblematic of the Bohras' melding of old ways with new: an electric generator supplying power to nine fluorescent tubes carried vertically by attendants like halberds of neon light. The loud chugging of the portable generator very nearly drowned out the music of the band, but the fluorescent glow through the unlit streets brought throngs of neighbors out to watch the shadi procession go by.

VARIATIONS IN THE MARRIAGE NORM

Mutaa

The institution of mutaa, or temporary marriage, is the most notable divergence between Shi'a and Sunni nikah practices. In theory, a mutaa follows the same pattern as that of a standard nikah in every respect except duration: it automatically dissolves after a specified period of time. The

mahr is agreed upon and given, the children of any such union are legiti-
mate, the wife cannot be with another man during the term of the mutaa,
and after the union ends the wife must observe *iddat* (as set out in the
Qur'an 2:228, a three-month term of celibacy). In practice, mutaa some-
times comes decidedly close to prostitution (from a Sunni viewpoint, at
least), with the term of the "marriage" set as brief as a single evening
and the mahr becoming in effect a payment for services rendered.
The textual foundation for mutaa is generally given as Qur'an 4:24; 23:1,
5–6; and 70:29–30.[58] Hadith literature contains traditions that support
mutaa, but others that clearly condemn it. The institution of mutaa pre-
dates Islam, and its justification seems to rest on the exigencies of Muslim
soldiers who had to spend long periods of time away from their wives
while on military campaigns. However it may have entered the practice of
the Muslim umma, mutaa was decisively forbidden by Caliph Umar and
has been deemed an invalid custom by Sunnis since. Because Shi'a con-
sider Umar to be an illegitimate usurper, his hukm carries no weight with
them and mutaa has continued to be practiced throughout the Ithna-
Ashari world.[59]

The Bohras, like other Ismailis, do not practice mutaa. Their avoidance
is based on teachings of the dawat (reportedly dating from Fatimid times)
rather than on Umar's decree, but it is similarly complete. This prohibition
is actual rather than merely theoretical—no source I consulted had ever
heard of it occurring in the community. Dawat attorney Abbasali Najafali,
writing in the late colonial period, cited mutaa as a forbidden practice.
Mian Bhai Abdul Husain, no dawat apologist himself, notes even in the
early twentieth century that mutaa was a custom alien to the Bohras.[60]

In avoiding the practice of mutaa, however, Bohras are well within the
mainstream of non-Bohra Indian Shi'a fitting their demographic profile.
The institution is only rarely practiced by Indian Ithna-Asharis, with a
mere 9% of Uttar Pradesh Shi'a surveyed acknowledging it. A close look
at the survey's demographic breakdown indicates that this custom is be-
coming increasingly anachronistic even among this segment of the popu-
lation: the men having practiced mutaa were almost all over fifty years old,
and overwhelmingly from the class of former *zamindars* (feudal aristo-
crats) made obsolete by the land reforms of Jawaharlal Nehru. Nationwide
figures are even more revealing. Hasnain and Husain found only 3.2% of
respondents having practiced mutaa, and the figures for the Bohras' home
states are lower still: 0.3% of Shi'a in Maharashtra and none at all in Gu-
jarat. Moreover, mutaa was approved of by 87.5% of Shi'a illiterates, but
this support decreased in direct proportion to the respondents' level of
education.[61] As a highly educated community living primarily in Maha-

rashtra and Gujarat, the Bohras are well in line with the mutaa avoidance of other Shi'a communities with similar demographics.

Divorce

In theory, divorce is as easy for Bohras (the men, at least) as it is for members of other Muslim denominations. Islam places few ironclad restrictions on the practice, and has permitted it without social stigma since the time of the Prophet.[62] As a matter of law rather than practice, divorce (talaq) throughout the Muslim world requires no clerical intervention. Since nikah is a civil contract, it can be dissolved without the involvement of any spiritual authority. In many Sunni communities, a "triple talaq"* is deemed legitimate even if the wife is not present, or if the husband is either intoxicated or speaking in jest. Whether the form of the talaq is *al-bid'a* (an "innovation," like the triple talaq) or *as-sunna* (spread out over the course of three months to permit an opportunity for reconciliation), it is strictly a matter between the couple involved. An Ithna-Ashari Shi'a divorce follows much the same pattern, except that it must be pronounced in the presence of the wife and two witnesses, in a specific formulation spoken in Arabic.[63]

In actual practice, however, social pressures make divorce a rare phenomenon among Indian Muslims. As Imtiaz Ahmad observes, "while Islamic law clearly makes a woman's position weak in respect of both polygamy and divorce, social practice in both these respects varies and differs widely from the provisions of the law."[64] This is no less true in the Bohra community—in fact, divorce may be even more stigmatized than in other Indian Muslim groups.

Whereas other groups lack any sort of centralized clerical authority to convey a sense of irrefutable moral opprobrium, the Bohra dawat generally bolsters the institution of marriage with all its spiritual authority. Just as nikah is not an entirely private contract for the Bohras, neither is talaq: both require the permission of Syedna or his representative. When an individual or couple requests such permission, the local amil will generally try all manner of counseling and moral suasion before granting the request. Talaq is only marginally more socially acceptable now than early in the last century, when Mian Bhai Abdul Husain wrote, "Divorce is allowed but it is very seldom resorted to and usually a woman, if divorced, is looked down [upon] in the community."[65]

*In order for a divorce to become final the talaq must be pronounced three times, preferably over a period of months. In many parts of the Muslim world it is considered highly inappropriate (although technically permitted) for a husband to pronounce all three talaqs (i.e., a "triple talaq") at once.

The dawat's authority in matters of divorce, however, can cut both ways. It generally discourages the practice, but if a husband or wife is seen as irredeemably noncompliant with Islamic norms the dawat may counsel the other spouse to dissolve the marriage. Syedna seldom (if ever) directly orders a divorce, but he seldom would need to. If a husband is placed under *baraat* (social ostracism), his wife can be stigmatized along with him; the marriage is not dissolved, but it becomes a hollow thing. Dissidents say the dawat has wielded the threat of de facto divorce via baraat to punish those who challenge Syedna's power.

Shaikh Najafali set out a number of circumstances under which a woman would be automatically entitled to a divorce. In all cases they boil down to a fraudulent contract: if the wife finds out that her new husband (whom she is presumed to have married sight-unseen) isn't all that she'd bargained for, she can trade him in for a better model. The conditions, however, are relatively limited. If the groom turns out to be insane, a leper, or afflicted with any of several dire communicable diseases, the new bride would have a fairly clear-cut case. If her mate is already married to a non-Muslim or a slave (it must be remembered that this is a Fatimid-era code), she can divorce him only if he doesn't give up his other wife. Another condition would presumably require external adjudication: if "the marriage guardian marries her with one who is inferior in social status to her and if the woman comes to know of this after her marriage, she is at liberty to revoke the marriage."[66]

One cause for automatic divorce takes up nearly half of Najafali's discussion: unconfessed impotence. The bride must have been unaware of the condition prior to marriage, and the threshold for return of merchandise is quite high. A wife cannot request a divorce on these grounds until a decent amount of time after the marriage, and once she makes her claim to the qadi she is obliged to give her husband a full year in which to disprove her assertion. At the end of the year, Najafali writes, "[t]he wife would not be entitled to divorce if even one successful act of intercourse is established."[67]

In a modern context, however, the wife's task is considerably easier. Her very claim might well prompt an unwilling husband to grant the divorce with no further discussion. In a patriarchal society, women find varied means of gaining control over their lives.

Polygamy

Like most Muslim communities in India, the Bohras accept polygamy in theory but practice it very rarely indeed. The late Syedna Taher Saifuddin

had one monogamous marriage and three polygamous ones (after the death of his first wife), but the current da'i has been married only once.

Those few Bohras who engage in polygamy generally do not describe it in idyllic terms. For the wives (Islam permits polygamy, but not polyandry) the inegality is obvious. For the husbands, the state falls far short of Western fantasy. "It is not a lifestyle I would recommend to others," says one Bohra polygamist, who had been happily married for years when he fell in love with another woman. He couldn't bring himself to carry on a secret affair, or to divorce his first wife in order to remarry. "My brothers and sisters, all my friends and relations tried to talk me out of it," he says, "but it seemed the only way to avoid misery while maintaining my obligations to my first wife and our children." He now divides his time between two households that are barely on speaking terms—an arrangement that leaves neither family particularly happy.

The primary textual justification for Islamic polygamy is the Qur'an 4:3: "[M]arry of the women, who seem good to you, two, three, or four." The context, however, is telling: this particular verse was revealed in the fourth year of Hijra shortly after the battle of Uhud, in which large numbers of Muslim men had been killed. Many scholars of Islamic history and theology contend the rationale of the verse is to insure that the widows and orphans of the soldiers slaughtered at Uhud would not be left without support and protection. From a Shi'a perspective, polygamy has the added stamp of approval of having been practiced by the ahl al-bayt. The Prophet himself married eleven times after the death of his first wife, Khadija, and all of these unions were polygamous. Ali, regarded even by Sunnis as among the most ascetic of the companions, had four wives and seventeen concubines, and is said to have remarried seven nights after Fatima's death. Ali's son Hasan is said to have married over 200 women (no more than four at any one time).[68] Monogamy is the norm in modern Bohra society, and has probably been the norm for most Bohras throughout history, but polygamy has always remained an option for some.

Current Bohra attitudes toward polygamy date at least as far back as the early twentieth century, when Abdul Husain reported: "Although four wives are allowed by law, a Bohra seldom marries more than one."[69] This is quite in line with the practices of other Indian Muslims. Imtiaz Ahmad notes that polygamy is practiced so infrequently that it is not significantly more common among Muslims (for whom it is legal) than among Hindus (for whom it is illegal).[70] In Hasnain and Husain's survey, only 6.2 % of respondents reported practicing any form of polygyny (that is, marriage, concubinage, or any other union between one man and more than one

woman). The only segment of society to report any significant occurrence was the class of former zamindars.

The most striking proof that the institution is on the wane is that out of one thousand respondents surveyed by Hasnain and Husain, there was not a single polygamist under the age of fifty. According to a report of the National Committee on the Status of Women published in 1974, at that time polygyny was practiced by 15.2% of tribal *adivasis,* 5.8% of Hindus, and only 5.7% of Indian Muslims. Even Jains and Buddhists had marginally higher rates of polygyny than Muslims did, despite the fact that only under the Muslim civil code are such unions officially recognized as legitimate.[71] The words of Hodkinson, applied to the subcontinental Muslim population as a whole, are equally applicable to the Daudi Bohras: "Given the actual incidence of polygamy in India and Pakistan today, the question is one of theoretical rather than practical importance for the majority of the Muslim population."[72]

DEATH

The next step after marriage (in a ritual sense at least) is death. The bulk of a Bohra's life is spent in the interim between wedding and funeral, but the religious events during this period are simply the same cycle of daily, annual, or occasional religious events that have been a part of his or her life up to this point. In theory the hajj is also a part of every Bohra's life cycle, but in practice far from all make the pilgrimage; it is therefore discussed in chapter 3, together with other annual rites.

Many of the ceremonies surrounding death are similar to those practiced by other Muslim communities, Shiʿa and Sunni alike.[73] Universal or unique, however, Bohra death rituals all require specific dawat approval, and are therefore a powerful tool in the maintenance of clerical authority. No member of the community can receive funeral rites or be buried in a Bohra cemetery without the explicit permission and blessing of the clergy, usually given through the local amil. Many dissidents who have lived at odds with the dawat for years, even those placed under official baraat, have reconciled themselves to clerical orthopraxy when confronted with the possibility of an excommunicate's death. Funerary rituals rank exactly in the center of priorities for the respondents to my survey. These ceremonies were cited fifth in a list of ten aspects of orthopraxy the respondents were asked to place in hierarchical order of importance. Had respondents been limited to the elderly or those with elderly relatives the ceremonies would probably have been ranked significantly higher.

When a Bohra seems to be approaching death, his relatives prop his

body up so that he is facing qiblah.[74] He is fed a spoonful of honey and a sip of water from the holy well of Zamzam (when performing hajj or *umra*, each Bohra pilgrim brings back a supply of Zamzam water for any elderly member of his extended family). During the deathbed vigil, family members recite verses from the Qur'an: the entire text if time permits, or only a few favored *surahs* if death comes quickly. The last words out of a Bohra's mouth should be the *kalama* (profession of faith): "There is no god but God, and Muhammad is Messenger, and Ali is the friend of God and the Wasi of His the Prophet."* The last words a Bohra hears when departing the world should be the same as the first ones he hears upon entering it: the adhan, whispered softly in his ear.[75]

After death, the body is taken to a masjid for the final *ghusl* (bath).[76]† Few families have a bathing chamber large enough to accommodate the corpse, several attendants, and a procession of relatives, so every town with a Bohra cemetery has at least one masjid with a *ghuslkhana* (special chamber for the ritual bath). The deceased is washed and perfumed with fragrant spices, either by elderly relatives or by a staff attendant of the masjid.

After ghusl, the deceased is dressed and brought out for public viewing. A cloth covering the face is removed, and for several hours (sometimes a whole day) mourners of both sexes can pay their respects and offer each other comfort, side by side. This is the last time that women will be a part of the funerary rites. Whether the deceased is male or female, the transportation of the body to the grave and the rituals at the cemetery are performed by men alone.[77]

The body is placed in its *jenazah* (coffin), which is attached to two poles and carried to the graveyard by at least four pallbearers. The Bohras maintain their own cemeteries separate from those of their Sunni or Ithna-Ashari coreligionists, and pay a special funerary tax to the dawat or local jamat for the maintenance of a graveyard near every population center. Before proceeding to the cemetery the pallbearers all perform *wuzu* (ritual washing) and go to the main chamber of the masjid for the deceased's final prayer (*jenanazani namaz*). The jenazah must be carried below shoulder level while inside the masjid, but is raised onto the pallbearers' shoul-

*This, of course, is the Shi'a version of the profession of faith. The Sunni *shahada* omits mention of Ali.

†Muslims engage in ritual ablutions before any religious ritual. Usually this consists merely of *wuzu*, the washing of one's face, mouth, nose, head, hands, and feet. When one is physically or ritually unclean (the pollutant can be biological or spiritual), a cleansing of the entire body (ghusl) is necessary before any rite can be performed. For ahadith on ghusl (and wuzu), see al-Bukhari 1986, 1:156–175; al-Muslim 1978: 147–205.

ders once the procession has moved outside. In towns where the ceme-
tery is walking distance from the masjid, the coffin is carried on shoulders
the entire distance. In Mumbai, however, the closest cemetery is more
than fifteen kilometers away from the nearest Bohra masjid. Here, as in
most other urban sites, the coffin is carried by shoulder from the mosque
to the street, then driven to the cemetery in a hearse, and then carried by
shoulder again from the road to the gravesite.

Jenazah ne kanda apvu ("to give a shoulder to the coffin") is an impor-
tant way for a Bohra man to show his respect for a fellow member of the
community and to gain spiritual merit as well.[78] Ideally, the crowd of
mourners will be so numerous that each member will remain stationary
and simply pass the jenazah from shoulder to shoulder all the way to the
grave. This ideal is often realized for particularly important and prominent
members of the community, and is always the method employed at the
funeral of a da'i or other high clerical official. In such cases pallbearers
are unnecessary, for the assembled multitudes can number in the tens
of thousands. The coffins of lesser figures are transported by a smaller
crowd, still passed from shoulder to shoulder rather than walked along,
but with men in the back running to the front of the pack as soon as they
have transferred the jenazah. In sites with very small Bohra populations,
the pallbearers will have to carry the coffin rather than pass it along.

Following the sunna of the Prophet,[79] Bohras consider it highly meri-
torious to help transport the coffin of a relative, friend, or complete
stranger: the more often one performs such a service for others, the more
pallbearers there will be to perform such a service at one's own funeral.
This is a matter of considerable importance, for an individual's standing
within the community is often measured by the number of men willing to
help shoulder his coffin. It is also a strong incentive to treat all members
of the community with kindness throughout one's life: There are tales of
Bohra misanthropes experiencing moral reformation late in life, each cur-
mudgeon spurred by the frightening image of his widow unable find any-
one to carry his coffin.

When the procession reaches the tomb site, a large *chader* (sheet) is
set up above the newly dug grave.[80] The chader is much like a large tarp,
and forms a symbolic barrier between the deceased and the elements.
The grave is typically six feet long and three feet wide, but can be larger if
necessary. Its depth is four feet, to prevent the corpse from being disin-
terred by animals. Under the symbolic screen of the chader, the body is
removed from the jenazah and lowered into the grave.[81]

The body is turned on its right side, in the direction of Mecca, with the
face oriented toward qiblah. The deceased is propped up with stones, so

he does not shift and roll on his back or stomach. Often a letter of prayer (*raqqa*) signed by the officiating amil is placed in the hand of the deceased; the raqqa may be given before or after payment of the death tax (*haqqun nafs*).[82] The face (up to now covered with a cloth) is unveiled, and the nose pressed right up against the stone wall of the qubba.[83] As prayers and Qur'anic verses are recited each mourner pours three double-handfuls of sand into the grave, and if necessary a sexton shovels more sand in to fill any remaining space. After the prayers are finished the mourners depart, leaving the sexton and other professionals to complete the construction of the *qubba* (tomb). This is a long process, generally taking more than six months—in the case of a marble qubba, up to a year. Once the burial is over, mourners can return to perform *ziyaret* (literally "visiting").

On the third day after death, the day on which the soul of the deceased is believed to be judged by God, the family holds a *suyyum* (wake). The only fully public ritual of death, the suyyum consists of a feast accompanied by prayers. Communal feasts are also given on the ninth day after death (*nomia*), the thirtieth day (*masma*), the fortieth day (*chehlum*), and the one-year anniversary (*varsi*). There will be no marriages in the family until at least the chehlum, sometimes not until the varsi.[84]

Once the qubba has been constructed and sealed, both men and women are free to visit it as often as they wish. Members of the deceased's family typically visit the gravesite every day during the period immediately following the completion of the qubba, then decrease their visits to once per week, then to the annual anniversary of the departed's demise, then (if they live in another city) to occasional ziyaret whenever they happen to be in town. In the Bohra worldview, every visit to a graveyard is a beneficial act: it reminds the visitor of the transitory nature of life and encourages repentance of sins while time still remains.

Rituals of the Daudi Bohra Year

The Bohras base their ritual calendar not on actual sighting of the new moon, but on astrological charts dating to the Fatimid caliphate. For this reason, Bohra observances of universal Islamic holidays do not correspond exactly with those of other groups; in recent years, they have preceded the Sunni and Ithna-Ashari dates by several days. The divergence of calendars further serves to emphasize the Bohras' unique identity and prevent assimilation to the mainstream of Islam. When other Muslims worldwide are fasting during Ramadan, performing hajj or commemorating Ashura, Bohras often have already completed their observance of these unifying annual rituals.

Of the most important Bohra rites, some are shared with Sunnis and other Shi'a, some with other Shi'a alone, and others (such as the death anniversary of Syedna Taher Saifuddin and the birth date of Syedna Muhammad Burhanuddin) are uniquely Bohra. The primary rituals are (1) *waaz:* a formal ceremony officiated by the da'i (or his local representative); the *khutba* (sermon) is delivered from a "throne" several steps above a raised platform known as a *tekhet;* and (2) *majlis:* less ceremonial than the waaz, sometimes without even the delivery of a khutba, a majlis is presented on the evening preceding the holy day in question. Syedna (or the local prayer imam) sits on a small *gadi* (couch) rather than a throne. In addition to Ismaili holidays, on the first of each month the da'i gives a fairly informal majlis and permits the faithful to seek his audience.

MUHARRAM

By far the most important annual ritual for Bohras, as for all orthodox Shi'a, is Ashura. As Keith Hjortshoj notes, "[D]uring Muharram the Shi'is do not define themselves as members of a sect or religious community but rather as the followers and family of Husayn at Kerbala."[1] The tenth of Muharram had been a pre-Islamic fast day, and for a time fasting on Ashura was obligatory for the early Muslim community; hadith literature

The Foremost Annual Rituals of the Daudi Bohras

Muharram	1: First day of the Islamic year, celebrated with a lavish feast.
	2–10: Ashura: daily waaz
	27: Shehadat (date of martyrdom) of Syedi Fakhruddin
Safar	20: Chehlum of Imam Husain
	26–27: Shehadat of Imam Hasan
Rabiul Awwal	12: Milad (birthday) of Prophet Muhammad
Rabiul Akher	4: Milad of Imam Tayyib
	20: Milad of Syedna Muhammad Burhanuddin
Jamadi Awwal	10: Shehadat of Fatima, daughter of the Prophet
Jamadi Akher	27: Urs (death anniversary) of Syedna Qutbuddin
	29: Pehli Rajab ("first of Rajab")
Rajab	13: Milad of Ali
	19: Urs of Syedna Taher Saifuddin
	27: Mebas marking Muhammad as natiq
Shaban	1: Zikra (also, start of Surat exams)
	15: Shabb-e-Baraat
Ramadan	19: Shehadat of Ali
	23: Lailat al-Qadr
Shawwal	1: Eid al-Fitr
Zilqaad	27: Milad of Syedna Taher Saifuddin
Zyl-Hajj	9: Day of Arafat (Hajj rite)
	10: Eid al-Adha (Bakri Eid)
	18: Ghadir Khumm (rite of mithaq)

Notes: In addition to these rites, the urs of all past daʿis and many syedis are observed at the sites of their shrines. Secondary rites are described in the text. *Sources:* My primary source for this, as for much of the ethnographic information in the preceding and following chapters, has been personal observation of rituals, combined with the instruction of dawat-affiliated authorities (most notably Mullah Shabbir M. Mansoorbhai Jamali and Shaikh Mustafa Abdulhussein), and the additional explication of Abduz-Zahir Bhaisaheb Mohyuddin and Tahera Behnsaheb Qutbuddin. My personal observation bears out the calendar highlights noted by recorded sources (Abdul Husain 1920: 109–111; Fyzee 1934a: 9; Hollister 1953: 303).

presents several versions of the origin of the date as an Islamic fast.[2] Since at least the fourth Islamic century (and probably much earlier) Ashura has honored the martyrdom of the Prophet's grandson Imam Husain. The earliest recorded observance of Ashura as a uniquely Shi'a ritual dates to the year 315/962 in Abbasid Baghdad, and the practice soon became standard in Fatimid Egypt.[3]

The event commemorated is the one defining moment in Shi'a history: the date on which Husain and seventy-two of his relatives and companions were slaughtered on the field of Kerbala. It was at this battle, fought in the year 61/680, that hopes for a Shi'a ascendancy throughout the unified Muslim umma were permanently dashed. David Pinault characterizes Ashura observances as an opportunity for Shi'a to atone for all the moral failings of the world: their own, those of their ancestors, and those of all mankind.[4]

The grief is overwhelming, and it serves to link humanity with transcendental spirituality. The *mu'mineen* (faithful; sing., *mu'min*) wail and beat their breasts to remind themselves of the agonies suffered by the ahl al-bayt: Imam Husain died for the sins of all mankind, and mankind can partake of his intercessionary aid by voluntarily recalling, accepting, and sharing his pain. The parallels with central aspects of Christian doctrine are obvious, and have been commented upon by such scholars as Talal Asad.[5]

The types of observance practiced throughout the Indian subcontinent (let alone throughout the Shi'a world) vary widely from place to place and community to community. Rituals include the breaking of glass bangles by women, construction of elaborate replicas of the tomb of Husain in Kerbala (*tazia*), establishment of sequestered mourning-houses (generally called *imambaras* or *ashurkhanas*), and a wide variety of emotionally charged parades or processions.[6] For all Bohras, by contrast, observance is focused on the waaz and majlis of the da'i. Here, as in all other aspects of life, the da'i is central to the spiritual life of the community.

More so than at any other time of the year, during Ashura the dawat solidifies and reifies Bohra group identity. The means by which it does this is simultaneously traditional and modern: direct, personal contact with the da'i, facilitated by any and every technological method available. Each year Syedna personally leads Ashura observance in a different city, and each year tens of thousands of Bohras fly in from all parts of the world to participate. Despite his advanced age (Muhammad Burhanuddin is in his mid-80s),[7] for more than a decade the da'i has made a point of spreading the sites of Muharram rites as widely as possible. In recent years he has held them as far afield as Mombasa, Colombo, Nairobi, and Dar-es-

Salaam.[8] Syedna keeps the site of each year's service secret from even his closest family members until a few weeks before the date: this serves to hold Bohras the world over in a state of readiness (no jamat wants to be caught unprepared to host Muharram), and limits the number of attendees to a barely manageable multitude.

No matter where Ashura is held, the dawat provides room and board free (or at nominal charge) for all Bohras who choose to attend. Transportation is paid by the individuals themselves, but travel agencies linked to the dawat make special provisions to get as many mu'mineen to the site as may wish to go. Here communications technology is absolutely vital: the mechanics of keeping all attendees housed and fed would be daunting enough, and trying to accomplish this task while running an elaborate series of religious programs requires every organizational tool available. When the 1994 ritual was held in Mumbai, over 200,000 Bohras from out of town all had to be accommodated in musafirkhanas, jamatkhanas, hotels, and private homes.[9]

The dawat also uses technology to minister to Bohras unable to attend Muharram rites in person. Since the late 1970s, the clergy has circulated videocassettes of khutbas and waaz of Syedna, and encouraged believers to purchase VCRs for home viewing. Those who cannot afford VCRs are urged to watch the tapes at their local jamatkhana; in recent years, videos of Syedna's daily service have been sent by air-courier to most of the 700 masjids and 400 jamatkhanas around the world so that worshipers could follow the service the very next day.[10] Since the early 1990s, Muharram services have been broadcast by telephone relay to Bohra congregations in London, Paris, Singapore, Cairo, Karachi, Stockholm, Jerusalem, Sanaa, and several cities in the United States.[11] In recent years, many jamats have used the Internet receive Ashura broadcasts: the rituals are recorded, converted to digitalized transferred audio files, and available for downloading almost immediately by any congregation—or any individual congregant—with a personal computer. Syedna's voice can be present, even if his body is thousands of miles away.

Several jamatkhanas even carried the rituals on closed-circuit television: "This arrangement," a dawat pamphlet notes, "was a sign of the community's awareness of the rapid technological advancement and the benefit to be derived from such advancement for the material and spiritual development of mankind."[12] The large majority of my survey respondents owned at least one item of technology enabling them to observe rituals from afar: 90.9% owned a television, over half owned a VCR, and more than three-quarters owned a radio.[13] Almost all respondents reported having observed Muharram rituals either by videocassette or radio relay.

Days of Muharram

Each of the first ten days of the month of Muharram has a special signifi-
cance—often, several different significances. In addition to retelling the
story of Kerbala, Bohras assign each day to a different devotional charac-
ter:

The first day of Muharram is the start of the Islamic year. In the evening
Bohras prepare for the somber days ahead with an epic feast: those who
can afford it lay out an array of fifty-two different dishes (one for each of
the fifty-two da'is). Families of more limited means prepare twenty-one
dishes (for the twenty-one imams), or seven (for the imams up to the pe-
riod of concealment), or any other odd number. All of the assorted curries,
sweets, and savories are squeezed onto one communal thal, and each
family member should eat at least a small portion of every dish.

On the second through the ninth days, a waaz is offered each morn-
ing. Generally it begins between 10 and 11 A.M. and lasts between two
and three hours, ending at midday (zuhr and ashr) namaz. On the tenth
of Muharram, the rituals last for most of the day: there is the usual waaz
in the morning, and another in the afternoon that lasts until evening
(maghrib and isha) namaz—more than eight hours in all.[14] As the week
goes on the emotional pitch of the observance increases in intensity. Some
Bohras fast for each day of Ashura, although this is not required. The ded-
ication of the daily waaz is as follows:

 2 Muharram: Adam
 3 Muharram: Nuh (Noah)
 4 Muharram: Ibrahim (Abraham)
 5 Muharram: Musa and Isa (Moses and Jesus)
 6 Muharram: Muhammad
 7 Muharram: Fatima
 8 Muharram: Ali
 9 Muharram: Hasan
 10 Muharram: Husain.

Regardless of which holy figure is celebrated, each day's waaz is de-
voted to retelling a portion of the Kerbala story. The tale is one thoroughly
familiar to nearly every Bohra long before he or she leaves childhood: the
courage of Husain and his companions, the lamentations of Hazrat Fatima
at the death of her son, the execution of Husain's six-month-old infant Ali
Asghar along with all the men, the decapitated corpses trampled under-
foot, the heads of the martyrs paraded through the streets of Baghdad on
the points of spears. Almost every Bohra child can conjure up the mem-

ory of the women and children of the Prophet's own family being dragged away into slavery.[15]

Bohra Ashura: Participant Observation

During my primary segment of Mumbai fieldwork, the Bohra tenth of Muharram fell two days earlier than the Ithna-Ashari date. The rituals I witnessed at Saifee Masjid and one other Mumbai masjid illustrate the paradigm of observance throughout the Bohra community.[16]

For most of the late morning and early afternoon, Saifee Masjid is filled to capacity. By the time I leave to observe rituals at the second site, the overcrowding has grown extreme even by the standards of this perpetually packed flagship of all Bohra houses of worship. In the heat of a sunny premonsoon day, only the most devout men are wearing formal *sherwani* jackets over their kurta pajamas. The fastidious have brought handkerchiefs to spread neatly beneath themselves as they kneel in prayer. The crush of devotees overwhelms the storage capacity of the shoe racks, so footwear is stowed haphazardly in every available nook outside the main chamber: sandals stuffed between the rungs of stairway guardrails or in the niches of walls, balanced on top of pediments, stashed in plastic bags hung on stray nails or tied to creaky wooden shutters.

The second masjid is not as large or as crowded as Saifee Masjid, but it too is filled to capacity. Three floors are packed with worshipers. The congregation here is slightly less strict in observance of dress codes than the worshipers at Saifee Masjid (the site of most of my prior ritual experiences) but the most noteworthy deviation from the norm is found on the men's chins: in all of the dozens of times I have been to Saifee and other important masjids I cannot recall having seen more than a very few men without beards. Here, however, something like one-quarter of the hundreds of men present are clean-shaven, wear only a mustache, or have beards that seem to be less than two weeks old. The divergence from orthopraxic norms may be due to the difference in the masjids' stature: people treat Saifee (the "cathedral" of Syedna; it is also known as Masjid al-Azam) with greater reverence, and when the da'i is out of Mumbai the waaz or majlis is always given by the mukasir or another top dawat official.

By the time we arrive the main floor is so full that masjid attendants have locked its doors to prevent other worshipers from forcing their way in, so we join the overflow audience accommodated on the third floor. This chamber (like that of the women on the second story) has a view of the main prayer area downstairs, but the service has to be piped in over loudspeakers. At several points in the ceremony the speaker system fails, and

the men leap up to cluster around the courtyard windows so as not to miss any of the rite. The ceremony here is substantially the same as that at Saifee. In a voice strangulated by emotion, the prayer imam reminds his audience of the tortures suffered by the martyrs at Kerbala. Sometimes he speaks in prose, sometimes in verses composed by Syedna Muhammad Burhanuddin or Syedna Taher Saifuddin. Often his words are interrupted by prolonged bursts of matam and shrieks of "Ya Husain!"

Posture as Penance

For many people, the first element of physical discomfort suffered during Ashura observance is that of posture: kneeling for several uninterrupted hours at a stretch can be truly excruciating. During any Bohra ritual it is considered bad form to sit cross-legged, resting one's back against a wall, or in any position other than what some refer to as a *bhaisaheb*[17] kneel— legs tucked completely under one's torso, with the only permissible concession being an occasional shift of weight from one side to the other. This posture has a practical utility of taking up a minimum of floor space, permitting greater numbers of devotees to squeeze into the room available. It can, however, be torturous—and not only for an uninitiated outsider, but also for a great many community members. In a hadith recorded by the Sunni compiler al-Muslim, an early member of the umma asks the companion of the Prophet Ibn Abbas about "sitting on one's buttocks in prayer." The questioner recalls, "We said to him: We find it a sort of cruelty to the foot. Ibn Abbas said: It is the sunnah of your Apostle (may peace be upon him)."[18] Modern translator Abdul Hamid Siddiqi adds an explanatory note: "There is a pressure on the feet which has been said as [sic] cruelty. Prayer is a training in patience and perseverance, and such a minor hardship is desirable."[19]

Most of the men in the overflow chamber today are cheating: in Saifee Masjid it is rare to see many worshipers breaking out of bhaisaheb posture, but here a majority are sitting cross-legged or leaning fully over on one side. Even among those segments of the Bohra community who manage to maintain proper position during all rituals, the effort required is a constant topic of comment: many thoroughly observant people have confided to me their inability to kneel for so long without terrible pain, and one of the most commonly noted examples of Syedna's miraculous spiritual power is his ability to kneel for hours at a time without any apparent discomfort.

On Ashura, even the torturous way of sitting is a tool for social cohesion: we are packed in like sardines, transformed figuratively (and, it feels, almost literally) into one organism. The shared pain is a bond between us.

Nor is this an accidental manifestation: since Fatimid times, one of the batin forms of prayer has been (as an Ismaili theologian of the classical era wrote) devotion "by the force of continuous meditation, or by the power of concentration . . . and exercise of self control in the most difficult and unpleasant situations of life, or fatiguing forms of worship. When one masters all this, he has really attained the desired attachment to God."[20]

Nearing the End of Fast

By late afternoon on Ashura observant Bohras have been fasting since dawn, after having attended an emotionally grueling cycle of daily rituals for the past ten days. This would be extremely demanding at any time of year, but during particularly hot weather it becomes a true test of any individual's strength of will. During my fieldwork, Ashura happened to fall at the very hottest time of year: the fortnight immediately preceding monsoon, the time when daytime temperatures in Mumbai seldom drop below 90 degrees and often surge well above 100. Since the Islamic practice of *sawm*[21] is a dry fast during daylight hours, a loyal Bohra cannot have so much as a sip of water until evening.

In the masjid at the culmination of Ashura rites, as each member of the congregation counts down the hours and minutes until sunset, jamatkhana attendants are busily preparing the *iftar* (fast-breaking) meal. They are clearly not Bohras: their lack of beards and choice of clothing mark them as Sunnis or Ithna-Asharis. The cooks and porters go about their tasks with apparent indifference to the ceremony being conducted around them. The chamber housing the overflow audience will become a dining hall as soon as the service is over, so the pace of the work is brisk. After maghrib namaz, worshipers will break their fast here before going home to feast the evening away. Four servants form a ring to carry out the enormous vats of food, each container far too heavy to be hauled by a single pair of arms; each man places one hand on the shoulder of the man to his side for balance, and with his free hand helps lift the massive urn. The food is simple: little more than *dal,* and a gruel called *kichero* that is said to be the food eaten by Husain and his family before Kerbala. This porridge of boiled and pounded wheat and mutton is the dish with which Bohras traditionally break their fast during Muharram; it is a poor substitute for the delicacies that follow—but to the devotees kneeling in anxious anticipation, the bland kichero gives off a fragrance as enticing as manna from heaven.

The act of fasting is meant to remind the worshipers of the agonies suffered by Husain and his family during their death-throes. Some of the more powerful tales of Kerbala concern the brutal thirst that the martyrs

suffered as they lay dying: the field of Kerbala was only a short distance from a rushing river, but the warriors had to fight, fall, and die within sight of the stream. As the congregants are singing a hymn whose words include the verse "Water, oh water, yet not a drop to drink," one of the cooks sticks his face under a tap and swallows a few deep gulps in full view of the worshipers. Whether or not his act is intentionally timed, all those who observe it shake their heads in woe.

Open-Hand Matam and Weeping

Throughout the week, and especially during the course of the afternoon's waaz, the pace and intensity of matam has steadily increased. During each service the congregants (both male and female) have been called upon to shed tears and engage in ritualized breast-beating to demonstrate their empathy with Husain and his companions. At first glance it is difficult to tell how much of the devotion is genuine and how much is stylized: the tears start flowing at all the proper moments, loud waves of sobbing roll through the masjid right on cue. A highly placed member of Qasr-e Ali (the clerical royal family) would later tell me that Syedna encourages the faithful to force themselves to cry at the correct moments: initially the responses might be artificial, but through repetition and devotion the tears will eventually well up from the heart of their own accord. Of course, my source notes, there are many attendees who have not yet reached the level of genuine empathy—their tears and their exuberant breast-beating are often intended less to demonstrate a bond with Husain than to impress their neighbors or members of the clergy.

An hour into the evening waaz, many of the men in the overflow hall have squeezed their way downstairs: a side stairway leading to the wuzu area allows access to the main prayer chamber by an unlocked gate. My friends and I join the main body of the worshipers for the final hour of the service. Matam down here is more intense, but still widely varied. Many attendees merely pat their right hands rhythmically against their chests, echoing the chants in a low voice. Many others go about their breast-beating with single-minded zeal, as if pounding out a powerful cadence on a kettledrum of bone and flesh. A new father teaches his young son how to perform matam—he cradles the child in his kneeling lap, and gently taps the boy's hand against his tiny chest.

Matam is a Shi'a institution that can easily appear exotic to outsiders, and is often put forward as an example of the supposed fanaticism of the denomination. To an outsider who happens to stumble upon a Muharram procession, the emotional pitch and intense devotion of matam can well be shocking—that has clearly been the reaction of many Christians, Hin-

dus, and even Sunnis. To participate in matam, however, is to understand its attraction and its spiritual utility, even for an individual who does not subscribe to its underlying doctrinal premises. As consultations with friends would later show, my experience is not wholly different from that of some of the younger, less spiritually committed members of the congregation.

By the late afternoon I am already faint with hunger, dizzy with thirst, and enervated with heat. Many of the other congregants seem equally weakened, some of them even slipping into the sort of semitrance observable in certain Sufi devotions. But some of the more zealous (or merely more youthful) devotees are slapping their chests with ever escalating vigor. Some beat their breasts with alternating whacks of balled left and right fists while gazing up at the heavens. Gradually, unconsciously, over the course of the day, I find myself starting to imitate them. My own matam shifts from the politely distant pats of an outside observer to the thoroughly engaged thumps of a participant. I become impatient during the khutba, the spoken exhortations: I welcome the hymns that are interspersed throughout the service because they are the cue for the matam. Pounding on my chest wakes me up, energizes me, gives me enough of an adrenaline rush to counter the weakness from the fasting and the heat. I find it both hypnotic and invigorating at the same time. Moreover, it establishes a bond between me and the rest of the congregation, a bond forged of pain and devotion. During the khutba I am an outsider, separated by language, ethnicity, and belief. During the matam, however, every man in the room is on an equal level. I may not know the words to every hymn, but I can beat my chest as heartily as anyone there.

Several of the friends who have brought me to this masjid are young men whose everyday life has little to do with Bohra orthodoxy. They speak Gujarati in their homes, but they too have difficulty following the arcane, Arabized language used in the service. What they can understand does not necessarily move them: like other teens and twentysomethings the world over, they find long-winded oratory less compelling than the unintellectual gut-level pull of a physical display. The more secular among them are bored by the speechifying, the more devout enjoy the opportunity to demonstrate their faith with actions rather than words. For all, matam is a welcome break from liturgy.

As the pace of the matam picks up, I find myself being carried along with the building emotion. When the prayer leader is giving a sermon I find myself champing at the bit, longing for the next break in oratory, itching for the chance to shout out "Ya Ali!" and pound away with gusto. The last half hour of the waaz is a nearly continuous marathon of matam, and

I find myself welcoming it, reveling in it, hoping it will continue to deepen in intensity. I channel all my thirst, all my hunger, all my discomfort into the matam, use it as fuel to drive me to a higher pitch. I feel the adrenaline surge through my veins: the same rush I've felt in a mosh pit, the same rush I've felt in a boxing ring. As in a mosh pit, as in a boxing ring, I welcome the pain: the impossible weariness in my arms and legs, the stinging smack after smack after smack, the dull bruise I feel forming on my chest, and a buoyancy of spirit that makes all the rest of the world slip away.

"Bloody" Matam

At the end of the Ashura ritual, I leave the role of participant and return to that of mere observer: in this particular masjid, about a dozen men engage in "bloody" matam, a custom frowned upon by the dawat but practiced surreptitiously nonetheless.

The last half-hour of the waaz is pure matam, uninterrupted by any direction or instruction. Some men drop to the ground and prostrate themselves, banging their heads and chests against the floor while others careen wildly about them. The main prayer chamber slips into a chaotic frenzy, and out of the chaos emerges order: matam circles form spontaneously, each composed of a small group of men and boys pounding themselves—and, vicariously, each other—into a higher level of devotion. Kurta buttons pop off, topis fall from heads, and droplets of tossed sweat whip through the air. One man, youngish but marked for piety by a particularly long black beard, faints dead away; he is eventually revived by three bystanders twirling sweat-soaked handkerchiefs around his face to create a soggy breeze.

The matam reaches its climax in the courtyard, in a rare display of devotion with ritual implements. A group of men scourge themselves with vicious flails: each weapon contains five double-edged blades as long and sharp as steak knives, attached to a wooden handle by metal chains. Each man tosses off his kurta and lashes his own back until blood flows in generous streaks, all the while continuing his chant of devotion. Once his skin has been crisscrossed by a series of red gashes, each man passes the scourge on to the next flagellant.

The entire operation seems to have been carefully planned and executed. The participants are all mature men rather than rash teenagers or boys: none seems younger than his late twenties, and most appear to be in their thirties or forties. As the men in the center of the courtyard lash themselves, a circle of others spray the flagellants' exposed backs with water or antiseptic from squirt-bottles. After each man finishes his matam,

someone gives his back a thorough dousing and helps him put his kurta back on. The courtyard's marble floor is soon running with spilled blood, red puddles turning pink when diluted with water from the wuzu enclosure. The rest of the worshipers have to walk barefoot through this area in order to reach the shoe rack and exit, so masjid attendants try to clean up even as the bloody matam is taking place. Although this is a practice officially shunned, there is no doubt that the men who engage in it earn great community prestige: each man whose pure white kurta has been reddened is treated as a hero, and the packed crowd reverently make way for him to pass.

After the matam ends, people pour out into the streets to break their fast. Some stay at the masjid to take advantage of the free meal, but many race to the first stall or shop where they can procure something to drink without waiting in line. A variety of charitable enterprises have set up stands to cater to the worshipers, and are handing out sherbet, tea, lassi, juice, and biscuits to all who can push their way to the front. The crowd is at the very limit of its physical tolerance, teetering between relief and exasperation. Beggars are thick and insistent: by their dress they are clearly not Bohras, most likely Sunnis from the other side of Muhammad Ali Road, but they cannily ask for alms "in the name of Imam Husain" nonetheless.

Too impatient to wait my turn at one of the charity stalls, I race into a local cold-drinks store and order a bottle of mineral water. The proprietor pulls one out from a cardboard box on the floor. It is warm, and there are several ants floating inside, so he offers to find me a colder, cleaner one in the back. *Koi bat nehin,* I tell him—it doesn't matter. I drain the entire tepid bottle in one long gulp, ants and all.

Bloody Matam: Comparison with Other Shi'a

According to dawat officials, the use of any sort of implement or weapon is strictly forbidden. Bloody matam is self destructive, one mullah explained to me, it is "like suicide, and God does not permit this." It is not routinely practiced, but the incident I witnessed is not an isolated one. Several informants mentioned having seen matam with bicycle chains or with *chaq chaqi*—wooden implements resembling nail-studded hairbrushes, held in the palm to turn open-handed matam into an excruciating exercise. One teenaged informant noted that groups of his friends sometimes seek out bloody matam by participating in Ashura rituals at Ithna-Ashari masjids. Such devotion seems to go on in Bohra circles more frequently than dawat authorities would wish: during Ashura, local steelmongers in the streets around Saifee Masjid and other Bohra neighbor-

hoods openly sell scourges identical to those described above, at Rs 90 for a simple flail and Rs 100 for one having longer, crueler, more devoutly devastating blades.

Among Ithna-Ashariyya, bloody matam is practiced more widely and with less secrecy than among the Bohras. In Northern India, devotees cut themselves with daggers or walk barefoot through fire while chanting the names of those martyred at Kerbala.[22] Scourges made of linked knives, like those employed at the observance I witnessed, are used from the seventh through the tenth days of Muharram at various places on the subcontinent.[23] One of the most complete discussions of bloody matam among Indian Shi'a is that of David Pinault, who has examined the customs surrounding Ashura in the city of Hyderabad. Pinault notes that matam is divided into *sineh-zani* (empty-handed breast-beating) and "with implements" (the English term is employed even by the Urdu speakers of the city, for reasons the author does not establish).[24] Even empty-handed forms of matam are highly complex, varying in cadence and intensity; one-handed matam, the type prevalent among the Bohras, is here reserved for the infirm or elderly. Women too perform matam (as they do among the Bohras), but only empty-handed and only in seclusion from the men. Implements used by men include the scourge, the chaq chaqi, razor blades, and knives or short daggers used for jabbing the scalp and chest.[25] Like the Bohra clergy, many Hyderabadi ulema frown upon displays of matam with implements: some consider it too close to the dancing and exuberance of Sufi devotion, others regard it as insincere competition.[26] Sociologist S. Mobarak Abbas likewise notes that significant numbers of Imami Shi'a clerics disapprove of "extreme reverence," seeing it as an orgiastic distraction from the prayer and soul-searching that are proper Ashura pursuits.[27]

Ashura Relations with Other Communities

Muharram is a time when intercommunal relations are both strengthened and weakened, depending on local circumstance and on unpredictable luck. In any community with a significant Shi'a population Ashura is a major event—and major events can be both good and bad things.

Throughout the subcontinent, Muharram is often marked by a high degree of intercommunal unity. As Hjortshoj notes, "In many areas Shi'is, Sunnis, and Hindus all participate in Muharram observances, together or separately, and no doubt for a variety of reasons."[28] He further reports that in one large procession in Lucknow, the bloody matam was led by a Sikh.[29] Pinault notes syncretic practices in Hyderabadi Muharram, with Hindu influences readily discernible.[30] A. R. Saiyid reports that among the Mahagir

fishing communities of the Konkan region, "some of the accretions surrounding the observance of Moharram are Hindu in origin, or at least are influenced by Hindu practices."[31] Such ecumenical practices include the seeking of *darshan* by Hindus at the tazia constructions, the playing of Hindi *filmi* music interspersed with Qur'anic verses, and even (amazingly) the serving of alcohol to Hindu guests at iftar meals.[32]

Among the Bohras such ecumenicalism is considerably more rare. During Ashura, as at all times, the Bohras tend to keep to themselves in religious matters, and in more than two years of fieldwork I observed virtually no other outsiders at Bohra rituals. What syncretism might occur seems to be at a less obvious level: the rhythmic chanting of the names of Husain and Ali may bear certain similarities to Sufi practice or to yogic mantras, and the use of coconuts and candy as ritual symbols of bounty and sweetness appear to be holdovers from Hindu custom.

While Muharram is often an occasion of neighborly amity, often it is also the spark of civil strife. In riot-prone Lucknow, for example, when violence between Sunnis and Shi'a erupts it is generally during Ashura.[33] Hyderabadi Muharram has seldom led to rioting in the postcolonial era, but in recent years the Bharatiya Janata Party and Vishwa Hindu Parishad have attempted to stir up conflict by scheduling provocative marches during the week when Ashura passions run high.[34] In Mumbai, policemen ring every mosque (Sunni and Shi'a alike) on Muhammad Ali Road and other Muslim neighborhoods during the first ten days of Muharram.

Among the Bohras, Muharram is the time of year when there is most risk of intercommunal strife. Part of the Bohra service, as is the case for most Shi'a, is the *lanat* (ritual cursing) of the usurper Yazid and various other historical figures. In Mumbai several years ago, the mukasir led the worshipers in a ritual condemnation of Abu Bakr, Umar, and Uthman, three figures regarded by the Sunnis as Rightly Guided Caliphs but reviled by Shi'a as thieves of the rule properly belonging to Ali. Then, as now, the waaz was broadcast into the streets to accommodate the overflow crowds unable to squeeze into Saifee Masjid. Most of the neighborhood's population is Sunni, so the incident led to violence. Different informants give different accounts of the strife: some say that Sunni bystanders attacked the Bohras at prayer, while others say teenaged Bohras became so enraged at the injustices inflicted upon Husain that they sought out street fights with Sunni boys. Regardless of that conflict's source, during my observance of Ashura all the lanes surrounding Saifee Masjid were lined with both police and the dawat's Saifee Guards.

MUHARRAM TO RAMADAN

The second through the eighth months of the Bohra calendar are of less ritual prominence than the months of Muharram, Ramadan, and zyl-Hajj. There are, however, three major observances during this period: the birth dates of the Prophet Muhammad and of Syedna Muhammad Burhanuddin, and the urs of Syedna Taher Saifuddin; in addition, the examination period at the Jamea tus-Saifiya in Surat—while not a religious ceremony per se, and not observed outside Surat itself—is a very important annual event. The significant holy days are as follows, with most observances taking place on the evening preceding the date in question:

Safar (The Second Month)

20: Chehlum for Imam Husain. A chehlum is a Shi'a rite commemorating the end of the obligatory forty-day mourning period after an individual's death. The chehlum for Husain is observed with a waaz.

26/27: Majlis for Imam Hasan, believed to have been martyred on this date.

Rabiul Awwal (The Third Month)

12: Milad of the Prophet Muhammad. This is a joyous occasion, much like Eid al-Fitr. Bohras observe this day also as the urs of Muhammad, holding that the Prophet died on the same date as the one on which he was born. The Prophet's birth date is celebrated throughout the Muslim world, although not always on the same day.

Rabiul Akher (The Fourth Month)

4: Milad of Imam Tayyib, the twenty-first and last imam before the period of concealment. A happy occasion, celebrated with a waaz.

20: Milad of Syedna Muhammad Burhanuddin. Another festive day. On this day Bohras throughout the world thank God for the guidance of Syedna, and for the happiness and prosperity of the community. At Burhani madrasas in India and abroad this date is the occasion for awards ceremonies and athletic competitions. During the year of my primary Mumbai fieldwork, Syedna Muhammad Burhanuddin's birthday fell during the annual pilgrimage to Kerbala, where it was celebrated by 8,000 pilgrims. This occurred during the time of bubonic plague scare in India, when Indian travelers throughout the Middle East were placed in quarantine and flights to or from the country were abruptly canceled. The dawat was under great pressure to provide housing, transportation, food, and preventative medical care for stranded pilgrims, and by all accounts did a

very good job managing the logistics—even providing assistance to offi-cials of the Indian government who were stuck in Iraq at the same time.

Jamadi Awwal (The Fifth Month)

10: Urs of Fatima. The shehadat of the daughter of the Prophet and pro-genitrix of the Fatimid line is marked with a majlis and a day of commu-nity mourning.[35]

Jamadi Akher (The Sixth Month)

2: Urs of Syedna Qutbuddin. The thirty-second da'i is buried in Ahmed-abad, so that is often the primary site of observance rituals. The date is marked by a majlis, unless Syedna is in Ahmedabad, in which case he de-livers a waaz.

29: Pehli Rajab, the eve of the first day of the month of Rajab. A spe-cial nighttime namaz is offered, consisting of twenty-four rak'ats. A rak'at is the cycle of prayer while standing, kneeling, kissing the ground, sitting, kissing the ground, and standing, as practiced in daily namaz. A break is taken between every two rak'ats, during which time the worshipers chant or call out devotional phrases while seated.

Rajab (The Seventh Month)

Fasting during the month of Rajab is not obligatory, but highly laudable. As in Ramadan, sawm consists of a daytime dry fast. Those choosing to fast during Rajab are strongly encouraged to commit to doing so for an entire decade. At the time of my fieldwork, for example, Mullah Shabbir M. Man-soorbhai Jamali had been fasting during Rajab for the past sixteen years: he had just completed a cycle of ten years' fasting when Syedna began a ten-year commitment of his own; like many devout Bohras, Mullah Shab-bir decided to undertake another fasting cycle in solidarity with the da'i.

13: Milad of Ali. The date (also observed by Ithna-Ashariyya)[36] is marked by a majlis. Since this is a fasting month—whether or not all of the faithful actually undertake sawm—celebrations are somewhat muted.

Days 13–15 of Rajab are called "the Days of Light," and many Bohras who do not fast for the entire month will practice sawm on these days.

15: Commemoration of an occasion on which Imam Jafar miracu-lously located a child who had been kidnaped. In a special service in the afternoon, Syedna recites ten of the most important surahs of the Qur'an.

19: Urs of Syedna Taher Saifuddin. Ever since the death of the fifty-first da'i in 1965, the event has been marked with a waaz in Mumbai. For more than a decade, since the construction of a spectacular marble mausoleum

there, Syedna Muhammad Burhanuddin has also made a special ziyaret to the *rauzah* of his father. Community devotion is intense, with 60,000 typically gathering to mourn the death anniversary.

27: Mebas (mabath). Commemoration of the date (also observed by Ithna-Ashariyya) on which Muhammad was given the title of Prophet. Bohra observance consists of an afternoon waaz and a daylight fast. This fast is practice for Ramadan: all children over the age of six months (and most adults as well) use the day to acquaint themselves with the rules of sawm, and build the self-discipline to follow them. The night preceding Mebas marks Miraj, when Muhammad ascended to heaven and brought a vision of Paradise back to the faithful. The event is commemorated by a prayer service of twenty-two rak'ats.

Shaban (The Eighth Month)

1: Zikra, a day on which the life and teachings of Syedna Taher Saifuddin are remembered. The breaking of the Rajab fast also marks the beginning of Jamea tus-Saifiya examinations in Surat. The da'i personally presides over the oral and written tests, which last between ten and twelve days. Syedna celebrates zikra with a majlis, for which many dignitaries from all over the Bohra world travel to Surat.

15: Shabb-e-Baraat, the longest individual namaz of the year. A nighttime prayer of only fourteen rak'ats, but each rak'at here takes almost twelve minutes to perform, so the entire ritual takes an hour and a half. By contrast, a typical namaz of twenty-four rak'ats can be performed in about fifteen minutes.

RAMADAN

The ninth month of the Islamic calendar is a period for fasting, spiritual self-examination, and the reinforcement of religious identity throughout the Muslim world. Like other Muslims, Bohras observe the fast with great rigor: from daybreak until sunset, not so much as a drop of water can enter their bodies. There are no half measures for the young or old or ill: one either fasts completely, or puts sawm off until such time as it can be undertaken wholeheartedly. There is no stigma attached to a sick or infirm person postponing sawm, but avoidance solely for personal comfort is strongly discouraged. The social pressure exerted by other community members during Ramadan is stronger than at most other times of the year, and it is for this very reason that many Bohras choose to live in predominantly Bohra mohallas or neighborhoods: it is much easier to do the right thing when everyone else around you is undergoing the same hard-

ship. The mutual reinforcement lightens the load, and serves as a powerful reminder not to shuck the burden surreptitiously.

The daily Ramadan schedule of most Bohras differs markedly from that of their Sunni neighbors.[37] The Sunnis of Muhammad Ali Road often reverse their day and nighttime schedules: they stay awake until three or four in the morning, eat a large dinner before going to bed, then sleep until noon and keep their shops open from three P.M. until midnight. Bohras are under no special dawat instructions as to how to fit their Ramadan observances into the course of their lives, but most follow a pattern similar to that of Zain Gunja. Like most Bohras, Zain tries to keep his work schedule as normal as possible. Each evening during Ramadan he goes to bed at nine o'clock rather than his customary 11 P.M. He rises at four o'clock in the morning and starts the day with a hearty meal: in order not to inadvertently mistime the beginning of his daily fast, he does not eat anything for a full hour before dawn. Zain goes to the masjid for morning namaz, and reaches his office at the normal time. While many Bohras go to masjid for the midday namaz as well, Zain says his midday prayers at his office. He closes up shop at 5:00 P.M. rather than his customary 7:00 P.M. and goes to the masjid for evening namaz and iftar. He arrives home around 7:30 and spends the remaining hour and a half with his family, or accepts invitations to celebrate a less hurried iftar with neighbors, friends, or relatives.

Ramadan is a time for settling financial obligations. Muslims typically pay *zakat* (Islamic poor-tax) during Ramadan, and Bohras are no exception. In addition, Bohras pay a range of other community fees and voluntary contributions during this month. In Mumbai, they will either give the money to their local amil, or go across town to deliver it to Syedna personally at his Saifee Mahal residence. During Ramadan the rich are under special obligation to give money to the poor: more so than at any other time of year, donations are considered the right of the deserving needy. Beggars from all parts of Mumbai converge on Muhammad Ali Road during Ramadan, and business is often exceptionally good. This is also the period in which Muslim employers typically give their workers a bonus. As a result, it is the only time of the year when many of the less advantaged members of the community have much disposable income. Ramadan is a time for haircuts and new clothes, for long-delayed household purchases and Eid gifts for the children. Bazaars are particularly vibrant during the evenings of Ramadan, especially as the holy month winds to a close.

In a paradox that is only initially surprising, the month of fasting is also the month of feasting. Every evening after namaz, all the major avenues of Muslim neighborhoods in Mumbai are filled with a rich profusion of food and drink. Traffic becomes even more intense than usual (if such a

thing can be imagined), with office workers from all parts of the city racing home to break the fast with their families. Street and sidewalk alike are packed with cars and motorbikes, with food sellers and food eaters, with toy vendors and eager-eyed children.

The largely Bohra streets surrounding Saifee Masjid are even more exuberant than most. On each Ramadan evening, but particularly on special nights such as the twenty-first and twenty-third, every thoroughfare and tiny alleyway is packed with vendors. From late afternoon onward there is a frantically festive atmosphere, with hundreds of chefs busily cooking to make sure their choicest delicacies are ready the moment namaz ends. Saifee Masjid is lit up in green and white lights, which illuminate the dusk as the sun slips away. About fifteen minutes after sunset the congregants pour out of the mosque, and the neighborhood erupts into an hour-long riot of consumption. Shoulder-to-shoulder stalls hawk enough types of food to satiate any fasting stomach: savory grilled morsels of chicken and lamb *tikka;* plastic bags full of *falooda,* the spaghetti-laced ice-cream beckoning with its neon orange, purple, blue, or yellow glow; piping hot *samosas* and *pakoras,* scooped from pans of wickedly bubbling oil; palmnuts, pineapples, strawberries, bananas, oranges, and other fresh fruit cascading out of their baskets and splattering on the ground; fried eggs, fried potatoes, and fried brains of various types of livestock; shallow earthenware bowls of white custard topped with a microthin layer of edible Mughlai silver leaf.

Ramadan Days of Special Ritual

Throughout the month of Ramadan, the da'i will say namaz publicly three times every day. Syedna Muhammad Burhanuddin has performed "imamate namaz" (congregational prayer, as opposed to the private saying of salat) three times daily during Ramadan for over thirty years; his father Taher Saifuddin maintained this practice for fifty-three years. The dates of special observance (the first three each marked with special night prayers of twenty-four rak'ats) are as follows:

17 Commemorates Amina, the mother of the Prophet Muhammad.

19 Waaz dedicated to Ali. This is the date of Ali's martyrdom (according to Bohra observance), and it also commemorates the mother of Ali.

21 Commemorates Khadija, the Prophet's first wife and the mother of Fatima.

23 Lailat al-Qadr: This ritual, the most important of Ramadan, commemorates the birth date of Hazrat Fatima.

Eve of Eid: A prayer of twenty-four rak'ats, followed by one of ten rak'ats.

These rituals have been institutionalized for at least the past century, as they are noted by Abdul Husain.[38]

Lailat al-Qadr

If a Bohra observes only one Ramadan ritual, this is the one.[39] Particularly devout Bohras spend the entire night at the masjid, while those who cannot come to the masjid typically stay awake all night in fasting and prayer at home. The date is often referred to by its Gujarati name of Jagvanirat. Typically Bohras say their isha prayers shortly after their maghrib ones, but on this night the isha namaz begins around 10:30 P.M. The highlight of the night is Syedna's *wasila* (set prayer for divine forgiveness), beginning around 2 A.M.

Competition for a space at all of the masjids is fierce. Any Bohra is permitted to attend any masjid at any time, but in order to prevent overcrowding, people are strongly encouraged to go to the mosque in their own neighborhood. Even local masjids, however, become overstuffed on a night such as Lailat al-Qadr: like Christians flocking to church on Christmas and Easter, many Bohras participate in community rituals only on Lailat al-Qadr and Ashura. Those who come to masjid week in and week out do not like to be displaced for part-timers, so there are informal rules about who has or has not earned the right to be present. At particularly crowded masjids the rights of attendance during special days, sometimes even rights to a particular spot in the chamber, are informally handed down from father to son. The man with whom I attended Lailat al-Qadr services during my fieldwork was a regular participant of services at Husaini Masjid, but on this day he did not have the quasi-hereditary right to attend; I, of course, was not even in the running. "We could show up," my friend told me, "but then somebody else would not be able to get in. It would not be very polite." He had arranged to pray at Qutbi Masjid instead. As a guest of the dawat I had been offered choice space in Saifee Masjid, but I decided it would be more politic to join the crowd in the street outside Badri Mahal.

The main offices of the dawat are not normally a major site of religious observance: the small masjid there is used by dawat officials, but anyone important enough to be working in Badri Mahal is also important enough to pray at the flagship Saifee Masjid. On this night, however, every available site had to be put to full use. The downtown colonial-era office building was strung with red and green lanterns, and all of the surrounding streets had been cordoned off by municipal police and Bohra security guards. Inside the building, kneeling space was limited to important indi-

viduals and early-birds. All the streets and alleyways outside, however, had been turned into an impromptu extension of the masjid.

Owing to strict municipal limits on the construction of new masjids or expansion of existing ones,[40] Muslims of all denominations (both in Mumbai and throughout India) must spill out onto the street during particularly busy holy days. On the night of Lailat al-Qadr, the overflow audience seemed to outnumber the tightly packed ranks inside Badri Mahal. The devout set prayer rugs, oilcloths, or layers of newspaper down on ground, while beggars from all over the city congregated around the congregants. The ritual followed the same basic patterns as those described above: namaz, matam, and hymns, building up to an emotional wasila delivered by the da'i in the early hours of the morning. It is said that fasting and prayer on Lailat al-Qadr are superior to the prayers and fasts of a thousand other months.[41] Such spiritual merit, perhaps, gives Bohras the will to spend all night kneeling in the soggy, unidentifiable muck of the alleyways of central Mumbai.

RAMADAN TO ZYL-HAJJ

Shawwal (The Tenth Month)

1: Eid al-Fitr. Like Muslims the world over, Bohras celebrate Eid al-Fitr as perhaps the most joyous festival of the year. The day begins with fajr namaz at sunrise, followed by the breaking of the night's fast with a dried date. During the day Bohras will typically visit neighbors and relatives, and eat festive foods such as sweetened milk or dried fruit. Traditionally families would send out greeting cards or letters, but today many use telephone, fax, or e-mail to wish their friends Eid Mubarak ("Happy Eid"—the Islamic "Season's Greetings").

Zilqaad (The Eleventh Month)

27: Milad of Syedna Taher Saifuddin. The only two da'is whose birthdays are celebrated are the current supreme pontiff and his predecessor; all other da'is are commemorated only by urs. Both birthdays are joyous occasions.

ZYL-HAJJ

For Bohras, as for all Muslims, the pilgrimage of Hajj is obligatory at least once in the life of every believer who is able to make such a trip. Respondents to my survey ranked this an aspect of orthopraxy second only to

contact with Syedna, and 89.4 % cited it as a fundamental obligation of the faith. Of my survey respondents who were questioned on the topic, 83.3 % reported having made use of the dawat's services in arranging their hajj and pilgrimage to Kerbala.

As at Ashura, the logistics of assembling, transporting, feeding, and housing such a large group of travelers would be impossible without modern communications technology. Moreover, without telephones, faxes, computerized plane reservations, and other modern tools, it would be very difficult to organize a large-scale cycle of hajj rituals at variance with the sequence undertaken by almost all other Muslims. As Barbara Metcalf notes, the experience of hajj is perhaps the greatest unifying ritual in Islam: "If a person is 'finding himself' he is doing so in a crowd, following a ritual program of dress and behavior meant precisely to obliterate the markers that make a believer distinct by class, race or region."[42] That Bohras keep themselves strictly separate even on hajj—the one rite that Muslims of nearly all nations and denominations can celebrate together— is both a marker of and a means for perpetuating their distinct identity.

Although the timing of Bohra rituals differs from that of other Muslims, the rites forming the pilgrimage experience are similar or (in many cases) identical to those of Sunnis and Ithna-Asharis.[43] The main differences are as follows:

—While most Muslims are free to undertake hajj on either an individual or a group basis, Bohras make their hajj in an organized group under the guidance of an *emir al-hajj* appointed by the dawat. Often during the twentieth century this duty fell to Syedna's brother, the late Syedi Saleh Bhaisaheb Safiyuddin; the mukasir and ex officio head amil of Mumbai, Syedi Saleh Bhaisaheb performed hajj thirty-seven times, pilgrimage to Kerbala more than forty times, and umra over one hundred times.[44]

—The dates of observance differ slightly, so Bohras generally begin their rituals a day or two earlier than Sunnis.

—Unless they have relations or friends living in Mecca, Bohras stay in private dawat-run musafirkhanas rather than in the hostels that Saudi authorities set up for hajj pilgrims.

—Bohras shave off *all* of the hair on their scalps after hajj, while some Sunni pilgrims interpret the direction more loosely.

—A ritual in which pilgrims hop on one leg is performed only by men among Bohra pilgrims, and by both men and women among Sunnis.

—In the "Stoning of the Devil" ritual,[45] each Bohra pilgrim throws precisely twenty-one stones at the symbolic boulder on the ninth of zyl-Hajj, and thirty-three stones on each of the next two days. Even the size of stone is carefully regulated: they should be modest, well-rounded pebbles. Sunni

pilgrims, in what Bohras consider an undisciplined display of violence, re-place the traditional number of stones with a bombardment of large rocks, sticks, and even sandals.

For those members of the community not traveling to Mecca, the month of zyl-Hajj contains two important dates:

10–12: Eid al-Adha (Bakri Eid). Day of sacrifice for all who have per-formed hajj.

18: Eid Ghadir Khumm. The day on which the oath of mithaq is made and reaffirmed by all members of the community.

Eid al-Adha (Bakri Eid)

The Bohra observance of Bakri Eid is basically the same as that of Sunnis and other Muslims. All hajjis are required to sacrifice a goat (hence the name of the festival, *bakri* = goat; other animals may be substituted, as described below) and use the meat to provide a feast for family members or alms for the poor. People who have not performed hajj are also welcome to sacrifice, and *hajjis* are free to pay a local butcher or some other proxy to sacrifice in their stead, but it is considered particularly appropriate to perform the sacrifice with one's own hands.[46] It is customary to prepare a lavish dinner featuring *pettar ka ghosht* (as the name implies, meat cooked on rocks), in some cases with stones brought from Mecca by a family member. Bohras are free to decide the logistics of their goat sacrifice in any way they see fit. Many perform the rite in their chawls, so that the en-tire family can watch and take part. Many others fulfill their obligation at the local jamatkhana: in that way they avoid arguments with non-Muslim neighbors, save themselves the problems of cleaning up the inevitable bloody mess, and keep away the kites, ravens, and rats that the fresh gore can attract.

Bohra organizations (both jamatkhanas and privately organized trusts) provide the infrastructure necessary to facilitate Bakri Eid: urban professionals are generally inexperienced in the techniques of slaughter and butchery, so in the modern age they often require the assistance of professionals with premodern expertise. These groups offer a sort of one-stop shopping for all of a person's sacrificial needs. Instead of finding and buying a goat, leading it to a decent slaughter-site, finding a few friends to help kill it, finding a person who reads Arabic to recite the appropriate verses, getting a sufficient supply of sharp knives and buckets of water, dismembering the carcass, dividing it into parcels of meat for distribution to the poor, and cleaning the site afterward—instead of performing all of these tasks himself, a hajji can simply go to the jamatkhana and purchase tickets to have any or all of them carried out by a proxy. Many Sunni and

Ithna-Ashari *waqfs* (trusts) perform a similar function, setting up chairs and booths on the streets during Eid, with the same air of casual camaraderie as Rotarians selling raffles for a church social. They are often distinguished by large piles of goatskins (like meat, a hajji donation) laid out beside their folding tables on the sidewalks of Muhammad Ali Road.

During the second year of my Mumbai fieldwork, Bohra Eid fell two days earlier than Sunni Eid. Since sacrifices can take place on any day within a three-day period, the rituals overlapped. Many Bohras put off their sacrifices owing to overcrowding at the jamatkhanas: the rite itself can take as little as fifteen minutes, but because of heavy demand the waiting lines begin forming well before dawn on the tenth of zyl-Hajj. Some families try to purchase their sacrificial animal ahead of time to avoid the last-minute buying rush and spike in prices, but others (in the interests of mohalla harmony) synchronize their butchering with that of their Sunni neighbors.

Ritual slaughter—whether performed by a hajji at Eid or a *halal* butcher at any time of year—should be carried out in accordance with a strict set of rules.[47] For a Bohra hajji during Bakri Eid, the main rules are as follows: (1) He should turn the animal's face toward qiblah, and recite the bismillah prayer. The purpose of the set phrase is to sanctify an action that would otherwise be profane: it is never right to kill any creature without a good purpose, so the butcher must note that he performs his duty out of obligation. (2) The knife used for the slaughter must be razor-sharp, since a sharp knife is less painful than a dull, blunted blade. (3) He must give the goat a final drink of water. This act of ritualized kindness, common to all Muslims, has special saliency for Bohras (and other Shi'a): like so many aspects of daily life, it brings to mind the sufferings of Imam Husain. As Husain lay dying on the fields of Kerbala, the Umayyads refused him even a sip of water—they gave him a worse death than they would have inflicted on an animal. (4) The sacrifice should be performed on soil rather than stone or concrete (as other Muslims often prefer, for ease of cleanup). If the rite takes place in a paved chawl, soil is brought in and spread on the ground, and afterward the blood-soaked dirt is thrown away.[48]

At the Eid I observed, all the streets surrounding Bhindi Bazaar and Muhammad Ali Road were full of Muslims of different denominations performing their sacrifices. The events I witnessed are typical both of Bohra and of Sunni or Ithna-Ashari rites.

From daybreak onward the neighborhood is packed with goats. Many have painted horns, wreathes of tinsel, or garlands of flowers around their necks to celebrate their status as victims-to-be,[49] and some have the Is-

lamic symbol of a star and crescent shaved or painted onto their hides. The animals bleat and grunt contentedly, oblivious to the carnage taking place all around them, unconcerned with the spectacle of so many other animals in various stages of bodily disassembly. Children happily pet the goats, feed them snacks, and then lead them to the slaughter.

On Bakri Eid, the streets and sidewalks of Bhindi Bazaar are turned into an open-air abattoir. The killing is constant, most concerted between dawn and late morning (10:30 A.M. or so), but a steady procession throughout the day. The actions are all in line with the ideal pattern, but the practice is much coarser than the theory.*

First the goat is led to a bucket of water, its head shoved inside for the last drink of mercy; invariably the animal panics, ignorant of the fact that the water is a gift while the real danger lies not in the bucket but the knife. After its final drink the goat is thrown to the ground and held firmly in place. For a tough animal this may require three strong men, as well as a fourth to slit its throat. Smaller animals may need only two men, if both are experienced: one man holds all four legs, the other clamps the goat's mouth shut with one hand while angling the head upward to expose the neck. Another man learned in Arabic recites a Qur'anic verse blessing the sacrifice. Often in Bhindi Bazaar one sees such men moving from one slaughter to the next, each man's religious stature marked by beard and skullcap, the sheet of paper from which he recites covered in a sheath of plastic to protect it from splattered blood. Sometimes he merely recites the prayer; sometimes he performs the actual slitting of the throat, and pockets a few coins or small bills before moving on to another sacrifice.

Children cluster around, watching the killings with a mixture of squeamishness and fascination. They push forward at the moment of incision, then jump back with cries of disgust and delight as geysers of blood shoot out. Each time the main artery is severed cleanly, a thin stream of blood arcs in a four-foot-long jet that soaks everything nearby. A goat whose throat has been slit expertly will die in a matter of moments (the rules of

*An observer with little personal experience of animal slaughter might be shocked at the festive atmosphere surrounding the matter-of-fact butchery: that was my initial reaction, and may well be the emotional response of many readers. But it took less than half an hour of direct observation for me to become thoroughly inured to the process, and I suspect many other outsiders would have a similar response. The phenomenon is oddly reminiscent of the Anthropology Goat Roast celebrated each year at Harvard's Peabody Museum: the animal butchered (with Neolithic tools, no less!) in the well-groomed courtyard has already been killed, gutted, and drained of blood, but the celebratory mood surrounding its dismemberment is remarkably similar to that on Muhammad Ali Road.

halal butchery are designed to minimize the pain of the animal), but a beast whose neck has been hacked at clumsily will suffer a long and agonizing death. One of the goats whose sacrifice I witnessed spent several lengthy minutes bleeding its life away: for the first thirty seconds it lay thrashing on the pavement, its throat gaping like a second mouth spewing yellow bile from its stomach, its head bent back at an angle nature never intended. Then the animal settled into a confused daze: still alive—but stunned to be staring directly at the hide covering its own spine. A few moments after the butcher had moved on to the next animal, the goat seemed to recover from its initial shock. Its nose began to twitch, its breathing became more labored, its legs began kicking with all their waning strength. The death-throes lasted at least two more minutes. Each time I thought the animal had finally sunk away, the nearly decapitated goat would start kicking again with renewed vigor, trying one last, fruitless time to scramble back into life.

At the busier sites of sacrifice the goats are laid in a row, like a factory assembly line in reverse. One animal will be held down for slaughter, the next will be on the ground dying, a third strung up in the process of dismemberment, a fourth already reduced to haunches of meat being cleaned and sorted. A trained butcher can skin, gut, and carve up a carcass in about ten minutes, but on this day there is a shortage of trained butchers and a surplus of amateurs. The butchering process becomes a social event, with overhelpful friends and onlookers offering competing advice on cutting techniques.

On Muhammad Ali Road, a goat's body is bled out before being cut apart for meat. Ideally the carcass will be hung up to drain, but if there is no space available it may simply be left on the pavement until much of the blood has flowed out. Sometimes the blood stains the ground a deep brown, other times the hyperoxygenated flow is so bright a shade of red that it looks artificial, like the stage blood used in a theatrical production. The heads are chopped off and stacked in a pile. Before they are skinned and prepared for sale, the severed heads can look completely alive: lips pulled away from the teeth in a final silent bleat, eyes not yet dull or glassy, the pyramid growing taller as the day goes on.

In order to be properly skinned and gutted the goat is strung up by its hind legs, usually suspended from a cord tossed over a high beam. This is a particularly good reason not to perform one's sacrifice at home: when the corpse is hung vertically, a steady stream of blood and partially digested food pours out of the goat's innards. Several men start to skin the animal at once, breaking a foot to begin the separation of flesh from hide.

They meticulously cut at the leg with small knives or razor blades, periodically splashing water into the skin to make it easier to peel away. When the bony forelegs have been skinned and chopped off, the butcher pulls off the rest of the hide almost in one piece. He leans against the carcass and yanks with all his might, while his assistants loosen stubborn bits with water and blades. The hide is peeled off like a scuba wetsuit, or a pair of Lycra biking shorts several sizes too small.

The goat's belly is then slit, and the internal organs plop to the ground. They lie there, among the remains of earlier sacrificial victims, swarmed by flies and picked over by cats. The huge gray stomach will usually be discarded, but the dark purple liver, pinkish intestines and other viscera will eventually be washed and prepared for sale. The butcher cuts out the heart, lungs, and esophagus and places them in a bucket of water. Once all the guts are removed from the carcass there seems to be little left: just a smallish sack of meat-covered bones, as if the whole animal had been composed of organs.

Once he has taken all of the innards out, the butcher cuts off the upper front legs, chops the ribcage in half, and in the case of larger carcasses may hack the front portion of the body cleanly off to be cut apart by an assistant. Paring scraps of flesh from bits of bone does not require the collaboration of strong men: young boys with dull, rusty knives finish the process of transforming bakri into ghosht—goat into meat.

All up and down the length of Muhammad Ali Road, from Crawford Market straight up to Mazgaon, people carry buckets full of severed heads and hooves, baskets of bloody haunches and bloody hides. A hundred impromptu butcher stalls pop up to dispose of the abundance of fresh mutton, equally willing to sell a whole lamb or just a limb. Sometimes the skinned, gutted carcass is taken home whole to be cut apart by the women of the household, sometimes it is parceled into its component parts and brought home in neat packages of plastic or oilskin. Goat torsos hang from meat hooks, their bushy tails the only skin left unshorn. Veteran butchers, inured through long decades of familiarity with the insides of animals, blow into lungs to inflate them for an easier sale. Gore-encrusted carving knives are brandished as casually as letter openers.

Despite the charnel-house atmosphere, the mood is one of celebration. Many girls (and even a few boys) have festive mehndi patterns painted on their hands. Vendors sell balloons, trinkets, and glittery toy swords, bows, or slingshots. Children in their finest dress-up clothing play giddy games of tag amidst the carnage, and go on pony rides through the gut-stained streets and alleyways. Garbage pickers examine the discarded goat stomachs for any overlooked bonanza: human scavengers poring

over the remains of animal scavengers to make sure no indigestible watch, ring, or necklace goes to waste.

Sometimes the Eid sacrifice turns into a particularly special occasion. At one butcher stall the crowd gathered is so thick that only those in the front can see the source of the commotion: the carcass being dismembered here is far too large to be that of a goat. In a city governed by the Hindu militants of Shiv Sena, the slaughter of a cow is a potentially explosive action. Onlookers divide their attention between the sacrifice being performed and the rumble of a mob they imagine approaching from Hindu neighborhoods nearby. Next to the slaughtering floor, a compact bullock with a garland around its neck chews its cud in placid boredom, completely oblivious to its impending fate.

A very rich hajji, or one wishing to make a special effort to impress his neighbors, may choose to sacrifice a camel. This custom is predictably rare in sites far from any desert. I witnessed only one instance of camel sacrifice in Mumbai (and then only the preparatory stages): like the aforementioned instance of cow slaughter, it was performed by a Sunni rather than a Bohra. The hajji paraded his camel through the streets of Bhindi Bazaar, attracting an ever larger crowd with every block. Few of the children would even have seen a camel before. There was robust speculation as to how and where the animal would be killed, but hopes of an unmatched Eid display were soon put to rest: the camel was only being shown off here, not butchered on the spot. Once he had gathered his glory, the hajji ordered his assistants to load the camel back into his truck, and carted it away to be sacrificed in private splendor.

The Bohra view of Eid sacrifice is considerably more complex than that of most mainstream Sunnis or Ithna-Ashariyya: it is a multilayered ritual that can be appreciated at levels ranging from the most straightforward to the most metaphysical. At its simplest, Eid sacrifice for the Bohras (as for other Muslims) is an act of charity, an occasion on which both hajjis and nonhajjis supply a feast of goat meat to the less-advantaged members of society. At a slightly more spiritual level but still within the sphere of *zahir* (open) knowledge, Eid is an annual remembrance of an important event in the development of Islam. Despite their nomenclature, Ismailis would have no more zahir stake in the tale of this Ismail than would any other Muslims: Bakri Eid commemorates Ismail ibn Ibrahim—known to Christians and Jews as Ishmael, son of Abraham—not Ismail ibn Jafar, the pivotal imam (or, to the Ithna-Ashariyya, non-imam) of Shi'ism.

At a deeper level, however, Ismail's rescue from sacrifice holds special symbolic meaning for Ismailis. The elements of Ismail ibn Ibrahim's story—a blameless individual facing unmerited execution, miraculously

saved at the last instant by divine intervention—would hold a natural appeal to members of a denomination that has faced religious persecution from fellow Muslims for over a thousand years.

For Bohras, however, these explanations only begin to scratch the surface. At a batin level, clerical sources have told me, the Eid sacrifice has another whole range of metaphysical interpretations. I (like the large majority of Bohras) am not privy to the deeper recesses of batini ta'wil. I was given vague hints about batini meanings, and was able to draw certain other inferences based on my reading of Fatimid texts, but only a person with access to gnostic teachings would be able to say how accurate these hints and inferences may be.

Briefly, Bohras view the killing of any animal as an event laden with spiritual meaning. What this meaning might be is a matter beyond the realm of zahir knowledge: as one clerical source put it, "We believe that what happens to the animal is a good thing. The animal will be rewarded. More than that I am not at liberty to say." The Fatimid theologians who crystallized much Ismaili doctrine were deeply influenced by neoplatonic ideas such as metempsychosis or transmigration of souls. The similarity of such ideas to Hindu concepts of reincarnation (which Bohras reject) suggests the rationale for keeping these metaphysical explanations limited to those community members able to appreciate the subtle distinctions.[50]

Regardless of their level of knowledge, Bohras understand that animal slaughter—whether the daily work of a halal butcher, or (far more powerfully) the hajji's sacrifice at Bakri Eid—is something deeper than the mere killing and consumption of one species by another. Most Bohras today may choose to delegate their Eid duty to a bloody-smocked professional, but they are strongly encouraged at least to witness the sacrifice. Most will not comprehend the deeper batini meanings of the rite being performed in their names, but they will know that they are partaking in something far greater than goat, far greater than man.

CHAPTER FOUR

Bohra Domestic Life: Kinship,

Sex, and the Status of Women

A nthropologists tend to find kinship structures interesting. Most other people, to put it mildly, don't. I present kinship data for the anthropological record, but a general reader may wish to skip directly to the second section of this chapter (p. 118).

KINSHIP

Despite their embrace of modernity in other aspects of life, when it comes to matters of kinship Bohras are highly traditional. The Bohras do not practice a prescriptive marriage system, but almost all unions within the community are arranged and endogamous. Out of 169 households in my survey, 99.4% reported that all members of their extended families had married partners within the community, and 96.8% said all family unions were both endogamous and arranged.[1]

These figures indicate that *qaum* endogamy (endogamy bounded by the community or sect) is somewhat stronger among the Bohras than among other Indian Shi'a groups. Hasnain and Husain's survey of Indian Shi'a breaks its results down by several prominent qaums, including Syeds, Sheikhs, Mughals, Pathans, and Khojahs; in matters of kinship, the respondent's qaum is a significantly better predictor of kinship attitudes than is the respondent's economic or educational level.[2] Of those surveyed, 87.1% practiced qaum endogamy when seeking a mate for their sons, while 95.4% did so for their daughters. The figures are only marginally lower than average for postgraduates and professionals, and unions with Sunnis are slightly higher than average at *both* ends of the educational spectrum (postgraduates and illiterates are closer to each than to the mean).[3]

While Bohras were not included in the Hasnain and Husain survey, much can be inferred from the responses of Khojahs: as a prosperous community of Gujarati Ismaili merchants based in and near Mumbai, Khojahs are closer to the Bohras in both religious experience and demo-

graphics than perhaps any other social group. It is noteworthy that Khojah respondents to the survey were significantly more endogamous than those of any other qaum. Every one of the Khojah respondents cited "family" as the prime factor to be considered when selecting a mate for their children.[4] Furthermore, not one of the Khojah respondents was willing to countenance a child's marriage to a member of any other sect or faith. By way of comparison, 40% of the Pathan (*Pukhtun*) respondents were willing to marry their sons to the daughters of Shi'a converts.[5]

Bohra and Khojah endogamy makes sense in both religious and cultural terms: ever since the end of the Fatimid caliphate Ismailis have kept themselves separate, both religiously and socially, from other Muslims. As in theology, so too in wedlock.

Kinship Structure

As Imtiaz Ahmad properly notes, the normative models of Islamic kinship are not always in accord with the on-the-ground facts of Muslim family life in India. Ahmad contends that some observers "have tended to disregard the possibility of a chasm dividing the stated ideals of Islam and social practices altogether or they ignore the deviations from the stated norms, wherever they occur."[6] Rather than present a wholly distinct kinship paradigm, Ahmad argues, Indian Muslims tend to follow the paradigms of their neighbors: "Muslim family norms in India correspond closely to those held among Hindus."[7] While Ahmad's observations may well hold true for Indian Muslims in general, their applicability to Shi'a in particular is less easily documented. The assessment of P. N. Chopra, in his overview of various religious minorities in India, seems hyperbolic when applying Ahmad's dictum to the Daudi kinship patterns: "In effect, the Bohras became something akin to a Hindu subcaste practicing endogamy, a hereditary occupation and the outcasting of rebels."[8]

Ahmad provides a valuable service by highlighting the limits of the Islamic kinship paradigm, and his edited volume presents many specific case studies, which document his critique.[9] But Bohra kinship patterns, like those of Indian Ithna-Asharis, seem to exhibit fewer Hindu traits than those of other syncretic Muslim communities. "Unlike Hindus, Shi'a maintain a narrow range of kinship," Hasnain and Husain write. Ties to both paternal and maternal consanguineous kin (kin by blood) are strong, but ties to affinal relatives (kin by marriage) are weak.[10] The Bohra pattern of kinship seems in closer accord with the Shi'a framework outlined above than to the patterns of Gujarati Hindus. As can be gauged from the terms used for various relatives, consanguineous kin are strictly differentiated into

those of the direct patrilineal branch and all others. In actual practice the lines are not quite as clear: I have seen many families in which ties to the maternal relatives seem to be at least as strong as ties to the paternal line.[11]

Household Type

Hasnain and Husain describe several interlocking types of familial living arrangement observed among Indian Shi'a: a nuclear family consists of husband, wife, and unmarried children; an extended family consists of a nuclear family, with the addition of several other relatives (whether male or female, from the mother's or the father's kin); and a joint family, consisting of a group of nuclear or extended families related patrilineally. Put within this framework, Bohra households are typically extended rather than nuclear or joint families. The largest percentage of households in my survey (66.3%) were families of between four and six members. Another 23.1% of the households had between seven and ten members, typically an extended nuclear family with several unmarried relatives. Only 7.7% of households were joint family structures of eleven to twenty members, and a mere 3.0% had fewer than four members. As a percentage of the survey population (1,068 individuals) rather than of households, the figures shift slightly toward units with more family members (this stands to reason: larger households contain more people), but the ratios remain roughly the same.[12]

The preference for joint families (even if this preference cannot be accommodated as often as in the past) is a trait commonly associated with Hindu Gujaratis as well. Leila Narayanan notes that Gujaratis in Madras are unusual among migrant communities in largely retaining the traditional joint family structure; nearly one-third of the households in her survey contained either parents with married sons and their families or several brothers with their families and unmarried siblings.[13] The preference for joint families is one area in which Imtiaz Ahmad's analysis of Muslim kinship patterns holds true for the Bohras. While such living arrangements are typically associated with Hindu society, such patterns are no less common among subcontinental Muslims. As George Conklin notes, "In terms of joint households, ideals of joint living, and in having sons actually stay home until the death of the father, the Muslims seem to be, in fact as well as in theory, identical to or more conservative than non-Muslims."[14]

Bohras likewise mirror their Hindu Gujarati compatriots in their pattern of moving from joint families to extended or nuclear families as their educational levels rise. In a survey of 467 families living in eleven Gujarati

CHART FOR BOHRA KINSHIP TERMS [15]

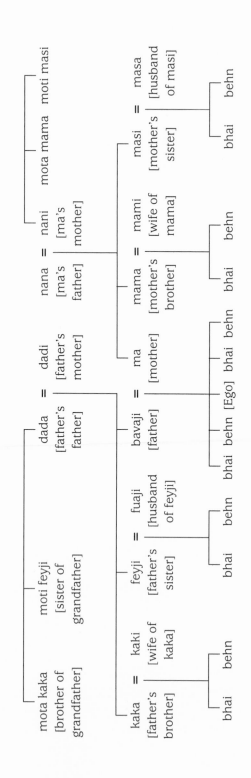

In this chart, Ego is presumed to be a man. Some terms would be different for a female Ego (see below), but in general Bohra kinship terminology differs with respect to the gender of the person described, not the person doing the describing.

The parents of Ego's wife are called *sasra* (her father) and *saso* (her mother). This is also the case in both Urdu and Gujarati. Likewise, the terms for Ego's paternal grandparents (*dada* and *dadi*) are almost identical to those in both Urdu and Gujarati. Other terms, such as those for Ego's mother (*ma*), maternal uncle and aunt (*mama* and *masi*) and their spouses (*mami* and *masa*) are the same as those of other Gujarati dialects, but not commonly used in Urdu. (For similarities among other Gujarati groups, cf. Misra 1964: 175.)

A wife calls her in-laws by the same names that her husband uses (e.g., her father-in-law's brother is *kaka*). A husband, however, refers to all of his in-laws as if they were members of his own mother's lineage (e.g., his mother-in-law's sister is called *masi*).

All male relatives of the same generation as Ego—whether brothers, first cousins, or kin so distant as to be utter strangers—are referred to as *bhai* (brother). All female relatives of the same generation as Ego are referred to as *behn* (sister). There is no separate term to distinguish elder from younger siblings. These same kinship terms are also used in reference to *any* member of the community, whether an actual relation or not. Bohras, like other Gujaratis, use *bhai* where Hindi or Urdu speakers might use the honorific -*ji*.

The siblings of Ego's father's mother are called by the same terms as the siblings of both of Ego's mother's parents: that is, all great-uncles (except the father's father's brothers) are called *mota mama*, and all great-aunts (except the father's father's sister) are called *moti masi*.

In more formal usage, the suffix -*ji* can be added to any of the above titles for Ego's elders. It is not uncommon for a Bohra to refer to his paternal grandfather (for example) as *dadaji*, or even *dadaji saheb*.

Usage displays considerable local adaptation. The use of predominantly Hindi kinship nicknames alongside Gujarati ones, for example, is not uncommon. The most widely used seem to be *chacha* (uncle), *chachi* (aunt), and *bobi* (brother's wife).

The terms *kaka/feyji, dada/dadi,* and *mota kaka/moti feyji* are used only for those kin in Ego's direct patrilineal line. All other relatives are called *mama/masi, nana/nani, mota mama/moti masi,* and so forth.

villages, Richard and Martha Anker examined the attitudes of both high-caste Patidars and middle-caste *banias*. They report:

> Desired family size was relatively small, and a majority of respondents said that economic factors were the reason for the small desired family size. . . . Level of education tended to be inversely related to family size preferences, actual family size and completed family size, and directly related to family planning acceptance.
> These findings are in general agreement with the findings of previous research in India and elsewhere.[16]

When compared specifically to other Shi'a communities, Bohras show greater similarity to Gujarati Shi'a than to Shi'a from different parts of the subcontinent. Overall, 56.7% of Shi'a surveyed by Hasnain and Husain lived in nuclear families, 33.8% in extended families, and 9.5% in joint families. In Gujarat, however, the figures are 32% in nuclear families, 52% in extended families (the Bohra norm), and 16% in joint families.[17] Wherever they live, Bohras have traditionally chosen to reside in close geographical proximity to each other. As Leila Narayanan notes, most ethnic or religious minorities tend to congregate in specific locales, but "Gujaratis particularly show a preference for settling along ethnic lines." Keralan migrants in Madras tend to move to the suburban Civil Lines as soon as they can afford to do so, but even wealthy Gujaratis prefer to remain near their shops in the central business district of Sowcarpet.[18]

Many well-to-do Bohras of Mumbai choose to live in the congested chawls and alleys of Bhindi Bazaar and Muhammad Ali Road rather than relocate to more spacious housing in the suburbs. In recent decades, technological innovation has permitted Bohras to spread throughout the city while still remaining in close touch with their own community: those who opt for upscale, ethnically and religiously mixed neighborhoods like Colaba, Cuffe Parade, or Malabar Hill (or more modest mixed neighborhoods like Santa Cruz and Bandra) maintain their social ties to the community with the help of telephones, public transportation, and now e-mail.

In matters of inheritance, Bohras have been adopting Qur'anic patterns with increasing regularity over the past two decades. Until the Islamization reforms of Syedna Muhammad Burhanuddin, Bohras had often followed the Hindu laws of inheritance. By observing traditional rules mandating specific inheritances for women, Bohras have very rapidly become significantly more "Islamic" than many other Indian Muslim groups: in a survey of family and kinship practices among Indian Muslims, Imtiaz Ahmad notes that with the exception of groups such as the Nimkhera Pukhtun (who, unlike Peshawar Valley Pukhtun, also follow

Qur'anic regulations), "women are excluded from inheritance except what their fathers set aside as a marriage portion. This seems to be the general practice among all the other communities on whom we have data." R. P. Khatana reports that Gujar Bakarwal women of Jammu and Kashmir receive only enough inheritance for their dowries (which will go to their husbands, in any case). Partap Aggarwal and A. R. Saiyid record the same situation for the Meos of Rajasthan and Koknis of Maharashtra respectively. In matters of inheritance, at least, Bohra practice seems to be both more Islamic and more egalitarian than those of many other Indian Muslims.[19]

On a broader level of social organization Bohra kinship patterns diverge markedly from those of their Hindu neighbors. Hindu kinship is generally based on bilateral jati ties, while the only comparable network in Shi'a kinship would be the *khandaan:* an aggregation of families traceable to a common village and capable of carrying out group action in certain circumstances. Khandaan networks may include kin from both the father's and the mother's families, but these units lack the cohesion and all-encompassing identity of a Hindu jati.[20]

The entire Bohra community is so tightly knit and (in most localities) so compact that there is little need for strong subcommunity kin-based institutions such as khandaan networks. Ancestral home, however, is a powerful determinant of marriage patterns. When seeking a match for their child, Bohra parents will generally look first among those Bohra families with an origin (even if many generations back) in the same Gujarati village that they themselves have come from. It is quite common to find Bohras who have lived for six decades in Calcutta (for example) forging a marriage union with Bohras whose grandparents emigrated to Bangalore in the late nineteenth century, simply for the reason that the ancestors of both families were originally from Dahod or Ahmedabad.

Of all the locally based kinship networks in the Bohra community, that of the Surtis is the most highly developed and dearly prized. Surat had been the seat of the dawat throughout the late eighteenth and early nineteenth centuries, and is still a site second in ritual importance only to Mumbai. Surtis regard themselves (and are regarded by other Bohras) as the aristocrats of the community: they are disproportionately represented not only in the dawat itself, but in all segments of the intellectual, professional, and economic elite. Among Surtis, by far the most important kinship unit is that of the Qasr-e Ali, within which the office of the da'i has been handed down for nearly a century and a half.

SEX AND MARRIED LIFE

Finding a Mate

Marriage is the normative state for Bohras, as for other Muslims.[21] If an individual (male or female) wishes to marry outside the community, the spouse is expected to convert. Such cases represent virtually all instances of conversion to the Daudi faith, and they occur more frequently among Bohras living far from a strong jamat than among those based in Indian cities with significant Bohra populations.[22]

The search for a spouse often begins shortly after mithaq. In previous generations, the parties themselves would have been largely removed from the decision-making process. Today, Bohras of both sexes have wide latitude in the choice of their mates. Family members and outside matchmakers will set up meetings between young people of compatible backgrounds, but the final decision is left to the youths themselves. One of the most common means of matchmaking is the circuit of jamat youth functions, at which boys and girls of marriageable age can mix freely under the eyes of vigilant chaperones. Such events are an important outlet, since unmarried Bohras living orthodox lifestyles typically have few opportunities to meet their counterparts of the opposite sex.

In the more cosmopolitan circles of Bohra society, it is not uncommon for youths in their late teens and early twenties to go out on dates without chaperones. This is a notable difference between Bohras and Shiʿa communities that are less urbanized or educated: as Abrar Husain notes of Shiʿa in Uttar Pradesh, "[C]ourtship and dating are alien notions among the Shiʿa of this region."[23] In the more cosmopolitan segments of Bohra society dating outside the community is not taboo, although such encounters are regarded as temporary dalliances not expected to lead to marriage. In fact, a surprisingly low percentage of my survey respondents listed "marriage ties to other Bohras" as a fundamental aspect of the faith: although almost all respondents reported universal endogamy in their own families, nearly half (43.7%) did not consider it to be one of the central facets of orthopraxy, and those who did rated it near the very bottom of the listed values.

All dating, whether within the community or outside it, is expected to be physically chaste. To a large degree this seems to be the actual practice as well as the mandated ideal. In numerous interviews with young adults of both sexes I found more than a few individuals willing to admit to consumption of alcohol, but none (in India) acknowledging premarital sex. A very small number who had grown up abroad admitted to premarital sex—but generally outside India and with partners outside the commu-

nity. This stands to reason: the Bohra community is so tightly knit that even the rumor of a sexual liaison could harm a young woman's marriage prospects irreparably, and few Bohra girls would take such a risk lightly.

Even the highly cosmopolitan youths who date outside the community generally return to the fold when it comes time to choose a spouse. As is the case in many other Indian groups (particularly Hindu ones), in arranging a match a girl's family might aggressively pursue likely prospects, while a boy's family is often content to choose among the array of requests. This is at variance with the Muslim ideal: "A marriage proposal from the girl's side is considered to be humiliating or indecent," Abrar Husain notes, "and therefore is always avoided."[24] Because of Hindu influence and the perceived shortage of eligible men in many Ithna-Ashari locales, however, increasing numbers of Indian Shi'a communities are seeing a rise in marriage initiative from the family of the girl rather than the boy.[25] The Bohras seem to display less squeamishness about this than do other Muslim groups: an unusually high standard of female education means that for a girl to find a mate with a suitable level of schooling (ideally superior to her own, or at least not much inferior) she will often have to put in considerable effort.

For the large majority of Bohras, however, dating is still an unfamiliar concept. As is the case for other Muslim groups, a great deal of the matchmaking is undertaken by elderly women, and matches between cousins are often the favored arrangement.[26] Most commonly, a suitable boy and girl will be paired up by their respective families, brought together several times (with or without chaperones), and if they seem compatible they will soon be engaged. Nizbat may take place while the couple are in their late teens, but marriage itself (at least among middle-class, urbanized families) typically is delayed until the parties are in their early twenties.

Family Planning

The first important decision a Bohra makes after marriage is when to start a family. Syedna encourages couples to have as many children as they can support—and no more. Contraception is not stigmatized, and is even (given the cramped urban areas in which many Bohras live) sometimes tacitly encouraged. The da'i does not often speak about the details of contraception, so the rules are somewhat fluid. No contraceptive method is forbidden, with the exception of abortion (which is forbidden at any stage in the pregnancy). Members of older generations, inhabitants of small towns, and other more traditional members of society tend to regard condoms, diaphragms, intrauterine devices, and hormonal pills as unnatural or invasive. For them 'azl (coitus interruptus) remains the primary form of

contraception, as it had been for most Bohras until recent decades. Residents of cosmopolitan cities like Mumbai, however, have few qualms about modern contraceptive methods. Both tubal ligation and vasectomies are permitted by the dawat—in fact, clerical sources report that men sometimes even ask Syedna to give them *raza* before going to the hospital for a vasectomy.

One measure by which actual practice (as opposed to orthodox ideal) can be gauged is the number of children born to a typical couple. In the Indian Shiʻa population as a whole, the trend is toward increasingly smaller families. In the Hasnain and Husain survey, over two-thirds of respondents had fewer than four children, and only 1.9% had more than six. The divergence is marginally more pronounced in the parts of India (Gujarat and Maharashtra) where most Bohras live.[27] This represents a complete inversion of the norms from the previous generation: in the same survey, not even one-third of respondents had fewer than four siblings. Where the vast majority of the previous generation lived in families of five or more children (the respondent plus four or more siblings), an equal proportion of today's households contain fewer than four.[28] With Indian infant mortality rates down considerably over the past three decades, the drop in average family size from about six children in the previous generation to fewer than four children in the current one strongly suggests widespread use of birth control (particularly of artificial methods not available to past generations) among Indian Shiʻa.

My research suggests that the preferred number of children in a Bohra nuclear family (at my test sites, at least) is two or three. In my survey nearly half (46.2%) of the households contained fewer than six members (i.e., a mother, a father, and no more than three children). Furthermore, 69.3% of households contained fewer than seven members, and since a typical Bohra household quite often includes at least one member outside the nuclear family (a mother-in-law, a widower father, an unmarried aunt) a great many of the six- and seven-member households (in all, 81.1% of households had seven or fewer members) would contain no more than three children).

Bohra attitudes and practices of birth control are well in line with those of other Muslim communities, both Sunni and Shiʻa. The basic Islamic uneasiness about birth control may stem from the early days of the faith, when there was no shortage of living space and the Prophet wanted the fledgling umma to grow as quickly as it could. The practice of ʻazl has a clear foundation in hadith literature but is treated as a problematic. Al-Ghazali, the great codifier of orthodoxy for Sunni Islam, regards ʻazl as *makruh*—that is, something better avoided, but permissible nonetheless.

He acknowledges that the opinion of the ulema on the subject ranges from complete acceptance to utter rejection, and (true to his customary preference for compromise and harmonious synthesis of competing ideas) he advocates a gradualist position: 'azl is bad, but not as bad as inducing a miscarriage, which in turn is not as bad as abortion, which in turn is not as bad as infanticide.[29] In other words, as the developing fetus matures it acquires increasingly more validity as a human being. Such a view is much closer to that of the modern liberal West than to the absolutist life-begins-at-conception position of many twentieth-century Muslim (or Christian) theologians.[30]

To the extent that Bohras might faithfully stick to the guidelines set forth by the dawat, their contraceptive practices would be considerably more traditional than those of other Indian Shiʿa. While it may safely be assumed that a great many Bohras follow the clergy's injunctions to the letter, the degree of actual compliance is a matter outside the scope of my research. By way of comparison, in the Hasnain and Husain survey, 34.2% of respondents reported using artificial methods of birth control (condoms, hormonal pills, intrauterine devices, etc.), while 65.8% reported using only natural methods (rhythm, ʿazl), or no birth control at all.[31] A breakdown of the data by educational level may give some hints about unacknowledged Bohra practice: there is a direct relation between the education of the respondents and their willingness to use artificial birth control. Fully 62% of postgraduates and professionals reported using artificial birth control, compared with a mere 17% of high-school dropouts and 5% of illiterates.[32] Since the Bohra community is one of the most highly educated Muslim groups in India, their use of modern forms of birth control may well be more common than many would admit.

Marital Intimacy

Within the context of matrimony, the Bohras (like other Muslims) see the taking of pleasure from physical intimacy as wholly legitimate and unblameworthy. Abdelwahab Bouhdiba goes so far as to argue that within Islam "the exercise of sexuality is a pious obligation."[33] Where some faiths (many strains of Hinduism and Christianity, for example) regard celibacy as the ideal and marriage as the accommodation made for human frailties, Islam regards marriage itself as the perfect human condition. Arguments are sometimes made that the Islamic ideal is monogamy (cf. Qurʾan: 4:3, "[M]arry of the women, who seem good to you, two, three or four; and if ye cannot do justice [to so many] then one [only]," taken with Qurʾan 4:129, "Ye will not be able to deal equally between [your] wives") and that polygamy is the accommodation made for excessive male ap-

petite. Others regard polygamy as the ideal, pointing to the example of the Prophet: at various points in his life Muhammad had nine, eleven, thirteen, and fourteen wives, and according to a famous hadith he was accustomed to visiting all of his wives in a single night.[34] The satisfaction of physical appetites is regarded as entirely proper, so long as such satisfaction is sanctioned by marriage.[35]

Lina Fruzzetti suggests that such a view represents only the male paradigm: Muslim and Hindu women alike (she writes) explicitly regard the purpose of marriage as procreation, particularly the procreation of sons.[36] While it is important to remember that textual sources tend to express the male paradigm, hadith literature demonstrates that the pleasures of matrimony were never intended to be one-sided: Islamic tradition specifies that physical gratification in marriage is owed to women as much as to men. Al-Ghazali cites ahadith outlining—in extremely explicit terms—a husband's duty to provide his wife full sexual satisfaction.[37]

Whether such exhortations are actually followed is quite another matter, but their normative status (at least in text) is clear. Within the Bohra community, however, the reciprocal nature of marital satisfaction is given an emphasis not commonly seen in many other Muslim communities. Both male and female informants report that the stereotypical paradigm of male gratification and female acquiescence has no place in Bohra teachings. If anything, such practice would be stigmatized rather than praised—and Bohra women would be little more likely to consider it acceptable than would their counterparts in the West. "Mutual pleasure is not merely permitted," one newlywed man in khidmat reported to me, "it is positively encouraged. The simple act of caressing one's wife or stroking her hair is regarded as meritorious."

Restrictions that the Bohras place on physical intimacy within the context of marriage are quite in line with those observed by other Muslim groups. A married couple is prohibited from having sex while facing qiblah (i.e., with their feet pointed in the direction of Mecca), but since it is *always* considered improper to point one's feet toward Mecca this prohibition is somewhat redundant. Of course, sex is utterly taboo while on hajj. Marital relations are forbidden during a woman's period of menstruation, and both man and woman should wash thoroughly before and after any sex act—in this the Bohras' customary emphasis on hygiene and cleanliness is particularly pronounced. Some informants note that couples are discouraged from having sexual relations while completely naked, during daylight hours, or with electric lights on, but others report that this discouragement (when it occurs) is quite mild; "There is nothing wrong in a

man being naked with his wife," said the newlywed cleric, "but he shouldn't . . . ogle her."[38]

By comparison, al-Ghazali notes that the companions of the Prophet did not face qiblah during sex, and speculates that having intercourse during or immediately after a woman's time of menstruation would lead to leprosy in the offspring. The prohibition of sexual relations during hajj and the exhortation to bathe after sex are common denominators in Muslim personal practice. Al-Ghazali notes that hadith literature describes Muhammad as covering himself during sex, and states, "A *khabar* says 'If one of you should have intimate relations with his wife, you should not denude yourselves completely like two onagers,' that is, two donkeys."[39]

Not long after marriage—there is no set time period, but most commonly within the first few years—a Bohra couple will typically eschew contraception and decide to have their first child. The sister-in-law may approach Syedna for a name, relatives will make preparations for the chatti ceremony, and the cycle of Bohra life begins once again.

STATUS OF WOMEN WITHIN THE BOHRA COMMUNITY

One of the most common misperceptions about Islam prevalent in non-Islamic circles is that the religion is fundamentally antagonistic to the freedom and high status of women. Harsh regulations imposed by such reactionary groups as the Taliban in Afghanistan are taken as indicative of the orientation of the whole faith, when in fact such strictures may well not represent the majority opinion even in the areas in which they are in force (at time of writing, most notably Afghanistan, Iran, Saudi Arabia, and Sudan—together representing not much more than one-tenth of the world's 1.1 billion Muslims). Even here the picture is more complex than is generally acknowledged. In revolutionary Iran, for example, women have often played a major part in politics: current president Muhammad Khatami, running on promises of liberalization of gender (and other) strictures against the united might of entrenched conservatives, was elected in May 1997 by a landslide coming in large measure from the votes of women. Female voters were similarly crucial to the reformists' overwhelming victory in the Majlis (Parliament) elections of February 2000. As the careers of such female mujtahids as Banu Amin of Isfahan (d.1983) demonstrate, even the area of religious interpretation is not an all-male preserve.[40]

Neighboring Pakistan is officially an Islamic republic, with a legal code containing harsh penalties such as stoning and whipping for sexual of-

fenses. But these *hudud* punishments are largely symbolic (there are very few cases in which they have actually been imposed), and popular attitudes in Pakistan do not conform neatly to Western stereotype. To mark the nation's fiftieth anniversary, the Karachi magazine *Herald* conducted what may have been the most extensive opinion poll in Pakistani history. Of the 1,260 adults surveyed in seven major sites around the country, 67% opposed restrictions on women similar to those instituted by the Taliban, 63% felt a woman's testimony should carry the same weight in court as that of a man, and 59% believed that men and women should have identical rights of divorce. On the broader question of whether political decisions should be influenced by religious groups, 72% felt that religious parties such as the Jamaat-i-Islami had done more harm than good, 74% said sectarian parties should be banned, and 81% believed that the imams of mosques should not give political khutbas.[41]

As the late Pakistani scholar Fazlur Rahman noted, many self-styled Islamic fundamentalists seem to have abandoned the fundamentals of Islam. The Qur'an, Rahman wrote, is a document for all ages, and must be considered in light of changing times. He rejected the "atomism" created by taking verses out of historical context, and urged a holistic approach rather than the "piecemeal, ad hoc, and often quite extrinsic treatment of the Qur'an" employed by obscurantists. In respect to women, Rahman noted, the Qur'an presents a set of social guidelines extraordinarily liberal for their time, considerably more liberal than those of premodern Europe.[42] Today's literalists ignore the entire outlook of the Qur'an if they fail to acknowledge the place and time of its revelation:

> The basic elan of the Qur'an—the stress on socioeconomic justice and essential human egalitarianism—is quite clear from its very early passages. . . . To insist on a *literal* [original italics] implementation of the rules of the Qur'an, shutting one's eyes to the social change that has occurred and that is so palpably occurring before our eyes, is tantamount to deliberately defeating its moral-social purposes and objectives. It is just as though, in the view of the Qur'anic emphasis on freeing slaves, one were to insist on preserving the institution of slavery so that one could "earn merit in the sight of God" by freeing slaves. . . . Or, again, to say that, no matter how much women may develop intellectually, their evidence must on principle carry less value than that of a man is an outrageous affront to the Qur'an's purposes of social revolution.[43]

The topic of women's place in Islam is, of course, far too large to be dealt with in the confines of this study. The following discussion is in-

tended merely to highlight the weaknesses of the prevailing Western pre-conceptions, and to suggest a fruitful area for other researchers to pursue in future. As Rahman, Fatima Mernissi, and others argue, the entire model of Islam as antagonistic to women's rights is highly problematic, if not out-right false. Even in cases where the prevailing paradigm seems to indicate a subordinate status, the underlying truth is often considerably more com-plex. In many Muslim cultures, the dynamic is similar to that described by Louis Dumont among Hindu Kallars: "[T]he subordination of the wife is more a matter of form, asserted at the beginning of the marriage, than a basic fact."[44] This is not to downplay the degradation imposed on women all too often in the name of Islam—merely to point out that such abuse is as abhorrent to many Muslims (of both genders) as it is to critics outside the faith.

The Bohra case study is particularly illuminating in that here, unlike in many other Muslim communities, one does not have to dig particularly deep to uncover evidence of female empowerment. Even for the Bohras this is a modern phenomenon. As recently as sixty years ago, Shaikh Na-jafali could write, "Just as a minor according to the law of contract is in-competent to make a binding contract, so is a woman according to the law of this sect of Islam incompetent to contract her marriage." Far from offer-ing this as criticism, Najafali (a dawat attorney) was expressing the clergy's own position when he described the exclusion of women from the deci-sion-making process in their own choice of mate as "the most outstanding feature of the law of marriage governing the Dawoodi Bohra Muslims."[45]

That was then, this is now. It should not be surprising that times have changed: when Shaikh Najafali wrote those words, American women had only recently won the right to vote (and African Americans of either sex would have to wait several decades more before they would freely be able to exercise this or other rights to which they were theoretically entitled). Today, a Bohra husband would treat his wife as an "incompetent minor" only at his own peril. The status of women within the community has risen markedly over the past half-century, a period corresponding closely with the increased availability of modern education. Whether or not a di-rect link is scientifically demonstrable, it does not seem coincidental that Bohra women are now among both the best educated and the highest-status women of any community on the Indian subcontinent.

EDUCATION AND STATUS OF WOMEN

One aspect of Western pedagogical philosophy that the Bohras have par-ticularly taken to heart is the emphasis on education of women. Bohra

women are quite often considerably better educated than the women of many other Indian communities,[46] and this has led to a level of power and respect atypical in traditional-minded societies (Muslim and non-Muslim alike).[47] Even the dissident writer H. S. Verdia noted—over two decades ago—that although "women were hardly educated [in the past], now higher education has become popular with them."[48] A colonial gazetteer reports Bohra girls routinely being given Qur'anic education in the nineteenth century,[49] and commitment to female schooling runs far deeper today.

The director of the entire Burhani madrasa system, for example (Ayman Behnsaheb Kalimuddin), is the sister-in-law of the da'i: a single order from her was sufficient to arrange the distribution of my survey questionnaire to all the Bohra madrasas, and insure that a good percentage of them would arrive back in Mumbai by the designated time. A psychologist named Rashida Mustafa crafted the madrasa system's curriculum in accordance with current child development theory, and uses her scientific training to supervise all the principals' efforts.[50] Many (if not most) of the teachers in Burhani madrasas are women, and more local schools seem to be run by headmistresses than headmasters. At the Jamea campuses in both Surat and Karachi, male and female students follow the same curriculum and make use of the same facilities: although segregated by gender, the student body is approximately 40 % female.

This embrace of coeducation extends well into the general Bohra population: 88.8 % of respondents to my survey reported full educational parity between the male and female members of their extended families. A closer look at the individual questionnaires reveals an even more striking revelation: a significant number of the "nonparity" households are ones in which the women actually have *higher* levels of education, so the figure for households in which women have educational levels equal to or higher than those of men is a stereotype-shattering 92.8 %.[51]

The link between women's education and women's status within other Indian Shi'a communities has been persuasively documented by Hasnain and Husain. "A very high rate of literacy among the Shi'a women," they note, "(in fact much higher than the national average) bears testimony to the growing consciousness among the Shi'a about the importance of secular education."[52] When asked who made important decisions for the household, respondents gave answers corresponding closely with educational levels.[53]

It is noteworthy, however, that even here the Bohra attitudes yield less restrictive views of a woman's place in society. In the Hasnain and Husain

survey, 93.7% of respondents felt that women should work only in the house, and this figure showed relatively little variation between respondents with less than a high school education (98% of whom agreed) and those with postgraduate degrees (87% of whom agreed).[54] In the Bhopal region, Doranne Jacobson reports that sequestration of women was on the rise among lower- and middle-class Muslims even before the Iranian Revolution: "Because of its previous association with the leisured and prosperous classes, the observance of purdah—or at least some of its obvious features—adds to the prestige of many low and middle status Muslims in their own circles."[55] While Bohra women tend to be homemakers, they are seldom stigmatized for working outside the house. In the middle and upper segments of Bohra society, professional careers are strongly encouraged.

Here too there is a strong parallel with the Khojah community, in which reforms begun by Aga Khan III in 1905 have given the women of the community an unusually high status.[56] An emphasis on female education is commonly found in other Gujarati communities, although seldom to the same degree as among the Bohras and the Khojahs. Of the younger generation of Gujarati migrants in Madras, Leila Narayanan found a slightly higher percentage of female graduates than male (55% versus 50%).[57] Jain migrants in particular considered female education desirable and prestigious, but only to a limited degree: education at the postgraduate level was believed to decrease a woman's marriage prospects as it limited her choices to men of an equal or higher level.[58]

Ayman Behnsaheb Kalimuddin, director of the Burhani madrasa network, described her institution's mission and purpose in the following words: "Which language a student speaks, which texts she studies is unimportant. What is important is how she thinks."[59] What is most illuminating about Ayman Behnsaheb's observation is her choice of pronoun: the student body of the Burhani madrasa system is at least half male, yet the director refers to a typical student with the feminine article. Such a nuanced approach to gendered language might be considered mildly progressive even in the West—from the highest authority of a madrasa with an avowedly traditional Islamic outlook and mission, it seems radical indeed. But once one has spent some time in the Bohra community, this brand of what Fatima Mernissi has described as "Islamic feminism"[60] can begin to look more like the norm than the exception. One female observer notes,

> In general, it can be said that the status of Bohra women is better
> in religious, social, economic and educational terms, compared to

> other Muslim women. . . . Unlike in a typical traditional Hindu
> family, the Bohra women mix freely with the menfolk in the joint
> family. They do not use purdah within the house.[61]

The openness to female education is facilitated by the Bohras' strictness in their avoidance of dowry (unlike many Muslim communities of the subcontinent). While this rejection of dowry was instituted in order to bring practice in line with traditional Islamic strictures, it has had the parallel effect of encouraging the education of women. Inee Faizulabhoy, a highly educated woman whose grandmother was one of the first Bohra women to take a double degree, notes that for the past few generations education (at least among the elite Surti circles) has been required for women as much as for men. She chalks this up partly to the practice of mahr instead of dowry: "There is still some son preference," she says, "but not to the extent found in other communities. We cherish our daughters, and regard their education as an investment. Communities that practice dowry see it as a waste of money—after all, every rupee you spend on schooling will only wind up raising the price of getting her married off."

Education, of course, is closely linked to class as well as to sex, so women in the lower socioeconomic strata of Bohra society will often display less independence of thought and action than those with the financial means to take advantage of educational opportunities. But strong-willed, straight-talking, self-aware women are so common among the Bohras as to be scarcely noteworthy, and one of the main reasons for this phenomenon seems to be the community's genuine embrace of female education. Among the middle and upper segments of Bohra society, at least, the mainstream opinion seems entirely in line with Mernissi's statement of purpose:

> We Muslim women can walk into the modern world with pride,
> knowing that the quest for dignity, democracy, and human rights,
> for full participation in the political and social affairs of our country, stems from no imported Western values, but is a true part of the Muslim tradition.[62]

PROFILES OF TWO BOHRA WOMEN

Discussions about the place of women in Islam, like most sociological discussions, tend to overlook one very important fact: human beings are individuals first, women or men second. Statistics and surveys are vital tools

of quantitative research, but they only draw the outlines of a society: all too often, one forgets that every society is made up not of paradigms, but of people. To fill in the detail, even to turn the sketch into living flesh and blood, one must actually get to know the individuals who make up a community. A book can give the reader little more than a fleeting glimpse at the real lives of real people—and an academic book, with issues of anthropological theory as its basis, is particularly ill suited to do even this. In a small attempt to add some color to the preceding black-and-white text, I here present brief character vignettes of two very different, and quite typical, Bohra women.

Zubeda Gunja

For the past thirty years Zubeda has been working as a tax adjuster for the Indian government. When she earned her bachelor's degree in sociology from Mumbai's prestigious St. Xavier's College, relatively few women of any community even considered a university education. For Zubeda, however, it represents one of her greatest sources of pride. She has her diploma and graduation photo displayed prominently above the doorway of her spare Muhammad Ali Road apartment—directly across from her photographs of Syednas Muhammad Burhanuddin and Taher Saifuddin.

"For Bohras, education has a special significance," she explains. "Boys and girls alike must learn the Arabic script, even if they learn nothing more; at the least, we have very few illiterates. Without this education, it would be too easy to slip back into the ways of our Hindu ancestors." Zubeda's sociology background comes out when she stresses the importance of early childhood training. The way to shape society is to focus on imprinting desired values on the young during their crucial formative years. "This is not a case of tradition versus modernity," she says. "The mullah and the psychologist reach the same conclusion."

The Bohras are not the only tightly knit community in India, but Zubeda feels that Syedna's presence helps them maintain their traditions better than other tightly knit communities in similar circumstances. "Other Gujaratis here in Mumbai—Jains, Hindus, Memons, what-have-you—can celebrate their religious holidays or not as they see fit, who's there to know? Each family can go its own way, there's nothing to hold them together. But we have Syedna to unify us, to serve as a gentle reminder of who we are."

Zubeda's one-room apartment is conveniently close to Bhindi Bazaar, but offers few other comforts. It is a fifth-story walk-up in an old, decaying building, barely insulated from the din of street traffic. A generation ago

the Gunja family occupied the entire floor of the building—ninety-two family members sharing fourteen rooms. With the price of downtown real estate skyrocketing, all except Zubeda and her brother (with his wife and son) have sold their shares and moved to more spacious quarters. Zubeda could easily afford a far more luxurious home, but she has no desire to leave. Virtually all of the other inhabitants of her chawl are Bohras, most of whom have been her neighbors since she was a little girl. Zubeda often feels lonely having a room all to herself, a room that didn't seem cramped when she used to share it with five relatives. If she had to live among strangers, she doesn't know how she'd bear it.

"Many Bohras live in mixed neighborhoods like Colaba," she says, "but I prefer life here. In a non-Bohra neighborhood, living properly is a lot more difficult. But here we all live the same way—we all fast during Ramadan, all go to masjid on the same days, all attend the same weddings, et cetera. There is no compulsion from Syedna—he reminds us of our duties, but everyone can choose for him or herself whether to follow his direction. Bohras in Malabar Hill or Cuffe Parade may have larger flats, but they must work harder to live right."

Zubeda never married, but it wasn't for lack of suitors. "I had many proposals," she says, "but they were all businessmen. So dull." Spinsterhood is very rare among Bohras, but Zubeda never suffered social ostracism because of her decision. If she had, it would have been the easiest thing in the world simply to move to a different neighborhood. "Most of my best friends are Hindus and Parsis," she says, a sentiment frequently voiced by Bohra men and women alike. "But I feel a closeness with other mu'mineen that goes beyond mere friendship. The other women here are like my sisters."

The status of Bohra women, she says, is much higher than that of Hindus or Sunnis she knows, and it disturbs her to see so many of her friends outside the community living in purdah.* "We have no purdah among the Daudis," she says proudly (using the term in its more restrictive sense). "Syedna has often preached in his khutbas that men and women are entirely equal." She notes that dowry is forbidden: "If offered at all, it is strictly *niche-niche*" (under-under, i.e., in secret). Syedna's own sister Shahzedi Sakina Behnsaheb (d.1999) had been a powerful (if soft-spoken) advocate for women's rights within the community. Ultimately, the high status and high educational levels of Bohra women are mutually reinforc-

*Bohras do not practice purdah as the term is generally understood: when used in a Bohra context, "purdah" refers to modest dress and demeanor, not to the sequestration of women.

ing: "We are more free because we are more confident, assertive, and educated," Zubeda says. "Also, we are more confident, assertive, and educated because we are more free."[63]

Diya*

Sipping her coffee in the lounge of the Taj Hotel, Diya is dressed in a short-sleeved T-shirt and defiantly tight jeans. She refers to Bohra women as "butterflies"—for their brightly colored *ridas* that flap in the wind—but she herself wears a burqa as infrequently as she possibly can. "Too hot," she says, "especially just before monsoon."

Diya lives with her family in the exclusive, cosmopolitan neighborhood of Cuffe Parade. All family members are "yellow card" holders[64]—they conform to all the major matters of orthopraxy, but are noncompliant on minor issues. Diya's father wears a beard and says namaz five times a day, but she, her mother, and her three sisters do not offer daily prayers. Diya doesn't enjoy paying dawat taxes, but (like taxpayers everywhere) regards it as a necessary evil: "They know exactly how much you make, and say, 'you must pay this sum.' Then you haggle, and they bring it down a bit. Unpleasant—but every community must pay taxes to support itself."

All family members wear community dress only when absolutely necessary. On their application for their orthopraxy certificates, Diya and her sisters bent the truth when answering more than a few of the questions. "Everybody does," she says, "otherwise hardly anyone would pass." Like the vast majority of unmarried women even in the most Westernized circles of Bohra society, Diya has never seriously considered moving out of the family home. She works in a travel agency not out of financial necessity, but to give herself something to do. "It's a bit dull," she says, "but I've been able to visit Britain, the Middle East, Malaysia, Singapore, and Sri Lanka."

Diya feels that Bohra women enjoy significantly more freedom and higher status than do women in other Muslim communities. She chafes at the inequality that still exists in Bohra society, but is content with her own lot: "Muslims—Sunni Muslims, that is—see a woman as property, a vehicle to bear their children and keep the house clean. They do not want her to be educated, certainly do not want her to have any fun. The man can run around with other women, but his wife is just expected to stay at home and wait."

Diya dated a Sunni man for about two years. He worked for an airline, so they met through work. He was insanely jealous, subjecting her to con-

*This is a pseudonym, to protect the woman in question from embarrassment.

stant interrogation if she so much as spoke with another man (including even her own cousins). He was constantly getting into fights, and would beat up any man who inadvertently brushed against her in the street. "One time, when we were in Abu Dhabi," she says, "someone pinched my bottom, and my boyfriend punched the man out on the spot. Then he claimed it was *my* fault, said it was because I was wearing jeans."

He always threatened that if she ever left him for another man he would kill her, kill him, and kill himself. When Diya ended the relationship he turned to drugs, and blamed her for it. Diya was amazed at his hypocrisy: "This man never drank, because the Qur'an forbade it, yet he used any manner of narcotics. That's the way the Sunnis think—what's set down in the Qur'an is all that matters." He wrote her a long, demented letter demanding that she come back to him—a letter written in his own blood. Diya's parents always disapproved of her boyfriend, and still take great pleasure in reminding her of the fiasco. But Diya has no regrets. "Youth," she says, "is a time for mistakes."

Mumbai is India's Gomorrah, the easiest place on the subcontinent for a young woman to be led astray. Discos at the Taj and the Oberoi, then after-hours pubs up in Breach Candy—the fast set of Bollywood, Channel V, and miscellaneous wannabes do their best to keep up with their counterparts in London, New York, or L.A. Most of Diya's friends are outside the community, but she's hardly the only Bohra to run with this crowd. At one club, nursing whiskeys long after midnight, Diya and I met up with another Bohra woman and her Hindu former boyfriend. Both were now happily engaged to other people within their respective communities.

"The old hens are always gossiping about me," Diya said while her friends were on the dance floor. "I have a reputation for wildness, but it's all talk. I know many girls who are far wilder than I am, yet they take care to hide their indiscretions." There are indeed Bohra women with an appetite for indiscretion. Another evening at another club, I saw an intoxicated young Bohra woman openly proposition a Bohra man she considered to be a good marriage prospect, and then hit two parked cars while driving home.

Wild or not, even the young Bohra women of Mumbai's jet set are looking for an arranged marriage. As an attractive, educated woman from a good family Diya has drawn her share of marriage feelers, but nothing particularly tempting. She's looking for a Bohra man with the proper family and proper education, but not so traditional as to cramp her lifestyle. "Marriage is no starry-eyed thing," she says; "it is a match for life. One is better off with somebody of compatible background." So the search goes on. Recently she went on an arranged date with a very traditional

young man, and made a point of slipping a burqa over her street clothes in the taxi to meet him. At the restaurant he kept asking questions about her family's level of piety, how often they prayed, whether they fasted every day of Ramadan. Eventually Diya lost patience. "Maybe you should be interviewing my grandmother rather than me," she said, and walked out.

Qasr-e Ali: The Royals

One of the defining characteristics of Shi'ism is a deep personal devotion to the ahl al-bayt, the family of the Prophet. This loyalty is often formulated as the paired obligations of *tawalla* and *tabarra:* to cherish the descendants of Muhammad through Ali and the succession of imams, and to shun all who reject or attack these descendants.[1] For scriptural support Shi'a cite the Qur'anic verse (42:23) in which Muhammad is told to demand no payment for his service except the loyalty of the umma to his family: "Say: I do not ask of you any reward for it but love for my near relatives."[2]

In the present-day Bohra faith, this loyalty is extended to the Prophet's spiritual rather than his strictly biological descendants—to the family of the da'i as successors to the family of the imams. The antiquity of this practice is very much open to debate: one of the foremost complaints articulated by dissident Bohras (and sometimes, quietly, by orthodox Bohras as well) is that too much power and privilege are concentrated among the blood relatives of the da'i. Dissidents such as Noman Contractor and Asghar Ali Engineer have charged that the institutionalization of a royal family is a nineteenth-century innovation rather than an integral part of Bohra tradition.[3] The dawat argues that top clerics earn their positions by merit rather than nepotism: since the da'i is the spiritual conduit linking humanity with the hidden imam, it stands to reason that his close relatives (by virtue of their daily contact with him) would display exemplary devotion to the faith. Neither position is wholly free of self-interest: the dissidents have no path to real influence so long as the upper reaches of the clerical hierarchy remain entirely hereditary, while the officials formulating dawat policy are themselves all members of the very family whose status they are attempting to justify.

Whatever the provenance of the custom, for at least the past century the Bohra royal family (as it is called by friends and foes alike) has enjoyed a place of unrivaled predominance in all community affairs. The most broadly defined unit of this clan is called the *bayt al-Zaini:* the descendents

of the forty-fifth da'i, Syedna Tayyib Zainuddin. Within this elite is a higher elite: the extended family (including siblings, half-siblings, nieces, nephews, and all their progeny) of the present da'i. This is the unit most commonly referred to when Bohras speak of the "royal family," and it goes by name of the Qasr-e Ali.

The term "Qasr-e Ali" may be translated (with apologies to James Clavell) as "Noble House." At the time of writing, the Qasr-e Ali consists of the children and grandchildren of the fifty-first da'i, Syedna Taher Saifuddin, along with their spouses and descendents. In all, there are upward of 200 members of the Qasr-e Ali. Just as the children of Fatimid imam-caliphs were princes and princesses in every sense of the word, so too are the children of da'is today. The sons and daughters of a da'i are given the titles of *shahzada* and *shahzedi* (prince and princess), respectively, and they represent the apex of the Bohras' clerical, social, and political hierarchy.

All members of the fifty-first da'i's lineage are given the honorific *bhaisaheb* (brother-sir) or, for women, *behnsaheb* (sister-madam).* While most Bohras address each other by their given names with an appended "bhai" or "behn," members of the Qasr-e Ali are addressed by their given names with an appended "bhaisaheb" or "behnsaheb." Since the royal family is so large, many Bohras address *any* social superior with the honorific: better to err on the side of flattery than give an unintended slight. The usage, therefore, is somewhat fluid, with the titles not limited to those technically entitled: when members of the bayt al-Zaini, nonaristocrats in khidmat, and other important commoners find themselves addressed with a *-saheb* after the *bhai-* or *behn-*, they do not always rush to correct the mistake.

ORGANIZATIONAL STRUCTURE OF THE DAWAT

The Bohra clergy is organized much like a Fatimid government-in-exile, although the exile is one of time rather than geography. The three highest officials have the same titles as those current when Imam Tayyib went into concealment: da'i al-mutlaq, mazoon, and mukasir. Paramount authority rests with the da'i, who serves as the earthly representative of the imam during the period of seclusion. Succession to this office is determined by nass: each da'i, inspired and guided by the hidden imam, appoints his own successor. Ideally, nass should be open and clear, like that which the Prophet Muhammad conferred upon his wasi Ali.[4] There is no inherent necessity for the title to be dynastic, but it has generally been so throughout

*Wives of the da'i are given the honorific of *aisaheba* instead of *behnsaheb*.

history; since the ascension of the forty-seventh daʿi Abdul-Qadir Naj-muddin (the great-grandfather of the present daʿi) in 1840 all daʿis have been members of the same extended family. The timing of nass is extremely variable: Syedna Taher Saifuddin designated his eldest son as his successor (and mazoon) three decades before his own death in 1965, while Syedna Muhammad Burhanuddin is eighty-five years old at the time of this writing and even his closest relatives say that he has given them no indication as to when his choice will be made.[5]

The daʿi's second-in-command bears the title of *mazoon saheb,* while the third official is titled *mukasir saheb* (both offices are currently held by brothers of the daʿi). These were the only top dawat posts (apart from that of the daʿi) noted in the first colonial gazetteer entry on the Bohras a century ago.[6] In Fatimid times there was a clear-cut distinction between the duties of these two subordinate offices, but today both officials have a wide array of overlapping functions. Both serve as aides to the daʿi in whatever capacity he may decide: leading the annual pilgrimage to Kerbala, conducting Muharram services at an important population center, attending ceremonial functions, or representing the daʿi in dealings with figures outside the denomination. By recent tradition (dating to the nineteenth century) the mukasir also holds the post of chief amil of Mumbai, but current practice does not imply a canonical responsibility.

This flexibility of job descriptions extends to the next level of dawat organization. Like a government, the dawat is divided into various departments or "ministries" with responsibilities for specific aspects of Bohra life. The education department, for example, oversees the Burhani madrasas, the Jamea tus-Saifiya academy, and many other scholastic institutions. The ministry of external relations operates much like the state department of an independent government, coordinating policies for all Bohra contact with other communities in India and around the world. But the boundaries between the ministries are often vague, with various officials shouldering many disparate responsibilities. The central headquarters of the dawat is Badri Mahal, a large Victorian edifice located between Victoria Terminus and Flora Fountain in downtown Mumbai.

There is no clear division between the clerical hierarchy and the family of the daʿi: All of the top clerics are brothers and sons of Syedna, and all of Syedna's brothers and sons are top clerics.* All bear the title of shahzada, but within this group there is a wide range of authority. There is

*Some are less actively engaged in dawat activities than others, but all are holders of the highest clerical titles available and all have had at least titular control over various aspects of dawat policy.

no direct correlation between title, job description, and de facto power. The two highest officials apart from the da'i, the mazoon and the mukasir, do not necessarily wield actual clout commensurate with their theoretical station.[7] All the rest of Syedna's brothers and sons are theoretically on a par, but some are clearly more influential than others. Most shahzadas have duties reaching across several departments: the delineation of duties was much sharper twenty years ago (sources say), but today it is less a tightly structured hierarchy than a shifting set of interlocking power rings. An individual shahzada's duties are largely a function of his closeness to Syedna and his political prominence at any given moment.

There are two titles awarded by Syedna: mullah and shaikh. Any man authorized to lead namaz is given the title of mullah; this title is automatically given to male graduates of the Jamea tus-Saifiya and teachers in Bohra schools. The higher title of shaikh is awarded by Syedna at his personal discretion, but it is generally given to those clerical officials who have put in at least ten years of meritorious service. Since khidmat (service) can refer to financial contributions as well as full-time clerical employment, the title of shaikh is sometimes awarded to individuals who have been particularly generous to the dawat. To distinguish clerical shaikhs from wealthy laymen, some Bohras use the title *miyasaheb* to address a shaikh who has earned his title by diligence and piety rather than an open wallet.

Central dawat policy is set by the clerics in Badri Mahal, often Surtis with close ties to Syedna's immediate family. Policy is implemented, however, by a network of amils who serve as Syedna's personal representatives in every Bohra community around the world. Amils perform a function roughly comparable to that of bishops in the Roman Catholic or Episcopal church, but their mandate covers all elements of secular as well as religious life. In places with relatively small Bohra populations a single amil may have jurisdiction over an entire nation, or even several nations lumped together. The usual pattern within India is for an amil to have charge of a particular city and its outlying suburbs.

In Mumbai the concentration of Bohras is so great that the city is divided into smaller administrative units with a chief amil supervising all. These units are called mohallas, a term that here connotes neighborhoods or sections of the city rather than the more common usage of apartment blocks. The entire cosmopolitan Colaba district, for example, is in the "Badri Mohalla." Each mohalla has its own amil, and is treated for administrative purposes as if it were a separate city. An amil's primary task is to serve as prayer leader at the local masjid, and to appoint a surrogate namaz imam when he is out of town. Leading prayers, however, is only one

of an amil's many duties. The amil of Hyderabad (Deccan) provides an example typical of others administering territories at a geographical remove from the center. "For members of the community here," he says, "I provide guidance on every aspect of life. Their spiritual lives, business practices, daily home life, everything."

In addition to the titles of mullah or shaikh (and the office of amil), Syedna sometimes awards a new surname to people who request one. The use of any surnames at all is a relatively recent innovation, and is still not a true part of Bohra nomenclature. Until the nineteenth century, Bohras (like many Indians) would typically be referred to by patronymic: "Tayyib, son of Idris," for example. As the community grew larger and more geographically dispersed, Bohras began using surnames (actually closer to nicknames) typically based on their trade or ancestral town. To distinguish himself from other men with the same name and same patronym, Tayyib ibn Idris might call himself Tayyib Dahodwala (if he happened to come from the city of Dahod) or Tayyib Kagezwala (if he happened to be in the stationery business: *kagez* = paper, *wala* = man).

Like the Parsis, Bohras in Mumbai adopted a wide array of highly untraditional surnames during the period of British colonialism: family names such as Lightbulbwala, Electricwala, and Rangoonwala are found throughout the Bohra community today. When an individual with a pedestrian surname distinguishes himself in khidmat, he is often granted a new appellation with explicitly religious overtones. If Tayyib Printingpresswala graduated from the Jamea academy and served the dawat loyally, he might be given permission to call himself Tayyib Saifuddin (Tayyib, Sword of the Faith). Perhaps he would soon find people addressing him not as Tayyib-bhai, but as Tayyib-bhaisaheb. He would correct them gently (if he possessed a proper sense of humility), but he might be secretly pleased nonetheless.

ZIYARET: PILGRIMAGE TO THE SHRINES OF DEPARTED DA'IS

One of the most important instruments of societal cohesion for the Bohras is the institution of ziyaret (pilgrimage: lit., "visiting"). This custom, greatly facilitated by modern communications technology, brings together community members from all over the world. In addition to hajj, Bohras perform ziyaret to the tombs of imams, da'is, and syedis in various parts of the Middle East and India. The current da'i and his predecessor both contributed significant sums for the restoration of shrines and the construction of *zerehs* (silver tomb encasements) in Egypt, Yemen, and Iraq. As in other Shi'a groups, the most important destinations for ziyaret are Kerbala

and Najaf in Iraq. The former, the site of Imam Husain's martyrdom in 681 C.E., is second only to Mecca in the sacred geography of faith. Every year a group pilgrimage led by a high cleric (organized much like the communal hajj) sets out for Kerbala, generally including other holy spots in Iraq, Egypt, and Saudi Arabia on the itinerary as well.

Burial places of da'is and imams in Egypt and Yemen have become important sites for ziyaret in recent decades, but the tombs of the Indian da'is have always been (and continue to be) the most widely visited shrines.[8] Ziyaret may be performed at any time of year (not unlike Sufi pilgrimage to the tombs of charismatic pirs), but is particularly auspicious on the death anniversary of the da'i in question. The most prominent sites for ziyaret are the seven cities that have served as the seat of the dawat in India, each of which houses rauzahs (mausoleums) of past da'is al-mutlaq:[9] da'is twenty-five to thirty-three in Ahmedabad; da'is thirty-four to thirty-six and thirty-eight in Jamnagar; da'i thirty-seven in Kutch-Mandvi; da'is thirty-nine, forty, and forty-seven in Ujjain; da'i forty-one in Burhanpur; da'is forty-two to forty-six and forty-eight to fifty in Surat.[10] In addition to these shrines, Cambay houses the rauzahs of the Musta'li Ismaili missionaries Abdullah and Ahmed; Aurangabad, the rauzah of the missionary Syedi Nuruddin; and Galiakot, the shrine of Syedi Fakhruddin, martyred during his missionary work among the Bhils in Rajasthan.[11] The only major shrine in Mumbai (there are several minor ones) is the Rauzah Tahera, the mausoleum of the fifty-first da'i, Syedna Taher Saifuddin. Opened on September 29, 1976, it is arguably the most impressive piece of Bohra architecture of recent centuries. It is built entirely of pure white marble from the same Rajasthani quarries that supplied the marble for the Taj Mahal, and its walls are engraved with the entire text of the Qur'an in gilded calligraphy.[12]

All Bohra shrines are open to and highly popular with women as well as men: at particularly busy ones such as the Rauzah Tahera in Mumbai there are even special visiting hours reserved only for women. This is in line with the findings of Nancy Tapper, who notes that in Turkey ziyaret is often particularly attractive to women as it provides a rare opportunity to travel, reach beyond their familiar environment, and mingle with people outside their immediate circle of family and neighbors.[13] At less frequented Bohra rauzahs, men and women often visit during the same hours. I visited the mausoleum of seven da'is in Surat in the company of a female pilgrim, who was pleased to find the tombs of several holy women in the sprawling enclosure—and irritated to discover that they were given less central placement than those of the men.

At every important place of pilgrimage, the dawat has established a

musafirkhana (traveler's lodge) for the use of any Bohra visitors—a total of 137 throughout the world.[14] Each musafirkhana provides comfortable rooms and Gujarati food, all at highly subsidized rates. In order to make use of the musafirkhanas (and to gain admittance to any Bohra shrine), a guest must present a certificate of orthopraxy from his or her local amil. As of 1920 there were Bohra musafirkhanas in Medina, Kerbala, Najaf, Cairo, Jerusalem, and several sites in India; some were built by popular subscription, some by the dawat, and some by the wealthy reformer Sir Adamji Pirbhai.[15] The proliferation of musafirkhanas within India both fueled and responded to growing demand in the last century, and limiting their use to properly documented mu'mineen is a recent innovation. Under Syedna Muhammad Burhanuddin the upkeep of musafirkhanas has been a high priority, and the threat of exclusion from this network is a strong incentive for believers to maintain orthopraxy. A resounding 86.6 % of my survey respondents reported using musafirkhanas, and more than one-fifth identified these lodges as one of the two most important dawat services. Ziyaret was cited as a prime aspect of orthopraxy by 82.1 % of respondents.

The experience of Mullah Shabbir M. Mansoorbhai Jamali is typical of Bohras performing ziyaret. After his daughter had been seriously ill with asthma for four years, Mullah Shabbir decided to take her on a pilgrimage to Ahmedabad, Jamnagar, and Surat. At every mausoleum, Mullah Shabbir performed wuzu and kissed the doors before entering. Inside, he recited the Yasin Surah of the Qur'an[16] and performed *sezda* (kissed the ground). He then kissed the *qabr* (coffin), asked the blessing of the da'i both for his daughter's health and his own spiritual well-being, and placed several roses on the gravesite. He ate a few petals from one of the flowers left by a previous pilgrim, and took some petals away as *berketi* (remembrance) for relatives back home. He kissed all four sides of the qabr, starting at the head and circumambulating counterclockwise.[17] Mullah Shabbir performed the same ritual at each qabr in the rauzah (the mausoleums in these cities each contain the tombs of several da'is), and at each rauzah in his pilgrimage. "Departed syednas and syedis are watching from heaven," he explains. "Syedna Taher Saifuddin used to say that if we came to pray at his tomb after his death he would help all who sought his assistance."

LIFESTYLES OF THE QASR-E ALI

The Bohra royals, like royals everywhere, attract both reverence and resentment. They are revered for their blood ties to Syedna and their work for the dawat, but they are sometimes resented for their comparative

wealth and luxurious lifestyle. That members of the Qasr-e Ali are supported by the taxes and contributions of every member of the community only adds to the resentment felt by some Bohras. The issue is a sticking point for dissidents, and sometimes the subject of whispered gossip among the orthodox. Rumors fly, but facts are few: those who really know how the royals live are, ipso facto, likely to be staunch defenders of Qasr-e Ali privilege; those who oppose such treatment are, ipso facto, unlikely ever to get a glimpse inside the palace gates. As perhaps the first non-Bohra with sufficient exposure to offer an impartial evaluation (the first anthropologist, at any rate), I can try to clear up a few misperceptions and provide an outsider's view of this contentious issue.

Ernest Hemingway famously noted that the very rich are different from you and me: they have more money. The Bohra royals are also different from you and me: they have more aristocratic relatives. This, rather than opulence of lifestyle, is the main distinguishing attribute of the Qasr-e Ali. It could even be argued that Bohras with a middle-class lifestyle in the United States or Europe probably enjoy greater material comfort than do members of Syedna's immediate family living in Saifee Mahal. After observing the royals at close quarters over the better part of three years, I do not consider their lifestyle to be more extravagant than that of a great many other Bohras of a similar socioeconomic background. Their privilege is generally more symbolic than material: access to Syedna, clerical titles, invitations to private religious functions, kneeling space at the front rather than the rear of the masjid.

The primary material benefit of royalty seems to be frequent travel, accompanying Syedna on his ceaseless globetrotting. Even here the myth is far greater than the reality: the Qasr-e Ali may be jet-setters, but they are not always flying high. Only the children and grandchildren of the da'i have their expenses paid directly by the dawat; other members of the retinue pay their own way, and are grateful for the honor of being invited. In a typical party of four dozen, only Syedna and one or two shahzadas will have first-class plane tickets. The other shahzadas will fly business class if they're lucky, or else they'll sit in coach with the remaining forty-odd members of the group. When they reach their destination, Syedna and his family seldom stay in a luxury hotel. The da'i and all members of his party stay in the homes of local Bohras: serving as host to Syedna or his relatives is a privilege for which mu'mineen engage in discretely ruthless bidding wars. The only time Syedna or those closest to him stay in a hotel is when they vacation at a remote resort—for any top royal to take a hotel room in a town with a single Bohra family would be a disgrace for the prince and for the local Bohra community alike.

The most august members of the Qasr-e Ali live and travel in ease and comfort—but no more so than any mid-level international businessman. This might be of little solace to a Bohra shopkeeper struggling just to put food on the table, but shopkeepers and street peddlers are seldom vocal critics of royal privilege. Most criticism (whether overt or secretly whispered) seems to come from the social class just below that of the royals: the upper and upper-middle segments of society, defined both by birth and by wealth, who feel shut out of the dawat's innermost circle.

The following glimpses of Syedna Muhammad Burhanuddin and members of his extended family are meant to provide what Clifford Geertz has termed "thick description."[18] They are offered not as a defense of the royals' lifestyle (the Qasr-e Ali is quite capable of defending itself without the assistance of an outsider) but as documentation of the central position that Syedna and his family occupy within the Daudi community. The vignettes that follow are ethnographic snapshots of a slice of Bohra society that most Bohras themselves see only at a distance, and through a reverent filter.

Syedna's Raza (Permission) and Du'a (Blessing)

The first time I saw Syedna Muhammad Burhanuddin was during the annual examinations at the Jamea tus-Saifiya in Surat.[19] After the day of oral questioning had concluded, Syedna left the crowded assembly hall and gave a series of audiences in a smaller chamber across the street. Here, as on every other occasion on which I have seen him, the da'i was surrounded by a phalanx of supplicants, relatives, and aides. It brings to mind the image of a president escorted by his secret service contingent, only without the glad-handing, grinning, or hearty waves.

As the da'i passed, every person in the multitude bowed, offered a joined-palm gesture of respect, reached out to kiss his hand or touch his clothing, asked for blessings with cries of, "Syedna, Syedna, du'a, du'a." At every step people surged forward, pressed as close to him as the other jostling supplicants would allow, seeking a mere instant of the da'i's attention to pose a private question, grasping for just a mere sentence, just a mere word. Commoners grudgingly made way for royals, but with so many assorted VIPs in attendance the whole procession soon became an unruly aristocratic mêlée. The only way to push through the throng was with the help of a powerful patron, so shahzadas and bhaisahebs of varying levels of importance vied to propel their chosen protégés closer to the da'i. The more ambitious favor-seekers worked their way up a chain of contacts to gain the support of one of the da'i's sons or brothers. Even with

the strenuous backing of several relatives of Syedna, I was initially unable to make much headway.

Out in the street, a crowd of thousands had been waiting over an hour for the brief instant when Syedna would walk from one building to the next. Men and women were mixed together somewhat indiscriminately, all clad in mandated community dress. Some raised cameras above their heads to snap a quick photo, some hoisted children onto their shoulders to give them a treasured memory, some climbed on top of an iron gate to gain a better view. As the time approached, aides laid a metal gangway across the alley so that Syedna would not have to descend to street level, and unfurled a red carpet stretching from one doorway to the other. When the da'i emerged, the crowd was held back by a thin line of Bohra security guards, all dressed in white trousers, white shirts, and pillbox topis. Each guard had a hefty black lanyard tied to his shiny leather belt, but the weapon at the lanyard's end was merely a small silver whistle.

Inside the private audience room, well insulated from the faithful masses in the street, the swirl of activity was no less frenzied. I was shuttled from one VIP to another in an effort to squeeze within talking range of Syedna. The combined efforts of several royals worked me up to the front ranks, just off to the pontiff's left side. Syedna was now seated, giving individual blessings to a long line of women: the crush of bodies that always materializes around Syedna would not make a seemly coed sport, so special segments of many appearances are set aside especially for women. Two attendants, their linked hands forming a human gateway, made sure that the line of women was orderly and sedate. Each supplicant (sometimes accompanied by a small child) was permitted to advance and kneel before Syedna, state her request, and then move on. All the while, a pack of men on Syedna's three other sides ceaselessly tried to gain his attention during the brief intervals between one woman's retreat and the next one's approach.

Finally, after the women's blessings had concluded and the throng of questioners had thinned out slightly, my patrons succeeded in winning me a hard-fought minute or two of Syedna's time. "Syedna saheb," I said, having prepared my statement in the most deferential Lisanu-Dawat* formu-

*Lisanu-Dawat is, by definition, the language spoken by the da'i. A highly Islamized version of the Bohras' native dialect of Gujarati, its propagation as the vernacular rather than solely the ritual language of the community is a significant element of Syedna's identity reification program. Since the vocabulary of Lisanu-Dawat tries to substitute Arabic, Persian, or Urdu words for Gujarati ones whenever possible, it is still noticeably different from the tongue of most Bohras outside clerical circles. Often the term "Lisanu-Dawat" is used to distinguish the written form of the language (in Arabic script) from the spoken form, but this usage is far from universal.

lations I knew, "I have traveled from America to study the culture of the Bohras, and would be exceptionally grateful for your du'a in this undertaking." If the da'i was surprised at my presence or my request, he engaged me in conversation without missing a beat. He asked a few polite questions about my background, my research, and my contacts within the community. Once he discovered that I had already been vetted by a range of authorities including one of his brothers and two of his sons, he gave his personal blessing for my fieldwork. He then reached under his seat and presented me with a prayer shawl as a token of his support: a plain buff-colored piece of cloth with a simple black-stitch design, it would be immediately recognizable by all community members as a mark of the da'i's special favor.

As soon as we had stepped away from the maelstrom, my royal patrons marveled at my good fortune: most Bohras consider themselves lucky merely to catch sight of Syedna, but to meet him face-to-face, to have an actual conversation with him, and to receive du'a at his own hand would be considered a once-in-a-lifetime event. To be given a prayer shawl (they explained) was very high honor indeed: even bhaisahebs with a lifetime of khidmat behind them might not receive such a gift. Since that day, every time I have attended an important Bohra function, I have come with the prayer shawl draped nonchalantly around my shoulders. In the stifling heat of a Mumbai summer it draws looks of surprise, but nods of bemused appreciation as well.

SYEDNA IN MUMBAI

The twenty-seventh of Zilqaad marks the birth date of Syedna Taher Saifuddin, the father of the current da'i. It is a holiday for the entire community, but for obvious reasons it holds particular importance for Syedna Muhammad Burhanuddin and the Qasr-e Ali. Because it is also the date of the current da'i's coronation, this day has become a celebration observed by Bohras all over the world.

At the ritual I witnessed during my fieldwork,[20] the crowd at Saifee Masjid was not as numerous as it had been at Lailat al-Qadr or would be during Ashura, but it was thick enough that a clerical friend advised me to carry my shoes with me in a sack. "If you leave them in the shoe rack," he warned, "you'll never see them again." The intricately carved dark wooden pillars of the main chamber were festooned with sweet-smelling wreaths of pale jasmine petals and bright strings of white lights. All of the many ancient ceiling fans were churning at full speed, and all were sorely needed. The chamber is surrounded by second- and third-floor purdah

galleries: women can watch and take part in all rituals, while maintaining a modest distance from the men packed in below. Since the wooden screens are often opened to provide adequate ventilation, visual segregation is not iron-clad.

The ceremony marking the Taher Saifuddin's birthday began immediately after maghrib namaz. Syedna (as the representative of his father) had his head circled three times with a thal containing coconuts and sweets: this is common practice at the birthday celebrations of many Bohras. A friend in the clergy describes this as a custom carried over from the Bohras' Hindu ancestors, noting that his own parents perform the same rite for him on his own birthday; the sweets ("today, often Cadbury chocolates") represent the hope of sweetness in life, while the coconuts (as has been noted often in anthropological literature) are a symbolic representation of fertility, longevity, and prosperity.

After the circling of the thal, a vessel of sherbet was passed around: first to Syedna, then to his brothers and sons. Even on this joyous occasion, however, the central aspect of ritual was commemoration of the martyrdom of Imam Husain. Syedna and other speakers retold episodes from the story of Kerbala, chanted hymns and recited poems about it, read sermons about it, and (as at all Bohra rituals) reminded their audience that the tale is the blueprint for all later human developments. Tonight's program was focused on Taher Saifuddin, with various poems or hymns composed by him, various others celebrating him—but the commemoration never strayed far from the topic of Ashura. Periodically the audience would break into loud cries of "Ya Husain!" and periods of hearty breast-beating matam. The majlis lasted a little less than two hours, after which Syedna and his close relatives crossed the street to perform ziyaret at Rauzah Tahera. There would be feasts later, but even on this day—one of the most joyous of the Bohra calendar—the mood was one of somber remembrance.

PALACE LIFE

Saifee Mahal

The primary residence for the close family of Syedna is the Saifee Mahal compound, near the hanging gardens on Malabar Hill in Mumbai. The main building is a very large, stately structure in the late colonial architectural style sometimes labeled Indian Gothic. It is of a piece with most of Mumbai's pre-Independence architecture, from the Parsi mansions of Colaba and Marine Drive to the countinghouses of Churchgate to the rococo

splendor of Mumbai University and Victoria Terminus; they are works of elegance and fine craftsmanship, though somewhat touched by the ravages of time. The royals who live in Saifee Mahal and work in Badri Mahal commute between two very similar structures: places of faded grandeur and peeling paint, of servants idly polishing marble floors, of rooms with little light or space, but beautifully ornate wainscoting. Places, in short, of quiet dignity rather than lavish extravagance.

The apartments in Saifee Mahal are rather modest, both in the old and the new parts of the compound. The newer buildings are clean and well maintained, but indistinguishable from other modern apartment houses found throughout middle-class Mumbai. The flats are more spacious than those of the older building, but it would be hard to describe them as overly luxurious. Even the apartments of Syedna's own children are considerably more modest than those of many of their Malabar Hill neighbors. The rooms in the main building are somewhat cramped and old-fashioned, looking much as they might have looked in the late nineteenth century, often stuffed with memorabilia of a past age. In the chambers of one elderly shahzedi (a daughter of Syedna Taher Saifuddin), the only evidence of modernity is the presence of a television, VCR, and a series of cartoon stickers—Mickey Mouse, Garfield, Teenage Mutant Ninja Turtles—plastered on a cabinet by the princess's great-grandchildren.[21]

Royal Homes in Surat

As the former seat of the dawat and the site of the Jamea tus-Saifiya, Surat is a place of tremendous importance to the Bohra community at large. As the city to which most of the aristocrats and all of the royals trace their ancestry, however, Surat has a particular significance for the Bohra elite. Most upper-crust families keep at least one house or apartment in Surat, and these domiciles range from faded grandeur to spartan simplicity. I have seen only a small fraction of these homes, but can attest to their wide variety.

At one end of the spectrum is Zaini Bungalow, Syedna's official residence in Surat. This spacious, baroque pavilion is set on a picturesque waterfront, but the city's industrial development has taken its toll on the river Tapi. At the bungalow's front gate an aged caretaker daubs a visitor's hand with strong perfume, as a precaution for when the wind blows from the direction of the water. Similar in appearance and style (but more salubrious in siting) is the residence of the late Shahzedi Sakina Behnsaheb, the da'i's daughter. Until her death in 1999 Shahzedi Sakina (like most shahzedis) spent considerable time teaching batini ta'wil classes for women. When in Surat she stayed in a Victorian mansion with lofty ceilings and palatial

drawing rooms: a mansion that is musty, dusty, a bit frayed at the edges, but still a place heavy with elegant grace.

The community's lesser aristocracy generally live in conditions that are decidedly middle-class. One apartment building in Surat is typical: a modern, somewhat dilapidated structure of concrete and cinderblock, it exhibits no external signs of being a royal residence. The flats themselves (I saw only a few, but they seemed to have a uniform pattern) are likewise thoroughly ordinary. Of the forty-eight residents listed in the building's directory, however, more than half are bhaisahebs and behnsahebs. The top three floors are occupied almost entirely by clerics in the upper reaches of the dawat.

Also typical is a household located a few blocks from the Jamea campus, on an upper story of a nineteenth-century row house shared by several old Surti families. This apartment is maintained as a pied-à-terre for visiting relatives, and a place for any family children to use while pursuing studies at the Jamea. At the time of my visit its occupants were four teenaged Jamea students, three boys and one girl, chaperoned by an elderly servant and his wife. The four cousins seemed much like any other Jamea students. When I arrived for lunch the two older boys were casually discussing their exam anxieties while busily ironing and starching their kurtas. At a wedding ceremony later that evening, I would see these teens and barely recognize them. At home they were ordinary high-schoolers sharing a cramped off-campus apartment, but in public, they would be transformed into three princes and a princess.

NIKAH RITES IN SURAT

A few days after I received du'a for my research I was invited to a celebration marking both the graduation of a dozen Jamea students and their joint nikah performed by Syedna himself. Ceremonies began just after evening namaz. Women could watch from a screened gallery, but (as was the case throughout most of the Jamea tus-Saifiya exam week) the main assembly hall was reserved for men. Many of the guests were themselves Jamea graduates, and wore distinctive red or green topped *pagris* (turbans). Others wore topis, or old-fashioned *fetas* of woven gold thread.

Trumpets and drums heralded the entry of the twelve grooms. Each graduate wore an academic pagri, with a single vertical feather to mark him as a bridegroom. The chamber was filled with swirls and eddies of activity, some guests following the rites with intense interest, others conducting private conversations in barely muted tones. In contrast to comportment during the examinations earlier that day or during namaz at

sunset, men felt little compunction about entering and leaving the chamber, shifting sitting positions, or engaging in small talk. Often the ceremony itself seemed only one among many focal points within the assembly hall.

At Syedna's entry, all conversation ceased. He made his way to a low throne by the qiblah niche, pressed at every step by the mass of devotees anxious to kiss his hand, touch his garment, receive his personal blessing. When the twelve grooms were brought before him they all began to weep copiously, lamenting that now they would have to leave their happy life at the academy. The public lamentation that is so central a feature of Shiʿa religious observance (Ashura, after all, is the pivotal event of the faith) is not far removed even from such joyous occasions as graduations and marriages. After permitting the grooms to finish their stylized sobbing, Syedna told them that now their education was complete and it was time for them to enter khidmat. One by one the grooms stepped forward to offer themselves, and presented Syedna with token gifts of dried fruits and nuts.

The nikah portion of the ceremony was more private. The microphone was turned off, and the guests freely carried on their own conversations. Men circulated through the hall passing out invitations for a large ziyafat to be given the next day for all past Jamea graduates; tonight's feast, invitees were reminded, would be hosted by the current Jamea graduating class in celebration of their classmates' wedding, and would begin immediately after the nikah. A chamberlain continually chided people to sit down and stop making a commotion, but his hectoring seemed to have little impact.

Three youths, their beards just starting to grow in, were bowed to and fawned over by men old enough to be their grandfathers. The boys with whom I'd shared lunch (I now learned) were great-grandchildren of Syedna Taher Saifuddin. On ceremonial occasions such as this, the general uniformity of Bohra dress gives way to subtle class distinction. Normally, a prince and pauper would dress in identical topis and kurtas. At religious events, however, royals are marked out by special finery. Even the youngest princelings can be seen in gilt-edged kurtas. After the age of mithaq, princes of particularly lofty lineage wear voluminous shawls of stiff white cloth with a texture similar to that of burlap, and my three lunchtime hosts now all were wrapped in such attire.

Every time a man passed one of these princes in the masjid, he joined all five fingertips of his right hand and shook them in front of his forehead three times. Such a gesture (while doubtless an obscenity in many a Mediterranean context) is a symbol of great respect among the Bohras. Called a *tasleem,* this gesture is the physical expression for salaam. It has

many of the same nuances as a Japanese bow: the more respect one wishes to display, the deeper the stoop and the more pronounced the shake. To see clerics with long, white beards offering the most deferential tasleem to youths barely out of puberty is to be reminded of the extent of the royal family's prestige.

During the nikah, meanwhile, relatives of the twelve couples clustered around the da'i to witness the signing of the marriage contracts by the grooms, the brides' fathers, two shahideen from each family, and Syedna. During this rather lengthy procedure the families of each couple exchanged gifts, after which Syedna recited several Qur'anic verses and presented each groom with a prayer shawl. The conclusion of the ceremony was marked with drums and trumpets, and Syedna departed the chamber in a crush of followers. The newlyweds, their relatives, and various royals retired to a private banquet room, while other guests hurried to the main dining hall for the celebratory feast.

After a meal of coriander-laced biryani and other wedding favorites (consumed, as is traditional, with all diners at the thal sharing dining utensils as well as dishes) I left the hall sated, and looked up at the screened-off enclosure where the royals were sitting at their own thals. It was about ten o'clock, and this was only their first ziyafat of the evening. There would be at least two more before they could return to their homes, and practically every day would bring a new round of ziyafats to attend. For many people, a surfeit of excellent food would hardly rank as one of life's great travails. But to endure feast after feast, night after night, month after month, year after year—it could be enough to make the heartiest royal trencherman lose his appetite.

Dumas: A Royal Family Picnic

Life in Qasr-e Ali circles is not always a press of ritual and stiff formality. The royal family, like all families, sometimes enjoys a private get-together outside the public eye. Unlike other families, however, the Qasr-e Ali has over 200 members; even an informal day in the country is a rather elaborate affair. I was fortunate enough to be invited to such an outing shortly after the joint nikah in Surat.

The royal retreat at Dumas is located about fifteen kilometers outside Surat, far enough away to be secluded from the less pleasant aspects of one of India's dirtiest cities.[22] It is a large park with several pavilions and bungalows, a site for day trips rather than a permanent residence. One could describe it as a well-tended garden stocked with peacocks and pure white doves, but such a description would be truthful without being wholly

accurate: the birds are confined to two rusty iron cages, a picture of bedraggled listlessness rather than the romance or opulence their names might conjure up. They serve as a reminder that the reality of royal life—for the Bohra royalty, at least—is far more mundane than it might appear when glimpsed from afar.

Syedna Taher Saifuddin is said to have advised his flock to divide each day into four parts: five hours for religious observance, eight for sleep, eight for earning one's living, three for enjoying what one has earned. The gathering at Dumas clearly fell into this last category. Several dozen family members relaxed in and around the central pavilion, talking in small groups while their grandchildren flew kites, played cricket, or queued up for rides on a tired pony and a painted elephant.

The bushes around the main villa were strewn with the kurtas of the young boys, who had all stripped down to their pajamas or underwear for a dip in a decorative marble pool. They splashed about merrily, dousing any gray-bearded shahzadas who happened to venture too close. Tens of thousands of Bohras would consider it an honor to kiss the hands of these reverend elders, but today the august clerics chuckled indulgently upon being soaked. When Shahzada Qaidjohar strayed within arm's reach of the boys they dragged him into the water as well; Syedna's eldest and most powerful son took the dunking with abundant good humor.

Unlike the formal ziyafats that are held for the royals in ceaseless succession, this barbecue was a rare casual buffet. Instead of the traditional Gujarati standards, diners could help themselves to *seekh kabab* grilled over charcoal, *bhel puri, naan* from a tandoor in the villa's kitchen, mangoes and coconuts, *kulfi* and *falooda,* or *barfi* in a rainbow of pink, blue, and yellow. A large mechanical press, the same sort found on many Mumbai street corners, ground long poles of sugarcane into stringy lumps of pulp to extract the sweet, green juice. Here, as in most other nonritual settings for the Bohras, it was virtually impossible to judge a person's social rank on the basis of appearance. During waaz in the masjid VIPs can be recognized by distinctive headgear or shawls, but outside of such occasions all Bohras (other than the da'i) follow exactly the same dress code. The sons of Syedna and the servants who wash their dishes all have the same white kurtas, the same topis, the same beards. It is an egalitarian touch quite in line with Bohra tradition; the custom of eating at the thal, for example, was introduced centuries ago specifically (Bohras say) to supplant Hindu exclusiveness with Muslim social unity. The symbolic egalitarianism implied by the dress code and thal, however, provide only a polite mask for the very real social divisions within the Bohra community. Even here at Dumas, Syedna and his very closest family members ate at

separate thals inside the central pavilion rather than dine with the rest of the crowd.

And even here, at a casual family outing, Syedna's appearance brought all other activity to an immediate standstill. The moment the da'i emerged from the pavilion for a brief stroll, every relative within eyesight or earshot abruptly dropped whatever he or she may have been doing and focused all attention on the pontiff. As at public functions, everyone around Syedna bowed when he passed, tried to touch the hem of his garment, jockeyed for position with anyone else standing nearby. The sons and brothers of Syedna dominated the tight-packed cluster directly surrounding him, and as at public functions a stream of favor-seekers tried to win the intercession of one of these inner circle relatives in order to gain a few precious moments of the da'i's attention. Syedna walked with a pronounced stoop, but appeared taller than anyone around him: every head in his vicinity is always reverently bowed in the da'i's presence.

The first time Syedna made a brief appearance, my patrons were unable to get me close enough to have my blessing from earlier in the week renewed: there was no need for a fresh du'a, they said, but one should never miss an opportunity all the same. The crush of petitioners here seemed barely less insistent than in public venues, but I was reminded that here Syedna's attention would be divided only among several dozen people rather than several thousand. The next time the da'i emerged from the pavilion, on the way to his car for the drive back to Surat, Syedna's son Qaidjohar secured me a brief conversation with him. I'd prepared a series of questions specifically bearing on my research, but it was quite obvious that this would be a du'a-opportunity rather than an interview—and that this would be the most prolonged exposure I'd be likely to receive.

I wasted several of my hard-won moments in the da'i's presence recapitulating my background, my purpose in being there, and the general thrust of my research. The summary may have been utterly unnecessary, since I'd told him these things at my first audience, and Syedna is commonly believed to have a photographic, encyclopedic memory. Community members sometimes tell stories (generally secondhand) of a relative of theirs who had exchanged only a sentence or two with the da'i in his or her youth, then met him again decades later to find that he had remembered every word from the first conversation. Despite these tales of superhuman feats of memory, with hundreds of different bits of personal information thrust at him every day—urgent requests from any number of important people—it hardly seemed reasonable to expect him to allot any memory space to the odd curiosities of a lowly (and poorly bearded) ethnographer.

The da'i gave no sign of whether he'd taken my recapitulation as old news or fresh information, an interesting diversion or an irrelevant annoyance. He asked a few general questions about my impressions of Surat and of the rituals, repeated his blessing for my endeavors, and got in the car to return to the city. His motorcade was worthy of a visiting head of state: six police officers in a jeep and a half-dozen Bohra security guards as motorcycle outriders formed a safety cordon on the highway. In the center of it all, however, the da'i traveled in an ordinary white Ambassador car. The only differences between Syedna's vehicle and those hired by visiting tourists were a gilt crown on the hood, and a small sign above the license plate reading "His Holiness."

Syedna Abroad: On Tour in New Jersey

During my fieldwork in Mumbai and Gujarat I attended a number of rites at which Syedna presided, most of them falling into a pattern similar to those described above. By way of comparison, I tried for a long time to attend one of the da'i's ceremonies outside India, to see what differences there might be between rituals in the home country and those of expatriate Bohra communities. In August 1996 Syedna made a visit to the United States, and I traveled to New Jersey to join the entourage.[23]

The site was a convention hall located in a strip mall off highway I–95, in a rather desolate industrial area near Passaic. The clash of cultures was evident in the parking lot: the hall was next to a glitzy suburban nightclub, so the congregation of over a thousand Bohras in conservative Islamic dress vied for parking spaces with teenagers who could have stepped directly out of *Saturday Night Fever*. The disco's bouncer—with his slicked-back hair, his mirrored sunglasses, his shirt open to display an assortment of gold chains—watched incredulously as the Muslim families emerged from their Chevrolet minivans,

Once inside, I met my close friend Abduz-Zahir Bhaisaheb Mohyuddin, a young businessman of Qasr-e Ali lineage who had recently married the daughter of the mazoon, and was thus doubly a member of the royal inner circle. For the past year we'd discussed Ismaili tradition while lifting weights or playing squash at the Harvard gym, and this was the first time I'd seen him in a ritual setting. In everyday life he maintains all aspects of Islamic orthopraxy, but is so modest about his stature within the community that a casual observer would never suspect him of being a closet aristocrat.

The hall was divided in half widthwise, with the men's and women's sections separated by a semiopaque curtain. Local jamat organizers had transformed the room into an impromptu masjid: floors covered with

plush carpets, walls decorated with Kufic-script calligraphy, doors and windows festooned with banners in green, red, and gold. At the front of the hall, on a slightly raised platform, was the seat from which Syedna would deliver his sermon. The convention hall's duty manager was no more comfortable with his patrons than the bouncer outside had been: a question about the timing of the waaz elicited the response, "Look, I don't know *nothing* about *none* of this."

Today was the milad of Imam Tayyib, the last of the Musta'li Ismaili imams before the period of concealment.[24] The evening's rituals began with maghrib/isha namaz at 8:00, with the waaz following at 8:30. It lasted until midnight—and this was only the first part of the night's observances. After leaving the hall, Syedna and his entourage went to private ziyafats lasting well into the early hours of the morning. A communal ziyafat for the rest of the assembled company had been scheduled as well, but the hall had been rented only until midnight and the manager gleefully stuck to the absolute letter of the arrangement. Jamat volunteers set up a makeshift cafeteria in the parking lot, and the congregation (much to the amazement of clubgoers exiting the disco) ate dinners of tandoori chicken and biryani off the hoods of their cars.

The most noteworthy aspect of the New Jersey ceremony, however, was how closely it mirrored similar gatherings in Mumbai. In matters of ritual and observance this might be expected, but even in such intangibles as mannerism or body language the mood was nearly identical. I'd expected the American Bohras to be far more Westernized than their Indian relatives—to seem ill-at-ease in their topis and kurtas, to make small talk in English rather than Gujarati or Lisanu-Dawat, to appear somewhat culturally alienated from the ceremony they were attending. This was not the case. The casual chatting of friends and relatives in the parking lot was almost all conducted in Gujarati. Even the physical gestures were the same: pressing one's forehead to the hand of a high-ranking cleric, three reverent shakes of the right arm when sitting down or standing up—all the ineffable elements of bodily carriage that mark a person indigenous to the community were displayed as fully in exile as on the home turf of Mumbai.

All but a few of the men present wore beards, and most of the beards were full enough to indicate long-standing orthopraxy. A higher percentage than might have been the case in India wore scraggly week-old chin-hair (possibly to be shaved off as soon as Syedna's plane left the tarmac), but these represented a small minority of attendees. The sheer intensity of devotion, moreover, far surpassed that of most Mumbai rituals I'd observed. The matam was vigorous and extremely physical, the shouts full-throated and piercing, the tears plentiful and prolonged. An observer can

only comment on exterior manifestations of devotion, but this milad seemed to have all the fervor of an Ashura rite.

After the service had ended, the mosh pit surrounding Syedna was more ferocious than just about any I had seen in India. I am told that this is not atypical, that the crush of people seeking blessings or advice is often more insistent overseas than at home. This stands to reason: in Mumbai, the da'i's appearance is an important event, but hardly an unusual one. Abroad, it is a matter to be particularly cherished for its rarity. To many of the faithful who had traveled from all across the United States to be here in New Jersey, the chance to come within an arm's reach of Syedna was a once-in-a-lifetime opportunity.

A View from the Bottom: How Royals Are Seen by Nonroyals

In the opinion of some Bohras, outward displays of devotion such as those described above are often hypocritical posturing, merely pieces of sycophantic showmanship by ambitious social climbers. In the view of these critics, the surface-level orthopraxy initiated since the late 1970s does not demonstrate an underlying reservoir of support for the dawat, merely a culture of fear, status-seeking, and blind obedience. That is the position of overt dissidents such as Asghar Ali Engineer, and a sentiment shared by at least some Bohras who outwardly comply with all dawat rules.

This study makes no claim to articulate the viewpoints of the entire Bohra population, or even (necessarily) of a majority of its members: when dealing with a community numbering in the neighborhood of one million, such a claim would be sheer hubris. Moreover, my fieldwork has focused on the dawat's top-down attempts to solidify mandated norms rather than on how this program has been perceived by people at the bottom of the social hierarchy. My personal contacts within the community are skewed toward elite Surti and Qasr-e Ali families, while my survey respondents (households with children attending Burhani madrasas) are representative of the more economically privileged and theologically orthodox segments of Bohra society. My observations on levels of public devotion in ritual settings are likewise incomplete: descriptions of the frenzied zeal displayed by those attending the da'i's services say nothing about Bohras who may have chosen to remain at home.

Nevertheless, this religious zeal and heartfelt commitment is hardly limited to elite circles. Quite the contrary: the large majority of people I have encountered casually at public rituals have been of thoroughly pedestrian socioeconomic backgrounds. Typical of these is a young couple with

whom I hitched a ride from the New Jersey waaz back to New York City: Salman and Alifiyah,* owners of a small hardware store in Brooklyn.

They'd emigrated from Kenya only six years earlier, but Alifiyah already spoke English with a thick Brooklyn accent. "I wouldn't want to live anyplace except New York," she said. "It's the capital of the world." Neither husband nor wife had ever been to India, and they interrogated me eagerly about the land of their ancestors. "We have relatives in Nagpur and in Hyderabad," Salman said. "Are these towns close to Mumbai?" Alifiyah asked about hygiene, and whether it was safe to drink the water.

Back in Mombasa, they said, the Bohra community is tight-knit and observant. Men wear topis with street clothes in nonritual settings, but women often wear burqas on a daily basis. Everyone they knew back in Kenya followed Syedna's guidelines—maybe not to the absolute letter, but closely enough to have clean consciences. Salman and Alifiyah's marriage had been arranged, but they had dated several times before agreeing to it. By the time they emigrated to the United States they had a son and a daughter, both now fast asleep next to me in the back seat of the car. Before each child's birth, Salman's sister had obtained chatti cloth from Syedna and a name selected by the da'i himself.

Both Salman and Alifiyah firmly believe in Syedna's ability to know what is best for every member of the community, and consider themselves fortunate to be guided by his instructions. Direction from the da'i is not something imposed upon them, they explain, but something they seek out and rely upon. Salman provided an example from the time before they left Kenya: "Back in Mombasa," he said, "my elder brother was running a hardware store. Business was not good, and he wanted to sell foodstuffs instead: people may not always need hardware, but they will always need food. My brother sent a letter asking Syedna for permission, but His Holiness would not allow the change. 'Stay in hardware,' Syedna said, and so my brother obeyed." Salman paused a moment before delivering the seal of his proof. "Business improved," he said, "and today my brother is a rich man."

Five months ago, Salman and Alifiyah opened their own hardware store. Back in Mombasa and then for nearly six years in the United States they had worked for relatives, but finally they'd saved enough money to set up a small business of their own. At the time of our conversation, the venture was struggling. Three times during the previous half year they'd

*These names have been changed, since the context of the conversation was not that of a formal interview: the couple had offered me a lift, not necessarily permission to be quoted in print.

solicited Syedna's blessings and advice; three times he had given his du'a and instructed them to stay the course. Each time the procedure had been the same: Salman contacted the dawat through a relative in Mumbai, then the Badri Mahal officials took the matter to the da'i and sent Salman a reply by fax. "It is difficult to keep the shop running," Alifiyah said, "and the rent is due every month, but we have no doubt it will be profitable soon. His Holiness has said so."

The fledgling hardware store has no staff other than the young husband and wife, who keep the store running every day of the week. We wouldn't reach New York until two o'clock in the morning, but the shop would be open for business less than seven hours later. The family had driven out to New Jersey each of the past three days for various ceremonies; the week before, Alifiyah had tended the hardware store alone while Salman flew to Houston for other stops in Syedna's tour. They couldn't easily afford the ticket, Alifiyah said, but the da'i's blessing would more than make up for the cost.

There are doubtless many Bohras who shed crocodile tears during Ashura, who find the rules of orthopraxy to be stifling rather than comforting, who follow the da'i's commands with resentment rather than joy. But there are also many Bohras like Salman and Alifiyah: people who hungrily seek Syedna's instructions, who consider themselves fortunate to be guided by the da'i in all aspects of life. This family's belief is sincere and unforced: it is credible precisely because it has no possible ulterior motive.

Salman and Alifiyah are not royals, not even VIPs. They don't travel in circles where their presence or absence at a community function would be a matter of praise or censure. Many of their friends are Bohras, but they don't take much part in jamatkhana activities, and have no interest in social climbing. Their goals are modest: to get their hardware business up and running, to pay off their debts, to provide a comfortable life for their children. It is a mark of their devotion to the religion that they sacrifice valuable work hours and savings to get Syedna's blessing—not once or twice, but each and every time they can. It is a mark of their religion's responsiveness that even believers of no great social standing can—if they try hard enough—have immediate and personal (if fleeting) access to the da'i, as frequently or infrequently as they choose to seek it out.

I asked the young couple to tell me their greatest dream. A smile crept over Alifiyah's mouth, the same sort of smile many of her neighbors might get when fantasizing about winning the lottery. "Someday," she said, hardly daring to articulate the wish, "if we're very lucky, perhaps we will be able to afford to host a ziyafat. That would be my dream—to have Syedna eat a meal in our very own home."

Syedna Muhammad Burhanuddin receiving *salaam*. (The first four pages of this photo
gallery, courtesy of Ayaz Shaikh, display the range of Bohra dress typical before the 1980s.
The following pages show the dress deemed normative for community functions today.)

Engagement rituals in the 1960s: The bride (Zaitoon Gunja) receives a blessing from her aunt (Zeni). In many Indian communities, the coconut (here pressed to the bride's forehead) is a symbol of fertility.

Marriage rituals: The bride's father (Huseni Gunja) hands her the *mahr* paid by the groom.

Marriage rituals: The bride gives
salaam to her mother (Ateka) . . .

. . . and to her father (Huseni).

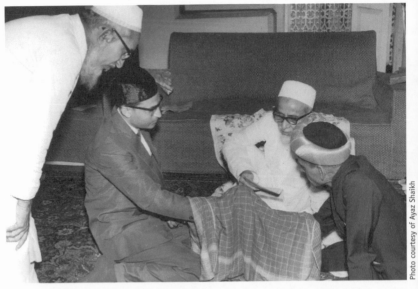

Nikah ceremony: The groom (Riaz Shaikh, seated left) and the father of the bride (Huseni Gunja, seated right) forge a family union, with the blessing of an amil (Mukasir Saleh Bhaisaheb Safiyuddin, seated center). A relative (standing) serves as *shaheed* (witness).

Nikah dinner for Riaz and Zaitoon. Male and female guests dine separately.

Syedna Muhammad Burhanuddin in procession for *Zikra* and start of annual examinations at the Jamea tus-Saifiya. Surat, 1995

Syedna (then Mazoon) Muhammad Burhanuddin, Indian Prime Minister Jawaharlal Nehru, and Syedna Taher Saifuddin at the Jamea tus-Saifiya in Surat

Syedna Muhammad Burhanuddin delivers 1994 Ashura *waaz* in Saifee Masjid, Mumbai.

Shadi customs, 1996: The groom (Ayaz Shaikh) rides to the wedding on a white horse. His parents (Zaitoon and Riaz) toss flower petals.

The author (left) with two sons of the da'i al-mutlaq: Shahzada Qaidjohar Bhaisaheb Ezzuddin (center) and Shahzada Malikul Ashtar Bhaisaheb Shujauddin (right), in 1995

Part II

Analysis

Maintenance of Spiritual

and Political Hegemony

The centrality and all-encompassing authority of the top clerics set the Bohras (and other Ismailis) apart from nearly all other Muslim groups. The daʻi is considered *kal maʻsum,* a state often described as infallible.[1] In the Sunni and Shiʻa mainstream, no single member of the ulema holds anything like the unchallenged sway over believers that the Bohra daʻi exercises.[2] A Sufi pir or shaikh will often wield such power over members of his tariqa, but this jurisdiction extends only to initiates and does not generally reach entire communities.[3] This extraordinary—almost unique—spiritual hegemony has given the Bohra daʻi virtual hegemony in the political realm as well. This central focus, perhaps more than any other factor, has enabled the Bohra clergy to promote modernization and reinstitutionalization of tradition at the same time.

The definition of kal maʻsum has caused much confusion over the past century. Dissidents blur the distinction between maʻsum and kal maʻsum, and even among the orthodox rank and file the difference is not always clear. Ismaili doctrine holds imams maʻsum: immaculate, infallible, and sinless (*ismat*). Nizari Ismailis consider the aga khan to be the *hazir* (present) imam, and therefore regard him as maʻsum.[4] Bohras see the daʻi as the imam's vice-regent, his stand-in, and therefore regard him as possessing a similar level of spiritual perfection. Kal maʻsum is generally explained as being "like" maʻsum, to recognize the imam's superior status. Dawat sources (in an interpretation hotly disputed by dissidents) describe the distinction as a theological technicality with little practical impact: the sole difference (in this view) is that the daʻi has maʻsum status only during the concealment of the imam, while the imam's status is inherent in his person.

To many, this is the Ismaili equivalent of debating the number of angels capable of performing pirouettes on a pin. Even Bohras consider this a fine point of *haqiqat,* something outside the realm of ordinary experience. But the issue is hardly frivolous: it is used by the dawat's opponents to accuse the daʻi of theological hyperbole—even (a charge launched by non-Bohras rather than by internal dissidents) of committing the blas-

phemy of claiming semidivine attributes for a human being. This subtle distinction was muddied, and then clarified, in colonial-era litigation. In the Chandabhai gulla case of 1921, the dawat's British attorney made exaggerated claims that Syedna Taher Saifuddin corrected when called to the stand. The daʿi is infallible (Syedna Taher Saifuddin testified) only when making pronouncements of dawat doctrine.[5] In this respect, the dawat's position is quite similar to that of the Roman Catholic Church, which considers the pope infallible only when making a theological pronouncement *ex cathedra*.

Competing moral paradigms of spiritual and political leadership are wholly absent among the Bohras. A comparison with the Pukhtun of the Swat Valley in Pakistan dramatically highlights the singularity of the Bohras' unified normative paradigm. As Fredrik Barth observed in his classic study, the qualities expected of Pukhtun political and religious leaders are diametrically opposed: "Pride, rivalry and virility are expected of chiefs," while "moderation, reasonableness and meekness" are the norm for holy men.[6] Moreover, it is the political rather than the spiritual model that is strongly privileged: Swat chiefs enjoy a virtual monopoly on social prestige. Barth notes that the mullah qaum is accorded a comparatively low social status, no more than two-thirds of the way up a hierarchical ladder that extends from pariahs to aristocratic khans.[7] Barth's observations have been seconded more recently by Charles Lindholm, who notes that "[t]he khan elite never intermarry with the mullahs." Families of mullah qaum themselves look down upon the imam of the local masjid; this occupation is stigmatized even by members of the hereditary religious caste, "and a landless mullah would consider it a shame to take up such work." The extent of respect accorded to spiritual norms—even among hereditary religious specialists—is that mullah families try to give one son a Qurʾanic education.[8]

While the Pukhtun are Sunni, even in comparison with other Shiʿa groups the level of spiritual authority enjoyed by the Bohra dawat is highly unusual. A Twelver mujtahid, like the Bohra daʿi, is expected both to guide his followers toward righteous actions (*amra-bil-maroof*) and steer them away from prohibited ones (*nahi-anil-munkar*).[9] But this spiritual leadership has always been far more diffuse than that of Ismailis. The Ithna-Ashari clergy has never spoken with a single voice, and even the paramount Ayatollah Ruhollah Khomeini was always an interpreter rather than a channel for doctrine. Since Khomeini's death, his successor Ayatollah Ali Khamenei has often seemed less of a supreme religious leader than the first among equals, his theological mandate challenged by Ayatollah Ali Montazeri and other respected mujtahids.[10]

Other surviving sects displaying a central focus similar to that of the Bohras tend to be small and somewhat marginalized non-Sunni groups: the Zaidis of Yemen, especially during the tenure of Imam Yahya; the Alawis of Turkey; the Druze of Syria and Lebanon; and the Ahmadiyya of Pakistan.[11] On the Indian subcontinent, the only large Muslim denomination displaying a similar level of centralization is the Khojahs, and the reasons for the crucial role played by the apex clerics of both surviving Ismaili schools are similar. Both trace their spiritual lineage to the Fatimid tradition of living imams governing as caliphs; both developed a tightly knit religiosocial structure to survive centuries of Sunni oppression; and both rely on an esoteric gnostic theology.

Shi'a theology in general (and Ismaili theology in particular) is based on ta'wil (esoteric interpretation of scripture).[12] In brief, this doctrine holds that beneath the zahir (apparent) aspect of revealed text and religious doctrine, a deeper and more important truth (batin) lies hidden. While any Muslim can try to learn the zahir by reading the Qur'an and other religious texts, only a mu'min can hope to uncover the batin with the guidance of the imam or his representative during concealment. Ismailis regard the entirety of the Qur'an as a text with hidden allegorical interpretations underlying even the most seemingly straightforward of passages.[13]

It is largely for this reason that Ismailis regard the teachings of a living, present human (whether the Bohras' da'i al-mutlaq or the Nizaris' aga khan) as more authoritative than unexplicated scripture or ahadith, a significant point of divergence from Ithna-Ashari Shi'a.[14] In the Bohra faith, not even devout believers are permitted to explore esoteric texts without the guidance of a master specially sanctioned by the dawat, and permission to delve into the deepest secrets is limited to a small group of highly trained clerics.[15] It is their unique access to batin knowledge—the true, inner meaning of the Qur'an, ahadith, and all scripture—that gives both the aga khan and the Bohra da'i their fundamental spiritual hegemony over their respective communities.

While the pronouncements of both the aga khan and the da'i al-mutlaq are taken as normative, their spiritual guidance does not have nearly the same manifestation. Recent aga khans have lived in Europe, married outside the community, and maintained a regal distance from the bulk of their followers. The da'i, however, is intimately linked to every aspect of Bohra life: the very essence of his office is to be physically present. While the imam lives in the world but not of it, guiding by inspiration rather than specific instruction, the da'i's role is to serve as a bridge between the hidden imam and the faithful. He *must* be part of his followers' daily lives: hegemonic oversight is his job.

ISMAILI THOUGHT AND DOCTRINE

In order to understand the nature of the spiritual and political hegemony enjoyed by Syedna, it is necessary to understand its source: both the dawat structure and the core doctrine of the Fatimid caliphate have survived intact (at the theoretical level, at least) among the present-day Daudi Bohras. Since the doctrine of taqiyya keeps the central batin knowledge of modern-day Bohras a matter of secrecy, an outsider's best window on Musta'li Ismaili theology can be found through the past rather than the present. In theory (if not in actual practice) there should be no difference between the two: historical conditions may vary, but the underlying theology and worldview are eternal. The Bohras regard and describe themselves as Fatimids, plain and simple. This doctrine, believed fervently by the devout and preached zealously by the clergy, underlies and explains the da'i's hegemony.

STRUCTURE OF THE FATIMID DAWAT BEFORE THE SECLUSION OF THE IMAMS

Supreme, unchallenged spiritual and political authority was vested in the person of the Ismaili caliph-imam, but this authority was exercised through an elaborate hierarchy of da'is spread throughout the Fatimid empire, and well into areas far beyond Fatimid political control. From the time of al-Hakim onward almost all imams were minors when they took office, so the institutional structure of the bureaucracy assumed even greater importance. The religious hierarchy of the dawat achieved its definitive form in the fourth/eleventh century under the leadership of chief da'i al-Muayyad f'il Din.[16] During classical Fatimid times, the hierarchy was as follows:

(1) Imam.

(2) Chief da'i. Also called *da'i al-dawat, bab* (door), or *bab al-abwab* (door of doors), this official was the supervisor of the entire religious structure and executor of the imam's commands. Often a powerful wazir (such as Badr al-Jamali) would hold the titles of bab, army commander, and chief qadi (judge) as well—effectively combining political, religious, military, and judicial authority in his own person.

(3) Hujja (proof). In pre-Fatimid times the title was given to dawat officials having contact with the hidden imam, or even (for the purposes of taqiyya) to the imam himself. Sometimes this official was referred to by the titles *naqib, lahiq,* or *yad.* In the classical Fatimid structure, the world was divided into twelve dioceses, called *jazair* (islands; sing., *jazira*). Each

jazira was under the supervision of a hujja. These districts are seldom clearly defined, but al-Nuʿman's *Taʾwil al-daʿaʾim* is one of the few texts to spell out exactly where the boundaries lay: there were separate jazair for al-Arab (Arabs), al-Rum (Byzantines), al-Saqaliba (Slavs), al-Nub (Nubians), al-Khazar (Khazars), al-Hind (Indians), al-Sindh (Sindhis), al-Zanj (black Africans), al-Habash (Abyssinians), al-Sin (Chinese), al-Daylam (Persians), and al-Barbar (Berbers). A list of a slightly later period is almost identical, but substitutes Turks for Nubians. Some sources mention twelve hujjas of the day and twelve of the night, possibly a reference to parallel overt and covert networks of proselytization.[17]

Each hujja was served by several daʿis, perhaps as many as thirty in the more important districts. There were two ranks of daʿis:

(4) *Daʿi al-balagh.* The duties of this office remain unclear. Like the offices of bab and hujja, this position has remained unoccupied for Mustaʿli Ismailis since the seclusion of Imam Tayyib (or by an alternate interpretation the holders of these positions have remained, like the imam, hidden in secrecy). At various times in Daudi Bohra history, pretenders have arisen claiming the office of daʿi al-balagh, hujja, or bab and using these titles as the grounds for challenging the authority of the Daudi daʿi al-mutlaq. None of these pretenders managed to build a significant, enduring following.

(5) *Daʿi al-mutlaq.* This title, of only intermediate rank in the Fatimid hierarchy, became the highest clerical authority in the Mustaʿli dawat after the seclusion of the last visible imam. It is the title held by current apex cleric Syedna Muhammad Burhanuddin, and by each of his fifty-one predecessors.

At least two ranks of officials served each daʿi. In Fatimid times there would have been many holders of either rank, just as there were many daʿis. In the present hierarchy of the Daudi Bohras, there is one holder of the following ranks:

(6) *Mazoon.* First assistant to the daʿi. This office and that of the mukasir are currently held by brothers of the daʿi.

(7) *Mukasir* (persuader). During the period of Fatimid proselytization, the job of a mukasir was to engage rival clerics in theological debate, win the support of important community members, and gain converts by a constant polemical campaign of propaganda. Mustaʿli Ismailis have generally refrained from proselytizing since the end of the Fatimid empire, so the duties of the mukasir have tended to blend with those of the mazoon. In the twentieth century, mukasirs have served as the chief amils of Mumbai.

It should be emphasized that this framework is merely the theoretical structure of the dawat, presented in Fatimid texts as normative rather than

necessarily actual. Not all of these offices were filled at all times, and some of them may never have been filled at all. It is unlikely, for example, that two completely separate networks of day (overt) and night (covert) missionaries were active in each of the twelve jazair. Since the seclusion of Imam Tayyib the hierarchy has been greatly simplified: there are no covert offices, and the only Fatimid titles in use are those of da'i al-mutlaq, mazoon, and mukasir. According to some interpretations, all of the top Fatimid hierarchy—twenty-five or twenty-six clerics outranking the da'i al-mutlaq—are in concealment along with the hidden imam, their offices (like that of the imam) having been handed down through all the generations in secret.[18]

During the high Fatimid period, missionary activity (both in Egypt and abroad) was one of the central functions of the state bureaucracy. Weekly sessions of public theological instruction were provided by the bab or hujja, and members of the general population were invited to attend as often as they wished. Both men and women would participate in these sessions, sitting separately but receiving the same lectures. Like Bohra men under post-1979 regulations, they dressed all in white.[19]

Before being sent out to the field, da'is during the high Fatimid period were given extensive training at the Dar al-Hikmat in Cairo. This training in some ways mirrored the training that present-day Daudi Bohra clerics receive at the Jamea tus-Saifiya in Surat or Karachi: it combined theological and worldly education together in a holistic package. According to Fatimid documents translated by Ivanow, all da'is were required to demonstrate credentials considerably more well-rounded than might have been expected for a medieval missionary. A candidate had to be spiritually irreproachable, but "[a]t the same time, he must have good knowledge of things belonging to secular education, *adab*, because . . . theological learning [that is] not accompanied by adab, deprives the man of the necessary polish, *rawnaq*, which evokes admiration and attracts people."[20]

FATIMID THEOLOGY AND PHILOSOPHY

The theology and philosophy of the Musta'li Ismailis today, far more than the structure of the dawat, is essentially that of the Fatimids. The most creative period of intellectual exploration ended with the line of the visible imams, and since the sixth/twelfth century, Musta'li Ismaili texts have been almost entirely works of recapitulation rather than of speculation.[21] The rediscovery of Fatimid documents in the twentieth century has cast light on the basic theology and philosophy upon which modern Daudi

Bohra ideology is premised. It should be remembered, however, that none of these recently disseminated texts are contemporary documents. According to authorized dawat sources, there is no divergence between current Bohra doctrine and the teachings of the Fatimid imams. Owing to the practice of taqiyya, however, nobody outside the highest ranks of the Daudi Bohra clerical hierarchy would be able to say with any authority how these texts fit in with modern batini thought.[22]

Central to Ismaili doctrine (and to the hesitancy any outsider must feel in venturing to write about it) is the nature of batini ta'wil. Since only the imam can provide the authoritative symbolic interpretation (ta'wil) necessary to understand either the zahir or the batin aspect of belief, the true core of Ismaili doctrine cannot be found in any book. The batin is knowledge far too precious to be disseminated carelessly throughout the world, or even throughout the believing community: the imam (or, during his seclusion, the da'i al-mutlaq) lets each individual know only as much of the inner batin truth as he considers that person prepared to receive.[23] Not only are the inner reaches of Bohra thought off-limits to outsiders, such spheres are off-limits to all but a few Bohras.

This is not, as some dawat opponents allege, merely a means of maintaining clerical hegemony. The da'i often encourages mu'mineen to learn as much batini ta'wil as they can, but such investigation must proceed only through authorized channels. Any Bohra is free to seek out instruction, and any mullah, shaikh, or amil can teach at least the introductory levels of esoteric doctrine. Many Jamea tus-Saifiya graduates run study groups and give individual lessons, not merely for khidmat candidates but for any interested laypeople who are willing to commit the required time and energy. The only absolute requirement for batin study is mithaq: in order to start on the path, one must first pledge loyalty to the da'i as gatekeeper.

Before exploring batin learning, a Bohra is expected to have a thorough understanding of the zahir texts, most notably, the *Da'a'im al-Islam* written by the Fatimid chief qadi and hujja Abu Hanifa al-Nu'man. While dabblers will not receive permission for further investigation, a serious student will generally be encouraged to probe deeper. Most observant Bohras gain a light smattering of batin knowledge simply by listening to Syedna's waaz, but only one out of five (a dawat source estimates) decides to pursue further esoteric learning.

The higher levels of batini ta'wil are called haqiqat, and dawat sources say fewer than 1 % of Bohras enter this elite sphere of scholarship. Within both the haqiqat and the larger area of batin knowledge there are innumerable gradations, a ladder of learning that anyone can climb with suffi-

cient devotion. Such knowledge, however, is too important to be disseminated carelessly. "I could tell you the answer," one clerical informant joked, when denying me information from time to time, "but then I'd have to kill you."

This cloak-and-dagger analogy is more apt than my friend may have realized. Most governments use a similar structure of progressively compartmentalized clearances to safeguard their most important national secrets. To use the U.S. government's system as an example, all potentially sensitive information is classified, and can be viewed only by candidates who have passed a rigorous background examination. Just as batin knowledge is restricted to Bohras who have taken the oath of mithaq, U.S. classified information is restricted to federal employees who have taken an oath to uphold the constitution of the United States. Within the sphere of classified information (as within the sphere of batin knowledge) there are ascending levels of secrecy: Confidential, Secret, Top Secret, and Codeword. Even at the Codeword level (and the comparable levels established separately for certain types of military and nuclear intelligence) all information is tightly compartmentalized on a need-to-know basis. Just as a student of haqiqat needs permission for each sensitive text he wishes to examine, a U.S. government employee must demonstrate an actual need for a specific document even if he or she possesses the requisite clearance.[24]

History demonstrates that the Bohra dawat's secrecy in matters of batini ta'wil is far from gratuitous. The danger of batin teachings when misapplied, and the justification for keeping such teachings jealously guarded from all but the most carefully prepared individuals, can be seen in the plethora of batini schismatic groups that have beset the orthodox community over time. Since the pre-Fatimid era, Ismaili emphasis of batin interpretation has been one of the prime generators of antinomianism and heresy. If the surface aspect of things is irrelevant to their inner truth (many have concluded through the centuries), all outward forms of worship and Islamic piety are unnecessary for a truly enlightened believer. This strain of the faith was strongest during the early years of the denomination. Countless radical or ghulat movements rose and fell before the Fatimid caliphate created a generally agreed-upon Ismaili orthodoxy. Ever since the early Fatimid period Ismaili theologians have cautioned adherents to give equal attention to the zahir as well as the batin, in order to avoid drawing false conclusions from teachings they cannot fully comprehend.[25]

The early twentieth-century Bohra dissident Mian Bhai Abdul Husain provides a jaundiced (and second- or thirdhand) account of these teach-

ings, and apparently accepts the depiction of esoteric antinomianism that Sunni polemicists have used to tarnish ghulat and orthodox Ismailis alike:

> They talk of essences, far-fetched analogies, quiddities, theoso-
> phies, speculation about names, letters & numbers in this connec-
> tion. This sort of hair splitting which they call Tavil and Haqiqat is
> unattractive and incomprehensible for a European reader but the
> Ismaili Shiʿa realizes their quiddities with astonishing tact and in-
> comparable skill . . . the candidate is taught the allegorical mean-
> ing of the rites and obligations of Islam such as prayers, alms, pil-
> grimage, fasting and the like and is persuaded that their outward
> observance is a matter of no importance and may be abandoned,
> since they were only instituted by wise and philosophical law-
> givers as a check to restrain the vulgar and unenlightened herd.[26]

The abstruse metaphysical ponderings referred to in the first part of Abdul Husain's statement are very much a part of Ismaili philosophy to-day, as they were in Fatimid times. The antinomian rejection of outer forms of worship, however, seems to be a reference more than nine cen-turies out of date. Not since the imamate of al-Hakim has such practice been ascribed to any legitimate dawat authority.* The rejection of sharia seems to have been characteristic of certain ghulat and Qarmati groups (although even here the documentary evidence comes largely from the enemies of such sects), but there is no evidence that such ideology has ever been countenanced by the Daudi Bohra clergy. Whenever advocates of apocalyptic antinomianism such as the Medhibaghwalas† have arisen within the community, they have been immediately excommunicated. While (as Ali Asani notes) modern-day Nizari Ismailis have "been con-spicuous for stressing the esoteric dimension of their faith over the exo-teric,"[27] the Bohra dawat has been actively working to strengthen rather than tear down all outward forms of Islamic orthopraxy.

Abdul Husain is correct, however, in noting that the Bohras (and all Is-mailis) regard the pillars of the faith in a different light than Sunnis do. Each pillar has a batin as well as a zahir interpretation. Since pre-Fatimid times, Ismailis (and other Shiʿa) have held to seven pillars rather than the Sunnis' five. Salat (prayer), zakat (alms), sawm (fasting), and hajj (pilgrim-age) are the same, but to these are added jihad (struggle) and tahara (pu-rity); walaya (devotion to the line of imams); the Sunni pillar of shahada

*Even al-Hakim is said to have vacillated between heterodoxy and hyperorthodoxy. Ismailis reject the implication that al-Hakim failed to uphold the norms of sharia.
†Late nineteenth-century followers of a schismatic who claimed to have received a rev-elation superseding sharia.

(witness to the unity of God) is regarded as the foundation on which the other pillars stand.[28]

The zahir aspect of each of these is straightforward, but the batin aspects have multiple interpretations. One symbolic meaning of salat might be individual meditation (in addition to ritual namaz); of zakat, teaching (i.e., the charitable gift of knowledge); of sawm, braving the hunger of individual speculation and being satiated by guidance of the da'i or imam; of hajj, the internal pilgrimage toward God; of jihad, the Greater Struggle against one's baser nature; of tahara, a faith untainted by the polluting contagions of doubt and pride; of walaya, devotion to the imam's message as well as his mere person.[29]

From the earliest times to the present, there has been very little Ismaili literature devoted to *tafsir* (external explication) of the Qur'an or other texts: the imam is regarded as a "speaking Qur'an" whose presence in the world makes tomes of ordinary exegesis unnecessary. During the imam's seclusion, such authoritative interpretation is carried out by his legitimately delegated da'is. One major result of this has been the liberation of Ismaili thought from the confines of strictly prescribed text: while Sunni intellectual debates have generally been bounded by the framework of the Qur'an and ahadith,* Ismaili speculation has been much less constrained. For the brief period of the Mu'tazila ascendancy during the Abbasid caliphate, Sunni intelligentsia experienced a similar burst of speculative energy. With the triumph of the Hanbalites and the "closing of the door of ijtihad," however, such experimentation fell into disfavor. In general Sunni intellectual exploration has been circumscribed by text and tradition, while Ismaili philosophy has been free to draw on a far wider range of sources (both internal and external) for inspiration.[30]

The most significant source of new ideas on which classical Ismaili thinkers drew was that of neoplatonism. They were hardly the only Muslim intellectuals to do so: both Aristotle and Plato were so revered by medieval Sunni philosophers that they were considered *hanifs*—true Muslims before the birth of Muhammad. Plotinus, the founder of neoplatonism, had a major impact on Sunni and Shi'a circles alike. Referred to as al-Shaykh al-Yunani, his work was translated into Arabic from the third/ninth century onward, and formed the basis of the work of such giants as al-Farabi (d.339/950) and ibn Sina. It was primarily through the writings of Plotinus that the thought of ancient Greece made its way into medieval Is-

*These comments do not apply as closely to Sufis or other Sunnis outside the textual ulema tradition.

lam (and through medieval Islam, back to modern Europe). While Islamic adoption of Platonic thought is most commonly associated with such Sunni Abbasid masters of *falsafah* (philosophy) as al-Farabi and ibn Sina, Ismailis were no slower in adopting such ideas. As Ismail K. Poonawala notes, "The introduction of neoplatonic philosophy into Ismaili circles is generally ascribed to Muhammad ibn Ahmad al-Nasafi," who died seven years before al-Farabi. During the early Fatimid period, prior to the transfer of the caliphal seat to Cairo, the locus of Ismaili neoplatonism was Persia rather than the Maghrib. During the reign of Imam al-Muizz, however, and particularly under the leadership of chief da'i al-Nu'man, it would become central to Fatimid ideology.[31]

Neoplatonism was attractive to Muslim thinkers of many stripes in part because of its argument that the supreme one is an entity wholly beyond human comprehension. Plotinus held that any attempt to describe this being would be an exercise in futility—an approach perfectly in line with the core Islamic tenet of *tawhid* (unity of God). Both neoplatonist and Islamic monotheist, therefore, faced the same problem: how to understand, or even discuss, an entity about whom any description would be either futility or blasphemy? The words of Syedna Idris Imad al-Din highlight the two camps' congruence:

> The Supreme God is beyond our comprehension and has no relation with the worlds. Nothing can be predicated to Him and no attributes are applicable to Him. He is above all definitions of existence (*ays*) and non-existence (*lays*). We know nothing about Him. The only possibility of recognition of His unity is to admit our inability to recognize Him. The nearest approach to the knowledge of the Supreme God (al-Mubdi) is only possible by the recognition of an intermediary."[32]

Special note may be paid to the penultimate sentence: the only thing we know is that we know nothing. Intentionally or not, Syedna Idris has given a nearly exact paraphrase of the words Socrates spoke at his trial in Athens: "I am likely to be a little bit wiser than he in this very thing: that whatever I do not know, I do not even suppose I know."[33] Perhaps there is some divine irony here: the very argument that condemned a hanif to death for blaspheming the pagan gods of Greece would be resurrected more than a thousand years later in support of the monotheism of Islam.

Another major neoplatonic concept transplanted to Ismaili doctrine is that of the transmigration of souls. While Ismailis do not believe in reincarnation per se, they hold to a complex ideology of souls being "purified"

after death and led to "higher levels" where they will inhabit other forms. The language used is often very similar to that of Plotinus's notions of emanations from the Universal Intellect creating the material universe, and all beings shifting from body to body in a ceaseless effort to reunify with this Universal Soul. Mystic numerology comes into play, both in Ismaili and in Greek gnosis. The specifics of Ismaili doctrine on spiritual transmigration are far from transparent. Noted Ismaili scholar Husain al-Hamdani observes, "This process seems to be similar to the gnostic doctrine of Metempsychosis; but the Ismailis emphatically dissociate themselves from it, drawing hair-splitting differentiations."[34] Parallels with Hindu concepts would have made such ideas seem natural to early Bohra converts.

The neoplatonic concept of a hierarchical chain of being finds its expression in the Ismaili concept of cyclical time. The idea has been explored and discussed extensively by Henry Corbin.[35] While the neoplatonic notion of cyclical emanation is abstract and universal, the Ismaili application of this principle is firmly grounded in Islamic mythopoetics. A single divine revelation, Ismaili doctrine holds, is not sufficient for the rapidly changing circumstances of the world and rapidly expanding reach of human understanding. Revelation is a continuing process, with each cycle of revelation initiated by a natiq (prophet). The natiqs of the past have included Adam, Nuh (Noah), Ibrahim (Abraham), Musa (Moses), Isa (Jesus), and Muhammad. Each prophet is assisted by a wasi (also called *asas*, "foundation," or *samit*, "silent one") whose job is to implement, enact, and safeguard the revelation that the natiq has brought. Adam had Shith (Seth) as his wasi, Nuh had Sam (Shem), Ibrahim had Ismail (Ishmael), Musa had Harun (Aaron) or Yusha (Joshua), Isa had Shamun al-Safa (Simon Peter), and Muhammad had Ali.

The natiq does not abrogate the teachings of past prophets, he merely updates the revelation as human conditions warrant. Each natiq and wasi pair is followed by six imams, who bring no new revelation (nor even a new interpretation), but who serve as authoritative interpreters of the existing revelation.[36] In pre-Fatimid doctrine, the seventh imam (Muhammad ibn Ismail) was held to have gone into concealment, and it was believed that he would reemerge as the final natiq, the Mahdi or Qaim, who would repeal the sharia of Muhammad and usher in the last cycle of mankind. Under the Fatimids this doctrine was changed to allow for a continuing line of imams, with continual doctrinal debate as to the significance of the seventh, fourteenth, and twenty-first of the series.[37]

Ismaili use of Western neoplatonic thought is particularly noteworthy in the context of the present study, for it shows the ancient provenance of modern-day Ismaili openness to intellectual borrowings from other cul-

tures. Whereas various Sunni and Ithna-Ashari schools have occasionally flirted with neoplatonism and other Western ideologies, few (if any) have embraced them so unreservedly or welcomed them so intimately to their hearts. This open-minded, intellectually omnivorous attitude is exemplified by an encyclopedic compendium of knowledge entitled *Rasaʿil Ikhwan al-Safa,* penned by unknown Ismaili authors before the Fatimid zenith. Syedna Idris Imad al-Din attributed it to hidden imam Ahmad ibn Abdullah ibn Muhammad ibn Ismail but modern scholars regard it as the collaborative effort of a group third/ninth-century Ismaili encyclopedists. While not particularly influential in its own time, the text became a central source during the Yemeni period of the Mustaʿli dawat, and has served as the basis for extensive Daudi Bohra commentary ever since its formal introduction to the Daudi canon by the second Yemeni daʿi al-mutlaq, Ibrahim al-Hamidi.[38]

The *Rasaʿil Ikhwan al-Safa* is composed of fifty-two epistles divided into four books. The first book deals with mathematical sciences, including astronomy, logic, geometry, and music; the second explores natural sciences, including physics, biology, and chemistry; the third concerns itself with philosophy, including eschatology and the intricacies of neoplatonic speculation; the fourth deals with theology. The authors consciously attempted to create a corpus of all the science known anywhere in the world—they drew information from all available sources of learning, whatever their basis or root culture. The encyclopedia borrowed from Babylonian astrologers, Christian and Manichaean gnostics, Jewish mystics, Greek philosophers of the Hermetic, Platonic, and Aristotelian as well as the expected neoplatonic schools. The text also brings in Hindu conceptions of reincarnation, and refers to Buddhist legends from ancient India.[39]

Even the *Rasaʿil*'s last book, the section on theology, includes wisdom from sources outside the Islamic tradition. The text, like Ismaili theology in general, accords divine inspiration (albeit corrupted) not only to the prophets of the Christians and the Jews but also to those of the Zoroastrians, Sabaeans, and other pre-Islamic societies.[40] When today's Daudi Bohras seek out not only the technology but the education and ideology of the modern West, therefore, they are merely following the example set by their spiritual forerunners. "Seek knowledge," runs a saying attributed to the Prophet, often cited by Syedna Muhammad Burhanuddin, "even if it be in China." Ismailis have been harmoniously integrating the ideas of traditional Islam with those of outside societies for at least the past millennium.

APPLICATION: CENTRALITY OF THE DAʿI TO MODERN BOHRA DAILY LIFE

When asked to select the most important aspects of their faith, an overwhelming 94.0% of my survey respondents cited direct, personal contact with the daʿi—for such services as *alamat,* duʿa, and the allocation of children's names—as among the most crucial. The category was ranked higher than any other element of orthopraxy, including hajj, pilgrimage to Kerbala, rituals of birth, mithaq, marriage, and death, eating halal food, personal ethics, ties with other Bohras (including endogamy), dress codes, or ziyaret. Contact with Syedna was not only deemed the most important aspect of orthopraxy in each site, it was rated number one by almost every respondent giving comparative rankings. Every time Syedna appears in public, he is mobbed by a continual stream of the faithful with requests for guidance on nuts-and-bolts issues of daily living. The situation described in a dawat encomium of 1975 is no less true today:

> It is not only spiritual guidance that he gives them but also his advice is sought by the followers on temporal matters. Even on such questions as the best course to adopt in an illness, the advisability of starting a new business enterprise or the way to reorganize an old one, or the choice of a partner for marriage, his judgment is always solicited. . . . The livelong day is absorbed in answering innumerable queries addressed personally to him or communicated through letters and telegrams.[41]

A dawat tract hardly overstates the case in asserting: "No loyal Dawoodi Bohra undertakes an important business assignment or any other work of his *Deen* and *Dunya* [i.e., spiritual or worldly life] without taking the *Raza* or advice from the Daʿi al-Mutlaq."[42]

The daʿi embodies personal charisma to a degree very rarely found in Islam outside of certain Sufi traditions. This charisma is transferable to a wide array of objects: any item touched by Syedna is believed to have ingrained merit.[43] Not only did 84.8% of my survey respondents report having asked the daʿi to name their children, but a great many seek scraps from his discarded clothing for their newborn babies' chatti garments. This personal charisma can also emanate (to a much lesser degree) from priestly subordinates of the daʿi.

Perhaps the most common manifestation of the daʿi's personal charisma is through photographic representation. While most Sunni Muslims (particularly those influenced by Wahhabi movements) shun pictorial representation of religious leaders, this ban does not extend to Shiʿa of ei-

ther the Ithna-Ashari or Ismaili denominations. The Bohras, however, go far beyond their Twelver counterparts in the embrace of devotional photographs. The display of a spiritual leader's photograph is quite permissible for Ithna-Ashari believers, but for observant Bohras it is virtually the norm. I do not think I have ever seen a home or office of an observant Bohra that did not have a photograph of Syedna (usually paired photos of Syedna Muhammad Burhanuddin and his father Syedna Taher Saifuddin) prominently exhibited.

This use of pictorial representation does not extend to such holy figures as the Prophet, Fatima, Ali, Husain, or any of the twenty-one imams. In this regard, Bohras are in accord with Sunni iconic avoidance.[44] Occasionally, however, figures of lesser stature than the da'i are portrayed; photographs of living or recently deceased syedis are sometimes seen, as are those of the mazoon or the mukasir. In the streets surrounding Mumbai's Saifee Masjid (or any important Bohra mosque), local vendors offer objects bearing Syedna's likeness on anything from pens to paperweights, from calendars and clocks to key chains. The image is believed to lend efficacy to the item in question: a pen bearing Syedna's likeness is said to help students in their schoolwork, for example, while a paperweight is believed to help keep office work organized.

Even the dissident Asghar Ali Engineer concedes that students often ask Syedna or one of his amils to breathe on their pens before an examination, and "[m]any Bohras, especially women, believe that certain diseases can be cured by drinking water from a bottle or a cup into which either the high priest or any other priest appointed by him has blown his breath."[45] Engineer reports that over half of the households in a survey he conducted had sought Syedna's blessing in matters of marriage, burial, pilgrimage, and zakat, while about half sought the da'i's advice when purchasing property or naming a child.[46] The figures are particularly noteworthy since Engineer's sampling necessarily excluded the more orthodox elements of society.

Nearly two-thirds (64.6%) of my respondents report regularly seeking the blessing of Syedna or his amil for their homes or businesses, through the ritual of *alamat*. The da'i confers this blessing by inscribing the word *bismillah* (Arabic for "In the name of God the Beneficent") or its numerical equivalent 786* on a plaque mounted on the wall of a new house or

*Every letter in the Arabic alphabet is assigned a numerical value (cf. Barker et al. 1967: 356–360) and the letters in the word *bismillah* add up to 786. The numeral is substituted to avoid the blasphemy of unintentionally showing disrespect to a word from the Qur'an (particularly a word such as *bismillah* that integrates the word *Allah*), since old ledger books will eventually find their way into the trash heap.

office, or on the first page of an account book for a new fiscal year. The most common time for a Bohra to seek alamat is the Hindu new year: for the purposes of business (and because of their mercantile orientation) Bohras, unlike most Indian Muslims, use Diwali rather than Muharram as the beginning of their fiscal (but not their religious) year.[47]

This close contact between the daʿi al-mutlaq and his flock is an essential element of Bohra identity, perhaps the strongest barrier against their assimilation to the mainstream of Indian Islam. Until the nineteenth century the Bohra community was small and compact enough for such direct contact to be relatively easy: the population was heavily concentrated in Mumbai and Gujarat, and most muʾmineen could have personal access to Syedna on a fairly regular basis. As the denomination grew larger and farther-flung, however, this direct access became increasingly difficult. By the late nineteenth and early twentieth centuries, daily contact had come to be monopolized by the coterie of Surti families with kinship ties to the royal lineage of the daʿis.

COMMUNICATIONS TECHNOLOGY AS A TOOL OF SOCIAL COHESION

Over the past two decades (if not longer), Bohras have used modern technology to recapture the close access to their daʿi that had been the hallmark of their sect in previous centuries. This effort has not been an accident: it has been carefully fostered by Syedna Muhammad Burhanuddin since the 1970s. Badri Mahal has eagerly latched onto every advance in communications: from telegram to telex, from fax to Federal Express, from transatlantic telephone to transpacific e-mail. A Bohra living in Calcutta, seeking advice on whether to expand his hardware business into electrical fittings, need only fax Badri Mahal to have his question relayed to Syedna for consideration. A Bohra living in Auckland, seeking a scrap of Syedna's used clothing for her new baby's chatti garment, can phone a Mumbai relative to have the cloth sent by the next morning's DHL.

The current daʿi, unlike all of his predecessors, can be physically present in every major Bohra community at one time or another. Air travel has shrunk the world, and Syedna has racked up enough frequent-flier mileage to make any globetrotter envious. In previous generations a Bohra wishing to have personal contact with the daʿi would have had to make a journey to Mumbai, Surat, or a Gujarati pilgrimage town. Today many, if not most, Bohras can wait for Syedna to come to them. The daʿi regularly jets from Delhi to Dhaka, from Lahore to London, from Hyderabad to Houston. In the words of one dawat publication:

In fact travel is a necessary and important factor in the duties associated with the office of the Daʻi al-Mutlaq. The faithful have been called to God and the path of As-siratul-Mustaqeem (the straight way). This naturally requires visits to various centres of the followers and imparting to them the teachings of the faith.[48]

This hypermobility gives almost all Bohras the opportunity to see their spiritual leader face-to-face at least once in their lives: the daʻi visits his flock, and his flock visits the daʻi. For the first time in history pilgrimage is now an activity well within the ability of most members of the community, and this activity has been radically affected by the advent of modern technology. More than two-fifths of my survey respondents reported using air travel, a figure that rose to a high of nearly three-quarters for respondents in relatively distant Karachi.[49] This mobility translates into increased opportunity for direct contact with the daʻi: 81.7% of my survey respondents had seen Syedna in person more than five times, and 59.1% listed the number of visits as "many," "very many," or "countless." Of current household heads, 80.4% reported at least as much contact already as their parents or grandparents had had in their whole lives.[50]

Even for those unable to see the daʻi on any given visit, Syedna's voyages have an impact far beyond the individuals directly affected. Muhammad Burhanuddin seldom announces his travel schedule more than a few weeks in advance, and frequently changes plans at the last minute. Whether or not this is a matter of strategy, it has the effect of keeping the worldwide community in a state of perpetual expectation. The mere possibility of a visit by Syedna—the fact that the daʻi could well show up in one's hometown with very little advance notice—is a powerful incentive to maintain rigid standards of orthopraxy. The amil of Hyderabad noted that prior to Syedna's three-week visit in 1994 nearly half of the city's families raised their level of orthopraxy high enough to earn green cards, with most of the rest of the community meriting orthopraxically acceptable yellow cards. During the three previous decades, the amil said, very few Hyderabadi Bohras had been in full compliance.

The Bohras are hardly the only Islamic group to embrace modern communications technology. As documented by Brinkley Messick, muftis in Yemen have used radio programs to provide *fatwas* (theological opinions) on a variety of topics for listeners at a geographical remove. Videocassettes of sermons by Ayatollah Khomeini and other prominent mujtahids provided a powerful catalyst to the Iranian Revolution. Within India, Ithna-Ashari identity has been solidified not only by the circulation of videocassettes, but also by the televised broadcast of Ashura majlis on the govern-

ment-run Doordarshan network. Based a few miles from al-Azhar University, an Egyptian company is marketing a CD-ROM version of the Qur'an formatted for computer karaoke.[51] David Edwards, following Benedict Anderson's observations on the role of print media in the fostering of a modernist ideology, notes that "the dynamic growth and institutional development of Hizb-i Islami Afghanistan was directly related to the ability of its leaders to harness and adapt new forms of political discourse and practice, in this case, pamphlets."[52]

What distinguishes the Bohras from groups such as these is the holistic nature of their modernization.[53] Some traditionalist groups regard modern technology with a great deal of suspicion: in their eyes it is a necessary evil, useful particularly for military operations, but a dangerous and potentially corrupting influence nonetheless. An image frequently broadcast on CNN is laden with symbolism: that of a pile of confiscated televisions, radios, and cassette players being crushed beneath the treads of a Taliban tank. Modern technology is used, but solely to combat other manifestations of modernity.

The Bohras, however, regard modern technology (and its accompanying ease of societal communication) as something beneficial even on its own merits. The enthusiastic embrace of communications technology for Muharram and hajj has been discussed earlier. This embrace extends to all aspects of dawat administration. New technologies are not adopted solely for the sake of novelty, but anything that brings the community closer— or simply makes life easier—is heartily encouraged.

The Bohras, wherever they live, seem to be taking this advice to heart. Nearly one-third of my survey respondents in Karachi and Mumbai reported owning microwave ovens, nearly three-quarters had satellite television dishes, and 85.4% owned washing machines.[54] Despite their embrace of material comforts, however, these respondents displayed no measurable difference in their answers to any of the questions relating to orthopraxy. One measure of the Bohras' high level of technology ownership is a comparison with minority groups in the United States: the percentage of my Mumbai respondents who owned a telephone (89.7%) was higher than the percentage that at least one researcher has reported for black and Hispanic Americans.[55]

Computers

The amil of Hyderabad credits technology for making the Bohras progressively more traditional over the past two decades. Once the program of Islamization had been initiated at the center, it was brought to Bohras living

at a great geographical remove from Mumbai by technologies hitherto unavailable. The amil has a cellular phone by his side, and several times during the course of our interview he is interrupted by calls from Surat, Ahmedabad, and Mombasa: clerical contacts organizing logistical details for the upcoming Ashura rituals.

An amil must know a great deal about the lives of every one of his charges: where they live, the names of their children, which dawat regulations they follow, how much money they earn. Even for a city like Hyderabad, which has a fairly small Bohra population, this means keeping tabs on 550 families. Today, increasing numbers of amils are turning to computers for help. "I have all the information on disk," says Hyderabad's amil. "There are simply too many people to keep track of in any other way. In the past we wrote it all down on paper, and even then an amil would have to have a very good memory. Today, all it takes is the touch of a button." Computerization of household information is a matter of convenience rather than dawat directive, and at the time of writing Badri Mahal did not have any centralized database. But the Jamea tus-Saifiya now stresses computer literacy in its education of future clerics, and many of the younger amils have received basic training. During the course of my fieldwork I had occasion to seek the guidance of mullahs at the Burhani Madrasa not only for questions of language, ritual, and culture, but also for technical advice when my laptop malfunctioned.

Computer ownership, use, and literacy are far more prevalent in the Bohra community than in most other segments of Indian society. More than one-seventh of my survey respondents had a personal computer in the household or office, and more than half of the remaining households expressed the desire to have one.[56] In 1997 (the last year of my fieldwork), the rates of computer ownership in several Asian countries considerably more technologically developed than India were estimated as follows: Indonesia, 0.7%; Thailand, 1.4%; Malaysia, 3.7%; Taiwan, 10.0%; South Korea, 11.0%; Japan, 15.0%; Singapore, 24.0%.[57]

The rate of computer ownership among the Bohra in my survey (14.5%), is therefore more than twenty times that of Indonesia, more than ten times that of Thailand, nearly quadruple that of Malaysia, about 50% higher than those of Taiwan and South Korea, and almost on par with that Japan. The rate for Karachi's Bohras was marginally higher than that of ultra-high-tech Singapore. India's national rate was 0.2%,[58] so the Bohras of India and Pakistan may be seventy-two times as likely to own a computer as their subcontinental neighbors. While my survey respondents were wealthier than the societal norm, their questionnaires had been turned in

two years before the publication of the international figures cited above; if the computer revolution continues to sweep through India, ownership among Bohras will continue to skyrocket.

One of the dawat's point men for computers and telecommunications is Abizer Bhaisaheb Husanmuddin, a grandson of Syedna Taher Saifuddin. A fair-skinned man with a graying beard and hazel eyes, he spent nearly a decade studying and teaching engineering in Europe. He is fluent in Russian and Serbo-Croatian, in addition to the expected English, Arabic, Lisanu-Dawat, Hindi, Urdu, and Marathi. While teaching in the former Yugoslavia, he would lecture in Slovene without having to translate in his head.

Abizer Bhaisaheb was responsible for linking all dawat houses in Surat through a high-tech intercom system. Municipal services in the city are so slipshod that telephones are unreliable at the best of times. Even when the rest of Surat is paralyzed by downed phone lines, the Bohras are still able to communicate with each other. Rapid as the dawat's progress has been, Abizer Bhaisaheb would like to see it proceed at an even faster pace. There is still no unified program for systematic computerization, no separate department at Badri Mahal, and Abizer Bhaisaheb wants to make sure that the Bohras get in the passing lane on the information superhighway. "What has held so many communities back is fear," he says. "Fear of change, fear of technology, fear of modern things in general. We Bohras have no such fear, and that is a large part of our success."

An incident at a former workplace reminds Abizer Bhaisaheb of the incongruity of his two worlds—and the prevalence of anachronistic misperceptions of traditionalist Muslims. He'd been assigned to give a visiting expert a tour of his engineering lab, and the visitor curtly sent him away to fetch some tea: seeing Abizer Bhaisaheb in his traditional topi and kurta, the computer scientist took him for a peon rather than a Ph.D.

Bohras on the 'Net

The latest technological device in the Bohra toolbox is the Internet. According to Shaikh Mustafa Abdulhussein, in fact, "Email has now become a primary method of seeking advice of Syedna."[59]

On January 25, 1995, three linked Bohra e-mail networks were initiated, and in their first year of operation grew to include several hundred subscribers in the United States, Canada, Hong Kong, Thailand, India, Saudi Arabia, Tanzania, Britain, and Egypt. One network was "a forum for mu'mineen professionals" to facilitate business ties; a second was for social or general messages; and the third was devoted to spiritual discussions.[60] While not officially set up by the dawat, the latter's stated purpose

is the dissemination of spiritual material: "Ijtemaa [the group's name, Arabic for "gathering"] is a religious mailing list with discussions that focus primarily on *deeni* [religious] topics. The list includes the presence of bhaisahebs and other knowledgeable people who have a lot of *ilm* [religious wisdom] and who can help guide discussions and answer any questions that may arise about our religion." All three lists continue to be monitored, and are explicitly committed to orthodoxy: "Any mail against the dawat and Aqa Maula (TUS) [the daʿi-al-mutlaq] will not be accepted." Dissident Web sites and chat groups also exist, giving the movement a powerful weapon in their battle against the dawat. But in the cyberworld, as in the physical one, orthodoxy seems entrenched firmly enough to withstand any challenge.

In the few years since India first gained Internet access, Bohra presence has grown exponentially. The giddy pace of change in cyberspace precludes any serious discussion of the topic here: developments may not come "@ the speed of thought" (as Bill Gates's hagiographic ghostwriter puts it), but they do come much faster than the speed of print. When I began my fieldwork, e-mail back in the United States was largely limited to computer scientists and Star Trek fanatics. For the entire time I lived in Mumbai, India remained essentially unwired. During my fieldwork in Pakistan I was first able to communicate with Bohras by e-mail—when phone lines, electricity, and Internet provider all happened to be functioning simultaneously. Since that time I have used e-mail to obtain information from Bohra sources in minutes that would previously have required weeks or months.

The Bohras were among the very first Muslim groups to take advantage of the Internet, but they have since been joined by countless others. Now even reactionary groups like the Taliban and Lashkar-e-Taiba have their own Web sites. How cyberspace shapes Islam will be truly fascinating to observe—and research data on the process will be obsolete long before it can be published by any peer-reviewed journal or press. I have no idea what impact the Internet will have on society in India or any other country, but I am confident that the Bohras will continue to explore its frontiers.

Technology has enabled the Bohras to recreate their own past. Modern societal mobility dispersed the community throughout the world, caused the faithful to lose touch with their spiritual touchstone, and led to widespread lapses in matters of both orthodoxy and orthopraxy. Modern tools of communication, however, have drawn the community together once again into a single virtual-reality village.

CERTIFICATES OF ORTHOPRAXY: ID CARDS AS A MODERN TOOL
FOR HEGEMONY

The dawat has long maintained its religious and political control by social pressure as well as persuasion. The threat of baraat (social ostracism) is a strong disincentive to theological revolt: not only is an excommunicate* unable to participate in any ritual of the faith, he or she is technically barred even from having the most casual contact with observant family or friends. Individuals associating with a person under baraat are themselves liable to be excommunicated, so any such contact is both clandestine and problematic. When faced with the inability to legitimize a daughter's marriage or perform a father's burial rites, many a passionate dissident has relented and taken the oath of mithaq.

The 1970s confrontation with the dissident community of Udaipur forced the dawat to create a system for separating orthodox community members from excommunicates. In previous generations no such system had been necessary: Bohra communities were sufficiently small and self-contained for religious authorities to have direct personal acquaintance with all the members. Increasing geographical mobility, and the increasing anonymity of modern life, prompted the dawat to craft a novel and entirely modern method of identity definition: the issuing of certificates of orthopraxy. A Bohra wishing to make use of any dawat services may be called upon to produce a document of compliance signed by the local amil. (In small towns the members of a local population still may be personally known to the amil and therefore permitted to dispense with formal proof, but absent such firsthand acquaintance the individual may have to produce a letter vouching for his or her good standing.) These certificates are commonly referred to as "cards," and they come in three varieties: green, yellow, and red.

A green card indicates that the holder is in full compliance with the dictates of Syedna on all matters public and private. Clerics, dawat employees doing khidmat, and members of the extended royal family are presumed to be green card holders ex officio, and any lapses of orthopraxy are quickly corrected by personal reprimands from other members

*Technically, baraat is not excommunication per se: a series of post-Independence court decisions, and the political considerations accompanying them, have made formal excommunication a problematic endeavor. Baraat is technically a social ostracism, but since this ban on contact with observant Bohras necessarily precludes participation in any religious ritual performed by orthodox clerics, it can amount to de facto excommunication in the spiritual as well as the social sphere.

of this elite group. Eban Faizulabhoy, an attorney who has represented dawat interests for decades, estimates that 20% of the community in Mumbai are green card holders. Many dawat VIPs (and most members of the Qasr-e Ali inner circle) are sufficiently well known throughout the community that they have never had to go through the formality of applying for a certificate—their status has never been in question, so it does not have to be demonstrated. Some members of Syedna's extended family to whom I spoke were only vaguely aware of the ID card system: everyone in their circle of acquaintance was sufficiently prominent never to have been asked for identification. Even nonroyals can bypass the card interviews if their daily conduct is clearly at a green card level. Mullah Shabbir M. Mansoorbhai Jamali of Mumbai's Burhani Madrasa did not have to apply for his green card until he made ziyaret to a distant shrine, because (he explained) "here in Mumbai, and at most of the places I travel, everyone in the community knows who I am."

One step down from a green card, a yellow card indicates that the bearer is in basic compliance with the most important requirements of the faith, but deviates from normative practice in one or more particulars. A typical yellow card holder might refrain from alcohol, keep a full beard, and pay all the appropriate dawat taxes, but might wear topi and kurta only in ritual settings, and fail to observe various fasts or important ceremonies. Depending on local circumstances and the strictness of the amil in question, possession of an interest-bearing bank account could be grounds for either yellow or red card status. Yellow card holders are considered respectable, upstanding (if imperfectly compliant) members of the community, and probably represent the majority of the Bohra population both in India and abroad.

The holder of a red card is still a legitimate member of the community, but a member who has strayed from Syedna's direction in one or more major areas. Reasons for red card status include drinking alcohol, failing to keep a beard, failing to keep a halal household, and being delinquent in taxes. According to one source, red card holders are typically "only obeying ten or fifteen per cent of Syedna's instructions." Red card holders are not stripped of the rights and privileges enjoyed by other community members, but they are regarded as probationers who will eventually be brought to a more complete level of compliance. Anyone who acknowledges Syedna's complete authority in both spiritual and worldly matters, and makes at least a token effort to live according to the rules of the dawat, is accepted as a full member of society. Even holders of red cards are not socially stigmatized, merely subjected to the persistent hectoring of their

local amil in an effort to improve their behavior. As one yellow card holder (with red card relatives) noted, "The color of the card is unimportant—but you must have the card."

The certificates of orthopraxy are theoretically required for every ritual in the Bohra lifecycle. To receive Syedna's blessing, take mithaq, solemnize a marriage, visit a shrine, stay in a musafirkhana, bury a dead relative, or host a ziyafat commemorating any major occasion, a Bohra must (if so requested) prove basic compliance with Syedna's teachings. Most Bohras apply for these certificates only when undertaking one of the above activities, but only a thoroughly nonobservant individual would be able to go his or her whole life without ever having to demonstrate orthopraxy.

There is considerable local variation in the requirements and even the physical description of the card itself. The choice of green, yellow, or red status is wholly up to the judgment of the local amil, so standards are not yet uniform from place to place. All cards must be updated periodically (usually every year or so), at which time the amil asks the cardholder a series of questions about his or her practices and beliefs. Such questions typically include: How often do you pray? Do you wear topi and kurta (for women, burqa and rida) all the time, or only in masjid? Do you drink alcohol or smoke tobacco? Do you have an interest-bearing bank account? How often do you read the Qur'an?*

The very notion of an identity card is a uniquely modern innovation, and the choice of green, yellow, and red as the categories is an unmistakably modern reference to Western traffic signals. The cards are often paper documents, sometimes of the appropriate color, but often merely signed certificates. In some localities (such as Mumbai) they include a photograph of the individual, while in others a photograph is not necessary. In Mumbai the cards are obtained from an office on the first floor of Badri Mahal, after examination by a dawat official to supplement initial screening at the mohalla level. In smaller cities and towns, the entire procedure is handled by the local amil. Even in the majority of Bohra centers in which dissidents have no significant presence, ID cards serve as a valuable tool in the perpetuation of orthodox hegemony. The introduction of the card system has enabled the dawat to measure adherence to the da'i's *hukums* (commands) in quantifiable, objective ways.

Within the Bohra community at large, there is a wide range of opinion about the ID card system. Dissidents, of course, regard it as an unwarranted innovation directed solely at separating them from their coreli-

*For the translation of a typical questionnaire, see Appendix 2.

gionists. Most mainstream Bohras to whom I spoke were considerably less troubled by it, considering it at worst a relatively minor annoyance. Some cosmopolitan, well-educated community members were concerned that the ID cards (and related orthopraxy reforms) could be the first steps down a path to an Iranian-style reactionary attitude: "These fundamentalists are far too rigid in their thinking," one woman (a yellow card holder) told me. "They are concerned only with the outward expressions, only with giving the right appearances. To me, the essence of faith is how you treat people, and what you have in your heart."

The woman's daughter agreed wholeheartedly: "This green card system forces people to be hypocrites," she said. "I admitted not wearing rida, skipping Ashura rituals sometimes, having a bank account—and was given a red card. The next time, I bent the truth a little bit and got a yellow. Perhaps if I'd been an even bigger liar I would have been given a green." The mother nodded her assent. "Everybody has to lie a little bit on the questionnaire," she said. "We're none of us perfect—but if you tell that to the amilsaheb, it's a license for him to badger and harass you all the day long."

Other Bohras, however, consider the ID card system a vital corrective to an overly lax societal atmosphere. One mullah, for example, regards the yellow card middle ground as a bit of a cop-out. "Either you are in compliance with Syedna's directives, or you are not," he said. "How can a person be *partly* loyal?" He says both yellow and red cards mean essentially the same thing: that the individual is not completely obeying the da'i's directives, and that improvement is necessary. The line between these categories is hazy, often arbitrary, and (in this mullah's opinion) close to meaningless. His position can perhaps be summarized in a formulation of seventeenth century European Calvinism: there are no little sins, for there is no little God to sin against.

Just as the uncompromising rigidity of Calvinism mellowed into more nuanced modern Protestant denominations, the Bohra dawat has made a realistic appraisal of what the community will and will not accept. When the ID cards were first introduced they came in only two varieties: "In full compliance," or "Not in full compliance." Very quickly, the intermediate category of yellow card was added, in response to community pressure. ID cards are a powerful tool for the maintenance of clerical hegemony— but the clergy has been savvy enough not to exercise this hegemony with too heavy a hand.

Specifics of Orthopraxy:

Dress and Economics

DISTINCTIVE CODES OF APPEARANCE AS MEANS OF
GROUP IDENTIFICATION

In the late 1970s and early 1980s Syedna Muhammad Burhanuddin issued several pronouncements setting out guidelines for dress and personal comportment by all observant Bohras. The two most important of these were: (1) a resolution of the Conference of Fatimi Knowledge (*al-Multaqa al-Fatimi al-Ilmi*), over which the da'i presided in January 1979 in Surat at the annual Jamea tus-Saifiya examinations; under the da'i's direction, the conference stated that male Bohras should wear a beard and female Bohras should dress in a burqa; (2) a *firman* (directive) delivered by Syedna during Ashura observances in Cairo in June 1981, setting the normative male dress code as white topi, kurta, and optional sherwani.[1]

The origin of this program seems more in accord with the paradigm of independently motivated Islamization in Tamil Nadu noted by Mattison Mines than that of Islamization in response to anti-Muslim harassment noted by Partap Aggarwal in Rajasthan and Haryana. Mines notes that Tamil-speaking Muslims "have tried to purify their ritual behavior and, through language and dress, to establish more clearly their distinct identity as Muslims. In so doing they have differentiated themselves from the Hindu population by Islamization."[2]

The Bohra community had always retained many cultural practices from its preconversion Hindu past, but such syncretism should not be viewed as a blurring of lines of identity: Talal Asad correctly notes that "heterogeneity in traditional practices is not necessarily an indication of the absence of an Islamic tradition."[3] While the community never gave up its Muslim identity, during the middle decades of the twentieth century it saw social ties to Hindus become increasingly common, rigid separation of genders relax, and a wide range of attitudes edge closer to the cultural mainstream of Indian society.

Theodore P. Wright, Jr., attributes this trend to the pressure of dissi-

dents: "[T]he criticism of group leadership by an internal reform movement stimulated the orthodox head of the sect reluctantly to modernize his followers in certain respects (e.g., purdah, banking)."[4] Whether or not one accepts this analysis (the shift seems to me rooted more in the outlook of Syedna Taher Saifuddin himself) it is clear that by the early 1970s the Bohra community was displaying definite assimilationist tendencies. It was partly to combat this trend that Syedna Muhammad Burhanuddin launched his program of Islamic reform.

It would be difficult to overemphasize the degree to which trends in an intensely centralized community such as the Bohras flow from the top down rather than from the bottom up: far more often than would be the case in less hierarchical societies, the personal outlook of the apex cleric can determine the entire spiritual orientation of the denomination. Consequently, the course of modernization and Islamization within the Bohra community is intimately linked to the priorities of Syednas Taher Saifuddin and Muhammad Burhanuddin.

Syedna Taher Saifuddin was, by all accounts, deeply interested in the world beyond the Bohra community. Over the course of his life, his fascination with modern ideas and Western customs continued to grow. It was he who truly opened up the community to outside influences, exposed it to a wide variety of changes. According to sources who knew him personally, not only did Taher Saifuddin consider such changes inevitable and necessary, but he found modern ideas personally fascinating. During the later part of his reign (inner-circle sources tell me) it was not uncommon for Qasr-e Ali women to dress in saris within the confines of Saifee Mahal. From Independence until the late 1970s, the Bohra community was considerably more assimilated to mainstream Indian society than it has been since the Islamization reforms put in place by Taher Saifuddin's successor. This does not imply that the former da'i was any less devoted to spiritual pursuits: Taher Saifuddin's extraordinary scholarship and piety are not disputed even by those who disagree with his overall outlook. For Taher Saifuddin, both the spiritual and the secular realms held a wealth of possibilities.

Syedna Muhammad Burhanuddin has never been as interested in secular affairs as his predecessor had been. Father and son share a profound religious sensibility, but the son has focused more specifically on matters of deen than of dunya. This difference in emphasis did not carry over to the larger Bohra community during the early years of Muhammad Burhanuddin's tenure, but over time the current da'i gradually reintroduced orthopraxic norms that had started to fade. According to attorney Eban Faizulabhoy, a generation ago few men outside the clergy wore

beards. Today, he estimates that 70% of the Bohra men in Mumbai are bearded—and of the remaining 30%, a very large number grow beards for Ashura or Ramadan.* In smaller cities (even those the size of Surat), Faizulabhoy estimates the rate to be closer to 95%, since in a small community the local amil is far more likely to know each member by sight. The change is primarily due to leadership from Syedna himself.

While the Islamization program was the product of internal rather than external motivation, it was given a new inspiration by the success of the Iranian ulema in institutionalizing Shi'a behavioral norms after the downfall of Muhammad Reza Shah. The 1979 revolution in Iran sparked a revival of interest in religious tradition among Indian Ithna-Asharis: "More Shi'as are growing beards and going to mosque," Hasnain and Husain reported nine years after Khomeini's return from exile, "and the size of Friday congregation has increased."[5] It is not surprising that Indian Twelvers should identify with their coreligionists in Iran. Historically, both the Deccan Sultans and the Nawab-Wazirs of Awadh maintained clerical ties with the religious authorities of Safavid Persia. Nor are such ties merely a thing of the past: when former Iranian president Hashemi Rafsanjani paid his first visit to India in 1994, a crowd of thousands turned out for his Lucknow rally at the imambara built by the Shi'a Nawab Asaf-ad-daulah. Keith Hjortshoj notes that Lucknow, capital once of Awadh and now of Uttar Pradesh, has traditionally been "a remote outpost of Iranian and Iraqi Shi'ism."[6] The response of the Bohra dawat, however, would have been far less predictable. As Ismailis with no ties to the Ithna-Ashari clergy and as Gujaratis with no ethnic ties to Iran, the Bohras eschew any direct linkage. The Iranian revolution, however, demonstrated the feasibility of reinstituting traditional (or neotraditional) practices and group identity.

DRESS

The most immediately noticeable manifestation of this newly forged traditional identity is the mandated code of personal appearance. The physical norms current in the late nineteenth and early twentieth centuries are described by Mian Bhai Abdul Husain. Within the home, men might typically wear a kurta reaching below the knee, a white cloth jacket, trousers of white or striped cotton cinched tightly around the ankles, and a white

*Among observant Bohras, as discussed below, I would suggest that the percentage of beard-wearing men is closer to 100%. While I have seen extremely few unbearded men at any community function, this observation is ipso facto applicable to members of the orthodox mainstream: Bohra men who do not choose to live within this mainstream simply stay home.

cotton skullcap; outdoors, men would wear a small white turban rather than a skullcap, with a Hindu-style overcoat and pointed "Ujjaini" shoes. Women would typically wear a red, dark blue, or yellow scarf of cotton or silk, with (in northern Gujarat) a tight silk bodice or (in southern Gujarat) a silk jacket, silk petticoat, and leather or wooden shoes; outside the house, women would wear a dark silk burqa covering the entire body, and a veil for the head and face with a small net opening through which to see.[7] In the late 1920s, traditional dress was still sufficiently ingrained to allow an observer to write of Bohra dissidents: "They shave their faces clean . . . [and] adopt the Western style of dress, which is most unusual among their people."[8] The typical dress immediately prior to the current program of standardization varied considerably from place to place and time to time. In Sri Lanka, for example, men wore a gold feta with a sherwani, while women dressed in what one observer called a "long skirt, blouse, and a flimsy shawl covering the head."[9]

The modern dress code is both a reaffirmation of preexisting practice and the introduction of novel elements to create a uniform, coherent "tradition" in place of a less standardized array of customs. Prior to the 1981 Ashura firman, for example, Bohra men had often dressed in white clothing and headgear, but equally often had worn black caps and dark clothing.[10] Since 1981, white kurtas and sherwanis—their color, like the uniform white of all Muslims when performing hajj, suggesting a state of spiritual purity—have been obligatory. But there is a deeper color symbolism here. During Fatimid times, black was the color of the Abbasids—armies of the Sunni caliphs marched into battle under a solid black banner. To indicate their polar opposition to their archrivals, Fatimid caliphs adopted white (said to be a color favored by the Prophet Muhammad) as their own symbolic hue. In a modern context, the Bohras' use of white makes them immediately distinguishable from Ithna-Ashari Shiʿa, who often favor black clothing for both men and women.

The Bohra male dress code leaves virtually no room for individual variation. All men are required to wear white pajama trousers with a white knee-length kurta, generally fastened by four tuxedo-style detachable studs, and (ideally) a white sherwani overcoat. Footwear generally consists of either *chappals* (sandals) or Western-style loafers. At all times, even in the privacy of one's own home, it is considered indecent for a man to display any part of his body between the waist and mid-thigh.

The only real differentiation comes in the style of the headgear, which often distinguishes a person of high status from one of ordinary position. The standard topi is a small pillbox-shaped cap. It is usually white with gold trim, but can also be gold with white trim. The pattern of the woven

design is a matter of individual taste, the one area of the Bohra dress code (much like the tie of a Western businessman) where personal esthetics are permitted free rein within tightly established boundaries. Even high-ranking Bohra men who are entitled to wear pagris (turbans) during certain religious services will wear an ordinary topi at all other times. Shahzadas are entitled to wear gold topis, as are shaikhs and amils when leading communal prayer.

Prior to 1981, Bohra headgear had not been uniform. In the nineteenth century there were four main types of turban worn: Ahmedabadi, worn by Syedna, a higher and looser style than those of laymen; Ujjaini, the smallest and most tightly wound style; Surti, higher and fuller than Ujjaini, but not so expansive as Ahmedabadi; and Kathiawari, conical, interwoven with a strip of gold thread. Boys' turbans were identical to those of adults, but of ochre or dark brown rather than white.[11] By the latter half of the twentieth century, however, turbans were being worn primarily by clerics, with laymen favoring smaller, less elaborate skullcaps. For ritual settings, however, laymen would generally wear a feta—a preshaped, permanently coiled turban of gold silk, now seen primarily among the older generation and in communities outside India. Part of the reason for the waning popularity of this type of headgear is its expense: in 1995 a feta cost between Rs 850 and Rs 1,000 (then equivalent to $30–$36; at current rates, $20–$23) compared with a topi's Rs 100–180 (then roughly $3). Moreover, in warm weather, particularly in a hot, densely packed masjid, a feta can quickly become rather uncomfortable. In any case, a feta is a supplement to rather than a replacement for a topi: it can be worn only during waaz or majlis, and therefore has largely fallen into disuse.

The primary designator of rank is the pagri, a turban whose use is strictly limited to graduates of the Jamea tus-Saifiya and other respected clerics. When leading imamate namaz Syedna wears a special conical turban of a style reserved for the use of Qasr-e Ali members, but all other Bohra males wear topi, feta, or pagri. Unlike the permanently formed feta, the pagri is a genuine turban: a strip of cloth about five meters long surrounding a red or green cap at the dome of the skull. It can take quite a considerable time to wind a pagri properly, so most wearers preserve the shape of their pagris by keeping the turbans coiled around a metal dish and wrapped in protective cloth. Typically, a pagri will be laboriously rewound only after being washed, or if it happens to come undone accidentally. Like a feta it may be worn only during waaz or majlis, so dawat VIPs come to masjid wearing their topis and change their headgear just before the highlight of a religious observance.

Bohra women actually have considerably greater latitude than Bohra men in matters of dress. Women are required to keep their bodies covered from ankles to shoulders with a burqa and to wear a special style of rida (veil).[12] A Bohra rida is less like a veil than like a bonnet: it covers the hair, neck, shoulders and upper chest, but leaves the entire face exposed. The rida has flaps on either side of the face, so that a woman can (if she is particularly scrupulous to detail) obscure her mouth and nose when eating or conversing with a man outside her family; this seems, however, to be more commonly practiced in the breach.

The burqa-rida combinations are of the same pattern, and this pattern can vary widely. It is generally brightly colored, often with elaborate woven designs, and leaves almost unlimited room for individual taste. Boutiques in many Bohra neighborhoods advertise a wide array of "fancy ridas" (as any rida with a colorful pattern is called), and this Technicolor exuberance of dress immediately sets Bohra women apart from those of most other Indian Muslim communities.[13] At important social or religious functions, it is not uncommon for a Bohra woman to go through three or four changes of fancy rida during the course of a day's varied activities. In a conscious attempt to distinguish themselves from the Sunnis and Ithna-Ashariyya, Bohra women seldom wear plain black clothing.

Prior to the firmans of the late 1970s and early 1980s, Bohra women often adopted the clothing styles of their Hindu neighbors. At midcentury, Hollister wrote that "Bohra women wear skirts and pardah [sic] is little observed among them,"[14] but his account is drawn from other sources (most notably Abdul Husain) rather than from direct observation. During the dissident battles of the mid-1970s (even before dress codes were instituted and therefore a marker of obedience) women in reformist circles can be seen in press clips wearing Hindu clothing: all of the brides photographed in press reports of the March 16, 1975, dissident joint nikah in Udaipur are wearing saris, as are the women photographed earlier as prospective brides. The same can be seen in the bridal photograph of Yasmin Contractor, daughter of the late reformist leader Noman Contractor.[15]

Both men and women are strongly encouraged to wear "community dress" not only for ritual occasions but at all times in their daily lives as well. In practice, however, such strict observance is generally limited to clerics, some members of Qasr-e Ali, officials of the sprawling khidmat bureaucracy, and a small minority of particularly devout laypeople. More commonly, outside a ritual setting women dress in a manner consistent with Islamic codes of modesty,[16] and men wear ordinary street clothes with a topi sometimes retained as a symbolic marker. Even at the dawat's

Badri Mahal headquarters, community dress is not universal: many of the support staff (secretaries, peons, watchmen) are Parsi, Sunni, Hindu, or Christian, and not expected to dress in Bohra clothing. The unique style of dress is a continual reminder of identity, and a great many Bohras make at least a token attempt to maintain dress orthopraxy on a daily basis. Even those who eschew community dress at other times quite often will make at least a symbolic gesture when praying or eating. A Bohra man (like most Muslim men) will cover his head to say namaz, and when he covers his head with a topi rather than a generic skullcap he is reminded of his community ties. Even an individual fairly lax in his or her observance will often put on his topi or drape a shawl over her head before sitting down for a meal. At least six times a day (morning, noon, and evening namaz, breakfast, lunch, and dinner) observant Bohras will have their identity reaffirmed.

In their evaluation of major points of orthopraxy, respondents to my survey ranked dress code surprisingly high. It was cited as a fundamental value by 88.7% of respondents: higher than any life ritual (birth, mithaq, marriage, death), higher than close ties or intermarriage with other Bohras, higher than personal ethics. Dress code was rated equal to ziyaret within India, behind only hajj/Kerbala pilgrimage and contact with Syedna.[17]

Gulshan-e Malumat as a Point of Comparison

Close examination of a 1975 Gujarati text entitled *Gulshan-e Malumat* yields an extremely valuable baseline for analysis of the dawat's dress code reforms. Privately published in a limited edition distributed to various dawat offices, the *Gulshan* is a Who's Who of important Bohra community leaders throughout the world. If such a work were published today, it is highly unlikely that any of the more than three thousand men pictured would present themselves without a beard or dressed in anything other than uniform topi and kurta. (As in most official or semiofficial Bohra texts, for reasons of modesty few, if any, photographs of women are printed). The snapshots of Bohra luminaries in the early 1970s, however, present a very different (and very illuminating) portrait.

The first third of the text is devoted to encomia of Syedna and various family members, while the remaining two-thirds is a directory with photographs of 3,177 men: 2,078 residing in India, 1,099 residing abroad. Of these dignitaries—who can be assumed to represent a higher-than-average level of orthopraxy—a mere 36.9% were in compliance with dress and appearance guidelines that are today deemed normative.

Nearly one-quarter (22.8%) of those living in India are shown in wholly untraditional ways (generally in Western clothing with no beard,

but occasionally in Indian garb unassociated with Bohras). Well over another quarter (29.3 %) wear Bohra headgear but no beard, indicating great potential mobility between the traditional and nontraditional worlds: all of these men could easily put on a topi for a photograph or for official occasions, but would blend perfectly well into the Indian or Western mainstream as soon as they removed their headgear. Together, more than half (52.1 %) of the most respected Indian Bohras of 1975—community leaders who can be assumed to be at least as traditional as the other members of their society, quite probably more so—chose to portray themselves in a way deemed nonconformist today.

For the expatriate Bohras, the figures were even more startling: over half (53.3 %) were directly nontraditional, and 83.9 % had a personal appearance that would today be deemed a grave breach of orthopraxy. Only 16.1 % of those living outside India had an appearance that would be acceptable today. When Indian and non-Indian figures are combined, the population of over three thousand individuals breaks down roughly into thirds: 36.9 % have a traditional appearance, 29.7 % have semitraditional appearance (community headgear, but no beards), and 33.4 % offer wholly nontraditional self-presentations.

The full range of Bohra dress and appearance evolution over the past half century can be seen by comparing post-1979 photographs with those in the *Gulshan-e Malumat,* and then contrasting both with a work that preceded the *Gulshan* by fifteen years. The *Bostan-e Daudi,* published in a limited run in 1960, is a Gujarati text with a format almost identical to that of the *Gulshan.* From internal evidence (years listed in personal biographies, for example) most of the photographs can be dated to the mid-1950s. What is noteworthy here is the radical shift in orthopraxic norms of appearance from the first edition of the Bohra Who's Who to the second. In the *Bostan,* about three-quarters of the men photographed have full beards and are dressed in a thoroughly traditional manner. Only about one in ten of the overall number are clean-shaven, have moustaches rather than beards, wear Western suits with ties, or otherwise present themselves in nontraditional ways.[18]

These photographs provide concrete evidence in support of an observation that many Bohras have made on an anecdotal basis. In less than two decades, from the 1950s to the early 1970s, the Bohra community experienced a dramatic loosening of long-standing custom in matters of personal appearance; and in less than a single decade, the 1980s, the community institutionalized dress and appearance codes that were wider-reaching and more thoroughly followed than at any point since the end of the colonial era.

Comparison with Other Communities

The mandating of specific visible markers has succeeded in sharpening the distinction between Bohras and members of other communities. When dressed in topi and kurta or burqa and rida, an individual is automatically identified as a Bohra by observers both within the denomination and outside of it. The sight of readily identifiable coreligionists is a daily reminder to Bohras of their identity and communal bonds. Fredrik Barth has demonstrated the importance of "overt signals or signs—the diacritical features that people look for and exhibit to show identity, often such features as dress, language, house-form or general style of life."[19]

The blurring of community borders is often a first step toward full assimilation, and it is this outcome that the Bohra dawat seeks to avoid by its dress code. Hasnain and Husain note that many Ithna-Asharis have begun to adopt the customs of their Sunni or Hindu neighbors, and as a result "it is very difficult to distinguish a Shiʿa in a crowd on the basis of his dress."[20] Likewise, Leila Narayanan describes the process of assimilation among Gujarati migrants in Madras: the newcomers typically eat rice, sambar, rasam, and appalam, with Gujarati food served only as special dishes; women take up Tamil styles of jewelry, and even the highly traditional Tanjore Brahmin men often wear their dhotis Tamil-style, sometimes even when presiding at Gujarati weddings or *pujas*. With increasing frequency, Narayanan reports, Tanjore Brahmins are mistaken for their Tamil counterparts.[21]

The same process of cultural assimilation was underway in the Bohra community, but the dress code mandated in the late 1970s and early 1980s has successfully reversed this tendency for the large mass of observant Bohras. Whether one supports or opposes this institutionalization of identity, one can hardly deny its efficacy. Like it or not (and Bohras fall into both camps), the program has clearly succeeded in its objectives.

BEARDS

More so even than dress, the wearing of beards by men of the community is a social marker par excellence. Individuals can move between different worlds by altering their dress, putting on and taking off various identities with each change of clothing, but the growth of a beard represents the forsaking of this symbolic mobility. Young Hindu and Jain men of cities like Mumbai tend to eschew beards (except, of course, *sadhus* and other renunciates), as do Parsis, Christians, and Buddhists. Even among Muslims of the urban centers where Bohras are likely to reside, the wearing of a

beard is often limited to men wishing to project a religious or spiritual image. In areas (like Kashmir) where the keeping of beards is a more common male norm, Bohras are generally rare or wholly absent.

The association of wearing a beard with the sunna of the Prophet Muhammad is well-established.[22] Syedna's injunction to wear a beard is clearly the institutionalization of a genuine Bohra tradition rather than the creation of an ersatz one. While significant numbers (*Gulshan* data suggest a solid majority) of Bohra men had stopped wearing beards by midcentury[23] this represents a sharp break with long-standing custom. Two incidents that led to lawsuits between the dawat and dissidents illustrate the point.

The first occurred in 1937, when the head amil of Mumbai refused to perform nikah for Abdeali Amiruddin and Fatima Chibawala on the grounds that the prospective groom was clean-shaven.[24] The second (and more contentious) episode occurred shortly thereafter, when a man named Idris Buxamusa was denied permission to marry on the same grounds. After much negotiation, the dawat agreed to sanction the wedding if the groom's father put up Rs 200 as a surety that Idris would grow a beard—which led to much argument over the precise definition of how much follicular growth constituted a full beard, to a promise that Idris's brother would grow a beard as well, and eventually to Civil Suit #7074 of 1941 in Mumbai's Court of Small Causes.[25] Whatever else these incidents may demonstrate about dawat-dissident relations, they clearly show that in mandating the wearing of a beard Syedna Muhammad Burhanuddin is upholding an authentic Bohra tradition of long standing. Even dissident leader Asghar Ali Engineer (a beard-wearer himself) agrees that this is the institutionalization of an authentic tradition rather than the creation of a new standard from scratch.[26]

The particular cut of the beard is highly regulated, in accordance with a style spelled out in the hadith recorded by al-Bukhari: "Narrated Ibn 'Umar: Allah's Apostle said, 'Cut the mustaches short and leave the beard (as it is).'"[27] The justification for this is explained in al-Bukhari's prior hadith: the Meccan pagans are said to have grown their mustaches and trimmed their beards, so the Prophet urged his followers to adopt the opposite style of facial hair in order to emphasize their difference.[28] In mandating this particular style of beard, the dawat is hearkening back to older Bohra tradition: according to the early twentieth-century account of Abdul Husain (a dissident community member), Bohra men "wear long thin beards and cut the hair on the upper lip close."[29] Coincidentally (but noteworthy nonetheless), both Hindus and Sunni Muslims in many urban areas populated by Bohras tend to favor a full mustache and shaved chin—

the exact opposite of the Bohra norm. As in the first days of Islam, a man's faith can be read right on his face.

By mandating that all Bohra men wear beards, therefore, Syedna accomplished two things: (1) the solidification of Bohra identity as something distinct from those of neighboring communities, and (2) the linkage of Bohra identity to a universalist sense of Islamic piety. Traditionally, in many Sunni and Shi'a communities throughout the world, wearing a beard has been customary for members of the ulema but not necessary for laymen uninterested in spiritual matters. Syedna's firman implicitly links *all* Bohra men to codes of behavior previously deemed appropriate for particularly religious individuals, thereby reinforcing the identification of the community as one centered around and founded upon a deeply spiritual core. The dawat uses physical appearance to make a profound symbolic statement: Bohras are both unique, and uniquely Islamic.

The only other major Indian community to mandate beards for all men is that of the Sikhs, and the parallels between the two groups are illuminating. On Baisakhi Day in 1699 Guru Gobind Singh established the code of physical comportment ("the five 'k's"—*kesh, kachcha, kara, kangha, kirpan*) still deemed normative for all Sikhs.[30] By forbidding Sikhs to cut their hair Gobind Singh associated the *khalsa* with ancient Hindu notions of the personal appearance appropriate for *rishis* and other spiritual figures. This reinforced early Sikh belief in a priesthood of all believers, a community entirely composed of sacralized individuals.[31] Moreover, the prohibition on trimming one's hair is perhaps the most effective barrier preventing Sikh assimilation: doctrinal differences alone would not automatically exclude Sikhs from the Hindu orbit.

Even the definition of Hinduism put forward by the right-wing Hindu revivalist group Rashtriya Swayamsevak Sangh includes Sikhs within the orbit of the faith. In the formulation proposed by V. D. Savarkar in his seminal work *Hindutva,* a Hindu is anyone "who regards this land of Bharatvarsha from the Indus to the Seas, as his Fatherland as well as his Holyland."[32] Theologians of both faiths have long argued about whether Sikhism is a Hindu sect or a wholly separate religion, and have still reached no universal consensus.[33] In the absence of any clear doctrinal demarcation, the community has been bounded by the five k's. As Khushwant Singh puts it, "We *are* Hindus, really, and well within the mainstream. The distinction between us and the rest is now little more than the beard, the turban, and the last name of Singh."[34]

Sant Jarnail Singh Bhindranwale, the militant preacher who used the Golden Temple as a base for violent agitation in the early 1980s, recognized the importance of the beard as a fundamental marker of identity:

his most ferocious denunciations were directed not at Hindus, but at Sikh men who were clean-shaven.[35] A beard can be cut off in an instant, but only grown to proper length over the course of years. A man can "become" a Hindu in a matter of seconds, but once he makes that choice he cannot regain his Sikh identity without a serious commitment of time.

The same rationale, I suggest, is at work among the Bohras: mandating the wearing of the beard forces all Bohra men to choose a single primary identity rather than shift between several of equal value. Wearing the beard does not separate a Bohra from mainstream society, but it does serve as an immediate identifier—a man can either be an undifferentiated member of secular Indian society or he can be an observant Bohra, but he cannot be both at once. If he ever chooses to give up the marker of his Bohra identity (and to be a true marker it cannot be a scraggly two-week Ashura beard) he will only be able to regain it slowly, gradually, through a transition visible to all his friends and neighbors.

Bhindranwale combined physical markers with physical violence as weapons to combat assimilation. He fueled a cycle of bloodshed in which Sikhs (easily identifiable by their beards and turbans) were singled out for retaliatory attacks, and were forced to rely all the more on their coreligionists for protection and group support.[36] Bohra leaders have sought to avoid rather than provoke sectarian conflict, but their mandated dress code has served to mark community members as Muslims in times of civil unrest. The process of identity solidification through shared physical threat has sometimes proceeded, tragically, in ways similar to those of the Sikhs.

ECONOMIC REFORMS

The Bohras are primarily a business community. Three-quarters of the households responding to my survey were headed by a businessman or shopkeeper, and this entrepreneurial orientation may be one of the prime reasons for the Bohras' openness to new ideas. It is particularly noteworthy, therefore, that the current program of Islamization has as one of its prime components the rejection of *riba*—technically usury, but in a strict interpretation encompassing all forms of financial interest. A non-Islamic banking system such as that of India leaves orthodox Muslims with few acceptable investment choices, so a cadre of young Bohras have been encouraged to get MBAs and explore modern investment strategies that are in accordance with Islamic principles. Such options include partnerships such as *modarbah*, stocks, mutual funds, and real estate.[37]

In Bohra economics, there are three permissible ways to deal with dis-

posable capital. In descending order of merit, they are: (1) give it to charity; (2) deposit it in a *qarzan hasanah* trust; or (3) invest it for profit, in a manner that does not violate Islamic orthopraxy. While Islam is not fundamentally antagonistic to the ideas of economic inequality or free enterprise, it does tend to view with suspicion some of the moral underpinnings of the framework of a "modern" economy.[38] The touchstone for determining whether an investment is "Islamic" is not potential for gain, but potential for loss.

Anything that guarantees the investor a set return without the real possibility of loss runs dangerously close to usury. What makes riba so offensive in Islamic terms is the inherently exploitative nature of the transaction: whether the borrower makes or loses money, he will still have to pay the lender back more than he has been loaned. The power relationship between lender and borrower is necessarily unequal: one of them *has* money, the other one *needs* it. In order to keep the haves from oppressing the have-nots, Islamic economic theory dictates that both parties share the risks as well as the rewards. In Muslim terms, a capitalist banker is little different from a loan shark: whether a defaulting debtor risks loss of his house or loss of his kneecaps, he has entered a financial arrangement based on intimidation rather than cooperation.

Since the global economic system is permeated by riba, a Bohra investor must be imaginative. Bonds, annuities, and other fixed-income instruments are *haraam* (impermissible). Stocks are acceptable, but only if they are traded honestly and not manipulated to return a riskless profit to insiders. Too much risk, however, is as problematic as too little: some stock investing, such as day-trading, might be considered haraam not as usury but as gambling. Certain types of stock options (including those commonly given to American corporate executives over and above their salaries) would be deemed haraam. If the CEO of Phatducats Industries were given a compensation package that included the option of purchasing stock at $10 a share and selling it back to the company at $20, he might well be accused of riba. On the other hand, if the same businessman decided to buy 1 million shares in the initial public offering of Phatducats.com, he could probably hold his head high. As the Bohra businessman and Harvard MBA Abduz-Zahir Mohyuddin puts it, "Equity financing is very Islamic."[39]

QARZAN HASANAH

The most important Bohra innovation here has been a network of credit unions to provide no-interest loans at the local level. The rules propagated

by the 1979 Conference of Fatimi Knowledge in Surat required "complete abstinence from any transaction which involved the element of interest."[40] The avoidance of riba is, of course, a Qur'anic principle (2:275–276) shared with other branches of Islam.[41] For the Bohras, however, this represented a major change from the practice of the recent past. In 1969 an outside observer could report that the Bohras "have retained a number of Hindu customs, such as the Hindu law of inheritance, [and] the practice of charging interest on loans."[42]

Syedna urged his followers to establish trusts to provide *qarzan hasanah* (interest-free loans; cf. Qur'an 73:20)[43] to fellow members of the community, noting that the lenders would earn spiritual merit far greater than the material profit they might otherwise collect. In 1981 he established the Burhani Qarzan Hasanah Trust with an initial capitalization of Rs 52 lakhs (about $120,000 at current rates),* and by 1988 had built the endowment to Rs 3 *crore* 34 lakhs; by 1992 it had climbed to Rs 8 crores ($1.8 million at current rates). Although intended mainly for Bohras, the trust provides loans to borrowers of all religions and communities. Among the intended beneficiaries of the trust are debtors hoping to pay off creditors without accumulating further interest charges; store employees hoping to set up their own shops; businesspeople wishing to expand operations; individuals needing money for weddings, hajj, or the purchase of a new home; and students seeking higher education.[44]

In the space of a few years, similar trusts have been created by local Bohra communities in Britain, Sri Lanka, Kenya, Pakistan, Tanzania, Dubai, and various localities within India. The dawat says that "The moral stamp of the community honour is so powerful and impressive that throughout the world there has not been a single serious case of failure to repay the loan."[45] While these claims must be taken with a certain degree of skepticism, it is worth noting that more than three-quarters of my survey respondents report using the institution of interest-free loans either as a lender or a borrower, and more than a third rate it one of the dawat's two most valuable services.[46]

The dawat's prohibition of interest led in 1982 to agitation against the Bombay Mercantile Co-operative Bank. Headquartered on Muhammad Ali Road and catering primarily to Muslims, the bank had been a largely Bohra-run institution since its 1939 incorporation. Its founder, Muhammad Ali Allabux, had once been a sufficiently strong supporter of the dawat to

*For the sake of comparability, conversion rates are those current at the time of the editing of this manuscript, per the *Financial Express,* January 28, 2000: $1 = Rs 43.6. Use of contemporary exchange rates is misleading because of the wide discrepancy between black-market and official rates prior to the 1990s.

earn the title of shaikh, and (according to his biographer Ambalal Joshi) to persuade Syedna Taher Saifuddin to waive his objection to the bank's levying of interest.[47] In 1955 he joined the dissident/reformist camp, but rejoined the orthodox fold eight years later when (it is said) he desired the dawat's blessing for a family marriage.[48] The Mercantile Bank, however, remained in Bohra hands throughout. At the time of the 1982 protest both its chairman (Husseini Doctor) and its managing director (Zain Rangoonwala) were Daudi Bohras. Syedna Muhammad Burhanuddin directed Bohras to sever all ties with the bank, and community members picketed branches located in Muslim (especially Bohra) neighborhoods. At the time this bank was the largest urban cooperative lending institution in India, with deposits of Rs 90 crore (more than $20 million at current rates).[49]

TAXES

An important part of the dawat's program of reinstitutionalizing Islamic norms has been the strengthening of collection of a variety of taxes and fees paid regularly by all observant Bohras. Not only do such taxes solidify the dawat's position as the "government" of the community, they also provide funding for various aspects of Islamization (the initial capitalization for the Burhani Qarzan Hasanah Trust, for example). In earlier decades collection of these levies had often been lax, and much of the opposition to the dawat's current Islamization programs is linked to a reluctance (quite understandable, of course) to pay taxes that had long been in abeyance.

The following information was provided, with dawat approval, by Mullah Shabbir M. Mansoorbhai Jamali. To the best of my knowledge, dawat figures for tax rates have never before been made public. Dissident sources have published estimates,[50] but these must be treated as partisan conjecture: the revenue estimates are extrapolations from figures that were rough guesses when originally published by other dissidents half a century earlier.

The three main taxes, generally paid to the local amil during Ramadan, are:

(1) *Zakat.* Like all Muslims, Bohras are obliged to pay 2.5% of their accumulated wealth every year.[51] Whereas in Sunni tradition the collection and allotment of zakat is generally left to a believer's individual arrangement,[52] in the Bohra community all distribution is through the dawat. Shibani Roy misidentifies this as "zakwa [sic]: The alms tax, one of the principal obligations of Islam. The tax is levied on definite kinds of property . . . given by every Bohra as 4 annas per head."[53] Setting aside the ob-

vious anachronism of citing a colonial-era unit of currency (*anna*) as modern usage,* Roy seems to have confused zakat (one of the central pillars of Islam) with *sila* (a levy unique to Ismailis). Her figures are unattributed, but 4 annas per head is exactly the rate that Abdul Husain (see below) gives for *zaka tus-salat* (i.e., sila) more than a quarter century before the end of colonial rule.[54] If this rate were still correct, then even if all one million (generously estimated) Bohras paid their taxes in full, the dawat's prime source of revenue would bring in a mere Rs 250,000 per year—less than $6,000 at current rates.[55]

(2) *Sila-Fitra.* These separate taxes (sila al-Imam, a uniquely Ismaili levy; fitra, a tax uniform throughout Islam) are generally paid together. During my 1995 fieldwork, the pair came out to about Rs 40 (then just under $2) per person, half for sila and half for fitra.[56] While fitra (Arabic: *fitr*) is obligatory and pegged to the rate of one gram of silver,[57] sila is technically voluntary, and the rate can vary. All Bohras pay these rather nominal taxes,[58] even a beggar who is a recipient rather than a contributor of zakat. Not even children (born or unborn) and the estates of those who have died during the past year are exempt from fitra, although they do not have to pay sila.

(3) *Sabil.* This tax is levied on households rather than individuals, at monthly rates of Rs 11, Rs 110, or multiples thereof depending on the family's resources. While assessed on a monthly basis, Sabil is generally paid in a lump sum once per year. The tax was instituted by Syedi Abdul-Qadir Hakimuddin (whose rauzah in Burhanpur is a major pilgrimage site) and goes to the local jamat rather than the central dawat or the coffers of Syedna. It is used solely for local programs such as joint nikahs for families too poor to afford their own celebrations.

In addition to these standard taxes Bohras are asked to make semivoluntary contributions to the dawat at certain occasions in their lives. The most notable are:

(1) *Haqqun-nafs:* a fee paid on the burial of a relative. The amount of this is Rs 119 (or any multiple thereof), or (in former times) the value of 119 gold sovereigns or gold mohurs (or any multiple thereof). It can be paid either before or after death.

(2) *Nikah:* a fee paid to an amil for officiating at a marriage. (Few observant Bohras neglect to make an offering on the occasion of the death of a parent or the marriage of a child.)

(3) *Salaam e-Syedna:* cash offering made to the da'i (through the local

* In colonial and early post-Independence coinage, 16 annas equaled 1 rupee, so 4 annas equaled 25 paise. On April 1, 1957, Indian coinage was decimalized and annas were taken out of use.

amil), generally on Syedna's birthday or other symbolic occasions. Unlike the preceding fees, this contribution is considered meritorious but wholly voluntary. A believer who has received a personal du'a (blessing), raza (permission), or bit of advice—even if the interaction lasted only a matter of moments—will typically offer salaam to demonstrate his gratitude. The amount of the salaam varies greatly, and is almost always considerably higher when tendered directly to Syedna than when given in his absence. Two of the most important sources of salaam revenue are alamat and ziyafat (hosting a feast for Syedna). Reformist estimates on alamat typically costing Rs 151–5,001[59] ($3–$115 at current rates) and ziyafat costing Rs 11,000–51,000[60] ($250–$1,100 at current rates) do not seem overstated, even when revised sharply upward to account for inflation since their publication in the 1970s. During my 1994–1997 fieldwork I heard many community stories of wealthy individuals paying $25,000 for the privilege of hosting a ziyafat, over and above all catering costs.

(4) *Nazar al-Maqam:* Offerings to the imam in concealment. These voluntary contributions to the dawat are proffered in times of special trouble or spiritual need.

(5) *Khums:* In the early days of Islam, this was one-fifth of all booty taken in raiding campaigns.[61] In modern times, it is interpreted as a semivoluntary 20% tax on capital gains.[62] Loyal community members are urged to donate one-fifth of any unexpected income they receive, whether it be an inheritance from a distant relative, windfall from a newly discovered resource, or extraordinary profit from an investment. Under this category also fall the payments made by wealthy individuals who cannot (or choose not to) perform fasts or sacrifices owing to ill health. According to Hasnain and Husain, Indian Ithna-Asharis treat khums as a poor-tax of one-fifth of a family's net savings after the deduction of legitimate expenses; any needy members of the Sadaat community (descendants of the Prophet) have the right to half of the funds from this tax, while the other half is kept by the local mujtahid for service to the imam.[63]

For Bohras, the one-fifth tax extends even to progeny: if a Bohra family is blessed with five sons, one of them will be "given" to Syedna for his personal service. In practice the gifting is largely symbolic, and reciprocal: throughout his life that son will have a special obligation (over and above that undertaken at mithaq) to provide Syedna any service at any time, and Syedna will likewise take a particular interest in the child's education and future welfare. The practice is reported in a nineteenth-century gazetteer: "Besides a fifth of their incomes, the head Mulla is said to have a right to the fifth of all property including sons, but not, it is said, daughters. The fifth child, if a boy, is either redeemed with money or made the Mullah's

servant."[64] The custom is very much alive today: during my second visit to Surat, I saw a family present its five sons to Syedna for his selection; with barely an instant's deliberation the da'i selected one of the middle boys and then moved on to the next set of supplicants.

While the structure of the dawat's tax system is known to all Bohras, the amounts raised are revealed to nobody outside the Badri Mahal inner circle. By way of (very inexact) comparison, the dissident writer Mian Bhai Abdul Husain reports the following figures for the earlier part of the early twentieth century: zaka tus-salat (described as a "poll tax," i.e., sila), of 4 annas per head (as of 1920, "recently" raised from 2 annas) brought in 1 lakh rupees per annum.[65] *Zakat al-fitra* (a "fasting tax," i.e., fitra, which is paid during Ramadan), also of 4 annas per head, brought in only Rs 50,000. Haqqun-nafs generated Rs 50,000, as did the fee of Rs 11 per nikah (with higher fees levied for a second or third marriage). Salaam-e Syedna raised Rs 175,000, and nazar-e muqam brought in Rs 125,000. By far the largest portion, however, came from zakat: 6 lakhs of rupees per year.[66] This represented over half of the total dawat funds: "The average annual income of the Head Priest is not less than Rupees 11 lacs a year."[67] While Abdul Husain's figures cannot be taken as anything other than extremely general estimates (as a source outside of and antagonistic to the dawat, he would not have had access to reliable information), the proportions seem to be in very rough accord with the impressions of dawat sources who have offered me estimates of modern-day distributions.

ECONOMIC THEORY

In his classic work *Islam et le capitalisme* (1966), Maxime Rodinson persuasively documents the problematic relationship between traditional Muslim ideology and Western capitalist theory. Muslim economics in general, and Bohra economics in particular, displays many points of congruence with Western-style capitalism, but is based on a different set of assumptions: rather than focus on the well-being and freedom of the individual, the Bohra dawat focuses on the economic well-being of the community as a whole.

The Bohra economic theory is sketched out by Shaikh Ali Asghar, professor of economics at the Jamea tus-Saifiya in Surat.[68] In brief, he explains, Bohras encourage expenditure but discourage frivolous consumption. "We reject the notion that the more you consume, the happier you are," Shaikh Ali Asghar explains, "and that is a premise on which most of Western economic thought seems to be based." Advertising is regarded with a great degree of distrust: "It creates false 'needs,' fuels materialistic

consumerism. We believe that mankind requires new resources, not new wants." Shaikh Ali Asghar identifies two concepts of Keynesian economics that underlie Bohra ideology:

(1) A free, but regulated, market. Socialist economists would rely on state planning to direct investment and spending, but Bohras reject heavy-handed intervention. Like other Indian businesspeople, they have strongly supported the Indian government's post-1991 economic liberalization initiated by former finance minister Manmohan Singh. The old Nehruvian socialist system exemplified by the "license-permit Raj" is regarded as unduly restrictive, but the Bohras are no laissez-faire absolutists. "We feel the market must be free, but regulated," Prof. Ali Asghar says. "Such regulation is vital in *keeping* the market free—without supervision, monopolies would quickly gain control." The crucial difference between Bohra economics and Western models of either leftist or rightist bent, it seems, is one of intent: in Bohra theory, economic principles should be based on moral principles rather than the other way around.

(2) Expenditure: Long before John Maynard Keynes, Bohras had recognized the importance of keeping as much money as possible in public circulation. "Islam has always discouraged the hoarding of resources," Shaikh Ali Asghar explains. He notes that the primary tax, now as in the days of the Prophet, is not a tax on income but on savings. "Marxists would deny individuals the right to earn and save. We encourage people to earn and to save—but while they are saving, to let the rest of society use any resources they themselves do not need." This is the basis for no-interest banking: money kept in a coffer or a safe-deposit vault is money that is idle; a far more efficient use of capital is to keep the money in constant circulation. Individuals should not have to be bribed into lending money with the promise of interest, which (in Qur'anic terms) is inherently exploitative owing to the power imbalance between lender and debtor. Instead, individuals should be willing to lend their surplus capital—money that by definition is above and beyond the amount required for their own immediate needs—in order to help other members of the community.

THEORY IN PRACTICE

Syedna frequently exhorts his followers to go into business for themselves rather than accept employment in large corporations or establishments owned and operated by non-Bohras. He emphasizes the personal benefits an individual enjoys by serving as his or her own boss, but also emphasizes the benefits to the community: economic independence is a bolster

for cultural and religious freedom, a bulwark against outside control, a foundation for self-pride and social revival. A community of small businesspeople will be rich in spirit as well as in cash. The dawat has recently established the Burhani School of Entrepreneurship to teach Bohras the basics of small business administration, and sought American professors of business management for its faculty.

Many Bohras hardly need such instruction. The community has been a mercantile one throughout its history, probably even before its conversion to Islam. The very name of the denomination comes from the Gujarati verb "to trade," and the mercantile orientation is in all likelihood a continuation of the group's pre-Islamic Vaishya ethic. In fact, three-quarters of the household heads in my survey listed their occupations as business, slightly up from 73.1 % for the previous generation of the same households. In Asghar Ali Engineer's survey of eighty dissident households,[69] 66.3 % of respondents were businesspeople.

Bohras overwhelmingly tend to make their livings as shopkeepers: only 4.2 % of my survey respondents described their line of work as "industry" (i.e., big business). The most popular trades include many of those customarily avoided by caste Hindus, but not considered seriously polluting. Hardware is a specialty particularly associated with Bohras, and other lines of trade popular among my survey respondents included glassware, metals, electrical supplies, cutlery, paper goods, printing, cloth, foodstuffs, cosmetics, hats, leather, and dyeing.[70]

While businessmen made up the overwhelming majority, 13.1 % of respondents listed khidmat as their line of work, 6.5 % cited various white-collar professions (accountant, engineer, lawyer, government clerk), and a smaller number mentioned teaching, housework, or manual trades (tailor, air-conditioning repairman, electrician, auto repairman). The percentages were virtually unchanged between the current generation and previous generations of the same families: in fact, very few respondents had chosen a profession different from that of their fathers and grandfathers.

In the course of writing on the wider issue of Muslims in Tamil Nadu, Mattison Mines notes that the Bohras of Madras "have an assistance programme for families at times of death, and encourage Bohra merchants to take in young boys of disadvantaged Bohra families as apprentices in order to teach them how to run a business."[71] The Bohras in my survey looked to the clergy for their financial as well as their spiritual well-being. Not only did 64.6 % of them ask Syedna (or his local amil) to bless their account books in the practice of alamat, but 42.7 % reported dawat assistance in forging business contacts.[72]

While most Bohras are small shopkeepers, some run far more exten-

sive operations. The hugely popular department-store chain Akbarally, for example, was founded by the Bohra magnate Akbarally Ebrahimji of Mumbai. The large downtown clothing store Zaibaish is owned and operated by Bohras, but it too caters to a mainstream clientele. The sales staff at Zaibaish wear ordinary Indian clothing (women generally in *shalwar qamiz* or saris, men in dress shirts and slacks) and the stock of merchandise is no different from that at other stores. Topis and burqas, either in showcases or worn by staff, are nowhere in sight. But photographs of Syedna Muhammad Burhanuddin and Syedna Taher Saifuddin grace the wall, prominently displayed beside a very large bismillah. On request, the staff produces an array of Bohra religious items for sale, ranging from canonical books to photos of the daʿi to items of community dress.

The entrepreneurial drive runs straight through Bohra society, from the wealthiest mogul to the humblest street vendor. Even financially disadvantaged Bohras are encouraged to go into business for themselves if at all possible. "It is very important to us that every Bohra be his own master," notes the amil of Hyderabad, "and you cannot truly be your own master if you are laboring for somebody else." The local qarzan hasanah trust helps even the poorest Bohras purchase sewing machines and gives a training course to equip them to work as tailors out of their own homes. For middle-class members of the community, the trust provides money for the initial expenses of opening a shop: in Hyderabad, most of the hardware and glassware stores are run by Bohras.

The Bohra work ethic would make Horatio Alger green with envy. Bohras often claim that no member of the community ever goes begging, and it is true that I have never seen a topi-wearing man with his hand out. There are beggars in Bohra neighborhoods, but they are generally easily identifiable by clothing or personal appearance as members of other communities. During important religious holidays professional mendicants often congregate outside Bohra masjids. During the month of Ramadan— especially during the few days when the Fatimid and mainstream observational lunar calendars do not overlap—Muslim beggars often move en masse from the neighboring Sunni and Ithna-Ashari areas of Muhammad Ali Road to the streets immediately surrounding the Bohras' Saifee Masjid. As members of a relatively well-to-do community, individual Bohras are singled out for particular attention throughout the year: anywhere in Mumbai, a man wearing a topi or a woman in a fancy rida can be a magnet for mendicants.

In Lisanu-Dawat, the generalized term for beggars is *mangwawalas,* literally "those who demand." This term is more commonly applied specifically to professional beggars— to people who harass passers-by on the

street—than to those truly in need. A *sayil,* by contrast, is a mendicant who is genuinely needy and grateful for whatever assistance may be offered. A *miskin*[73] is much like a sayil, but he will not even ask for donations, merely accepting whatever coins may be dropped in his lap. The term *fakir* has definite spiritual overtones, but for the Bohras (unlike, for example, members of many Sufi *tariqa*) there is no recognized class of holy mendicants.

All Bohras are exhorted to treat beggars with kindness, since there is no way of telling which might be a con artist and which might be an angel sent by God to test the charity of the faithful. In the Bohra view, *sadaqa* (voluntary charity, over and above zakat) is more of an obligation than a meritorious deed. When any supplicant comes to the da'i seeking advice for a problem or charismatic blessing for a physical ailment, part of the solution or cure offered by Syedna will be instruction for the afflicted to perform sadaqa.

COMPARISON WITH OTHER GROUPS

In their economic outlook and practices, Bohras seem to display greater similarity to other Gujarati communities than to other Indian Shi'a denominations. The mercantile orientation of many Gujarati groups of various religions is well documented: whether Jain banias, Parsis, Sunni Memons or Ismaili Khojahs, Gujaratis have a well-earned reputation for business acumen. Of Gujaratis in Madras studied by Narayanan, over 90% (apart from Tanjore Brahmins) of the household heads either owned their own shops or were employed in shops owned by other Gujaratis.[74]

The mainstream of Indian Shi'a (mostly Ithna-Ashari), by contrast, display considerably less entrepreneurial activity. In the Hasnain and Husain survey, slightly fewer than one-third of respondents described themselves as small businessmen. Almost half of respondents earned less than Rs 1,000 per month, and only 6% earned more than Rs 5,000. Even here the results are skewed by the disproportionate presence at the upper income levels of Gujarati Khojahs and Shi'a Kutchi Memons; apart from these groups, most communities studied were more economically backward than their neighbors. As is the case for the Bohras, "it may be said that Shi'as have been, and still are, an 'urban phenomenon' because the majority of them have traditionally been living in towns and cities."

In the nawabate of Awadh and the sultanates of the Deccan there had been a long-standing tradition of Shi'a *zamindars, taluqdars, jagirdars,* and other rural landowners, but since the abolition of the *zamindari* system very few Shi'a have made their livings from agriculture. A small but signif-

icant number (7.5%) of Hasnain and Husain's respondents were farmers, compared with not a single one of my Bohra respondents and a mere 3.8% of the previous generation in my respondents' households. The geographical breakdown of the Hasnain and Husain survey is illustrative. Overall only 42.5% of respondents wanted their children to go into business, but the figure was significantly higher in Maharashtra (62%) and highest of all in Gujarat (65%).[75] Even where Bohras share an entrepreneurial outlook with other Muslim groups (Khojahs or Memons, for example), the tie seems to have more to do with a common Gujarati Vaishya ethic than with a common Islamic set of values.

This business outlook and mercantile orientation may, in fact, be one of the prime reasons for the Bohras' comfort with and ready use of modern technology and ideology. The qualities of a successful entrepreneur are particularly well suited to promoting smooth, frictionless modernization: a small businessperson must be adaptable to new circumstances, open to new ideas and novel methods of production, flexible and forward-thinking enough to stay one step ahead of the competition. It is an axiom of business that one can buy in any language but must sell in the language of the customer. As a community that makes its living by selling products to members of other communities, the Bohras have always needed to understand and work within the confines of the larger mainstream culture. Whether in Hyderabad or Houston, Bohras have proven themselves unusually adept at adapting to local circumstances. Wherever they have settled they have had to learn a new language, a new culture, a new way of doing business. Bohras have been intellectual *bricoleurs* throughout their history, and it stands to reason that they would continue their handiwork with whatever tools might be at their disposal. As retired accountant Zubeda Gunja says: "We've always been comfortable with outside influences and customs. After all, we've *had* to be."[76]

Education ---

I n no area, perhaps, is the Bohras' melding of tradition and modernity more striking than in the field of education. The dawat has adopted much of the curriculum and pedagogical ideology of the West, and has done so with genuine enthusiasm rather than grudging acquiescence. These teaching practices have been formulated not merely to promote the students' material advancement in secular society, but to bolster traditional customs, ideology, and identity. Such scholars as Dale Eickelman and Fazlur Rahman have rightly noted the central place of educational policy in programs of cultural revival throughout the Islamic world,[1] but few such movements balance old and new as thoroughly as that of the Bohras.

The use of modern technology is not uncommon among fundamentalist Muslim groups ranging from the Wahhabis in Saudi Arabia to the Taliban in Afghanistan to the Jamaat-i-Islami in Pakistan.[2] As Margaret Mead noted in a more general context, "Technical change is as old as civilization, and since time immemorial the ways of life of whole peoples have been transformed by the introduction of new tools and new technical procedures."[3] In some Muslim countries (most notably Turkey and prerevolutionary Iran) Western education has been used by secularizing Muslims to downgrade the position of Islam in society. The use of modern pedagogy and a Western intellectual framework for education, however, is far less common among traditional Islamic groups,[4] and this is perhaps the most noteworthy and unusual part of the Bohra identity program.

The Bohras are unusual among Indian Muslims in placing far higher emphasis on modern education than the mainstream of Indian society does.[5] There is some evidence suggesting that Indian Shi'a in general have higher educational levels than the Indian norm: of Hasnain and Husain's survey respondents, more than one-third had been educated up to the secondary level, nearly another third were graduates, and only 4% were illiterate.[6] The authors conclude that "the rate of literacy among the Shi'a is quite high despite their economic backwardness."[7] Among Ismaili Shi'a in their survey, however, this trend seems more pronounced than for Ithna-

Asharis: Khojahs display a devotion to modern education on par with any subcontinental group.[8]

While Bohra dawat claims of 100 % literacy in the community[9] must be regarded as inflated, the actual figure is surely well above the Indian average of 52 %.[10] Satish Misra, in his section on Bohras in a larger work examining Gujarati Muslim communities, estimated three decades ago that more than three-quarters of Daudi Bohras had at least a primary education.[11] When asked to state the highest level of education attained by any member of their households, 91.0 % of my survey respondents cited levels of secondary school or higher—a huge increase over 58.2 % of previous generations reported in the same families. The difference of a single generation is quite stark: for current heads of household, 70.6 % reported education up to Standard XII or higher (roughly equivalent to an American high-school diploma), while 29.4 % reported dropping out at the secondary-school level or below. When questioned about the education of their parents, the ratios were almost completely reversed.

Slightly more than half of respondents had degrees of higher learning (whether bachelor's, master's, or higher), compared with 14.2 % in the previous generation. Only 1.3 % reported "little or no" formal education, down from 14.9 % in their parents' day. Mumbai showed significantly higher educational levels than even this impressive baseline. An overwhelming 92.3 % of respondents had Standard XII or higher education, nearly triple the level of the previous generation. No respondent had less than elementary school training. Karachi respondents were also somewhat above the norm, with Calcutta and Nagpur respondents slightly below.

Since the survey was distributed to parents of children in madrasas, one surprising result was the infrequency of religious education among respondents themselves. A mere 4.4 % reported madrasas or the Jamea tus-Saifiya academy as their terminal point of education, down from 11.2 % in past generations. This does not preclude the possibility of respondents taking primary education in madrasas and moving to secular schools for their secondary and higher education, nor does it take account of those individuals who attended madrasa as a supplement to their secular education (a practice analogous to Sunday school for Christians). It is interesting, however, that Mumbai respondents—the most highly educated both in the current and in previous generations—were the most likely to have had a religious education: 7.7 % of respondents in the current generation had finished their education in madrasas or the Jamea, down from 16.7 % in past generations; these figures are above those at all three other sites.

Such emphasis is a particularly effective way to shape attitudes: sev-

eral Indian studies have suggested that schooling influences a student's outlook at least as powerfully as societal context or family background. Bachan Lal Jindal, after extensive research in Haryana schools, states, "[N]either the mass media (composite) nor any one of its channels was found significantly related to student modernity," and goes on to argue that "it is not the family, but the school which is a more powerful predictor of student modernity."[12] Jindal's survey population wound up adopting a modernist attitude in secular matters while retaining traditional attitudes toward religious issues; the Bohra dawat, however, has achieved similar results through conscious, concerted effort.

Prior to the mid-twentieth century, Bohras (like other Muslims) had to choose between the competing philosophies of Islamic and Western education. The former generally meant: (1) at a rudimentary level (maktab), rote memorization of portions of the Qur'an and enough familiarity with the Arabic or Gujarati script to claim functional literacy in either the textual or vernacular language;[13] (2) at a more advanced level (madrasa), full command of written (and possibly spoken) Arabic, Persian, and/or Urdu; intellectual familiarity with the Qur'an and the scriptural writings of imams, da'is, and syedis; and a broad-based understanding of the zahir aspects of Ismaili history, philosophy, and theology; (3) at the higher clerical levels, access to batin knowledge and interpretations of scripture and text shielded from the mass of uninitiates. Like other systems of Islamic education, the Bohra structure left relatively little room for modern innovation. As the Muslim traveler Muhammad Shibli Nu'mani wrote of Sunni practice during an 1892 trip to Cairo, "[T]hose people who have been once as much as touched by traditional education remain forever irreconcilably estranged from modern learning."[14]

In the late nineteenth and early twentieth centuries several movements of educational reform appeared in various parts of the Muslim world, most notably those of Sir Syed Ahmad Khan, Muhammad Abduh, Nemik Kemal, and Maulana Abul Kalam Azad. All attempted to reconcile Islamic ideology with modern thought and reinterpret traditional concepts in the light of Western science. The solutions covered a wide ideological range, from Kemal's neotraditional defense of traditional orthodoxies to Abduh's rejection of medieval cosmology coupled with retention of neo-Mu'tazila philosophy, to Khan's radical "proof" of Islam through rationality and implicit acceptance of modern science as the standard by which human beliefs may be judged.[15] Such movements paved the way for the Bohras' own program of educational reform.

The traditional educational structure of maktab and madrasa, while adequately serving the needs of the denomination in a premodern soci-

ety, did not address the changing requirements of a mercantile community in a rapidly evolving cultural milieu. From the nineteenth century onward, a thorough grounding in such Western subjects as English language, math, and science gained increasing importance in Mumbai's cosmopolitan business environment. Bohras were slower to adapt than were fellow Gujarati merchants such as the Parsis, Jain banias, and Khojahs, but they had adapted informally even before such changes were institutionalized in the educational system.[16] As a community disproportionately made up of purveyors of hardware and general goods, the Bohras had little choice but to keep up with societal transformation ushered in by the Raj. The British influence is readily apparent in the prevalence of modern-day Bohra surnames such as "Shipchandlerwala," "Merchant," "Cutlerywala," "Doctor," and "Bootwala," not to mention the surnames of dissident leaders Asghar Ali Engineer and Noman Contractor. The growing importance of a modern education to Gujarati mercantile communities is noted by Narayanan, who observes that among the older generation of her informants education was not considered particularly vital but "today it is considered essential for a Gujarati male to qualify for a degree even if he ultimately is going to enter the family business."[17]

The current dispute between the dawat and dissidents like Engineer has its roots, to a large degree, in educational philosophy. In the late nineteenth and early twentieth centuries members of the Bohra intellectual elite, like those of other Indian Muslim groups, wrestled with the issue of educational reform. Traditionalists clung passionately to a heritage that had served the community quite well for centuries, while Western-educated modernists pointed to the rapid societal advancement that non-Muslim groups had been steadily making during the period of British rule. In the Indian Sunni mainstream the case for adapting a Western curriculum was put forward most strongly by Sir Syed Ahmad Khan, whose efforts led to the foundation of Aligarh Muslim University over the objections of the traditionalist Deoband ulema.* In the Bohra community, the reformists established a school (the Madrasa-i Hakimiya) in 1901 that aimed to teach English and several other Western subjects alongside traditional ones, to the consternation of the conservative fiftieth da'i Abdullah Badruddin.[18] Arguments over control of this school (as well as control of community finances, which soon became a more pressing issue) led to lawsuits against the da'i, pronouncements of baraat, and a rift that has grown ever wider over time.

*In a stroke of poetic irony, the honorary chancellor of Aligarh Muslim University appointed in 1999 was none other than Syedna Muhammad Burhanuddin.

The core of the dispute, then as now, has been the issue of clerical authority: who should decide what to teach Bohra children, and what ideas should be inculcated as the basis for orthodox identity? Ironically, while the issue of control is little closer to resolution now than in 1901, the dissidents' original pedagogical demands have long been integrated into the dawat's own educational program: since the reign of Syedna Abdullah Badruddin's successor Syedna Taher Saifuddin, the Bohra clergy has actively provided Western as well as Islamic education.

The late da'i Syedna Taher Saifuddin began promoting modern education over half a century ago, and he is generally credited for the attitudinal sea change on Western pedagogy that has swept the community since that time.[19] There are currently more than 350 Bohra schools throughout the world, all of them operating under the late da'i's educational philosophy.[20] Some of these, like the Burhani College of Commerce and Arts in Mumbai, are unequivocally modern in outlook and approach. As a recipient of government funds, the college educates both Bohra and non-Bohra students on equal footing. Bohras wear topi and kurta or burqa and rida and pray at regular times, but most of the non-Bohra male students dress in jeans and Western-style shirtsleeves, the non-Bohra female students in skirts or saris. Classrooms are segregated by sex, but boys and girls mix and socialize freely in the hallways, courtyards, cafeteria, and everywhere else throughout the campus. A further marker of the college's modernist orientation is its incorporation of the Burhani Computer Technical School. Right next door to the Burhani College of Commerce and Arts, however, is Mumbai's Burhani Madrasa, an institution that illustrates the dawat's attempt to forge an identity that is simultaneously modernist and traditionally Islamic.

BURHANI MADRASAS

Under Taher Saifuddin's successor Muhammad Burhanuddin, the dawat has established an entire network of schools whose mission is to teach modern and traditional subjects side by side, with grades ranging from nursery school through the equivalent of American high school. There are currently sixteen of these Burhani madrasas, located in cities including Mumbai, Bangalore, Nasik, Surat, Hyderabad (Deccan), Madras, Calcutta, Dhaka, Dar es Salaam, Mombasa, Nairobi, and Karachi.[21] The combined enrollment of these madrasas is over 1,500, with all students following the same curriculum and all held to the same exacting standards.

Like India's most elite Western-oriented private academies and convent schools, in the upper grades Burhani madrasas teach all the curricula

necessary for matriculation in American or European universities. In 1995 the Mumbai madrasa was the only school in the city (and one of only five in all of India) to prepare students for the International Baccalaureate.[22] To insure uniform standards at all madrasas and safeguard against inadvertent divergence from orthodoxy, teachers are brought to the central headquarters in Mumbai for training whenever possible and teams of examiners are sent out every year to make spot-checks on various local campuses.

There are no restrictions on the religious or community backgrounds of members of the madrasa teaching staff. Most teachers are Bohras, but there are many Christians, Parsis, Hindus, and Sunni Muslims as well. This is particularly true in cosmopolitan Mumbai, where the local madrasa's administrator is a woman of mixed Goan Christian and Sinhalese Buddhist parentage who is married to a Parsi and is raising her own son in that faith. While the students are all Bohra and all wear Bohra community dress, the teachers have no such restrictions. All are expected to dress modestly and comport themselves in accordance with norms of propriety, but they are not expected to dress or act like Bohras. According to the Mumbai chief administrator, the community background of teachers is seldom considered when making hiring decisions—if anything, Parsi and Christian staff members are particularly sought-after for their superior fluency in English.

Most students at the Mumbai madrasa are admitted at the nursery school level, because after this point they may lag behind in Arabic language. Admission criteria vary little from those of other elite Mumbai nurseries: teachers will have a brief conversation with the child, and ask him or her to perform simple tasks such as identifying colors or stringing beads. As at any nursery school, however, "merit" selection of toddlers can go only so far. Family background plays a part, and since Burhani madrasas (particularly the Mumbai one) are prime feeders for the Jamea academies in Surat and Karachi, the competition is sometimes intense. Financial considerations also affect the composition of the student body: while the dawat subsidizes all madrasas (the Indian government provides no funding), it does not provide free tuition.

The nursery section of the madrasa contains 90 children aged two-and-a-half to three-and-a-half. At first glance it seems indistinguishable from any nursery school in the West: miniature chairs and tables, walls decorated with finger painting and collages of dry macaroni, spelling posters of household objects and barnyard animals. Little girls and boys are acting like little girls and boys—piling up houses of wooden blocks and knocking them down, playing an impromptu game of tag when the teacher's back is turned, or shyly retreating into a corner to wait until nap

time. But even at this early age there is a clear religious bent; the poems and stories told generally contain spiritual messages, and the first half hour of the day is spent listening to a cassette of daily prayer so that the children will learn to say namaz properly. They are introduced to the Arabic script and begin learning simple Arabic words by rote. The kids sitting in the miniature chairs around the miniature tables are all dressed in miniature topis, kurtas, and burqas.

Emphasis throughout the younger grades is on cultural instruction. The students are taught how to dress, eat, speak, pray, and comport themselves like Bohras, so that by the time they reach puberty their personal identities have been shaped largely in accordance with the values of the dawat. Whatever other influences the children may be exposed to at home or in the street, at school they will be taught to internalize all the doctrines and practices deemed normative by the clergy. By the time they graduate (it is hoped), they will view all details of orthopraxy as second nature. The specific practices inculcated include:

(1) Dress: Boys are put in the habit of wearing topi and kurta and girls of wearing burqa and rida from the earliest ages. This is done to instill lifelong habits rather than for reasons of modesty: until they reach the age of mithaq, children are not separated by gender either in the classroom or in the larger Bohra society. By the time they reach adulthood (the dawat reasons) students will be thoroughly accustomed to wearing community dress on a daily rather than occasional basis.[23]

(2) Food: At the Burhani madrasas, students not only are taught the basic Islamic dietary classifications of halal and haraam types of food,[24] they are also taught Bohra dining etiquette at child-sized thals. The thal has created a dining etiquette with its own rules and prohibitions. Utensils are not used, every morsel of food must be consumed, and each diner customarily takes a pinch of salt before and after the meal.* It is interesting to note that 82.1 % of my survey respondents noted "way of eating" as one of the basic elements of orthopraxy, ranking it fourth out of ten. Eating at the thal and keeping halal were deemed more important than rituals of marriage, death, or mithaq.

Dining customs are particularly important, as almost every religious or social observance in the community is marked by a lavish feast. In fact, communal meals are given in many Bohra jamats on an almost daily basis. Occasionally these are ziyafats (formal functions held for the da'i or any other important figure), but more often they are feasts known as *niyaz*

*This practice, sometimes followed even by nonobservant Bohras, is said to ward off seventy sicknesses, including leprosy and elephantiasis.

(when held in honor of Imam Husain) or simply *jamat*. Individuals compete to sponsor the most sumptuous meals, and even the simplest events will typically combine lengthy prayers and prodigious consumption into a program that can last many hours. Invitations are utterly superfluous: while members of the Qasr-e Ali are limited by protocol in their attendance at "casual" dinners, all other community members (except those under baraat) are welcome to attend any jamat function.

Although communal meals were instituted partly to break down Hindu taboos against interdining, traces of Gujarati Vaishya concern for ritual purity seem to have been transferred to an Islamic context. Diners sit with legs tucked under their bodies, or at least with one leg bent and the other sole pressed compactly against the raised thigh, but never with legs crossed or stretched out. The prohibition stems partly from convenience (in close quarters such postures might inconvenience other diners) but more from a sense of respect: meals are a vital social bond rather than mere physical sustenance. For Bohras (as for their Vaishya ancestors) food has an aura tinged with religious sentiment, and it should not be consumed while lounging in a posture of disrespectful indolence. In implicit recognition of the quasi-sacral character of a meal, Bohra men and women alike are required to keep their heads covered while eating.

(3) Prayer: At a young age all madrasa students learn the proper ritual for saying namaz. The order of standing, kneeling, and prostration, accompanied by the appropriate recitations in Arabic, is a complex sequence without which no Bohra can take full part in the religious life of the community. Students are also habituated to sitting in "bhaisaheb" position (a kneeling posture with torso erect and legs half folded underneath the body) required at religious ceremonies.

(4) Personal comportment: Islam is not merely a faith, but a unified, holistic manner of living. The Bohra interpretation of this way of living is inculcated at the madrasa, right down to the most minute details of daily routine. Rules of hygiene are emphasized early, not merely for reasons of health but because the Bohras consider tahara (cleanliness) as one of the seven pillars of the faith.[25] While acknowledging that other Muslims place a high normative value on cleanliness,[26] the Bohras believe that they honor this value more scrupulously than their Sunni coreligionists do. As one observer notes, "[T]he religious tenet of tahara (cleanliness) is all-pervasive and has blended with the Bohra lifestyle."[27] This Ismaili emphasis (common to Bohras and Khojahs) is a continuation of Fatimid doctrine, but may also have the additional cultural force of meshing with preconversion Vaishya ideals of ritual purity.

At the more advanced grade levels, the Burhani Madrasa provides the

fullest possible range of facilities for a modern, Western education. The Mumbai madrasa, for example, has well-equipped chemistry, physics, and biology labs, a library full of texts on a variety of Western and Islamic subjects, and a computer room (fully operational on my first visit early in 1995) with a small array of desktop PCs, printers, and even a mainframe-type integrated system. Equal emphasis, however, is placed on subjects not offered at any secular school: Bohra history and culture, Musta'li Ismaili philosophy and theology, classical Arabic language, and calligraphy in the Fatimid Kufic script.

The state-of-the-art language lab would be the envy of most subcontinental universities, let alone secondary schools. Fifteen soundproofed booths with a centrally controlled and monitored Tandberg system allow students to practice their English, French, German, and Spanish as well as colloquial Arabic, Hindi, and Marathi. There are tapes of plays by Shakespeare and Molière, poems by Rabindranath Tagore, and mellifluous recitations of the Qur'an. Only vocal popular music is excluded from the tape library, on grounds that it violates the spirit of Islam.

Sports facilities are similarly ecumenical. In addition to the normal range of school team sports, madrasa students can learn Filipino stick-fighting and Okinawan karate. Since the later involves a high degree of physical contact, the madrasa employs a husband-and-wife team to teach boys and girls separately. Gender segregation, however, does not lead to an atmosphere of oppressive grimness. "The twelve-year-old girls are the naughtiest group in the school," says one teacher, with amusement. "Often they'll be peeking through a crack in the wall while the boys change into their athletic gear for gym or karate. Some people complain, but I tell them not to get upset over such little things." From her light tone of voice, it is unclear whether she is referring to the act or the object of the girls' illicit spying.

The philosophy and outlook of the Burhani madrasa system as a whole is summarized in the words of Ayman Behnsaheb Kalimuddin, director of the worldwide network of madrasas and sister-in-law of Syedna Muhammad Burhanuddin:

> We are trying to foster an Islamic way of thinking about all aspects
> of learning—geography, history, math, all of it. If we teach chil-
> dren about monsoons, we not only teach them the scientific
> causes for such weather conditions, but also the Qur'anic verses
> describing heavy rainfall as a sign of God's power. We do not see
> modern Western education as being antithetical to Islam at all: in
> today's world, a person must be thoroughly grounded in every

form of knowledge in order to function in a wider society. But we try to give our students the Islamic basis to underlie this education.[28]

JAMEA TUS-SAIFIYA

After leaving madrasa, the best students will go on to the highly competitive academy Jamea tus-Saifiya, located in Surat with a satellite campus in Karachi. The program of study lasts up to eleven years, with some students entering as young as twelve and others joining and graduating at various later stages. During the first four years students are drilled in Arabic language (both spoken and written), Islamic history, law, and theology, and such modern topics as English language, humanities, and science (both social and natural). Graduates are given the degree *mubtaghi al-ilm,* "seeker of knowledge," approximately equivalent to a secular high-school diploma. The next five years are equivalent to a university bachelor's degree program. In addition to a deeper exploration of the topics studied up to this point, students are taught such subjects as psychology, philosophy, and theology. The degree awarded is *al-faqih al-mutqin,* "perfect jurist." The final two years are graduate-level work, which can be undertaken in a variety of traditional and Western subjects. The diploma (*al-faqih al-jayyid,* "accomplished jurist") is regarded by Karachi University and other institutions as the equivalent of a master of arts degree.[29]

The Jamea tus-Saifiya in Surat is the apex of the Bohra educational system, and it produces the lion's share of the clerics who serve in the dawat. Founded in 1814 as a theological seminary named *El-Dars-el-Saifi,* for much of the nineteenth century it was an academy where "150 to 200 boys are clothed, fed and taught Arabic, geometry, logic, and law," drawing students from all over the subcontinent, and even from Arabia.[30] By 1897, however, it was "on a greatly reduced scale, and kept up at a yearly charge of about Rs 10,000," and by 1919 it had deteriorated to the point where it was providing little more than primary-level religious education.[31] Syedna Taher Saifuddin gave the academy a new name, new mission, and new outlook. Contemporary dissidents charged the school with serving only the interests of the hidebound clerical reactionaries, and in retrospect the dawat now seems to agree: Taher Saifuddin "initiated a fresh educational upsurge," wrote Yusuf Najmuddin, late brother of the current da'i, "and freed it from the clutches of the so-called self-styled Ulema."[32]

This transformation of the Surat academy marks the beginning of a transformation of Bohra education overall. Until the second quarter of the

twentieth century, dawat officials concede, members of the community were actively discouraged from learning English and other Western subjects. A nineteenth-century gazetteer noted that "besides the central college, every Daudi settlement has its school, where, under the charge of the Mulla and generally by a Sunni Musalman teacher, boys and girls are taught to read the Kuraan . . . [but] they seem little inclined to teach their children English or to take other than their hereditary calling of trade."[33]

Under Syedna Taher Saifuddin, however, this policy changed. One dawat publication states that "His Holiness had not only taken the initiative and undergone considerable expenditures in establishing schools of the modern type," but made English compulsory for all Jamea students.[34] Dr. Najmuddin (himself a son of Taher Saifuddin) notes that the current da'i's sons and daughters are "all graduates and well qualified even by Western standards," thus providing "a worthy example of how secular education should be blended with Islamic lore."[35]

Like the Burhani madrasas, the Jamea offers a full range of both Western and Islamic subjects at a university level. The campus (extensively enlarged by Syedna Muhammad Burhanuddin) compares quite favorably with many centers of higher learning in India. An honest description of the Jamea sounds embarrassingly similar to a college recruitment pamphlet: it has spacious, well-constructed buildings impeccably maintained, voluminous libraries, impressive athletic facilities, fully stocked labs for various sciences, comfortable, uncrowded dormitories, and a thoroughly dedicated, professional faculty. While not solely a training academy, the Jamea has a curriculum geared toward students planning a career in the dawat. Because dawat service is not an exclusive arrangement, however, it is quite common for individuals to hold important clerical positions while running a small business or taking part in family commercial endeavors.

By providing a first-rate modern education (and providing it essentially free, for both male and female students)[36] the Bohra dawat avoids the brain drain that has afflicted so many other Indian communities. The Jamea not only insures that the brightest minds of the faith remain grounded in Islamic values throughout their intellectually formative years, it effectively draws much of the cream of the crop into khidmat. An educational system stressing only Islamic subjects would drive many of the brightest students to convent schools or private secular institutions, but the dawat's open attitude toward all types of modern learning has enabled it to co-opt most aspects of Western culture while excluding only those elements directly in conflict with religious values.

The student body of the Surat Jamea consists of approximately 600 men and 300 women from the elite of Bohra youth throughout the world. At the time of my first visit to Surat, there were students in residence from Bangladesh, Sri Lanka, Kenya, Tanzania, Madagascar, Egypt, Kuwait, Saudi Arabia, Yemen, Britain, and the United States. During their stay at the Jamea all expenses are paid by the dawat: tuition, housing, food, books, sports facilities, laundry—everything is provided gratis. The expectation is that Jamea graduates will repay their debt by entering khidmat, or helping to educate the next generation in turn.

"We don't believe in a rigid division between science and social science," explains Shaikh Ali Asghar, a professor at the Jamea for the past twenty years. "There is no conflict whatsoever between science and faith—after all, science is merely the sum total of observation and common sense." All of the Jamea's instructors are required to be fully versed in both traditional and modern subjects, and many are experts in several widely disparate fields. Shaikh Ali Asghar, for example, teaches both economics (in which he has a doctorate) and chemistry. "Too often modern academia means knowing more and more about less and less," he says, "until eventually you know everything there is to know about nothing at all.[37] This is what we try to avoid." The Jamea, he explains, has a different educational philosophy: "Knowledge is like a tree, with different branches spreading out in all directions, growing organically off one another, all organically linked, all part of the same living entity."

The Jamea's dual emphasis on traditional and modern learning is apparent in its educational facilities. The Surat academy not only possesses one of the world's richest collections of Ismaili theological literature, but also boasts three separate up-to-the-moment laboratories for biology, chemistry, and physics. The sophistication of instruction in math and sciences can be gauged by the exam required for Standard III (i.e., students less than eleven years old). In the version offered January 7, 1995, students were asked to explain why "when different allotropes of an element are burnt in oxygen they produce different amounts of heat energy," to "describe with a labeled diagram the structure and working of a human heart or kidney," and to answer a variety of other technical questions that would utterly stump at least one Harvard Ph.D. triple their age.

The school's multistory library has an enviable range of texts on scientific, literary, and zahir theological topics in its open shelving—and a wealth of batini texts in closed shelving that is accessible only with the consent of the proper spiritual authorities. The languages of instruction at the Jamea typify the institution's outlook. Most students arrive speaking Gujarati as their first language, but by graduation all are fluent in Arabic,

English, and Lisanu-Dawat* as well. As the instructions for the English portion of the Standard III exam note, "Acquiring mastery over the English language is *essential* [original emphasis] for a *Talib-e-Ilm* [student of religious knowledge] to keep himself abreast of all learning so as to compete and achieve this distinction in all fields."

The teaching staff at the Jamea is predominantly Bohra, but many non-Bohra instructors are employed to teach specialized subjects. The custodial staff (*dhobis*, sweepers, and servants) is predominantly non-Bohra, mostly Hindu. In accordance with traditional Bohra custom students and teachers take their meals together, with eight or nine diners sharing a huge metal thal. Most students live in dormitories on the Jamea campus, in rooms that are simple but immaculately maintained and considerably more comfortable than typical Indian university hostels. Students from Surat sometimes live with their families, and old Surti families who emigrated to other cities generations ago sometimes retain a Surat residence specifically for the use of family members at the Jamea. Members of Syedna's extended family generally do not live in the dormitories, in order to maintain a dignified distance from the general student body. Off-campus students are entitled to free food from the Jamea's kitchens, so long as they send an attendant over to fetch it daily. In order to maintain some measure of egalitarianism, the maximum spending-money allowance that Jamea students are permitted to receive from their families is Rs 300 per month.

Life in the student dormitories is comfortable, if circumscribed. Every floor has a large color television set equipped with satellite receiver and videocassette recorder. The channel selection, however, is centrally controlled by house proctors, who make sure that all programs broadcast are wholesome and at least marginally educational. At the time of my first visit to the Jamea the system had just been hooked up to receive BBC broadcasts and other satellite programming, but proctors were waiting for approval from Badri Mahal in Mumbai before airing these shows. The Jamea runs its own in-house audio news service, preparing a daily summary of world events of special note to the Bohra community. Some of the items are the same sort of general news that one might find in a Doordarshan or BBC broadcast, but the stories are selected to give particular emphasis to news from the Muslim world or relating to uniquely Islamic subjects. This summary, drawn from the Associated Press, Reuters, and a wide variety of other news sources, is broadcast in Arabic throughout the cam-

* As noted earlier, Lisanu-Dawat is the name given to the highly Islamized version of the Bohra dialect. Sometimes the term refers only to the written language, but in common parlance it is often used for the Arabized spoken language as well.

pus buildings on a custom-built sound system imported from the Netherlands.

Jamea students are not generally permitted to go to the cinema, so proctors broadcast a different video film for entertainment each week. The video library includes over a thousand titles, most of them English-language documentaries on scientific or cultural subjects, but with Arabic and Urdu offerings as well. In selecting their movies, proctors give a wide berth to Hollywood and Bollywood alike: if anything, Hindi films are subjected to even greater scrutiny than English ones. The most unwholesome influence seems to be not merely the violence and sexual laxity of the Mumbai cinema, but the *filmi* music: "Hindu boys are always walking around whistling," one student explained, "always singing 'Chole Ke Piche Kya Hai' ['What's under the Blouse?'—a popular, mildly risqué *filmi* song]. But we do not want to be distracted from our studies."

One area in which students are not only permitted, but encouraged, to take a break from their studies is in the realm of athletics. The Jamea has excellent sports facilities, including squash courts, volleyball/basketball courts, badminton courts, an airy, high-domed free-weight room, a recreational area for table tennis, practice rooms for Shotokan karate and other martial arts, two large swimming pools (with separate hours for male and female students), and even a nearby cricket pitch. The Jamea tries to foster physical as well as intellectual vigor. There are no elevators anywhere on campus: during the Jamea's 1970s renovation several were planned, but when Syedna Muhammad Burhanuddin toured the construction site he overruled the architects; young people, he said, should have the energy and fitness to climb five flights of stairs.

On the roof of the boys' dorm are both a solar-powered laundry and a garden. The terrace is a pleasant, leafy oasis, a place where students can relax, enjoy the warm weather, and (when Surat's air pollution permits) watch the sun set over the entire city. The garden is seen not as an escape from theological pursuits, but an extension of them—a metaphor for the intellectual delights of study. Not even esthetics are removed from the sphere of religion. The dominant architectural motif at Surat's Jamea is the hexagon: it can be seen on walls and banisters, floor tiles and ceiling tiles, doorjambs and window grills. This is done deliberately, to give the campus the subtle appearance of a great beehive: the Qur'an refers to knowledge as the sweetest thing in creation. "Knowledge is the sweet honey," one student explains, "and we are the busy bees whose job it is to collect it."

The Jamea's Karachi campus, home to 325 boys and 175 girls, is also a beehive of learning. This branch of the academy was opened in 1983 by the da'i, who appointed his brother Yusuf Najmuddin rector and tasked

him with overseeing the Jamea's modernization.³⁸ The walls and windows here are decorated with the same honeycomb motif as those in Surat, and the physics and chemistry labs here are just as well equipped. The language lab uses the very same high-tech Scandinavian equipment installed in the language lab at Harvard. In a display of both modernism and traditional Ismaili tahara, the Jamea gives its tap water antibacterial and ultraviolet treatment—it is said to be safer than bottled mineral water available elsewhere in the city.

If the science labs emphasize a forward-looking approach, the academy's physical setting highlights its ties to tradition. One enters the campus through an enormous stone portal, a full-scale replica of the Fatimi Gate in old Cairo. Inside, a delicate sandstone minaret (for symbolism rather than use by a muezzin) recreates another celebrated Fatimid monument. Nearby is a garden that Jamea officials say may be the only one of its kind in the world: in it grow every type of fruit and plant mentioned in the Qur'an. The collection includes such delicacies as figs, dates, bananas, grapes, and pomegranates. Since the soil and climate of Karachi are quite different from those of Arabia, coaxing all the different crops from the earth represents a considerable achievement in horticulture.

The traditional and modern dual emphases are integrated in the Karachi Jamea's libraries. In all of these archives, the subject matter is primarily theological, but the means of access and preservation are thoroughly up-to-the-moment. The photography library, for example, contains over four thousand images of the da'i and other high clerics, with each picture individually catalogued, filed, and carefully preserved in heat-sensitive storage. Nearly half of these photos (1,500 in November 1997, and the progress continues daily) have had all their data computerized for easier access, and there are plans to have the entire collection image-scanned onto compact discs.

The video and audio archives are similarly advanced. Every one of Syedna's waaz for the past twenty years has been videotaped, and all are available here. There are more than 700 tapes on file. The da'i delivers a waaz nine times each year (in addition to the daily service for the first nine days of Muharram), and to this number are added several hundred less formal khutbas on various occasions. For the viewing of these videocassettes the Jamea has its own screening room. With three dozen seats as plush as those in the first-class compartment of an airplane, the viewing room would hardly look out of place in the office of a Hollywood mogul.

The audiocassette library is even more extensive than the video collection: 16,000 tapes, each ninety minutes long, containing khutbas delivered by the various shahzadas. Each tape is color-coded both by speaker

and by subject: green for Syedna himself, red for Muharram, and so forth. All of the data are computerized and cross-referenced. If a listener requests a sermon delivered by Shahzada Qaidjohar Bhaisaheb on the topic of the dangers of riba, for example, it would all be available at the touch of a button. The audiovisual center is also the place from which a real-time telephone relay of the Surat exam questioning is broadcast on a public address system throughout the Karachi campus. Technical experts are trying to set up a videophone link for exams and religious services in the near future.

The library of zahir texts looks very much like the library of any small college in the United States. It has open stacks, and is organized on the Dewey decimal system. There are sections on many secular fields of study: literature, hard sciences, politics, even anthropology. There is also a good collection of general works on Islam, and such aspects of the faith as are shared with members of other denominations. Since hadith literature is not a major part of Bohra doctrine, I was surprised to see on these shelves the very same editions of al-Bukhari and al-Muslim that I had used in my own research. Shaikh Murtaza Africawala (the head administrator of the Karachi campus) assured me that hadith study is indeed an integral part of Bohra religious instruction, and that these two great compilers of tradition are studied despite their Sunni provenance.[39] In a glass-fronted cabinet toward the back of the room, ancient texts and antique manuscripts were being fumigated with insecticide to prevent their destruction by silverfish.

The greatest pride of the Karachi Jamea, however, is its collection of batini texts. This archive is said to be second in importance only to that of the Surat Jamea. Access to the collection is tightly controlled, and students at the academy are not permitted to study the texts stored here without specific permission. While Shaikh Murtaza was kind enough to show me this library, he did not (and I did not ask him to) open any of its batini texts for examination.

The archive is structured like a shrine, with (appropriately enough) the Qur'an at its very center. In fact, the shelving that houses the collection of Qur'ans is itself built in the form of a domed monument. Among the many editions contained inside are versions of the holy scripture in more than forty different languages, and a copy of the "Alifiya Qur'an" (this edition, the copyright of which was bought by Syedna Taher Saifuddin, is laid out in such a way that every line of the entire text begins with the letter "alif"). The library's high-vaulted ceiling is reminiscent of that of a rauzah: the batin library subtly (and simultaneously) conveys the symbolism of both the exterior and the interior of a Bohra holy site.

Starting in the left-hand corner of the chamber, the texts are arranged chronologically as the visitor circumambulates counterclockwise: the direction in which Bohra pilgrims circle the shrines of past da'is and syedis when performing ziyaret. The divisions of the batin texts surrounding the central collection of Qur'ans are as follows: (1) works written by imams prior to the concealment of Imam Mastur; (2) works written during the first period of concealment (dawr al-satr) in the second-fourth/eighth-tenth centuries; (3) texts written by the Fatimid imam-caliphs; (4) texts of Musta'li Ismaili da'is and syedis in Yemen; (5) works of da'is and syedis in India, up to Syedna Taher Saifuddin; (6) works of Syednas Taher Saifuddin and Muhammad Burhanuddin, as well as clothing and personal effects of these da'is; among the most highly prized texts are several *rasa'il* (epistles) displaying Taher Saifuddin's extraordinary mastery of classical Arabic, including one text written wholly without use of the letter "alif," another excluding any letter with dots (i.e., such letters as the Arabic equivalents of p, sh, x, b, n, z, f), and a third omitting both alifs *and* dotted letters; (7) rare manuscripts: only a few of the most prized texts are displayed here, often fine examples of Kufic calligraphy.

Jamea Exams

The Jamea's impact is not limited to the students themselves. Every year, in one of the most important rituals of the Bohras' annual cycle, the da'i uses Jamea graduation examinations as an opportunity to reassert the centrality of orthodox teachings to mu'mineen everywhere. Tens of thousands of believers converge on Surat every year to watch the candidates from both the Surat and Karachi academies prove their command of traditional and Western subjects alike. The description that follows is drawn from personal observation of the January 1995 examinations.

The exam period begins with a joyous parade through the neighborhood streets and into the Jamea's masjid. The procession is led by two brass bands, followed by half a dozen men brandishing drawn swords to remind the observers of their duty to defend the faith against all attacks. Next comes Syedna, carried on a wooden palanquin covered with flowers, beneath an enormous green umbrella. Hundreds of men march in front, in back, and on all sides of the palanquin as it weaves through the streets of the mohalla. Men, women and children line the parade route, bowing deferentially when the da'i draws near. Syedna blesses the onlookers, then enters the masjid to bless the students.

The Jamea students write seven papers in seven days: two in English (on social sciences and English language) and five in Arabic (on Fatimid history, law, literature, philosophy, and theology). The boys and girls sit

their exams separately; women may watch the boys' examination from a viewing gallery, but men are not permitted to watch the girls' exam. Students fill the masjid and the adjoining assembly hall, writing their essays on the floor rather than at desks. From a screened chamber above, Syedna provides spiritual guidance without which (a Jamea official tells me) the students would not be able to succeed.

The community element is strongest during the oral exams in theology. Syedna personally poses questions to students, and all the gathered audience members are called upon to put their own orthodoxy to the test along with the young men and women in the spotlight. All Jamea students write their exams during this week, but only a thrilled, terrified few are chosen for public interrogation by Syedna himself. Kneeling before the daʿi and four other examiners, speaking into a microphone that will broadcast their responses to an audience of thousands, the candidates know that they can be asked any question on any topic. The examiners have before them the full file on each candidate for a degree—often several dozen pages detailing everything from what grades he has received in chemistry to how clean he keeps his quarters to whether he has ever been absent from Muharram services. Said one student, with a tone of awe rather than paranoia, "The Jamea keeps better records than the CIA and the KGB combined."

In the lavishly decorated main hall of the masjid, its walls and ceiling engraved with the shahada, the names of all twenty-one imams and fifty-two daʿis, and stars composed of the names of the Prophet and his wasi in 24-karat gold calligraphy, each candidate silently prays to be delivered from the disaster of an unintentional misstatement. Each student addresses his responses directly to Syedna, pressing his palms together all the while in a gesture of deference. The Jamea's rectors do most of the interrogation, but the daʿi occasionally interjects a question of his own.

To be asked a question by Syedna himself is the greatest honor most of these youths could dream of, and each one both dreads and relishes his moment in the spotlight. For a few minutes, he is the center of attention for the entire Bohra community. The questions range from specific, technical queries about the nature of Imam Tayyib's veiled satr to deceptively simple invitations to describe the impact of Ashura on one's own life—blistering curveballs you can barely see coming, and lofted grapefruits you'd damn well better hit out of the park.

One student I observed had been asked to relate the story of the martyr Abbas in his own words, in Lisanu-Dawat rather than Arabic to insure a more spontaneous response. At several points in the narration, the examinee and the audience members alike broke into a passionate display of tears, chest-beating matam, and loud cries of "Ya Husain!" Students di-

rectly in Syedna's line of sight pounded their breasts with both fists and shouted at the top of their lungs, while some of those in the corners and behind pillars contented themselves with less vociferous forms of expression. This ritualized mourning, a staple of Muharram observance, occurred whenever an examinee's response dealt with some aspect of the Kerbala tragedy. Another candidate was asked to read a passage from the writings of Syedna Taher Saifuddin, whose collected works are a mainstay of the Jamea education. The student was told to recite the passage, and then translate it into Lisanu-Dawat. He gave his translation in rhyming couplets, a feat far beyond what he had been required to do. The audience swelled with low murmurs of appreciation.

The last day's oral exams were concluded with a bit of comic relief. An amil whose jurisdiction at that time included much of the Northeastern United States presented a parody of a cocksure trans-Atlantic student trying to impress his examiners with flashy answers. In a speech sprinkled with humorous Lisanu-Dawat malapropisms, the amil painted a picture of an American Bohra caught between two cultures, so enthralled with his Western education that he has forgotten the essence of his faith and culture. For the first time since exams began the audience erupted in waves of laughter, but the interlude served to instruct as well as entertain. Whatever else the Jamea examinations do, they force all in attendance to examine their own beliefs and reaffirm their own personal orthodoxy. Each year's orals are a test not merely of the students, but of the community as a whole. Each year's exuberant graduation festivities are a celebration not merely of individual triumph but of communal triumph as well.

PROFILES OF JAMEA STUDENTS

Khuzema

Khuzema* is a nineteen-year-old with a peripatetic past: he was born in Calcutta, to a family originally from the Gujarati town of Sidhpur, and grew up in Bangalore speaking Kannada as his primary language. Coming to the Jamea had always been a dream of his, but a dream that seemed unlikely ever to come true. Khuzema took the entrance exam fifteen times, and failed it the first fourteen. "Some students get in on the first try, some take the test again and again and again and never succeed," he says. "It took a long time, but in the end I was lucky."

After graduation, almost all students are offered jobs somewhere within the dawat network. Some become *jenabs* (teachers; lit., "masters")

*The names of these students have been changed.

at a madrasa or at the Jamea itself, some work in Badri Mahal, some train to be amils. In each case it is the dawat that decides which path any candidate will follow. "Syedna has full access to our records," Khuzema says, "and we know he will be able to make a better decision than we could make ourselves."

As an only child, Khuzema feels pressure to return to Bangalore and help run the family hardware store. Khidmat can be burdensome, especially for less privileged families—that's why it is called "service" rather than "reward." More than a few students must drop out of the Jamea in order to help support their parents. Khuzema hopes the dawat will be able to find work for him to do back in Bangalore, and he knows that if he does not like his initial posting he will be able to request a transfer after a year or two. But whatever job he is offered, he will gratefully accept. "I feel so lucky to be here," he says, "that I will eagerly repay Syedna in whatever way I can."

Qasim

A fifteen-year-old with a wispy mustache and a mouth full of orthodontia, Qasim insists on speaking to me in English. Although born in Sri Lanka and once fluent in Sinhalese, Qasim has lived in London for most of his life and relishes English conversation with what he calls "a native speaker." He expresses an intense distaste for most aspects of Indian life outside the walls of the Jamea, and eagerly looks forward to spending the upcoming Ramadan vacation back home in England. "So dirty and crowded here," he says, in an accent right off the BBC, "and any time you wish to go anywhere you've got to dicker with the rickshaw driver." What does he miss most about home? "Going out with friends—not doing anything bad, you understand, just going out. And all the luxury goods that are unavailable here, chocolate and the like. Having a bedroom to myself. Corn flakes for breakfast." He pauses, and sums it up in a word: "Living."

Despite the hardships and the homesickness, however, Qasim finds life at the Jamea itself to be surprisingly congenial. "Here it's so easy to live properly—it's all planned for you, no fuss and no bother." Back in London he always had to explain to his mates why he couldn't join them when they'd sneak a beer, or go to a rock concert, or stop for sausage and chips after school. Every time he'd slip away from class or a Saturday football match to say midday namaz, Qasim had heard all the snickers behind his back. "At the Jamea, life is so simple. I don't always have to be planning and balancing, don't have to justify myself to teachers, friends, or anybody. Syedna has laid out the proper path, and all we have to do is follow it."

Most fifteen-year-old boys spend a fair portion of their waking hours thinking about fifteen-year-old girls. Qasim and his Jamea classmates are no exception: "Once we are older, the dawat may help arrange a marriage—sometimes it helps the families introduce suitable partners, but then it is up to the boy and girl to see whether or not they like each other. For now, we have very little contact with the girls." I point out that several girls are walking across the courtyard, not far from where we are standing, and ask whether our very proximity might be deemed inappropriate. It all depends, Qasim says, what is in the heart: "There is no harm in seeing girls, or talking with them, but there is a danger. If we were looking at them in a lustful manner, that would be wicked. Only God knows what is in a person's heart, but at Judgment Day we all will know." Does that stop the boys from talking about girls? "Oh, no, we talk about them," he says. "So long as it is only talk."

For all his Westernized tastes, Qasim has no doubt that the Jamea is the right place for him to be. The regimentation of life here is an effective barrier against adolescent angst. All that is necessary is to follow Syedna's directions without question. No untrained mind could hope to understand the faith, or life itself, but the Jamea provides all the training a student could need. The dangers of rebellion are great indeed: Qasim notes that an acquaintance of his once read esoteric batin texts without permission and nearly went insane. "Only by confessing his sin to an amilsaheb was he able to restore his sanity," the transplanted Londoner says with a look of utter solemnity.

Abbas

A cold-drinks shop across the street from campus serves as the Jamea's version of a student brew house or *ratskeller*. The clientele here are all adolescents, and all wear community dress. The densely packed establishment is full of Bohra boys and girls sitting at separate (but closely adjoining) tables, never talking to each other, but more than occasionally sneaking a just-too-long peek.

Abbas is a large, hulking young man whose family runs a successful import-export business in Kenya. He carries himself not with the diffidence and shyness common to many Indian college students, but with a confident, self-assured swagger that makes him seem like an Australian outback rancher wearing a fake beard and Islamic costume for a Halloween party.

"From Harvard?" he asks. "Well, you must have an IQ of about 2,000." He says it without the least sense of intimidation, but also without an overtone of contempt. I assure him that Harvard accepts many people of sub-

average intellect, and that he may be speaking to one right now. Abbas seems unsurprised.

"Still," he says, "I guess that still means you're set for life." And you're not? I shoot back. "Yes," he concedes, "so long as I want a khidmat job. The dawat takes care of us pretty well, I suppose." Abbas tells me of the quick action taken by the authorities when the plague had hit Surat less than two months before.

In the fall of 1994, all of India fell into a panic over widespread outbreaks of the bubonic and pneumatic plague. In a few weeks the casualty rate had soared above a thousand, and India had been placed under international quarantine. The epidemic's epicenter was Surat, a place long labeled "India's Filthiest City." From the very first days of the outbreak, all Jamea students were forbidden to leave the campus: the streets of Surat might be choked with the rotting, waterlogged corpses of dead cattle, but the Jamea tus-Saifiya had always been a clean, modern, hygienic oasis in the middle of one of the subcontinent's worst urban wastelands. For the duration of the plague panic, all food and water were trucked into the Jamea from outside the city limits. The dawat rushed four doctors up from Mumbai, and all students were given doses of tetracycline as prophylaxis.

"As far away as Delhi and Calcutta," Abbas noted, echoing numerous press reports, "mobs had cleaned out all the chemists' supplies of tetra, but the dawat managed to secure enough for us all." In the following weeks experts would caution that this plague may not actually have been pneumatic plague after all, and that tetracycline used as prophylaxis can do more harm than good. But regardless of the medical community's post-crisis second-guessing, the dawat had provided what was at the time considered (locally, at least) to be the most effective, modern treatment available anywhere in the world—and had done so with a level of efficiency that put all the civil authorities of Surat to shame.[40]

For Abbas, the dawat's response to this crisis is powerful evidence of Syedna's power and wisdom. It is yet another reason for him to trust the da'i's direction, another argument for him to stay the course. Apart from his beard and clothing, Abbas gives the impression of being a young man who'd feel most comfortable with a pint of ale in one hand and a cigarette in the other, chatting up the barmaid at his local pub. I ask him what he most enjoys doing when he takes a break from his studies.

"I like to swim in the pool," he says, "or perhaps enjoy a cold Pepsi."

Dissidents and Control

DETERMINING COMMUNITY BOUNDARIES

One of the first tasks any anthropologist undertakes in conducting field-work is that of determining the boundaries of the community to be studied. As it happens, determination of boundaries is at the heart of the most important internal struggle to beset the Bohra community in more than a century. In a nutshell, the dawat defines the community as all individuals who accept Syedna's absolute authority over both spiritual and secular aspects of life. A small but persistent group of dissidents challenges this boundary, arguing instead for a definition that allots the da'i full sway over purely theological matters but denies his authority on any issue not directly linked to religion.

In my own fieldwork I have chosen to follow the realist rather than the nominalist definition of boundaries:[1] to me, it seems both more respectful and more accurate to use the subjects' own mental framework than to impose an arbitrary set of guidelines upon the community from outside. In accepting the subjects' own definitions, however, one must be aware that there are at least three overlapping definitions present within the Bohra community itself: (1) the dawat's theologically based definition; (2) the dissidents' culturally based definition; and (3) a loose amalgam of both definitions that is probably (I would suggest) the informal boundary set by most members of the community.

THE DAWAT POSITION: A COMMUNITY DEFINED BY THEOLOGY

The dawat, quite naturally, defines the community in strictly religious terms. In the view of the clergy, the society is bounded by the oath of mithaq: those individuals who take it and keep it are Bohras, those who do not are not. Any definition based on ethnicity or culture is explicitly rejected: "Membership is not inherited by birth," one dawat publication states. "The child, after reaching puberty, has to receive the religious oath

of fealty (misaq) to be enrolled as a follower." Fundamental to this enroll-
ment is acceptance of Syedna's dominance, without reservation or abridg-
ment: "The Dawoodi Bohra believes in the complete authority of the Dai
over all areas of his life."[2]

Community membership requires total subordination, yet such sub-
ordination (the dawat argues) is itself totally voluntary. Syedna Muham-
mad Burhanuddin emphasized this point in a ceremony at his father's
mausoleum in 1983, shortly after the orthopraxic directives discussed in
chapter 7 were put in place. Quoting surah 2:256 of the Qur'an, he said,
"We believe in and practice the Qur'an's directive '*la ikraha fi-al-deen*,'
which means that there is no force or coercion in religious matters. Who-
ever does not like or agree with our way of life, he can part with us. Nei-
ther do we forcibly take anyone into our fold, nor do we forcibly keep any-
one in our fold."[3]

Far from attempting to keep dissidents within the community by co-
ercion, the dawat has long encouraged them to make the schism official.
Anyone who objects to the da'i's pronouncements (their argument goes),
is perfectly free to seek religious leadership elsewhere. Syedna's nephew
Badrul Bhaisaheb Jamali told an Indian journalist, "Nobody is compelled
to give this misaq. If you want to give it, you give. If you don't, you don't
. . . And if you don't like this system, who's compelling you to remain a
Dawoodi Bohra?"[4] As one dawat tract notes, the community has survived
schism before: the united Ismaili denomination split into Nizari and
Musta'li factions (today's Khojahs and Bohras) during Fatimid times; the
ascension of the twenty-sixth da'i led to a parting of ways between the
Daudi and Sulaimani Bohras. These need not be the last such splits:

> The dissenters cannot, according to the basic tenets of the Bohra
> creed, challenge the authority of the Dai. Instead of creating
> painful conflicts in the community and harassing the faithful, they
> are free to follow the example of earlier dissenters and form an or-
> ganisation in tune with their own beliefs and in keeping with their
> hearts' desires.[5]

DISSIDENT DEFINITION: A COMMUNITY DEFINED BY ETHNICITY AND CULTURE

The dissident/reformist group, currently led by the scholar and journalist
Asghar Ali Engineer, puts forward a definition of community based on
shared custom, ethnicity, kinship, and broad underlying beliefs rather
than on a shared set of strictly delineated theological doctrines. As the late

reformist leader Noman Contractor put it, "Previously a person by birth was accepted as a Bohra and the oath of allegiance was merely a symbol of attaining an age to be able to know one's duties."[6] Engineer accepts Syedna's authority in the spiritual sphere while rejecting it in all other arenas: "He can tell me the meaning of the Qur'anic verse, fine. He can tell me how to pray, fine. He can tell me how nikah should be done, fine. But how can he interfere with my secular matters?"[7]

The disagreement, therefore, is enmeshed in a catch–22. The self-styled reformists claim to accept the daʿi's paramountcy on all points of faith—but reject the daʿi's authority to decide what these points of faith might be. Since the dawat regards absolute subordination to the daʿi in all aspects of life to be a central and irreducible tenet of the religion, the dissidents are drawing a distinction that the dawat regards as meaningless. Reformists say they follow the daʿi on all matters of religious dogma—they merely disagree with his interpretation of what constitutes religious dogma.

In the opinion of the reformists, it is they who are holding to traditional Bohra doctrine and the dawat that has strayed from age-old custom: "We are great inheritors of Fatimi Daʿwah and its glorious traditions," Engineer writes. "Unfortunately we have forgotten these traditions and are not even aware of our intellectual heritage."[8] The dissidents accuse the dawat of deliberately twisting doctrine to suit its own needs: "Syedna has been distorting and misinterpreting the Islamic principles."[9]

Engineer himself is a cordial, erudite, good-natured figure, not at all the bogeyman conjured up by orthodox rumor. He wears large-framed glasses, and keeps a whitening beard that would not look out of place on the most respectable of bhaisahebs. He outlined his basic position in a personal interview:

> The reformers are not challenging any religious tenet, we believe
> in all the tenets of the Bohra faith. Our society is mainly against
> dictatorship and unaccountability toward the community. These
> are our main planks. We don't even challenge the position of the
> daʿi, it is fine for the daʿi to be there, but he must govern according
> to the norms laid down for a daʿi. Our complaint is that Syedna
> has strayed from these norms . . . I am trying to reform, not
> leave.[10]

Highest among the dissidents' complaints are: (1) use of baraat to enforce compliance with dawat orders; (2) misuse of dawat funds; (3) monopolization of power by Syedna's family. All of these complaints have been voiced by mainstream orthodox Bohras as well, forcing one to probe

deeper for the precise point of irreconcilability. It seems to come not over any specific norm the da'i has established, but over the da'i's absolute right to establish such norms at all.

Despite protestations of loyalty to the da'i as supreme spiritual leader, the reformists appear to regard Syedna more as a teacher, one whose pronouncements are ideally worthy of respect but not necessarily obedience. This is in direct conflict not only with the position put forward by the dawat, but with that held (publicly, at least) by the mainstream of Bohra society. In some of his writings Engineer rejects the very idea of a formalized clergy, a concept central to Ismaili doctrine. He describes the requirement that nikahs and burials be conducted by amils as "un-Islamic practice,"[11] arguing that "[i]n Islam there is no concept of priesthood."[12]

Engineer's descriptions of the da'i and dawat are also difficult to reconcile with his professions of spiritual loyalty: "Muhammad Burhanuddin totally lacks any intelligence and leadership qualities," he said in an interview. "If Syedna has done anything, it is deviating Bohras from the true Islamic course, because he introduced many practices which have nothing to do with Islam."[13] In his writings Engineer has been similarly vehement: "Metaphorically speaking, the Bohra priesthood is a colonizer and the Bohras a colonized people. The priesthood humiliates, insults and tortures them and treats them as slaves."[14] The dawat is equally bitter in its criticism of Engineer. Pamphlets describe the rebel camp as "a ragbag element"[15] with virtually no roots in the Bohra populace, as "only a minuscule group"[16] that has "failed miserably to enlist the support of the community."[17] In private conversations, many orthodox Bohras are even less restrained. Whatever the rights or wrongs of the situation may be, the split seems to extend far beyond a mere disagreement over how to enforce an agreed-upon orthodoxy.

Dissidents claim to have the tacit encouragement of a majority of the community, but acknowledge that they have little overt support. When asked for an estimate of the movement's strength, Engineer replied, "All told, not more than 25,000 open members. I can say that secretly a large proportion, more than 60%, of the Bohras are having sympathy with us."[18] A dawat-affiliated source places the dissident strength at "as much as 2 percent."[19] This figure is quite in line with Engineer's tally of open membership.[20] The claims of the previous leader were even more modest. During the mid-1970s, when the city of Udaipur was in open rebellion, Noman Contractor wrote, "The Bohra reformist movement in Bombay has, as yet, a rather small following. It has about 200 members."[21]

It is unclear, also, how much contact Engineer has with any Bohras not explicitly linked to his group. He has been under official ostracism since

the 1970s, and any observant Bohra so much as speaking with him would face grave social consequences. The Central Board of Dawoodi Bohra Community (the main organization for the reformist movement) is largely a paper society operating out of Engineer's modest office in the Mumbai suburb of Santa Cruz.* In his 1989 survey of Bohras, Khojahs, and Memons (the only one of his works to present specific statistical evidence on the Bohras), Engineer publishes the results of a "representative" sample population, but this sample is limited (by the very fact of their participation) to nonorthodox households. Of the eighty Daudi families interviewed, few (if any) could be deemed strict observers of orthopraxy. Only nineteen of fifty households in Gujarat and one of thirty in Mumbai attended masjid on a regular basis. In all, 21.3 % of the respondents never went to masjid at all, and 15 % never prayed even in their own homes. Engineer admits that he encountered great resistance while conducting the survey, and that most potential respondents refused to participate without the permission of their amil. Such permission, not surprisingly, was unforthcoming.[22]

Relations between the dawat and the dissidents are so bad that I delayed interviewing Engineer until well after I had established my bona fides with the orthodox camp. "You have spoken with Syedna," a member of the da'i's immediate family advised me; "you have seen what sort of man he is. Now go talk with Engineer, and judge for yourself." I took the advice, but I leave the judgment to members of the community. Throughout the course of this study I have focused on the orthodox paradigm—in part because it has never been thoroughly articulated outside the Bohra community itself, while the dissidents have needed no interlocutor. Engineer has been a tireless and effective advocate of his positions: his writings present the reformist/dissident position with enough thoroughness to make extensive recapitulation in this study superfluous.

Owing in no small part to Engineer's own energy, in fact, the reformist camp has been very successful at dominating discussion of the Bohras in the wider Indian society. Indeed, virtually every mention of the Bohras made by outside writers, whether popular or scholarly, is traceable to dissident rather than orthodox sources. As Engineer notes, "The media has also played its role in widening the base of the reform movement."[23] Whenever the community is mentioned in a newspaper article, magazine feature, or academic conference, the angle is almost invariably that of the

*At the time of my visit in mid-1995, the same two-room walk-up (overflowing with books, newspaper clippings, and computer printouts) also served as headquarters for Engineer's Center for the Study of Society and Secularism and his Islamic Research Institute.

dissidents. The dawat's own policy is a contributing factor: the clergy has consistently shunned public debate, preferring instead to address Bohras with authoritative directives while building support outside the community through private discussions with political or religious leaders. On occasion the dawat has expressed its position in the Gujarati or Urdu press, but has made little effort to influence the perceptions of Indian society at large.

From the earliest days of the movement, a disproportionate number of the reformists have been Western-educated, cosmopolitan, and trained in modern professions like law, medicine, academia, accountancy, or journalism; it is perhaps no coincidence that the two most prominent leaders of the movement have had the surnames Contractor and Engineer. This outlook has made it easier for the reformists to gain support from members of the Indian intelligentsia outside the community. As Theodore P. Wright, Jr., notes, "Their aim, it would seem, has been to goad the Indian authorities into action favorable to their cause as much as it is to convince their co-religionists."[24] One petition of support for the dissidents was signed by 480 intellectual figures (214 of them academicians), including such fixtures of the all-India *bhadralok* as justices Krishna Iyer and V. M. Tarkunde, scholars Romila Thapar, Bipan Chandra, K. N. Panikkar, Ram Gopal, Syed Wahiuddin, and Uday Mehta, and writers Ali Ashraf and Iqbal Masud.[25]

As both a scholar and a journalist Engineer has been indefatigable in defense of his cause. In his capacity as an academic, he has written at least thirty-four books and countless pamphlets on Islamic topics, many of which contain at least passing critiques of the Bohra dawat. In his capacity as a journalistic commentator he has not only penned innumerable columns in a variety of publications, but established himself as the only Bohra source regularly consulted by Indian reporters. In a review of several hundred articles from the Indian media dealing with Bohra issues, I found Engineer quoted considerably more frequently than any other source, including Syedna himself. Apart from these two, no figure inside or outside the dawat was cited more than a few times; the da'i, in almost every case, was quoted from a press release rather than a personal interview. The dissidents may not have attracted much overt support within the community, but they have been winning the public relations war outside it.

The newsmagazine *India Today*, for example, which is generally considered one of the nation's most responsible and professional publications, described mithaq as "obnoxious," Syedna's rule as a "dictatorship," and dawat policies as "atrocities" in the space of a single article.[26] Another

article asserts that the da'i "has 28 brothers,"[27] an error blatant enough to indicate that no dawat source was even consulted. Press accounts often lift their text from dissident publications virtually word for word. To cite just one example, *Bombay* magazine's description of royal privilege ("every member of the family gets Rs 4,000 a month in addition to furnished flats, chauffeur-driven cars, servants and food from a central kitchen")[28] is taken essentially verbatim (and without attribution) from Noman Contractor's pamphlet *The Bohras.*[29]

Engineer contends that the power traditionally exercised by past da'is had never been regarded as absolute until the twentieth century, and that the scope of obedience demanded by the current mithaq oath is a modern innovation. He cites a version of the mithaq oath allegedly dating from 560 A.H. (a version he says was compiled by the third da'i, Syedna Hatim ibn Ibrahim, from pre-Fatimid texts) in which no such scope is claimed.[30] He asserts that Syedna Taher Saifuddin accepted a recently revised version of the text of the mithaq to expand his own area of control, and that Syedna Muhammad Burhanuddin has continued to use this allegedly fraudulent text.[31] The dawat, of course, strenuously rejects this interpretation, and argues that it is unsubstantiated by any documentary evidence.

Even as late as the nineteenth century, Engineer argues, da'is did not claim unfettered control over the secular lives of community members. In cases where da'is happened to exert such control, he says, it was a matter of policy rather than doctrine:

> As for the secular authority, the Syedna has no religious jurisdiction. It may be argued that the dais in the past did exercise secular authority also, and there is some truth in this assertion. But it should also be understood that exercise of secular authority by the dais in the past was part of their social contract with the community. In other words it was done with the unspoken consent of the community, not against its will.[32]

It is unclear why such control should be deemed legitimate when exercised with the "unspoken consent" of the group, yet illegitimate when (as is the case today) all observant Bohras give their explicit, verbal consent both at the taking of mithaq and at its reaffirmation every year.

HISTORICAL BACKGROUND OF REFORMIST AGITATION

The issues that motivate the dissidents today are in large measure the same issues that motivated the original group of reformists early in the last century: clerical privilege, dawat control of community financial re-

sources, and the enforcement of dawat policy by means of rigid social sanctions. The issues of financial control and baraat warrant further discussion here.

The current dissident movement had its genesis in a wide-ranging power struggle between Syedna Taher Saifuddin and the sons of the Bohra business tycoon Sir Adamji Pirbhai.* During the latter half of the nineteenth century, following a bitter internal dispute over succession, the da'is had seen their wealth and societal authority decline markedly. Toward the end of the century this power vacuum was partly filled by Pirbhai, a self-made industrialist who amassed a fortune as a contractor for the British army in India. He served as sheriff of Mumbai in 1897–1898, and rivaled the da'i in influence (although never challenging his authority) until his death in 1913. The demise of Pirbhai, the ascension of Taher Saifuddin in 1915, and a financial boom fueled by World War I trading profits all served to strengthen the dawat's hand in its bid to reclaim community predominance. The first test came almost immediately after Taher Saifuddin's installation: Bohras fleeing sectarian violence in Bhopal sought shelter in Ujjain, and both the dawat and Pirbhai's sons struggled to gain mastery of the relief efforts. Since Bhopal was a nominally independent princely state, the three-sided negotiations over the aid (and the credit that would accrue to whoever provided it) proved highly complex.

The refugees had barely been returned home when another conflict broke out, the most important milestone in the reformist/dissident movement until the 1970s. In 1917 the da'i purchased several parcels of real estate, including properties that now make up dawat head offices at Badri Mahal in downtown Mumbai. The funds used for the purchase were said to have come from the *gulla* (donation box) at the nearby mausoleum of Seth Chandabhai.† Ibrahimji Adamji and his brothers (the sons of Sir Adamji) filed a lawsuit, claiming that gulla funds belonged to the community at large and could not be spent by the da'i without community permission. By the time the case was heard, the sons and their prime supporters had been excommunicated.

The central issue in the case was that of Syedna's degree of control: the plaintiffs argued that the da'i had narrowly circumscribed rights over community property and narrowly defined jurisdiction over secular matters.

*The struggle began under Taher Saifuddin's two immediate predecessors: Syedna Muhammad Burhanuddin ibn Abdul-Qadir (the forty-ninth da'i) and Syedna Abdullah Badruddin (the fiftieth da'i), but became considerably more entrenched during the early twentieth century. The early reformist leader's name is sometimes spelled Adamjee Peerbhoy.
†Also spelled Chandabhoy.

Syedna's attorneys argued that the oath of mithaq and long-standing Bohra tradition gave the da'i virtually unlimited control over all aspects of believers' lives. The text of mithaq seems to support them: in the version cited in court, all oath-takers must agree when told that "you shall accept the order of the Dai of the Imam in all things."[33] The judgment rejected the absolutist claims made by the da'i's British attorney, but the dawat's appeal was settled in December 1921 by a consent decree. The da'i was permitted to place another set of gullas at Bohra shrines with plaques clearly advising donors that the money would be entirely at the disposal of Syedna.[34] Legal niceties aside, the dawat seemed to have won the battle on the ground: Syedna bought and moved into the Pirbhai family's Malabar Hill mansion.[35]

The next major court battle was the Burhanpur durgah case of 1925. Ever since the reign of the fiftieth da'i, Syedna Abdullah Badruddin, the dawat and reformist dissidents had been wrangling over the management of Burhanpur's Madrasa-i Hakimiya. By the 1920s relations had soured to the point that many key opposition figures had been excommunicated, and a group of students and trustees were prevented from visiting the *durgah* (mausoleum) of Syedi Hakimuddin. The dissidents sued, charging that their excommunications were invalid and that they had been illegally denied permission to visit an important community shrine. When the ruling was finally delivered in 1931, both sides again claimed victory.[36] As in the Chandabhai gulla case, there were elements of the judgment to both please and disappoint either side. It is hardly coincidental, Theodore Wright correctly notes, that the dawat-dissident controversy should flare up—and find its expression in litigation—during the period of British colonialism. He quotes an observation of Bernard Cohn on the Thakurs and notes its applicability to the Bohras: "With the coming of the British . . . the basis of the solidarity of the group was cut away; they no longer had to cooperate from fear of outside subjugation . . . The courts provided an excellent battleground in which to carry out a fight."[37] In fact, Abbasali Najafali's tract on Bohra marriage law (one of the very few books by a dawat-affiliated author meant for distribution beyond the community) implicitly acknowledges this phenomenon: "The recent frequent tendency of the malcontent members of the Dawoodi Bohra community to have recourse to the Law Courts necessitates that special features of the law applicable to the Dawoodi Bohras should be stated as based on their authoritative texts."[38]

The mood of the dissidents during this early period can be judged from the only major reformist text to have been published at the time.[39] In the *Gulzare Daudi for the Bohras of India* (1920), author Mian Bhai Mullah Abdul Husain is motivated largely by the issues of educational control at

stake in the Madrasa-i Hakimiya dispute. "It is true that Bohras are industrious and enterprising," he states, "yet 95 p.c. of them are bigoted religionists, superstitious, and ignorant [sic], the priest class though partially educated in Arabic support the reactionary movement against education, saying that the study of English conduces to the loss of faith in Islam."[40] He urges educational reform "so that they may keep pace with the advancing world," and asks the da'i to "raise his followers in the estimation of their fellow brethren of other communities by encouraging secular education amongst his followers and spending a few lacs out of his ten to 13 lac income on education."[41]

Dissidents expressed concern about the dynastic privileges of Syedna's extended family. Abdul Husain reproached "[t]he dai or the Head priest who lives luxuriously in palaces,"[42] noting that "[a]s outsiders were not allowed to compete for this coveted high post since 1256 A.H. (i.e., for the last 80 years) there has been unusual agitation, heart burning, and discontentment amongst the Bohra learned Mashaikhs, and the present troubles at Bombay and Ujjain originate from a similar motive."[43] The author of the *Gulzare Daudi,* however, is careful not to challenge the da'i's religious authority directly: "In these days of liberty, freedom and democracy the bona-fide reformers do not claim any rival spiritual position or divine inspiration as Jafer, Ali, Suleman, Hibtulla, or Abdulhussain of Nagpore did,[44] but respectfully and humbly pray Syedna to restore the systematic teaching of the Esoteric doctrines of the Fatimid Lodge, as his predecessors did."[45] In fact, Abdul Husain regards the da'i's unlimited authority as a potential vehicle for the cause of reform:

> The progressive party of the Bohras welcome the autocratic spiritual rule of their Head priest, for they fully realise that this power if well & rightly directed will accustom the rude followers of his faith to the manners of Islam and the bigoted Bohras will gladly take to secular training in the primary and secondary schools if the training is combined with religious training.[46]

Over the course of the following decades, Syedna Taher Saifuddin wound up enthusiastically endorsing the very same program of educational modernization shunned by his predecessor. The issues at the heart of the Madrasa-i Hakimiya dispute have gone from dissident demand to dawat orthodoxy. But on the larger issue—degree of control legitimately exercised by the da'i over the lives of believers—modern-day reformers hold a position quite similar to that of the first dissidents. The tone of debate, however, has coarsened considerably: whereas Abdul Husain had described the da'i as a figure "for whose long life I as his humble follower

always pray,"[47] the dissident H. K. Sanchawala wrote in a forward to the 1977 reprinting of the *Gulzare Daudi* that the text had been a bid "for freedom from the clutches of the absolute and despotic and exploitative powers of the Mullaji Saheb."[48]

For a brief time in 1936 a reformist group coalesced in the Gujarati town of Dahod,[49] but the next milestone in the movement did not come until after Independence. In keeping with the traditional Bohra policy of political quietism, the dawat gave little support to the Indian National Congress during the movement to end colonial rule. To the extent that the da'i became entangled in politics, it was to provide measured backing to the Muslim League or (until very late in the colonial period) to British institutions of government. While this stance stemmed from religious doctrine more than political motives, it provoked retaliation from Congress during the early years of the new republic. Home Minister Morarji Desai piloted the Prevention of Excommunication Act through the Bombay Legislative Assembly. In debates he described excommunication as "a monstrous thing for any Government to tolerate."[50]

The act establishes the following definition: "'[E]xcommunication' means the expulsion of a person from any community of which he is a member by depriving him of rights and privileges which are legally enforceable by a suit of civil nature by him, or on his behalf as such a member."[51] The pivotal portion of the act is section 3: "Notwithstanding anything contained in any law, custom or usage for the time being in force to the contrary, no excommunication of a member of any community shall be valid and shall be of any effect."[52] Although the act did not specify the Bohras by name, there was no other denomination for whom excommunication was a salient issue in Mumbai in the 1950s, and the Bohras were the only group to challenge the act in court.

Even Engineer concedes that Congress was motivated in part by desire for payback: "The Congress leaders, partly inspired by the ideals and partly by way of political vendetta, decided to legislate against the practice of excommunication."[53] The act was upheld by the Bombay High Court in 1953, but overturned by the Supreme Court of India in 1961 on the grounds that it interfered with the free practice of religion. A denomination could not excommunicate its members over purely nonspiritual arguments, the court ruled, but the government had no standing to prevent religious groups from establishing and enforcing theological bases for membership. Justice C. J. Sinha wrote, "As the Act invalidates excommunication on any ground whatsoever, including religious grounds, it must be held in clear violation of the right of the Dawoodi Bohra community under Article 26(b) of the Constitution."[54]

Since the case first made its way though the courts, however, the dawat has replaced excommunication with baraat: a form of social boycott that is technically distinct from theological excommunication but achieves virtually the same result. In either instance, the individual under sanction is barred (in practice, at least) from access to religious services or contact with orthodox members of the community.

In the 1960s the reform/dissident movement, now working under the name Pragati Mandal, was revitalized under the leadership of Noman Contractor. A self-made industrialist, he was the first figure to bring protest to a critical mass since the challenges of the Pirbhai brothers forty years earlier. During this period the Gujarati city of Godhra became a hotbed of dissent: some rebels even performed nikahs and funerary rituals without the permission or blessing of the dawat.[55]

Dissidents in the Bohra community of Tanzania managed to cause considerable embarrassment to Syedna Muhammad Burhanuddin in 1968. The previous year, in a reversal of the measured laissez-faire policy maintained by Syedna Taher Saifuddin in his later years, the new da'i's brother Yusuf Najmuddin had traveled to East Africa in order to bring the Bohra populations of Kenya, Tanzania, and Uganda into closer compliance with dawat policies. When Syedna Muhammad Burhanuddin paid a visit to East Africa the dissidents struck back: in response to their pressure, the government of Tanzania expelled the da'i for allegedly violating foreign-exchange regulations in the purchase of air tickets for his entourage. The sequence of events remains murky, but the fact that Contractor was in East Africa at the time fueled suspicions of his involvement.[56]

Contractor severed his ties with Pragati Mandal after this incident and for a time retired from active opposition to the dawat,[57] but returned to a leadership position during the "Udaipur rebellion" to come. The issues raised by Contractor during the 1960s and 1970s were the same ones that had been raised by the Pirbhais: Syedna's control over secular life, de facto excommunication, financial accountability, and royal privilege. Contractor portrayed himself as upholding the traditional position and outlook of the dawat from Fatimid times to the mid-nineteenth century. In his view all da'is up to the forty-seventh (Abdul-Qadir Najmuddin) had been righteous, but "from the time of the forty-seventh Dai onward the members of the Dai's family appear to have developed a lust for power and wealth."[58] In 1978 he estimated the da'i's income at Rs 43 million in India and Rs 31.3 million from abroad, plus Rs 18 million in India and Rs 12 million abroad from gullas whose ownership had been clarified since the Chandabhai gulla case: "A metal plate is fixed on these charity boxes stating that this collection is the personal perquisite of the Head Priest as the Dai of the community."[59]

Contractor's accusations of clerical privilege, like his revenue figures, must be examined closely. He asserts that "the family members total 182, and style themselves Shahzadas and Shahzedis" although "[n]one of the family members except two holds any religious office in the religious organization."[60] Each family member, he charges, receives Rs 4,000 per month, a free bungalow or apartment, a chauffeur-driven car, a central kitchen and servants.[61] In fact, only twenty-four members of the family (fifteen shahzadas and nine shahzedis)[62] are called "princes" and "princesses," titles reserved for the sons and daughters of a da'i. While the core members of the family are housed in Saifee Mahal and have access to a central kitchen and servants (but not a chauffeured car each), the level of material privilege here is overrated by a writer who is unlikely ever to have set foot inside the compound. The assertion that no family members (his two exceptions are presumably the mazoon and the mukasir) are clerics is quite false: nearly *all* of Syedna's closest family members hold clerical titles, and most are deeply engaged in dawat affairs. Members of the Qasr-e Ali run the madrasa program and the Jamea tus-Saifiya, dispense batin theology, and officiate at countless rituals. A more accurate charge would be that the royal family *monopolizes* religious office than that they avoid it.

CONFLICT IN UDAIPUR

The most recent and most dramatic major challenge to dawat authority came during the 1970s, in the city of Udaipur. Located in Rajasthan, Udaipur has no Bohra pilgrimage sites, but a very large Bohra population. Contemporary sources estimated the number of Bohras living here at 15,000–20,000 concentrated largely in four adjoining neighborhoods.[63] Amazingly for a Bohra community, throughout much of the 1970s and 1980s Udaipur was in a state of open rebellion against the dawat's authority.

The issue here was one of power more than of money. After some initial hostility in the immediate post-Independence years, the dawat had been a steady supporter of the Congress Party since the 1950s. In Udaipur, as elsewhere, local dawat authorities urged Bohras to vote for Congress candidates and supported the candidacy of Bohras on Congress slates for local offices. The city flared into disputation during the course of a municipal election in 1970, when the candidates selected by the amil in the four Bohra-dominated wards were challenged by a group called the Bohra Youth Association. The election turned into a power struggle between the popular, left-leaning "Youthis" and the dawat loyalists ("Shababis"), with

the Bohra population of Udaipur forced to declare its loyalty to one camp or the other. The Youthis gained the upper hand, and won election in all four wards. When they extended their reach from the political to the religious sphere and gained control of all the Bohra mosques in Udaipur, they were placed under baraat.[64]

Three years later Syedna sent his eldest son, Shahzada Qaidjohar Bhaisaheb Ezzuddin, to try to bring the Youthis back into the flock. What actually happened next is open to multiple interpretations. In the dawat's version of events, a violent Youthi mob besieged Qaidjohar Bhaisaheb, kept him trapped in his lodging without food and water for three days, and caused him to flee the city for refuge in the town of Galiakot seventy-five miles away. In the dissidents' version, Youthis told Qaidjohar Bhaisaheb of their displeasure with the local amil and other dawat officials—perhaps quite forcefully: Contractor concedes that "a thousand members of the Bohra Youth Association gheraoed* the Shahzada"[65] but says they did not mistreat him. In Galiakot, Qaidjohar Bhaisaheb joined his father and other Bohra pilgrims who had assembled to observe the urs of Syedi Fakhruddin at the martyr's durgah.

Among the pilgrims were many of the wives of Udaipur Bohras, who had come to the holy town ahead of their husbands in order to secure space in Galiakot's limited accommodations. In some dissidents' version of events, dawat officials incited other pilgrims to attack the Udaipur women. Many of the women, these sources allege, were beaten and humiliated right outside the lodging of the da'i himself.[66] In the versions presented by other dissidents, the outrage is significantly less extreme. Contractor describes the riot with barely a sentence: "[S]ome supporters of the Bohra Youth Association were beaten at Galiakot."[67] In the dawat's version, it was Youthi men who initiated the riot in Galiakot, and loyalist pilgrims who were the primary victims.

The Youthis' break with the dawat was unequivocal, but many (possibly most) dissidents maintained at least a nominal respect for Syedna's authority. The dawat's actions at Galiakot were blamed not on the da'i himself but upon his relatives:

> It is alleged that all important decisions are taken by Yusuf Najmuddin and a small coterie of other brothers around him . . . It is also maintained by some people that the high priest himself is in favour of following a soft-line towards the reformist section but Dr. Najmuddin . . . advocates hard-line and his voice is decisive.[68]

*In common Indian parlance, a *gherao* is a vociferous protest—often bordering on a riot—generally directed toward a government official or other officeholder.

This conspiracy-theory interpretation of the da'i's actions enables dissidents to oppose acts taken in the name of Syedna, even to reject pronouncements made by the da'i before witnesses, yet still maintain at least the semblance of respect. In the 1970s Noman Contractor asserted that dawat policy was set not by Syedna but by his brothers, Shahzadas Yusuf Bhaisaheb Najmuddin, Shabbir Bhaisaheb Nuruddin, and Qasim Bhaisaheb Hakimuddin. "The hierarchy," Contractor wrote, "has reduced the internal position of the Dai to such an extent that he is financially and otherwise dependent on the sweet will of the hierarchy."[69]

From 1973 onward, every person with any tie to the Youthis was placed under baraat. The number of those boycotted has been put at 10,000,[70] which would mean (if the estimates given above are accurate) that between one-half and two-thirds of the population of Udaipur was under baraat. The ban was so widespread that the copy of *Gulshan-e Malumat* that I borrowed from a mullah in Mumbai had been disfigured: in this directory of Bohra notables throughout the world, every VIP in Udaipur had had his name obscured and his face scratched out.

A system of identity cards was instituted in order to distinguish loyalists from rebels. Even after religious services were resumed, entry was strictly limited to inhabitants with the proper papers. Engineer (who joined the ranks of the dissident leadership at this point, helping found a Mumbai group to support the Udaipur rebels) claims that loyalists initially were only 5% of the Bohra population of Udaipur, but grew more numerous when faced with the prospect of baraat. H. S. Verdia, another dissident source, writes that the Youthis comprised 85% of the local populace; both estimates, of course, must be treated as partisan claims.[71] Youthis and loyalists engaged in pitched battles throughout the Bohra mohallas of Udaipur, and in 1976 civil authorities had to impose curfew to restore order.[72] Soon the rebels established themselves as the dominant party and continued to hold de facto power for many years. With the Youthis in control, it was impossible for the dawat to separate them out for punishment without imposing sanctions on the community as a whole: all religious observances were suspended in Udaipur for several years. Youthis tried to turn the dawat's ban against the clergy itself: they brought in reporters to interview and photograph about 200 dissident couples unable to have nikah performed for two years. On March 16, 1975, 106 of these couples were united by non-Bohra qadis imported from Mumbai in a joint ceremony arranged by Noman Contractor.[73]

Only gradually, over the course of the 1980s, have the Bohras of Udaipur rejoined the rest of the Bohra community. Generally this has involved individual and group reassertions of loyalty, repledging of mithaq,

and (in many cases) unconditional apology for past actions. In 1983 the Youthis were still in control. Badrul Bhaisaheb Jamali, nephew of the daʿi, told an interviewer, "In Udaipur I am not in a position to go for ziyaret to our cemetery. If I go they'll throw stones at me. Even today."[74] Later that year an attempt by Mazoon Saheb Khuzema Bhaisaheb Qutbuddin to bring breakaway Youthis back to the fold was unsuccessful.[75]

In three brief research expeditions to Udaipur (in November 1993, March 1995, and October 1997) I observed no signs of open discord. Some sources have told me that the Youthi/Shababi divide is still alive, and that the Youthis today are merely more discreet about challenging the dawat head-on. As recently as 1995 Engineer claimed that the dissidents were still in full (if covert) control of Udaipur.[76] In March 1998, however, Syedna made his first visit to Udaipur in thirty-two years, and according to dawat source Shaikh Mustafa Abdulhussein, "many of the dissidents, including some of their leaders, have now returned to the fold."[77]

NATHWANI COMMISSION

Meanwhile, in Mumbai, the Janata Dal victory in the 1977 national elections gave new life to the dissident cause in the dawat's own backyard. When the Congress Party was defeated in the first elections after Indira Gandhi's Emergency, the orthodox Bohras were left without their customary bastion of political support. The reformists had always maintained contacts with the more left-leaning circles of the Indian intelligentsia, so when Janata Dal came to power they found they suddenly had old friends in high places.

The oldest friend in the highest place was Prime Minister Morarji Desai, whose efforts to outlaw dawat excommunication were not forgotten by any parties to the conflict. Desai now remained aloof from the dispute, however, for fear of alienating the Muslim electorate. The reformists quickly enlisted the support of the populist leader Jayaprakash Narayan, whose advocacy group Citizens for Democracy established a commission specifically at the dissidents' request[78] to study what the report's very title describes as "the alleged infringement of human rights of reformist members of the Dawoodi Bohras in the name of the High Priest." Narayan himself, however, disavowed the commission before it even got underway:

> I had never associated myself with the so-called inquiry and further make it clear that politicians and political considerations should not be allowed to infringe upon religious susceptibilities or wound them in any way. Every religious community must have

the freedom to resolve its internal religious affairs according to the dictates of its faith and beliefs.[79]

Nonetheless, the Dawoodi Bohra Commission was formed by Narayan's Citizens for Democracy, and issued its report in 1979. Popularly known as the Nathwani Commission after the name of its chairman Narendra Nathwani, it was composed of three Hindus, two Muslims, and one Parsi (Aloo Dastur, who withdrew before the report was filed). None of the commission members were Bohras.[80]

As the report's authors acknowledge, the information supplied to the Nathwani Commission came almost entirely from dissident sources: "The Syedna Saheb . . . decided to boycott the Commission and to dissuade the orthodox members of the community from co-operating with the Commission."[81] Opposition was intense: in April 1978, ninety-two orthodox Bohras were injured during a protest that degenerated into a scuffle with police.[82] The Nathwani Commission claimed to have received questionnaires from 1,075 individuals out of the 5,000 solicited,[83] but the Bohra community at large does not seem to have welcomed the commission's intrusions. V. M. Tarkunde, a commission member and for a time its chairman, admitted that even as early as 1977 he had received "thousands" of telegrams and letters opposing the investigation,[84] which would mean that many more Bohras actively rejected the commission's survey than chose to participate. For a time, protests were coming at a rate of 300–400 letters and 600 telegrams per day.[85]

Unsurprisingly, the commission's report turned out to be a virtual recapitulation of the principal dissident complaints. On the issue of Qasr-e Ali privilege, the report charged, "The family at present has 188 members and each member of the family behaves as a Chhota [little] Potentate."[86] The commission's information is often drawn directly from dissident pamphlets: on finances, for example, the Nathwani report uses reformist estimates for dawat resources without acknowledging the source of these figures. The report cites rates for the sila-fitra tax as Rs 5.74 per adult, Rs 2.87 per child or fetus in the womb.[87] Since fitra is pegged to the market price of silver and consequently fluctuates on a regular basis, it hardly seems coincidental that the rates quoted are exactly those cited—five years earlier—by Noman Contractor in the polemical pamphlet *New Quest 7*.[88] The commission certainly relied on this issue of *New Quest* for other material, as it cites the publication elsewhere.[89] Figures for haqqun nafs and ziyafat contributions likewise seem to be borrowed without attribution.[90] The report's authors state their opposition to the very idea of dawat taxation: "[W]e are satisfied that at least three imposts namely Zaka [zakat], Sila Fi-

tra and Haqqun Nafs are being collected as compulsory exactions, and that even the other collections are not entirely voluntary."[91]

The commission's harshest words, however, are reserved for the institution of mithaq. The version cited in the Nathwani report, as the authors acknowledge, is taken directly from *New Quest*.[92] Of the mithaq oath, the Nathwani authors are unsparing: "This document is virtually a charter of slavery . . . unabashed inhumanity"; "atrocious and monstrous"; "Misaq in its present form is absolutely oppressive, harsh and inconsistent with human rights."[93]

Ironically, the Nathwani authors concede the very point at the heart of the orthodox/reformist dispute over mithaq—the report considers the text to be genuine, and not a nineteenth- or twentieth-century revision as alleged by dissidents.[94] The report, while denouncing mithaq's impact, implicitly accepts the dawat's interpretation of the oath's scope and meaning:

> Paragraph 4* makes it clear that obedience to the order is demanded not only in religious matters but "in all things," that is to say, in all the secular affairs also. This para leaves the oath-maker in no doubt about the consequences of breaking the oath. As soon as he breaks the oath, he automatically places himself outside the pale of religion.[95]

After recognizing mithaq as an oath of total submission, the report rejects it in its entirety: "It is difficult to see how a human being with any sense of self-respect can take such [an] oath, or having taken it when he was a minor can ever think of respecting it."[96] The Nathwani report recommends that the oath either be drastically rewritten or outlawed by the government.[97] In any case, the commission urges, "Baraat or social boycott should be made illegal and penalised as an offence."[98]

As an extragovernmental commission with no official standing, the Nathwani Commission was unable to put its recommendations into force. Neither the Janata Dal government nor the Congress one that soon un-

*"And you shall accept the order of the Dai of Imam in all things. And you shall not use that thing which the Dai shall forbid you, and you shall not take steps (toward it). You shall love him whom the Dai loves. You shall be enemy to him with whom the Dai is hostile. You shall war against him against whom the Dai makes war. Any person transgressing those engagements to the Dai he is outside the pale of religion. Whether he be great or small, whether he is a close relation or a distant one you shall not have any intercourse with him. You shall not correspond with him openly or secretly. You shall not do any act calculated to be friendly to him. And by no manner or means or pretence shall you see the enemy of the Dai. The enemy of the Dai is your enemy" (Nathwani 1979: 21). Dawat sources note that this translation omits a vital component: all versions of the *mithaqnama* use the formulation "imam and his da'i" wherever the above translation uses "da'i" alone.

seated it took any action on the report, a fact that left the reformists demoralized and greatly weakened. In 1980 A. B. Shah charged in his introduction to Contractor's collection of essays that "political parties in India have no conscience and . . . any government formed by them is bound to be devoid of integrity and the courage of conviction."[99]

Over the past two decades, legal battles have died down to an occasional skirmish. Dawat attorney Eban Faizulabhoy notes that until a generation or two ago very few Bohras went to law school, and those few were often affiliated with the dissident camp. (Prominent orthodox Bohra attorneys have included Abbasali Najafali, who represented the dawat in the Burhanpur durgah case; Shaikh Yusuf Muchhala, who dealt with most of the Udaipur litigation; and Shaikh Aziz Ahmedi, India's last chief justice of the twentieth century). Ever since the Chandabhai gulla case the dawat has relied heavily on Parsi attorneys, generally from the preeminent Mumbai firm of Mulla & Mulla. Faizulabhoy, now a partner at Mulla & Mulla himself, was mentored by the Parsi lawyer who had handled many dawat cases in the early years of Indian independence. An urbane, sophisticated man who would seem quite at home in the most cosmopolitan circles of Mumbai, Delhi, London, or New York, Faizulabhoy regards dissidents like Asghar Ali Engineer with the same professional detachment he would regard any legal adversary. "There's still plenty of work," he says, "but it's not like the hectic times of the 1970s."

Since the early 1980s the dissident movement (under the leadership of Asghar Ali Engineer) has contented itself with steady, low-key opposition rather than outright rebellion as in Udaipur. The relative lack of open conflict between the two camps, however, does not indicate a softening of mutual distrust and harsh sentiments. Contractor's collection, published a few years before his death, is directed "to those who have not yet completely gone over to the Devil in the name of religion."[100] In 1995 Engineer said that he had been assaulted by dawat supporters four times during the 1970s and badly beaten in Egypt in 1983, but that he had had no violence directed at him since then. He noted the sharp contrast in dawat responses to reformist conferences over the course of a decade: A convention in 1981 was disbanded (he said in an interview) when "we were surrounded on all sides by fanatical wolves." Ten years later, at the eighth All-World Conference in Mumbai, "not a stone was thrown. Not even five persons gathered to oppose us. This is the [only] difference between the seventies, early eighties and the nineties: the violence has stopped."[101]

The fragility of this détente was shown on February 13, 2000. In an unlucky coincidence, Engineer and Syedna Muhammad Burhanuddin happened to be traveling on the same flight from Indore to Mumbai. By Engi-

neer's account, Syedna delayed the plane's departure by half an hour to suit his own schedule, and did nothing to restrain his followers from berating the dissident leader throughout the flight; on arrival, Engineer was attacked by three Bohra men and sent to the hospital. His home and office were ransacked, something that had never happened in previous flare-ups.[102]

The dawat's account is quite different. Engineer stirred up the passengers to protest the delay (dawat sources say), and physically attempted to prevent Syedna from boarding the aircraft. Throughout the flight, they say, Engineer continued to abuse Syedna verbally (even before this latest incident, the dissident leader had not been shy about labeling Syedna "just a dictator" at the head of a dawat "reeking of corruption").[103] The beating of Engineer and vandalism of his house, dawat sources say, were regrettable acts of a few individuals who had been stirred up by insults directed at their spiritual leader.[104]

As ever, the dispute between the orthodox and the dissident camps resembled a scene from *Rashomon:* the parties experienced the same events, but saw them from entirely divergent perspectives. Engineer, and his supporters in the Indian press, demanded that Syedna be held liable for the actions of his followers. Orthodox Bohras saw themselves as the aggrieved party, and staged *bandhs* (shop-closings) in several cities to protest the treatment of their da'i.[105] There was no replay of Udaipur, nor the grinding litigation of the early twentieth century. But both camps may wish they'd decided to take a different flight.

PROFILE OF A FAMILY NOT OBSERVING DAWAT NORMS OF ORTHOPRAXY

While most Bohra households are in broad compliance with dawat guidelines and do at least the minimum necessary to maintain their standing in the community, a number (how many is difficult to determine) live quite happily outside the dawat's sphere of control. They are not necessarily politicized dissidents like Asghar Ali Engineer, but are merely families who choose to circumvent dawat restrictions rather than either submit to them or challenge them openly. Such a policy would be virtually impossible in towns or small cities, but the anonymity of a sprawling metropolis like Mumbai lets families live under the dawat's radar screen.

One such household consists of Zulfikar, his wife Khadija, and their two children Latifa and Hasan.* They live in a modest middle-class apartment, in a modest middle-class suburb, enjoying such comforts and conven-

*The names of the members of this family have been changed, for obvious reasons.

iences as a car, a television, VCR, microwave oven, computer, and two phone lines. They have no live-in servant, but a woman comes in daily to take care of the housework. Like the homes of more orthodox Bohras, the apartment is immaculate. There is, however, one glaring difference: unlike orthodox homes, this flat has no picture of Syedna. "We refuse to put up a photo of the high priest," says Khadija, "because Islam prohibits the reverence of idols." It is noteworthy that she refers to the da'i as "high priest" rather than with the usual Bohra appellations of "Syedna" or "His Holiness."

Heavyset, light-skinned, her hair braided in a queue reaching all the way to her waist, Khadija wears a sari instead of a burqa. She considers the burqa and rida to be hypocritical: "If it were true purdah it might serve some purpose," she says. "When the face is covered at least it preserves a woman from the stares and abuse of men in the street; it insures that an old grandmother and a pretty young virgin will be treated exactly the same. But Bohra clothing leaves the face wholly exposed, and 'fancy ridas' are the height of vanity. You're supposed to keep your head covered while eating, but so many women just lightly drape the fringe of their rida over their hair and pretend not to notice when it 'happens' to slip off. I prefer to dress comfortably, and be honest about it."

Zulfikar, an engineer, runs his own consulting company with a Hindu, a Christian, and a Parsi for partners. He has a graying mustache, but no beard. Wearing topi and kurta to work, he says, would be professionally disastrous: "Clients would lose all confidence in me, regard me as a backward fundamentalist." When he does wear a topi, at community functions where it is unavoidable, he invariably stands out because of his lack of a beard. But he knows more than a few other Bohra men without beards—and many other men who wear beards but tear the topis off their heads the moment they step out of the masjid.

"Fundamentalism is rising in all groups," he says, "Sunnis, Shi'a, Christians, even Hindus. To me, fundamentalism means following a set of rules without understanding the meaning. We Bohras have more in common with Jains or Parsis than with the Sunnis, so why should we follow *their* example?" Zulfikar is, however, quite willing to follow Islamic practices that make sense to him personally. Ramadan is only a week away, and he plans to keep the fast.

Latifa and Hasan, both in their early twenties and still living at home, agree with their parents' outlook. Latifa, who is studying computer programming, wears a sari and feels uncomfortable in a rida. Hasan, a biomedical technician, has no beard or mustache, and resents being lectured when he attends a community function. "I am doing nothing wrong," he says, "so what gives them the right to criticize me?"

The family does not pay dawat taxes, a fact that in itself would make them liable for red card status (if not outright social baraat). They get away with it by keeping a low profile. The local amil doesn't know them, and they are very discreet about attending functions where they might be noticed. They turn down invitations to most Bohra weddings, all except the shadis of close friends and relatives. Many of their friends within the community tend to be similarly inclined: avoiding taxes whenever possible, generally noncompliant in matters of dress and appearance, seeking to evade rather than outright challenge dawat strictures.

Both Khadija and Zulfikar come from aristocratic Surti families. Residents of five particular mohallas in Surat (including theirs) all claim descent from converted Brahmins rather than converted banias, and this fuels much of the Surti snobbery. But the social round of elite Surti functions has never been to the couples' taste. Their family backgrounds would have justified an enormous wedding, perhaps even with the nikah performed by Syedna himself, but Khadija and Zulfikar opted instead for a simple civil ceremony overseas.

The family members do not have ID cards, and have been able to get by without them, but social situations are always a bit precarious. Cards are generally not needed for social functions at a jamatkhana or religious observances at a masjid, and the services for which certificates are required (staying in musafirkhanas, receiving alamat, having Syedna select children's names) are not services for which the family has much desire. Situations like marriage are somewhat trickier. A civil ceremony or a non-Bohra nikah can be hidden from the dawat, but any celebration to which large numbers of Bohras will be invited is sure to be noticed by the authorities. In these cases the host must have a valid certificate, but (Khadija says) many people simply have the party "officially" hosted by a friend or relative with valid credentials. Several of Khadija's close friends hold green cards, so the social barriers between orthodox and unorthodox Bohras are not as tight as either dawat or dissident sources might indicate.

Despite their rejection of the da'i's identity solidification program, nobody in the family says anything derogatory about Syedna himself. This is quite typical of almost all the nonobservant Bohras I have met: even those with little use for the da'i's rules maintain a certain degree of respect for his person. One woman who habitually bemoans the nosiness and harassment of clerics, the intrigues and greed of Qasr-e Ali members, and the heavy-handedness of dawat restrictions, has only words of praise for Syedna himself. Her view of the faith is indicative of Khadija's, and of many other members of the Bohra community: "I believe that the heart of all religion is ethics, and love for all. You can't love God unless you first love

your neighbors, and you can't love your neighbors unless you first love yourself—right down to your very toenails."

ANALYSIS OF THE DISSIDENT-DAWAT DISPUTE

SECULARISM

At its heart, the debate between the dawat and the dissidents is one over secularism. Orthodox Bohras regard all aspects of life as a holistic package, with the spiritual and the mundane inextricably linked. In this view, Islam (and the Daudi Bohra interpretation of it) is not merely a set of beliefs, but an integrated manner of living. There is no way of drawing a line between areas in which an individual is obliged to obey spiritual directives and areas in which no such obedience is necessary.

The dissident view, however, is based on a modernist distinction between the spiritual and the secular spheres. Such a distinction, as T. N. Madan and Ashis Nandy eloquently argue,[106] is largely a Western intellectual construct that may be at odds with the mindset traditionally held by Indians of all religious backgrounds. The introduction of Western-style secularism (as opposed, for example, to a less absolutist Gandhian style of secularism) by Jawaharlal Nehru may be a major factor in the rise of both Hindu revivalism and Islamic fundamentalism. As Madan writes,

> Contrary to what may be presumed, it is not religious zealots alone who contribute to fundamentalism or fanaticism, which are a misunderstanding of religion, reducing it to mere political bickering, but also the secularists who deny the very legitimacy of religion in human life and society and provoke a reaction.[107]

One need not accept the Madan-Nandy critique of secularism in its entirety to accept the premise that Nehruvian secularism has not been a perfect fit for Indian society. On the fiftieth anniversary of India's Independence, the Bharatiya Janata Party—the primary political arm of the Hindu nationalism movement—was the largest single party in Parliament, and its leader Atal Bihari Vajpayee by far the most popular politician in the entire country. Even in the midst of celebrations marking the creation of India as a secular state, a poll of 12,651 respondents found Vajpayee more popular than founding father Nehru himself.[108] Less than a year later Vajpayee was prime minister, and the antisecularist BJP was the governing party of the Indian state. By the turn of the millennium the BJP had again trounced Congress (led by the mother of Nehru's great-grandchildren) and

could plausibly claim to have supplanted Nehru's party as the voice of the Indian mainstream.

The Bohra dissidents' modernist vision of society may well be where India is heading over the long run, but it is not where India is now. The dawat's holistic concept of a life permeated by spiritual obligations seems wholly in keeping with traditional concepts—although traditions change, and the ways of the past might not be the ways of the future. Throughout this study I have argued that the dawat's overall outlook is simultaneously traditionalist and modern, but on the question of secularism the two viewpoints may well be irreconcilable. Whenever possible, the dawat seeks to combine tradition with modernity and accept the best of both. When the two conflict, however, the Bohra clergy opts for the former. Modernity can support tradition, but here tradition will trump modernity.

EQUILIBRIUM

Another major factor underlying the dawat-dissident conflict is the mutual misapprehension that Bohra society (or any society) is a static entity. Both the dawat and the dissidents put forward a normative model based on the status of clerical power at a specific moment in time. For the dissidents that moment seems to be the late nineteenth century; for the dawat, a period nine centuries earlier. Each camp assumes that its own golden age represents the right and proper level of clerical control, while neither camp seems to acknowledge that Bohra society—like every society—is, has been, and will always be in a constant state of flux.

Edmund Leach, in his classic study of political organization in highland Burma, described the Kachins' vision of their society as a static structure composed of *gumsa* and *gumlao* in a state of perpetual equilibrium.[109] This view of society as an eternally changeless creature—an assumption largely unquestioned during the early decades of the development of anthropology—has been thoroughly discredited by the work of Leach and other social scientists. Any vision of society, whether the nominally objective research of an ethnographer or the normative evocations of an engaged social actor, are of necessity no more than snapshots of an instant in time.

The dissidents take as their normative starting point a time when the da'i was extremely weak. Engineer notes that the forty-ninth da'i, Syedna Muhammad Burhanuddin ibn Abdul-Qadir Najmuddin, made far less extensive claims to power than his twentieth-century successors have. This appears to be so, but emphasis on one historical moment overlooks the fact that the forty-ninth da'i did not have the ability to exercise as much

control as many of his predecessors or successors. The institution of the dawat had been badly shaken by a bitter controversy over the nass of his father, the forty-seventh da'i Syedna Abdul-Qadir Najmuddin, and by the time of his own reign the clergy lacked the resources to challenge the community standing of a powerful industrialist such as Sir Adamji Pirbhai.[110]

The dawat, for its part, seems to take as normative the level of clerical control enjoyed by the immediate successors to the Fatimid caliphs.[111] This choice of framing is similarly incomplete and self-selective. The power exercised by the early da'is owed much to their status as vice-regents for a hidden imam who had only recently gone into concealment. The Fatimid imams had been full-fledged political potentates, ruling a vast empire with unchallenged authority; mu'mineen considered it only natural to follow their directives in all aspects of life, since the spiritual and temporal leaders were one and the same. Separation of "church" and state, arguably a modern concept anywhere, would have been inconceivable to most Fatimid Ismailis: while the caliphs generally permitted freedom of worship to the Sunnis, Christians, and other groups that composed the majority of their population, they left no doubt that their regime and the Ismaili dawat were essentially coterminous. The early da'is, therefore, enjoyed wide-ranging political power by association with this tradition.

During the centuries since the satr of the twenty-first imam, succeeding da'is reigning first in Yemen and later in India have exercised widely varying degrees of sociopolitical control over the community. There has never been an equilibrium position, never a condition of perfect, normative stasis. Both today's dawat and today's dissidents are right in their conjuring up of historical support for their present-day positions—but wrong in attempting to claim the exclusive backing of history for their individual claims.

A PAPAL COMPARISON

Both the dawat and the dissidents have compared the da'i's status to that of the pope of the Roman Catholic Church. It is not an exact analogy, but close enough to highlight various aspects of the competing positions. In one polemical dawat tract entitled "Believers and Yet Unbelievers!" the clerical author notes that when Martin Luther and John Wycliffe rejected the pope's status as sole spiritual authority, they were intellectually honest enough to form their own separate churches. That Protestant denominations disagree with Catholic teaching on such matters as birth control and priestly celibacy, the author notes, has not caused the pope to alter church doctrine.[112]

Engineer has made the same comparison,[113] but does not develop from it an argument that would bolster his rhetorical position: there are and have always been considerable numbers of Catholics who reject the pope's authoritative judgments on a variety of theological or social issues, yet consider themselves (and are often considered by many of their peers) to be loyal members of the church. In the early centuries of the church, the Bishop of Rome was often considered *primus inter pares* rather than an unchallenged superior. During the "Babylonian Captivity" of 1308–1377, such eminent Franciscans as William of Ockham and Marsilius of Padua were vehement critics of papal supremacy while zealously defending what they regarded as Catholic orthodoxy.

The Council of Constance (1414–1418), ending the Great Schism of 1378–1417, represented perhaps the high-water mark of the conciliarist movement. In a declaration agreed to by the papacy of the time, it held the authority of the council actually superior to that of the pope. In modern circumstances, the very fact that so many American Catholics reject papal doctrine on such matters as birth control and divorce—yet still remain full members of the church—is an argument in favor of Engineer's claim that he and his fellow dissidents can reject Syedna's rulings in secular matters and still reserve the right to call themselves Daudi Bohras.

On the other side of the equation, a comparison with Catholicism highlights the hollowness of a prime dissident argument, that of grass-roots dissatisfaction with clerical behavior delegitimizing the institution as a whole. Anticlericalism need not indicate a rejection of the authority of the supreme pontiff. Many European and Latin American communities have long traditions of anticlerical attitudes, coupled with deep devotion to and respect for the Roman Catholic Church. Just as it is quite possible for villagers of Salerno or Chiapas to hate their priests yet love their pope, so too is it possible for loyal, orthodox Bohras to grumble about money-grubbing *chamchas* in the dawat bureaucracy, yet have nothing but respect and reverence for Syedna.

POTENTIAL FOR SCHISM

The central aspect of the Bohra faith (as distinct, say, from the Bohra culture more broadly defined) is the belief that every mu'min requires constant, personal direction from Syedna over almost all aspects of daily life. Not even the critics within the mainstream community seem to challenge this premise; they merely object to the rigidity of clerical control, the toadying politics, and the rising cost of dawat services. After all, a person is hardly likely to be annoyed about the price of the da'i's blessing and guid-

ance unless he or she feels the actual *need* to be blessed and guided by the da'i.

Dissidents like Engineer, however, appear to have taken a radically different view. They see Syedna as a purely spiritual leader rather than the central focus of every believer's life. This outlook has obvious similarities with that of Sunni Islam, as well as a modernist secular outlook inspired (as Weber argues) by the ethos of Protestant Christianity.[114] Musta'li Ismaili belief regards constant direct contact with the da'i as an absolute necessity, to prevent deviations from the doctrinal path. The dissidents have lost this contact, and have indeed deviated from (at very least) the doctrines deemed normative for the past century. The difference in theology is itself a tautology: orthodox doctrine requires total submission, in large part to prevent spiritual deviation; the spiritual deviation of the dissidents stems from (and largely consists of) a rejection of total submission.

Engineer argues that it is the dawat that has deviated from traditional Ismaili practice and from core Islamic values.[115] I make no attempt to evaluate the competing theological claims of the two parties: as an ethnographer rather than a theologian, I try not to stray outside my limited range of abilities. The whole question of whether the dawat or the dissident camp is more in line with the "true" Musta'li Ismaili tradition is a topic I leave to writers who possess a far deeper spiritual expertise than mine. On the likelihood of this debate leading to doctrinal schism, however, I can offer a simple observation while making no claims to special authority: A doctrinal schism, it seems to me, has already occurred.

The normative side of the equation—whether the dawat or the dissidents represent the "true" path—is a matter that each Bohra will decide for himself or herself. On such a question the opinion of an outside researcher would be presumptuous and inappropriate. I have sought to report the facts of the situation as impartially as possible (while acknowledging that no researcher is free of subjectivity) and to let members of the community themselves decide what interpretation to draw from these facts.

OVERALL ASSESSMENT AND SUMMARY

Engineer and his allies acknowledge their lack of widespread overt support within the Bohra community, but claim to speak for the majority of the believers who they contend have been cowed into silence by threat of baraat. Such an assertion is impossible either to prove or disprove, but this outside researcher has seen little evidence of broad-based theological discontent. Many of the critiques made by the dissidents are indeed echoed by members of the mainstream Bohra community: complaints of in-

creasing commercialization in the dawat, of ever higher clerical demands for money, of restrictions on personal expression ushered by the post-1979 program of identity reification. These complaints, however, are generally leveled not at Syedna himself but at the clerics and bureaucrats charged with carrying out his commands. Instead of criticizing the da'i's policies directly, Bohras will sometimes criticize the overzealousness with which low-level officials carry out these policies.

Overall, community response to the dawat's identity program seems to be positive and uncoerced. Virtually every Bohra household prominently displays photographs of Syednas Muhammad Burhanuddin and Taher Saifuddin, indicating a widespread acceptance of the da'i's centrality to the believers' lives. While full compliance with every priestly instruction may be difficult, a level of compliance necessary for yellow card status is not particularly onerous for most believers.

The only Bohras who need apply for a card at all, in fact, are those who see value in the rituals of the faith. Any member of the community who does not feel the need for clerical approval when marrying, burying a relative, or performing any other ceremony need never justify his or her lifestyle to a censorious amil. The dawat does not generally hunt down and hound out Bohras who choose to lead nonobservant or unorthodox lives. It is only when making use of dawat services that an ID card is required. In an analogy employed by the orthodox (and rejected by the dissidents), if you want to exercise the privileges of membership in a club, it stands to reason that you pay your dues and abide by the rules.

Nor are dawat taxes per se a source of much complaint offered to an outside observer. Those who consider these levies overly burdensome simply do not pay, and do not make use of dawat services. The main tax, zakat, is leveled at the same 2.5% mandated by the Qur'an and regarded by all Muslims as a central pillar of the faith; there may be discontent over how zakat funds are used, but even individuals who resent having to pay would have difficulty challenging the scriptural legitimacy of this tax. Other taxes, such as sila-fitra, are more or less nominal. According to Contractor's own calculations,[116] sila-fitra for a typical family came to less than Rs 32—less than one dollar at present-day exchange rates, no more than a few dollars at exchange rates of the time.

Moreover, criticism of clerical financial practices is hardly unique to the Bohras. Hasnain and Husain report many internal complaints among Indian Ithna-Asharis of clerics attempting to squeeze excessive sums of money for such rituals as khatna and nikah.[117] These writers—among the foremost modern scholars on Shi'a in India—point out the "continuing rampant corruption and mismanagement" of Twelver clerics, and make

sweeping condemnations of the mujtahid hierarchy: "[I]t may be inferred with a fair degree of accuracy that the majority of religious preachers and Ulema have reduced Shiaism and Islam into a body of lifeless rituals and rendered them quite incapable of facing modern challenges."[118]

The experience of a young Mumbai woman I'll call Ateka is perhaps typical of many mainstream Bohras who support the da'i and consider themselves loyal members of the community, but share many of the same concerns as the more militant dissidents. While dissident criticisms of Qasr-e Ali privilege and clerical restrictions ring true for Ateka, the stridency and schismatic tendencies of the movement do not appeal to her. She has few kind words for Asghar Ali Engineer: "That man has it in for Syedna. Motivated by malice, he is—for him, this is merely a personal grudge." Ateka's protest is limited to private acts of subversion: while having her identification picture taken for her (yellow) card of orthopraxy, just before the photographer snapped the shot she pushed her rida back to let a scandalous shock of hair escape onto her forehead.

Perhaps the most powerful argument for the legitimacy of the da'i and the dawat is the outpouring of passionate devotion (to all appearance, quite genuine and unforced) that can be witnessed any time Syedna makes one of his frequent public appearances. Whenever the da'i officiates at any rite the mass of attendees typically overflows the masjid or ziyafat hall. Whenever he travels outside Mumbai, hordes of followers come by train, car, plane, and bus just to be near him. For clerics and members of the royal inner circle such devotion may have ulterior motives; some members of Syedna's entourage, no doubt, engage in a lavish show of loyalty for the sake of personal advancement. But the vast mass of the Bohra population has nothing material to gain by displays of deep piety, and nothing to lose by just staying home.

If, as the dissidents allege, the dawat were keeping the populace in check merely by the threat of baraat, there would be no incentive for Bohras to turn out in the thousands for every waaz and every majlis. No attendance is taken, no summonses issued, no points are tallied or prizes awarded to the person who sheds the most copious tears at Ashura. In the opinion of this field researcher, the outward displays of piety by members of the mainstream Bohra community most commonly reflect a genuine inner belief—a belief that is both exhibited and solidified by these examples of loyalty. As Clifford Geertz has noted, orthopraxy leads to orthodoxy.[119] The path has been carefully laid out by the dawat, but the journey is one most Bohras seem to undertake quite willingly.

Conclusion

I n the preceding pages I have attempted to do several things:

(1) Present a basic ethnography of a community numbering up to one million, yet never before examined by an outside researcher (chapters 1 through 5).

(2) Describe the pivotal position of the apex cleric, suggest that this extraordinary centrality has greatly facilitated the promotion of both Islamic and Western-inspired modernist values, and examine the modernist means by which the dawat has reinforced its spiritual and political hegemony (chapter 6).

(3) Outline the program by which a (neo)traditionalist cultural and identity has been instituted through the concerted application of centrally mandated codes of orthopraxy, most notably in the areas of dress, physical comportment, and personal finance (chapter 7).

(4) Highlight the denomination's educational system, both as a foundation for and expression of the dual Islamization/modernization program (chapter 8).

(5) Discuss the most noteworthy internal challenge to the dawat's hegemony: the movement of dissidents/reformists who speak for an unknown number of Bohras within the orthodox fold, but who are teetering on the brink of outright schism (chapter 9).

In simpler terms, I've tried to provide a rough sketch of Bohra society, show that traditionalist Islam is quite compatible with an open-minded, twenty-first century outlook, and describe how one community has used the very tools of Western modernity to combat the dangers of Western modernity.

DEFINITIONS OF MODERNITY

When seeking to probe such issues as these, one must first ask just what is meant by "modernity." Max Weber rightly noted that economic forces

alone cannot adequately explain the congregation of ethical and intellectual values commonly associated with post-Enlightenment society in the West, but his positing of a causal relationship between Protestantism and the rise of modern liberal bourgeois values[1] can provide only tangential answers in the Asian context. Nor is such a Eurocentric line of analysis limited to the distant past. A variant of these Weberian concepts has recently been put forward by the historian David Landes,[2] and one need not search particularly hard to find other examples of self-congratulatory triumphalism in American intellectual circles.

Regardless of the genesis of much-vaunted entrepreneurial values, they have taken root in soil far removed from any putative Protestant homeland. It is worth noting, also, that the Bohras—every bit as much as sixteenth-century European Calvinists—are a mercantile community with a powerful work ethic and a marked avoidance of spendthrift ostentation. Had history worked out only a little bit differently, perhaps Weber's groundbreaking work would have been entitled *The Ismaili Ethic and the Spirit of Capitalism.*

Even in a strictly Western context, the concept of modernity is rather elusive. J. C. Heesterman notes,

> [S]uccessful modernity does not mean the supersession of tradition or the superimposition on it of a different order. It means that the inner conflict of tradition is now fought within the confines of an expanded reality . . . In contradistinction to tradition, modernity must valorize change because the authority of its code of abstract rules and principles no longer transcends reality.[3]

The very ellipticality (perhaps even impenetrability) of the above quotation highlights the slipperiness of the term. As Yogendra Singh noted three decades ago, the division between the modern and premodern mindset is difficult to pin down. One common dividing line, the reliance on science rather than religion for certainties, is of limited value: "[T]he world-view [of science] itself is not less abstract than the traditional and, consequently, is understood only by a few, the rest claiming it on the basis of mere hearsay."[4] Singh cites the political scientist Edward Shils:

> No good purpose is served by making it appear as if there is an unbridgeable gap between "traditional society" and "modern society" or even the more recent variant of the latter, "mass society." The "traditional society" is by no means entirely traditional, "modern society" is by no means free of tradition.[5]

In an Asian context, the definition of modernity becomes even more problematic. As Theodore P. Wright, Jr., properly notes, "It is incumbent upon a scholar employing the term modernization to define it in a way distinguishable from Westernization."[6] The definition he adopts is that of John Kautsky: "the process by which a society comes to be characterized by a belief in the rational and scientific control of man's physical and social environment and the application of technology to that end."[7] As noted by Singh, as well as by Clifford Geertz,[8] such a rigid dichotomization into the religiously based premodern and scientifically based modern mindset seems less and less applicable in a rapidly changing world. A valuable corrective is voiced by Seyyed Vali Reza Nasr; writing on Pakistan's Jamaat-i-Islami, Nasr argues that the group's fundamentalist Islamic orientation does not prevent it from adopting certain modernistic approaches:

> Modernization can no longer be regarded as a process that automatically produces secularization, privatization of faith, and the rejection of old values. Nor can religion any longer be seen merely as a set of traditional rites and beliefs, impervious to change and irrelevant to modernization. The task therefore becomes one of reconciling anachronistic values and loyalties with time-honored assumptions about the content, nature, and direction of modernizing change.[9]

I noted above that a researcher investigating the topic of modernization in a traditional society must ask what "modernity" is. *Ask,* but not necessarily *answer:* any definition one might be tempted to cobble together would almost inevitably be either so restrictive as to omit vast areas of study, or so broad as to be virtually meaningless. Can the Bohras be regarded as modern simply because they use computers? Such a standard would not distinguish them from groups like the Taliban. Can the Bohras be deemed antimodern because their social structure is rigidly hierarchical and faith-based rather than internally democratic and secular? Such a definition seems narrowly Eurocentric, making Western society the yardstick by which all other communities are measured. In my theoretical analysis I have taken note of the definitions discussed above, and a great many others, but I do not claim to shine any light on this particular area of shadow. Ultimately, perhaps one must define modernity in the same manner that Justice Potter Stewart defined pornography: you know it when you see it.

In the course of this study, I have focused less on what modernity *is*

than on what modernity *does*. And, more to the point, what the Bohras have done with modernity. One of the central arguments I have attempted to put forth is that modernity need not stand in polar opposition to tradition—in fact, that it can reinvigorate long-standing customs, beliefs, and practices.

The hunt for a perfect, pristine "tradition" is somewhat akin to the medieval search for a unicorn: what one finds are only relics, and these may turn out to be no more authentic than the horn of a beached narwhal. Just as Benedict Anderson and Ernest Gellner have highlighted the artificiality of modern national identities, Eric Hobsbawm and Terence Ranger (among others) have pointed out the artificiality of modern formulations of "tradition."[10] As Paul Brass persuasively argues, ethnic traditions and identities are always somewhat fluid, always subject to manipulation by elites for reasons of self-interest.[11] Richard Gombrich and Gananath Obeyesekere note that many new cultural expressions are presented (and regarded) as the resurrection of an older heritage, and an anthropologist must be cautious in labeling such expressions ersatz:

> The new movements get their legitimation from tradition: each is explicitly perceived as a re-creation of a lost tradition or simply as an old tradition continuing. . . . Sometimes the invented tradition bears little or no relation to the past as we see it; yet protagonists see it very differently. For them it is the re-creation or an expression of the past in the present. Is there any way in which we could legitimately discriminate between our sense of tradition and theirs?[12]

In his classic study of caste and kinship in Sri Lanka, Nur Yalman comments on the difficulty of capturing this elusive unicorn of tradition. The quarry seems to evade not only anthropologists, but members of the communities they study: "It is a curious feature of ethnographic accounts," Yalman writes, "that many peoples speak of such a 'traditional' period which is presumed to have existed about seventy to a hundred years ago. Ethnographers are sometimes taken in by this, and write neat accounts of the 'traditional' structure."[13]

Throughout the preceding study I have used the words "tradition" and "modernity" as shorthand, to refer to concepts that are not nearly as distinct as such neatly packaged terms might suggest. But one must not make the mistake of assuming that any clear-cut, night-and-day division can exist between the two. A careful researcher, when viewing a horse, ought not take it for a modernized unicorn.

MODERNITY AND ISLAMIC FUNDAMENTALISM*

One of the underlying premises of this study has been a belief in the potential for peaceful coexistence between traditionalist Islam and Western-style modernity. Sadly, such a premise stands in marked contrast to the prevailing popular attitude both in the West and in many Muslim circles. Westerners with little knowledge of Islam often reflexively judge it solely by its most militant, rejectionist elements: the Taliban, hard-line Iranian ayatollahs, or self-described mujahideen of various extremist (even terrorist) organizations. These elements represent only a tiny fraction of world Muslim opinion, yet all too often in the West they are presumed to be the legitimate voice of the entire community. The Muslim world, for its part, is equally quick to take Western actions out of context: there are those who may be profitably reminded that the term "modern values" is not necessarily an oxymoron, and that Western civilization does not find its definitive expression in *Baywatch*. As a citizen of the West, however, it is not my place to tell Muslims what they should and should not believe about my culture. I will therefore comment (very briefly) on misperceptions that Westerners have about Islam, and leave Muslim writers to balance the other side of the equation.

Talal Asad, in his *Genealogies of Religion,* highlights a particularly blatant (but not atypical) example of the prejudice prevalent even in Western intellectual circles: "The Bible, in its entirety," writes the novelist and social critic Fay Weldon (quoted by Asad) "is at least food for thought. The Koran is food for no-thought. It is not a poem on which a society can be safely or sensibly based."[14] Such an attitude could be dismissed as mere bigotry if it were not so thoroughly indicative of mainstream Western views. Even in academic and policy-making circles, Islam is today's bogeyman of choice: Samuel Huntington's positing of an Islamic bloc irretrievably hostile to everything the West represents[15] is only one among many prominent expressions of this outlook. When Thomas Carlyle described the Qur'an as a work of "insupportable stupidity,"[16] he was expressing the prejudices of an unenlightened colonialist power. One might have hoped Western society would have become more open-minded in the century and a half since.

*As noted in the introduction, the term "fundamentalist" is problematic: it has been used to describe groups ranging from orthodox traditionalists to revolutionary militants. Throughout this study I use the term primarily in the former sense: the hijacking of the term "fundamentalist" by groups that are actually more radical than traditional is a linguistic appropriation which too many Westerners have aided and abetted.

Observers such as Edward Said sometimes portray Western misrepresentation of Islam as a deliberate or quasi-deliberate act, stemming (at least subconsciously) from a neocolonialist desire for political and cultural hegemony: "[B]ecause of Orientalism the Orient was not (and is not) a free subject of thought or action. . . . European culture gained in strength and identity by setting itself off against the Orient as a sort of surrogate and even underground self."[17] Said's *Orientalism* is a useful reminder of the depth and long history of Western misrepresentation of "the East" (a concept which, as Bernard Lewis points out, Said seems to collaborate in essentializing),[18] but as a charge sheet of Western intellectual larceny with malice aforethought, it seems more polemic than proof. Lewis, with more than half a century of scholarship behind him, has the credentials to launch an eloquent counterattack: "The implication would seem to be that by learning Arabic, Englishmen and Frenchmen were committing some kind of offense," he writes. "For Mr. Said, it would seem, scholarship and science are commodities which exist in finite quantities; the West has grabbed an unfair share of these as well as other resources."[19]

An explanation for Western misperceptions more convincing than intellectual hegemony or theft is, perhaps, simple ignorance. Most Westerners know virtually nothing about Islam, so they form their impressions on the most lurid, shocking, and exotic images presented to them. There is nothing unique in this: as Xiaomei Chen notes, in the non-Western world (she writes with particular reference to China, but her observation is valid elsewhere) "Orientalism, or the Western construction of the Orient, has been accompanied by instances of what might be termed Occidentalism."[20]

While Said seems to regard studying another culture as an act of intellectual imperialism,* I suggest that what is needed is *more* cultural outreach rather than less. The best way to defeat ignorance is through knowledge, imperfect as such a search may be. If Fay Weldon had actually taken the time to read the Qur'an, it is difficult to believe she would have come away with all her biases and preconceived notions about Islam intact. Here social anthropology can serve a useful purpose: as David Maybury-Lewis notes (in a reference to the thought of Claude Lévi-Strauss that could equally well apply to many other anthropological works), "It forces us to recognize that we in the West, despite a temporary scientific advantage, have no basis for claiming intellectual superiority over the rest of the world."[21]

*A mystifying attitude, considering that Said's own field of academic specialization is not his native Palestine, or any aspect of Middle Eastern studies, but the literature and arts of Western Europe.

Islam is far too varied and complex to have a single, authoritative position on the topic of modernity. For every hidebound Taliban zealot who condemns television or female education as *bid'a* (innovation), there are tens of thousands of other Muslims who do not. By what standard is he more "Islamic" than they? An excellent case could be made that it is the literalists themselves who are outside the mainstream of contemporary Islam. To step away from Bohras and the Indian subcontinent for a moment, two Islamic leaders in Indonesia admirably demonstrate the point.

Even before becoming president of the world's largest Muslim nation, Abdurrahman Wahid (better known by the nickname of Gus Dur) had led the world's largest Muslim organization. The Nadhlatul Ulama is a group over seven decades old, with more members (nearly forty million) than the populations of Saudi Arabia and all the Gulf emirates combined.[22] As head of the Nahdlatul Ulama, Gus Dur strongly opposed making sharia the law of the land. His vision of Islam is based on ethics and universal tolerance: "There is no monopoly of Islam on goodness," he said in an interview. "[We] can never impose any kind of belief. . . . Islam respects plurality more than anything else." His prediction for the future stands in sharp contrast to that of the essentialists: "I don't think the Taliban's version of Islam will stick, or be preserved in history for long."[23]

These sentiments are echoed by Amien Rais, head of the twenty-eight-million-strong Muhammadiyah organization and now speaker of the Indonesian Parliament. Even before he assumed political office after helping lead the movement that dislodged the dictator Suharto in 1998, he and Gus Dur together had about as many followers as the entire population of Iran, about three times as many as that of Taliban-held Afghanistan.[24] Often described as more conservative than the Nahdlatul Ulama leader (and often displaying less tolerance toward minority communities at the political rather than the theological level),[25] Rais regards himself as equally "open and receptive to other people and other ideas" as Gus Dur. The holder of a Ph.D. in political science from the University of Chicago, Rais dresses in Western clothing—a crisply ironed white shirt and unloosened tie at the height of the Javanese hot season. "We must respect and tolerate others, so that all may enjoy the practice of their respective religions," he says. Rais has no wish to resurrect the lifestyle of a time long past: "As a Muslim, I see no obstacle to enjoying the modern world."[26]

The late Fazlur Rahman, once head of Pakistan's Central Institute of Islamic Research, saw the entire resurgence of literalist Islam not as a homegrown return to tradition, but a twisted reaction to modernity. Foreshadowing Madan and Nandy's antisecular critique of Hindu revivalism, Rahman advocated that Islam find its own path to the future:

Thus, while the modernist was engaged by the West through attraction, the neorevivalist is equally haunted by the West through repulsion. The most important and urgent thing to do from this point of view is to "disengage" mentally from the West and to cultivate an independent but understanding attitude toward it. . . . So long as Muslims remain mentally locked with the West in one way or the other, they will not be able to act independently and autonomously.[27]

Rahman urged his coreligionists to "distinguish clearly between normative Islam and historical Islam,"[28] and reject the notion that the way something was done in the distant (or recent) past is somehow closer to the authentic core of the faith. A trained Qur'anic scholar with far more right to the title of *alim* than many of his theological opponents, Rahman described Islam not as an impediment to progress, but as its source: "[T]he Muslim modernists say exactly the same thing as the so-called Muslim fundamentalists say: that Muslims must go back to the original and definitive sources of Islam and perform *ijtihad* [theological interpretation] on that basis."[29]

Foremost among Rahman's opponents, and among the foremost Islamic fundamentalist voices worldwide, was Maulana Abul Ala Maududi. As much as any other single individual in the twentieth century, Maududi helped shape and promote modern-day Sunni Islamic revivalism.[30] It is noteworthy that Maududi's title of Maulana was bestowed by his followers rather than the ulema, whether of India, Pakistan, or any other country: Maududi did not have much formal religious training, and could not truly be considered a traditional clerical authority. Of his more than 120 publications, only one is on a purely theological topic.[31] The champion of Islamic fundamentalism began his career in a very modern occupation indeed: he started out as a journalist.

Maududi founded the Jamaat-i-Islami in 1941 as a political and social advocacy organization; from very early in its history to the present day it has been led by, composed of, and oriented toward laypeople rather than ulema.[32] The parallels between this foremost revivalist organization in the Islamic world and contemporaneous Hindu revivalist groups is obvious: the Rashtriya Swayamsevak Sangh (RSS) and its collateral organizations are primarily cultural and political groups rather than strictly "religious" ones.[33] RSS founder Keshav Baliram Hedgewar was in no meaningful sense a spiritual figure; current Bharatiya Janata Party ideologue L. K. Advani is publicly agnostic; and the legendary Hindu Mahasabha president (indeed, the intellectual progenitor of Hindu nationalism itself) Veer

Savarkar was a self-avowed atheist.* Just as life-long scholars of Hinduism have sharply challenged the RSS interpretation of the faith, Rahman writes that "not one of Mawdudi's followers ever became a serious student of Islam, the result being that, for the faithful, Mawdudi's statements represented the last word on Islam—no matter how much and how blatantly he contradicted himself."[34] When self-styled fundamentalists profess to present a "true" version of Islam, such claims must be treated with extreme caution—both in the Muslim world and in the West.

Yet not even the outlook of Maududi himself, while generally regarded as traditionalist and reactionary, is void of modernist elements. His *Risala-e-Diniyat,* published first in Urdu in 1932 and translated into English as *Towards Understanding Islam* (1940), is a defense of religious doctrine on wholly rationalistic terms. In this important work, Maududi makes an eloquent, logical, and persuasive case for Islamic orthodoxy, using modernist skepticism and speculative detachment as his outlook and frame of reference. A Muslim accepts his creed on faith, Maududi argues, but even if this truth were not available in the form of revealed text, it would be an eminently rational—even scientific—explanation for the mysteries of life. Agree or disagree, one can hardly accuse him of being stuck in the seventh century.

A thorough discussion of Islam and modernity would fill several bookshelves. I have raised the topic merely to indicate a few premises underlying this study, in brief:

(1) Western perceptions of Islam in general, and Islamic fundamentalism in particular, are based upon the views of a small, unrepresentative sampling of Muslim attitudes and beliefs.

(2) Even these self-styled spokesmen of Islamic traditionalism are often less categorically hostile to modernist ideas than is generally recognized.

(3) There are tremendous numbers of wholly orthodox Muslims, both individuals and entire communities, living their lives in strict accordance with a traditionalist interpretation of the faith, yet displaying few (if any) of the anti-Western, antisecular, antimodern attitudes commonly associated with this level of Islamic devotion.

(4) Misportrayals of Islam can become self-fulfilling prophecies. The West singles out peripheral figures for condemnation, and inflates barely known terrorists into world-renowned champions of "Islamic jihad." This

*The only major Hindu nationalist group oriented toward religious specialists is the Vishwa Hindu Parishad, which was created by RSS leader (and former religious specialist) Madhav Sadashiv Golwalkar.

grants prominence to militants who might otherwise have struggled in obscurity, and legitimizes extremist views that might otherwise have been shunned by mainstream Muslims. How did Usama bin Laden, a man with little theological training and no status to issue a fatwa on any aspect of the faith, come to be seen—both in the West and, increasingly, in the Muslim world—as a spokesman for Islamic values? He has such status, at least in part, because America gave it to him.[35]

It is my hope that the portrait of the Bohra community presented in this study will help dispel some commonly held misperceptions about fundamentalist Islam. I do not argue that traditional Muslim values are identical (or even particularly similar) to those of modern Western society—merely that they can be *compatible* with so-called modern Western values. I would argue that the values Western triumphalists like to claim as their own (respect for human and civil rights, pursuit of social justice, equality of sexes, promotion of liberal education, aptitude for technology) are hardly limited to the West. And "modernity" (whatever its definition may be), is something far broader than a taste for sex, drugs, and rock 'n' roll. As one of my Bohra friends asked me, "A Mormon in Salt Lake City can work as a computer programmer, help with the housework when his wife is at the hospital practicing neurosurgery, and refrain from liquor, tobacco, and R-rated movies. Why should I be more of an anomaly than him?"

Why, indeed. My friend is somewhat of an anomaly (at least compared with most of the world's one billion Muslims)—but there is no reason he has to be. And in the Bohra community, he is becoming less and less anomalous every day.

Are the Bohras themselves an anomaly among Muslims? Whether or not they are representative of Islam's future, the Daudi Bohras shatter stereotypes about traditionalist Islam today. As a community of up to one million devout Shi'a whose faith is every bit as fundamental to them as it is for Afghans, Saudis, or Iranians, they present an example that must be taken seriously. While adhering faithfully to traditional Islamic norms, the Bohras eagerly accept most aspects of modernity, strongly support the concept of a pluralist civil society, boast a deeply engrained heritage of friendly engagement with members of other communities, and have a history of apolitical quietism stretching back nearly a thousand years.

Not all traditionalist Muslims are like the Daudi Bohras—but not all are so very different.

ISLAM, IDENTITY, AND SECTARIAN VIOLENCE

One tragic byproduct of identity reification through physical markers has been the increasing degree to which Bohras have been drawn into larger Hindu-Muslim conflicts. In the Mumbai riots of 1993 Bohras were often targeted specifically because of their unabashedly Muslim personal appearance. Paradoxically, Bohras were sometimes attacked because they looked more "Muslim" than the Sunni Muslims protesting the destruction of Babri Masjid in Ayodhya. Prior to the Islamization program of Syedna Muhammad Burhanuddin, Bohra identity often veered closer to that of non-Muslim Gujarati mercantile communities such as the Parsis or Jain banias than to that of other Muslim groups. The communal polarization of the past two decades, however, has driven a wedge between the Bohras and the majority population, and forced them out of necessity to identify with other members of the besieged Muslim minority. It was an unintended consequence of the codes of personal appearance, but a consequence nonetheless. Their Islamic identity has not only been strengthened by internal clerical regulation, it has been simultaneously reinvigorated by heightened tension with various elements in the wider Indian society.

Subaltern Interpretation of Sectarian Violence

Before discussing the impact of sectarian conflict on the Bohra community in particular, a few remarks are warranted on the larger topic of communal violence in India. In recent years a great deal has been written on the causes and consequences of communalism, the genesis of Hindu revivalism, and the outlook for secularism on the subcontinent. A thorough review of the literature, let alone a comprehensive discussion of the issues involved, would constitute an entire monograph in itself. I mention only a few aspects of this important and all-too-salient topic.

Until the middle of the twentieth century, historians generally subscribed to James Mill's view of communal divide on the subcontinent: that Muslims and Hindus were two groups predestined for conflict by the nature of their respective cultures and the teachings of their respective faiths. It is worth remembering that Mill, whose *History of British India*[36] formed the basis of historical education in India for well over a century (not only for the colonizers, but for many of the colonized as well), never set foot anywhere near the Indian subcontinent. While mainstream historians in the years since Independence have steadily eroded the absolutism of this communal divide, since the 1980s the Subaltern historians have provided a valuable service by hammering nails into Mill's intellectual coffin. It is

now more or less generally accepted that divisions between Muslim and Hindu communities have never been quite as clearly defined as had previously been assumed, and that present-day violence owes much to colonial legacies. Gayatri Chakavorty Spivak rightly notes that a careful researcher must always be wary of official documents on matters of communalism, because the authors of these texts often saw what they had been preconditioned to see.[37] Partha Chatterjee points out that many riots had socioeconomic causes that were overlooked by colonial observers predisposed to fit every disturbance into a Hindu-Muslim model.[38]

Gyanendra Pandey, perhaps the foremost Subaltern historian, argues that at the local level Hindus and Muslims as late as the nineteenth century identified more strongly with their individual jati or qaum than with their larger religion.[39] Romila Thapar, while not a part of the Subaltern school, likewise notes that the description of many events was colored by the British colonial tendency to regard Islam and Hinduism as fundamentally irreconcilable and immutably hostile.[40] Pandey provides several specific examples where such misinterpretation clearly seems to have occurred. His strongest case, perhaps, is that of a riot in Varanasi on October 21, 1809. Official documents described it as a Muslim-Hindu conflict sparked by a Muharram procession, a version that remained unchallenged through the years. Merely by checking a calendar, Pandey showed that in the Islamic lunar year in question Muharram did not fall until February 1810.[41]

Without detracting from the Subalterns' contributions, one must ask whether this is truly a separate school of historiography, or merely the same sort of good, solid historical research that many other scholars have been undertaking without a fashionable label. As Chris Bayly notes, "What appears mainly to distinguish the subalterns from their predecessors and co-workers in the field of popular and rural history is a rhetorical device, the term 'subaltern' itself, and a populist idiom."[42] An ideological orientation in favor of the downtrodden might prompt a researcher to look with particular zeal for facts shedding light on the lives of the unchronicled poor—but one would hope that the same zeal could be found in any responsible social historian with a scholarly passion for the topic. And just as lines of religion are not as sharp as colonial historians believed, neither are lines of class clearly chiseled in granite: "Down almost to the very bottom of society," Bayly observes, "every subaltern was an elite to someone lower than him."[43]

The Subalterns, I would argue, are caught between a truism and a false-ism. The truism is that communal divisions were deepened by colonial policies of divide-and-rule, then exaggerated both by the biased de-

scriptions of official documents and a century of view-from-above sec-
ondary-source histories. The false-ism, however, is that such divisions are
entirely (or even primarily) the creation of colonialism. From the times of
Mahmud of Ghazna and Muhammad of Ghur straight through to those of
Shivaji and Aurangzeb, Indian Hindus and Muslims have been aware of
their differences. Subaltern historians who overstate their case fall quickly
into the false side of the equation. The stance of historians such as Fran-
cis Robinson demonstrates that the debunking of antiquated notions is
not wholly complete: Robinson's view of a fundamental cleavage between
the Hindus and Muslims of the subcontinent is so clear-cut that it almost
seems to put the two faiths in hermetically sealed containers.[44] But, by and
large, both Subaltern and non-Subaltern researchers seem to have made
the case against essentializing the two religions persuasively enough to
have swayed a critical mass of scholarly opinion.

Peter Van der Veer strikes a valuable corrective note to the excesses of
the Subaltern and postmodern schools of historiography. Colonialism and
orientalism played a significant part in widening the communal divide, he
writes, but by overstating the impact of Western imperialism the Subal-
terns wind up denigrating the very downtrodden communities they aim
to represent. To chalk sectarian conflict up to colonialism—more than half
a century after the end of colonial rule—robs Indians of all agency over
their own lives.[45] To blame modern communal strife on long-dead impe-
rialists turns the British into fiendishly powerful puppet masters, and turns
Indians into woefully feeble puppets.

Secularism and Sectarianism

Another factor fueling the rise of modern sectarianism, scholars such as
T. N. Madan and Ashis Nandy argue, is the parallel rise of modern secu-
larism.[46] In the mindset of the vast majority of the inhabitants of the sub-
continent, the argument goes, any division between the spiritual and the
temporal spheres is artificial, contrived, and false—and it is the imposi-
tion of this modernist division upon India that has sparked a backlash in
the form of both Islamic fundamentalism and Hindu revivalism. Madan
writes:

> I submit that in the prevailing circumstances secularism in South
> Asia as a generally shared credo of life is impossible, as a basis for
> state action impracticable, and as a blueprint for the foreseeable
> future impotent. . . . and it is impotent as a blueprint for the fu-
> ture because, by its very nature, it is incapable of countering reli-
> gious fundamentalism and fanaticism."[47]

The strict Nehruvian secularism enshrined in the Indian constitution (championed today, appropriately enough, by scholars at Jawaharlal Nehru University) has much natural appeal to those comfortable with Western norms, but little resonance with the bulk of the Indian population. Even in the Christian West (as Max Weber rightly noted) such a separation between faith and policy did not come until the rise of Protestant capitalism, possibly as late as the eighteenth and early nineteenth centuries.[48] Nehru personally saw organized displays of faith as an anachronism. In *The Discovery of India,* he wrote:

> Religion, whether it was Hinduism or Islam or Buddhism or Christianity, did not attract me. It seemed to be closely associated with superstitious practices and dogmatic beliefs, and behind it lay a method of approach to life's problems which was certainly not that of science. There was an element of magic about it, an uncritical credulousness, a reliance on the supernatural.[49]

Nehru felt vaguely embarrassed that most of his countrymen did not share his skepticism, conceding only that "religion had supplied some deeply felt inner need of human nature, and that the vast majority of people all over the world could not do without some form of religious belief."[50] He hoped that over time this "superstition" would fade away.

Such denigration of popular piety could hardly fail to spark an intense reaction. In the view of Madan and Nandy, it has contributed directly to the rise of Hindu revivalist groups like the Rashtriya Swayamsevak Sangh, the Bharatiya Janata Party, the Vishwa Hindu Parishad, Bajrang Dal, and Shiv Sena, not to mention such pre-Independence bodies as the Hindu Mahasabha. Nandy writes, with some justification, that "the RSS is an illegitimate child of western colonialism."[51] He rightly notes that the beliefs and practices advocated by the Hindutva movement represent a radical departure from previous tradition, although he may employ more than a shade of hyperbole when he argues that "whatever the revivalist Hindu may seek to revive, it is not Hinduism."[52]

This revivalism—among Hindus and Muslims alike—has often led to intercommunal conflict. As Mark Juergensmeyer notes with reference to the revivalist Sikh followers of the slain militant Sant Jarnail Singh Bhindranwale, the aim of those perpetrating religious violence is often something more cultural and political than strictly religious: "Their purpose is to awaken good folk, mobilize their community, insult the evil forces, and perhaps even to demonstrate dramatically to God himself that there are those who are willing to fight and die on his side, and to deliver his judgment of death."[53]

Nor is such revivalism limited to India. Pakistan and Bangladesh have both seen rising support for Islamic fundamentalist groups, while Sri Lanka has witnessed the growing politicization of a movement (begun in the nineteenth century) termed "Protestant Buddhism" by Gananath Obeyesekere.[54] Not even the Bohras of Sri Lanka have been untouched by the tide of revivalism in that country: Anagarika Dharmapala, the foremost architect of "Protestant Buddhism," singled them out for special condemnation. Gombrich and Obeyesekere note that Dharmapala's "politicization of Buddhism involved castigating all the non-Sinhala communities in Sri Lanka, but he directed his fiercest vituperation at Indian merchants (Bohras and Parsis), Muslims (whom he contemptuously referred to as 'hambayo') and 'filthy Tamils' (hadi demalu)."[55]

In other writings I have discussed the Madan-Nandy critique of secularism, the broader Hindu-Muslim dynamic in modern India, and the rise of the Hindu right with reference to the Babri Masjid/Ramjanambhumi controversy in Ayodhya,[56] so I will refrain from rehashing my comments on these topics. The preceding paragraphs are intended to provide a backdrop to the sectarian conflicts of contemporary India, as a basis for examining the impact of such conflicts upon the Bohra community. The paramount theoretical issue here seems to be the reification of societal boundaries through civil disorder. As Stanley J. Tambiah has noted, riots and communal bloodbaths not only arise from societal identities, but also serve to reinforce, refashion, and even (sometimes) create them anew.[57] This highlighting of sectarian identities because of sectarian conflict—part of the phenomenon earlier described by Tambiah as the "politicization of ethnicity"[58]—is itself a condition of modernity. Whether such violence is viewed as a uniquely modern phenomenon, as an ancient one, or as a modern manifestation of underlying social cleavages, it is also a *response* to plainly modern social dislocations.[59] What Tambiah has termed "a form of modern political Ludditism"[60] represents explicit rejection of some of the basic tenets of the "modern" social contract.

Bohra Legacy of Apolitical Quietism

Traditionally the Bohras have shunned political, religious, or sectarian agitation—both as an article of faith and as a practical necessity for survival. During the early post-Fatimid period in Yemen, several da'is were called upon to take up arms against Zaidi (and other) political rivals. There are several early instances of assassination reportedly used as a dawat tactic: most notably, the killing of Jafar Patani in the year 845/1441, but also that of the renegade Maulana Tahir, who was murdered in 986/1578 for aiding the

suppression of Shi'ism.[61] Even when faced with such oppression as that meted out by Mughal emperor Aurangzeb, however, the Bohras have almost always resorted to taqiyya rather than revolt.[62] Bohra dissidents such as Engineer contend that the dawat has used deliberate mob violence against advocates of reform, but even if such charges are true, intracommunal and intercommunal strife are two radically different phenomena.[63]

Much of this goes back to broader Shi'a customs of secrecy, quietism, and avoidance of all political activism. The concept of taqiyya is common to both Ismaili and Ithna-Ashari branches of the faith, and is based on Qur'anic verses 3:28 and 16:108. In brief, it is the doctrine permitting (even encouraging) a believer to disguise his faith in the face of oppression.[64] With such notable exceptions as Fatimid Egypt, Iran from Safavid times onward, and several Indian principalities (the Deccan sultanates, the Nawabate of Awadh), Shi'a have in almost all places and times lived under the political domination of Sunni authorities. In most places they have been a small minority with justifiable fear of the Sunni mainstream. Several of the imams held in common by Twelvers and Ismailis temporarily went into hiding, and both Ithna-Asharis and Musta'li Ismailis believe that the last visible imam entered seclusion to escape the dangers of a hostile world.[65]

Some Shi'a groups, from anti-Umayyad cliques to backers of the Abbasid coup d'etat, have pursued the opposite course of political intrigue and rebellion. Such efforts, however, were generally crushed with brutal efficiency by Sunni authorities, forcing entire Shi'a communities to suffer for the plotting of a few members.[66] The rejection of political action eventually became enshrined as an article of doctrine: quietism became not only prudent, but theologically mandated. This quietism has been at least as pronounced in the Ismaili as in the Ithna-Ashari tradition. Since Fatimid times (Nikki Keddie and Juan R. Cole note), both the Musta'li and Nizari camps "became increasingly quietistic politically" and "have remained generally nonrebellious."[67] The apolitical nature of postmedieval Ismaili communities has often gone unnoticed by Western observers. As Etan Kohlberg points out, historians and other scholars basing their judgments on medieval extremist groups such as the Assassins and ghulats have sometimes tended to regard the Ismaili faith as an incubator of rebellion.[68] Keddie and Cole note that this misperception lasted all the way up until the Iranian Revolution: "[M]any scholars treated the Ismailis as radicals and the Imami Twelvers as moderate or middle of the road, but clearly this typology is false for the twentieth century, and in many instances for some centuries before that."[69]

For the Bohras, this long tradition of quietism has the parallel support of demographics. As Ismailis within the framework of Shi'a Islam in a larger context of predominantly Hindu India, Bohras are a minority of a minority of a minority. Their position has always been far too tenuous to allow for confrontational sectarianism. It is for both theological and commonsensical reasons, therefore, that the Bohras have remained aloof from political entanglement. As a matter of policy the dawat has given its support to the government of the day, and instructed all believers to do the same. Syedna Taher Saifuddin offered public prayers for the smooth operation of the British Raj until nearly the end of colonial rule, but after Independence he was quick to offer prayers for the newly formed government as well.[70]

Syedna Muhammad Burhanuddin has continued this policy of supporting any legitimately constituted government. The issue has growing importance, as the Bohra community continues to spread throughout the world. Wherever they settle, Bohras are urged to be loyal and patriotic. The current da'i expressed this sentiment very clearly to Bohras living in Nairobi, Kenya, during a visit on May 3, 1992: "My advice to the followers is but one. Be faithful to the country of your birth and adoption; serve the nation with all your might; work for its prosperity. This is the teaching of our Prophet (SA) *Hubbul Watan minal Iman*. To love your country is a part of your Deen [faith]."[71]

A student at the Jamea tus-Saifiya in Surat (originally from Kenya himself) expressed the same sentiment in slightly more cynical terms: "We don't care who the government is. We'd support the BJP, Shiv Sena, whoever gained power. *All* politics is dirty, so why get involved? Besides, it's not honest to oppose a government while enjoying its protection and benefits." This statement very succinctly encapsulates two of the primary moral foundations for Bohra (and, more generally, Shi'a) apolitical quietism:

(1) In the absence of a visible imam all temporal governments are inherently imperfect, and therefore equally morally suspect. Bernard Lewis notes that this rationale has undergirded Shi'a avoidance of politics throughout the centuries: if the only legitimate rule is that of a present imam, during the period of concealment there is no basis for preferring one illegitimate government to another.[72]

(2) If a government is so oppressive that mu'mineen cannot in good conscience support it, the only moral (and pragmatic) course is to leave the country and oppose it from exile. This, it may be noted, was the course of action followed by Ayatollah Khomeini and other clerical opponents of Shah Muhammad Reza Pahlavi, rebels who planned and largely brought about the Iranian Revolution from exile in Paris and Iraq.

While Indian Shiʿa tend not to be highly politicized, the Bohras maintain their attitude of apoliticality considerably more scrupulously than do Twelvers. In Hasnain and Husain's survey of Ithna-Asharis, 94.3 % of respondents favored active participation in politics, an overwhelming majority that crossed all educational and class lines (90 % of illiterates, 99 % of highly educated). This politicization, however, was not strictly communal: 85.9 % favored joining different political parties rather than forming a single Shiʿa party or voting as a bloc.[73]

The Mumbai Riots and Other Conflicts

The Bohras avoid sectarian violence as an article of faith, but sometimes sectarian violence does not avoid *them*. They suffered continuous persecution from Sunni authorities for much of the Mughal period, and are now (like other Muslims) under increasing threat from the Hindu Right. The rioting that engulfed Mumbai in January 1993 was some of the bloodiest civil strife to hit India in the half century since Partition. More than 500 were reported killed in the Mumbai phase of the post-Ayodhya rioting while nationwide estimates of casualties for the December 1992–March 1993 communal strife are conservatively placed between 1,200 and 1,700. Reputable unofficial death tolls run as high as 3,000, and a majority of the victims seem to have been Muslim.[74] Two years after the destruction of Babri Masjid, the government's Srikrishna Commission still had not been able to explain a two-month casualty toll it placed at 872 dead, 1,829 injured, and 443 "missing."[75] With the municipal government of Mumbai securely in the hands of Shiv Sena, there have been numerous, credible reports of police collusion with (and even active participation in) attacks on Muslims. At a bare minimum, Lise McKean seems correct in her statement that during the 1992–1993 riots "the police and military killed many more Muslims than Hindus."[76] As Tambiah notes, "The Bombay riots present us with the worst instances of active police participation in the shooting of victims."[77]

Particularly troubling to Bohras and other Muslims has been the rise to power of Shiv Sena, first in Mumbai and since 1995 in the entire state of Maharashtra. Bal Thackeray, the founder and self-styled "Supremo" of the Marathi chauvinist organization, has made his political career by scapegoating all residents who are not Hindus and native Marathi-speakers, with Muslims singled out for special abuse.[78] While secularists often slap the label of "fascist" on the entire Hindu nationalist movement, Shiv Sena is one member of the Hindu revivalist family to which that appellation (for reasons of structure, tactics, and ideology) seems singularly appropriate.

Thackeray is quite open in his admiration for European fascist leaders, and has advocated the use of their "solutions" for India's "Muslim problem." In an interview with the Marathi newspaper *Nawa Kal* as far back as August 19, 1967, Thackeray said, "Yes, I am a dictator. Why should we have so many rulers? It is a Hitler that is needed in India today."[79] He has made similar statements on many occasions, up to the present. In clarifying his remarks, Thackeray told an American researcher in 1971 that he simply admired Hitler's decisiveness, and that other examples of a similarly "enlightened dictator" would be Kemal Ataturk and Gamal Abdel Nasser.[80] It is interesting that the two men he selected were both ardent secularists—and both Muslims.

At a superficial level, Bohras sometimes maintain that not even the political dominance of Shiv Sena can influence their attitude of apoliticality. In 1999 Bal Thackeray paid his respects to Syedna Muhammad Burhanuddin on the occasion of Eid al-Fitr, despite the da'i's outspoken condemnation of Shiv Sena for the Mumbai riots.[81] Some Bohras claim that their community has been largely untouched by sectarian violence. As one young man said, "The Hindus know we aren't involved in Babri Masjid, so they have no quarrel with us. When they see the topi, they leave us alone. In past riots, the *goondas* [thugs] have even broken into a house, seen the photograph of His Holiness on the wall, and immediately left—with apologies!"

Much of the violence between Hindus and Muslims has been highly organized,[82] particularly in sites such as Mumbai. During the 1993 riots, much of the bloodshed was due to rival underworld gangs (and their police or Shiv Sainik allies) using the breakdown of civil order to settle a range of private scores that had nothing to do with religion.[83] In the case of organized violence, Bohras may well have been protected by their neutral status: criminal dons would have had little reason to target them, and there is speculation that the dawat paid protection money to assure some level of safety. Even so hostile an observer as Engineer, writing several years before the Mumbai riots, states that the dawat promulgated its dress code reforms in part to *avoid* (rather than provoke) sectarian abuse: "The religious leadership enforced the use of the Bohra cap for Bohra men and the ridah (veil) for their women in order that they were not made targets of attack by Hindus during communal riots."[84]

The reality, unfortunately, has been more tragic. Bohras may not have been attacked by underworld-led gangs, but their quietism provided no protection from the disorganized violence of unruly mobs on a rampage. In their beards or burqas, they were easily identifiable as Muslims—while many Sunnis could blend effortlessly into the Hindu mainstream, Bohras

had marked themselves out by intentional design.* And as a community composed largely of petty shopkeepers, their stores presented attractive targets for the stones and petrol bombs of mobs marauding down Muhammad Ali Road or Bhindi Bazaar. In material terms (at the very least), by virtue of both their appearance and their profession Bohras bore a disproportionate share of the damage.

A dawat publication of 1994 acknowledges as much. An encomium for Mukasir Syedi Saleh Bhaisaheb Safiyuddin notes that the late cleric provided shelter and food to community members whose houses had been torched "during the evil communal holocaust of last year."[85] Engineer notes that Bohras had previously suffered in the Ahmedabad riots of 1969 and the Nagpur violence of 1986.[86] Even before the bloodshed of 1993, 26.7% of his respondents in Mumbai and 60% of those in Gujarat had seen riots, while 16.7% of those in Mumbai and 50% of those in Gujarat (37.5% of the total pool) had been personally affected.[87]

My Mumbai fieldwork was conducted between 1993 and 1995, and almost all of the people I interviewed had some direct, personal experience of rioting. Nearly all expressed shock, surprise, and mystification. As a general rule, Bohras tend to enjoy closer social relations with Hindus than they do with Sunnis, so they were entirely unaccustomed to the shift of alliances. One family, living in the cosmopolitan, religiously integrated Colaba section of the city, recalled the reaction of their Hindu friends with a combination of gratitude and sadness. First the Hindu friends counseled them to leave town for a few days, then (when the family stood firm) advised them to at least take the nameplates off their front door, and finally (when reports of mob violence began to exceed anyone's wildest fears) insisted on giving them refuge in their own homes until the rioting had ceased. "We were glad we had such true friends, who would protect us at great risk to their own lives," the father said, "but we are heartbroken to now live in a world where such protection is needed."

The Bohra population of Karachi has also found itself caught in the communal crossfire. The second largest concentration of Bohras in the world, the community of Karachi numbers approximately 40,000: of these (local sources say), about 30,000 are dues-paying members of the jamat, while the rest live without formal affiliation. There are seventeen Bohra masjids in the city, and relations with civic authorities are so good

*The ease with which many Sunnis could disguise their communal identity led to one of the more bizarre tragedies of the 1993 Mumbai riots. According to popular reports, some Hindu gangs seized any man not personally known to them and forced him to disrobe in order to determine his religious affiliation; uncircumcised men were released, while circumcised Muslims were subjected to a variety of tortures.

that the municipality named all of the streets in Shabbirabad (one of the primary Bohra neighborhoods) after past Bohra daʿis.

Despite their steadfast avoidance of political entanglements, however, the Bohras of Karachi have not been able to stay wholly clear of the rampant sectarian violence that periodically ravages this Pakistani city. The alliances and fault lines shift regularly, with Sindhi-Muhajir and (to a lesser extent) Sunni-Shiʿa battles a continuing fact of life. While the Bohras are an easily identifiable segment of both the Muhajir and the Shiʿa communities, they seem to suffer more from the general atmosphere of lawlessness than from any sectarian targeting. "The *dacoits* [bandits] have gotten completely out of hand," one Karachi Bohra told me. "They are the cronies of the police, so they don't even bother with stealth. They knock on your door in broad daylight, guns drawn, and you have no choice but to give them everything you own."

Their markers of identity may single the Bohras out, but for reasons of expediency rather than ideology: as members of one of the city's wealthier groups, some particularly well-to-do Bohras attract repeated visits from dacoit bands. But the highly organized nature of much of Karachi's violence may have lessened the impact. At the Jamea tus-Saifiya, Mullah Husaifa Saifuddin credits the charismatic spiritual mantle of Syedna for keeping both bandits and mobs away: "We have always been safe from communal strife," the teacher says, and notes that in a city whose residents are armed to the teeth, the campus *chowkidars* (watchmen) carry no firearms. Other sources say the relatively gentle treatment of the Bohras is due less to spiritual than to financial protection: here, as in Mumbai, there is talk of dawat contributions to the political patrons of the local gangs.

Whatever the source of the Bohras' comparative shelter, this field researcher was fortunate enough to benefit from it. On November 12, 1997, Karachi gunmen assassinated four American businessmen and their Pakistani driver, in retaliation for the murder convictions of Pakistanis Mir Amal Kasi and Ramsi Yousef by courts in the United States. On November 13, I was scheduled to fly out of Karachi to attend an anthropological conference. The U.S. embassy advised Americans throughout Pakistan to avoid leaving their homes, and particularly urged those in Karachi to batten down until the crisis passed. Threatening new graffiti appeared on the walls of the city overnight: "Love Islam, Hate America," and scrawled sketches of burning U.S. flags. Since the paper I was scheduled to present highlighted the success of the Bohras in handling a variety of modern social and political problems, there would have been a cruel irony in being derailed by the particularly modern problem of political terrorism.

As it happened, however, friends within the Bohra community provided me sanctuary—quite literally, they protected me with tradition. I was instructed to wear my topi and kurta/pajamas, and spend all of the following day hiding in plain sight. On the campus of the Jamea tus-Saifiya, friends made sure I was always surrounded by diligent eyes and ears. My beard may have been somewhat more blonde than those of the other students, but a Shiʿa theological academy was one of the last places any potential terrorist might have thought to look for an American target. At considerable potential risk to their own safety, the Daudi Bohras of Karachi provided me better protection than a phalanx of bodyguards with flak jackets and AK-47s.

Relations with the Larger Muslim Community

Despite generally warm social relations with other bania groups, the Bohras have traditionally distrusted and kept themselves removed from Sunnis. This is partly the legacy of several centuries of persecution at the hands of Mughals and local Gujarati vassals to Mughal rule, but also the outgrowth of basic doctrinal differences: the central, defining religio-historical event for Bohras (as for all Shiʿa) is the martyrdom of Husain and his companions at Kerbala, and the betrayal of the House of Ali by the Sunni Umayyads.

Abdul Husain, writing in the early twentieth century, noted that even then Bohras and Sunnis had a long heritage of hostility and mutual ill will: "Bohras consider themselves superior to other Mohammadens and are taught to live separate from them."[88] Bohras sometimes seem uncertain about whether or not they belong to the same umma as Sunnis. Like other Shiʿa, they often use the term "Muslims" to mean Sunnis alone, while reserving for themselves the term muʾmineen ("the faithful"). Engineer observes, "Muslims are generally despised both by the Khojahs and Bohras, and they are referred to as 'miyabhais,' a word of contempt. They are considered of lowly origin, backward and aggressive."[89]

Today, Bohras sometimes blame Sunnis for the rise in communal tensions. The issues that motivate Sunni agitation (Shah Bano and Babri Masjid, for example) are not issues of concern to the Bohras, and they resent being drawn into other peoples' battles. For their part, Sunnis sometimes accuse Bohras of cowardice for their apolitical quietism, and call them "idol worshipers" for their intense devotion to Syedna. Such a charge, of course—in theological terms, shirk—is one of the very worst accusations that can be leveled against a devout Muslim.

The words of a young Bohra woman who works in the travel industry are indicative of wider community attitudes. She has spent considerable

time in Dubai and therefore has wider exposure to Sunnis than do many of her peers, but her opinions and preconceptions have been reinforced rather than dismantled by personal contact: "The Muslims are so militant, so fanatical, so violent," she says; "with them everything is a fight. They look only to the Qur'an for all answers in life, as if the book could not be read in a variety of ways. They are always full of pride, think only *they* know the right answers, so they're quick to argue, quick to anger, quick to start a brawl."

Cooperation with Sunni Political Leaders

Despite mutual antipathy between the communities on a social level, on a political level the dawat has made a common cause with the leadership of Sunni (and some Ithna-Ashari) Muslim groups. Syedna Taher Saifuddin contributed generously to Aligarh Muslim University, and he was rewarded for his scholarly endeavors with the school's honorary chancellorship (an honor recently bestowed on the present da'i as well). Although Bohras had no direct stake in the Babri Masjid or Shah Bano controversies, Syedna Muhammad Burhanuddin came out squarely on the side of the Sunni ulema in these cases. In political terms this was partly a deposit in the favor bank, and partly repayment of a previous withdrawal: many Sunni clerics had supported the Bohra dawat when the dissident-launched Nath-wani Commission released its report in 1979. In religious terms, the da'i shared the Sunnis' discomfort at having non-Muslims interpret Islamic law by unmediated reference to the Qur'an: even the haughty proconsuls of the British Raj eventually realized that they had to defer to the ulema in determining the application of sharia.[90]

Such cooperation between Bohras and other Muslims is not entirely new. Immediately prior to Partition, Syedna Taher Saifuddin issued a fatwa to Bohras residing in the Mumbai city constituency from which Muhammad Ali Jinnah was running for a seat in the Central Assembly to cast their votes for the Muslim League leader. Bohras made up a major electoral bloc in the constituency, so Syedna's fatwa was crucial.[91] Jinnah's opponent was a Khojah, Husainbhoy Lalji, who as a fellow Gujarati Ismaili could be presumed to have enjoyed a certain level of sympathy and support among Bohra voters. Jinnah himself would have been a less immediately sympathetic figure: an Ithna-Ashari (rather than Ismaili) Khojah by birth, he had let both his ancestral religion and his ancestral language lapse to the point that Muslim leaders berated him for not knowing how to pray namaz, and Mahatma Gandhi gently urged him to learn Gujarati and Hindi "as soon as possible."[92] Despite this, and despite the fact that the Muslim League was an overwhelmingly Sunni organization, with Taher

Saifuddin's backing Jinnah won the seat handily. From the time of Independence until the present, and increasingly over the past two decades, the Bohra dawat has sought to solidify ties with other Muslim leaders while maintaining a wide social distance at the popular level.

These ties have shown themselves most notably during the controversy over the Hindu revivalist demand for a uniform civil code, which came to a head in the Shah Bano case during the mid-1980s. Shah Bano, an elderly woman divorced by her husband after more than forty years of marriage, took the highly unusual step of suing for alimony in India's civil courts. Historically, Muslims in India have been governed by Islamic rules of marriage, divorce, and all other "personal laws." From the Delhi sultanates until the end of the Mughal empire, of course, such shariat had been the law of the land (for Muslims, at least). During the colonial period, members of each religious community were governed by standardized versions of their own personal laws, administered by the British judicial system. Since Independence, Indian Muslims have been exempt from the uniform personal laws in force for other communities; they are governed by the same standardized version of Islamic shariat put into practice during the time of the Raj.[93]

The Supreme Court's ruling in favor of Shah Bano sent shock waves throughout the Muslim community of India. The judgment was deemed particularly offensive in that the chief justice (like all five members of the bench, a Hindu himself)[94] backed up his reasoning with the assertion that the Qur'an mandated alimony, and that Muslim opponents of this view were not sufficiently versed in their own scriptures. Prime Minister Rajiv Gandhi supported the Supreme Court's decision, but quickly reversed course when faced with the prospect of losing Congress's Muslim vote bank. He pushed the Muslim Women's (Protection of Rights upon Divorce) Act through Parliament in 1987, which effectively overruled the Supreme Court and restored the status quo ante. This quieted Muslim opposition, but suspicion still ran (and still runs) very high.[95]

On the issue of a uniform civil code the Bohra dawat has been particularly active, although it is of little direct concern to Bohras themselves. Yusuf Najmuddin, the late brother and foremost counselor to Syedna Muhammad Burhanuddin, served as treasurer of the Muslim Personal Law Board, a group working against the promulgation of a uniform civil code. Even the respondents to Engineer's survey (a self-selecting group ipso facto somewhat alienated from dawat positions) report that the Shah Bano judgment had no impact on them, as their local jamat took care of the maintenance of divorcées in need.[96] Nevertheless, Syedna Muhammad Burhanuddin has probably been more vocal in his opposition to a uniform

civil code than on any other political topic. The Bohra dawat's veering into electoral activism here stands in marked contrast to the attitude of the Ismaili Khojahs. Under express firman of the aga khan, Khojahs are forbidden to engage in political agitation on Babri Masjid, uniform civil code, or any of the other concerns roiling the larger Muslim community.[97]

A FEW QUESTIONS AND POSSIBLE ANSWERS

In the course of my study on the Bohras I have raised questions that may, in many cases, have much broader social applicability. The following are several of the more immediately pertinent questions, and some thoughts drawn from the Bohra experience that may be of theoretical interest to those pursuing similar topics in other societies.

WHAT ELEMENTS OF BOHRA SOCIETY HAVE FACILITATED THE SMOOTH AND EFFECTIVE INTEGRATION OF MODERN IDEOLOGY AND TECHNOLOGY?

Centralization. Once the dawat made the decision to modernize traditional practices (a course initiated by Syedna Taher Saifuddin and continued by Syedna Muhammad Burhanuddin), this program immediately had the force of religious doctrine. The uniquely hierarchical structure of the denomination makes it particularly well suited to top-down innovation and rapid, coordinated change. There is no need to build grassroots consensus in order for a policy to be carried out effectively. The lines of control among Daudi Bohra are close to unidirectional.

Business orientation. Ease of communication (whether linguistic or technological) is vitally important to small businesspeople, so new technologies have been eagerly absorbed and utilized. Merchants must adapt quickly to changing market circumstances to avoid losing out to competitors, and this necessity spills over into noncommercial facets of everyday life. In a market economy (and, as shopkeepers rather than industrialists, Bohras operated in a market economy even during the "license-permit Raj" of 1947–1991) economic deadwood is generally swept away. The coziness of a social cocoon is a luxury that the Bohras (or any mercantile community) can never afford.

Cultural distance. The Bohras have been influenced both by mainstream and by other minority cultures, but have never been ideologically wedded to any them. They have no sentimental attachment to the Hindu heritage(s) of the Indian majority, nor to the Mughal countertradition upheld by Sunnis of the subcontinent, nor even to the Ithna-Ashari Shi'a tra-

ditions of Awadh and the Deccan sultanates. They are less likely to be held back from innovation by the burden of nostalgia. Quite the contrary—they enjoyed their greatest prosperity and security since Fatimid times under British and postcolonial rule. Not only did Mughal oppression cease under the Raj, but the Bohras (like other Gujarati traders) were able to grow rich serving as intermediaries between East and West. Like the Parsis, Khojahs, and Jain banias, they became comfortable with Western modernity and used this facility to take part in the meteoric rise of Mumbai as a commercial center.

Ideological receptivity. Shi'a theologians have often been more open to outside influences than their Sunni counterparts, even when these influences have come from the alien West. While the Sunni world had a brief, brilliant flirtation with Hellenistic thought during the Abbasid caliphate, once the Mu'tazila school lost favor the door to ijtihad slammed shut. Since the death of Imam al-Ghazali in 1111 C.E., Sunni orthodoxy (outside the realm of Sufism, at least) has generally been welded to the ideas directly expressed in the Qur'an and ahadith. Shi'a orthodoxy, based on the interpretation of the imams and their successors, is less rigid.

Ismaili orthodoxy is even more flexible than that of the Ithna-Ashariyya. Thoroughly grounded in neoplatonic metaphysics, it relies on a living, present, unchallengeable source for the articulation and interpretation of doctrine. While Ithna-Asharis have many mujtahids all competing for the mantle of most orthodox and all liable to be attacked if they stray far from established custom, Ismailis take their guidance from a single apex cleric. For Ismailis the word of the leader carries more weight than mere text, so there is greater leeway for modernist reinterpretation of orthodoxy. It is no accident, I would contend, that the Bohras and their fellow Ismailis the Khojahs are two of the most modern, forward-thinking groups in the Muslim world.

WHY HAVE BOHRAS, UNLIKE SOME OTHER SHI'A GROUPS, SHUNNED POLITICAL VIOLENCE?

Potential answers to this question seem to dovetail with those of the previous one:

Centralized structure. Any community with the Bohras' highly disciplined, hierarchical structure would have to either take up political violence as a tightly controlled guerrilla militia, or not take it up at all. The centrality of the da'i and the all-encompassing nature of his control leave little opportunity for random, centrifugal violence. Sects with more diffuse power structures lend themselves far more easily to sporadic, unmoni-

torable outbursts of sectarian hostility. Even the Ithna-Ashari mujtahids of Iran speak with many voices rather than one. For every reformist cleric like President Muhammad Khatami or Ayatollah Ali Montazeri favoring an easing of political violence there is a conservative like Supreme Leader Ali Khamenei or Ayatollah Taqi Mesbah-Yazdi unwilling to accept moderating influence.[98]

The hierarchical structure of the Bohra community does not preclude political violence, but it discourages the sort of small-scale, uncontrollable hostilities that have plagued many other communities. Dissidents claim that the dawat has used violence to suppress their movement, and over the course of the twentieth century there have been more than a few cases of unarmed scuffles between orthodox and dissident partisans. But the very fact that dissident leader Asghar Ali Engineer lives and works without any bodyguards or elaborate safety precautions in a Mumbai suburb populated by many orthodox Bohras is testament to the dawat's basically quietistic attitude.[99]

Business outlook and minority status. Political violence is all but incompatible with the lifestyle of petty shopowners—their stores make far too easy a target for any counterattack. As a community largely located in urban areas, possessing immovable property and livelihoods, the Bohras do not have the option of engaging in violence and then taking refuge in the hinterland. In order to engage effectively in sectarian conflict the Bohras would first have change their entire economy and style of life. Moreover, their business outlook is not merely an economic veneer thinly overlying wholly different core values: the Bohras are a community converted from Hindu Vaishya castes. The prevailing ethos, from the centuries prior to conversion right up to the present, has been that of the mercantile Vaishya rather than the martial Kshatriya varna. Moreover, as shopkeepers they have of necessity lived as a relatively small minority amidst far more numerous populations of other communities. They have been both economically dependent upon the goodwill (not to mention the business) of their neighbors, and numerically in no position to engage in sectarian conflict. Like the Khojahs, they have historically had little choice but to come to terms with the local ruling powers of the day.

Ideology. Two long-standing Shi'a doctrines bear directly on the issue of political violence and practice of quietism: (1) since the only truly legitimate temporal rule would be that of the imam, during the period of seclusion all mu'mineen should avoid political engagement and refrain from political agitation; (2) the concept of taqiyya (dissimulation) permits Shi'a to accept the dictates of temporal masters outwardly while secretly maintaining their own true agendas and beliefs. This doctrine has been even

more prominent among Ismailis than mainstream Twelver Shi'a, since (with the exception of Fatimid Egypt) they have often had to suffer persecution not only from Sunni rulers, but from Ithna-Ashari local officials as well. If the Bohras have chosen to maintain their culture and identity through taqiyya and careful protection of gnostic batin knowledge rather than through sectarian violence, they are following a long historical and ideological tradition.

WHAT LESSONS CAN OTHER TRADITIONAL CULTURES LEARN FROM THE BOHRAS' EXAMPLE?

Anthropology is a discipline that can (and, in my opinion, should) have real-world applicability as well as more narrowly focused scholarly interest.[100] It is my hope that this case study of the Daudi Bohras will not only make some contribution to the sphere of academic knowledge, but in so doing may provide data relevant to a much wider audience. This was the rationale behind the dawat's decision to sanction my research: the possibility that other traditionalist communities (Muslim and non-Muslim alike) might find some benefit from the study of the Bohras' effort to maintain their cultural and spiritual identity. This study is not meant to be a platform for activist concerns, but it gives rise to certain observations that may profitably be explored in other venues.

Modernity is inevitable. As the Anglo-Danish king Canute famously demonstrated, nobody can turn back the tide. Modernity will come, the only question is when, how, and with what sort of impact. A society may retain greater control over its traditional culture by riding the wave of modernity than merely by waiting for it to crash.

Modernity is divisible. A society can accept certain elements while rejecting others, and can even use certain elements of modernity to protect itself from others. This need not be (indeed, perhaps cannot be) limited to the technological sphere alone. Qing mandarins and Ottoman sultans of the nineteenth century attempted to accept Western technology while rejecting Western ideology, and discovered the difficulty of such wholesale division. At the time of writing, Iranian clerics may be learning the same lesson. But even in the ideological realm there are many intellectual tools that can help premodern societies defend their core values. The Bohras' holistic approach to modern and traditional education, for example, can serve as a model for other communities.

An effective harnessing of modern forces and technologies does not come by accident. The Bohras have succeeded because they have had a unified game plan, and strict dawat control insures coordinated application.

Other cultures with more diffuse structures will be less easily able to control their modernization—they may well consider coordinating their response, forging intrasocietal bonds to prepare a common and unified approach. There is great strength in societal unity, against a human enemy or one so nebulous as the forces of modernity. Whether the agent of change is a logging consortium in the Amazon or an oil company in coastal Nigeria (pick your villain—there are plenty to go around), examples of premodern cultures dismembered by the divide-and-conquer policies of transnational corporations and other modern forces are too numerous to cite. There is power in diversity of opinion, but there is also power in solidarity of purpose.

Symbiosis is key. The Bohras have been able to integrate and utilize modernity because they regard it as a friend rather than a foe. When modernity is cast as the obstacle to be overcome, the battle is already more than halfway lost. By reorienting the mindset of the community, the dawat has succeeded in reorienting modernity to serve as a bolster for the group's fundamental traditions. The Bohras regard deen and dunya (spiritual and temporal concerns) as two halves of an integrated whole: it's not an either-or proposition, but a way of looking at both religious and everyday concerns in a holistic manner. In the meeting of heritage and humanism, there need be no victor or vanquished.

CLOSING THOUGHTS

When guardians of tradition set up a dichotomy between group identity and "modern" identity, it is generally group identity that will lose out. If being a good Bohra means living in exactly the same way one's grandfather and great-grandfather lived, eschewing Western education and the material comforts that come with it, shutting one's eyes to an exciting and rapidly changing world—if this is what it means to be a good Bohra, there will be fewer and fewer good Bohras with every passing year. The Daudi clergy has skillfully avoided this pitfall. The dawat's success comes from its ability to break down the false dichotomy between modernity and tradition, to let members of the community revel in both. This approach permits them to enjoy the benefits of modern life while solidifying an identity that is both thoroughly Islamic and uniquely Bohra. The program has been so successful that an overwhelming 90.1% of my survey respondents reported traditional values stronger today than in previous generations, and said modern educational and technological methods had strongly aided in this revival.

Lévi-Strauss noted the importance of "intellectual '*bricolage*'" (handi-

work) in the maintenance of traditional systems of "mythical thought."[101] I suggest that the Bohras—a highly cosmopolitan group whose *pensée* is in no way *sauvage*—have become masterful *bricoleurs* indeed. Some of the elements that have made their program a success may be unique to the Bohras, but there is much that other traditional-minded minority communities can borrow in their own attempts to balance ancient custom with modern innovations. As Fredrik Barth notes, the mission of anthropology extends beyond the mere cataloging and analysis of societal practices: "[W]e should not seek a fictitious cultural authority in others—we should engage them in an interchange of knowledge and judgment. . . . Our relativism should be located in the humility to learn and to engage."[102]

Such an interchange with the Daudi Bohras, a community never before engaged by outside scholars, should prove fruitful indeed. A vibrant traditional culture can enrich the life of a society, but when ancient customs are seen merely as quaint anachronisms they are in danger of being cast off as the detritus of history. The Daudi Bohras, however, have succeeded in chipping the rust off their rituals, keeping their core values and beliefs functional through careful rehabilitation and reformulation. By using all the modernist tools in their technological and intellectual toolbox, the Bohra *bricoleurs* have maintained their cultural heritage in full working order.

Can other traditional societies reconcile the legacy of the past with the demands of the future? One way or another, all will have to. The Daudi Bohras, a vulnerable minority throughout their existence, have always managed to adapt to the world around them without losing their souls. Modernity, for them, is nothing new.

Appendixes

1. LINE OF MUSTAʿLI TAYYIBI ISMAILI IMAMS

1. Hasan ibn Ali ibn Abi Talib (40–49/661–669)*
2. Husain ibn Ali ibn Abi Talib (49–61/669–680)
3. Ali Zain al-Abidin ibn Husain (61–95/680–714)
4. Muhammad al-Baqir ibn Ali Zain al-Abidin (95–114/714–732)
5. Jafar al-Sadiq ibn Muhammad al-Baqir (114–148/732–765)
6. Ismail al-Mubarak ibn Jafar al-Sadiq†
7. Muhammad al-Maktum ibn Ismail al-Mubarak†
8. Abdullah ibn Muhammad†
9. Ahmad ul-Wafi ibn Abdullah†
10. Husain-ut Taqi ibn Ahmad (d.268/881)†
11. Abu Muhammad Abdullah al-Mahdi ibn Husain (268–322/881–934)
12. Abul-Qasim Muhammad al-Qaim ibn Abdullah (322–334/934–946)
13. Abu Tahir Ismail al-Mansur billah ibn Muhammad (334–341/946–953)
14. Abu Tamim Muayid al-Muizz li-Din Allah (341–365/953–975)
15. Abu Mansur Nizar al-Aziz billah ibn Muizz (365–386/975–996)
16. Abu Ali al-Mansur al-Hakim bi-Amr Allah ibn Aziz (386–411/996–1021)
17. Abul-Hasan Ali al-Zahir li-Izaz Din Allah ibn Mansur (411–427/1021–1036)
18. Abu Tamim Maad al-Mustansir billah ibn Zahir (427–487/1036–1094)
19. Mustaʿli billah ibn Mustansir (487–495/1094–1101)
20. Al-Amir bi-ahkam Allah ibn Mustaʿli (495–524/1101–1130)
21. Tayyib ibn Amir (entered concealment 526/1132)

Sources: Dawat interviews and texts, corroborated in Abdul Husain 1920: 4–5; Daftary 1990: 551; Poonawala 1977: 363.

*In Bohra (as opposed to Ithna-Ashari Shiʿa) doctrine, Ali ibn Abi Talib is regarded not as the first imam, but as Wasi to the Prophet Muhammad.

†Ismaili opinion has been divided as to the date of Imam Ismail's death. Some theologians have placed Ismail's death around the year 136/754, while other sources describe this as an event staged for reasons of taqiyya.

†Hidden imams (no reliable dates).

2. LINE OF DAUDI BOHRA DA'IS

Musta'li Da'is in Yemen

1. Dhuaib ibn Musa 546/1151*
2. Ibrahim ibn Husain al-Hamidi 557/1162
3. Hatim Shamsuddin ibn Ibrahim al-Hamidi (son of da'i 2) 596/1199
4. Ali ibn Hatim al-Hamidi Shamsuddin (son of da'i 3) 605/1209
5. Ali ibn Muhammad ibn al-Walid 612/1215
6. Ali ibn Hanzala 626/1229
7. Ahmad ibn Mubarak ibn Muhammad ibn al-Walid (nephew of da'i 5) 627/1229
8. Husain ibn Ali ibn Muhammad ibn al-Walid (son of da'i 5) 667/1268
9. Ali ibn Husain ibn Ali ibn M. al-Walid (son of da'i 8) 682/1284
10. Ali ibn Husain ibn Ali ibn Hanzala (grandson of da'i 6) 686/1287
11. Ibrahim ibn Husain ibn Ali ibn M. ibn al-Walid (son of da'i 8) 728/1328
12. Muhammad ibn Hatim ibn Husain ibn al-Walid (nephew of da'i 11) 729/1329
13. Ali Shamsuddin ibn Ibrahim ibn Husain (son of da'i 11) 746/1345
14. Abdul Muttalib Najmuddin ibn Muhammad ibn Hatim (son of da'i 12) 755/1354
15. Abbas ibn Muhammad ibn Hatim (brother of da'i 14) 779/1378
16. Abdullah Fakhruddin ibn Ali ibn Muhammad (nephew of da'i 15) 809/1407
17. Hasan Badruddin ibn Abdullah Fakhruddin (son of da'i 16) 821/1418
18. Ali Shamsuddin ibn Abdullah Fakhruddin (brother of da'i 17) 832/1428
19. Idris Imad al-Din ibn Hasan Badruddin (son of da'i 17) 872/1468
20. Hasan Badruddin ibn Idris Imad al-Din (son of da'i 19) 918/1512
21. Husain Husamuddin ibn Idris Imad al-Din (son of da'i 19) 933/1527
22. Ali Shamsuddin ibn Husain Husamuddin (son of da'i 21) 933/1527
23. Muhammad Ezzuddin ibn Hasan Badruddin (son of da'i 20) 946/1539

Daudi Bohra Da'is in India

24. Yusuf Najmuddin ibn Sulaiman 974/1567
25. Jalal Shamsuddin ibn Hasan 975/1567
26. Daud Burhanuddin ibn Ajabshah 999/1591
27. Daud Burhanuddin ibn Qutbshah 1021/1612†

*Dates listed are those of death. Sources for succession of da'is in Yemen and India: Dawat interviews and texts. Cf. Fyzee 1934a: 11–12, 13–14; also cf. Abdul Husain 1920: 24–28; Hollister 1953: 266–267, 275.

†Sulaimani Bohras have a separate line from the twenty-seventh da'i onward.

28. Shaikh Adam Saifuddin ibn Tayyibshah 1030/1621

29. Abdul-Tayyib Zakiuddin ibn Daud ibn Qutbshah (son of daʿi 27) 1041/1631

30. Ali Shamsuddin ibn Husain ibn Idris (Yemeni grandson of daʿi 19) 1042/1632

31. Qasim Zainuddin ibn Pirkhan 1054/1644

32. Qutbkhan Qutbuddin ibn Daud ibn Qutbshah (son of daʿi 27) 1056/1646

33. Pirkhan Shujahuddin ibn Ahmedji 1065/1655

34. Ismail Badruddin ibn Mulla Raj (first Rajput daʿi) 1085/1674

35. Abdul-Tayyib Zakiuddin ibn Badruddin (son of daʿi 34) 1110/1699

36. Musa Kalimuddin ibn Zakiuddin (son of daʿi 35) 1122/1710

37. Nur Muhammad Nuruddin ibn Kalimuddin (son of daʿi 36) 1130/1718

38. Ismail Badruddin ibn Syedi Adam (cousin of daʿi 37) 1150/1737

39. Ibrahim Wajihuddin ibn Abdul-Qadir Hakimuddin 1168/1754

40. Hibtullah Muayidfuddin ibn Wajihuddin (son of daʿi 39) 1193/1779

41. Abdul-Tayyib Zakiuddin ibn Badruddin (son of daʿi 38) 1200/1785

42. Yusuf Najmuddin ibn Zakiuddin (son of daʿi 41) 1213/1798

43. Abdul Ali Saifuddin ibn Zakiuddin (brother of daʿi 42) 1232/1817

44. Muhammad Ezzuddin ibn Shaikh Jiwanji Aurangabadi 1236/1821

45. Tayyib Zainuddin ibn Shaikh Jiwanji Aurangabadi (brother of daʿi 44) 1252/1837

46. Muhammad Badruddin ibn Saifuddin (son of daʿi 43) 1256/1840

47. Abdul-Qadir Najmuddin ibn Zainuddin (son of daʿi 45) 1302/1885

48. Abdul-Husain Husamuddin ibn Zainuddin (brother of daʿi 47) 1308/1891

49. Muhammad Burhanuddin ibn Najmuddin (son of daʿi 47) 1323/1906

50. Abdullah Badruddin ibn Husamuddin (son of daʿi 48) 1333/1915

51. Taher Saifuddin ibn Burhanuddin (son of daʿi 49) 1385/1965

52. Muhammad Burhanuddin ibn Saifuddin (son of daʿi 51) present daʿi

3. QUESTIONNAIRE USED FOR ISSUING CERTIFICATES
OF ORTHOPRAXY

This translation of a Lisanu-Dawat original was made by Jonah Blank, under the guidance of Mullah Shabbir M. Mansoorbhai Jamali. The form is the one used by the Hyderabad (Deccan) jamat; each local jamat is free to devise any form it wishes in order to elicit the necessary information, or to make its determination of eligibility for green, yellow, and red ID cards by an oral examination. The form that follows is typical of those used in many jamats throughout the Bohra world, but there is considerable local variation. [Bracketed text is the translator's comment]

Place: Hyderabad.
Amil present _____
 [Sometimes the card is issued by a person other than the usual amil; another trusted member of the jamat can stand in during the amil's absence.]

Salaam Aleikum. The blessings of God be upon you [i.e., the amil]. Having blessed the name of God, I also thank Ali and the family of Ali by saying salawat [sɛlɛwat] upon them. I have faith in Ali and his family, I love them in my heart, as I love the present daʿi, the 52nd daʿi His Holiness Muhammad Burhanuddin. I love him, submit to his firman, and pledge to act according to his instructions. I am a mumin, I believe in Islam and the Imams, and this [i.e., faith] is something God gave me without my asking him. For all this, I thank God. And these are the details [of my petition]:

Male/Female
 [Petitioner circles one; the term for "male" is *mamuluk,* lit. Arabic for "manservant," i.e., manservant of God. The term for "female" is *ahmat.*]

Purpose [In seeking card; petitioner circles one or more.]
 (1) Hajj. (2) Ziyaret [including permission to stay in musafirkhanas]. (3) Marriage of son. (4) Marriage of daughter. (5) Audience with Syedna. (6) Salawat [inviting people to a feast in praise of members of ahl-e bayt; card issued when this act is performed out of town, since within the community everybody would already know the individual throwing the feast]. (7) Fatiyah [when a relative dies in another city, and survivors must go there to perform rituals]. (8) Other.

Name _____

Father's name _____
 [This is for men, or adult unmarried women. Generally all members of a household are listed on the same card, filled out by the household head. Children under the age of mithaq do not need a card.]

Mithaq [Petitioner circles one.]
 Given in presence of Syedna.
 Given in presence of another member of Qasr-e Ali.
 Given in presence of the amil or other local official.

Religious Titles

	Yes	No	Year given
Mullah			
Shaikh			
Other title			

[Other titles include those given to individuals active in local jamat.]

Committee Memberships [Circle all that apply, now or in the past.]
 Jamat
 Shabab [for young adults, approximately 25–40 years old]
 Madrasas
 No-interest loans
 Savings bank [This is different from loans. Here individuals deposit money
 and withdraw it just like in any public bank, but receive no interest.]
 Women's Committee
 Burhani Women's' Association [A committee for women over the age of 50.
 Until her death in August 1994, headed by the daʻi's wife.]
[Then follow seven blank spaces for other committee names. The committees
listed above are the ones on the Hyderabad form; other localities would have a
slightly different selection.]

Jamat title [Check whichever applies.]
 Wali mullah [Can substitute for amil when the amil is out of town.]
 Treasurer [In charge of financial dealings with the Mumbai dawat. He sends
 zakat to the daʻi, and handles major finances rather than daily expendi-
 tures.]
 Trustee
 Vice-president [His duties are more like those of an assistant administrator.]
 Secretary
 Assistant secretary
 Accountant [Handles the local, day-to-day jamat expenditures.]
 Assistant accountant
 Member

Professional office [That is, title in the secular world. This lets the jamat keep
track of which judges, lawyers, policemen, doctors, professors, etc. are available
for service.]
 General office _____
 Political office _____
 Academic office _____

Namaz

	Regularly	Sometimes	Never
In masjid			
At home			

23rd of Ramadan

	In masjid	Home with family	Alone
First half of night			
Second half of night			

Eid [i.e., Eid al-Fitr]	In masjid	Home with family	Alone

Other Eids [incl. Bakri Eid]	In masjid	Home with family	Alone

During namaz at masjid, do you stay to the end?

Fasting

	All days	Some days	No days
Ramadan			

	Fasted	Did not fast
13–15 of Rajab		
27 of Rajab		
18 of zyl-Hajj		

Tahara
wuzu [washing before namaz]
gusl [bathing at home]
[Check whether one is careful about cleanliness before coming to masjid.]

Prohibitions

	Never	Sometimes, but trying to phase out	Often
Interest			
Liquor [sherab]			
Gambling			
Tobacco			
Other [includes adultery, drugs, etc.]			

Personal dress/cleanliness

	Always	Sometimes	Never
Wear dhari [beard]			
Wear topi			

	Always	Only sometimes
Keep body clean		
Wear clean clothes		

Explanation [If petitioner works in an auto garage, for example, it is understandable that his cleanliness would not be perfect at all times]

Taxes

	Paid every year	Not paid every year
Zakat		
Sila/fitra		

Have you kissed the hand of Syedna? Yes/No

Have you had an audience with Syedna? If so, when? _____

Pilgrimages [Ziyaret; check those that apply]

	Yes	No
Hajj		
Umra		
Medina		
Najaf [Iraq]		
Kerbala [Iraq]		
Cairo		
Yemen		

Majlis

	On time	Early	Late	Not attended	Partly attended
Muharram					
Urs					
Teachings					
Other programs					

Charitable donations

	Often	Occasionally	Never
Dinners [salawat]			
Majlis [paying for one in a relative's honor]			
Construction of buildings			
Other charity			

Do you pay your jamat tax regularly?
[This is often nominal, as little as Rs. 20 per household per month, but can be much higher for wealthy families.]

I hereby request Syedna's blessing. I will follow sharia, in accordance with his instructions. By so doing, I know I will live happily in this life, and in the next I will reach Heaven.

Signature _____

4. ANALYSIS OF *GULSHAN-E MALUMAT* DATA

In examining the 3,177 photos of community leaders published in the *Gulshan-e Malumat* (Raik 1975), I have divided the individuals into three groups: traditional, semitraditional, and nontraditional. In an attempt to make the division as objective as possible I have used the following guidelines:

> Traditional: Subject is wearing a beard and Muslim headgear (feta, topi, etc.).
>
> Semitraditional: Subject is wearing Muslim headgear, but not a beard.
>
> Nontraditional: Subject wears neither a beard nor Muslim headgear.

In assessing overall appearance, I have tried to make my judgments conservative: I include as Muslim headgear not only traditional Bohra feta (golden turban) and white pillbox topi, but also black topi or similar cap, and any turban more compact than the large Rajasthani headgear generally associated with Hindu Rajputs. Several men were judged traditional even if they did not have full beards: if the rest of their dress was traditional and they appeared not to be intentionally shaven, I judged the lack of facial hair to be follicular rather than ideological. The only cases in which I judged a bearded man to be nontraditional were those in which he was wearing a business suit and no headgear.

About three quarters of the nontraditionalists could never be mistaken for orthodox traditionalists: they are clean-shaven and wearing a suit or shirtsleeves with a tie. The other quarter wear Indian clothing not generally associated with Bohras: Nehru suits, Maharashtrian headgear, even high-piled Rajput turbans. If any element of the individual's dress or appearance was traditional I excluded him from the nontraditional group.

The semitraditional men appear much closer to the nontraditionalists in general bearing than to the traditionalists: most of them wear Western or modern Indian clothing, often suits or shirtsleeves rather than kurtas. Those who have facial hair have a mustache or close-trimmed goatee rather than a full beard. It is quite possible, perhaps even likely, that many of these individuals would be indistinguishable from the nontraditionalists in daily life, but chose to wear a topi for their official photograph.

Data from all sites was tabulated to produce the tallies below. The chart below provides data for sites with twenty-five or more community leaders photographed. Pilgrimage towns, where the level of orthopraxy would presumably be higher than average, are denoted by an asterisk.

Analysis of *Gulshan-e Malumat* data

	Traditional	Semitraditional	Nontraditional
India totals (510 sites)	996	608	474
(2,078 profiles)	(47.9%)	(29.3%)	(22.8%)
Non-India totals	177	336	586
(1,099 profiles)	(16.1%)	(30.6%)	(53.3%)
Combined totals	1,173	944	1,060
(3,177 profiles)	(36.9%)	(29.7%)	(33.4%)

	Traditional	Semitraditional	Nontraditional
Sites in India:			
Ahmedabad*	26	22	3
Aurangabad	6	9	10
Bhopal	18	8	7
Calcutta	23	29	17
Dohad	46	28	10
Godhra*	17	17	17
Hyderabad	6	4	37
Indore	30	27	12
Jamnagar*	8	14	9
Madras (Chennai)	19	19	21
Mumbai*	76	43	45
Nagpur	11	21	45
Pune	24	17	19
Raipur	9	13	8
Rajkot	19	6	6
Rampura*	26	2	2
Siddhpur*	20	5	1
Sunel	26	5	4
Surat*	65	7	19
Udaipur*	19	11	3
Ujjain*	34	35	17
Foreign countries:			
Bangladesh	6	10	55
Dubai	4	6	19
Indonesia	1	23	18
Iraq	3	21	26
Kenya	24	17	55
Kuwait	7	15	64
Madagascar	28	83	83

Malaysia	6	12	19
Pakistan	22	49	21
Sri Lanka	31	15	7
Singapore	2	13	39
Tanzania	24	43	82
Thailand	6	5	19
USA	0	0	12

*Pilgrimage towns

5. KINSHIP TIES OF THE DAUDI DAʿIS

Dhuaib ibn Musa (daʿi 1) 546/1151 [no kinship ties]

The transferral of the dawat to India severed the dynastic link with Yemeni families (except, briefly, for Ali Shamsuddin (daʿi 30) 1042/1632, a descendant of Syedna Idris). The daʿis of this time without dynastic ties were: Yusuf Najmuddin (daʿi 24) 974/1567; Jalal Shamsuddin (daʿi 25) 975/1567; Daud Burhanuddin ibn Ajabshah (daʿi 26) 999/1591; Shaikh Adam Saifuddin (daʿi 28) 1030/1621; Qasim Zainuddin ibn Pirkhan (daʿi 31) 1054/1644; and Pirkhan Shujahuddin ibn Ahmedji (daʿi 33) 1065/1655.

Daud Burhanuddin (daʿi 27) 1021/1612

Abdul-Tayyib Zakiuddin
(daʿi 29) 1041/1631

Qutbkhan Qutbuddin
(daʿi 32) 1056/1646

[break in dynastic line]

Ismail Badruddin
(da'i 34) 1085/1674

Abdul-Tayyib Zakiuddin
(da'i 35) 1110/1699

Musa Kalimuddin
(da'i 36) 1122/1710

Nur Muhammad
(da'i 37) 1130/1718

Syedi Adam

Ismail Badruddin
(da'i 38) 1150/1737

Abdul-Qadir Hakimuddin

Ibrahim Wajihuddin
(da'i 39) 1168/1754

Hibtullah Muayidfuddin
(da'i 40) 1193/1779

Abdul-Tayyib Zakiuddin
(da'i 41) 1200/1785

Yusuf Najmuddin
(da'i 42) 1213/1798

Abdul Ali Saifuddin
(da'i 43) 1232/1817

Current Dynasty:
Shaikh Jiwanji Aurangabadi

Muhammad Ezzuddin
(da'i 44) 1236/1821

Tayyib Zainuddin
(da'i 45) 1252/1837

Muhammad Badruddin
(da'i 46) 1256/1840

Abdul-Qadir Najmuddin
(da'i 47) 302/1885

Muhammad Burhanuddin
(da'i 49) 1323/1906

Taher Saifuddin ibn Burhanuddin
(da'i 51) 1385/1965

Muhammad Burhanuddin
(da'i 52) present da'i

Abdul-Husain Husamuddin
(da'i 48) 1308/1891

Abdullah Badruddin
(da'i 50) 1333/1915

(*Sources:* Assembled primarily from information in Mausam-e bahar; also Ali 1954, Abdul Husain 1920, Fyzee 1934a, Hollister 1953, Ismailji 1937)

Bibliographical Discussion

An academic researcher seeking to study the Daudi Bohras through texts faces a challenge not often encountered in modern times: primary-source documents are almost entirely off-limits, and nonpartisan secondary sources are almost nonexistent. The dawat's strict control over access to the community has kept the Bohras free from the ravages of anthropological study, so a scholar seeking background must become an omnivorous scavenger of information. Available material falls into several categories:

HISTORICAL WORKS ON ISMAILIS

While early Orientalists such as de Sacy, de Goeje, Lane-Poole, O'Leary, Casanova, and Massignon had to make do with second- or thirdhand speculation about early Ismaili practices, modern scholars are now able to examine many documents in something close to their original form. The titan in this field was Wladamir Alekseevich Ivanow (d.1970), a Russian émigré who spent most of his life unearthing, translating, and publishing long-secret Ismaili texts in Central Asia, Yemen, Mumbai, and the Nizari hill country of Chitral, Gilgit, and Hunza. In the middle decades of the twentieth century, Henry Corbin, Bernard Lewis, and Samuel Stern brought a new level of scholarship to the field, while A. A. A. Fyzee and Husain F. al-Hamdani were among first Ismaili writers to study their community from a strictly historical rather than devotional viewpoint. While these and most of the other internationally known Ismaili historians have been Sulaimanis or Khojahs, several Daudi Bohra scholars have also made contributions to the study of Fatimid texts: S. T. Lokhandwalla edited an edition of Qadi al-Nuʿman's *Kitab Ikhtil afusul al-madhahib,* while Shaikh Yunus Shakib Mubarakpuri translated al-Nuʿman's *Daʿaʾim al-Islam* into Urdu and Gujarati, and wrote a 3,000-page Urdu history of the Fatimid caliphate.[1] The most comprehensive and useful modern survey of Fatimid and pre-Fatimid Ismailism (with what post-Fatimid information can be

gleaned from less plentiful sources) is probably that of Farhad Daftary, who draws the available scholarship together in a unified, authoritative study.

In sharp contrast to source material for the Fatimid period, or even the later history of the Nizaris, texts dealing with Musta'li Ismaili history are exceptionally sparse. For the very earliest years of the dawat in Yemen, information can be gathered from the *Tarikh al-Yaman* of Najmuddin Umara ibn Ali al-Hakami (d.569/1174). The most important source for events of the sixth-ninth/twelfth-fifteenth centuries is the history written by the nineteenth Tayyibi da'i, Syedna Idris Imad al-Din (Qureshi) ibn al-Hasan (d.872/1468). A scion of the al-Walid clan of Yemeni Quraish who led the dawat for the first three centuries of its post-Fatimid operation, Idris was a noted warrior and administrator as well as the dawat's most celebrated historian. His *Uyun al-akhbar wa funun al-athar* (1975) is the most valuable source on the dawat prior to its transferal to India.

The next major documentary source does not arrive for more than 400 years: the *Mausam-e bahar*. This text, written in Gujarati in Arabic script, remains the single most important work of Bohra history. Its author was Muhammad Ali ibn Jiwabhai, a dawat official under the forty-seventh da'i, Syedna Abdul-Qadir Najmuddin.[2] The first two volumes are accounts of the prophets and the imams, ending with the imamate of Tayyib. The third volume contains the history of the Bohras in India. This tome, completed in 1882 and published in several Gujarati editions since, is generally deemed authoritative by both the dawat and dissidents alike. During the Burhanpur durgah case of the early twentieth century, both parties accepted the chronicle as reliable.[3] It has been only rarely available, however, since it contains a discussion of the controversy surrounding the nass of Syedna Abdul-Qadir Najmuddin, a topic of great sensitivity to dawat officials. (While no copies are available in any of the major university libraries of India, I have located two in libraries in the United States.)

There has been no significant attention paid to the Bohras even by the limited cadre of scholars (Ismaili and Western alike) working on Fatimid doctrine. Daftary notes, "Western Orientalists and Ismaili specialists have not so far produced major works on Musta'li Ismailism, particularly the history of the Tayyibi dawa in India, owing mainly to the scarcity of reliable sources."[4] Likewise, the late Ismaili scholars Fyzee and Husain al-Hamdani (as well as the latter's son Abbas, and more recently Ismail Poonawala) have provided important works on Fatimid history, but little on more recent centuries. Several Daudi Bohra writers have provided historical accounts in Gujarati and Urdu, but these consist almost entirely of

uncritical recapitulation and condensation of the information in the *Mausam-e bahar* rather than independent analysis.[5]

WORKS PUBLISHED BY THE BOHRA CLERGY

Although the dawat libraries contain great literary treasures, these texts are not available to researchers outside the community—a matter of considerable disgruntlement among scholars of Ismailism.[6] Access to all such works—including many zahir texts as well as the esoteric batin ones—is strictly limited to individuals who have taken the oath of mithaq. Bohras themselves are permitted to study the deeper reaches of Ismaili theology only under careful supervision, and each text requires special authorization.* Because of taqiyya and the fundamental nature of batini ta'wil, outside scholars would have a very difficult time interpreting such works properly even if they were permitted access: Ismaili doctrine reaches far beyond words on a page. In any case these works, and the limited number of zahir texts that are more widely available, deal strictly with theology (dawat sources have told me),† and would be of considerably more interest to a student of religion than of anthropology.

Virtually all other dawat texts are either devotional tracts or polemical pamphlets. This is to be expected: the Vatican press similarly prints works that conform to Roman Catholic orthodoxy. The Bohra dawat's Department of Statistics and Information has issued dozens of brief pamphlets (often little more than press releases) by such authors as Shaikh Yusuf Bekhud and the late Shaikh Tyebally Davoodbhoy or merely credited to the Dawat-e-Hadiyah. The institutional outlook of these publications is readily apparent. In 1943, an informative tract on Bohra marriage codes by dawat attorney Shaikh Abbasali Najafali was published posthumously.

*In recent years the dawat has made access to batin texts considerably easier than it had been for past generations. While such works are still available only to Bohras who have taken mithaq, and are generally taught in carefully monitored study groups rather than opened for unsupervised individual research, this represents a significant easing of restrictions. Reportedly, not even the higher reaches of haqiqat (the upper levels of batini ta'wil) are off-limits to ordinary laypeople who have demonstrated loyalty to the dawat and a serious will to learn. The da'i has often encouraged his followers to pursue as much batin knowledge as they can. It may be of small comfort to scholars of Ismailism who are outside the community, but among the Bohras themselves exploration of batini ta'wil may well be more widespread than at any time since the fall of the Fatimid caliphate.

†There is, of course, no way to be certain. I have been in libraries where some of these texts are stored, but did not request (and would not have been granted) permission to study them.

Perhaps the most useful orthodox publication (not printed or commissioned by the dawat, but circulated with its approval and under its aegis) is S. Kikabhai Raik's *Gulshan-e Malumat* (1975), which includes (after 300 pages of devotional material) a Who's Who of prominent Bohras throughout the world prior to the issuing of various orthopraxic reforms in the late 1970s and early 1980s. A similar work, the *Bostan-e Daudi,* had been published in 1960. In 1998 a dawat-affiliated author (Shaikh Mustafa Abdulhussein) contributed three brief entries on Bohra-related topics to the *Oxford Encyclopedia of the Modern Islamic World,* entries that fully meet the standards of academic impartiality; while I myself am hardly impartial on the subject of Dr. Abdulhussein's impartiality (he was kind enough to review my manuscript for accuracy prior to publication), I can attest to his keen appreciation of the standards and requirements of modern scholarship.

WORKS WRITTEN BY BOHRA DISSIDENTS

Owing largely to the dawat's long-standing policy of keeping internal matters strictly internal, publicly circulated texts dealing with the Bohras are generally the work of dissidents—usually dawat opponents who have been placed under baraat. The most prolific of these authors is Asghar Ali Engineer, the current leader of the dissident camp, whose influence throughout the spheres of Indian academia and journalism is described in chapter 9.* Several sources not officially affiliated with the reformist Bohras must be treated as de facto dissident sources, as they draw most (in some cases, all) of their material directly from dissident texts. The most important of these is the Nathwani Report, the dissident provenance of which is described earlier. There is also a monograph by Shibani Roy: while Roy is not herself a party to the controversy, she relies almost entirely on Engineer (and, through him, Abdul Husain) for her cultural, historical, and religious material.[7] Any information not taken from Engineer or Abdul Husain is based on observations made in Udaipur during a period when that city's congregation was excommunicated from the worldwide Bohra community. Her study has been called into question by its author's primary authority: Engineer described Roy's work as "highly misleading," and noted that "she did not know the languages or the original sources."[8]

*Dr. Engineer, it should be noted, is an academic scholar rather than a mere polemicist. He has authored a wide variety of books on Islam, politics, and culture. When discussing the Bohra community he writes as a partisan rather than a dispassionate outsider, but on many other topics his academic detachment is not in dispute.

REFERENCES TO BOHRAS IN WIDER WORKS

Academic texts on Indian Shiʿa of any denomination are quite rare,[9] and the only monograph on them to discuss the Bohras is that of John Norman Hollister (1953). Daftary provides a brief discussion of the Bohras in his history of Ismailis, but he (like Hollister and, indeed, almost all other sources) draws his material from secondhand reports. Satish Misra's survey of Gujarati Muslims (1964) includes useful chapters on the Bohras and the Khojahs, as well as less extensive treatments of sixty-seven other communities. P. N. Chopra (1982) and other authors deal with Bohras briefly in the larger context of Indian Muslim groups. Theodore P. Wright, Jr., has written two valuable pieces, both of them chapters of edited books about larger issues: the first deals with struggles between the Daudi Bohra dawat and dissidents/reformists in the context of "competitive modernization" (1975); the second discusses kinship ties of a prominent family of Sulaimani Bohras (1976). John Mansfield, meanwhile, has used the Bohras' Chandabhai gulla and Burhanpur durgah litigation to examine issues of sectarian extralegality in Indian jurisprudence (1993). In the hard sciences, the Bohras' strict endogamy has prompted several biological researchers to use them as the subjects of genetic study.[10]

So successful have the Bohra dissidents been in controlling the tenor of discussion that the few outside scholars to take passing notice of the denomination have almost invariably relied on dissident rather than orthodox sources not only for their information, but for their analytical outlook as well. Hollister, for example, editorializes: "The future is with this reforming element. Bohra leadership, it would seem, has fallen far below its true heritage in needing such prodding from its friends."[11] Daftary (one of the most respected and authoritative historians of Ismailism alive today) follows Engineer's interpretation of events even when the latter departs from the historical record; for example, Daftary writes that the daʿi "is considered to be maʿsum, sinless and infallible,"[12] while Bohras reserve this status for the imam (the daʿi is considered kal maʿsum—a subtle, yet important, distinction). Moreover, the dissident materials (generally Abdul Husain when not Engineer) on which Daftary bases his Bohra observations are in many cases nearly a century out of date. He states that there are normally eighteen individuals holding the title of shaikh,[13] for example, when the actual number is perhaps 100 times as great; he writes that "a few hundred [Bohras] have emigrated to Europe and America in recent decades,"[14] when the Bohra population of the United States alone probably numbers in the tens of thousands. It is somewhat suspect, therefore, when Daftary

concludes that "The majority of the Daudi Bohras, traditional in their ways and outlook, continue to be apathetic and submissive to their da'i."[15]

A SINGLE SOURCE FOR ALL TWENTIETH-CENTURY MATERIAL

Perhaps the most remarkable fact about printed material on the Bohras is that nearly all ethnographic* references published anywhere, at any time in the past hundred years, ultimately revert back to a single source: Mian Bhai Mullah Abdul Husain of Rangoon, a Daudi dissident writing in the late nineteenth and early twentieth centuries. Publishing under his own name, Abdul Husain wrote the *Gulzare Daudi for the Bohras of India* (1920). This book provides the ethnographic backbone of all later works. None of the outside scholars (Hollister, Daftary, Misra) who describe the Bohras in texts on larger Muslim communities conducted firsthand fieldwork in the community, so all rely heavily on Abdul Husain for their primary data. Abdul Husain is also the baseline source for cultural material in all later accounts by Bohra dissidents (notably Engineer and Noman Contractor, both of whom were cut off from their community by de facto excommunication). The extent of such reliance can be readily gauged by a quick glance at the text citations in these works.

Less immediately apparent, however, is the degree to which Abdul Husain shaped not only the accounts that followed his book, but even those that *preceded* it. His cultural descriptions date to the late nineteenth century, since many of them appear verbatim in a colonial gazetteer of that time.[16] Take the following passage in his *Gulzare Daudi:*

> Though active and well made, few Dawoodi Bohras are muscular or even robust . . . They shave the head, wear long thin beards and cut the hair on the upper lip close. Many of the women are said to be beautiful and fair-skinned with delicate features. Following the precept and to some extent the example of the Prophet, they are careful to keep their eyelids penciled with missi, an astringent powder, and the palms of their hands and the soles of their feet reddened with henna.[17]

This very passage, word for word, also appears not only in a colonial gazetteer of the same year,[18] but also in a gazetteer published two decades earlier.[19] The verbatim repetitions among the three works are too numerous to cite—in fact, there is very little material in either the 1899 gazetteer

*As distinct from purely historical, religious, or polemical accounts. As noted above, historical and religious texts are considerably more plentiful.

edited by James Campbell or the 1920 edition by R. E. Enthoven that cannot also be found (often word for word, frequently with only minor alterations) in Abdul Husain. Clearly Abdul Husain is either a plagiarist or the author of the earlier gazetteer entries. As a Daudi Bohra himself, he would have been far more likely to be the ultimate source of ethnographic details about his community than would Campbell, who as editor of the volume makes no claim to have ever conducted fieldwork. Fortunately for the *Gulzare Daudi* author's reputation, Campbell acknowledges his source (although hardly confessing the extent of the borrowing) in a grudging footnote: "Certain historical and other parts of the Bohora account are taken from papers prepared by Mr. Mirza Abdul Husain of Rangoon."[20]

Campbell's account was essentially written by Abdul Husain, and Enthoven's account is lifted almost in its entirety from Campbell. These three pre-Independence authors are in reality one author, and from this one author stem nearly all later cultural accounts. Hollister's sources are Abdul Husain, Enthoven, and Campbell.[21] Misra's sources are these original three, plus Hollister. Engineer's sources are these four, plus Misra.* Daftary relies on the previous five, plus Engineer. Virtually all of the ethnographic material yet published thus ultimately boils down to the single nineteenth-century account of Mian Bhai Abdul Husain, whether first-, second-, third-, fourth-, or fifthhand.

This reliance on a single source would be problematic enough in itself, but the difficulties are magnified by the fact that this source is hardly a disinterested observer of facts: Abdul Husain was an active member of the dissident group, a public opponent of the clerical hierarchy, and made no claims of impartial scholarship. In his *Gulzare Daudi* he labels his coreligionists "superstitious,"[22] and writes that since the term of Syedna Najmuddin eighty years earlier "there has been unusual agitation, heart burning, and discontentment among the Bohra[s]."[23] Abdul Husain even accuses the dawat of fostering antinomianism through batini ta'wil,[24] a charge seemingly drawn from anti-Ismaili canards circulated by Sunni heresiographers for over a millennium. While his writings provide a valuable glimpse of Bohra life in the late nineteenth century, they should be treated as partisan observations. When it comes to previous Bohra ethnography, Abdul Husain remains an irreplaceable source simply because he is (quite literally) the *only* source.

*Engineer also makes selective use of several Gujarati texts (such as the *Mausam-e bahar*) and his own personal experience, but since he is the leader of the movement challenging dawat authority his works on the Bohras must be considered advocacy rather than independent ethnography.

Notes

Introduction

1. Throughout this study, except where otherwise noted or implied, the terms "Bohra" and "Daudi Bohra" are used interchangeably. This is the usage employed by the Daudi Bohras themselves and that prevalent in Mumbai society at large. While non-Daudi groups of Bohras exist, they make up less than 10% of the total number, and were not the community in which my fieldwork was conducted. Just as no true ethnography of the Daudi Bohras has previously been published, no study of the Sulaimani, Alia, or various splinter sects has yet been made.

2. Davoodbhoy 1992a: 4.

3. Quoted in *Dawn*, November 11, 1994, 1.

4. Hobsbawm and Ranger 1983.

5. Anderson 1983; Gellner 1983, 1994.

6. The Subaltern works to which I refer include Chatterjee 1982; Guha 1982, 1983; Pandey 1983, 1990a, 1990b; Spivak 1988. On Ataturk and Reza Shah Pahlavi: Keddie 1981; Okyar 1984; Rahman 1984; Yalman 1991. On Taliban and Iranian clerics: Akhavi 1987; Fischer 1980; Ghani 1987; Rose 1983; Tabari 1983. On Sir Syed Ahmad Khan and Muhammad Abduh: Haq 1979: 461–469; Rahman 1982a: 31–39.

7. Geertz 1968: 103–105.

8. Lindholm quotation: 1986: 61. Syncretic theorists: Ahmad 1976, 1983; Madan 1981; Das 1984. Robinson quotation: 1983: 201. Das quotation: 1984: 294.

9. Khare 1988: 163; Weber 1958a, 1965. On Weber and Islam, cf. Peacock 1978: 1–22; Turner 1974.

10. Dumont 1970: 17; On Khojah modernization: Asani 1987, 1994.

11. This mandated quietism does not apply to the Fatimid caliphate or other periods of Ismaili political ascendancy.

12. Nandy 1988: 83.

13. Huntington 1996.

14. Statistical breakdown: Of 121 households responding, 109 (90.1%) stated

that values were stronger today than in previous generations, and that modern technology and education had strengthened rather than weakened them. Seven (5.8%) reported values weaker or no different today, or reported that modern causes had weakened or had no effect on values; five (4.1%) gave ambiguous responses or said that they did not know. The remaining participants did not answer, provided illegible responses, or were siblings within the same family who provided duplicate answers. "A little leaven leaveneth the whole lump": Galatians 5:9.

15. Banks 1996: 189.

16. Duʿa was obtained January 10, 1995, at the Jamea tus-Saifiya in Surat.

17. The dissident Bohra leader Asghar Ali Engineer has included Bohras of various denominations—together with Khojahs and Memons—in a survey of Gujarati Muslims (1989). Since orthodox Daudi Bohras are forbidden to have any contact with Engineer, however, the respondents to his survey are ipso facto unrepresentative of mainstream (let alone strictly orthodox) Bohra opinion. The results are illustrative of dissident outlook, but do not speak to the views and practices of the mass of Bohras: Engineer himself numbers his open followers only at 25,000 out of a population he has estimated at between 560,000 and one million (sourcing below). While he claims that more than half of the overall population secretly support his movement's goals, his survey data must be taken as indicative only of the views of the small cadre (less than 5% of the population, by Engineer's own reckoning) of active dissidents.

18. Cultural reportage: Blank 1992, 1993, 1999, and in press (a). Sociology of religion: Blank 1994, in press (a) and (b).

Chapter One. Historical Background: The Roots of the Faith

1. On 470 communities in forty nations: Davoodbhoy 1992a: 4. One million population: dawat sources: Abdulhussein 1995a: 225; Davoodbhoy 1993a: 1; Niazi 1992: 1; dissident sources: Contractor 1980: 5; Engineer 1995: i; Nathwani 1979: 7.

2. On 1931 census and Shiʿa underreporting: Hollister 1953: 293. At the end of the nineteenth century, the Bohra population of Gujarat was said to number 142,767. While this figure (like all colonial census figures) is far less reliable than its degree of specificity might suggest, it provides a general idea of how Bohra numbers compared with those of other communities: in the same survey, Memons were tallied at 88,582; Khojahs at 46,353; and all Gujarati Muslim communities combined at 1,113,000 (Campbell 1899: 1). Bohras, therefore, were deemed more populous than the other two largest Gujarati Muslim trading communities combined, and were estimated to comprise just over 10% of the entire population of Gujarati Muslims. In the 1901 cen-

sus of the Bombay presidency, Bohras were numbered at 118,307, with a distribution of 60,363 female Bohras and 57,944 male (Enthoven 1920: 197).

3. Population figures: 317,844: Raik 1975: 350; 560,000: Engineer 1993: 144; 300,000: "Judgment" 1931: 1,068; Hollister 1953: 293; Najafali 1943: 9. Population distribution: dawat source: Niazi 1992: 1; dissident source: Engineer 1989: 51. Shi'a as one-fifth of Indian Muslims: Abbas 1991: 40; Djalili 1981: 29; Rizvi 1984: 2. Muslims as about 12% of the Indian population: Brass 1994: 231. Percentages of Indian Muslims and Shi'a are based on a 1997 Government of India/United Nations estimate of 967 million for the total population of India. If the total Indian population of Bohras is 500,000 (a rather conservative estimate), they would form 2.2% of Indian Shi'a and 0.4% of Indian Muslims. If the total Indian population of Bohras is one million (an upper-limit figure), they would comprise 4.3% of Indian Shi'a and 0.9% of Indian Muslims. The estimates above are, like all figures relating to the Daudi Bohras and most other Indian Muslims, by no means a scientific reckoning.

4. *Ajlaf/ashraf:* cf. Asani 1987: 31. *Vohrvun* as source of name: Abdul Husain 1920: 1; Abdulhussein 1995a: 224; Campbell 1899: 24; Chopra 1982: 204; Enthoven 1920: 197; Hollister 1953: 272; Najafali 1943: 8; Schimmel 1980: 71. Several other explanations of the name have been offered, including derivations from Gujarati, Arabic, and even Persian words for "right way," "many paths," "prudent," and "businesslike," but a gazetteer of the early twentieth century was probably correct to dismiss such theories as "fanciful and unlikely" (Enthoven 1920: 197n). Vaishya descent: Jhaveri 1933-1935: 37-52; Misra 1964: 8-10; Qureshi, 1985: 41-45; Schimmel 1980: 70. All of the Shi'a communities of Bohras are mercantile, but a group that split from the Bohra mainstream adopted both Sunnism and agriculturalism in the ninth-tenth/fifteenth-sixteenth centuries (see Campbell 1899: 58-61; Lambat 1976: 49-53). Theoretical Brahminical descent: Campbell 1899: 24; Enthoven 1920: 197.

5. The early history of Islam is sufficiently well known not to require extensive documentation. Some sources for this and the following paragraphs are Djalili 1981: 13ff.; Jafri 1979: 58-79, 117-123; Karandikar 1968: 31ff.; Lewis 1940: 12ff.; Tabataba'i 1975: 194-203.

6. Goldziher 1981: 30-66; Schimmel 1992: 59-72.

7. Jafar al-Sadiq: Daftary 1990: 84-88. Present imam: al-Nu'man 1961, 1:1-98. Theological points summarized in the paragraph: Hollister 1953: 198-199; Jafri 1979: 1-23, 289-312; Karandikar 1968: 92ff.; Misra 1964: 15-16; Pinault 1992: 25. Inlibration: Wolfson 1976: 244ff.; see also Lawson 1997.

8. Daftary 1990: 58; Jafri 1979: 269-270.

9. Karandikar 1968: 97; Messick 1993: 38; Tabataba'i 1975: 76-77.

10. Jafar as instructor of Abu Hanifa al-Nu'man and Malik ibn Anas: Daftary

1990: 83. Jafar and nass: Jafri 1979: 289–300. ". . . dies as an unbeliever": quoted in Daftary 1990: 86.

11. *Kitab al-rushd wa'l-hidaya* and *Kitab al-alim wa'l-ghulam:* Daftary 1990: 92; ibn Hawshab 1955; Jafar ibn Mansur 1955. *Uyun al-akhbar* and *Iftitah al-dawa:* Daftary 1990: 92; Idris 1975; al-Nuʿman 1970.

12. Lewis quotation: 1940: 92. Hollister quotation: 1953: 203. Ivanow quotation: 1942: xxii. Congruence of al-Nuʿman and Jafar: Fyzee 1934a, 1974; Ivanow 1936: 7; al-Nuʿman 1961. Twelver claims to al-Nuʿman: Ivanow 1933: 37.

13. Daftary quotation: 1990: 93. Fatimid theologian: Jafar ibn Mansur 1942: 94; trans. in Ivanow 1942: 291. Dating of Ismail's death: dawat sources, and Ali 1963, 1:41–43.

14. Modern sources: Mustafa Abdulhussein, personal communication, May 31, 2000. Syedna Hatim quotation: from 117th Majalis, translated in Ivanow 1942: 306. Hasan ibn Nuh quotation: from the sixth volume of the *Kitab'ul-azhar,* translated in Ivanow 1942: 30.

15. The anachronism of placing Musa's emergence prior to Jafar's death can be explained by the fact that Idris was writing 700 years after the event. I use the transliteration "Imad al-Din" rather than "Imamuddin" (the style more familiar to most Bohras and the one I have used for other daʿis) to avoid confusing readers who may have encountered Idris in Arabic histories.

16. Idris Imad al-Din quotation: 1942: 47, 51; trans. in Ivanow 1942: 232–233, 235. Jafar ibn Mansur quotation: 1984: 258; 1942: 98, trans. in Ivanow 1942: 275–276. "Proving" Ismail's death: Idris 1975, 4:334; 1942: 47; trans. in Ivanow 1942: 234; Jafar ibn Mansur 1984: 262; 1942: 103–104, trans. Ivanow 1942: 301–302. Curing the paralytic: Idris 1942: 48, trans. in Ivanow 1942: 235.

17. Charges of drunkenness: al-Kashshi 1969: 473–474. Refutation of charges: Lewis 1940: 38–39; Ivanow 1946: 159. Links to, and cursing of, Abu al-Khattab: Daftary 1990: 88–89; Ivanow 1940: 57n; al-Kashshi 1969: 354–356; Lewis 1940: 33–37. Ghulat theology and death of al-Khattab: Corbin 1953: 14ff.; Ivanow 1946: 113–137; Jafar ibn Mansur 1984: 256–257; 1942: 95–96, trans. in Ivanow 1942: 292–293; Lewis 1940: 32–44.

18. Daftary 1990: 60; Ivanow 1955: 24.

19. Idris 1975, 4:351–356; 1942: 53–58, trans. in Ivanow 1942: 240–248; see also: Ivanow 1940: 60–63; Jafar ibn Mansur 1984: 259; 1942: 99, trans. in Ivanow 1942: 296.

20. Reliable historical dates are unavailable for the hidden imams. When such dates are provided by much later sources, they are essentially arbitrary.

21. Articulation of hidden imamate, and Bedouin roots: Daftary 1990: 126, 124. Imam Abdullah al-Mastur: Ali 1963, 1:43; Idris 1942: 59, trans. in Ivanow 1942: 249; Hollister 1953: 207.

22. Abu Abdullah al-Shii: Ali 1963, 1:43. Syedna Idris quotation: Idris 1975, 4:357; 1942: 36; Ivanow 1940: 63.

23. Hollister 1953: 210–211.

24. Non-Ismaili historians sometimes refer to this imam as Ubaidallah al-Mahdi; the Daudi Bohras refer to him as al-Mahdi, or Abdullah al-Mahdi.

25. Dachraoui 1981: 25–36: 224–231; Idris 1975, 5:44–112; Hollister 1953: 211.

26. Daftary quotation: 1990: 126. Al-Mahdi details: Ali 1963, 1:74–75; al-Hamdani 1958a: 10–13; ibn Hawshab 1955: 201, trans. in Ivanow 1955: 46; Jafar ibn Mansur 1952: 97–104.

27. Malahida: Daftary 1990: 5. Sabiyya: Ivanow 1933: 8n. Qarmatis as "Seveners": Stern 1961: 102–103; 1983: 47–53. Discussion of nomenclature: Daftary 1990: 93; Fyzee 1965: 233; al-Hamdani 1934: 320–322; ibn Hawshab 1955, trans. Ivanow 1955: 40ff.; Ivanow 1933: 5–8; 1941: 12–18; Lewis 1948: 597–598; Stern 1961: 100.

28. Derivation of "Qarmati": Daftary 1990: 116. Qarmati egalitarianism and alleged antinomianism: Lewis 1940: 96, 99–100.

29. Al-Mahdi quotation: Lewis 1940: 81. Qarmati and Zanji history: Lewis 1940: 80; de Goeje 1886; Hollister 1953: 218–220; Ivanow 1940; Massignon 1922.

30. Abu Tahir's heresies: Daftary 1990: 163 (also cf. sources from previous note).

31. Daftary 1990: 64–67. The Ismaili doctrine of concealment (satr) differs from the Twelver concept of occultation (ghayba) primarily in that it does not posit a superhuman lifespan for the secluded imam. During the pre-Fatimid era, various Ismaili groups espoused ghayba or similar ideas.

32. Quoted in Karandikar 1968: 108.

33. English renditions: 3.28 from Shakir 1983: 47; 16.106 from Pickthall 1953: 202.

34. Corbin 1972, 1:6, 87, 117; Filippani-Ronconi 1973: 22–44; Kohlberg 1975: 395–402; Tabataba'i 1975: 223–5.

35. Hasan 1964: 117–122.

36. Ali 1963, 1:116–124; Dachraoui 1981: 57–96, 122–132; al-Hamdani 1933: 366–370; Hasan 1964: 80–92; Idris 1975, 5:112–190; 1942: 70–72, trans. in Ivanow 1942: 263–266; Lewis 1940: 86; al-Nu'man 1970: 249–282; Stern 1983: 96–145; Tabataba'i 1975: 81–82.

37. Ali 1963, 1:138–145; Dachraoui 1981: 188–206; Hollister 1953: 225; Idris 1975, 5:172–198; Lewis 1940: 87; al-Nu'man 1978: 113–114, 336–337.

38. Fyzee 1934b: 11, 22–32; 1969, 1974; al-Hamdani 1933: 369; Hollister 1953: 255; Idris 1975, 6:38–50; Ivanow 1936: para. 44; al-Nu'man 1960, 1961, 1970, 1978; Poonawala 1973: 109–115; 1974: 572–577.

39. Control of holy places: Daftary 1990: 174; Hasan 1964: 152–155. Al-Muizz: Ali 1963, 1:148–166; Dachraoui 1981: 219–255; Hasan 1964: 122–151; Idris 1975, 6:22–173; Lewis 1940: 81–82; Stern 1955: 14–22.

40. Ali 1963, 1:189–205; Daftary 1990: 184; Hasan 1964: 156–163.

41. Ali 1963, 2:111–112, 130–131; Hasan 1964: 270–272; Poonawala 1977: 78–79.

42. Daftary 1990: 185; Hollister 1953: 229.

43. Daftary 1990: 188; Hollister 1953: 231–232.
44. Ali 1963, 1:206–261; Daftary 1990: 189; Hasan 1964: 205–209, 428–445; Idris 1975, 6:248–304.
45. Abdulhussein 1995b: 238; Davoodbhoy 1994: 16.
46. Al-Hakim remains a highly controversial figure, and information on his reign comes from sources of uncertain reliability. Since none of the official Fatimid chronicles of the period have survived, the only Ismaili account available is that of Syedna Idris Imad al-Din's *Uyun al-akhbar*, written three centuries after the fall of the caliphate. The only contemporary account comes from an Arab Christian named al-Antaki. It should be noted that al-Hakim's harsh policies ebbed and flowed: despite his anti-Sunni attitudes, for example, he established a Sunni academy at Fustat under the direction of two Maliki scholars, and kept it open for three years before experiencing a change of heart. On al-Hakim: Ali 1963, 1:244–261; Daftary 1990: 183–196; Goldziher 1981: 222; al-Hamdani 1933: 375–378; Hodgson 1962: 5–20; Hollister 1953: 230–237; Schimmel 1992: 96.
47. Daftary 1990: 197–199; Filippani-Ronconi 1973: 91–105; Hodgson 1962: 5–20; Hollister 1953: 235–237.
48. Ali 1963, 1:262–272; Hasan 1964: 445–448; Idris 1975, 6:304–322.
49. Daftary 1990: 202; Lewis 1940: 68.
50. Daftary 1990: 203–207; Hasan 1964: 210–211; Hollister 1953: 239–242; Idris 1975, 6:322–334.
51. Daftary 1990: 223; Hasan 1964: 259–261; Idris 1975, 6:334–348.
52. Ali 1963, 1:116–118; Corbin 1953: 25–39; Daftary 1990: 214–217; Idris 1975, 6:329–359; al-Hamdani 1933: 375–377; 1932: 129–135; Hasan 1964: 492–500; Poonawala 1977: 430–436. Ibn Sina's Ismaili ties: Daftary 1990: 212.
53. Fakhr 1940: 87–98; Jhaveri 1933–1935: 37–52; al-Hamdani 1934: 321–324; al-Mustansir 1954: 203–206.
54. Ali 1963, 1:324–332; Hasan 1964: 171–173; Hollister 1953: 242–243; Karandikar 1968: 97; al-Mustansir 1954: 109–118; Schimmel 1980: 70; Tabataba'i 1975: 81–82. Nizar's sister's testimony: Daftary 1990: 265.
55. Hichi 1972: 85–102. An additional murder, that of Kansuh al-Ghuri in 922/1516, is separated from the others by so much time—two and a half centuries—that it seems clearly the product of mythical association.
56. Lewis 1967: 11–12; 1971: 575–576. For a complete account of the Assassins, see Lewis 1952, 1953.
57. Fraser reports the event as having taken place in 1822. In actuality, Shah Khalil Allah was killed in a Yazd riot in 1817. Fraser 1825: 377. Nizari distribution: Asani 1987: 32; Filippani-Ronconi 1973: 113–115; Nanji 1978: 3–6; Tabataba'i 1975: 82.
58. Ali 1963, 2:13–22; al-Hamdani 1932: 128; Hasan 1964: 173–176; Hollister 1953: 244–245; Karandikar 1968: 97; Stern 1951: 193ff.

59. Ali 1963, 2:36–66; Daftary 1990: 268; Hasan 1964: 179–201; Schimmel 1980: 70; Tabataba'i 1975: 81–82.

60. Since the Tayyibis were the only Musta'li branch to survive in any significant numbers beyond the fall of the Fatimid caliphate, I generally describe the Bohras simply as Musta'lis rather than by the more precise (and more pedantic) term Tayyibi Musta'li Ismailis. On al-Malika al-Sayyida: Daftary 1990: 284; Hamdani 1971: 271; Stern 1951: 221, 227–228. Satr in Yemen: Ali 1954: 44–66; 1963: vol 2: 25–28; Hamdani 1976: 92–99; 1985: 151–155; Ivanow 1942: 37–38; Stern 1951: 199–202, 232–233.

61. Abdulhussein 1995b: 237.

62. While sources for Fatimid history and doctrine are relatively plentiful, documents relating to Musta'li Ismailis after their fall from power in Egypt are much more rare. On the nine-hundred-year history of the dawat in India, source material—whether primary or secondary—is exceptionally sparse indeed. For a more extensive analysis of documentary material (and lack thereof), see the Bibliographic Discussion.

63. Misra 1964: 15.

64. Hamdani 1956: 3–9; 1967: 185–187; Khan 1975: 36–57; Misra 1963: 21; Stern 1949: 302–306. Khutba in name of Fatimid caliph: Muqaddasi 1877: 481.

65. Al-Hamdani 1934: 317ff.; Hollister 1953: 241.

66. Abdul Husain 1920: 30–32; Ali 1963, 2:80–82; Campbell 1899: 26; Enthoven 1920: 199–200; Ismailji 1937: 53–58; Jhaveri 1933–1935: 37–52; Khan 1924: 270ff.; Mausam-e bahar 1884: 328–345; Misra 1963: 21; 1964: 8–10; Qureshi 1985: 41–45.

67. Ali 1963, 2:82–86; Ismailji 1937: 58–60; Jhaveri 1933–1935: 41; Khan 1924: 277; Mausam-e bahar 1884: 343.

68. Ismailji 1937: 221; Khan 1924: 277; Mausam-e bahar 1884: 327. Siddharaj as Shaivite: Misra 1964: 12. While Nizari Khojahs claim that their community dates to the time of Bharmal, Sunni Khojahs claim that the first conversions were made by the Sunni missionary Pir Sadruddin in the early fifteenth century (Merchant, Banatwalla, et al. 1969: 1).

69. Ali 1954: 292–293; Campbell 1899: 26n; Desai 1989: 92ff.; Engineer 1993: 110–111; Enthoven 1920: 203; Hollister 1953: 271; Ismailji 1937: 61–64; Lambat 1976: 49–53; Mausam-e bahar 1884: 117–123; Misra 1964: 22–23; Qureshi 1985: 65; Schimmel 1980: 71. Eighty percent of population converted: Abdul Husain 1920: 29–30. 1.2 million: Khan 1924: 316–317.

70. Abdul Husain 1920: 45; Abdulhussein 1995a: 224; Ali 1954: 292–293; Campbell 1899: 34; Enthoven 1920: 204; Hollister 1953: 276; Ismailji 1937: 64–66; Lambat 1976: 53–55; Mausam-e bahar 1884: 123–127; Misra 1964: 22–23.

71. Colonial gazetteers: Campbell 1899: 58–61; Enthoven 1920: 205–206. Modern scholarship casting doubt on this: Lambat 1976: 49–68. In the early eighteenth century, a substantial section of the Sunni population of Ahmed-

316 NOTES TO PAGES 40–45

abad, Patan, Surat, and Baroda became followers of the Sufi pir Sayyid
Muhammad Shah, and no contemporary mention seems to have been made
of cleavages within the Sunni Bohra community (Desai 1989: 92).

72. Herklots's Jafar Sharif quotation: Sharif 1832: 12–13. Abdul Husain quota-
tion: Campbell 1899: 34.

73. Ali 1954: 576ff.; 1963, 2:195–210; Corbin 1951: 192–217; 1954: 162–172;
1957: 126–133; 1984: 124–136; al-Hamdani 1937: 210–220.

74. Ismailji 1937: 93–94.

75. Ali 1963, 2:74–77; Hamdani 1971: 271–286; 1985: 151–160; Ismailji 1937:
85–86; Ivanow 1933: 52–54; Misra 1964: 25–26; *Mausam-e bahar* 1884:
46–56; Poonawala 1977: 137–143, 151–155; Stern 1951: 244–249.

76. Abdul Husain 1920: 30; Campbell 1899: 27; Engineer 1993: 117–122; Hollis-
ter 1953: 272–275; Ismailji 1937: 144–162; Khan 1924: 312–314; *Mausam-e
bahar* 1884: 174–228; Misra 1964: 26–30; Najafali 1943: 8.

77. Misra 1964: 28n, from statement made to Misra by the Sulaimani wali for
India, Maulana Muhammad Shakir of Baroda; for succession of Sulaimani
da'is, see Poonawala 1977: 364–369.

78. Campbell 1899: 33; repeated verbatim, supposedly as current information,
in Enthoven 1920: 204–205.

79. Chopra 1982: 216; Engineer 1989: 109–118; Hollister 1953: 300; Schimmel
1980: 72, 213.

80. Abdul Husain 1920: 31, 46–47; Ali 1954: 293–294; Campbell 1899: 27; En-
gineer 1989: 131–138; 1993: 122; Enthoven 1920: 201; Hollister 1953: 277;
Ivanow 1933: 109–111; Khan 1924: 314; Misra 1964: 31; Najafali 1943: 8. For
a list of Alia da'is, see Poonawala 1977: 369–370. Nineteenth-century ac-
count: Campbell 1899: 33. Currently 5,000: Abdulhussein 1995a: 225.

81. Abdul Husain 1920: 31; Campbell 1899: 27; Enthoven 1920: 204; Hollister
1953: 277; Khan 1924: 314.

82. Abdul Husain 1920: 31; Daftary 1990: 306; Engineer 1993: 122; Enthoven
1920: 204; Hollister 1953: 277; Khan 1924: 314; Misra 1964: 31. Four house-
holds in 1897: Campbell 1899: 33.

83. *Mausam-e bahar* 1884: 280–296.

84. Abdul Husain 1920: 20–21, 38–39; Commissariat 1957, 2:127, 207–208; En-
gineer 1993: 122–124; Karandikar 1968: 115; *Mausam-e bahar* 1884: 214;
Misra 1964: 32–38; Schimmel 1980: 72. Deccan sultans: Pinault 1992: 60.

85. Commissariat 1957, 2:429–430.

86. Abdul Husain 1920: 31, 49; Ali 1954: 294–295, 662; Daftary 1990: 309–310;
Hollister 1953: 278; *Mausam-e bahar* 1884: 440–456; Misra 1964: 41–43;
Poonawala 1977: 204–206. On Shaikh Hibtullah and Shaikh Ismail as
sources for Ivanow: Daftary 1990: 309n; Ivanow 1933: 93–94. The bibliogra-
phy in question would become Ivanow 1963.

87. Abdul Husain 1920: 49.

88. Abdulhussein 1995c: 360; Campbell 1899: 32; Daftary 1990: 310; Misra 1964: 44. On Virji Vora: Misra 1961: 23.

89. Misra 1964: 45–46.

90. Even more uniformly, perhaps, than Hinduism or Buddhism, Jainism has made *ahimsa* (nonviolence) central to its belief system since the earliest days of the faith. Recorded examples of Jains instigating, or even being provoked into, sectarian violence are very rare indeed.

91. Mercantile niches: Chopra 1982: 205. IIC quotation: Misra 1961: 24.

92. Katzenstein 1979: 40, 43.

93. 1808 records: Douglas 1893, 2:130. Banking and larger industry: Katzenstein 1979: 42, 44. Khojah population in 1840: Merchant, Banatwalla, et al. 1969: 2–3. Colonial gazetteer quotation: Campbell 1899: 24.

94. Quoted in Hay 1988: 180.

95. Syed Amir Ali: Karandikar 1968: 215–218. Muhammad Iqbal: quoted in Karandikar 1968: 223.

96. Campbell 1899: 29n.

97. Some Bohra dissidents (Engineer 1993: 135–136) and outside historians (Daftary 1990: 310–311) contend that the nass was indeed challenged at the time of the forty-sixth da'i's death. (Engineer, it should be noted, does not himself reject the legitimacy of the nass: personal interview, June 2, 1995). According to this interpretation, the nass had not been made because the imam's return was imminent; Abdul-Qadir (who had been serving as mukasir) was appointed caretaker until the imam himself should appear. The dawat's position (set out for me by Tahera Behnsaheb Qutbuddin and Shaikh Mustafa Abdulhussein, in communications of January 16, 2000, and April 18, 2000, respectively) is that the nass had not been publicly announced, but that it had been implied on numerous occasions and explicitly pronounced before four witnesses in private (an accepted means of designation that previous da'is had employed). The dispute (these sources say) arose only after the witnesses had died, and dissenters claimed that Syedna Muhammad Badruddin had been murdered to prevent him from changing his mind. For details of this controversy, see Ali 1954: 295–297; Ismailji 1937: 362–364; "Judgment" 1931: 30; Wright 1975: 153; *Mausam-e bahar* 1884: 693–767; Poonawala 1977: 219–228. Ground diamonds: *Mausam-e bahar* 1884: 717.

98. *Mausam-e bahar* 1884: 738–739; cf. Daftary 1990: 311; Engineer 1993: 136; Ismailji 1937: 362–363; Misra 1964: 48.

99. Najmuddin 1992: 13; cf. Abdul Husain 1920: 52; Campbell 1899: 32. Tahera Qutbuddin, niece of Dr. Najmuddin as well as of the current da'i, disputes the contention that the Jamea had suffered such a decline (personal communication, January 16, 2000).

100. Daftary 1990: 312; Engineer 1993: 137–138; Misra 1964: 50.

101. An overwhelming 86.6% of the respondents to my survey report using musafirkhanas, and 21.7% cite it as one of the top two dawat services.

102. Abdul Husain 1920: 84. Since this section also appears in Campbell's gazetteer, it (along with other portions of the 1920 account) clearly dates to a period contemporaneous with the tenure of Syedna Abdul-Husain Husamuddin.

103. Dissident sources (and those following them) even claim that the da'i was compelled to sign a document acknowledging that he and his two predecessors were and had been merely caretakers (*nazim*) rather than full spiritual leaders (Daftary 1990: 312; Engineer 1993: 138–139; Poonawala 1977: 14, 238–239). Daftary states (1990: 667–668) that this document, called the *Ahd-nama,* was later destroyed; he cites a work entitled *Aqida-yi Burhaniyya* (Surat, 1966) by Fayd Allah as providing the Gujarati text and analysis. I have been unable to locate any copy of this work. The dawat strongly objects to the implication that any da'i ever signed such a document. Shaikh Mustafa Abdulhussein states: "This supposed document has never been proven authentic. I do not believe the scholars Poonawala and Daftary have seen the document in question, nor has any research authenticated it, though it is often mentioned as a valid document. The only place it has been examined is the Chandabhai gulla case. On page 985 of the judgment, Justice Marten declares the document invalid. The handwriting does not even match that of Syedna Burhanuddin [the forty-ninth da'i, not the fifty-second da'i of the same name]. And the witness himself was declared unreliable in this matter" (personal communication, May 11, 1998).

104. Abdul Husain 1920: 49–53; Ali 1954: 295; Daftary 1990: 313; Engineer 1993: 138–139; Ismailji 1937: 378; "Judgment" 1931: 37–38; Najafali 1943: 8–9. References to the Medhibaghwalas, like those to other splinter sects, are somewhat dated.

105. Campbell 1899: 24–35.

106. Ibid., 30; identical passage in Enthoven 1920: 202.

107. Campbell 1899: 32.

108. Head Mulla: In colonial times, the da'i was often referred to by sources outside the community as the "Head Mulla" or "Mullaji Saheb." Such usage is still heard occasionally, but not from orthodox Bohras: believers see the da'i as an authority far greater than a mere mullah. The title of this book, I should reemphasize, does *not* refer to the da'i al-mutlaq.

Chapter Two. Rituals of a Daudi Bohra Life

1. The gazetteer is Campbell 1899 (The spelling of the title of the work published under Abdul Husain's own name is that used by Abdul Husain himself—i.e., *Gulzare* rather than *Gulzar-e.* Secondary texts generally refer to

this work as the *Gulzare,* without separating out the Arabic possessive). Non-Bohra writers: Enthoven 1920; Hollister 1953; Misra 1964; Roy 1984. For example of verbatim language, compare Campbell 1899: 28, with Abdul Husain 1920: 77. See Bibliographical Discussion for details.

2. The dawat officials upon whose guidance I relied most consistently included Shabbir Muhammad Mansoorbhai Jamali, the mullah at the Mumbai Burhani Madrasa who instructed me in Lisanu-Dawat and provided basic cultural information with the kind permission of Ayman Behnsaheb Kalimuddin and Shahzada Shabbir Bhaisaheb Nuruddin; Shaikh Mustafa Abdulhussein, whom Shahzada Qaidjohar Bhaisaheb Ezzuddin assigned to facilitate the integration and correction of my data; and my good friend Abduz-Zahir Bhaisaheb Mohyuddin. All errors, of course, are my own.

3. Honorific titles of the da'i include Syedna, Maulana, and His Holiness. The letters "T.U.S." are appended to written mentions of his name, for Tawwalullahu Umroho Sharif: "May God prolong his noble life."

4. Ahadith on proper Muslim names: Cf. al-Bukhari 1986, 7:273ff.; al-Ghazali 1971, 2:48; al-Muslim 1978: 1170. In the Khojah community, the aga khan performs a similar service. It is not unknown for people wholly outside the Bohra community to seek names from Syedna: on one occasion (a clerical source told me) a Hindu man entered Saifee Mahal during one of Syedna's public audiences, and approached the da'i to ask a name for his expected baby. The assembled Bohras were thrown into confusion, but Syedna gave the man an immediate answer: he suggested Ram or Sita, popular male and female Hindu names drawn from the Sanskrit epic *Ramayana.*

5. Out of 169 households in the survey universe, 165 answered this question; 144 provided rankings of dawat services; 27 Mumbai households were given a slightly different questionnaire, which asked whether the respondents had used various dawat services but did not ask them to rank them in order of importance.

6. The percentage of households receiving children's names is slightly higher in Mumbai (92.0%) than in Karachi (86.4%), Calcutta (85.0%), or Nagpur (80.4%). The rankings of importance likewise show no direct relation between distance and emphasis: in Nagpur, 3.6% rated naming children as the most important dawat service, and 8.9% rated it one of the top two; in Calcutta, the figures were 5.0% and 25.0% respectively; in Karachi, 2.3% and 15.9%. Phone ownership: Nagpur: 56.6%, vs. 68.4% in Calcutta and 82.2% in Karachi.

7. Cf. al-Muslim 1978: 1172; al-Ghazali 1971, 2:48, with date given to the baby.

8. For Gujarati examples, see Misra 1964: 79ff. Hadith on Hasan: quoted in al-Ghazali 1971, 2:48. Bengali practice: Fruzzetti 1982: 18.

9. Fruzzetti 1982: 18.

10. Forty-five of those responding to the question had been given questionnaires including the category of birth rituals, while 106 returned forms without the cat-

egory listed; among those whose forms listed the category, 64.4% acknowl-
edged birth rites one of the top ten values, but respondents ranked it only sev-
enth out of ten. Among the larger group it received no write-in citations.

11. Cf. Bouhdiba 1985: 176–177.

12. Cf. al-Ghazali 1971, 2:48, recommending circumcision on the seventh day
 after birth.

13. Bombay census: quoted in Enthoven 1920: 202n. There are occasional cita-
 tions in the Indian press referring to the custom (*Times of India,* November
 20, 1994, 1, for example), but in all instances I have seen these are sourced
 to dawat opponents such as Asghar Ali Engineer. Contacts within the com-
 munity have told me compelling stories of the continuation of the practice,
 but none have been willing to give their testimony in public or provide de-
 tails for publication.

14. Bohra usage of these terms differs slightly from those of other Indian groups.
 A chawl is the courtyard of a housing complex, but a mohalla can be a hous-
 ing block, a collection of nearby buildings, a neighborhood, or an entire sec-
 tion of a city.

15. Al-Ghazali 1971, 2:48.

16. Aqiqa ahadith: al-Bukhari 1986, 7:272–276. Al-Ghazali citation: 1971, 2:48.

17. Cf. Lévi-Strauss 1966: 109–133; 1963: 210–230. While Lévi-Strauss is pre-
 sumably sincere in arguing for the rationality of so-called primitive belief
 systems, his reliance on grand armchair theorizing about cultures he had
 never visited raises questions about the true extent of his appreciation for
 the intellectual agency of peoples he sometimes described as "shaggy and
 corpulent savages" (1966: 89, in reference to indigenous Australians). One
 might wish the discipline's most famous theoretician had taken his own
 words to heart: "[N]o one should be entitled to teach anthropology unless he
 has carried out considerable field research. It is sheer illusion that anthropol-
 ogy can be taught purely theoretically" (1963: 372).

18. Cf. al-Ghazali 1971, 2:48, noting hadith of teaching kalama as first words, a
 custom also practiced among Bohras.

19. Ahadith: al-Bukhari 1986, 1:313; 2:111, 118–119. Ithna-Ashari custom:
 Tabataba'i 1975: 231.

20. Shi'a view of Ghadir Khumm: Abdul Husain 1920: 61; Ali 1954: 378–379. Cf.
 Hollister 1953: 266; for Sunni hadith parallels: al-Bukhari 1986, 4:128–129;
 9:236–242.

21. A few nonclerical sources have suggested an alternate meaning: the Arabic
 letters "nun,""alif" (or "'ain"), and "mim," say these sources, comprise the
 entire first verses of some surahs of the Qur'an, and therefore have deep
 mystical significance known only to Syedna and other initiates. This expla-
 nation would be in keeping with Bohra gnosticism, but does not seem to fit
 the actual text. While it is true that many Qur'anic surahs have an initial

verse composed of several cryptic letters, scholarly opinion is divided on whether these letters have a mystical pre-Islamic significance, or are merely a notation of the scribe who wrote down the Prophet's oral dictation (Pickthall 1953: 34n.). Regardless of their meaning, however, the letters "nun," "alif," "mim" do not begin *any* Qur'anic verse. This appears, therefore, to be a case of pseudognosticism: some members of the community regard their vocalization of the word "nam" as participation in a gnostic ritual—but the ritual in question would seem not actually to exist.

22. Identical (or nearly identical) versions of the oath: Abdul Husain 1920: 125–138; Ali 1954: 326–329; "Judgment" 1931: 50–53; Hollister 1953: 282–284; Nathwani 1979: 21–25. The text was provided by dissident plaintiffs in the Burhanpur durgah case initiated shortly after the First World War and stalled in litigation for many years ("Judgment" 1931), which in turn relied on the version of Abdul Husain. The Nathwani Commission cites the dissident journal *New Quest* (issue 7: January-February 1978) as its source, and *New Quest* in turn cites both the court records and Abdul Husain. In the Burhanpur durgah case, the dissident plaintiffs alleged that Syedna Taher Saifuddin imposed this version of mithaq in the early twentieth century, replacing a less restrictive version that had been instituted around the year 560/1182 (they claimed) by the third da'i, Syedna Hatim, in the book *Tuhfat al-Qulab*. Modern dissident Asghar Ali Engineer cites what he says is the text from the Tuhfat al-Qulab, as entered into the book of exhibits of the case in the Privy Council on Appeal from the High Court of Judicature at Nagpur, pp. 835, part 2 (full text quoted in Engineer 1993: 158).

23. Slightly over half of my survey respondents cited it as a bedrock component of the faith.

24. Ahadith: al-Bukhari 1986, 7:3–70; al-Muslim 1978: 702–752. Contractual: Bouhdiba 1985: 98–99. Traditional Bohra practice: Najafali 1943.

25. Hodkinson 1984: 92. Child marriage was practiced in the Sunni Vohra community (as noted earlier, a group that may share distant ancestry with the Daudi Bohras) until at least the beginning of the twentieth century, but by the 1970s it had already faded into anachronism; Lambat (1976: 54) reports elderly Vohras telling stories of their child marriages, and of being informed that they had been married only when they were old enough to understand the concept.

26. Husain 1976: 57.

27. Najafali 1943: 27.

28. Seventy percent listed 18–23 as the optimal age for girls, with a significant minority (22%) opting for ages 15–17 (Hasnain and Husain 1988: 81). Hasnain and Husain's *Shi'a and Shi'a Islam: A Study in Society and Culture* and Abrar Husain's *Marriage Customs among Muslims in India* (1976) are probably the most authoritative sources available on marriage and kinship patterns

for Indian Ithna-Ashari Shiʿa. I have used these texts as a baseline for comparison with my own observations on the Bohras.

29. Hasnain and Husain 1988: 82.

30. Husain 1976: 58–59.

31. Sought dawat assistance: 32.3%; guesthouses: used by 86.6% of respondents, ranked one of top two services by 21.7%; naming children: 84.8% and 16.0% respectively; no-interest loans: 75.6% and 35.0%; business contacts: 42.7% and 6.3%. Considered dawat useful: 26.2%; considered modern technology useful: 72.4%; explicitly noted technology more useful than dawat: 52.3%.

32. Cf. Qurʾan 2:229; 2:237; 4:4; 4:20–21.

33. Esposito 1982: 87.

34. Hadith: al-Muslim 1978: 717. Bride-price: Hodkinson 1984: 132 (the term is sometimes applied to mahr, but such usage is inaccurate and misleading). Disincentive for divorce: Husain 1976: 119. Among Bohras: "The bride, in order to counter-balance the power of the husband to divorce her, can demand any dower she likes" (Najafali 1943: 53).

35. Najafali 1943: 53–54.

36. Lambat 1976: 67n. Lambat also notes that when Sunni Vohras emigrate to other countries, they give a mahr of whatever sum in local currency is exactly equivalent to Rs 127.50 (1976: 67n).

37. Misra 1964: Chhaparbandhs: 86; Mansuri-Tantgaras: 101; Bhands: 82; Dhobis: 87; Khatris: 97; Hajams: 95; Maliks: 98; Marwadis: 102. These sums are now purely symbolic; Rs 127 is the equivalent of less than three dollars.

38. Husain 1976: 125.

39. Sharia-mahr: Hasnain and Husain 1988: 70; Rs 1,100: Husain 1976: 129.

40. National figures: respondents paying Rs 1,100: 67.8%; those paying Rs 1,100–50,000: 18.5%; Rs 50,000–100,000: 9.6%. (The heading of the chart's second column reads "1,100–5,000," but since the next column is "50,000–1 lakh" this appears to be a misprint.) Maharashtra figures: 1,100: 75%; Rs 1,100–50,000: 20%; Rs 50,000–1 lakh: 4%; more than 1 lakh: 1%. Gujarat figures: Rs 1,100: 80%; Rs 1,100–50,000: 12%; Rs 50,000–1 lakh: 8%; over 1 lakh: 0%. Hasnain and Husain 1988: 98.

41. Ibid., 99.

42. Hodkinson 1984: 109–110; Karandikar 1968: 297. The provisions of the Special Marriages Act are clarified in a 1976 amendation (s.21A). Some other minority groups are given similar dispensations, although the controversy over Shah Bano and subsequent legislation casts a shadow of uncertainty over the entire issue of personal laws.

43. Ahadith: al-Bukhari 1986, 7:1–127.

44. Husain 1976: 41.

45. Najafali 1943: 43.
46. Hodkinson 1984: 114.
47. Ibid., 89; Husain 1976: 42–43.
48. Quoted in Najafali 1943: 66.
49. Najafali 1943: 24. Shaikh Najafali specifies that "a Nikah which has not been performed by the true and rightful Qazi is null and void." During the seclusion of the imam the true qadi is the daʻi, who can authorize a deputy to sanction marriage and divorce in his stead (Ibid., 37–39).
50. The kinship view of nikah is clarified by the precedence of *vakils* (trustees) for the bride. According to Najafali, "the father and the grandfather . . . are marriage guardians of equal degree but it is preferable that, when both of them are present in the Majlis of Nikah, the grandfather should officiate in preference to the father" (Ibid., 29). This indicates that the vakil's role is not merely to fulfill the necessity of maintaining the bride's purdah. Further evidence of this is the fact that changes in purdah definition have not removed the vakil from the ritual. In the mid-twentieth century, Najafali could write, "As women observe purdah generally, the bride does not appear before the Qazi to give her consent to the marriage" (Ibid., 43). In modern Bohra practice, the bride generally *does* appear before the daʻi or his amil, and provides this assurance without any intermediary. Whatever the symbolic meaning of keeping nikah an all-male ceremony, it does not seem that maintenance of strict purdah is an adequate explanation.
51. Husain 1976: 132.
52. According to Shaikh Najafali's account, rites were almost identical several generations ago. The groom would say to the bride's father or guardian, "In the name of God and according to the holy Shariat you marry [name of the bride who has attained puberty and whose marriage guardian you are] . . . who has duly constituted you as Vakil for giving consent for marriage on her behalf, on a dower of Rs [. . .], prompt or deferred as the case may be, with me." Then the guardian would say the inverse formula, and the ceremony would be complete. Najafali 1943 42–43.
53. Ahadith: al-Bukhari 1986, 5:189; 7:70.
54. Ahmad 1976: xxv.
55. Husain 1976: 113–115.
56. Chopra 1982: 204.
57. Gujarat: Cf. Misra 1964: 80–125. Uttar Pradesh: Husain 1976: 105. Hasnain quotation: Hasnain and Husain 1988: 205–206. Many Hindu-inspired urfi customs such as *mangni, manjha, salaam, chauthi,* and *chalas* were introduced to North Indian Shiʻa by the court of the Shiʻa Nawabs of Awadh in the eighteenth and nineteenth centuries. Hindu-tinged marriage practices still in place there include: (1) such Rajput customs as mock battles and bride-thefts, including a symbolic food fight (chauthi); (2) the blessing of the union

by *hijras* (a caste of eunuchs), who are given money and gifts in return; (3) sanchaq, a prewedding rite in which such Hindu wedding symbols as a *nuth* (nose ring), *tikka* (forehead ornament) and *matki* (jar of curd) are exchanged; (4) draping of the groom and his brother-in-law in *sehra* (veils of flowers); (5) *kheer chatai,* a social custom in which the bride and groom feed each other *kheer* (sweet milk pudding) (Husain 1976: 107–108, 192). Some of these (such as sehra) are widely practiced by Bohras, some (such as kheer chatai) are practiced occasionally, and some (such as the blessing by hijras) are practiced seldom, if ever.

58. Qur'an 4:24: "And all married women are forbidden unto you save those (captives) whom your right hands possess. It is a decree of Allah for you. Lawful unto you are all beyond those mentioned, so that ye seek them with your wealth in honest wedlock, not debauchery. And those of whom ye seek content (by marrying them), give unto them their portions as a duty. And there is no sin for you in what ye do by mutual agreement after the duty (hath been done). Lo! Allah is ever Knower, Wise" (Pickthall 1953: 82). Qur'an 23:1, 5–6: "Successful indeed are the believers . . . who guard their modesty—save from their wives or the (slaves) that their right hands possess, for them they are not blameworthy" (Pickthall 1953: 248). Qur'an 70:29–30: "And those who preserve their chastity, save with their wives and those whom their right hands possess, for thus they are not blameworthy" (Pickthall 1953: 414). Abrar Husain states that mutaa was not permitted in the Muslim umma prior to Hijra, but that the pressures of lengthy military campaigns far away from home led Muhammad to allow his soldiers to contract temporary unions with women in foreign lands. This argument would be more convincing if applied to the immediate Sunni successors of the Prophet than to the Prophet himself: it was not until the reign of Caliph Umar that military campaigns became truly protracted events in far-flung territories. Be that as it may, hadith literature portrays the Prophet himself as sanctioning mutaa. One tradition has a companion named Abdullah ibn Masud stating: "We represented (to the Holy Prophet) whether we should emasculate ourselves. He prevented us from this (course) and then permitted us to resort to Mutaa . . . Some of us used to marry a woman for a specified time by giving her a piece of cloth."

59. Ahadith on mutaa: al-Muslim 1978: 705; mutaa and iddat: Husain 1976: 172. Mutaa predating Islam: Hodkinson 1984: 115. Forbidden by Umar: Farah 1984: 14; Hodkinson 1984: 115.

60. Abdul Husain 1920: 73; Najafali 1943: 61; cf. Hollister 1953: 302.

61. Rarely practiced by Ithna-Asharis: Hodkinson 1984: 115. In Uttar Pradesh, 9%: Husain 1976: 175. Nationwide figures: Hasnain and Husain 1988: 94–95.

62. Ahadith: al-Bukhari 1986, 7:129–199; al-Muslim 1978: 755ff.

63. Triple talaq: Hodkinson 1984: 220; Ithna-Ashari talaq: Hodkinson 1984: 247.

64. Ahmad 1976: xxvii.

65. Abdul Husain 1920: 73.

66. Najafali 1943: 62.

67. Ibid., 63.

68. Widows after Uhud: Pickthall 1953: 79n. Ali's wives and concubines: Farah 1984: 51. Hasan's marriages: al-Ghazali 1971, 2:27.

69. Abdul Husain 1920: 73. The same is true for Sunni Vohras: Lambat reports that monogamy is the rule, with the few exceptions occurring when a first wife is barren—and even in these cases a first wife will generally ask for a divorce if her husband marries another woman (1976: 54).

70. Ahmad 1976: xxv–xxvi.

71. Only significant for former zamindars: Hasnain and Husain 1988: 93. No polygamists under fifty: Ibid., 66; National Committee on Status of Women report: cited in Ibid., 65.

72. Hodkinson 1984: 108.

73. Ahadith relating to burial: al-Bukhari 1986, 2:186–270; al-Muslim 1978: 436–464.

74. A Bohra will normally have his bed oriented so that the head rather than the foot faces Mecca; only a deathbed is turned the other way around. This allows the dying person to sit up (when he is able) and offer prayers in the proper direction. It is the only time when it is not merely acceptable but laudable for a Bohra to point his feet toward qiblah. My information on death rituals comes not from personal observation but from the accounts of informants. Much of the information is in accord with the early twentieth-century account of Abdul Husain (1920: 73–74).

75. Ibid., 73.

76. Ahadith: al-Bukhari 1986, 2:194; al-Muslim 1978: 445.

77. Ahadith: al-Muslim 1978: 445.

78. Ahadith: al-Bukhari 1986, 2:225; cf. al-Ghazali 1971, 2:162.

79. Ahadith: al-Bukhari 1986, 2:230; al-Muslim 1978: 449.

80. *Qubba* is the word used both for a completed tomb and for the grave over which the tomb will be built.

81. When asked about the purpose of the chader, some clerical sources explained that it serves to keep the deceased from "seeing" the sky, while others speculated it was for reasons of modesty. For similarities to funerary rites of Gujarati Maliks and other groups, see Misra 1964: 99ff.

82. Abdul Husain 1920: 73; Chopra 1982: 204.

83. Hadith: al-Muslim 1978: 458.

84. Abdul Husain 1920: 74; Engineer 1993: 152.

Chapter Three. Rituals of the Daudi Bohra Year

1. Hjortshoj 1987: 302.

2. By one tradition (transmitted by Aisha, and therefore deemed credible by Sunnis but not by Shiʻa), the Quraish tribe used to fast on this date, and the Prophet carried this practice over to Islam until the Qurʾanic revelation of Ramadan fasting prompted him to downgrade Ashura fasting to the status of optional (Ahadith: al-Bukhari 1986, 2:388; 3:65; al-Muslim 1978: 548, 569). By another tradition (with an isnad acceptable to Sunni and Shiʻa alike), the Prophet was first introduced to the practice by the Jewish tribes of Medina, who observed the date as one on which the prophet Musa (Moses) had fasted. According to a hadith transmitted by Ibn Abbas, "The Prophet said, 'We have more claim over Moses than you.' So the Prophet fasted on that day and ordered (the Muslims) to fast (on that day)" (Al-Bukhari 1986, 3:124).

3. Abbas 1991: 41.

4. Pinault 1992: 56, 106.

5. Asad 1993.

6. Hasnain and Husain 1988: 145.

7. Syedna Muhammad Burhanuddin was born on March 6, 1915.

8. Mombasa and Dar-es-Salaam: Davoodbhoy 1990: 4; 1993a: 1–8; 1993b. Nairobi and Colombo: Personal communication with Abduz-Zahir Bhaisaheb Mohyuddin, January 1, 2000.

9. Bekhud 1994a: 4.

10. Davoodbhoy 1992a: 4.

11. Bekhud 1994a: 8.

12. Ibid.

13. TV ownership: 96.6% in Mumbai, 94.7% in Calcutta; VCR ownership: 54.4% overall, 75.6% in Karachi; radio ownership: 77.3%.

14. Bekhud 1994a: 11.

15. The captives included one male adult: Husain's son Imam Ali Zain al-Abidin, whose illness kept him from fighting at Kerbala—and thus saved the line of imams from destruction.

16. Because of my witnessing of "bloody matam" at the second site I refrain from naming the masjid in question: since the practice of matam with instruments is forbidden by dawat authorities, identification of the site could bring social chastisement upon people not necessarily aware that their actions were being observed by an anthropologist. The site, however, is one specific urban masjid rather than a composite of several masjids.

17. Members of the clerical royal family are given the honorific of *bhaisaheb* (brother-sir; the female equivalent is *behnsaheb*), a term commonly used in other communities without special significance, but among the Bohras a tightly regulated title; men of ordinary rank are called "bhai" (brother).

18. Al-Muslim 1978: 271.

19. Ibid., 271n.

20. Muhammad ibn Tahir, quoted in Ivanow 1936: para. 76.

21. On the tenth of Ashura the fast is called *lagan,* a remembrance of Husain, but its requirements are the same as those of sawm.

22. Hasnain and Husain 1988: 146.

23. Abbas 1991: 42.

24. Pinault 1992: 109.

25. Ibid., 114.

26. Ibid., 148–150.

27. Abbas 1991: 42.

28. Hjortshoj 1987: 292.

29. Ibid., 302.

30. Pinault 1992: 61–62.

31. Saiyid 1981: 115.

32. Ibid., 121–123; Madan, ed., 1991: 250–255. Darshan, seeking spiritual merit through the viewing of a holy image, is of course a Hindu rather Muslim practice—as incongruous here on a doctrinal level as the serving of alcohol is at the level of culture.

33. Hjortshoj 1987: 289.

34. Pinault 1992: 148–150.

35. Many Ithna-Ashariyya commemorate the urs of Fatima on the third of the following month, and celebrate her birth on the twentieth of that month. On the fifteenth they celebrate the birth date of the fourth imam, Zain-ul Abideen. Likewise, many Twelvers observe the birth date of the Prophet Muhammad on the seventeenth of Rabiul Awwal, the same date that they mark the birth of Imam Jafar al-Sadiq.

36. On the first of the month Twelvers (and some Bohras) mark the birth date of the fifth imam, Muhammad al-Baqir.

37. Ahadith: al-Bukhari 1986, 6:28; al-Muslim 1978: 533.

38. Abdul Husain 1920: 109–111; see the Bibliographical Discussion on the nineteenth-century provenance for much of Abdul Husain's text; see also Fyzee 1934a: 9; Hollister 1953: 289.

39. Cf. al-Muslim 1978: 570.

40. Since the Hindu militant party Shiv Sena gained political control of Mumbai in the 1970s, it has consistently denied building permits to masjids and other Muslim institutions (cf. Katzenstein 1979).

41. The basis for this belief, and for the all-night prayer, are the Qur'anic verses 97.1–3, 5: "Surely We revealed it on the grand night. And what will make you comprehend what the grand night is? The grand night is better than a

thousand months. . . . Peace! it is till the break of the morning" (translation: Shakir 1983: 627).

42. Metcalf 1990: 101.

43. For Sunni and Shi'a hajj rites, see al-Bukhari 1986, 2:344–475; al-Muslim 1978, 2:578–700; Peters 1994.

44. Bekhud 1994b: 8. During the central year of my fieldwork in Mumbai (after Syedi Saleh's death in 1994) Syedna's fourth son, Shahzada Idris Bhaisaheb, served as hajj emir.

45. Ahadith: al-Muslim 1978: 652–654.

46. Cf. al-Muslim 1978: 1087.

47. For the theological explanation of ritual elements of Bohra sacrifice, I am indebted to Mullah Shabbir M. Mansoorbhai Jamali. Cf. general Islamic practice as outlined in ahadith: al-Bukhari 1986, 7:322–334.

48. The rationale for using soil rather than pavement is batin—hidden. As one clerical source joked, "I'd like to tell you, but I'm afraid you don't have the clearance." This is a good example of the difficulties that batin ideology presents to an outside researcher. I had earlier been told by another source that the reason for sacrificing on soil rather than stone was simple cleanliness (*tahara*, one of the pillars of the Ismaili faith). Was this informant unaware of the batin interpretation, or was he intentionally keeping it from me? Or was my later informant merely pulling my leg? Since I know the second informant quite well I am inclined to believe that a batin interpretation exists—but how many other times in the course of my fieldwork have I accepted an offered zahir explanation without knowing that a batin one was intentionally withheld?

49. Cf. al-Muslim 1978: 632.

50. On Ismaili neoplatonism and exploration of metempsychosis, see Corbin 1957: 122–139; Ivanow 1936: paras. 34–37; al-Hamdani 1958b: 220ff.

Chapter Four. Bohra Domestic Life: Kinship, Sex, and the Status of Women

1. Endogamy, in this context, meaning that the whole Daudi Bohra community is treated as the bounded kinship group, in the same way a jati would function within a Hindu kinship pattern. Survey figures: 95.8% unambiguously stated that all members of their extended families had married Daudi Bohras; 90.4% unambiguously reported all unions in their families to be both endogamous and arranged. If the eleven ambiguous responses are excluded from the sampling, the numbers become even more striking (as cited in the main text): three of the eleven ambiguous responses occupy a difficult-to-classify middle ground between support for and rejection of marriage norms; each of these respondents said that "all but one" member of their extended families conformed with the norm, raising the question of

whether a single black sheep has any bearing on the *mores* of the rest of the family. Only one respondent acknowledged a nonendogamous relationship in his extended family, while five noted nonarranged marriages. By way of comparison, an Ahmedabad University master's thesis on Bohra architecture puts the rate of endogamy at "almost 90 %" (Desai 1992: 30), although this figure is sourced only to the estimate of dissident leader Asghar Ali Engineer.

2. Hasnain and Husain 1988: 86–87.

3. Marginally lower than average: 84 % for sons, 94 % for daughters; over 90 % limited marriage to members of their own *khandan* (kin group). A mere 3.8 % reported any intermarriage with Sunnis during the past quarter century: 5 % for illiterates, 6 % for postgraduates/professionals. Intermarriage with non-Muslims was exceptionally rare indeed: 0.7 % reported intercommunal matches within their extended families at some point in the past twenty-five years, a rate virtually the same (0.92 %) for postgraduates but slightly higher (2.5 %) for illiterates. No respondents were willing to marry their children to Hindus, Parsis, Christians, or Jews, but 6.7 % were willing to let a son marry the daughter of Sunni parents or of converts to Islam, 7.9 % were willing to let a son marry the daughter of a convert to Shi'ism, and 3.9 % were willing to let a daughter marry the son of a convert to Shi'ism (Hasnain and Husain 1988: 88–91). The chart is somewhat ambiguous here: it is broken down by qaum, by denomination of marriage partner, and within denomination of marriage partner by son or daughter. It is not absolutely clear, either from the chart or the analysis in the text, whether the "son" or "daughter" referred to is that of the respondent or that of the other party. Since the figures are all markedly higher for "daughter" than for "son," and since in other charts the survey respondents show considerably more conservative marriage preferences for their daughters than their sons, I am assuming that a table listing such as "Hindu: daughter" refers to a union with the daughter *of* a Hindu rather than to the union of the respondent's daughter *to* a Hindu).

4. Hasnain and Husain 1988: 84–85.

5. Ibid., 91.

6. Ahmad 1976: xvii.

7. Ibid., xxi.

8. Chopra 1982: 204.

9. Aggarwal 1976: 265–296; Conklin 1976: 127–140; Saiyid 1976: 239–265.

10. "An uncle or maternal uncle are one's secondary consanguineous kin but their wives' parents, brothers and sisters have nothing to do with a Shi'a unless he has developed some personal relationship. . . . Thus we may conclude that among the Shi'as those kinship ties coming into being out of consanguine relationships may stretch up to tertiary and even quarternary degrees but the affinal ones do not, usually, stretch beyond secondary stage" (Hasnain and Husain 1988: 107–108).

11. A hint of kinship practices of the distant Bohra past may be gained by look-
ing at the kinship practices of the Sunni Vohras of Gujarat, an agricultural
group that has had no significant interaction with Shiʿa Bohras for at least
400 years (if, indeed, even then). Ismail Lambat (1976: 54–56) describes the
modern-day Sunni Vohras as strictly endogamous, though holding no restric-
tions on village exogamy. Virilocality is the rule, although uxorilocality occurs
as well. Levirate is permitted (with the widow almost always marrying her
deceased husband's younger rather than elder brother), as is sororate (partic-
ularly if the wife dies before bearing children). In the modern Daudi Bohra
community virilocality is more common than uxorilocality, but in an urban
setting (where the large majority of Bohras live) such an issue is far less
salient. Neither levirate nor sororate has been practiced within living mem-
ory.

12. Percentages of total survey population: 52.6% lived in families of between
four and six members; 28.6% in families of seven to ten members; 17.6%
lived in joint family structures of eleven to twenty members; 1.2% lived in
small nuclear families of fewer than four members. There was a limited de-
gree of regional variation: in Nagpur, 22.6% of the survey population lived in
joint families, and Calcutta households also tended to be slightly larger than
the norm (35.0% of households had between seven and ten members).
Mumbai households, by contrast, were markedly smaller: 86.6% contained
six or fewer members, and only 6.7% were true joint families with more
than ten members. This is most likely a reflection of the cramped quarters in
which most Mumbai residents live: it would be very difficult to cram a joint
family into the tiny, overstuffed apartments of the Bohra mohallas on
Muhammad Ali Road and Bhindi Bazaar. By way of comparison Asghar Ali
Engineer's survey of reformist Bohras indicated that 55.3% of households in
Mumbai and 62% of those in Gujarat contained more than six members,
while 6.7% and 12% respectively contained more than eleven members
(Engineer 1989: 55).

13. Narayanan 1989: 56.

14. Conklin 1976: 133.

15. My guide through the kinship maze was Mullah Shabbir M. Mansoorbhai Ja-
mali.

16. Anker and Anker 1982: 126, 129.

17. These figures, it should be noted, may say as much about variation among
cities as among regions: the survey was conducted in ten urban centers (a
reasonable siting, as Indian Shiʿa tend to live in urban rather than rural areas),
but the cities have radically different costs of living and real-estate values. The
regions with the five highest levels of nuclear family and lowest levels of joint
family occurrence were Maharashtra, Delhi, Karnataka, Tamil Nadu, and West
Bengal, but the surveys in these regions were distributed in Mumbai, Delhi,
Bangalore, Madras, and Calcutta—five of the most crowded, most expensive

cities in India. The regions with the five highest levels of joint family occurrence and lowest levels of nuclear family occurrence were Jammu & Kashmir, Gujarat, Bihar, Uttar Pradesh, and Andhra Pradesh, but the surveys in these states were limited to Srinagar, Ahmedabad, Patna, Lucknow, and Hyderabad—five cities considerably more conducive to larger families than those listed above. Therefore, while the Bohra results are thoroughly in line with the survey results for other Gujarati Shiʿa, this correlation cannot be taken as wholly conclusive without factoring out the differences inherent in the cities involved. It is hardly surprising that in congested Mumbai only 1 % of respondents live in joint families, while in sprawling Srinagar 38 % do (Hasnain and Husain 1988: for family type and figures, 110; survey sites, 15).

18. Narayanan 1989: 65, 31.

19. Bohras following Hindu rules of inheritance: Ahmad 1969: 161. Ahadith on mandated inheritance for women: al-Muslim 1978: 854–855. Pukhtun: Jacobson 1976: 186. Imtiaz Ahmad quotation: 1976: xxviii. Khatana quotation: 1976: 110. Meos: Aggarwal 1976: 281ff.; Koknis: Saiyid 1976: 260.

20. Hasnain and Husain 1988: 108.

21. Cf. al-Bukhari 1986, 7:3; al-Ghazali 1971, 2:20–29; al-Muslim 1978: 702.

22. My presence at Bohra functions both in Mumbai and Surat was the source of widespread community speculation, and a great many observers (I was informed) assumed that I was a convert married or engaged to a Bohra woman. Unions with Christians, Parsis, or Hindus are exceptionally rare, but not wholly unknown. In East Africa, intermarriage occurs frequently enough to be the subject of occasional discussion in Indian circles. This may say more about racial attitudes within the community than the actual frequency of such unions, since the few African converts are not always welcomed enthusiastically. The rarity of conversions from East Africa may be gauged not only by the fact that I never met or saw such an outsider, but also that none of the Bohras with whom I discussed the topic had ever met or seen one either. So nebulous were the notions of outside converts that I (light-haired and melanin-impaired) was mistaken for an African on at least one occasion.

23. Husain 1976: 90.

24. Ibid., 94.

25. Ibid., 96.

26. Cf. Ibid., 90.

27. Nationwide: Fewer than four children, 71.5 %; four to six children, 26.6 %; more than six, 1.9 %. Gujarat, fewer than four, 75 % ; four to six, 25 %; more than six, none; Maharashtra, fewer than four children, 83 %; four to six, 16 %; more than six, 1 % (Hasnain and Husain 1988: 192).

28. Only 30.7 % of respondents had fewer than four siblings, 57.2 % had four to six, and 12.1 % had more than six brothers or sisters (Ibid., 192).

29. Need for early umma to grow: cf. Khan 1979: 20–33. Ahadith on birth control: al-Bukhari 1986, 7:102–103; al-Muslim 1978: 732, 735. 'Azl as makruh: al-Ghazali 1971, 2:44–47; cf. al-Bukhari 1986, 3:237. Gradualist position: al-Ghazali 1971, 2:45.

30. Nor does al-Ghazali regard birth control as appropriate only in dire circumstances. He states that 'azl would be permissible not only to preserve the wife's health from the ravages of childbirth, but to preserve her beauty as well. He also considers 'azl legitimate when its aim is to prevent the financial ruin of a family overburdened with children, or to prevent the birth of a child to a concubine who would then have to be manumitted. The only two motives for birth control that al-Ghazali specifically labels impermissible are (1) the avoidance of female progeny, which he likens to fi qatlihim al-'inath (the pre-Islamic practice of burying female newborns), and (2) mere convenience, in order "to keep her [the wife] neat and clean and to save her from maintaining children" (Al-Ghazali 1971, 2:46). The attitudes of al-Ghazali on 'azl are indicative of mainstream attitudes throughout many (if not most) schools of Islamic thought (Bouhdiba 1985: 125–126).

31. Hasnain and Husain 1988: 194.

32. Ibid.

33. Bouhdiba 1985: 13.

34. Visiting all wives in one night: al-Bukhari 1986, 1:166; 7:106. On the number of wives, I follow Farah 1984: 77, 77n. She provides no specific citations, but attributes nine wives to an al-Bukhari hadith, eleven wives to a different al-Bukhari hadith, thirteen wives to an unsourced hadith, and fourteen wives to a hadith sourced to Ibn al-Jawzi.

35. Apart from certain Sufis and members of related ascetic movements, this attitude runs straight through almost all branches of Islam. Al-Ghazali recalls the statement of the Prophet: "He who marries fulfills half his religion" (1971, 2:21). The archtraditionalist Ahmad ibn Muhammad ibn Hanbal, the jurist and philosopher who founded what is perhaps the most straightlaced of the four Sunni schools of holy law, remarried the second day after the death of his wife; at the time, he is said to have commented, "I detest spending the night as a celibate" (quoted in Farah 1984: 51). His rationale sums up the generally accepted Muslim view on the matter: sexual urges are natural and inevitable, and therefore it is unnatural and unholy to be celibate; no man can be immune to these temptations, but only an unmarried man would lack the legitimate means of expressing them. It is for this reason that the philosopher and legal codifier al-Ghazali writes, "God created pleasure of the world with this object that if the people have pleasure they will be eager to have lasting pleasure of the next world" (1971, 2:26). In many Muslim communities the maximum period of abstinence before a marriage is deemed invalid is 120 days (Bouhdiba 1985: 18).

36. Fruzzetti 1982: 17.

37. Al-Ghazali 1971, 2:43.

38. Hadith: al-Muslim 1978: 192. Cf. Bouhdiba 1985: 38. The only exception to the prohibition on pointing one's feet in the direction of qiblah is for a person on his deathbed.

39. Not facing qiblah: al-Ghazali 1971, 2:43. Not during menstruation: Farah 1984: 107. "Two donkeys": Quoted in Farah 1984: 106; cf. al-Ghazali 1971, 2:43. 'Iraqi attributes this hadith to 'Atabah in a weak transmittal via Ibn Majah (Farah 1984: 106n).

40. Hasnain and Husain 1988: 134.

41. *India Today,* August 18, 1997, 69.

42. Changing times: Rahman 1982a: 20. Atomism: Ibid., 2. "piecemeal . . . ," comparison with premodern Europe: ibid.

43. Ibid., 19.

44. Dumont 1986: 229–230.

45. Najafali 1943: 26.

46. A major Haryana school study, for example, showed far lower educational levels for the subjects' mothers than fathers (Jindal 1984: 84–85).

47. Cf. Beck and Keddie 1978, Bhowmick 1984, Esposito 1982, Jacobson 1976, Metcalf 1984, Michaelson 1983, Rahman 1982b, Tapper 1990.

48. Verdia 1974: 13.

49. Campbell 1899: 32.

50. Ms. Mustafa is the wife of Shaikh Mustafa Abdulhussein, one of the dawat sources on whom I have relied heavily.

51. Mumbai has the highest levels of female education (96.4% reported parity, 100% parity or female superiority), and Calcutta has the lowest (82.4% reported parity, 85.3% parity or female superiority).

52. Hasnain and Husain 1988: 206–207.

53. Table from Ibid., 111: Who Makes Important Family Decisions.

Respondent's educational level	Eldest male	Eldest female	Adult males	Several people
Illiterate	75%	7.5%	17.5%	
Below high school	80%	3.0%	12.0%	5%
Undergraduate	56%	4.0%	33.0%	7%
Postgraduate	15%	2.5%	42.0%	40.5%

54. Ibid., 112.

55. Jacobson 1976: 209.

56. Asani 1994: 20–22; Merchant, Banatwalla, et al. 1969: 66.

57. Narayanan 1989: 53.

58. Ibid.

59. Personal interview, April 4, 1995.

60. Mernissi 1975, 1987, 1991a, 1991c.

61. Desai 1992: 32-33.

62. Mernissi 1991b: viii.

63. Personal interview, March 12, 1995.

64. See chapter 6 for description of orthopraxic identity cards.

Chapter Five. Qasr-e Ali: The Royals

1. Hasnain and Husain 1988: 139-140.

2. English rendition: Shakir 1983: 481.

3. Contractor 1980: 6; Engineer 1993: 156.

4. Ali 1954: 378-379.

5. Syedna Muhammad Burhanuddin was born March 6, 1915. He received nass on the twenty-seventh of Rajab, 1352 A.H. (Najmuddin 1992: 7). On hereditary succession: throughout the Yemeni period the da'iship generally remained in the hands of one family; of the first twenty-two da'is, no fewer than seventeen belonged to the same lineage. In India, nine da'is of the Rajput dynasty reigned between 1085/1674 and 1256/1840.

6. Campbell 1899: 32.

7. Shahzada Qaidjohar Bhaisaheb, the eldest son of Syedna, is generally regarded as one of the most powerful individuals in the dawat. While holding no title comparable to those of Mazoon Saheb and Mukasir Saheb, Shahzada Qaidjohar cannot be considered less influential than these top officeholders. When asked what specific department Qaidjohar controls, an informed dawat official responded, "What department *doesn't* he control?" This day-to-day management of affairs, however, does not imply that Qaidjohar will succeed his father as da'i al-mutlaq. In fact, his strong command over operational minutiae leads most observers to downplay his odds of succession. Syedna Muhammad Burhanuddin is said to view the da'i's spiritual role as taking precedence over his more mundane tasks, and therefore observers see his second son Shahzada Mufaddal Bhaisaheb Saifuddin (who devotes more time to strictly religious pursuits rather than on-the-ground implementation of policy) as a more likely candidate for succession.

8. Campbell 1899: 30n; Hollister 1953: 289-290.

9. Bekhud 1994c: 9. The term *rauzah,* in Bohra usage, is applied only to the mausoleums of da'is and syedis: for all other individuals, the more generalized term *qubba* is used instead. Within the rauzah the *kebbeh* (sarcophagus) is covered with a *chettri,* an awning or umbrella of green cloth.

10. Abdul Husain 1920: 81.

11. Ibid., 81-82. In modern practice, the most important shrines include Rauzah Tahera in Mumbai; Qubbah Qutbi in Ahmedabad; Mazar-e-Saifee in Surat; Mazar-e-Noorani in Kutch-Mandvi; Mazar-e-Najmi in Ujjain; Mazar-e-Hakimi

in Burhanpur; Mazar-e-Fakri in Galiakot; and Qubbah Badriyah in Jamnagar (Davoodbhoy 1993b: 2).

12. Zaidi 1988: 17–19.

13. Tapper 1990: 236–255.

14. Davoodbhoy 1992a: 4.

15. Abdul Husain 1920: 81.

16. This surah is closely associated with death rituals and remembrances.

17. The direction of circumambulation shows an appropriately Islamic (rather than syncretic) tendency: Muslim circumambulation is counterclockwise, while Hindu and Buddhist circumambulation is clockwise.

18. Geertz 1973: 3ff.

19. January 10, 1995.

20. The celebration I observed took place on April 25, 1995.

21. The occupant of the apartment in question has since passed away. The politics of Saifee Mahal are said to be highly byzantine. Syedna Taher Saifuddin had four wives—Husena Aisaheba, Fatima Aisaheba, Vazira Aisaheba, and Amina Aisaheba—and the children and grandchildren of these wives are said to share close bonds on the basis of maternity. Syedna Muhammad Burhanuddin (the eldest son), the late Shahzedi Asma Behnsaheb (the eldest child), and Mukasir Saheb Husain are the children of Husena Aisaheba; Shahzada Shabbir Bhaisaheb and Mazoon Saheb Khuzema are sons of Amina Aisaheba. As in any large family, personal grudges may be trumped by loyalty to the clan.

22. Surat boosters note that the city has become considerably cleaner in the intervening years.

23. August 17, 1996.

24. As noted earlier, Hafizi Musta'lis recognized a different line of imams, but this sect did not last long after the fall of the Fatimid caliphate.

Chapter Six. Maintenance of Spiritual and Political Hegemony

1. Ali 1954: 252–254; "Judgment" 1931: 55–56; Najafali 1943: 7, 15–16.

2. Schimmel 1980: 71; Esposito 1988: 162–169.

3. Eaton 1978, 1984; Gaborieau 1986: 110–119; Goldziher 1981: 116–166; Shah 1971: 322–346; Trimingham 1971: 218–244. It is noteworthy, perhaps, that Surat has traditionally been a center of great religious importance not only to Bohras and Parsis, but also to the Sufi Rifa'i tariqa that still flourishes there today (Van der Veer 1992: 549, 562).

4. Asani 1994: 17; Hollister 1953: 379.

5. Marten 1921: 12–37.

6. Barth 1959: 133. As David B. Edwards notes (1998: 712–715), Barth's inter-

pretation has come under fire from critics such as Talal Asad (1972), Akbar S. Ahmed (1976), and Michael Meeker (1980). Whatever the merits of these critiques, they do not challenge Barth on the issue of political and religious paradigms standing in near polar opposition. Edwards rightly notes, however, that the war in neighboring Afghanistan may have turned some of the observations of both Barth and Lindholm into historical rather than contemporary ethnography (Edwards 1998: 714–716, 727).

7. Barth 1960: 113–145.

8. Lindholm 1982: 93.

9. Hasnain and Husain 1988: 139–141.

10. Amanat 1988; Arjomand 1988a; Cole and Keddie 1986: 2; Cottam 1986: 57; Jafri 1979: 3–23. Shortly before the February 2000 majlis elections, Ayatollah Montazeri stated that Khamenei (who had supplanted him as heir apparent to Ayatollah Khomeini and placed him under house arrest) has "no right to exercise absolute power" (*New York Times*, January 24, 2000).

11. Zaidis: Pinault 1992: 44; Tabataba'i 1975: 76. Alawis: Kramer 1987; Yalman 1969. Ahmadiyya: Ali 1973; Friedmann 1989.

12. Djalili 1981: 14–15; Feki 1978; Pinault 1992: 31.

13. Corbin 1984: 136–139; Pinault 1992: 33; Walker 1993: 26–29.

14. Borthwick 1990; Makarem 1972.

15. Abdul Husain 1920: 42 (confirmed to me by dawat authorities).

16. Daftary 1990: 228.

17. Al-Nu'man's *Ta'wil al-da'a'im:* 1972, 3:48–49. Listing of jazair: Fyzee, 1934b: 12; Poonawala 1973: 109–115; 1974: 572–577. Turks for Nubians: Daftary 1990: 228. Twelve hujjas of the day and twelve of the night: Jafar ibn Mansur 1984: 216–217.

18. On Fatimid and post-Fatimid clerical hierarchy: Abdul Husain 1920: 37; Abdulhussein 1995a: 225; Ali 1963, 2:99–103; Corbin 1954: 178–184; 1982: 103–106; Dachraoui 1981: 279–395; Hamdani 1976: 85–114; al-Hamdani 1933: 377; Hasan 1964: 279–305; Ivanow 1938: 62ff.; 1939: 1–35; 1942: 189; Najafali 1943: 7; Stern 1983: 234–253.

19. Abdul Husain 1920: 13, 22, 37; Hollister 1953: 263; Misra 1964: 15–16. The current dress code for Bohra men is all white; women have considerably more leeway.

20. Ali 1954: 299–330, 317–319; Ivanow 1939: 20–21; see also Engineer 1993: 24–25.

21. Ivanow 1933: 22–23; Hollister 1953: 246; cf. Poonawala 1977. The writings of Syedna Idris Imad al-Din, while still works of recapitulation, are the most noteworthy post-Fatimid texts.

22. Mustafa Abdulhussein notes: "There is scrupulous adherence to the batini thought laid out by the books of the Fatimid period and their summaries written by the early da'is of Yemen. Any deviation from this is regarded as

sinful. A study of the Fatimid and early Yemeni books thus gives a complete picture of modern batini thought" (personal communication, April 9, 2000).

23. Corbin 1980: 183–196; Djalili 1981: 14–15; Goldziher 1981: 221–224; Ivanow 1936: para. 60; 1952: 33–36; Karandikar 1968: 97; Tabataba'i 1975: 78–79.

24. Just as classified U.S. government information can be shared with members of foreign intelligence agencies or other outsiders under careful supervision of properly constituted authorities, a limited amount of batin knowledge can sometimes be shared with outsiders who have been granted special permission. I gained a new perspective on the American government's version of batini ta'wil when I underwent clearance procedures for the Senate Foreign Relations Committee staff, but Mustafa Abdulhussein warns against taking the comparison too far. "Your government's secrecy is for the protection of the government itself," he said. "Ours is for the protection of the individual. Exposure to batin knowledge before the zahir has been assimilated would be like feeding a newborn infant heavy, indigestible food instead of milk."

25. As long as the human soul is trapped in its body, the zahir is as necessary as the batin for an individual's salvation. On zahir and batin: Daftary 1990: 232; Ivanow 1952: 31–36; al-Nu'man 1960: 347; 1961, 1:53; 1972, 1:69–71.

26. Abdul Husain 1920: 44, 50. (Some typographical errors in original text have been corrected).

27. Asani 1994: 17.

28. Abdulhussein 1995a: 225. Daftary makes an uncharacteristic error when, after correctly listing the seven Ismaili pillars, he states: "The Fatimid Ismailis, as Shi'is, had thus added walaya and tahara to the five pillars recognized by the Sunnis" (1990: 250). Jihad, while a vital component of Sunni doctrine, is not generally acknowledged as one of its five pillars (shahada, salat, zakat, sawm, and hajj) (see al-Muslim 1978: 9).

29. Corbin 1972, 1:235–284; 1984: 78–92; Hollister 1953: 257–259; Tabataba'i 1975: 78–79.

30. Corbin 1953: 112–128; 1954: 193ff.; Daftary 1990: 239–241; Filippani-Ronconi: 75ff.; Najafali 1943: 14.

31. Corbin 1982: 116ff.; 1957: 114–120; 1984: 118–124; Goldziher 1981: 219–223; Makarem 1972: 44–67; Walker 1978: 14ff. Poonawala quotation: 1970: 278; cf. Stern 1960: 79; 1961: 107.

32. Syedna Idris Imad al-Din, quoted in al-Hamdani 1958b: 212–213.

33. West and West 1984: 70.

34. Transmigration of souls: Corbin 1957: 122–139; Hollister 1953: 251; Ivanow 1936: paras. 34–37. Numerology: Corbin 1984: 111ff., 204–207. Husain al-Hamdani quotation: 1958b: 220.

35. Corbin 1951, 1954, 1980, 1982. The concept is still readily discernible in twentieth-century Western philosophy: cf. Ridenhour and Shocklee: "Cycles, cycles—Life runs in cycles" (1987).

36. Al-Hamdani 1958b: 215; Idris 1942: 54–55, trans. in Ivanow 1942: 242; Ivanow 1932: 71n.

37. Ali 1954: 576ff.; Corbin 1982: 39–69; Jafar ibn Mansur 1952: 113–114, 132–138; al-Nu'man 1960; Stern 1983: 3–16, 53–55; Walker 1978: 355–366.

38. *Rasa'il Ikhwan al-Safa* (Beirut, 1957). Attributed to Imam Ahmad ibn Abdullah ibn Muhammad ibn Ismail: Idris 1975, 4:367ff.) Collaborative effort: Daftary 1990: 247; Stern 1946: 367–372.

39. Ali 1963, 2:226–249; Corbin 1984: 190–194; Daftary 1990: 248–249; Ivanow 1933: 91; Poonawala 1977: 360.

40. Corbin 1951: 155–161; 1982: 203–208; Ivanow 1946: 87–89; Stern 1983: 30–42. The inclusion of Christians and Jews is less surprising than that of members of other religions, since practitioners of the other two Abrahamic (or, in this context, Ibrahimic) monotheisms are specifically described as *ahl al-kitab,* "people of the scripture," in the Qur'an (3:113–115, 29:46).

41. Dawat-e-Hadiyah 1975: 60.

42. Niazi 1992: 11.

43. The transferal of charisma has been given its definitive explication by Stanley J. Tambiah in the context of Buddhist forest saints and amulets in Thailand (1984).

44. Ahadith: al-Muslim 1978: 1157.

45. Engineer 1993: 152.

46. Engineer 1989: 67.

47. The percentages for alamat-seekers are higher in Nagpur (83.6%) and Calcutta (72.5%) than in more cosmopolitan Mumbai (52.0%) and Karachi (40.9%). On alamat: Dawat-e-Hadiyah 1975: 98. For alamat on Diwali prior to orthopraxic reforms: Ahmad 1969: 161.

48. Dawat-e-Hadiyah 1975: 32.

49. Respondents using air travel: 43.6%; of Karachi respondents: 71.1%.

50. The figures were, understandably, higher in Mumbai than in sites at a greater distance: every one of the Mumbai respondents reported five or more times in Syedna's presence, and 96.7% fell into the too-many-to-count category.

51. Radio fatwas: Messick 1996. Khomeini's videocassettes: Esposito 1988: 177. Ashura on Doordarshan: Abbas 1991: 43. Qur'an karaoke: Reuters, *Asian Age,* April 29, 1995, 1. (The fountain of Sunni orthodoxy for many centuries, al-Azhar was itself founded by the Bohras' Fatimid Ismaili ancestors.)

52. Edwards 1993: 610, following Anderson 1983: 37–46.

53. A few groups, most notably the Khojahs, the Ahmadiyya, and the Baha'i, share the Bohras' holistic approach to modernity and modern technology, though not necessarily the accompanying zeal for Islamization. The heterodox Ahmadi clerical mission, for example, transmits a live radio (and, in some places,

television) broadcast for twelve hours daily, its programming simultaneously translated into Urdu, Bengali, Arabic, English, French, German, Russian, and Dutch, beamed from London throughout the world by a system of four orbiting satellites (*Times of India,* December 8, 1994). This passion for modernization, however, has brought them no closer to Muslim orthopraxy (at least in the eyes of their coreligionists): in Pakistan, for example, the Ahmadiyya are legally defined as a denomination wholly outside the fold of Islam.

54. Microwave ownership: 29.9%; satellite TV: 72.9%; washing machines: 85.4%. These items were listed only on the questionnaires distributed in Mumbai and Karachi, not on the general form distributed to all Nagpur and Calcutta respondents as well as three Mumbai respondents and twenty-three Karachi respondents. There were forty-eight respondents for microwave, satellite TV, and washing-machine questions.

55. Philip Bereano, professor of technical communication at the University of Washington, personal communication, March 9, 1999.

56. Desire for computer ownership: 46.7% of total, 51.1% of those who do not have or use one (the slight divergence in figures is due to the overlap of five respondents who marked both categories, either because they wanted a second computer or shared ownership of the first). There was considerable regional variation among the sites: ownership ranged from a low of 3.8% in relatively slow-paced Nagpur to 13.2% in Calcutta, and highs of more than one-fifth (20.7%) of respondents in Mumbai and nearly one-quarter (24.4%) of those in cosmopolitan Karachi.

57. *India Today,* July 29, 1997, 13.

58. Ibid., In fact, the rate of computer ownership among my Karachi respondents (24.4%) is only marginally lower than that of African Americans (29.0%: *New York Times,* April 17, 1998).

59. Personal communication—by e-mail, May 13, 1998.

60. All quotations are taken from the introductory posting, dated 1995 by Yusuf Goolamabba and Zakir Haveliwala. Since this is a closed list with access strictly limited to Daudi Bohras, I refrain from giving the address. My own occasional access to the network has been only by the permission of clerical authorities.

Chapter Seven. Specifics of Orthopraxy: Dress and Economics

1. The sherwani (or *saya*) is a white overcoat that had previously been normative (rather than merely customary) only for clerics. While institutionalizing a standardized community dress, both at the Conference on Fatimi Knowledge and in the Cairo Ashura firman, Syedna gave equal emphasis to other elements of Islamic orthopraxy: namaz, daily reading of the Qur'an, avoidance of riba, and upholding of shariat.

2. Mines 1981: 66. For a contrasting model, see Aggarwal 1973.
3. Asad 1986: 16.
4. Wright 1983: 85. Cf. Wright 1975.
5. Hasnain and Husain 1988: 211.
6. Hjortshoj 1987: 305.
7. Abdul Husain 1920: 77.
8. Lane-Smith 1928: 160.
9. Mahroof et al. 1986: 8.
10. See Raik 1975.
11. Abdul Husain 1920: 78.
12. Cf. al-Bukhari 1986, 7:460.
13. Beck and Keddie 1978: 5–20; Jacobson 1976; Mutahhari 1988.
14. Hollister 1953: 294.
15. Joint nikah: *Current,* March 29, 1975, 4. Prospective brides: *Hindustan Times/Evening News,* November 8, 1974, 1; Yasmin Contractor: *Times of India,* October 30, 1973.
16. Cf. Mutahhari 1988: 73–77.
17. Ethics and birth rites were categories only on the Mumbai and Karachi forms, given to forty-five responding households. In Nagpur dress orthopraxy ranked fourth, after death rites, but in Mumbai it was cited by 92.9% of respondents and in Calcutta it was mentioned by 92.1%, earning a higher ranking (second place) than that of Hajj; in Karachi it tied hajj for the second-ranked practice.
18. *Gulshan-e Malumat* data is taken from Raik 1975 (more complete details provided in Appendix 3). *Bostan-e Daudi* data is taken from *Bostan-e Daudi* 1960. I have done a rough tally rather than a precise frame-by-frame tabulation of the *Bostan* photographs, since the focus of this chapter is contemporary rather than historical.
19. Barth 1969: 14.
20. Hasnain and Husain 1988: 206.
21. Narayanan 1989: 84–85. Cf. Kalka 1990 on Gujaratis in Britain.
22. Al-Bukhari 1986, 7:517ff.
23. On post-Independence beard wearing, see also Chopra 1982: 206.
24. Engineer 1993: 197. Engineer argues that the real impediment was that the bride was the daughter of reformist figure Abdulali Chibawala. Whether or not this was the underlying reason for the amil's refusal, the incident shows that beards were deemed normative in the 1930s.
25. Hollister 1953: 299; *Statesman,* February 4, 1940, 9; March 29, 1940, 6.; Engineer 1993: 198.
26. Personal interview, June 2, 1995.

27. Al-Bukhari 1986, 7:517.

28. Ibid, 7:516.

29. Abdul Husain 1920: 77.

30. Singh 1963: 84; Uberoi 1969: 127ff.

31. Uberoi 1969: 127; 1991: 324-329; Fox 1985: 109, 236n.

32. Quoted in Gold 1994: 549.

33. See Fox 1985: 185-211; Kapur 1986: 7-57; Pettigrew 1995; Van der Veer 1994: 53-56.

34. Personal interview, quoted in Blank 1992: 190-191.

35. Juergensmeyer 1988: 78-80; Pettigrew 1995: 143-187.

36. Juergensmeyer 1988: 82-85.

37. For elaboration of Islamic investment, see Siddiqui 1992.

38. Cf. al-Bukhari 1986, 3:148-241.

39. Personal communication, January 16, 2000.

40. Dawat-e-Hadiyah 1985: 4ff.

41. Al-Bukhari 1986, 6:49; al-Muslim 1978: 831, 839.

42. Ahmad 1969: 161.

43. The Qur'an language is not specific. Shakir translates *qardan hasana* as "a goodly gift" (1983: 587), while commentator Bahadur Altaf Ahmad Kherie translates it as "a beautiful loan" (1992: 378).

44. Spiritual merit: Dawat-e-Hadiyah 1985: 2. Capitalization figures: Zaidi 1988: 9; Niazi 1992: 11. Loans to all communities: Niazi 1992: 11.

45. Dawat-e-Hadiyah 1985: 5.

46. Respondents using the service: 75.6%; those rating it one of the top two services: 35.0%.

47. Wright 1975: 176. The text cited by Wright for foundation is *Sheikh Mohammedali Allabux* (Mumbai, 1968).

48. Wright 1975: 164, 176.

49. *Sunday Observer,* May 30, 1982, 1. Calculation of current rates based on Rs 43.6 = $1, as of January 28, 2000.

50. Contractor 1980: 38-41; Engineer 1993: 159-161; Nathwani 1979: 117-119.

51. Rate of zakat: al Bukhari 1986, 2:308; There is a certain amount of disagreement over the definition of "accumulated wealth." This is perhaps inevitable, given the language of the Qur'an and ahadith. In a hadith reported by Abu Said al-Khudri, the Prophet said that no zakat was owed "on less than five camels" (Ibid., 302), while Abu Huraira reported that no zakat was owed on a horse or a slave (Ibid., 314; al-Muslim 1978: 467), but this guidance would be difficult to extrapolate into stock portfolios. Abdul Hamid Siddiqi, translator of al-Muslim's collection of ahadith, defines accumulated wealth as that "which is left over after passage of a year," with animals and agricultural pro-

duce excluded (Al-Muslim 1979: 466). Among my Bohra sources, Shaikh Ali Asghar cited the one-year accumulation as a benchmark, while Abduz-Zahir Bhaisaheb Mohyuddin tried to place the traditional exhortations in a modern context; zakat would be levied, in his judgment, on a person's nonessential assets: cash and investments, for example, but not one's home or money needed to provide for one's family (personal communication, January 16, 2000).

52. Al-Bukhari 1986, 2:271–275, 308–338; al-Muslim 1978: 470–474.

53. Roy 1984: 35–36.

54. Abdul Husain 1920: 65ff.

55. 1,000,000 Bohras, each paying one-quarter of one rupee (4 annas) = Rs 250,000 = $5,732 by current rates.

56. As of February (i.e., Ramadan) 1995, according to dawat sources.

57. Al-Bukhari 1986, 2:339–342; al-Muslim 1978: 468.

58. In the five years since, the rupee has dropped precipitously against the dollar. By exchange rates of January 2000, Rs 40 comes out to just under one dollar.

59. Contractor 1980: 41.

60. Nathwani 1979: 118. At exchange rates of January 28, 2000, Rs 51,000 = $1,169.

61. Qur'an 8:41; al-Bukhari 1986, 1:44; 2:335; 4:222.

62. Shibani Roy misidentifies this also: "Khums: property of a lone man is taken by the 'dawat'" (1984: 36).

63. Hasnain and Husain 1988: 139–141.

64. Campbell 1899: 33n.

65. If this information is accurate, it would help establish a number for the Bohra population: 400,000, as of 1920. It must be noted, however, that the amount of revenue raised seems to be pure guesswork on the part of a writer who had no access to genuine dawat records, and even this guess may date back at least two decades prior to publication (see Bibliographical Discussion).

66. Abdul Husain 1920: 65–68.

67. Ibid., 68.

68. Personal interview, January 11, 1995.

69. Engineer 1989: 70. He does not identify the participants as dissidents per se, but since orthodox Bohras are forbidden to have any contact with Engineer (who is under baraat), his survey participants are ipso facto self-selected dissidents.

70. Respondents for this question were the family breadwinners. While 11.9% listed their professions as hardware, the actual percentage is probably significantly higher: more than half (52.4%) of respondents listed "business" as

their profession, without further detail and it is likely that many of these respondents were in the business of hardware.

71. Mines 1983: 113.

72. In Nagpur, more than half (56.4%) used the dawat to network for business opportunities.

73. Cf. al-Muslim 1978: 496.

74. Narayanan 1989: 67.

75. Small businessmen: 32.5%; earning less than Rs 1,000/month: 49.0%; Hasnain and Husain 1988: 18. Non-Gujaratis more backward than neighbors: Ibid., 21, 114. Shiʿa agriculturalists: Ibid., 113–114, 118. National figures vs. Maharashtra and Gujarat: Ibid., 125.

76. Personal interview, March 12, 1995.

Chapter Eight. Education

1. Eickelman 1992: 643–655; Rahman 1982a: 140.

2. Ahmad 1994: 509; Edwards 1993, 1995; Sachedina 1994: 410–420; Voll 1994: 347–368.

3. Quoted in Singh 1965: 52.

4. Turkey and Iran: Winter 1984. Western intellectual framework: cf. Eickelman 1992.

5. On mainstream Indian society and education, see Jain 1986; Jindal 1984; Rudolph and Rudolph 1987: 290–311.

6. Up to secondary level: 36%; graduates: 32.5%. Hasnain and Husain 1988: 20.

7. Ibid., 114.

8. Asani 1987; Daftary 1990: 545–548; Merchant, Banatwalla, et al. 1969.

9. Niazi 1992: 11.

10. Hardgrave and Kochanek 1993: 22. A breakdown of the 1991 census figures by gender reveals that only 39% of Indian women and girls above the age of seven are literate (Drèze and Sen 1996: 112).

11. Misra 1964: 70.

12. Jindal 1984: 98, 106.

13. Cf. Eickelman 1992: 644; Fischer 1980: 41; Metcalf 1982: 100–125; Mujeeb 1967: 404.

14. Nuʿmani 1961: 285–286.

15. Ahmad 1967: 260–273; Krishna 1976: 154; Rahman 1982a: 51.

16. Mercantile requirements: Shahabuddin and Wright 1987: 166. Mumbai environment: Hardy 1972: 205. Adaptation vis-à-vis other banias: Katzenstein 1979: 44, Michaelson 1976: 289–293.

17. Narayanan 1989: 50.

18. Engineer 1993: 166. Dawat sources argue that the issue was control rather than curriculum.

19. Abdulhussein 1995a: 225; Anjuman-e-Burhani 1965: 8; Najmuddin 1992: 13.

20. Davoodbhoy 1992a: 4.

21. The Burhani Madrasa of Karachi, for examples, operates on the same principles and maintains the same academic standards as the Mumbai flagship. The Karachi school is located near the Saifee Cooperative Housing Society, a Bohra housing complex of 1,400 private homes and nine apartment buildings, all oriented toward a central masjid.

22. *Indian Express*, February 18, 1995. This pre-university degree is based on a uniform syllabus taught at more than 600 schools worldwide.

23. Cf. Mutahhari 1988, in an Ithna-Ashari context.

24. Ahadith: al-Bukhari 1986, 7:219–270.

25. Bohras, like other Ismailis, number the pillars of Islam at seven rather than five.

26. Ahadith: al-Bukhari 1986: bks. 3, 4, 5; al-Muslim 1978: 147–171.

27. Desai 1992: 120.

28. Personal interview, April 4, 1995.

29. Abdulhussein 1995c: 361.

30. Campbell 1899: 32n.

31. Abdul Husain 1920: 52.

32. Najmuddin 1992: 13.

33. Campbell 1899: 32–33.

34. Anjuman-e-Burhani 1965: 8.

35. Najmuddin 1992: 19.

36. Not only is tuition paid by the dawat, but board and lodging are free as well (Abdulhussein 1995c: 361).

37. The shaikh reached this conclusion, moreover, without ever having read *American Ethnologist*.

38. Abdulhussein 1995c: 361. Shaikh Murtaza Africawala, head of the Karachi Jamea's administrative department, and Mullah Husaifa Saifuddin, one of the academy's instructors, were kind enough to show me around the campus.

39. While al-Bukhari and al-Muslim are themselves respected, the standards by which Bohras (and other Shi'a) assess the reliability of ahadith differ from the standards used by Sunni scholars. A hadith is judged reliable not on the basis of its isnad, but if it has been accepted by an imam.

40. For a journalistic rather than a scholarly account of the plague, see Jonah Blank, "Bombay's Rat Patrol Takes on the Plague," *US News and World Report*, October 10, 1994, 14.

Chapter Nine. Dissidents and Control

1. To use the argot of sociological discourse, the realist (or phenomenalist) stance adopts the vantage point of the social actors themselves, while the nominalist position consciously sets its own framework for the study. Examples of the former include Weber (1947: 145) and Barth (1960), while the later is exemplified by Parsons (1951, 1961). The realist tact is generally regarded as closer to the modern anthropological norm (Burt, Minor, et al. 1983: 22).

2. Davoodbhoy 1992a: 2, 4. Nor is this a new position. Half a century earlier, dawat attorney Abbasali Najafali had written, "It being essential for a Dawoodi Bohra to owe allegiance to the Dai-ul-Mutlaq of his time, anyone who challenges the position and the authority of the Dai-ul-Mutlaq goes out of the fold and forfeits his right to all the privileges that are available to a member of the community" (1943: 9).

3. Dawat-e-Hadiyah 1983: 2.

4. *Week,* March 20, 1983, 36.

5. Dawat-e-Hadiyah n.d.: 4.

6. Contractor 1980: 7.

7. Personal interview, June 2, 1995.

8. Engineer n.d.: 7–8.

9. Engineer 1989: 63.

10. Personal interview, June 2, 1995.

11. Engineer 1993: 314.

12. Engineer 1995: i.

13. Personal interview, June 2, 1995.

14. Engineer 1993: 317.

15. Davoodbhoy 1992a: 10.

16. Dawat-e-Hadiyah n.d.: 3.

17. Ibid., 1.

18. Personal interview, June 2, 1995.

19. Abdulhussein 1995a: 225. (Shaikh Mustafa is writing here as an independent source rather than a dawat spokesman).

20. Engineer, like the dawat, most recently calculates the total number of Daudi Bohras at one million (1995: i). In previous writings he has calculated it at 560,000 (1993: 144 [same figure in edition originally published 1980]). As he rightly points out there, all estimates of Bohra population involve a large degree of guesswork. A very low estimate of 500,000 would place the dissidents' overt strength at 5% of the populace, while the more commonly cited one million would place the figure (by Engineer's tally) at 2.5%.

21. Contractor 1980: 25 (essay written before 1978).

22. Figures for masjid attendance and home prayer: Engineer 1989: 19, 66; most potential respondents refusing to participate: Ibid., 21.

23. Engineer 1993: 315.

24. Wright 1975: 164.

25. List of signatories in Engineer 1990: 14–18.

26. *India Today,* May 31, 1979, 15.

27. Ibid., July 15, 1983, 116.

28. *Bombay* magazine, January 21, 1984, 73.

29. Contractor 1980: 6, exact wording cited in main text below.

30. Engineer 1993: 157.

31. Ibid., 157–159.

32. Engineer 1991: 3.

33. Nathwani 1979: 21.

34. The judgment was handed down by Justice J. Marten, in suits nos. 918 and 941 of 1917 in the High Court of Judicature at Bombay on March 19, 1921. The dawat's appeal was no. 42 of 1921. For helping me unravel the complex legal tangles of the reform movement I am indebted to John Mansfield of Harvard Law School, who is perhaps the only legal scholar outside India to study the issue in depth.

35. Nathwani 1979: 17; Wright 1975: 153–154.

36. Engineer 1993: 182.

37. Cohn 1959: 93, quoted in Wright 1975: 154.

38. Najafali 1943: 16. Shaikh Najafali had direct experience battling the dissidents in court: he served as the dawat's attorney in the Burhanpur durgah case of the 1930s. In his tract on Bohra marriage, Najafali notes that prior to 1917 very few Bohras resorted to the British judicial system; those who appeared before colonial magistrates were judged by the shariat of Ithna-Ashari Shi'a, since no Bohra law texts were publicly available (Ibid., 10, 16). Access to British courts fueled the dissident movement, and the dissident movement necessitated access to British courts.

39. At least, the only text distributed widely enough to have been mentioned in later works. It was reprinted by the revitalized dissident group in 1977, but had been widely discussed and cited during the intervening half century. Portions of the text—those segments dealing with cultural description—date back to the nineteenth century, as some of them appear verbatim in Campbell's 1899 gazetteer (see Bibliographical Discussion).

40. Abdul Husain 1920: 54.

41. Ibid., 87, 63. (Typographical errors in original corrected).

42. Ibid., 65.

43. Ibid., 41.

44. The individuals cited were all schismatics who had split from the Bohra community over issues of nass.

45. Abdul Husain 1920: 63.

46. Ibid., 55.

47. Ibid., 87.

48. Ibid., ii.

49. Engineer 1993: 194.

50. Quoted in Nathwani 1979: 109.

51. Bombay Act XLII of 1949, Bombay Code III, 1949–1954, p. 3045. The text from which I quote is a photocopy of the statute book kindly supplied by John Mansfield. I have not been able to locate an original edition of the book itself.

52. Ibid.

53. Engineer 1993: 201.

54. Sardar Syedna Tahir Saifuddin Saheb v. State of Bombay, AIR 1962, S.C. 853. As above, my source for this citation is a photocopy provided by Professor Mansfield rather than the law text in its original form.

55. Nathwani 1979: 36.

56. Wright 1975: 159.

57. *Bombay Samachar,* September 24, 1968, cited in Wright 1975: 175.

58. Contractor 1980: 6.

59. Ibid., 38. These calculations, however, must be viewed with a certain degree of skepticism: they were arrived at by assuming a total Bohra population of one million and an average family as consisting of three adults, two children, one fetus in the womb, and two adults deceased during the previous year (Ibid., 41; the fetus and deceased family members are included in Contractor's calculation because they are assessed for fitra [though not sila]). As a measure of what these figures would mean to an Indian audience, Contractor's estimates (by exchange rates of January 28, 2000) translate to about $986,000 collected from taxes in India and $718,000 from abroad; $413,000 from gullas in India and $275,000 from gullas abroad. (As noted above, the use of contemporary exchange rates is misleading because of the difference between official rates and black-market rates prior to currency reforms of the 1990s.)

60. Contractor 1980: 6.

61. Ibid., Rs 4,000 = $92 by current exchange rates.

62. At the time of Contractor's writing, there would have been twenty-nine: three shahzadas and two shahzedis have passed away since then.

63. 15,000: Wright 1975: 167. 20,000: Verdia 1974: 13–14.

64. The facts of the Udaipur revolt are very much in dispute. Written accounts can be found primarily in reformist sources: Engineer 1993: 218–247; Verdia 1974: 13–17; Contractor 1980: 20–25; Nathwani 1979: 37, 62; Wright 1975: 167–168 (Wright himself is a nonpartisan observer, but—as he told

me in personal communication—because of dawat noncooperation throughout his research he was forced to rely on dissident sources for his information). I have drawn information also from conversations with Engineer (personal communication of June 2, 1995), and with various dawat officials.

65. Contractor 1980: 20.

66. Engineer 1993: 226.

67. Contractor 1980: 20.

68. Engineer 1993: 233, quoting a document of the time. Yusuf Najmuddin died in 1986.

69. Contractor 1980: 6–7.

70. Nathwani 1979: 37.

71. Engineer joining movement: Engineer 1993: 236. His estimates of loyalist strength: Ibid., 228. 85% of population: Verdia 1974: 17.

72. *Times of India,* May 19, 1983. Both dawat and dissident sources agree that such incidents occurred, although they disagree about who were the victims and who were the provocateurs. Engineer's assertion that the loyalists had virtually no local support is cast into doubt by his claim that the Youthis were routinely victimized by loyalist mobs (1993: 229–231). It is unclear which assertion is true and which is false, but the dissidents are unlikely to have been on the losing end of mob violence if they comprised 95% of the population.

73. Two hundred couples: Shaikh Mustafa Abdulhussein, personal communication, April 19, 2000. Report placing number at 300: *Hindustan Times/Evening News,* November 8, 1974; 1975 joint nikah: *Current,* March 29, 1975.

74. *Week,* March 20, 1983.36.

75. *Times of India,* May 19, 1983.

76. Personal interview, June 2, 1995.

77. Personal communication, May 19, 1998.

78. Nathwani 1979: 1.

79. *Bombay Samachar,* quoted in Engineer 1993: 264.

80. Nathwani 1979: 2.

81. Ibid., 4.

82. *Times of India,* May 1, 1978, 2.

83. 1,075 received: Nathwani 1979: 5. 5,000 solicited: *Hindustan Times,* April 17, 1979.

84. *Bombay Samachar,* October 22, 1977, quoted in Contractor 1980: 26.

85. Ibid.

86. Nathwani 1979: 34.

87. Ibid., 117.

88. *New Quest 7* (1978); reprinted in Contractor 1980: 40–41.

89. Nathwani 1979: 21.

90. Compare Nathwani 1979: 117-118 with Contractor 1980: 40-43.

91. Nathwani 1979: 120.

92. Ibid., 21; identical English texts presented in Nathwani 1979: 21-25, and Contractor 1980: 30-34; the source cited by Contractor as the basis for the *New Quest* text is another dissident publication: *Secularist,* January-February 1974.

93. Nathwani 1979: 25, 26, 32.

94. Text deemed genuine: Nathwani 1979: 30-31. Dissident claim of fraud: Engineer 1993: 157-159.

95. Nathwani 1979: 25.

96. Ibid., 28.

97. Ibid.

98. Ibid., 135.

99. Contractor 1980: 3.

100. Ibid.

101. Personal interview, June 2, 1995.

102. *Hindu* (Mumbai), February 15, 2000.

103. Personal interview, June 2, 1995.

104. Shaikh Mustafa Abdulhussein, personal communication of March 2, 2000 (relaying the accounts of several dawat-affiliated participants); *Hindu* (Chennai), February 15, 2000. Dawat sources say Syedna told his entourage to ignore the dissident's provocations, and they insist that the da'i was not present when the assault on Engineer occurred.

105. Pro-Engineer editorials and columns: *Hindu* (Chennai), "Increasing Insensitivity," February 29, 2000; and "A Long Winter Ahead," March 3, 2000; *Statesman* (editorial), "For God's Sake," February 17, 2000; Prem Shankar Jha, "Save Asghar Ali Engineer," *Outlook,* February 28, 2000; Anand Patwardhan, "Invisible Hijack," *Hindu* (Chennai), March 12, 2000. Dawat bandhs: *Hindu* (Mumbai), February 15, 2000; *Hindu* (Coimbatore), February 16, 2000.

106. Madan 1987; Nandy 1988.

107. Madan 1987: 757.

108. *India Today,* August 18, 1997, 44.

109. Leach 1990.

110. Engineer's assertion about the forty-ninth da'i's claims: Engineer 1993: 137. Nonpolemical source in basic agreement: Poonawala 1977: 14. (The forty-ninth da'i, Syedna Muhammad Burhanuddin ibn Abdul-Qadir Najmuddin, should not be confused with the fifty-second da'i, Syedna Muhammad Burhanuddin ibn Taher Saifuddin.)

111. The dawat avowedly does not regard any particular period as normative, seeking normative guidance in the Fatimid texts themselves.
112. Dawat-e-Hadiyah n.d: 4.
113. Engineer 1993: 314.
114. Weber 1947: 279.
115. Personal interview, June 2, 1995, and throughout his writings.
116. Contractor 1980: 41.
117. Hasnain and Husain 1988: 115–116.
118. Ibid., 118, 116.
119. Geertz 1968: 100.

Chapter Ten. Conclusion

1. Economic definition inadequate: Weber 1947: 279. Impact of Protestant ethic: Weber 1958b: 13–46.
2. Landes 1998.
3. Heesterman 1985: 25.
4. Singh 1965: 59.
5. Quoted in Ibid., 47.
6. Wright 1983: 83.
7. Quoted in ibid.
8. Geertz 1968: 103ff.
9. Nasr 1994: xiii.
10. Anderson 1983; Gellner 1983, 1994; Hobsbawm and Ranger 1983.
11. Brass 1991.
12. Gombrich and Obeyesekere 1988: 241.
13. Yalman 1967: 75.
14. Weldon 1989: 6; quoted in Asad 1993: 276–277.
15. Huntington 1996.
16. The full citation is even more egregious: "I must say, it is as toilsome reading as I ever undertook. A wearisome confused jumble, crude, incondite; endless iterations, longwindedness, entanglement; most crude, incondite;—insupportable stupidity, in short! Nothing but a sense of duty could carry any European through the Koran" (Carlyle 1841: 104). But even Carlyle may have been more open-minded than many Western critics today: he devotes nearly an entire chapter of *On Heroes, Hero-Worship, & the Heroic in History* to a discussion of the Prophet Muhammad, and his tone is laudatory (albeit rather patronizing). Modern detractors might benefit from Carlyle's admonition: "The lies, which well-meaning zeal has heaped round this man, are disgraceful to ourselves only" (Ibid., 70).
17. Said 1978: 3.

18. Lewis 1993: 112ff.

19. Ibid., 108.

20. Chen 1992: 688.

21. Maybury-Lewis 1988: 95.

22. Figures for 1999: Saudi Arabia, 21.5 million; United Arab Emirates, 2.3 million; Oman, 2.4 million; Kuwait, 2.0 million; Qatar, 0.7 million; Bahrain, 0.6 million. Total: 29.5 million (Central Intelligence Agency 1999: 423, 503, 369, 268, 397, 38). I have used CIA population figures, since as of April 2000 they are more up-to-date and accurate than available United Nations estimates.

23. Personal interview, January 14, 1998.

24. Based on 1999 figures of 65.2 million in Iran and 25.8 million in Afghanistan (Central Intelligence Agency 1999: 231, 1). The Taliban holds about 90% of Afghanistan, so the population it controls can be roughly calculated at 23.2 million.

25. While Amien Rais has generally worked for cooperation between different religious communities, he has also made statements that helped fuel sectarian violence. During the January 2000 rioting between Muslims and Christians in Lombok and other sites, Rais was quoted as advocating armed action against the Christian minority (Associated Press, January 18, 2000). Abetting bloodshed must always be condemned, but there is an important distinction between communal violence based on religion per se and that based on ethnic background, economic status, and political power. The rioting described as "Muslim-Christian" in Mataram, Ambon, and other parts of Indonesia is often, in fact, violence between Javanese (or other groups indigenous to the Indonesian archipelago) and ethnic Chinese (generally a merchant class, who have suffered considerable persecution on political and economic grounds since the days of President Sukarno). Stirring up communal discord is always blameworthy, but it is not necessarily indicative of religious intolerance.

26. Personal interview, January 16, 1998.

27. Rahman 1982a: 136–137.

28. Ibid., 141.

29. Ibid., 142.

30. In the Ithna-Ashari world, Ayatollah Khomeini and Ali Shariati would be claimants for this distinction.

31. Ahmad 1994: 464.

32. Nasr 1994: 84.

33. Cf. Tambiah 1996: 244–246.

34. Rahman 1982a: 116.

35. As Bernard Lewis correctly notes, there is a vital distinction to be made be-

tween raw terrorism and religiously inspired acts of unconventional warfare. For a discussion of the rationale underlying the bin Laden–sponsored fatwa, see Lewis 1998: 14–19.

36. Mill 1975.

37. Spivak 1988: 3–32.

38. Chatterjee 1982: 9–39.

39. Pandey 1983: 60–129; 1990a: 198–200.

40. Thapar 1989: 209–231.

41. Pandey 1990a: 34–36.

42. Bayly 1988: 112.

43. Ibid., 119.

44. Robinson 1983: 185–203.

45. Van der Veer, 1994: 20–21.

46. Madan 1987; Nandy 1987, 1988.

47. Madan 1987: 748.

48. Weber 1958b.

49. Nehru 1991: 26.

50. Ibid.

51. Nandy 1988: 83.

52. Ibid.

53. Juergensmeyer 1988: 88. For a discussion of a similar tendency among Islamist militants in Kashmir, see Blank 1999: 42–47.

54. Obeyesekere 1970.

55. Gombrich and Obeyesekere 1988: 13; quoting Dharmapala 1963: 61ff.

56. On Madan-Nandy critique: Blank 1994; on broader Hindu-Muslim questions: Blank 1999; on Babri Masjid–Ramjanambhumi controversy: Blank 1993, 1994.

57. Tambiah 1996: 31–32, 145–147, 266–268, 293–296.

58. Tambiah 1989: 340.

59. Uniquely modern phenomenon: Chatterjee 1982; Guha 1982, 1983; Pandey 1983, 1990a, 1990b; Spivak 1988. Ancient phenomenon: Robinson 1983. Modern manifestation of underlying cleavages: Bayly 1985, 1988; Blank 1994, 1999; Brass 1991, 1994; Van der Veer 1994; Varshney 1993.

60. Tambiah 1990: 749.

61. Ismailji 1937: 95; *Mausam-e bahar* 1884: 346ff.; Misra 1964: 24.

62. One of the only recorded instances of outright rebellion occurred in 1730, when an uprising against Sarbuland Khan in Ahmedabad and scattered other sites was quickly and brutally crushed. Commissariat 1957, 2:429–430.

63. Cf. Tambiah 1989, 1990, 1996.

64. Keddie and Cole 1986: 28–29.

65. Shaikh Mustafa Abdulhussein notes that Imam Tayyib went into seclusion for esoteric rather than purely practical reasons (personal communication, May 19, 1998). Nizari Ismailis believe that the current imam is manifest in the world, in the person of the aga khan.

66. Lewis 1993: 157–165.

67. Keddie and Cole 1986: 4–5.

68. Kohlberg 1987: 31–41.

69. Keddie and Cole 1986: 5.

70. According to an account related to me by Mullah Shabbir M. Mansoorbhai Jamali, at Partition, Muhammad Ali Jinnah tried to persuade Taher Saifuddin to emigrate to Pakistan along with all of his community. Although the two men had cordial relations, Taher Saifuddin refused. Jinnah is even said to have offered him a post in the cabinet, but the da'i would not be budged. To abandon one's homeland in its hour of crisis would have been (Maulana explained) *dhwkvu:* to betray one's friends (and, by extension, one's countrymen). The Gujarati word has connotations of dragging a person down from behind, or stabbing in the back. Those Bohras living in Pakistan were urged to support Pakistan, those living in India were urged to support India.

71. Quoted in Davoodbhoy 1992b: 4.

72. Lewis 1987: 21–30.

73. Hasnain and Husain 1988: 166.

74. Mumbai death toll: Tambiah 1996: 253. Nationwide 1992–1993 toll: Reuters, March 27, 1998. Most victims Muslim: McKean 1996: 317.

75. *Times of India,* December 5, 1994, 3. The commission excluded from this tally all casualties from the March 1993 bloodshed, sparked by bombings that have been blamed variously on crime lord Ibrahim Dawood, Middle Eastern terrorists, and the Pakistani secret service.

76. McKean 1996: 317.

77. Tambiah 1996: 254.

78. Cf. Ibid., 254–256.

79. Quoted in Katzenstein 1979: 128n.

80. Ibid., On the rise of Shiv Sena, see Weiner 1978.

81. Mustafa Abdulhussein, personal communication of April 26, 2000. According to Asghar Ali Engineer (personal interview, June 2, 1995; I have not been able to confirm this report independently), Syedna had officially congratulated Thackeray after a Shiv Sena electoral victory on at least one occasion.

82. Tambiah 1996: 257–265.

83. Although the most notorious Muslim don at the time (and putative culprit of the March 1993 bombings) was named Dawood Ibrahim, there seems to have been no significant public confusion between the Dawoodi gang and the Dawoodi (alternate spelling of Daudi) Bohras.

84. Engineer 1989: 60.

85. Bekhud 1994b: 10.

86. Engineer 1989: 9.

87. Ibid., 66.

88. Abdul Husain 1920: 75.

89. Engineer 1989: 8.

90. During the late colonial period, four decades before the Shah Bano case, Shaikh Najafali cited the grounds on which the Bohra dawat and Sunni clerics alike would object to the Supreme Court's decision: "It is an accepted principle of law as laid down by their Lordships of the Privy Council in Aga Mohammad Jaffar vs. Koolsumbibi, I. L. R. 25 Calcutta 9 and I. L. R. 25 Allahabad 236, that, for ascertaining the law applicable to the Muslims of a particular sect recourse should not be had to the primary sources, namely the Qur'an or the Precepts or the Sayings of the Imams, but reference should be made to the secondary sources, namely to the interpretations of the commentators who are recognised as authoritative by that sect of Islam." (1943: 21).

91. Wright 1975: 158; and dawat sources.

92. Gandhi 1990: 133.

93. Hasnain and Husain 1988: 183.

94. Mansfield 1993: 164.

95. Brass 1994: 233. The name of the bill struck many as Orwellian: it seemed to offer Muslim women "protection" by denying them the right to sue for alimony. Supporters argued that divorcées like Shah Bano were entitled to maintenance under Islamic law, and that Rajiv's legislation prevented Muslim husbands from using the civil code to evade their shariat obligations.

96. Engineer 1989: 9.

97. Ibid., 15.

98. Ayatollah Taqi Mesbah-Yazdi is representative of the harder-line reactionaries. While campaigning for the February 2000 majlis elections, he went so far as to openly advocate political violence against moderate reformists: "If someone tells you he has a new interpretation of Islam," the ayatollah is quoted as having said during a Friday khutba, "punch him in the mouth" (Reuters/New York Times, January 2, 2000).

99. The February 2000 assault on Engineer and ransacking of his office were the first such incidents in seventeen years.

100. Cf. Maybury-Lewis 1997. Cultural Survival, founded by Maybury-Lewis to help empower indigenous peoples, is one of the most successful examples of such a project.

101. Lévi-Strauss 1962: 26–47.

102. Barth 1995: 67.

Bibliographical Discussion

1. Lokhandwalla 1972; Mubarakpuri 1964, 1966 (Urdu translation of the *Da'a'im;* I have not been able to locate a copy of the Gujarati version). Lokhandwalla is also author of a general article on the Bohra community published in *Studia Islamica* (1955) shortly after Indian independence. In addition to the works cited, Mubarakpuri wrote a devotional work presenting brief Urdu biographies of the Bohra da'is (1978). Most other Daudi Bohra writers have either limited themselves to devotional works, or have cast off dawat supervision and allied themselves with the dissident camp; of the dissident writers, few other than Asghar Ali Engineer have produced books of scholarship rather than polemic.

2. The *Mausam-e bahar* borrows material from an unpublished Arabic-language history written half a century earlier: *Muntaza'al-akhbar,* by the Daudi Bohra writer Qutbuddin Sulaymanji Burhanpuri (d.1241/1826) (cf. Daftary 1990: 259).

3. "Judgment" 1931: 20.

4. Daftary 1990: 260. Fewer than forty-one pages (282–323) of his own book are devoted to the nearly 900 years of Musta'li history since the concealment of Imam Tayyib, with barely twenty pages (303–323) given to the Bohras in India.

5. The most notable of these writers are Hasan Ali Badripresswala Ismailji, Zahid Ali, Abu Zafar Nadvi, and Najm-ul Ghani Khan (a more up-to-date work will soon be published by Mustafa Abdulhussein). Noteworthy Urdu histories of the Fatimid period include works by Qudrat Allah Khan and S. Ahmad Jafari. Ismail Poonawala (1977) provides an excellent summary of primary source material available to historians researching the history of Musta'li Ismailis: on Fatimid and pre-Fatimid texts, 31–132; on Musta'li Tayyibi sources during the Yemeni period, 133–183; on Daudi Bohra sources from 946/1539 to the present (many of them not available to researchers outside the community), 184–241. He also provides a list of sources on Sulaimani Bohras in Yemen and India: 242–250.

6. Daftary 1990: 315. Hollister 1953: 301. Ivanow lamented: "According to the latest customs which are strictly followed by those concerned, every orthodox Bohra's private library is confiscated on his death and goes to this library . . . Very unfortunately, a library so unique in the world is entirely inaccessible not only to an outsider but even to the faithful themselves" (Ivanow 1933: 25).

7. Roy 1984: 194ff. Another source that must be placed in the de facto dissident camp is Saifuddin Insaf (1987), who is a close associate of Engineer. His book is useful, however, as it assembles many press clippings on the dissident movement.

8. Personal interview, June 2, 1995.

9. Keith Hjortshoj notes that apart from Awadh and the Deccan sultanates Shi‘a are virtually absent from the historical record, in large measure because of the practice of taqiyya (1987: 290–291). Nadeem Hasnain and Abrar Husain, on publishing what they describe as the first "'full-fledged' sociological study of the Shi‘a in India," lament the near absence of prior material: "The paucity of any sociological-anthropological data on Indian Shi‘as may be gauged from the fact that when researchers try to get references for possible use they get a pleasant surprise even if they get hold of a few" (1988: 14, i).

10. Basu and Gupta 1982; Basu and Jinal 1983.

11. Hollister 1953: 304.

12. Daftary 1990: 315.

13. Ibid., 316.

14. Ibid., 314.

15. Ibid., 313.

16. Campbell 1899.

17. Abdul Husain 1920: 77.

18. Enthoven 1920: 201.

19. Campbell 1899: 28.

20. Ibid., 24n.

21. Hollister also cites Faradi, editor of another edition of the gazetteer whose Bohra material is likewise a verbatim recapitulation of Campbell.

22. Abdul Husain 1920: 34.

23. Ibid., 41.

24. Ibid., 50.

Glossary

Throughout this work, I have tried to balance clarity against exactitude in the transliteration of Arabic, Lisanu-Dawat, Gujarati, and Urdu or Hindi words. To avoid the pedantic clutter of massed diacritical marks, I have opted for simplified forms in most cases. Rather than follow a rigid system of transliteration, I made my decisions word by word: I included diacriticals when I thought they wouldn't cause undue confusion (Shiʿa, for example, or Qurʾan), but excluded them for terms that a reader already familiar with Islamic topics might recognize if shorn of the marked hamzas, long vowels, or elided alifs. The process, like most transliteration, was sometimes arbitrary. Too much simplification leads to the appearance of dilettantism, too little leads to sentence like "The Shīʿī Ismāʿīli dāʿī is comparable to a ṣūfī pir, a qāḍī relying on aḥadīth, or the ʿulamāʾ in agreement on a point of sharīʿa." Over the course of several hundred pages, it would become tough sledding indeed. This glossary provides some alternate spellings for various words, but makes no claim to provide authoritative (or even systematic) transliteration.

Note: * denotes a uniquely Bohra term, or a term with a Bohra usage different from that prevalent in other Muslim communities.

Adhan/azan: Call to prayer, issued before salat (namaz) five times each
 day.
Adivasi: Member of one of India's aboriginal ("tribal") communities.
Aga khan: The leader of Nizari Ismailis. While Bohras believe that the
 imam is in concealment, Nizaris believe that the aga khan is the
 hazir (present) imam.
Ahl al-bayt: "People of the household." The family of the Prophet
 Muhammad, especially his descendents through his daughter Fatima
 and son-in-law Ali. Bohras, like all Shiʿa, feel a direct personal loyalty
 to the ahl al-bayt.
Ahl al-kitab: "People of the Book," that is, members of faiths with a re-

vealed scripture (specifically Christians, Jews, Sabaeans, and Zoroastrians. Considered dhimmis, people under protection).

*Aisaheba: Title given to the wife of a da'i al-mutlaq.

Ajlaf/ashraf: Two categories of subcontinental Muslims. Ajlaf communities (the overwhelming majority, a group that includes the Bohras) are descendents of indigenous converts; ashraf communities are descendents of Afghans, Persians, Arabs, or other Muslim ruling elites from outside the subcontinent.

*Alamat: Bohra ceremony in which the da'i provides an inscription of "bismillah" to a devotee, either as a plaque for the home or written on the first page of a business's annual account book.

*Amil (pl. ummal): Deputy. Cleric in the Bohra hierarchy who serves as the da'i's personal representative in a given locality. The title is often translated as "priest," a term that would be out of place in almost any Islamic context other than an Ismaili one.

Aqiqa: Islamic childhood ritual involving the sacrifice of a flawless goat, and occasion of a child's first haircut.

Asas: Foundation. In Ismaili theology, every natiq (prophet) is succeeded by an asas who imparts the batin knowledge that the natiq has revealed (cf. wasi).

Ashura: The tenth day of the Islamic month of Muharram, this is the holiest time of the Shi'a year. Ashura rituals, culminating on the final day of the observance, commemorate the martyrdom of Imam Husain on the field of Kerbala in year 61/680.

Ayatollah: The highest rank of Ithna-Ashari clerics.

*Badri Mahal: The office in downtown Mumbai from which the Bohra dawat administers affairs of the community.

Badshah: Emperor (title of Mughal rulers of India).

Bania: Member of a Gujarati mercantile caste or community. Bania communities include Bohras, Khojahs, Memons, Parsis, and various subgroups of Jains and Hindu Vaishyas.

*Baraat: Social ostracism imposed by the Bohra dawat. Since outright excommunication is a legally precarious practice in modern India, the dawat relies on baraat to achieve the same purpose. Orthodox Bohras are forbidden to have any contact with a person placed under baraat. (Not to be confused with similar words meaning "wedding party" or "India.")

*Batin (adj. batini): Secret theological doctrines, esoteric meaning underlying the surface interpretation of the Qur'an and other sources of Islamic orthodoxy. In Ismaili practice, the deeper recesses of theology are open only to mu'mineen with special instruction.

*Behn(saheb)/(saheba). Behn = sister, the appellation given to every

Bohra woman. Behnsaheb (or behnsaheba) is a title reserved for women of the Qasr-e Ali.

*Bhai(saheb): Bhai = brother, the appellation given to every Bohra man. Bhaisaheb is a title reserved for men of the Qasr-e Ali.

Bidʻa: Innovation. Orthodox Muslims regard bidʻa in matters of theology to be a form of heresy.

*Bismillah: Lit. "In the name of God." Generally used as shorthand for *bismillah ar-rahman ar-rahim,* "In the name of God, the Compassionate, the Merciful." Statement often uttered by Muslims before any undertaking, great or small. For Bohras, the word "bismillah" is written in calligraphic script and given as a blessing by Syedna to a devotee in a practice known as alamat.

Brahmin/Brahman: The highest of the four varnas (classes) in the Hindu caste system. Several Bohra families claim descent from priestly Brahmins rather than mercantile Vaishyas.

*Burqa: Modest dress worn by traditional Muslim women. For Bohras, the wearing of a burqa is a central part of the current Islamization program.

Caliph: (Arabic: khalifa, "successor," i.e., successor to the Prophet). Title of the leaders of early Muslim umma, later assumed by various Sunni and Shiʻa rulers. The eleventh through the twentieth Ismaili imams (as reckoned by the Bohras) ruled the Fatimid empire with the title of caliph.

Chamcha: Lit. "spoon." Indian slang, equivalent of "tool" in American English: derogatory term for an officious bureaucrat or self-important functionary with no independent power.

Chatti: Sixth-day ceremony, a rite in which a Muslim child is named. For Bohras, the baby's name is often selected by the daʻi.

Chawl: In Indian towns, a housing complex or apartment building.

Crore: An Indian mathematical unit: 10 million.

*Daʻi: "Missionary." In Fatimid usage, a cleric involved in the propagation of the faith. In modern Bohra usage, shorthand for the daʻi al-mutlaq.

*Daʻi al-mutlaq: The apex cleric of the Bohra community. The daʻi al-mutlaq is believed to be in contact with the hidden imam. This title was of only intermediate rank in the Fatimid hierarchy. All orthodox Bohras pledge to obey the dictates of the daʻi al-mutlaq in both spiritual and temporal matters—the main point of contention between the orthodox and dissident camps. The daʻi is commonly referred to by his honorific (Syedna).

*Dawat/dawa(h)/daʻwa(h): "Mission." In Bohra terms, the clerical hierarchy of which the daʻi al-mutlaq serves as head. The formal term for the Bohra clergy is al-dawa-al-hadiyah: "the rightly guided mission."

*Dawr al-satr: Period of concealment, during which the imam lives in the world but is hidden away even from his own followers. Ismailis of both the Nizari and Musta'li branches believe a dawr al-satr encompassed the reigns of the seventh to the tenth imams (148–268/ 765–881). Bohras believe a second dawr al-satr began when the twenty-first imam entered concealment in 526/1132, and continues to the present. The Ismaili concept of satr is analogous, but not identical, to the Ithna Ashari doctrine of occultation (ghayba).

Deen: Matters of spiritual (as opposed to strictly temporal) concern.

Devanagari: The writing system used for Sanskrit and several modern Sanskritic languages (such as Hindi).

Diwali: The Hindu celebration marking each New Year.

*Du'a/duwa: Blessing, prayer. In Bohra usage, du'a is a blessing conferred by the da'i, and is eagerly sought by the faithful at every opportunity.

Dunya/duniya: Matters of worldly (as opposed to strictly spiritual) concern.

*Durgah: Mausoleum. In Bohra usage, typically the mausoleum of a da'i or syedi.

Eid al-Adha/Bakri Eid: Celebration on the tenth of zyl-Hajj, during which hajjis (people who have performed pilgrimage to Mecca) sacrifice a goat and use the meat to provide a feast for the needy.

Eid al-Fitr: The celebration marking the end of Ramadan.

Fakir: Holy mendicant. Bohras may contribute money to fakirs, but these beggars tend to be Sunni (generally members of Sufi orders) rather than Ismailis.

Falsafah: Philosophy; particularly neoplatonic speculation drawn from Greek sources and put into an Islamic intellectual framework.

*Fatimi/Fatimid: Spiritual descendent of Fatima (the Prophet's daughter). The Fatimid empire, based in Cairo and at its height including most of North Africa and the Near East, was the most powerful and historically significant example of an Ismaili state. For Bohras, "Fatimi" is a formal term of cultural self-description. Bohras regard themselves as the spiritual and cultural inheritors of the Fatimid caliphate, and guardians of the Fatimid tradition.

Fatwa: Ruling on a matter of Islamic law or doctrine, issued by a member of the ulema (generally a Sunni mufti or Ithna-Ashari mujtahid.) In the Bohra community, only the da'i is authorized to issue a fatwa.

*Feta: A prewound turban of gold silk, worn by some Bohras instead of a topi.

Fiqh: Islamic jurisprudence, the science of law.

Firman: Royal directive. For Bohras, a directive from the da'i.

*Fitra: Islamic tax. Among Bohras, paid together with sila during Ramadan.

*Ghadir Khumm (Ghadir-e Khum, Ghadir i-Khumm): The eighteenth of zyl-Hajj, when Shi'a believe Muhammad declared Ali his successor. Bohras mark the date with an annual reaffirmation of communal mithaq, the oath of allegiance.

Ghulat (sing. ghali): "Exaggerators." Theological extremists, historically a term applied to various fringe groups of Ismailism (especially by the denomination's Ithna-Ashari adversaries).

Ghusl: "Bath." Ritual ablution of the entire body after a major pollution.

Hadith (pl. ahadith): A saying attributed to the Prophet Muhammad. Two compilers of ahadith, al-Bukhari and al-Muslim, are regarded as the most authoritative by Sunnis. For Bohras (as for other Shi'a), a hadith can be the report of an imam as well as of the Prophet, and is deemed reliable not on the basis of its isnad (chain of transmittal), but on the judgment of an imam. An anecdote about the Prophet is called a *khabar* rather than a hadith, but the latter term is commonly (if imprecisely) used in reference to deeds as well as words.

Hafiz: One who knows the Qur'an by heart

Hajj/hajji: Pilgrimage to Mecca undertaken during the month of zyl-Hajj. All observant Muslims are required to perform hajj at least once, if they are able. A person who has completed hajj is a hajji.

Halal/haraam: Two categories of activity or item: halal acts and items are permitted by Islam, haraam ones are forbidden.

Hanif: Believer in God's unity prior to Muhammad's prophecy.

*Haqiqat/haqiqa(h) (sing. haqa'iq): Truth, reality. The higher reaches of Ismaili gnostic learning. A subsection of batini ta'wil.

*Haqqun nafs: Fee paid to the Bohra dawat on the death of a relative.

Hijab: Veil. Often used as shorthand for purdah.

Hijra: The flight of the Prophet Muhammad and his companions from Mecca to Medina in 622 C.E., an event that marks the beginning of the Islamic calendar.

Hudud (sing. hadd): Offenses for which the punishment is laid out in the Qur'an. Often used to refer to Islamic criminal (as opposed to personal) law.

*Hujja: "Proof." One of the highest titles of the early Ismaili clerical hierarchy. The title has not been used since the Fatimid empire.

Hukm: Official command. In Bohra usage, a directive from the da'i.

Iddat: Mandated period of celibacy for a newly divorced woman.

Iftar: Meal breaking a dry fast (sawm).

Ijma: Consensus of the ulema on a point of Islamic law or doctrine. The third element of fiqh.

Ijtihad: Interpretation of religious doctrine by a qualified authority.

Imam (pl. a'imma): Spiritual leader. In Sunni usage, the term is generally applied to the prayer leader at a local mosque. In Shi'a usage it can have this meaning, but is more significantly applied to one of the infallible intermediaries between God and man. Ithna-Ashari Shi'a recognize twelve imams before the period of occultation, while Bohras recognize twenty-one before satr.

Iman: Faith (not to be confused with imam).

Ismaili/Isma'ili (pl. Ismailiyya/Isma'iliyya): One of the two major surviving branches of Shi'ism. Bohras, like other Ismailis, recognize Ismail ibn Jafar as imam instead of his brother Musa (the imam recognized by the Ithna-Ashariyya).

Ismat: Sinless, an attribute of imams. Da'is are regarded as kal ismat, a distinction similar to than between ma'sum and kal ma'sum.

Isnad: Chain of transmittal by which a hadith has been passed down.

Ithna Ashari (pl. Ithna Ashariyya): The predominant Shi'a denomination. Also called Twelver, or Imami, Shi'ism.

Jahiliya: Pre-Islamic "time of ignorance."

*Jamat/jama'a: Assembly. In Bohra usage, a local Bohra community.

*Jamatkhana: The building that serves as the social and cultural (as opposed to spiritual) center for a local Bohra community.

Jati: Caste. Hindus belong to one of several thousand geographically and occupationally specific jatis, all within the framework of four varnas (and the outcastes beneath this traditional structure).

Jihad: "Struggle." A term commonly mistranslated (and misunderstood) as "holy war." Jihad can be an intellectual and spiritual struggle for individual or communal improvement (the Greater Jihad, in classical Sunni terminology), or it can be a physical struggle to defend the Muslim community from oppression (the Lesser Struggle, in classical terms). For Bohras, jihad is one of the seven pillars of the faith.

Jizya: Poll tax historically levied on non-Muslims living in Muslim countries, in lieu of military service.

*Kal ma'sum: The spiritual state of the Bohra da'i al-mutlaq. The difference between kal ma'sum and ma'sum (immaculate and infallible, the spiritual state of an imam) is subtle, but important.

*Khak-e-shifa mahti: Soil from Kerbala. Also, the ritual in which an infant is fed a pinch of this soil on each of the first three days after birth.

Khalsa: In the Sikh faith, the community of baptized believers.

Khatna: "Cutting," i.e., circumcision. The term is applicable to both male and female procedures.

*Khidmat: "Service." For the Bohras, serving as part of the clerical hierarchy. Khidmat can also mean financial service (generous contributions to the dawat).

Khojah: Indian Nizari Ismaili, recognizing the aga khan as the living imam. The Khojahs, like the Bohras, are a community of Gujarati banias centered in Mumbai.

*Khums: Tax of one-fifth of any unanticipated bonanza. For Bohras, this extends to progeny: A family with five sons will "give" one of them to the dawat for special service.

*Khutba: Sermon. For Sunnis, typically part of the Friday noon prayer. For Bohras, a khutba may be delivered during any number of religious ceremonies.

Kshatriya: In the Hindu caste system, the varna (class) of kings, aristocrats, and warriors.

*Kurta: A white cotton shirt, reaching down to about the knees. For Bohras, an essential part of the male "community dress" instituted by Syedna Muhammad Burhanuddin in 1981.

Lailat al-Qadr: The twenty-third of Ramadan, the night on which Muhammad received his first Qur'anic revelation. For Bohras, as for all Muslims, one of the most important commemorations of the year.

Lakh/lac: An Indian mathematical unit: 100,000.

Madhhab: School or tradition of Islamic jurisprudence. The four major Sunni schools are Hanafi, Hanbali, Maliki, and Shafi'i, while the Ithna-Ashariyya follow the Jafari madhhab.

*Madrasa/madrassa: Islamic school providing higher education than a maktab. Traditionally, a school teaching Qur'anic rote memorization and other religious subjects. The Bohra network of Burhani Madrasa combine Islamic and Western subjects in the same curriculum.

Mahdi/al-Mahdi: "Rightly Guided One." The Muslim equivalent of the Judeo-Christian concept of Messiah.

Mahr: Dower. The sum given by a groom to a bride at their wedding.

*Majlis: Council. In Bohra terminology, a religious ceremony less formal than a waaz.

Maktab: A rudimentary Islamic school.

Masjid: Mosque.

*Ma'sum: Infallible and immaculate. In Bohra doctrine the imam is ma'sum, while the da'i is kal ma'sum ("like" ma'sum).

Matam: Ritualized breast-beating and self-flagellation undertaken by

Shiʿa at Ashura (and by Bohras at religious rituals throughout the year).

*Maulana: An honorific title given to Muslim clerics. In the Bohra community, the title is reserved for the daʿi al-mutlaq.

*Mazoon/maʾdhun: The second-highest cleric in the Bohra hierarchy, an office currently held by a brother of the daʿi al-mutlaq.

*Milad/maulud: Birth date of the Prophet, an imam, or (for Bohras) a daʿi.

*Mithaq/misaq: Oath of allegiance to God and the daʿi al-mutlaq, undertaken by all observant Bohras upon reaching puberty. The prime rite of passage, and an oath repeated annually during the month of zyl-Hajj.

*Miyasaheb: Honorific given to a Bohra shaikh who has earned his title through piety and devotion rather than financial contributions.

*Mohalla: In Bohra usage, a neighborhood or administrative unit for dawat organization.

Mufti: A Sunni jurist qualified to issue authoritative fatwas.

Muharram: The first month of the Islamic year. For Shiʿa, the tenth day of Muharram (Ashura) is the most solemn and important observance of the annual ritual cycle.

Mujahid (pl. mujahideen): A warrior undertaking jihad.

Mujtahid: A cleric authorized to conduct ijtihad (interpretation of religious doctrine). For Ithna-Ashari Shiʿa, the highest rank a mujtahid can attain is that of ayatollah. (Among Bohras the term is not commonly used.)

*Mukasir: The third-ranking cleric in the Bohra dawat. By custom the mukasir is also the chief amil of Mumbai. The current officeholder is a brother of the daʿi al-mutlaq.

*Mullah: In Bohra usage, the title given to any man authorized to lead namaz. The title of mullah is lower than that of shaikh or amil, and is awarded to graduates of the Jamea tus-Saifiya and to teachers at Burhani madrasas.

*Muʾmin (pl. muʾmineen): "Faithful." In general Islamic usage, a Muslim. In Bohra usage, the term is reserved for members of the Mustaʿli Ismaili community: a Bohra is a muʾmin, while all other members of the larger faith are referred to simply as Muslims.

*Musafirkhana: Pilgrims' lodge maintained near a Bohra shrine.

*Mustaʿli (pl. Mustaʿliyya): One of the two surviving branches of the Ismaili faith. Bohras represent the only significant group of Mustaʿli Ismailis in the modern world.

Mutaa: Ithna-Ashari practice of temporary marriage.

Nafs: Soul, self (lower soul, as opposed to higher principle of God).

Namaz (Arabic, salat): One of the pillars of the Muslim faith.

*Nass: Designation of an imam or (for Bohras) daʿi al-mutlaq by his predecessor.

Natiq (pl. nutaqaʾ). Prophet, sent to deliver a new revelation. In Ismaili belief, each age is ushered in by a natiq, who is followed by an asas establishing the esoteric interpretation of the law the natiq has brought, and a succession of imams to transmit this teaching to every generation. The natiq of the current age is the Prophet Muhammad.

Nikah: Marriage. For a Bohra nikah to be recognized, both parties must renew their mithaq oaths.

Nikahnama: Contract setting out the terms of a marriage.

Nizari (pl. Nizariyya): One of the two major branches of Ismailism. The Nizariyya are today represented by the Khojahs and other followers of the aga khan.

Nizbat: Engagement.

*Pagri: Turban. In the Bohra community, only certain dignitaries (such as graduates of the Jamea tus-Saifiya academy) are authorized to wear a pagri.

Puja: Hindu religious ceremony; can be an elaborate ritual at a temple, or a very simple daily rite performed at home.

*Purdah: For Bohra women, purdah (seclusion) is considerably less restrictive than for the women of many other communities. It primarily consists of avoiding physical contact with or revealing hair and body contours to men other than one's husband or blood relatives.

Qaʿba/Qaba/Qaaba/Kaaba: The holiest site in the Islamic world. The black stone structure in Mecca toward which Muslims orient themselves when making their daily prayers.

Qadi/qazi: Judge of religious law.

Qaim/al-Qaʾim: "Riser." Term for the Mahdi preferred by Ismailis.

*Qarzan hasanah: Trust for no-interest loans. Syedna Muhammad Burhanuddin has made this system of Islamic finance an important component of the Bohra identity program.

*Qasr-e Ali: The clerical "royal family" of the Bohra community.

Qaum: Community. In Indian terms, roughly the Muslim equivalent of a Hindu caste.

Qiblah: Direction of Muslim prayer.

Qiyas: Analogy. One of the tools in Sunni fiqh.

Qurʾan/Quran/Koran: The revealed scripture of Islam.

*Qurʾan-i natiq: Speaking Qurʾan—in Ismaili terms, the imam.

Rai: Opinion. One of the tools in Sunni fiqh.

Rak'at/rak'a(h): Cycle of movements and recitations in ritual prayer.

Rauzah: Mausoleum, especially (in Bohra usage) that of an imam or da'i.

*Raza: Permission. In the Bohra community, mu'mineen often ask the raza of the da'i for any type of action undertaken.

Riba: Usury. More broadly, giving or taking financial interest.

*Rida(h): Veil. Bohra women wear a rida that covers the hair, neck, and chest, but not the face.

Risala (pl. rasa'il): Epistle, treatise, or learned discourse on a theological subject.

Rupee: Indian unit of currency. As of January 2000, Rs 43 = $1.

Sadaqa: Voluntary charity, over and above mandatory zakat.

Sadhu: Hindu renunciate, often belonging to an ashram or holy order.

Saheb: Lord, sir.

*Saifee Mahal: Mumbai compound in which members of the Bohra Qasr-e Ali live.

Saivite/Shaivite: Hindu devotee of the god Shiva.

*Salaam/salaam-e Syedna: Ceremony in which Bohras pay homage to the da'i al-mutlaq.

Salat: Prayer, offered five times daily (Arabic equivalent of the Urdu/Persian/Turkish word "namaz").

Sawm: Dry fast during daylight hours.

Sayyid/Syed/Saiyid: Direct descendant of the Prophet.

*Shadi: For Hindus, marriage. For Bohras, the social (as opposed to religious) aspects of a wedding celebration.

*Shahzada/shahzedi: "Prince/Princess." Title given to the sons and daughtes of a Bohra da'i.

*Shaikh/shaykh (pl. mashaikh): "Elder." A title given by the Bohra da'i al-mutlaq to individuals who have provided loyal dawat service. Also, leader of a Sufi order (tariqa).

Shalwar qamiz: Type of dress commonly worn by men and women of northern India and Pakistan.

Sharia/shariah/shari'a: Islamic religious law.

Shariat: Islamic personal law (governing marriage, divorce, and other noncriminal matters).

Sharif: "Noble." Adjective applied to anything having to do with the Prophet Muhammad. Also, the title given to the custodian of the holy places in Mecca.

*Sherwani (also called saya): Long white overcoat, a part of the male dress code for Bohras.

Shiʿa/Shia/Shiʿi/Shiite: Abbreviation of Shiʿat ʿAli, Party of Ali. The two main branches are the Ithna-Ashariyya and the Ismailiyya.

Shudra: The lowest (and most populous) of the four varnas (classes) of the Hindu caste system.

*Sila: Ismaili tax, paid by Bohras at the same time as fitra.

Sufi: The mystical strain of Sunni Islam. A Sufi master is known as a shaikh in Arabic or pir in Persian, and leads an established order (tariqa).

Sulaimanis: A denomination of Bohras that split from the Daudi mainstream in the sixteenth century C.E.

Sunna(h): Custom or path of the Prophet Muhammad.

Sunni: The main denomination of Islam, historically opposed (at various points) to Shiʿa adherents.

*Surti: Resident of the Gujarati city of Surat, or descendent of a Surat native. Among the Bohras, a de facto aristocratic class.

*Syedna: Honorific title by which the Bohra daʿi al-mutlaq is commonly known.

Tabarra: Also called lanat. Shiʿa custom of cursing the first three Sunni caliphs, regarded as usurpers.

Tafsir: Explication of the Qurʾan or zahir (open) religious texts. This external commentary is at a more accessible level than the esoteric batini taʾwil.

*Tahara: Cleanliness, purity. For Ismailis, one of the seven pillars of the faith. Like all pillars, it can be understood in zahir (apparent) or batin (esoteric) terms.

Talaq: Divorce. Must be pronounced three times to take effect.

Taqiyya/taqiya(h): Dissimulation. A right (even an obligation) of Shiʿa when faced with religious oppression. Practiced by Bohras throughout much of their history.

Tariqa: "Path" of Sufi devotion.

Tawhid: The unity of God. A fundamental belief of all Muslims.

*Taʾwil: Search for the batin meaning that underlies the zahir (apparent) explanation of doctrine. Esoteric exegesis, the practice of which among the Bohras is strictly limited by dawat authorities.

*Tayyibi: The sole surviving school of Mustaʿli Ismailism, named for the last imam (Tayyib) recognized by adherents. In theological terms, Bohras are Tayyibi Mustaʿli Ismaili Shiʿa Muslims.

*Thal: Metal plate. For Bohras, a large communal plate, shared by up to eight diners.

*Topi: "Hat." For Bohras, a unique pillbox skullcap that must be worn by

all men during religious services (and which ought to be worn at other times as well).

Ulema/ulama (sing. alim): Religious scholars, men learned in ilm (spiritual knowledge). In the Sunni world, the closest approximation to a bounded clergy.

Umma: Community, especially the community of all mu'mineen.

Umra: Lesser pilgrimage to Mecca, performed at a time other than the month of zyl-Hajj.

*Urs: Death anniversary. For Bohras, particularly the death anniversary of a da'i al-mutlaq.

Vaishnavite: Hindu devotee of the god Vishnu.

Vaishya: The lowest of the three "twice-born" varnas in the Hindu caste system (Shudras are not considered twice-born). The mercantile class, to which the ancestors of the Bohras belonged prior to conversion.

Varna: "Color." Varnas are the four classes (Brahmin, Kshatriya, Vaishya, and Shudra) that make up the Hindu caste system. (Dalits, tribal adivasis, and other people formerly deemed "untouchable" are technically below the varna system altogether.)

*Waaz: Formal Bohra ritual, in which the da'i delivers a sermon from a ceremonial throne.

*Walaya(h): Devotion to the family of the Prophet. One of the seven pillars of Shi'ism.

Wali: Legatee or stand-in.

*Wasi (pl. awsiya): Immediate successor of a prophet. Also called the asas, the wasi sets forth the esoteric meaning of the natiq's law.

Wazir/vizier: Prime minister of a caliph or other Muslim ruler.

Wuzu: Ritual ablution performed before prayer.

*Zahir: Open or literal interpretation of religious texts. Exterior aspects of faith, as laid out in the apparent meaning of the Qur'an and sharia.

Zakat: Obligatory charity, one of the pillars of both Sunni and Shi'a practice. Generally assessed at 2.5% of accumulated wealth.

*Ziyafat: Among the Bohras, a lavish feast given in honor of Syedna or another high cleric.

*Ziyaret: "Visiting." Can be mean a visit to the grave of a relative, or a pilgrimage to the tomb of a deceased da'i al-mutlaq.

Bibliography

Books and Articles

Abbas, S. Mobarak. 1991. Sociocultural Implications of Muharram Observance: A Study in Rural North Bihar. South Asian Anthropologist 12 (1–2): 39–44.

Abdul Husain, Mian Bhai Mullah. 1920. Gulzare Daudi for the Bohras of India. Ahmedabad. Reprint, Surat: Progressive Publications, 1977.

Abdulhussein, Shaikh Dr. Mustafa. 1995a. Bohras. *In* Oxford Encyclopedia of the Modern Islamic World. John Esposito, ed., pp. 224–226. New York: Oxford University Press.

———. 1995b. Sayyidna Muhammad Burhanuddin. *In* Oxford Encyclopedia of the Modern Islamic World. John Esposito, ed., pp. 237–238. New York: Oxford University Press.

———. 1995c. al-Jami'ah al-Sayfiyah. *In* Oxford Encyclopedia of the Modern Islamic World. John Esposito, ed., pp. 360–361. New York: Oxford University Press.

———. 2000. al-Dai al-Fatimi, Syedna Mohammed Burhanuddin: A Biographical Sketch in Pictures. London: al-Jamea tus-Saifiya.

Aggarwal, Partap C. 1973. The Meos of Rajasthan and Haryana. *In* Caste and Social Stratification among the Muslims. Imtiaz Ahmad, ed., pp. 21–44. New Delhi: Manohar Books.

———. 1976. Kinship and Marriage among the Meos of Rajastan. *In* Family, Kinship, and Marriage among Muslims in India. Imtiaz Ahmad, ed., pp. 265–296. New Delhi: Manohar Books.

Ahmad, Aziz. 1967. Islamic Modernization in India and Pakistan: 1857–1964. London: Oxford University Press.

———. 1969. Studies in Islamic Culture in the Indian Environment. Oxford: Clarendon Press.

Ahmad, Imtiaz, ed. 1973. Caste and Social Stratification among the Muslims. New Delhi: Manohar Books.

———. 1976. Family, Kinship, and Marriage among Muslims in India. New Delhi: Manohar Books.

————. 1981. Ritual and Religion among Muslims in India. New Delhi: Manohar Books.

————. 1983. Modernization and Social Change among Muslims in India. New Delhi: Manohar Books.

Ahmad, Mumtaz. 1994. Islamic Fundamentalism in South Asia: The Jamaat-i-Islami and the Tablighi Jamaat of South Asia. In Fundamentalisms Observed. Martin E. Marty and R. Scott Appleby, eds., pp. 457–530. Chicago: University of Chicago Press.

Ahmed, Akbar S. 1976. Millennium and Charisma among Pathans. London: Routledge and Kegan Paul.

Akhavi, Sharough. 1987. Iran: Implementation of an Islamic State. In Islam in Asia: Religion, Politics, and Society. John Esposito, ed., pp. 27–49. New York: Oxford University Press.

Ali, Maulana Muhammad. 1973. Tahrik-i Ahmadiyyat (The Ahmadiyyah Movement). S. Muhammad Tufail, trans. Lahore: Ahmadiyyah Anjuman Isha'at. 1st Urdu ed. 1931.

Ali, Zahid. 1954. Hamare Ismaili madhhab ki haqiqat aur uska nizam/The Origins of Our Ismaili Creed and Its System. Hyderabad (Deccan): Academy of Islamic Studies.

————. 1963. Tarikh-i Fatimiyyin-i Misr. 2nd ed. Karachi: Nafis Academy.

Amanat, Abbas. 1988. In between the Madrasa and the Marketplace: The Designation of Clerical Leadership in Modern Shi'ism. In Authority and Political Culture in Shi'ism. Said A. Arjomand, ed., pp. 98–124. Albany: State University of New York Press.

Anderson, Benedict. 1983. Imagined Communities: Reflections on the Origin and Spread of Nationalism. Reprint, London: Verso and NLB, 1993.

Anjuman-e-Burhani (Calcutta Dawoodi Bohra Jamaat Organization). 1965. In Reverential Memory of His Holiness Dr. Syedna Taher Saifuddin Saheb. Calcutta: Nilhat Press.

Anker, Richard, and Martha Anker. 1982. Reproductive Behavior in Households of Rural Gujarat: Social, Economic, and Community Factors. New Delhi: Concept Publishing.

Arjomand, Said Amir. 1988a. The Mujtahid of the Age and the Mulla-Bashi: An Intermediate Stage in the Institutionalization of Religious Authority in Shi'ite Iran. In Authority and Political Culture in Shi'ism. Said A. Arjomand, ed., pp. 80–92. Albany: State University of New York Press.

————, ed. 1988b. Authority and Political Culture in Shi'ism. Albany: State University of New York.

Asad, Talal. 1972. Market Model, Class Structure, and Consent: A Reconsideration of Swat Political Organization. Man, n.s. 7 (1): 74–94.

———. 1986. The Idea of an Anthropology of Islam. Washington: Center for Contemporary Arab Studies.

———. 1993. Genealogies of Religion: Discipline and Reasons of Power in Christianity and Islam. Baltimore: Johns Hopkins Press.

Asani, Ali Sultaan Ali. 1987. The Khojahs of Indo-Pakistan: The Quest for an Islamic Identity. Journal of the Institute of Muslim Minority Affairs 8 (1): 31–41.

———. 1994. The Impact of Modernization on the Marriage Rites of the Khojah Ismailis of East Africa. Journal of Turkish Studies 18: 17–24.

Baird, R., ed. 1993. Religion and Law in Independent India. New Delhi: Manohar Books.

Banks, Marcus. 1996. Ethnicity: Anthropological Constructions. London: Routledge.

Barker, Muhammed Abd-al-Rahman, Hasan Jahangir Hamdani, et al. 1967. Spoken Urdu. Montreal: Institute of Islamic Studies (McGill University).

Barth, Fredrik. 1959. Political Leadership among Swat Paths. London: University of London Press.

———. 1960. The System of Social Stratification in Swat, Northern Pakistan. In Aspects of Caste in South India, Ceylon, and North-West Pakistan. Edmund Leach, ed., pp. 113–145. Reprint, Cambridge: Cambridge University Press, 1979.

———. 1969. Ethnic Groups and Boundaries: The Social Organization of Cultural Differences. Boston: Little, Brown.

———. 1995. Other Knowledge and Other Ways of Knowing. Journal of Anthropological Research 51 (1): 65–68.

Basu, Salil Kumar, and Pravita Gupta. 1982. Trend of Menarche and Menopause among Inbred Muslim Shia Dawoodi Bohras of Udaipur (Rajasthan). South Asian Anthropologist 3 (2): 35–38.

Basu, Salil Kumar, and Anil Jinal. 1983. Genetic Aspects of Myopia among the Shia Muslim Dawoodi Bohras of Udaipur, Rajasthan. Human Heredity 33 (3): 163–169.

Bayly, Christopher A. 1985. The Prehistory of "Communalism": Religions in Conflict in India, 1700–1860. Modern Asian Studies 19 (2): 177–203.

———. 1988. Rallying Round the Subaltern. Journal of Peasant Studies 16 (1): 110–120.

Beck, Lois, and Nikki Keddie, eds. 1978. Women in the Muslim World. Cambridge: Harvard University Press.

Bekhud, Shaikh Yusuf. 1994a. Tragedy at Kerbala: The Days of Sorrow and Revival. Mumbai: Dawat-e-Hadiyah, Department of Statistics and Information. Pamphlet.

————. 1994b. Mukasir-e-Dawat Syedi Salehbhaisaheb Safiyuddin S. D. T.: An Appreciation. Mumbai: Dawat-e-Hadiyah, Department of Statistics and Information. Pamphlet.

————. 1994c. A Chronicle of the Mausoleum: The Heritage and the Dedication. Mumbai: Dawat-e-Hadiyah, Department of Statistics and Information. Pamphlet.

Bhowmick, Samita Manna. 1984. Attitude of Rural Women towards Modernity: A Case Study of a Village in Midnapore. Journal of the Indian Anthropological Society 19 (1): 1a–4a.

Blank, Jonah. 1992. Arrow of the Blue-Skinned God: Retracing the Ramayana through India. Boston: Houghton Mifflin.

————. 1993. Arrow of the Blue-Skinned God: Retracing the Ramayana through India. Rev. ed. New York: Doubleday/Image.

————. 1994. "Ram and Ram Rajya: The Babri Masjid/Ramjanambhumi Dispute and the Politicization of a Divinity." Journal of Vaisnava Studies 2 (4): 159–174.

————. 1999. "Kashmir: Fundamentalism Takes Root." Foreign Affairs 78 (6): 36–53.

————. In press (a). Arrow of the Blue-Skinned God: Retracing the Ramayana through India. Rev. ed. New York: Grove/Atlantic Monthly Press.

————. In press (b). "Annual Rites of the Daudi Bohras: Islamic Identity as Universal and Unique." Eastern Anthropologist.

Borthwick, Bruce. 1990. The Ismailis and Islamization in Pakistan. Washington: American Council for the Study of Islamic Societies Newsletter.

Bostan-e Daudi. (No author.) 1960. Ujjain: India Kalima Kutubhkhana.

Bouhdiba, Abdelwahab. 1985. Sexuality in Islam. Alan Sheridan, trans. London: Routledge and Kegan Paul.

Brass, Paul. 1991. Ethnicity and Nationalism: Theory and Comparison. New Delhi: Sage Books.

————. 1994. The Politics of India since Independence. Cambridge: Cambridge University Press.

al-Bukhari, Muhammad ibn Ismail. 1986. Sahih al-Bukhari. Muhammad Muhsin, ed. and trans. Lahore: Kazi Publications.

Burt, Ronald S., Michael J. Minor, et al. 1983. Applied Network Analysis: A Methodological Introduction. London: Sage Publications.

Campbell, James M., ed. 1899. Gazetteer of the Bombay Presidency. Vol. 9, pt. 2: Gujarat Population: Musalmans and Parsis. Mumbai: Government Central Press. Reprinted as: Muslim and Parsi Castes and Tribes of Gujaret. Gurgaon: Vintage Books, 1990.

Carlyle, Thomas. 1841. On Heroes, Hero-Worship, & the Heroic in History. London: James Fraser.

Casanova, Paul. 1897. Les derniers fatimides. In Mémoires de la mission archéologique française du Caire 6 (1897): 415–445.

Central Intelligence Agency. 1999. The World Factbook. Washington, DC: Central Intelligence Agency.

Chatterjee, Partha. 1982. Agrarian Relations and Communalism in Bengal, 1926–1935. In Subaltern Studies I: Writings on South Asian History and Society. Ranajit Guha, ed., pp. 9–39. Delhi: Oxford University Press.

Chen, Xiaomei. 1992. Occidentalism as Counterdiscourse: "He Shang" in Post-Mao China. Critical Inquiry 18 (4): 686–712.

Chopra, P. N. 1982. Religions and Communities of India. Delhi: Vision Books.

Cohn, Bernard S. 1959. Some Notes on Law and Change in North India. In Economic Development and Cultural Change 8.

Cole, Juan R., and Nikki Keddie, eds. 1986. Shi'ism and Social Protest. New Haven: Yale University Press.

Commissariat, Khan Bahadur Menekshah Sorabshah. 1957. A History of Gujarat: Including a Survey of Its Chief Architectural Monuments and Inscriptions. Mumbai: Orient Longmans. Originally published 1938.

Conklin, George H. 1976. Muslim Family Life and Secularization in Dharwar, Karnataka. In Family, Kinship, and Marriage among Muslims in India. Imtiaz Ahmad, ed., pp. 127–140. New Delhi: Manohar Books.

Contractor, Noman L. 1980. The Dawoodi Bohras. Pune: New Quest Books.

Corbin, Henry. 1951. Le temps cyclique dans le Mazdéisme et dans l'Ismaélisme. Eranos Jahrbuch 20: 149–217.

———. 1953. Étude préliminaire pour le "Livre réunissant les deux sagesses" de Nasir-e-Khosraw. Teheran: L'Institut Franco-Iranien.

———. 1954. Épiphanie divine et naissance spirituelle dans la gnose Ismaélienne. Eranos Jahrbuch 23: 141–249.

———. 1957. De la gnose antique à la gnose Ismaélienne. Oriente ed Occidente nel medio evo: Atti del XII convegno Volta, pp. 105–143.

———. 1972. En Islam Iranien: Aspects spirituels et philosophiques. Paris: Gallimard.

———. 1980. Temple et contemplation. Paris: Gallimard.

———. 1982. Temps cyclique et gnose ismaélienne. Paris: Gallimard.

———. 1984. Histoire de la philosophie islamique. Paris: Gallimard.

Cottam, Richard R. 1986. The Iranian Revolution. In Shi'ism and Social

Protest. Juan Cole and Nikki Keddie, eds., pp. 55–87. New Haven: Yale University Press.

Dachraoui, Farhat. 1981. Le califat Fatimide au Maghreb, 296–365 H./909–975 JC. Tunis: al-Sharikah al-Tunisiyah lil-Tawzi.

Daftary, Farhad. 1990. The Ismailis: Their History and Doctrines. Cambridge: Cambridge University Press.

Das, Veena. 1984. For a Folk-Theology and Theological Anthropology of Islam. Contributions to Indian Sociology, n.s. 18 (2): 293–305.

———, ed. 1990. Mirrors of Violence: Communities, Riots, and Survivors in South Asia. Delhi: Oxford University Press.

Davoodbhoy, Shaikh Tyebally A. 1990. In the Footsteps of a Glorious Tradition. Mumbai: Dawat-e-Hadiyah, Department of Statistics and Information. Pamphlet.

———. 1992a. Faith of the Dawoodi Bohras. Mumbai: Dawat-e-Hadiyah, Department of Statistics and Information. Pamphlet.

———. 1992b. Historic Visit to the Republic of Madagascar. Mumbai: Dawat-e-Hadiyah, Department of Statistics and Information. Pamphlet.

———. 1993a. Barakate Azae Moulanal Imam Husain (AS) 1414 A.D.: The Mombasa Experience. Mumbai: Dawat-e-Hadiyah, Department of Statistics and Information. Pamphlet.

———. 1993b. A Historic Dedication: Fulfillment of Spiritual and Religious Aspirations. Mumbai: Dawat-e-Hadiyah, Department of Statistics and Information. Pamphlet.

———. 1994. Compendium of Unalloyed Reverence. Mumbai: Dawat-i-Hadiyah, Department of Statistics and Information. Pamphlet.

Dawat-e-Hadiyah (Daudi Bohra dawat, no author noted). 1975. A Treasury of Reminiscences: His Holiness Dr. Syedna Mohammed Burhanuddin, Fifty-second Da'i-al-Mutlaq. Mumbai: Dawat-e-Hadiyah, Department of Statistics and Information. Pamphlet.

———. 1983. Fatimi Heritage. Mumbai: Dawat-e-Hadiyah, Department of Statistics and Information. Pamphlet.

———. 1985. A Golden Chapter in Islamic Economy. Mumbai: Dawat-e-Hadiyah, Department of Statistics and Information. Pamphlet.

———. n.d. Believers and Yet Unbelievers!. Mumbai: Dawat-e-Hadiyah, Department of Statistics and Information. Pamphlet.

Defremery, M. C. 1856. Histoire d'ismaeliens. Journal asiatique 8.

Desai, Madhavi. 1992. "The Traditional Houseform of Bohras in Gujarat: Architectural Response to Cultural Ethos." Masters' thesis, Ahmedabad University, Department of Art and Architechture.

Desai, Z. A. 1989. The Major Dargahs of Ahmadabad. In Muslim Shrines

of India: Their Character, History, and Significance. Christian W. Troll, ed., pp. 76–96. Delhi: Oxford University.

Dharmapala, Anagarika. 1963. Dharmapala Lipi/Dharmapala Letters. Ananda W. P. Guruge, ed. Colombo: Government Press.

Djalili, Mohammad-Reza. 1981. Religion et Revolution: L'Islam Shi'ites et l'Etat. Paris: Economica.

Douglas, James. 1893. Bombay and Western India, vol. 2. London: Sampson Low, Marston and Co.

Drèze, Jean, and Amartya Sen. 1996. India: Economic Development and Social Opportunity. Delhi: Oxford University Press.

Dumont, Louis. 1970. Religion, Politics, and History in India: Collected Papers in Indian Sociology. Paris: Mouton.

———. 1986. A South Indian Subcaste: Social Organization and Religion of the Pramalai Kallar. M. Moffat and L. Morton, trans. New York: Oxford University Press.

Eaton, Richard Maxwell. 1978. Sufis of Bijapur 1300–1700: Social Roles of Sufis in Medieval India. Princeton: Princeton University Press.

———. 1984. The Political and Religious Authority of the Shrine of Baba Farid. In Moral Conduct and Authority: The Place of Adab in South Asian Islam. Barbara Daly Metcalf, ed., pp. 333–356. Berkeley: University of California Press.

Edwards, David B. 1993. Summoning Muslims: Print, Politics, and Religious Ideology in Afghanistan. Journal of Asian Studies 52 (3): 609–628.

———. 1995. Print Islam: Media and Religious Revolution in Afghanistan. Anthropological Quarterly 68 (3): 171–184.

———. 1998. Learning from the Swat Pathans: Political Leadership in Afghanistan, 1978–97. American Ethnologist 25 (4): 712–728.

Eickelman, Dale. 1992. Mass Higher Education and the Religious Imagination in Contemporary Arab Societies. American Ethnologist 19 (4): 643–655.

Eickelman, Dale, and James Piscatori, eds. 1990. Muslim Travellers: Pilgrimage, Migration, and the Religious Imagination. Berkeley: University of California Press.

Engineer, Asghar Ali. 1983. Ismaili 'aqa'id par ek nazar. Mumbai: Institute of Islamic Studies.

———. 1989. The Muslim Communities of Gujarat: An Exploratory Study of Bohras, Khojas, and Memons. Delhi: Ajanta.

———. 1990. The Reformist Bohras: Their Problems and Demands. Mumbai: Central Board of the Dawoodi Bohra Community. Pamphlet.

————. 1991. The Issues in the Bohra Reform Movement. Mumbai: Central Board of the Dawoodi Bohra Community. Pamphlet.

————. 1993. The Bohras. Rev. ed. New Delhi: Vikas. Originally published in 1980.

————. 1995: The Bohra Clergy and Religion. Mumbai: Central Board of the Dawoodi Bohra Community. Pamphlet.

————. n.d. The Problems of the Bohra Community: What Is to Be Done? Mumbai: Central Board of the Dawoodi Bohra Community. Pamphlet.

Enthoven, R. E. 1920. The Tribes and Castes of Bombay, 1. Mumbai: Government Central Press.

Esposito, John. 1982. Women in Muslim Family Law. Syracuse: Syracuse University Press.

————. 1988. Islam: The Straight Path. New York: Oxford University Press.

————. 1995. Oxford Encyclodia of the Modern Islamic World. New York: Oxford University Press.

————, ed. 1987. Islam in Asia: Religion, Politics, and Society. New York: Oxford University Press.

Fakhr, H. M., ed. 1940. al-Tarjama al-Zahira li-firqat Bohrat al-bahira. Journal of the Bombay Branch of the Royal Asiatic Society, n.s. 16: 87–98.

Farah, Madelain. 1984. Marriage and Sexuality in Islam. Salt Lake City: University of Utah Press.

Feki, Habib. 1978. Les idées religieuses et philosophique de l'Ismaelisme Fatimide. Tunis: Université de Tunis.

Filippani-Ronconi, Pio. 1973. Ismaeliti ed 'Assassini.' Milan: Editiones Basilienses.

Fischer, Michael M. J. 1980. Iran: From Religious Dispute to Revolution. Cambridge: Harvard University Press.

Fox, Richard G. 1985. Lions of the Punjab: Culture in the Making. Berkeley: University of California Press.

Fraser, James Baillie. 1825. Narrative of a Journey into Khorasan, in the Years 1821 and 1822. London: Longmans, Hurst, Rees, Orme, Brown, and Green.

Friedmann, Yohanan. 1989. Ahmadiyya Movement: A Historical Survey. In Prophesy Continuous: Aspects of Ahmadi Religious Thought and Its Medieval Background. Yohanan Friedmann, ed., pp. 1–46. Berkeley: University of California Press.

Fruzzetti, Lina. 1982. Food and Worship: An Account of Hindu and Muslim Birth Rituals. Journal of the Indian Anthropological Society 17 (1).

Fyzee, Asaf Ali Asghar. 1934a. A Chronological List of the Imams and

Dais of the Mustalian Ismailis. Journal of the Bombay Branch of the Royal Asiatic Society, n.s. 10: 8–16.

———. 1934b. Qadi al-Nu'man, the Fatimid Jurist and Author. Journal of the Royal Asiatic Society of Great Britain and Ireland: 1–32.

———. 1965. The Study of the Literature of the Fatimid Dawa. In Arabic and Islamic Studies in Honor of Hamilton A. R. Gibb. G. Makdisi, ed., pp. 232–249. Leiden: E. J. Brill.

———. 1969. Compendium of Fatimid Law. Simla: Indian Institute of Advanced Study.

———. 1974. The Book of Faith (partial translation of al-Nu'man's Da'a'im al-Islam). Mumbai: Nachiketa Publications.

Gaborieau, Marc. 1986. Les ordres mystiques dans le sous-continent indien: Un point de vue ethnologique. In Les ordres mystiques dans l'Islam: Cheminements et situation actuelle. Alexandre Popovic and Gilles Veinstein, eds., pp. 105–129. Paris: Recherches d'Histoire et de Sciences Sociales.

Gandhi, Rajmohan. 1990. Understanding the Muslim Mind. New Delhi: Penguin India.

Geertz, Clifford. 1968. Islam Observed. Chicago: University of Chicago Press.

———. 1973. The Interpretation of Cultures: Selected Essays. New York: Basic Books.

Gellner, Ernest. 1983. Nations and Nationalism. Ithaca: Cornell University Press.

———. 1994. Encounters with Nationalism. Cambridge: Blackwell.

Ghani, Ashraf. 1987. Afghanistan: Islam and Counterrevolutionary Movements. In Islam in Asia: Religion, Politics, and Society. John Esposito, ed., pp. 79–95. New York: Oxford University Press.

al-Ghazali, Abu Hamid. 1971. Ihya' 'Ulum-ud-din [The Revival of Religious Learning]. Maulana Fazal-ul-Karam, trans. Lahore: Kazi Publications.

de Goeje, Michael J. 1886. Mémoire sur les Carmathes du Bahrain et les Fatimides. 2nd ed. Leiden, E. J. Brill.

Gold, Daniel. 1994. Organized Hinduisms: From Vedic Truth to Hindu Nation. In Fundamentalisms Observed. Martin E. Marty and R. Scott Appleby, eds., pp. 531–593. Chicago: University of Chicago Press.

Goldziher, Ignaz. 1981. Vorlesungen uber den Islam (Introduction to Islamic Theology and Law). Andras and Ruth Hamori, trans. Princeton: Princeton University Press. Translation of 1910 edition.

Gombrich, Richard, and Gananath Obeyesekere. 1988. Buddhism Transformed: Religious Change in Sri Lanka. Princeton: Princeton University Press.

Guha, Ranajit, ed. 1982. Subaltern Studies I: Writings on South Asian History and Society. Delhi: Oxford University Press.

———. 1983. Subaltern Studies II: Writings on South Asian History and Society. Delhi: Oxford University Press.

Guha, Ranajit, and Gayatri Chakavorty Spivak, eds. 1988. Selected Subaltern Studies. New York: Oxford University Press.

Gupta, Raj, ed. 1983. Urban India. New Delhi: Vikas.

Hamdani, Abbas. 1956. The Beginnings of the Ismaili Dawa in Northern India. Cairo: Sirovic Books.

———. 1967. The Fatimid-Abbasid Conflict in India. Islamic Culture 41.

———. 1971. The Daʿi Hatim ibn Ibrahim al-Hamidi (d.596H/1199A.D.) and his book Tuhfat al-Qulub. Oriens 23–24: 258–300.

———. 1976. Evolution of the Organisational Structure of the Fatimi Dawah. Arabian Studies 3: 85–114.

———. 1985. The Tayyibi-Fatimid Community of the Yaman at the Time of the Ayyubid Conquest of Southern Arabia. Arabian Studies 7: 151–160.

al-Hamdani, Husain F. 1932. History of the Ismaili Dawat and Its Literature during the Last Phase of the Fatimid Empire. Journal of the Royal Asiatic Society of Great Britain and Ireland: 129–135.

———. 1933. Some Unknown Ismaili Authors and Their Works. Journal of the Royal Asiatic Society of Great Britain and Ireland: 359–378.

———. 1934. The Letters of al-Mustansir billah. Bulletin of the School of Oriental and African Studies 7: 307–324.

———. 1937. A Compendium of Ismaili Esoterics. Islamic Culture 2: 210–220.

———. 1958a. On the Genealogy of the Fatimid Caliphs. Cairo: American University of Cairo.

———. 1958b. A Compendium of Ismaili Esoterics. Islamic Culture 9.

Haq, S. Moinul. 1979. Islamic Thought and Movements in the Subcontinent: 711–1947. Karachi: Pakistan Historical Society.

Hardgrave, Robert L., Jr., and Stanley A. Kochanek. 1993. India: Government and Politics in a Developing Nation. New York: Harcourt, Brace, Jovanovich.

Hardy, Peter. 1972. The Muslims of British India. Cambridge: Cambridge University Press.

Hasan, Hasan Ibrahim. 1964. Tarikh al-dawla al-Fatimiyaa. 3rd ed. Cairo.

Hasnain, Nadeem, and Sheikh Abrar Husain. 1988. Shias and Shia Islam in India: A Study in Society and Culture. New Delhi: Harnam.

ibn Hawshab, Mansur al-Yaman. 1955. Kitab al-rushd wa'l hidaya/The Book of Righteousness and True Guidance. In Studies in Early Persian

Ismailism. W. Ivanow, ed. and trans., pp. 29–59. 2nd ed. Mumbai: Ismaili Society.

Hay, Stephen, ed. 1988. Sources of Indian Tradition, vol. 2. New York: Columbia University Press.

Heesterman, J. C. 1985. The Inner Conflict of Tradition. Chicago: University of Chicago Press.

Hichi, Selim Hassan. 1972. La communauté des Isma'ilites de l'époque des Mamaliques à nos jours. Beirut: N.p.

Hjortshoj, Keith. 1987. Shi'i Identity and the Significance of Muharram in Lucknow, India. In Shi'ism, Resistance, and Revolution. Martin Kramer, ed., pp. 289–308. Boulder: Westview Press.

Hobsbawm, Eric, and Terence Ranger. 1983. The Invention of Tradition. Cambridge: Cambridge University Press.

Hodgson, M. G. S. 1962. al-Darazi and Hamza in the Origin of the Druze Religion. Journal of the American Oriental Society 82: 5–20.

Hodkinson, Keith. 1984. Muslim Family Law: A Sourcebook. London: Croom Helm.

Hollister, John Norman. 1953. The Shia of India. London: Luzac and Co.

Huntington, Samuel. 1996. The Clash of Civilizations and the Remaking of World Order. New York: Simon and Schuster.

Husain, Abrar. 1976. Marriage Customs among Muslims in India: A Sociological Study of the Shia Marriage Customs. New Delhi: Sterling Publishers.

Idris Imad al-Din (Qureshi) ibn al-Hasan. 1942. Zahr al-ma'ani. In Ismaili Tradition Concerning the Rise of the Fatimids. W. Ivanow, ed. London: Oxford University Press.

———. 1975. Uyun al-akhbar wa-funun al-althar. M. Ghalib, ed. Beirut: Dar al-Andalus.

Insaf, Saifuddin, ed. 1987. The Bohra Controversy as Reflected through Newspapers. Mumbai: Central Board of Dawoodi Bohra Community Publications.

Ismailji, Hasan Ali Badripresswala. 1937. Akhbar al-duat al-akramin. Rajkot: Badri Press.

Ivanow, Wladimir. 1932. An Ismaili Interpretation of the Gulshani Raz, Journal of the Bombay Branch of the Royal Asiatic Society, n.s. 8.

———. 1933. A Guide to Ismaili Literature. London: Oxford University Press.

———. 1936. A Creed of the Fatimids. Mumbai: Qayyimah Press. Summary of Taj al- 'aqa'id by Ali al-Walid.

———. 1938. A Forgotten Branch of the Ismailis. Journal of the Royal Asiatic Society of Great Britain and Ireland: 57–79.

————. 1939. The Organization of the Fatimid Propaganda. Journal of the Bombay Branch of the Royal Asiatic Society, n.s. 15: 1–35.

————. 1940. Ismailis and Qarmatians. Journal of the Bombay Branch of the Royal Asiatic Society, n.s. 16: 43–85.

————. 1941. Early Shiite Movements. Journal of the Bombay Branch of the Royal Asiatic Society, n.s. 17: 1–23.

————. 1942. Ismaili Tradition Concerning the Rise of the Fatimids. London: Oxford University Press.

————. 1946. The Alleged Founder of Ismailism. Mumbai: Ismaili Society.

————. 1952. Brief Survey of the Evolution of Ismailism. Leiden: E. J. Brill.

————. 1955. Sources in Early Persian Ismailism. Mumba: Ismaili Society.

————. 1963. Ismaili Literature: A Bibliographic Survey. Teheran: N.p.

Jacobson, Doranne. 1976. The Veil of Virtue: Purdah and the Muslim Family in the Bhopal Region of Central India. In Family, Kinship, and Marriage among Indian Muslims. Imtiaz Ahmad, ed., pp. 169–215. Columbia, MO: South Asia Books.

Jafar ibn Mansur al-Yaman, Abul-Qasim. 1942. Asrar al-nutaqa. In Ismaili Tradition Concerning the Rise of the Fatimids. W. Ivanow, ed. London: Oxford University Press.

————. 1952. Kitab al-kashf. R. Strothmann, ed. London: Oxford University Press.

————. 1955. Kitab al-ʿalim waʾl-ghulam/The Book of the Teacher and the Pupil. In Studies in Early Persian Ismailism. W. Ivanow, ed. and trans., pp. 61–86. 2nd ed. Mumbai: Ismaili Society.

————. 1984. Saraʾir wa asrar al-nutaqa. M. Ghalib, ed. Beirut: Dar al-Andalus.

Jafari, S. Ahmad. 1965. Tarikh-i dawlat-i Fatimiyya. Lahore: Idarah Shirkat-i Mussaniffin.

Jafri, S. Husain. 1979. Origin and Early Development of Shia Islam. London: Longmans.

Jain, Sushila. 1986. Muslims and Modernisation. Jaipur: Rawat Books.

Jhaveri, K. M. 1933–1935. A Legendary History of the Bohras. Journal of the Bombay Branch of the Royal Asiatic Society 9: 37–52.

Jindal, Bachan Lal. 1984. Schooling and Modernity. New Delhi: Inter-India Books.

"Judgment 1931" 1931. Judgment in Civil Suit #32 of 1925 in the Court of First Class Sub-Judge, Burhanpur. Burhanpur: Tayebali Mahomedali Bhamgarhwala. [Ruling in the Burhanpur Durgah case].

uergensmeyer, Mark. 1988. The Logic of Religious Violence: The Case of the Punjab. Contributions to Indian Sociology 22: 66–88.

Kalka, Iris. 1990. Attachment to the Mother Country: Image and Reality. Ethnic Groups 8 (4): 249–265.

Kapur, Rajiv. 1986. Sikh Separatism: The Politics of Faith. London: Allen and Unwin.

Karandikar, Maheshwar. 1968. Islam in India's Transition to Modernity. Mumbai: Orient Longmans.

al-Kashshi, Abu Amr Muhammad ibn Umar. 1969. Ikhtiyar ma'rifat al-rijal. Hasan al-Mustafawi, ed. Mashhad: N.p.

Katzenstein, Mary Fainsod. 1979. Ethnicity and Equality: Preferential Policies in Bombay. Ithaca: Cornell University.

Keddie, Nikki. 1981. Roots of Revolution: An Interpretive History of Modern Iran. New Haven: Yale University Press.

——, ed. 1983. Religion and Politics in Iran: Shi'ism from Quietism to Revolution. New Haven: Yale University Press.

Keddie, Nikki, and Juan R. Cole. 1986. Introduction. In Shi'ism and Social Protest. Juan R. Cole and Nikki Keddie, eds. 1–29. New Haven: Yale University Press.

Khan, A. Z. 1975. Ismailism in Multan and Sind. Journal of the Pakistan Historical Society 23: 36–57.

Khan, M. E. 1979. Family Planning among Muslims in India. New Delhi: Manohar Books.

Khan, Najm-ul Ghani. 1914. Daudi Bohron-ki Tarikh. Moradabad: N.p.

——. 1924. Madhahib al-Islam. Lucknow: N.p.

Khan, Qudrat Allah. 1962. Fatimi khilafat-i Misr. Karachi: N.p.

Khare, Ravindra. 1988. India's Modernity: Some Preliminary Notes and Comments. South Asian Anthropologist 9 (2): 163–170.

Khatana, R. P. 1976. Marriage and Kinship among the Gujar Bakarwals of Jammu and Kashmir. In Family, Kinship, and Marriage among Muslims in India. Imtiaz Ahmad, ed., pp. 83–126. New Delhi: Manohar Books.

Kherie, al-Haj Khan Bahadur Altaf Ahmad. 1992. A Key to [the] Holy Qur'an: Index-cum-Concordance for the Holy Qur'an. Delhi: Adam Publishers.

Kohlberg, Etan. 1975. Some Imami-Shii Views on Taqiyya. Journal of the American Oriental Society 95: 395–402.

——. 1987. Western Studies of Shi'a Islam. In Shi'ism, Resistance, and Revolution. Martin Kramer, ed., pp. 31–41. Boulder: Westview Press.

Kramer, Martin. 1987. Syria's Alawis and Shi'ism. In Shi'ism, Resistance,

and Revolution. Martin Kramer ed., pp. 237–252. Boulder: Westview Press.

———, ed. 1987. Shi'ism, Resistance, and Revolution. Boulder: Westview Press.

Krishna, Gopal. 1976. Piety and Politics in Indian Islam. *In* Muslim Communities of South Asia: Culture and Society. T. N. Madan, ed. New Delhi: Vikas Publishing House.

Lambat, Ismail. 1976. Marriage among the Sunni Surati Vohras of South Gujarat. *In* Family, Kinship, and Marriage among Muslims in India. Imtiaz Ahmad, ed., pp. 49–81. Columbia: South Asia.

Landau, Jacob M., ed. 1984. Ataturk and the Modernization of Turkey. Leiden: E. J. Brill.

Landes, David. 1998. The Wealth and Poverty of Nations: Why Some Are So Rich and Some So Poor. New York: Norton.

Lane-Poole, Stanley. 1901. A History of Egypt in the Middle Ages. London: Methuen & Co.

Lane-Smith, N.J. 1928. The Bohras of Bombay. Indian Witness, March 7, 1928.

Lawson, Todd. 1997. "The Dangers of Reading: Inlibration, Communion, and Transference in the Qur'an Commentary of the Bab." *In* Scripture and Revelation. Moojan Momen, ed., pp. 171–215. Oxford: George Ronald.

Leach, Edmund R. 1990. Political Sytems of Highland Burma: A Study of Kachin Social Structure. London: Athlone Press. Originally published 1954.

———, ed. 1979. Aspects of Caste in South India, Ceylon, and North-West Pakistan. Cambridge: Cambridge University Press.

Lévi-Strauss, Claude. 1962. La pensée sauvage. Paris: Librarie Plon.

———. 1963. Structural Anthropology. Claire Jacobson and Brooke Grundfest Schoepf, trans. New York: Basic Books.

———. 1966. The Savage Mind. Chicago: University of Chicago Press.

Lewis, Bernard. 1940. The Origins of Ismailism: A Study of the Historical Backround of the Fatimid Caliphate. Cambridge: Cambridge University Press.

———. 1948. Ismaili Notes. Bulletin of the School of Oriental and African Studies 12.

———. 1952. The Sources for the History of the Syrian Assassins. Speculum 27: 475–489.

———. 1953. Saladin and the Assassins. Bulletin of the School of Oriental and African Studies 15: 239–245.

———. 1968. The Assassins: A Radical Sect in Islam. New York: Basic Books.

———. 1971. Assassins of Syria and Ismailis of Persia. Accademia Nazionale dei Lincei, Atti del convegno internazionale sul tema: La Persia nel mediovo: 573–580.

———. 1987. The Shi'a in Islamic History. In Shi'ism, Resistance, and Revolution. Martin Kramer, ed., pp. 21–30. Boulder: Westview Press.

———. 1993. Islam and the West. Oxford: Oxford University Press.

———. 1998. "License to Kill: Usama bin Laden's Declaration of Jihad." In Foreign Affairs 77 (6): 14–19.

Lindholm, Charles. 1982. Generosity and Jealousy: The Swat Pukhtun of Northern Pakistan. New York: Columbia University Press.

———. 1986. Caste in Islam and the Problem of Deviant Systems. Contributions to Indian Sociology 20: 61–73.

Lokhandwalla, S. T. 1955. The Bohras: A Muslim Community in Gujarat. Studia Islamica 3: 117–135.

———, ed. 1972. Kitab Ikhtil afusul al-madhahib lil-Qadi al-Nu'man. Simla: al-Mahad al-Hindi lil-Dirasah al-Mutaqaddimah.

Madan, T. N. 1981. Religious Ideology and Social Structure: The Muslims and Hindus of Kashmir. In Ritual and Religion among Muslims in India. Imtiaz Ahmad, ed., pp. 21–64. New Delhi: Manohar Books.

———. 1987. Secularism in Its Place. Journal of Asian Studies 46 (4): 747–759.

———, ed. 1976. Muslim Communities of South Asia: Culture and Society. New Delhi: Vikas Publishing House.

———. ed. 1991. Religion in India. Delhi: Oxford University Press.

Mahroof, M. M. M., Marina Azeez, et al. 1986. An Ethnological Survey of the Muslims of Sri Lanka. Colombo: Sir Razik Fareed Foundation.

Makarem, Sami. 1972. The Doctrine of the Ismailis. Beirut: Arab Institute for Research and Publishing.

Makdisi, G., ed. 1965. Arabic and Islamic Studies in Honor of Hamilton A. R. Gibb. Leiden: E. J. Brill.

Mansfield, John H. 1993. The Personal Laws or a Uniform Civil Code? In Religion and Law in Independent India. R. Baird, ed., pp. 139–177. Delhi: Manohar Books.

Marten, J. [Justice]. 1921. Judgment in Suits no. 918 and 941 of 1917 in the High Court of Judicature, Bombay (Ruling delivered on March 19).

Marty, Martin, and R. Scott Appleby, eds. 1994. Fundamentalisms Observed. Chicago: University of Chicago Press.

Massignon, Louis. 1922. Esquisse d'une bibliographie Qarmate. In A Volume of Oriental Studies Presented to Edward G. Browne. T. W.

Arnold and R. A. Nicholson, eds., pp. 329–338. Cambridge: Cambridge University Press.

Masud, Muhammad Khalid, Brinkley Messick, and David Powers, eds. 1996. Islamic Legal Interpretation: Muftis and Their Fatwas. Cambridge: Harvard University Press.

Maududi, Sayyid Abul Ala. 1940. Towards Understanding Islam (Risala-e-Diniyat). Abdul Ghani, trans. Lahore: Muhammad Ashraf.

Mausam-e bahar [Muhammad Ali ibn Jiwabhai, author]. 1884. Mausim-e bahar fi akhbar al-tahirin al-akhyar, vol. 3. Mumbai: Hyderi Press.

Maybury-Lewis, David H. P. 1988. Claude Lévi-Strauss and the Search for Structure. Wilson Quarterly (1): 82–95.

———. 1997. Indigenous Peoples, Ethnic Groups, and the State. London: Allyn and Bacon.

McKean, Lise. 1996. Divine Enterprise: Gurus and the Hindu Nationalist Movement. Chicago: University of Chicago Press.

Meeker, Michael. 1980. Islam and Resistance in Afghanistan. New York: Columbia University Press.

Merchant, Salim Mahomedbhai, Usman Ismailbhai Banatwalla, et al. 1969. An Account of the Khoja Sunnat Jamat. Karachi: Oxford Book House.

Mernissi, Fatima. 1975. Beyond the Veil: Male-Female Dynamics in a Modern Muslim Society. Cambridge: Schenkman Publishing.

———. 1987. Harem politique: Le Prophete et les femmes. Paris: Albin Michel.

———. 1991a. Le monde n'est pas un harem. Paris: Albin Michel.

———. 1991b. The Veil and the Male Elite: A Feminist Interpretation of Women's Rights in Islam. English rev. ed. of Harem politique. Mary Jo Lakeland, trans. New York: Addison-Wesley.

———. 1991c. Women and Islam: An Historical and Theological Enquiry. Mary Jo Lakeland, trans. Oxford: Basil Blackwell.

Messick, Brinkley. 1993. The Calligraphic State: Textual Dominion and History in a Muslim Society. Berkeley: University of California Press.

———. 1996. Media Muftis: Radio Fatwas of Yemen. In Islamic Legal Interpretation: Muftis and Their Fatwas. Muhammad Khalid Masud, Brinkley Messick, and David Powers, eds. Cambridge: Harvard University Press.

Metcalf, Barbara Daly. 1982. Islamic Revival in British India: Deoband, 1860–1900. Princeton: Princeton University Press.

———. 1984. Islamic Reform and Islamic Women. In Moral Conduct and Authority: The Place of Adab in South Asian Islam. Barbara Metcalf, ed., pp. 184–195. Berkeley: University of California Press.

———. 1990. The Pilgrimage Remembered: South Asian Accounts of the Hajj. *In* Muslim Travellers: Pilgrimage, Migration, and the Religious Imagination. Dale F. Eickelman and James Piscatori, eds., pp. 85–107. Berkeley: University of California Press.

———, ed. 1984. Moral Conduct and Authority: The Place of Adab in South Asian Islam. Berkeley: University of California Press.

Michaelson, Karen L. 1976. Patronage, Mediators, and the Historical Context of Social Organization in Bombay. American Ethnologist 3 (2): 281–295.

———. 1983. Education and the Reproduction of the Social Hierarchy: Bombay. *In* Urban India. Raj Gupta, ed., pp. 325–355. New Delhi: Vikas Books.

Mill, James. 1975. The History of British India. Chicago: University of Chicago Press.

Mines, Mattison. 1981. Islamization and Muslim Identity in South India. *In* Ritual and Religion among Muslims in India. Imtiaz Ahmad, ed., pp. 65–89. New Delhi: Manohar Books.

———. 1983. Kin Centres and Ethnicity among Muslim Tamilians. *In* Modernization and Social Change among Muslims in India. Imtiaz Ahmad, ed. New Delhi: Manohar Books.

Misra, B. B. 1961. The Indian Middle Classes: Their Growth in Modern Times. London: Oxford University Press.

Misra, Satish Chandra. 1963. The Rise of Muslim Power in Gujarat. New York: Asia Publishing House.

———. 1964. The Muslim Communities of Gujarat. Baroda: Asia Publishing House.

Momen, Moojan, ed. 1997. Scripture and Revelation. Oxford: George Ronald.

Mubarakpuri, Shaikh Yunus Shakib. 1964. Da‘a’im al-Islam. Surat: Idarahyi Adabiyat-i Fatimi. Urdu translation of Qadi al-Nu‘man's text.

———. 1966. Fatimi akabir. Surat: Idarahyi Adabiyat-i Fatimi.

———. 1978. Bohrah da‘i-yi mutlaq Bare Mulla Ji ka naya Islam. Delhi: Kitabvala.

Mujeeb, M. 1967. The Indian Muslims. London: Allen & Unwin.

Muqaddasi, Shams-ud-din Muhammad ibn Ahmad Bashshari. 1877. Ahsan al-taqasim. M. J. de Goeje, ed. Leiden: E. J. Brill.

al-Muslim, ibn al Hajjaj. 1978. al-Jami-us-Sahih, Abdul Hamid Siddiqi, trans. New Delhi: Kitab Bhavan.

al-Mustansir billah, Abu Tamim (Imam). 1954. al-Sijillat al-Mustansiriyya. Abdul Munim Majid, ed. Cairo: Maktabat al-Anjul al-Misriyah.

Mutahhari, Murtaza. 1988. The Islamic Modest Dress. Laleh Bakhtiar, trans. Albuquerque: Abjad.

Nadvi, Abu Zafar. 1975. ʿIqd al-javahir fi ahval al-bavahir: tarikh-i Daudi Bohra. Karachi: A. M. N. Rajokotwala (original edition: 1936).

Najafali, Abbasali. 1943. Law of Marriage Governing the Dawoodi Bohra Muslims. Mumbai: Times of India Press.

Najmuddin, Yusuf. 1992. al-Daʿi-al-Mutlaq the Fifty-second: Seventy-five Momentous Years. Mumbai: Dawat-e-Hadiyah, Department of Statistics and Information. Pamphlet.

Nandy, Ashis. 1988. The Politics of Secularism. Alternatives 13: 68–93.

———, ed. 1987. Tradition, Tyranny. and Utopias: Essays in the Politics of Awareness. New York: Oxford University Press.

Nanji, Azim. 1978. The Nizari Ismaili Tradition in the Indo-Pakistan Subcontinent. Delmar: Caravan.

Narayanan, Leila. 1989. Ethnicity in Urban Context: The Gujaratis of Madras City. Jaipur: Rawat.

Nasr, Seyyed Vali Reza. 1994. The Vanguard of the Islamic Revolution: The Jamaat-i-Islami of Pakistan. Berkeley: University of California Press.

Nathwani, N. P., chair. 1979. Dawoodi Bohra Commission: Report of Investigation Conducted by the Commission Appointed by the Citizens for Democracy into the Alleged Infringement of Human Rights of Reformist Members of the Dawoodi Bohras in the Name of the High Priest. Ahmedbad: Nathwani Commission.

Nehru, Jawaharlal. 1991. The Discovery of India. New Delhi: Oxford University Press.

Niazi, Maulana Kausar. 1992. Heir to a Great Spiritual Heritage. Mumbai: Daudi Bohra Dawat, Department of Statistics and Information. Pamphlet.

al-Nuʿman ibn Muhammad, al-Qadi Abu Hanifa. 1960. Asas al-taʾwil. Arif Tamir, ed. Cairo: N.p.

———. 1961. Daʿaʾim al-Islam. A. A. A. Fyzee, ed. Cairo: N.p.

———. 1970. Iftitah al-dawa. W. al-Qadi, ed. Beirut: N.p.

———. 1972. Taʾwil al-daʿaʾim. M. Hasan al-Azami, ed. Cairo: Dar al-Maʾarif.

———. 1978. al-Majalis waʾl-musayarat. al-Habib al-Faqi, I. Shabbuh, and M. al-Yalawi, eds. Tunis: al-Jamiah al-Tunisiyah.

Nuʿmani, Muhammad Shibli. 1961. Safarnama. Lahore: Ghulam Ali and Sons.

Obeyesekere, Gananath. 1970. Religious Symbolism and Political Change in Ceylon. Modern Ceylon Studies 1 (1).

Okyar, Osman. 1984. Ataturk's Quest for Modernism. *In* Ataturk and the Modernization of Turkey. Jacob M. Landau, ed., pp. 45–57. Leiden: E. J. Brill.

O'Leary, De Lacy. 1923. A Short History of the Fatimid Khalifate. New York: E. P. Dutton & Co.

Pandey, Gyanendra. 1983. Rallying Round the Cow: Sectarian Strife in the Bhojpuri Region, c.1888–1917. *In* Subaltern Studies II: Writings on South Asian History and Society. Ranajit Guha, ed., pp. 60–129. Delhi: Oxford University Press.

———. 1990a. The Construction of Communalism in Colonial North India. Delhi: Oxford University Press.

———. 1990b. The Colonial Construction of "Communalism": British Writings on Banares in the Nineteenth century. *In* Mirrors of Violence: Communities, Riots, and Survivors in South Asia. Veena Das, ed. Delhi: Oxford University Press.

Papanek, Hanna, and Gail Minault, eds. 1982. Separate Worlds: Studies of Purdah in South Asia. Delhi: Chanakya Press.

Parsons, Talcott. 1951. The Social System. Glencoe, IL: Free Press.

———. 1961. Class Structure in the Social Consciousness. London: Routledge and Kegan Paul.

Peacock, James L. 1978. Muslim Puritans: Reformist Psychology in Southeast Asian Islam. Berkeley: University of California Press.

Peters, F. E. 1994. The Hajj: The Muslim Pilgrimage to Mecca and the Holy Places. Princeton: Princeton University Press.

Pettigrew, Joyce J. M. 1995. The Sikhs of the Punjab. London: Zed Books.

Pickthall, Mohammed Marmaduke, trans. 1953. The Meaning of the Glorious Koran. New York: Mentor Books.

Pinault, David. 1992. The Shiites: Ritual and Popular Piety in a Muslim Community. New York: St. Martin's Press.

Poonawala, Ismail K. 1970. al-Sijistani and His Kitab al-Maqalid. *In* Essays on Islamic Civilization. Donald Little, ed., pp. 274–283. Leiden: E. J. Brill.

———. 1973. al-Qadi al-Nu'man's Works and the Sources. Bulletin of the School of Oriental and African Studies 36: 109–115.

———. 1974. A Reconsideration of al-Qadi al-Nu'man's Madhhab. Bulletin of the School of Oriental and African Studies 37: 572–579.

———. 1977. Biobibliography of Ismaili Literature. Malibu, CA: Undena Publications.

Popovic, Alexandre, and Gilles Veinstein, eds. 1986. Les ordres mystiques dans l'Islam: Cheminements et situation actuelle. Paris: Recherches d'Histoire et de Sciences Sociales.

Qureshi, Ishtiaq Husain. 1985. The Muslim Community of the Indo-Pakistan Subcontinent (610–1947). Delhi: Renaissance Books.

Rahman, Fazlur. 1982a. Islam and Modernity: Transformation of an Intellectual Tradition. Chicago: University of Chicago Press.

———. 1982b. The Status of Women in Islam: A Modernist Interpretation. In Separate Worlds: Studies of Purdah in South Asia. Hanna Papanek and Gail Minault, eds., pp. 275–310. Delhi: Chanakya Press.

———. 1984. Muhammad Iqbal and Ataturk's Reforms. Journal of Near Eastern Studies 43 (2): 157–162.

Raik, S. Kikabhai, ed. 1975. Gulshan-e Malumat. Ujjain: Kalim Kutub Khana.

Ridenhour, C., and H. Shocklee. 1987. Timebomb. In Yo! Bum Rush the Show. New York: Def Jam Recordings.

Rizvi, Irshad Hussain. 1984. Hindustan ke Subon ki Shi'a Abadi. Banares: Aljawad/Arabic College.

Robinson, Francis. 1983. Islam and Muslim Society in South Asia. Contributions to Indian Sociology 17 (2): 185–203.

Rodinson, Maxime. 1966. Islam et le capitalisme. Paris: Editions du Seuil.

Rose, Gregory. 1983. Velayat-e Faqih and the Recovery of Islamic Identity in the Thought of Ayatollah Khomeini. In Religion and Politics in Iran: Shi'ism from Quietism to Revolution. Nikki Keddie, ed., pp. 166–188. New Haven: Yale University Press.

Roy, Shibani. 1984. The Dawoodi Bohras. Delhi: B. R. Publishing.

Rudolph, Lloyd I., and Susanne Hoeber Rudolph. 1987. In Pursuit of Lakshmi: The Political Economy of the Indian State. Chicago: University of Chicago Press.

Ruthven, Malise. 1984. Islam in the World. New York: Oxford University Press.

Sachedina, Abdulaziz A. 1994. Activist Shi'ism in Iran, Iraq, and Lebanon. In Fundamentalisms Observed. Martin Marty and R. Scott Appleby, eds., pp. 403–456. Chicago: Chicago University Press.

Said, Edward. 1978. Orientalism. New York: Pantheon Books.

Saiyid, A. R. 1976. Purdah, Family Structure, and the Status of Women: A Note on a Deviant Case. In Family, Kinship, and Marriage among Muslims in India. Imtiaz Ahmad, ed., pp. 239–264. New Delhi: Manohar Books.

———. 1981. Ideal and Reality in the Observance of Moharram: A Behavioral Interpretation. In Ritual and Religion among Muslims in India. Imtiaz Ahmad, ed., pp. 113–142. New Delhi: Manohar Books.

Schimmel, Annemarie. 1980. Islam in the Indian Subcontinent. Leiden: E. J. Brill.

———. 1992. Islam. Albany: State University of New York Press.

Shah, A. B., and C. R. M. Rao, eds. 1965. Tradition and Modernity in India. Mumbai: Manaktalas Books.

Shah, Idries. 1971. The Sufis. Garden City, NJ: Doubleday/Anchor Books.

Shahabuddin, Syed, and Theodore Paul Wright, Jr. 1987. India: Muslim Minority Politics and Society. *In* Islam in Asia: Religion, Politics, and Society. John L. Esposito, ed., pp. 152–176. New York: Oxford University Press.

Shakir, M. H., trans. 1983. Holy Qur'an. Elmhurst, NY: Tahrike Tarsile Qur'an.

Sharif, Jafar [presumed]. 1832. Qanun-i-Islam/Islam in India: The Customs of the Musalmans in India. G. A. Herklots, trans. Rev. ed.: William Crooke, ed. London: Oxford University Press, 1921. Reprint, New Delhi: Oriental Books, 1971.

Siddiqui, Nejatullah. 1992. Banking Without Interest. Mumbai: Taj Publishers.

Singh, Khushwant. 1963. A History of the Sikhs. Princeton: Princeton University Press.

Singh, Yogendra. 1965. Traditional Culture Pattern of India and Industrial Change. *In* Tradition and Modernity in India. A. B. Shah and C. R. M. Rao, eds., pp. 47–69. Mumbai: Manaktalas.

Spivak, Gayatri Chakavorty. 1988. Subaltern Studies: Deconstructing Historiography. *In* Selected Subaltern Studies. Ranajit Guha and Gayatri Chakavorty Spivak, eds., pp. 3–32. New York: Oxford University Press.

Stern, Samuel M. 1946. The Authorship of the Epistles of the Ikhwan-as-Safa. Islamic Culture 20: 367–372.

———. 1949. Ismaili Propaganda and Fatimid Rule in Sind. Islamic Culture 23: 298–307.

———. 1951. The Succession to the Fatimid Imam al-Amir, the Claims of the Later Fatimids to the Imamate, and the Rise of Tayyibi Ismailism. Oriens 4: 193–255.

———. 1955. Heterodox Ismailism at the time of al-Muizz. Bulletin of the School of Oriental and African Studies 17: 10–33.

———. 1960. The Early Ismaili Missionaries in North-West Persia and in Khurasan and Transoxania. Bulletin of the School of Oriental and African Studies 23: 56–90.

———. 1961. Ismailis and Qarmatians. *In* L'élaboration de l'Islam, pp. 99–108. Paris: Colloque de Strasbourg.

————. 1983. Studies in Early Ismailism. Leiden: E. J. Brill.

Tabari, Azar. 1983. The Role of the Clergy in Modern Iranian Politics. *In* Religion and Politics in Iran: Shi'ism from Quietism to Revolution. Nikki Keddie, ed., pp. 47–72. New Haven: Yale University Press.

Tabataba'i, 'Allamah Sayyid Muhammad Husayn. 1975. Shi'ite Islam. Seyyed Hossein Nasr, trans. Albany: State University of New York.

Tambiah, Stanley J. 1984. The Buddhist Saints of the Forest and the Cult of Amulets: A Study of Charisma, Hagiography, Sectarianism, and Millennial Buddhism. Cambridge: Cambridge University Press.

————. 1989. Ethnic Conflict in the World Today. American Ethnologist 16 (2): 335–349.

————. 1990. Some Reflections on Communal Violence in South Asia. AAS presidential Address. Journal of Asian Studies 49 (4): 741–760.

————. 1996. Levelling Crowds: Ethnonationalist Conflicts and Collective Violence in South Asia. Berkeley: University of California Press.

Tapper, Nancy. 1990. Ziyaret: Gender, Movement, and Exchange in a Turkish Community. *In* Muslim Travellers: Pilgrimage, Migration, and the Religious Imagination. Dale F. Eickelman and James Piscatori, eds., pp. 236–255. Berkeley: University of California Press.

Thapar, Romila. 1989. Imagined Religious Communities? Ancient History and the Modern Search for a Hindu Identity. Modern Asian Studies (May): 209–231.

Trimingham, J. Spencer. 1971. The Sufi Orders in Islam. Oxford: Oxford University Press.

Troll, Christian, ed. 1989. Muslim Shrines in India. Delhi: Oxford University Press.

Turner, Bryan S. 1974. Weber and Islam: A Critical Study. London: Routledge and Kegan Paul.

Uberoi, J. P. S. 1969. Sikhism. Patiala: Punjab University Press.

————. 1991. Five Symbols of Sikh Identity. *In* Religion in India. T. N. Madan, ed., pp. 320–332. Delhi: Oxford University Press.

Ullrich, Helen, ed. 1975. Competition and Modernization in South Asia. Delhi: Abhinav.

Van der Veer, Peter. 1992. Playing or Praying: A Sufi Saint's Day in Surat. Journal of Asian Studies 51 (3): 545–564.

————. 1994. Religious Nationalism: Hindus and Muslims in India. Berkeley: University of California Press.

Varshney, Ashutosh. 1993. Contested Meanings: India's National Identity, Hindu Nationalism, and the Politics of Anxiety. Daedalus (Summer): 227–255.

Verdia, H. S. 1974. "The Pains of Modernization: A Case Study of Bohras

in Udaipur." The Secularist (Pune), January-February 1974. Reprinted in The Dawoodi Bohras. Noman Contractor, ed. pp. 13–18. Pune: New Quest Publications, 1980.

Voll, John O. 1994. Fundamentalism in the Sunni Arab World: Egypt and Sudan. *In* Fundamentalisms Observed. Martin E. Marty and R. Scott Appleby, eds., pp. 345–402. Chicago: University of Chicago Press.

Walker, Paul Ernest. 1978. Eternal Cosmos and the Womb of History: Time in Early Ismaili Thought. International Journal of Middle East Studies 9: 355–366.

———. 1993. Early Philosophical Shiism: The Ismaili Neoplatonism of Abu Yaqub al-Sijistani. Cambridge: Cambridge University Press.

Weber, Max. 1947. Social and Economic Organization. A. M. Henderson and Talcott Parsons, trans. New York: Free Press.

———. 1958a. The Religion of India. H. H. Gerth and D. Martindale, trans. Glencoe, IL: Free Press.

———. 1958b. The Protestant Ethic and the Spirit of Capitalism. Talcott Parsons, trans. New York: Charles Scribner's Sons.

———. 1965. The Sociology of Religion. London: Methuen.

Weiner, Myron. 1978. Sons of the Soil: Migration and Ethnic Conflict in India. Princeton: Princeton University.

Weldon, Fay. 1989. Sacred Cows. London: Chatto and Windus.

West, Thomas G., and Grace Starry West, trans. 1984. Plato and Aristophanes: Four Texts on Socrates. Ithaca: Cornell University Press.

Winter, Michael. 1984. The Modernization of Education in Kemalist Turkey. *In* Ataturk and the Modernization of Turkey. Jacob M. Landau, ed., pp. 183–195. Leiden: E. J. Brill.

Wolfson, Harry A. 1976. The Philosophy of the Kalam. Cambridge, MA: Harvard University Press.

Wright, Theodore P., Jr. 1975. Competitive Modernization within the Daudi Bohra Sect of Muslims and Its Significance for Indian Political Development. *In* Competition and Modernization in South Asia, Helen Ullrich ed., pp. 151–178. Delhi: Abhinav.

———. 1976. Muslim Kinship and Modernization: The Tyabji Clan of Bombay. *In* Family, Kinship, and Marriage among Muslims in India. Imtiaz Ahmad, ed., pp. 217–238. Columbia, MO: South Asia Books.

———. 1983. Inadvertant Modernization of Indian Muslims by Revivalists. *In* Modernization and Social Change among Muslims in India. Imtiaz Ahmad, ed., pp. 83–98. New Delhi: Manohar Books.

Yalman, Nur. 1967. Under the Bo Tree: Studies in Caste, Kinship, and Marriage in the Interior of Ceylon. Berkeley: University of California Press.

———. 1969. Islamic Reform and the Mystic Tradition in Eastern Turkey. Archives Européenne de Sociologie 10: 41–60.

———. 1991. On Secularism and Its Critics: Notes on Turkey, India, and Iran. Contributions to Indian Sociology, n.s. 25 (2): 233–266.

Zaidi, B. H. 1988. The Fatimi Tradition. Mumbai: Dawat-e-Hadiyah, Department of Statistics and Information. Pamphlet.

Indian and Pakistani newspapers and magazines cited

Asian Age (Mumbai).

Bombay magazine (Mumbai).

Bombay Samachar [Gujarati] (Mumbai).

Current (Mumbai).

Dawn (Karachi).

The Hindu (Chennai, Mumbai, Coimbatore).

The Hindustan Times (Mumbai).

India Today (New Delhi).

Indian Express (Mumbai).

New Quest (Pune).

Outlook (New Delhi, Mumbai).

The Secularist (Pune).

The Statesman (Calcutta, New Delhi).

The Sunday Observer (Mumbai).

The Times of India (New Delhi, Mumbai).

The Week (Mumbai).

Index

Uthman (Sunni caliph), 15, 16
Uttar Pradesh
 Ithna-Ashari courtship in, 118
 Shi'a marriage customs in, 72–73
Uyun al-akbar (Idris Imad al-Din ibn
 Hasan), 20, 302

Vaishya, 14, 33, 38, 40, 203, 206, 214,
 284
Vajpayee, Atal Bihari, 251
Van der Veer, Peter, 270
Vishwa Hindu Parishad, 95, 271
Vohras, 67, 321n25, 322n36, 330n11
Vora, Virji, 46

waaz, 82, 85, 86, 87, 90, 92, 96, 150, 153,
 165, 188, 221, 257
Wahhabis, 48, 49
Wahid, Abdurrahman ("Gus Dur"), 264,
 351n24
walaya, 167, 168, 337n28
wali, 38
waqf, 105, 197
wasi, 79, 135, 170, 224
wazir, 29
Weber, Max, 259, 260
Western Ismailis, 33. *See* Bohras
Westernization, 49, 260. *See also* Bohras,
 and assimilation
women, Bohra
 careers encouraged among, 127
 clothes prescribed for, 189–90
 Diya, 131–33
 education of, 126, 333n51
 educational parity among, 125–26
 segregation of, 59, 62, 69–70, 127,
 130n, 215

status of, 123–28
 ziyaret participation of, 139
women and Islam, Western perceptions of,
 123, 125
Wright, Theodore P., Jr., 184, 234, 260, 305
wuzu, 79, 79n

Yahya (Zaidi *imam*), 161
Yalman, Nur, 261
al-Yaman ibn Hawshab, Mansur, 20
Yazid ibn Muawiya, 17
yellow card. *See* certificates of orthopraxy
Yemen, 14, 20, 23, 25, 33, 36, 38, 39, 40,
 41, 42, 138, 139, 161, 171, 175, 218,
 223, 253, 272
"Youthis." *See* "Udaipur rebellion"
Yusuf Najmuddin ibn Sulaiman (24th *da'i*),
 41
Yusuf Najmuddin ibn Zakiuddin (42nd *da'i*),
 46

Zafar Khan Muzaffar, 38
zahir, 109, 110, 161, 165, 166, 168, 209,
 218, 222
al-Zahir (17th *imam*), 31–32
Zaidis, 19, 40, 161, 272
Zaini Bungalow, 146
zakat, 167, 168, 198–99, 341–42n51
zamindars, 74, 78
Zamzam, 25, 79
Zanj rebels, 25
al-Zanji, Ali ibn Muhammad, 25
Zikra, 98
ziyafats, 1, 47, 50, 72, 148, 149, 150, 153,
 156, 182, 200, 213, 246
ziyaret, 81, 98, 138–40, 145, 172, 181, 190,
 223, 244, 334–35n11